MANUAL OF ENTOMOLOGY,

TRANSLATED FROM THE GERMAN OF

DR. HERMANN BURMEISTER.

BY

W. E. SHUCKARD, M.E.S.

WITH ADDITIONS BY THE AUTHOR, AND ORIGINAL NOTES AND PLATES
BY THE TRANSLATOR.

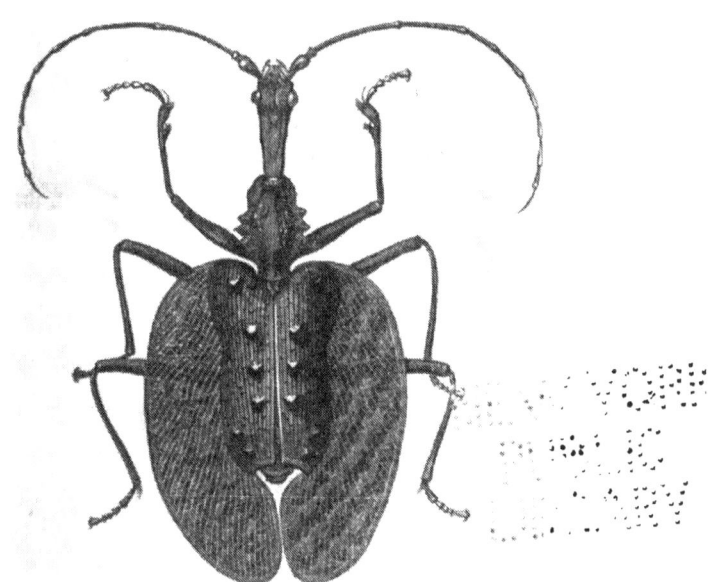

MORMOLYCE PHYLLODES.

LONDON:
EDWARD CHURTON, PUBLIC LIBRARY, 26, HOLLES STREET.

1836.

LONDON:
BRADBURY AND EVANS, PRINTERS, WHITEFRIARS.

PREFACE.

Upon completing the Translation of this 'Manual,' it is incumbent upon me to thank the press generally for the very favourable reception it has obtained throughout its progress. It was undertaken with the view to contribute to the advancement of the study of Entomology, by giving a wider circulation to its elementary principles; and it is hoped that its interesting details will tend to diffuse a taste for its more general cultivation.

Amidst a multitude of original experiments and observations, in addition to its numerous other scientific claims, this work will be found to comprise, in its anatomical and physiological departments, a generalisation of the host of facts elicited by the laborious investigations of Straus Durckheim, Müller, Suckow, Leon Dufour, Nitzsch, &c. &c., up to a very late period. It is confidently believed, that a book combining the researches of such eminent men must necessarily become extremely useful, not only to the entomological but also to the physiological student, and to the scientific man in general.

The advantages to be derived from the study of natural history are manifest. One of its most conspicuous merits, and that upon which the immortal Cuvier particularly dwelt, is its tendency to methodise the mind, by impressing it with a habit of order and precision; thus, having all the effect, but under a more alluring mask, of the abstract mathematics, and the logic of the schools. This character attaches more peculiarly to that portion of natural history upon which this work exclusively bears—namely, the STUDY OF INSECTS. Their great multitude and diversity, their brilliancy of colour, eccentricity and extreme elegance of form, their metamorphoses, complexity of structure, and peculiarities of habits, always adapted to the purposes they have to accomplish in the economy of nature, altogether unite to give an intense interest to this delightful pursuit.

Having thus summarily shown the value of the work, and the utility and pleasure to be derived from the study of the science, it only remains for me to add my best thanks to DR. BURMEISTER for the promptitude with which he spontaneously supplied me, upon hearing of my undertaking, with the new MS. of several portions wherein his opinions had become modified or changed.

THE TRANSLATOR.

TABLE OF CONTENTS.

	PAGE
Introduction—Definition and Compass of Entomology, §§ 1—4	1

FIRST DIVISION.

GENERAL ENTOMOLOGY.

FIRST SECTION.—ORISMOLOGY.

Its Definition and Compass, §§ 5—7	5

FIRST CHAPTER.

General Principles, §§ 8—13	7

SECOND CHAPTER.

General Orismology, § 14	11
I. Form, §§ 15—21	11
II. Quality, §§ 22—24	16
III. Clothing, §§ 25, 26	19
IV. Colour, §§ 27—38	20
V. Measure, §§ 39—42	26
VI. Affixion, Direction, §§ 43—45	28

THIRD CHAPTER.

	PAGE
Partial Orismology, §§ 46, 47	30
I. The Egg, §§ 48—50	31
II. The Larva, §§ 51—58	33
III. The Pupa, §§ 59—64	43
IV. The Imago, § 65	48
1. The Head, §§ 66—72	49
The Mouth, §§ 68—70	51
The Eyes, § 71	62
The Antennæ, § 72	63
2. The Thorax, §§ 73—78	71
Organs of Motion on the Thorax.	
A. The Wings, §§ 79, 80	91
B. The Legs, §§ 81—83	100
3. The Abdomen, §§ 84, 85	108

SECOND SECTION.—ANATOMY.

Idea and Subdivision of it, §§ 86—90 114

FIRST SUBSECTION.—VEGETATIVE ORGANS.

Their general Character, §§ 91—94 117

FIRST CHAPTER.

THE ORGANS OF NUTRITION.

I. The Intestinal Canal and its Appendages, §§ 95—114	119
II. The Fatty Substance, § 115	151
III. The Blood-vessels, §§ 116—121	153
IV. The Organs of Respiration, §§ 122—130	158

SECOND CHAPTER.
THE ORGANS OF GENERATION.

	PAGE
Their general Character, §§ 131—134	181
I. Female Organs of Generation, §§ 135—145	184
II. Male ditto, §§ 146—152	200
III. Development of the Sexual Organs during the Metamorphosis, § 153	220
IV. Conformity of the Female and Male Sexual Organs, § 154	222

SECOND SUBSECTION.—THE ANIMAL ORGANS.

Their general Character, §§ 155—157 224

THIRD CHAPTER.
THE ORGANS OF MOTION.

I. Of the Horny Skeleton, §§ 159—168	226
II. The Muscular System, §§ 169—181	247

FOURTH CHAPTER.
THE ORGANS OF SENSATION.

Their general Division and Character, § 182	269
I. The Brain, §§ 183—185	272
II. The Ventral Cord, §§ 186—188	277
III. The Sympathic System, §§ 189—191	286
IV. The Organs of the Senses, §§ 192—198	289

THIRD SECTION.—PHYSIOLOGY.

Its idea and subdivision, §§ 199—200 302

FIRST SUBSECTION.—SOMATIC PHYSIOLOGY.

Its idea, § 201 304

FIRST CHAPTER.

	PAGE
Of Generation, §§ 202—213	306

SECOND CHAPTER.

Of Nutrition.

Its general character and kinds, §§ 214—216	344
I. Digestion, §§ 217—225	347
II. Respiration, §§ 226—236	384
III. Circulation of the blood, §§ 237—243	403

THIRD CHAPTER.

The Metamorphoses, §§ 244—260	414

FOURTH CHAPTER.

The Muscular Motion, §§ 261—267	445

FIFTH CHAPTER.

The Sounds emitted by Insects, §§ 268—271	466

SIXTH CHAPTER.

Of Sensation and the Senses, §§ 272—278	474

SEVENTH CHAPTER.

The Luminousness of Insects, §§ 279—282	490

SECOND SUBSECTION.—PSYCHOLOGICAL PHYSIOLOGY.

The Nature and Object of Instinct, §§ 283—286	498

EIGHTH CHAPTER.
THEIR SELF-PRESERVATION.

I. Means of Defence, § 288	504
II. Instinct of Nutrition, § 290	511

NINTH CHAPTER.

THEIR MEANS FOR THE CONSERVATION OF THE SPECIES.

	PAGE
Sexual Instinct, § 291	513
I. The Copulative impulse, § 292	513
II. Affection for their young, §§ 293—299	515

THIRD SUBSECTION.—RELATIONS OF INSECTS TO THE EXTERNAL WORLD.

Compass of this relation, § 300 537

TENTH CHAPTER.

IN RELATION TO OTHER ORGANIC BEINGS.

To Plants, §§ 301—306	538
To Insects, § 307	552
To Birds, § 308	554
To Mammalia, § 309	556
To Man, § 310	558

ELEVENTH CHAPTER.

Relation to the Elements and Seasons, §§ 311—313 . . 565

TWELFTH CHAPTER.

Relation to the Antediluvian World, §§ 314—317 . . 574

FOURTH SECTION.—TAXONOMY.

FIRST CHAPTER.

General ideas—Nature of Artificial and Natural Divisions, §§ 318—321	582
I. Idea of Species, §§ 322—324	588
II. Idea of a Genus, §§ 325—331	590
III. Idea of the Higher Groups, §§ 332—336	594

SECOND CHAPTER.
HISTORY OF THE PRINCIPAL SYSTEMS.

	PAGE
Earliest essays, Aristotle, § 337	597
More recent ones, §§ 338—343	598
Zootomical systems, §§ 344—349	608
Physiological systems, §§ 350—352	617

THIRD CHAPTER.

Nomenclature, §§ 353—363	624

INTRODUCTION.

DEFINITION AND COMPASS OF ENTOMOLOGY.

§ 1.

NATURAL HISTORY has for its object the inquiry into the being of natural bodies and their thorough investigation in reference to their various qualities, and the relative functions of their component parts. Understood in this extent, it presents us with a distinct unique entirety, which treats the natural body as complete, but gradually perfected; and at the same time seeks to discover the means whereby it attained its completion and perfection. Natural History, therefore, is no mere description of form,—no description of nature, as it has been, latterly, very incorrectly considered, but a true, and pragmatical history, developed from its own fundamental principles.

ENTOMOLOGY is that branch of this extensive science, which treats of the Natural History of Insects.

Insects are animals with articulated bodies divided into three chief portions, the head, thorax, and abdomen; they have three pairs of legs, and generally two pairs of wings, and, to acquire this structure, pass through several transformations and changes, called their metamorphoses.

The object of Entomology, consequently, is to investigate the nature of insects; its design is to show how the insect is organised and formed, and why it was obliged to adopt this particular conformation and internal structure; and when this is accomplished, it proceeds to the generalisation and development of the various vital phenomena observable in the class. Its view is, however, not limited here to show the mere general form of the body of the insect, but it also displays how this general form varies in the several orders of insects, and how far this transformation and change may extend without destruction to its identification.

This comprises, therefore, a summary of the essential purpose of the science. The chief incentive to our study, and investigation, of natural bodies in general, is the instinctive impulse of the human mind towards progressive information, and the extension of the circle of its knowledge; but, in this pursuit, a multiplicity of useful discoveries are made, which are applicable to daily life, and which distinctly show the evident advantages of the science, although their elicitation can never be considered the primary object of scientific research. The study of insects will likewise be found rich in similar results, which I shall state in its appropriate place.

§ 2.

Thus, the Natural History of Insects falls into two great divisions—viz. the introductory, or general portion, and the particular, or systematic Natural History of them.

The former, or general division, acquaints us with insects with respect to their exterior construction, and with regard to their interior organisation; it also instructs us of the various phenomena displayed by this class of animals; and lastly, developes the principle upon which insects must be arranged, and naturally subdivided. The following divisions are thence deduced:—

1. The ORISMOLOGY, generally called the Terminology*, which contains the various technical terms used in explaining the perceptible differences in the body of an insect, and at the same time acquaints us with its exterior visible parts in the several periods of its existence, until its full and perfect development.

2. The ANATOMY, or, as it has been called, in reference to the dissection of insects, ENTOMOTOMY, which acquaints us with their internal construction, and with the form as well as texture of their organs.

3. In their PHYSIOLOGY we learn the functions of these organs. Besides which, it generalises the multifariously varied phenomena displayed by these animals, and re-examines, under a general view, those to which we are accustomed to apply the name of instinct.

---

* Kirby has introduced the term ORISMOLOGY in lieu of the hybrid compound TERMINOLOGY, but which being derived from 'ορισμος (*terminus, definitio*) should be written Horismology. But as it is not unusual to reject the *spiritus asper*, we have retained his orthography.

INTRODUCTION.

4. This is succeeded by their TAXONOMY, or principles of arrangement, which, after giving its general rudiments, proceeds with a critical survey of the most remarkable Entomological systems.

§ 3.

The second or particular division of Entomology, contains merely the description of the insect world, from their highest to their lowest sub-divisions, in the mode most consonant with system and their scientific definition. It is this portion which is generally called systematic Entomology, or plainly Entomology, and which is both the most comprehensive, and most varied portion of the whole science.

§ 4.

These, therefore, are the several divisions of which the complete Natural History of Insects consists; they are all closely connected together, and produce, only by their strict union, that harmonious entirety of which the science boasts; whereas, the several parts, considered separately, form but dislocated fragments, each of which, without the elucidation of the rest, must frequently remain incomprehensible. The subdivision of insects into orders, groups, and families, does not properly belong here, but will find its true situation much lower, where we purpose passing to the particular description of the individuals of this class; but as, in the course of the following treatise, we shall so frequently have occasion to refer to the several orders, it will perhaps be considered not inapposite, particularly as it may assist the judgment of Tyros, if we here lay down the distribution into groups. It may remain here merely intercalated by anticipation.

The commencement of this introduction has already defined what an insect is; all animals comprised in it may be thus classed into

A.—Those with an imperfect metamorphosis, *i. e.* larva, pupa, and perfect insect, strongly resembling each other, the pupa possessing locomotion and eating.

   a. having a suctorial mouth.

      1. ORDER.—HEMIPTERA.—(*Cimices, Bugs, &c.*)

   b. having a masticatory mouth.

      a. Four unequal wings, the superior ones pergameneous, the inferior generally larger, and membranous; the latter are folded in repose.

2. ORDER.—Orthoptera.—(*Locusts, Grasshoppers, &c.*)

  b. Four sometimes equal, sometimes unequal membraneous wings with reticulated nervures, but never folded.

3. ORDER.—Dictyoptera.—(*Cockroaches.*)

B.—Those with a perfect metamorphosis. The larva is a long maggot, caterpillar, or wornil. The pupa generally quiescent, and does not eat.

  a. Some have a suctorial mouth.

    a. Insects with two naked transparent wings.

4. ORDER.—Diptera.—(*Flies.*)

  b. Insects with four large wings, covered wholly, or partially, with broad scales.

5. ORDER.—Lepidoptera.—(*Butterflies, Moths.*)

  b. The others have a masticatory mouth, or at least visible mandibles and palpi.

    a. Four equal wings, with reticulated nervures.

6. ORDER.—Neuroptera.—(*Dragon Flies, &c.*)

  b. Four unequal wings, with the nervures variously branching.

7. ORDER.—Hymenoptera.—(*Bees, Wasps, Ichneumons, &c.*)

  c. Four unequal wings, the superior ones consisting of a corneous case.

8. ORDER.—Coleoptera.—(*Beetles.*)

Note.—Throughout almost all the orders there are apterous families, genera, and species, which are very easily referred to their orders from their metamorphosis, and the structure of their mouths, but they never form correctly a distinct one, as Latreille insists, and which he calls Aptera.

FIRST DIVISION.

GENERAL ENTOMOLOGY.

FIRST SECTION.

ORISMOLOGY.

ITS DEFINITION AND COMPASS.

§ 5.

In a science, which, like Natural History, has to distinguish such multifarious, and, frequently, such closely approximate forms, it is of great importance that the differences perceptible to the eye should be explained by a suitable selection of precise terms, and in a clear, concise, and readily comprehensible language. Since the recognition of this principle, a kind of conventional agreement has been aimed at, whereby the Latin language still retains, at least in the descriptive natural history of the animal and vegetable kingdoms, that degree of importance which it acquired by its introduction as the universal language of the learned. The technical language of natural history thus therefore originated; for, in the course of progressive investigation, new terms were required to characterise the newly discovered parts.

§ 6.

Following the example of early writers, whenever the Latin language is deficient in the characteristic expression, we apply to the Greek, and endeavour to derive from it an appropriate name, or form one from it by composition. From the euphony of its words, and the fulness of its tone, it is peculiarly adapted to the construction of permanent names of general importance, and has therefore found a suitable application in the naming of newly discovered orders, families, and genera. In the construction of these names, however, we must be exceedingly careful not to wound the spirit of the language by barbarisms, grammatical inaccuracies, and hybrid compounds (*e.g. Bitoma, Biphyllus, Taxicornes*, &c.), of which, unfortunately, too many disagreeable examples could be cited. But it is decidedly wrong to retain these inaccuracies, although such words may have derived a certain authority from their age, from the mere accident of the inadmissible nature of their composition not being previously discovered. The love of truth and correctness demands that such blemishes should be expunged, wherever they are found, and they can never be subject to other considerations; for esteem for their authors, which they may, in other respects, justly merit, must not prejudice us in their favour.

§ 7.

The technical language of Entomology is subdivided into three parts, which may be here concisely indicated.

The FIRST chapter contains the important and indispensably necessary general rules and principles for properly naming newly discovered parts.

The SECOND chapter treats of the general qualities of all, or many organs, which are comprehensible without a knowledge of their peculiar forms; but, on the contrary, in the description of the latter, must be frequently referred to. The differences of colour, and of clothing, annex themselves hereto. GENERAL ORISMOLOGY.

In the THIRD chapter I shall explain the various parts and organs of the body of an insect, as well as their peculiar differences. PARTIAL ORISMOLOGY.—(*Kirby's Exterior Anatomy.*)

FIRST CHAPTER.

GENERAL PRINCIPLES.

§ 8.

Although we here, at once, declare ourselves opposed to an unnecessary multiplication of orismological terms, yet we do not mean that the determinate distinction of particular parts should be rejected, whenever they are decidedly important. On the contrary, it is the very first requisite of a precise orismology to apply an exclusively proper term to each constantly distinct and peculiar part. It will certainly appear often difficult to restrain oneself within exact limits, particularly as there are but few other general principles to guide us than a certain, judicious, and intuitive tact. We will, however, commence by endeavouring to lay down a few principles as rules to be observed.

§ 9.

I.—Every decidedly different organ, or, where it appears necessary, every portion of an organ, should receive a name exclusively peculiar to itself.

II.—This naming, however, must not be arbitrarily exercised; but the organs of the superior animals must be consulted, and their analogical structure examined in the insect *.

---

* The greatest mistakes have, at all times, been made in opposition to this principle, and yet it is as absolutely necessary, and as strictly founded in the very nature of the thing, as any. It has doubtlessly occasionally proceeded from an ignorance of the anatomy of the higher animals; perhaps, also, from the love of innovation of many writers, that the most singular interpretations have been made,—names having been applied to parts, or merely portions of organs, which, strictly, could be applied only to very different organs. To call that part, the neck (collum), which bears the legs, is absolutely absurd. Even Fabricius's division of the body of an insect into *caput*, *truncus*, and *abdomen*, is wrong, as every one who knows anything of anatomy must admit that the *truncus* includes the abdomen. In the course of our observations we shall detect many similar inconsistencies, but we have generally considered it unnecessary to take further notice of them, confiding in the correct judgment of the reader. We have, indeed, endeavoured to retain, as far as was possible, what has been already done; but we make it a rule to adopt nothing that is false, whatever may be its antiquity, and notwithstanding its toleration by the great masters of the science.

§ 10.

III.—Great caution must be exercised in the naming of different parts in the several orders, as, frequently, the same organ in the different groups takes a very different form. If particular names were applied to such modifications, it would tend to mislead, by giving the appearance of different parts to one and the same. Nor is the reverse of this admissible, for different organs must not bear the same name *.

§ 11.

IV.—The names of parts should be derived, in prefereuce, from Latin, but it is advisable in those parts which have always been signified by Greek terms, to retain them, and introduce new Greek ones whenever new parts are discovered within the limits of the particular organs †.

V.—Peculiar organs, which, nevertheless, can only be considered as variations of a long known typical form, are best distinguished by an adjective expressive of the peculiarity.

E. g. The legs are called *pedes;* when adapted to the seizing of prey they are suitably called *pedes raptorii,* not arms (*brachia*) according to Kirby. The idea of arms presumes a certain organisation which is never found in insects, although the raptorious legs of insects may possibly be analogous in their functions. But it is certainly incorrect to call the anterior legs of insects in general arms; we might just as rationally call the fore legs of quadrupeds arms. Swimming legs are thus called *pedes natatorii,* but not fins (*pinnæ*).

---

* Fabricius made a mistake of this kind, in applying to what he had called *truncus,* in the Coleoptera, the name of *thorax,* in the Hymenoptera and Diptera; and, in calling by the latter term the anterior portion only of the same part, in the Coleoptera, Hemiptera, and Orthoptera. As in each of the orders of insects, the thorax consists of three parts, which have been distinguished as prothorax, mesothorax, and metathorax, it is evidently incorrect to call that *collare,* in the Hymenoptera, which is called *prothorax* in the Coleoptera, Hemiptera, and Orthoptera; for the same orismology must be applied to every order. Reasoning upon the same principle, we cannot see why that portion of the head should be called *hypostoma,* in the Diptera, which, in the other orders, has long been indicated by the name of *clypeus.*

† It consequently appears preferable to us to call the first segment of the *thorax* the *prothorax,* rather than *collare,* exclusive of the greater precision and comprehensibility of the first term.

VI.—In many such cases, however, where the substantive is borrowed from the Greek, a new word is formed by the compounding of two, e. g. hemelytra, prothorax, &c.

§ 12.

VII.—All fluctuating qualities of one and the same part are distinguished by adjectives, and indeed by such as, according to grammatical use, are customarily applied to such variations.

But the form of the adjectives, which express particular kinds of qualities, vary chiefly in their terminations. The following are important for our use:—

1. The termination in *atus* and *itus*, shows merely the existence of something in general : for ex. *antennatus*, provided with antennæ; *alatus*, winged ; *sulcatus*, with longitudinal furrows ; *auritus*, furnished with ears (two little appendages).

2. The terminations in *aceus* and *icius* express a resemblance to a material; those in *eus* indicate the material itself: for ex. *membranaceus*, resembling skin; *membraneus*, skin itself; *coriaceus*, leathery; *latericius*, resembling bricks (in colour).

3. The termination *osus* expresses fulness, or the abundant presence of a quality : for ex. *pilosus,* covered with much hair; *setosus,* covered with stiff bristles ; *squamosus,* covered with scales.

4. The termination *ius* expresses the uses or aptness of an organ : for ex. *raptorius*, adapted to seize prey ; *fossorius,* fitted for digging; *natatorius*, suited to swim, &c.

5. The deficiency of a usually present quality is indicated by placing in front the *a* privative in the Greek, and the preposition *e, ex,* or *in,* in Latin words: for ex. *apterus,* without wings ; *escutellatus,* without a scutellum ; *inermis,* unarmed.

6. To express quantity or particular distinctness, the superlative degree of comparison is used, or the words *valde, maxime, distincte,* are prefixed : for ex. *squamosissimus,* densely covered with scales; *rugosissimus,* very uneven ; *distincte-punctatus,* very clearly covered with punctures.

7. The indistinctness of a quality is expressed by prefixing the word *obscure,* or by uniting the preposition *sub* to the adjective. But diminutives are not unfrequently used : for ex. *obscure-æneus,* of an indistinct bronze colour ; *subpunctatus,* slightly punctured ; *substriatus,* slightly striated; *hirsutiusculus,* somewhat hairy.

8. To express a quality which is directly the reverse of the usual signification of the term, the particle *ob* is added, and we say, for ex. *obconicus*, of the shape of a reversed cone; viz., when a part, instead of running from the base upwards to a point, runs from the apex downwards to the point; *obovatus* is used in the same way to express its being of a reversed egg-shape.

9. Qualities which consist of the conjunction of two generally separated peculiarities are also expressed by the union of both the adjectives. In composing these words we must be particularly cautious in the succession of the united terms, as it is by no means indifferent. The word expressive of the dominant quality stands last, and that made to precede it is merely its modification: for ex. *punctatus* indicates being covered with punctures; *striatus*, having linear longitudinal impressions. By the various compounding of these two words, very different ideas are formed, according to their precedence. *Striato-punctatus* indicates a surface which is merely punctured, but the punctures whereof are placed in rows; *punctato-striatus*, on the contrary, is a surface which has distinctly impressed lines with punctures within.

§ 13.

VIII.—Parts which discover a certain resemblance of form with objects, which, by their application, or uses in common life, are sufficiently known, are suitably named from what they accord with. Many adjectives thence occur in Orismology which require no further explanation. This is not so usual in the terms expressive of colour, and particularly where it is desirable to explain the multifarious transitions of one into the other, we meet with difficulties in the selection of the exactly appropriate word, so that peculiar orismological terms are requisite for their correct definition.

SECOND CHAPTER.

GENERAL ORISMOLOGY.

§ 14.

This portion of Orismology has not the advantage of a consecutive arrangement derived from the nature of the objects contemplated, for it can be regarded only as consisting of a mass of equivalent ideas, with their applicable and variable attributes. But the best arrangement appears to be that of passing from the most general to the more partial terms; we have thought, therefore, but without wishing to prescribe it as necessary, that the most agreeable mode would be to proceed from the general form of parts to the differences of colour, clothing, size, direction, &c.

I.—The Form.

§ 15.

The differences of form may be considered, doubtlessly, as the most multifarious throughout the whole class of insects; it will not therefore surprise that this portion of Orismology is very rich in terms. But even this very great diversity leads us to conclude that certain forms are peculiar to a few organs only. All distinctions, therefore, which have merely this restricted application, are necessarily excluded from our immediate general consideration.

§ 16.

If we take any part and contemplate it in its natural connexion with the rest of the body, the following portions may be clearly distinguished in it :—

Base (*basis*), that portion whereby it is affixed to the body.

Apex (*apex*), that which is opposed to the base.

Contour (*peripheria*), a portion whereof is the margin (*margo*). According to its situation, this is distinguished into anterior margin, that which is directed towards the head of the insect; posterior margin, that directed towards its tail; and lateral margins, those intervening between the anterior and posterior.

SUPERIOR SURFACE (*superficies externa*), the INFERIOR SURFACE (*sup. interna*), the centre of the superior surface or DISC (*discus*), the border surrounding the disc or LIMB (*limbus*).

ANGLE (*angulus*), is that portion where two parts or the margins of one meet; SINUS (*sinus*), is a curved break in an otherwise straight margin; KEEL (*carina*), is a sharp, longitudinal, gradually rising elevation upon the inferior surface.

§ 17.

Besides these general definitions, which may be applied to all or very many organs, the differences of form may be contemplated under the following heads:—

1.—*Differences of Surface.*
2.—*Differences of Solids.*
3.—*Differences of Margin.*
4.—*Differences of Apex.*
5.—*Differences of Base.*

§ 18.

Figure of the Superficies.

CIRCULAR (*rotundum, circulare*), is a round surface with its diameter equal on all sides.

ROUNDED (*rotundate*), when the margins pass gradually into each other, and not meeting in sharp angles.

OVAL (*ovale*), a rounded surface, its two right angular diameters being of an unequal length, so that its longest transverse diameter does not pass through the middle of its longitudinal diameter, but lies nearer to one end.

ELLIPTICAL (*ellipticum*), allied to the preceding, but differing, inasmuch as that its greatest transverse diameter passes through the centre of the longitudinal.

LANCEOLATE (*lanceolatum*), when the base is not so broad as the centre, and the lateral margins slightly, but equally, swollen, gradually tapering towards the apex, where it terminates in a point, and the longitudinal diameter more than three times the length of the transverse.

LINEAR (*lineare*), a figure having the lateral margins very close together, and parallel throughout.

HALF-MOON SHAPED (*lunare*), a figure formed by the portion of a circle cut off by the segment of a larger circle.

HEART-SHAPED (*cordatum*), a triangular figure, having its base emarginate, lateral angles rounded, and lateral margins slightly swollen.

KIDNEY-SHAPED (*reniforme*), is a half-moon shaped figure, with its angles rounded, and its concave margin emarginate.

TRIANGULAR (*triangulare*), when the margins meet in three angles.

SQUARE (*quadratum*), when the four straight parallel margins are of equal length.

QUADRANGULAR (*quadrangulare*), when two of the margins are of unequal length.

OBLONG (*oblongum, parallelogramum*), a square with two of the parallel margins equal, but longer than the other two equal parallel ones.

ANGULAR (*angulatum*), when the angular margins do not exclusively elbow outwards, but also inwards.

FALCATE (*falcatum*), a figure formed by two curves bending the same way, and meeting in a point at the apex, the base terminating in a straight margin, resembling a sickle.

SPATULATE (*spatulatum*), a figure commencing with a narrow base, gradually widening by the lateral margins sloping out, and terminated at the extremity by a sudden straight line, (the antennæ of many *Tachina* and other *Diptera*).

LOZENGED (*rhomboidal*), a quadrangular figure, with two opposite angles acute and two obtuse.

§ 19.
Forms of Bodies.

SPHERICAL (*globosum, sphæricum*), a round body, having all its diameters equal.

HEMISPHERICAL (*semiglobosum, hemisphæricum*), a round body, terminated on one side by a flat circular surface.

LENTICULAR (*lenticulare*), a round body, with its opposite sides convex, meeting in a sharp edge.

CONICAL (*conicum*), a round body, the base of which is a flat circle and the apex a point.

SUBULATE (*subulatum*), a long thin cone softly bent throughout its whole course.

COLUMNAR (*teres*), a form the circumference of which is always circular, but its thickness indeterminate.

CYLINDRICAL (*cylindricum*), a body with its circumference round, of indeterminate length, but equally thick throughout.

ATTENUATE (*attenuatum*), a cylinder having its transverse diameter much narrower in one part.

EQUAL (*equale*), a substance of variable longitude, but the transverse diameters of which are equal.

INCRASSATE (*incrassatum*), much swollen at one portion of its length.

CLUB-SHAPED (*clavatum*), a form which gradually increases in thickness towards its apex, where it is obtuse.

PEAR-SHAPED (*pyriforme*), a similar shape, but with this difference, that its longitudinal section is spatulate.

FUNNEL-SHAPED (*infundibuliforme*), resembling the last in exterior form, but scooped out at its apical margin.

FORNICATE (*fornicatum*), concave within and convex without.

KNOTTED (*nodosum*), a longitudinal body swollen at one or more parts.

ANGULAR bodies are distinguished by the number of their sides, viz. three sided (*triquetrum*), four sided (*tetragonum*), &c.

PRISMATIC (*prismaticum*), an angular body of indeterminate length but equal thickness.

PYRAMIDAL (*pyramidale*), a triangular body, the angles of which all meet in one point.

WEDGE-SHAPED (*cuneatum*), a body whose horizontal longitudinal section is quadrate, and perpendicular transverse section triangular.

§ 20.
Differences of Margin.

ENTIRE (*integer*), a plain, flat, straight, or bowed margin, without angle or incision.

ARCHED (*arcuatus*) a margin in the form of a bow.

SINUATE (*sinuatus*), a margin with a rounded incision.

WAVED (*undulatus*), a margin with a series of successive arched incisions.

SERRATE (*serratus*), with jagged incisions, like the teeth of a saw.

CRENATE (*crenatus*), a margin with indentations, the exterior whereof is rounded.

DENTATE (*dentatus*), when the incisions are larger, causing the margin to stand forth free and direct like teeth.

CILIATE (*ciliatus*), when it is occupied with short stiff hairs.

LOBATE (*lobatus*), when the margin is divided by deep undulating and successive incisions.

EROSE (*erosus*), when from the irregularity of its incisions it appears gnawed (the margins of the wings of many butterflies).

TENTACULATE (*tentaculatus*), when soft tensile excrescences are found upon the margin (*Cantharis, Malachius*).

CALLOUS (*callosus*), a margin which resembles a thick swollen lump.

MARGINATE (*marginatus*), is when the sharp edge is margined, and surrounds the surface with a narrow border.

DEFLEXED (*deflexus*), when this sharp edge is bent downwards.

DILATED (*dilatatus*, or *amplificatus*), when the sharp marginal edge extends beyond its usual limits.

INCRASSATE (*incrassatus*), a margin whose edge is not sharp, but rounded, and somewhat swollen.

§ 21.
Differences of Base and Apex.

The few distinct differences of the base refer merely to its greater or smaller width, and robustness.

ANGUSTATE (*angustatum*), or COARCTATE (*coarctatum*), is where a part begins with a narrow base, and then dilates and thickens.

DILATED (*dilatatum*), a distended part, the transverse diameter of which is much longer at one particular part, and this peculiarity is generally found near the base.

The differences of apex are much more varied; we may enumerate the following as particularly important.

TRUNCATED (*truncatum*), when a part is limited at the end by a straight line or surface.

ROUNDED (*rotundatum*), when the end takes the form of a segment of a circle.

PREMORSE (*præmorsum*), when the end appears bitten off or splintery.

EMARGINATE (*emarginatum*), when the end has an obtuse incision.

RETUSE (*retusum*), when the terminal margin has an obtuse impression.

OBTUSE (*obtusum*), indicates a rounded termination.

ACUTE (*acutum*), when it becomes regularly narrower and terminates in a point.

ACUMINATE (*acuminatum*), when this decrease is very gradual, becoming thereby much longer.

MUCRONATE (*mucronatum*), when from an obtuse end a fine point suddenly proceeds.

CUSPIDATE (*cuspidatum*), when this pointed process is very much extended, becoming almost setiform.

II.—QUALITY.

§ 22.

Although the investigation into structure, and the consequential qualities of the organs, is more restrictively the object of anatomy; yet the precise definition of their various distinctions is of importance to descriptive entomology. We must not, therefore, omit defining orismologically these peculiarities of the structure of the parts, and the more so, as they are chiefly superficial. Under this head we shall accordingly treat particularly of the differences of substance, and of those of superficies, excluding however from this chapter those arising from individual substances springing from, or reposing upon the surface of bodies, such as hair, scales, &c. &c.

§ 23.
Differences of Substance.

MEMBRANOUS (*membranaceum*), is a delicate, flexible, transparent, thin, superficially distended substance.

CORIACEUS (*coriaceum*), is also a thin, flexible, distended substance, but is somewhat thicker, and opaque, resembling leather.

CORNEOUS (*corneum*), a thicker, harder, entirely opaque, and scarcely flexible substance, resembling horn.

CARTILAGINOUS (*cartilagineum*), is a substance combined of the qualities of membrane and horn; it is thicker than the latter, but somewhat transparent, flexible, and always whitish.

SOLID (*solidum*), is a substance consisting of one mass, with no vacant interstices.

POROUS (*porosum*), when small interstices or holes are observable upon the surface.

SPONGY (*spongiosum*), when soft and intersected by small channels throughout its substance.

TUBULAR (*tubulorum*), when a longitudinal cylindrical body is hollow throughout its whole length.

VENTRICOSE (*ventricosum*), when this tubular pipe suddenly distends into a large cavity.

FLEXIBLE (*flexilis*), a substance possessing elastic properties.

RIGID (*rigidum*), when it will not bend without breaking.

§ 24.
Differences of Surface.

SMOOTH (*læve*), a surface without either impressions or elevations.

LEVIGATE (*lævigatum*), a smooth surface, somewhat shining.

SHINING (*nitidum, politum*), when a smooth surface reflects, as if formed of metal.

LUCID (*lucidum*), possessing this quality in a high degree, reflecting with the brilliancy of a mirror.

SCABROUS (*scabrum*), a surface covered with small and slight elevations.

ROUGH (*asperum*), when these elevations are more perceptible.

VERRUCOSE (*verrucosum*), a surface beset with large smooth elevations, resembling warts.

TORULOSE (*torulosum*), when there are but few elevations spread about, but these of considerable size.

GRANULATED (*granulatum*), when small roundish elevations are placed in rows; MURICATE (*muricatum*), when dispersed elevations rise in sharp points; ECHINATE (*echinatum*), when they rise higher, and are thinner; CATENULATED (*catenulatum*), when longitudinal elevations are connected like the links of a chain, and are placed in rows; INTRICATE (*intricatum*), when the elevations and depressions are placed without any regularity, but close to each other; PAPILLULATE (*papillulatum*), when the dispersed elevations or depressions have a smaller elevation in their centre.

LINEATE (*lineatum*), when there are fine longitudinal elevated lines; COSTATE (*costatum*), when these lines are stronger, and the intervals between them wider; FURROW (*sulcus*), is such an interval.

TESSELATE (*tesselatum*), when the lineate surface is intersected by similar transverse elevated lines, as it were chequered (it is also used to indicate square scales); RETICULATED (*reticulatum*), when the stronger lines intersect each other like the meshes of a net.

STRIATED (*striatum*), when there are parallel longitudinal shallow impressions; SULCATE (*sulcatum*), when these impressions are broader and deeper than the preceding, or rather when they are of the same width as the interstitial elevations; whereas, when striate, these interstices are much wider; PORCATE (*porcatum*), on the contrary, when the sulcations are deep, and very much broader than the intervening elevated ridges; CANALICULATE (*canaliculatum*), is a surface, which has in its centre a broad, but not very deep longitudinal furrows; EXARATE (*exaratum*), when several such furrows with perpendicular margins, and wide, elevated intervals, run parallel to each other; ACICULATE (*aciculatum*), when many fine, frequently undulating striæ running either parallel, or interweaving each other, make the surface appear as if scratched with a needle.

PUNCTURED (*punctatum*), a surface covered with small impressed punctures; VARIOLUS (*variolorum*), when larger depressions are isolated, and resemble the marks of the small-pox; FOVEOLATE (*foveolatum*), or SCROBICULATE (*scrobiculatum*), when somewhat deeper impressions become narrower towards their bottom; CLATHRATE (*clathratum*), when such foveoles are placed in rows, having elevated longitudinal lines between them; FAVOSE (*favosum*), when these depressions stand close together, so that the surface resembles a honey-comb; ENGRAVED (*exsculptum*), when a variety of irregular longitudinal depressions cover the surface; VERMICULATE (*vermiculatum*), when the depressions are longitudinal and tortuous, like a worm-eaten stem.

The following distinctions are made with respect to the convexity or concavity of a surface:—

PLANE (*planum*), when the whole surface is of an equal height.

CONVEX (*convexum*), when a surface rises gradually to its centre, which becomes thus the highest of the whole.

CONCAVE (*concavum*), when the surface gradually declines towards its centre, thus becoming the deepest.

EXCAVATED (*excavatum*), a depression, the section of which is not the segment of a circle.

GIBBOSE (*gibbosum*), when separate parts rise higher than the rest; GIBBOUS (*gibbum*), on the contrary, is a surface, the section of which is not the segment of a circle; TUBERCULATE (*tuberculatum*), when the whole surface rises conically; RUGOSE (*rugosum*), when longitudinal elevations are placed irregularly like coarse wrinkles.

The inequalities, caused by a production of the true surface, are thus distinguished:—

ACULEATE (*aculeatum*), with slender pointed processes; SPINOSE (*spinosum*), covered with solitary, thicker, and frequently bowed processes.

UNARMED (*muticum, inerme*), when no such processes exist. The first word is generally used when terminal processes are wanting, where they are usually present.

III.—CLOTHING.

§ 25.

Having thus explained the differences of surface produced within itself, we have yet to notice those caused by individual substances lying upon or attached to it.

GLABROUS (*glabrum*), is a uniform surface, without this distinction, when according to rule hair (*pili*) clothes it.

PILOSE (*pilosum*), when covered with dispersed, somewhat long and bent hairs.

HAIRY (*hirtum, hirsutum*), when densely covered with short stiff hairs.

VILLOSE (*villosum*), when densely covered with long slender hairs, which rise upright.

PUBESCENT (*pubescens*), when the hair is soft, short, and decumbent.

CRINITE (*crinitum*), when the hair is very long, slender, and dispersed.

SERICEOUS (*sericeum, holosericeum*), when short shining hairs lie closely to the surface, resembling silk or satin in splendour.

LANUGINOSE (*lanuginosum*), when longish curled hair is dispersed over the surface.

TOMENTOSE (*tomentosum*), when longish curled hair stands densely and interwoven.

SETOSE (*setosum*), with dispersed long stiff hair.

CILIATE (*ciliatum*), when fringed with short stiff hair.

PINNATE (*pinnatum*), when stiff hairs, or thorny processes, occupy the opposite sides of a thin shank.

SQUAMOSE (*squamosum*), when covered with small broad scales which lap over each other; such a scale with a short stalk is called squama. When these scales are square the surface is called TESSELATED (*tesselatum*), PRUINOSE (*pruinose*), when covered with minute dust, scarcely discoverable by the lens; FARINOSE (*farinosum*), when the dust is more perceptible, resembling flour, and removed by the least touch; POLINOSE (*polinosum*), this dust, when yellow, like the pollen of flowers; PULVERULENT (*pulverulentum*), RORULENT (*rorulentum*), express very similar, scarcely precisely distinguishable qualities; LUTOSE (*lutosum*), apparently or absolutely covered with dirt*; NAKED (*nudum*), a surface without either a scaly or dusty covering.

* Many beetles that live upon a clay soil are always thus covered with dirt; for example, the species of the genera *Arida, Meleus variolosus*.

§ 26.

If the clothing be placed isolated, leaving free spaces between it, or if present upon only certain parts of the body, the following terms are used to distinguish these differences:—

FASCICULATE (*fasciculatum*), is a surface covered with dispersed bundles of long hair; a solitary one is called a FASCICULE (*fasciculus*); CIRRUS (*cirrus*), is a curled lock of hair placed upon a thin stalk; BRUSH (*scopa*), when the hair is short, stiff, and of equal length; SCOPATE (*scopaceum*), is a surface entirely covered with such a brush.

COMATE (*comatum*), when the upper part of the head or vertex alone is covered with long hairs.

BARBATE (*barbatum*), when a part, chiefly an opening, as the mouth, &c., is surrounded by long hairs.

PENCILLATE (*pencillatum*), when long flexible hair is placed upon a thin stalk.

FIMBRIATE (*fimbriatum*), when a part is fringed with hair of irregular length.

JUBATE (*jubatum*), when fringed with long pendent hair (intermediate legs of the male of *Anthophora retusa*).

IV.—COLOUR.

§ 27.

Colour succeeds to form, and the various qualities of surface, as the next most important character for distinguishing insects. Even in groups where colour cannot be used as a specific character, from its great and frequent variation in the same species (as *Coccinella variabilis*, Illig.), it then becomes important to notice precisely its differences for the requisite separation of the varieties of the species. In order to explain distinctly these differences of colour, terms expressive of the multitudinous gradations of tint produced by the various admixture of the several primary colours are necessary. But as we have not yet arrived at a general unanimity, which may be readily perceived by the comparison of the descriptions of the same insect by different authors, it is vain to hope that we shall here solve the problem of reducing the system to universal harmony. Clearly perceiving these difficulties, Lamarck, and after him Latreille[*], proposed a peculiar method for the definition of colour, whereby he thought he had removed every possible doubt.

[*] P. A. Latreille, Histoire Naturelle des Crust. et des Insectes. Paris, an. XII. Vol. i. p. 331, &c.

He considered three of the seven prismatic colours as simple primary colours; viz. blue, red, and yellow, and adopted them as the basis of his whole system, seeking their correspondent affinities in nature. Blue conducts on the one side to black, yellow to white. From the admixture of equal parts of the approximate colours, two new ones arise; viz. violet, from blue and red, and orange, from red and yellow; green is excluded, it being treated as the unnatural and irregular union of two colours removed from their true places (!). Thence we have the following series:—

Black, blue, violet, red, orange, yellow, white.

This series he inscribes upon a scale, divided into sixty equal parts; he places white at 0, and proceeding from 10 to 10, consecutively arranges them all. The modification, in the union of two approximate colours, is determined by their relative numerical power; for example, five parts black, and five blue, give black-blue; eight parts black, and two blue, give a very deep black-blue (bleu noir triple), &c. By this means, he obtains sixty different gradations of colour, which, we admit, frequently suffice for the description of natural colours, but do not certainly extend to all, for all unions of black and red, red and white, black and white, are wanting. This table is also rendered excessively defective by the entire omission of green, one of the most prevailing colours, and in the most variable gradations, throughout nature.

§ 28.

Eight primary colours are generally adopted in Natural History; viz. white, grey, black, brown, red, blue, green and yellow. Each of these colours admit of being mixed with others, and even some of those named are produced by the union of two of the rest. It is, therefore, evident, how excessively variable must be the effect of such mixtures of colours, and how very closely they approach to and pass into each other, so that the precise distinction of each change would be an ungrateful and useless task.

The degrees and intensity of colour are also very variable.

The following terms are in use to express some of them:—

DEEP (*saturate*), when colour is very intense or thickly laid on.

PALE (*dilute*), when but slightly coloured.

BRIGHT (*lætc*), when the colour is clear and vivacious.

FADED (*obsolete*), when it appears as if faded by the air.

SORDID (*sordide*), when the colouring is impure, and as if clouded by the admixture of another.

§ 29.

WHITE (*albus*), a pure plain white.
NIVEOUS (*niveus*), the purest, dazzling white of snow.
LACTEOUS (*lacteus*), white, with a bluish tint like milk.
CRETACEOUS (*cretaceus*), white, with a yellowish tint like chalk.

§ 30.

GRISEOUS (*griseus*), a mixture of black and white.
HOARY (*canus, incanus*), grey, with the white prevailing.
CINEREOUS (*cinereus*), a dark grey, in which the black prevails.
MOUSE-COLOURED (*murinus*), grey, with a yellowish tint.
FAWN-COLOURED (*cervinus*), grey, with a reddish-brown tint.
SMOKY (*fumatus*), grey, inclining to dark-brown, like the colour of smoke.

§ 31.

BLACK (*niger*), pure black, the colour of fresh garden-earth.
BLACKISH (*nigricans*), a bright black, inclining to grey.
ATROUS (*ater, aterrimus*), the purest, most intense black.
COAL-BLACK (*anthracinus*), a deep shining black, with a bluish tint.
PICEOUS (*piceus*), a bright black, with a greenish tint.

§ 32.

FUSCUS (*fuscus*), dull brown, a plain mixture of black and red.
BROWN (*brunneus*), a pure bright brown.
CHESTNUT (*castaneus*), a bright red-brown, the colour of the fruit of the horse-chestnut.
BAY (*badius*), a clearer lighter brown than the preceding.
FERRUGINOUS (*ferrugineus*), a brown, wherein red prevails, resembling the rust of iron.
FULIGINOUS (*fuliginosus*), a very deep dark brown, the colour of soot.
UMBER (*umbrinus*), a bright dark brown, with some yellow
FULVOUS (*fulvus*), a light brown, with much yellow.

§ 33.

RED (*ruber*), the usual red; the colour of burnt tiles.
MINIATOUS (*miniatus*), the colour of red lead.
LATERICEOUS (*latcricius*), the yellow-red of yellowish bricks.

Sanguineous (*sanguineus*), a deep red, with a dash of blue, the colour of fresh blood.

Purple (*purpureus* or *puniceus*), a bright red, with a violet tint.

§ 34.

Blue (*cyaneus*), pure dark blue of Indigo.

Azure (*azureus*), a clear brilliant blue, viz. wings of *Lycæna*.

Sky-blue (*cæruleus*) a pale blue, like the colour of the sky.

Violet (*violaceus*), a blue, with a reddish tint.

Pruinose (*pruinus, pruinosus*), a reddish blue, with a whitish covering, like the bloom of ripe plums.

Glaucous (*glaucus*), a bright blue, with a strong admixture of white, inclining to grey.

Cæsious (*cæsius*,) a greenish, grey, sordid blue.

Dark-blue (*atroceruleus*), a dark, deep blue, inclining to black.

§ 35.

Yellow (*flavus*), most beautiful, and purest in the colour of sulphur, thence sulphureous (*sulphureus*).

Stramineous (*stramineus*), a pale, less brilliant, but pure yellow of the colour of straw.

Saffron-coloured (*croceus*), or Orange (*aurantiacus*), yellow, with an admixture of red.

Ochraceous (*ochraceus*), a similar but sordid yellow, inclining to brown, the colour of ochre.

Luteous (*luteus*), a brownish yellow, the colour of clay.

Lurid (*luridus*), a dirty yellow, more inclining to brown.

Livid (*lividus*), a palish yellow, with a blue tint.

Testaceous (*testaceus*), a dull, yellow brown.

§ 36.

Green (*viridis*), the mixture of blue and yellow, the prevalent colour of the leaves of plants.

Œruginous (*æruginosus*), a bright green, inclining to blue.

Prasinous (*prasinus*), a light green, inclining to yellow.

Olivaceous (*olivaceus*), a green, with an admixture of brown.

Yellow-green (*flavo-virens*), a bright green, with the yellow predominant.

§ 37.

Besides the above terms, expressive of colour, several are used derived from natural objects, or from those in daily use.

HYALINE (*hyalinus*), expresses a transparent, colourless part.

PELLUCID (*pellucidus, diaphanus*), a coloured but transparent part.

OPAQUE (*opacus*), a clouded, not transparent part.

The brilliant or glittering colours are derived chiefly from metals or other minerals, to which they are exclusively peculiar.

OPALINE (*opalinus*, or *opalizans*), the prismatic reflection of the opal.

MARGARITACEOUS (*margaritaceus*), reflecting the prismatic colours like mother of pearl.

CRYSTALLINE (*crystallinus*), the pure transparency of crystal.

AMETHYSTINE (*amethystinus*), the brilliant colour of the amethyst.

SMARAGDINE (*smaragdinus*), the brilliant green of the emerald.

SILVERY (*argenteus*), the metallic white of silver.

GOLDEN (*auratus*, or *inauratus*), the metallic yellow of gold.

AURICHALCEOUS (*aurichalceous*), the metallic yellow of brass.

CUPREOUS (*cupreus*), the metallic red of copper.

ÆNEOUS (*æneus*), the green metallic colour of bronze.

CHALYBEOUS (*chalybeus*), the metallic blue of case-hardened steel.

PLUMBEOUS (*plumbeus*), the pale blue grey of lead.

FERREOUS (*ferreus*), the metallic grey of polished iron.

SPLENDENT (*splendens*), any colour having a metallic splendour.

§ 38.

There are also peculiar terms to express the painting of parts.

SPOT (*punctum*), a small roundish dark spot upon a plain surface; these spots must be distinguished from impressed punctures, but the latter are sometimes differently coloured from the rest of the surface.

ATOMS (*atomi*), are points not proceeding from the colour of the surface, but applied to the surface; they must, however, be so large and distinct that each can be clearly recognised.

PUSTULE (*pustula*), a point of larger circumference.

MACULA (*macula*), is a tolerably large angular spot, of a dark colour, upon a uniform surface.

GUTTA (*gutta*), is a light spot upon a light ground, viz. white upon yellow.

LITURA (*litura*), an indistinct spot, paler at its margins.

PLAGA (*plaga*), a longish spot of irregular form.

LINE (*linea*), a very slight, generally straight, but also sometimes gently bent, differently coloured stripe.

VITTA (*vitta*), a broad longitudinal stripe.

STRIGA (*striga*), a transverse band.

FASCIA (*fascia*), a broad transverse band.

ANNULET (*annulus*), a narrow differently coloured circle upon a surface, or upon the circumference of a part.

LUNULET (*lunula*), a half-moon shaped spot of a different colour.

OCELLUS (*ocellus*), a coloured ring, with a similarly or differently coloured centre. In the latter case this point is called the PUPIL (*pupilla*), and the space between it and the ring the IRIS.

From these terms are derived the adjectives of a similar signification, as *Elytra vittata*, &c. Besides these, many adjectives are used to express similar, but less peculiar painting, such as,—

IRRORATE (*irroratus*), when a space is covered with the above described atoms.

NEBULOSE (*nebulosus*), when a surface has different, lighter and darker and paler markings resembling the irregular colouring of a cloud.

SIGNATE (*signatus*, or *notatus*), is a part with distinct markings.

DISPERSED (*adspersus, conspersus*), when these markings consist of small spots standing close together.

FENESTRATE (*fenestratus*), is a dark surface, with one or more transparent spots.

MARMORATE (*marmoratus*), when the markings are variegated like marble.

TESTUDINATE (*testudineatus*), when the surface resembles the back of a tortoise.

UNDULATE (*undulatus*), when the markings are waved either longitudinally or transversely.

UNICOLOR (*unicolor*), a part uniformly coloured.

CONCOLOROUS (*concolor*), when resembling in colour to any other part of the same insect.

VERSICOLOURED (*versicolor*), when a part displays several different colours, indeterminately restricted.

DISCOLOURED (*discolor*). when the same part of an insect has different colours. (For example, legs are called discoloured when the anterior are red and the posterior black.)

IRIDICOLOR (*iridicolor*), a surface reflecting the prismatic hues.

V. Measure.

§ 39.

A universally known measure,—the Paris line,—the twelfth part of an inch, has been adopted as unit for the determination of the length of insects. This character is of considerable importance from the very constant uniformity of size, not only of the parts of the same individual, but also of all the individuals of the same species*; and thus the length of every possible part can be as precisely ascertained as the purpose in view may require. This mode of measuring has by far the advantage, and must consequently never be omitted when a species is named and published. The difference of size which immediately catches the eye is frequently the first best character whereby we are enabled, at the very first glimpse, to separate two, or more, closely related species.

§ 40.

Besides this universally applicable, absolute measure, there is another relative one. A portion of the insect is adopted as the unit, and by means of it, the length of the remainder is determined, or two or more parts are compared together, and thereby a proportional relation formed. This plan is also useful particularly when given in conjunction with its absolute length. The following is the mode of proceeding to the precise determination of the longitudinal proportions.

We must commence by measuring the whole length of the body and giving it, and then the length and breadth of the different divisions must be placed as in the following table:—

HEAD.		THORAX.		ABDOMEN.	
Length.	Breadth.	Length.	Breadth.	Length.	Breadth.
0,70	1,0	1,80	2,10	3,50	2,40

Such a table immediately gives the relative proportions of each

---

* This is liable to innumerable exceptions, but a familiarity with insects soon gives an idea of the range that it may be allowed, as it varies considerably in different species. It can never be permitted alone to determine a difference, unless supported by other characters which, in themselves, sometimes (particularly in colour) would scarcely suffice for a separation. Its use is consequently of importance for identification, exclusive of its value in determining the effects of climate and temperature.—Tr.

chief division to the other; and it is very easy, by a comparison with these, to indicate sufficiently the length of the limbs; as, for example, we might say of the antennæ, as long as head and thorax together; or of the wings, they are one-half longer than the abdomen. And the length of the legs, and their several joints, may also be thus shown.

Hausmann[*] was the first, as far as we are aware, who applied this method to insects, and A. Ahrens followed him, and which all writers of Monographs should likewise do. But it can scarcely be adopted in a complete system of insects (the want of which is now so strongly felt upon all sides) by reason of its too great prolixity. In such a work, the mere length must suffice, but which must never be omitted.

§ 41.

This precise and elaborate measuring of the parts has been endeavoured to be dispensed with by the introduction of a comparison with universally known objects. The width of the thumb (an INCH, *pollex*) has served for the determination of the length of large individuals. Half that length is indicated by the adjective HALF (*dimidius*), which is universally used to indicate half the size. We thus say half as large, *dimidio minus;* by one-half larger, *dimidio majus;* by one-half broader, *dimidio latius*, &c. In the same manner the comparative numerals are applied, *triplex, quadruplex*, &c. Thus, one-third as large, *triplo-minus;* three times as large, *triplo-majus;* one-fourth as large, *quadruplo-minus;* four times as large, *quadruplo-majus*. *Quincuplex* and *sextuplex*, are also, but very seldom, used.

§ 42.

EQUAL size is indicated by the adjective *æqualis;* a more considerable size is given generally without precise determination, or by the expressions *superans* and *excedens*. Very variable size, as well as the variableness of colour, are indicated by the words *variabilis, mutabilis.*

---

[*] Illiger's Magazine, vi. 229.
[†] Neue. Schreften der Hallis. naturf. Gesellschaft, i. 3.

VI.—AFFIXION, DIRECTION.

§ 43.

We have but few generalities to give upon affixion and direction, insects having but few exterior organs, and those applied in a uniform manner to the same place. But there are a few phenomena of greater universality, which we shall now refer to.

§ 44.

Affixion is of a double kind. ADNATE (*adnatum*) are those parts which form an immediate continuation of the base upon which they repose, and are besides immoveable. ARTICULATE (*articulatum*), are those parts which stand in connexion with the body merely by a flexible membranous medium, as sinews, &c., and possess a greater or less degree of motion.

Processes such as SPINES (*spinæ, aculei*); HORNS (*cornua*), or plainly processes, forms, merely distinguished from each other by their size, and often indifferently applied, require no general notice of their affixion, it being precisely the same in all.

In the ARTICULATION (*articulatio*), we distinguish the ball and socket (*Arthrodia*), whereby motion is possible in every, or very many ways (for example, between the head and prothorax), and the gynglimous (*gynglimus*), which admits merely of the flexion and extension of the two united parts.

§ 45.

With respect to the direction of parts, we distinguish—

ANTERIOR (*anticum*), lying near the head.

POSTERIOR (*posticum*), that approximate to the end of the body.

SUPERIOR (*supra*), placed upon the back.

INFERIOR (*infra*), attached to the ventral portion of the body.

BOTH SIDES (*utrinque*), indicates a quality or peculiarity found on each side of the body, and indeed at the same place.

BASAL (*basales*), are parts or organs arising from the base of another.

TERMINAL (*terminalis*), such as arise from its apex or end.

AXILLARY (*axillares*), are those which spring from the point of union of two others.

ERECT (*erectus*), a part which stands perpendicular upon another.

ADUNCOUS (*aduncus*), a part which gradually bows from the direct line.

NUTANT (*nutans*), a perpendicular part, the apex of which bends over.

DEPRESSED (*depressus*), a part which appears to have been pressed from above.

COMPRESSED (*compressus*), on the contrary, when the pressure seems to have been made from the sides.

REFLEXED (*reflexus, reclinatus*), when the margin of a part rises upwards; DEFLEXED (*deflexus*), when it bends downwards.

REVOLVED (*revolutus*), and INVOLVED (*involutus*), are also thus distinguished, but they indicate a greater degree of it—an absolute rolling up.

COMPLICATED (*complicatus*), is a part laid longitudinally in folds; REPLICATE (*replicatus*), when the apex bends round, and the part is thereby refolded.

A part prolonged or distended most considerably from front to back, is called STRAIGHT (*rectus*); when its greatest distension, however, is at right angles with the length of the body, it is called TRANSVERSE (*transversus*).

Note. Many of the general terms of other writers, of Kirby, for instance, are passed over, as their signification may be found in any Latin dictionary.

THIRD CHAPTER.

PARTIAL ORISMOLOGY.

§ 46.

HAVING thus concluded the examination of the general differences observed in all, or the majority of the organs, it now remains for us, as the subject of the following chapter, to describe the insect body in its separate periods of existence, and all the thence perceptible differences of its various organs. The illustration of its several stages of development first claims our attention.

§ 47.

Commencing our investigation with the first beginning of insects, we may lay it down as a universal law, that all insects originate from EGGS (*ova*). With the exception of the few instances, wherein the egg is hatched in the body of the mother, and the young thus born more fully developed, a species of propagation to which the ancients applied the name of *Insecta ovo-vivipara* (*Musca carnaria*, &c.), all insects are truly *animalia ovipara*. We must here indeed mention a second exception, comprising those *Diptera* which are retained in the body of the mother, until transformed into pupæ, and are excluded in an apparent egg-shell, but which is, in fact, the pupa-case. This species of developement is peculiar to a single family, which has thence received the name *Diptera pupipara*. Exclusive of these very rare anomalies, we may observe four distinct periods of existence in every insect, namely, those of the EGG, the LARVA, the PUPA, and the IMAGO, or PERFECT INSECT. In each of these states they are subject to manifold differences, arising from the various groups to which they belong, and to the contemplation of which we now pass.

I.—THE EGG (*Ovum*).

§ 48.

The shape of the egg in the several classes of animals is in general so exceedingly uniform, that a peculiar expression has been thence deduced for its definition. Indeed, in the class of insects, the majority of eggs are OVAL (*ovale*); but their shape is subject to so many differences, that it is necessary to enumerate the chief.

Perfectly GLOBOSE (*globosum*) they are very frequently, particularly in several families of *Lepidoptera*.

SEMIGLOBOSE (*semiglobosum*), likewise in several *Lepidoptera*; for example, in *Harpya vinula* (pl. i. f. 1).

CONIC (*conicum*) also among *Lepidoptera*, as in *Pontia Brassicæ* (pl. i. f. 2)

CYLINDRICAL (*cylindricum*), chiefly in such insects which lay them in numbers, and close together (*Gastrophaga Neustria*, pl. i. f. 3).

LENTICULAR (*lenticulare*), depressed, circular, and frequently ribbed eggs, as in the moths (pl. i. f. 6).

Other forms are TURBAN-SHAPED (*tiaratum*, pl. i. f. 11); MELON-SHAPED (*cucurbitaceum*); PEAR-SHAPED (*pyriforme*); BARREL-SHAPED (pl. i. f. 5).

Many eggs are placed upon long, straight (*Hemerobius perla*, pl. i. f. 14), or shorter, bent (*Ophion luteus*, pl. i. f. 16), footstalks, and are thence called PETIOLATED (*ova petiolata*). Others have at one end particular appendages; for ex. the EARED-EGGS (*ova aurita*, pl. i. f. 17) of *Scatophaga putris*, which, just before their apex, are furnished with two short oblique appendages, that they may not sink too deep in the matter whereon the insect deposits them; or CROWNED (*ova coronata*, pl. i. f. 19) of the water scorpion (*Nepa cinerea*), which are surrounded at their superior extremity with a circle of strong spines, for the reception of the following egg, whereby they hang in a row together, and do not inaptly represent the small, short-limbed branches of the horse-tailed grass (*equisetum*).

§ 49.

With respect to the surfaces of eggs, they are generally smooth (*o. glabra*), but also frequently uneven, or covered with a variety of regular sculpture. Some are provided with lateral wings (*ova alata*);

others with short ribs extending from one pole to the other (*ova costata*, pl. i. f. 5); others with delicate filaments, which show the segments of the embryo* (*Attacus paphia*). Other eggs display upon their surface cross lines and sculpture, which gives them a reticulated appearance (*ova reticulata*), *Hipparchia Hyperanthus* (pl. i. f. 13); in others these lines take a curve, so that the egg appears as if covered with tiles (*Hipp. Jurtina*); others, lastly, have decided knobs, making the surface rough and uneven (*Pont. Brassicæ*). We also occasionally observe in eggs irregular wrinkles and impressions, but which do not proceed from the sculpture of the superficies, and are accidental, arising from their drying after being laid.

The colour of the eggs of insects is, notwithstanding their great variety, not so variable as in the class of birds. White, yellow, and green, are the chief colours, indeed almost the only ones; for the few others, as brown in *Harp. vinula*, or green (*Cimex baccarum*), or banded (*Gastr. quercifolia*, p. l. f. 1), import but little, considering the greater universality of the before-mentioned colours. We occasionally observe very dark ones, even a black brown (*Culex pipiens*).

§ 50.

It is also interesting to observe the way in which the eggs are deposited.

Some lie solitary, and dispersed upon the plants and shrubs which nourish the young (*ova solitaria*.) Others, which are deposited within the substances, which serve the young as food, are called (*ova imposita*); for ex. the eggs of the *Ichneumons* in the bodies of caterpillars. The eggs of *Gastr. neustria* are placed in a spiral line around the young shoots of the plant that feeds the caterpillar (*ova spiraliter deposita*, p. l. f. 15); others form irregular heaps, which the mother secures from cold, and other prejudicial influences, by means of the hair of her body (*ova pilosa*, p. l. f. 4), for ex. *Liparis chrysorrhea, fascelina, dispar;* others again are concealed in lumps of dung (*ova glebata*, for ex. *Gymnopl. pilularius*); others are formed in the galls of plants (*gallæ*), occasioned by the punctures of the mother (*ova gallata*, for ex. *Cynips, Diplolepis, Trypeta*); many, lastly, are placed in close cells formed by the parents for this purpose (*ova favosa*, for ex. *Apis, Vespa, Pelopæus*). All these eggs adhere by a peculiar gummy secretion, and are thence called *ova*

---

* Lin. Tr. vii. 34.

gummosa; but such eggs as lie dispersed in any substance, as, for ex. the eggs of the house fly (*Musca domestica*), in dung, are called naked (*ova nuda*).

Besides those above indicated, there are many other differences, with respect to their mode of being deposited, which, as they are peculiar to certain genera or families, we can take notice of only in the natural history of such groups.

II. THE LARVA.—(*Larva.*)

§ 51.

As soon as the young insect breaks through the egg-shell, it is called either LARVA, CATERPILLAR, or MAGGOT. In this state it frequently appears in the shape of a long, more or less cylindrical, ringed worm, either apparently without a head and feet, or having a head only, or else provided with several (at least six) feet. In other, but less numerous instances, the young assumes the form of the parent, although necessarily much smaller, and always destitute of wings, whether the parent insects possess them or not. Both kinds of metamorphosis thus evidently differ considerably from each other from the mere form of the young itself; and in the progress of their development this difference becomes still more perceptible; for whilst, in the latter instance, the young one gradually attains both the size and perfect form of its parents by a frequent change of skin only, in the former species of development we observe, also after successive changes of skin, a state of repose, in which the insect neither takes food nor, in the generality of cases, moves—a period of its life distinguished by the name of PUPA STATE; and at the completion of this stage of its existence only, is it that the PERFECT INSECT, or IMAGO, bursts forth in all its beauty.

It was in reference to the actual differences of these modes of development, that the names were applied which are used to distinguish them. Taken collectively, they are called METAMORPHOSES; the application of which name may, doubtlessly, be justified by the decided dissimilarity of the same individual insect in its several stages of existence. The last kind of metamorphosis is called COMPLETE (*metamorph. completa*), because in it alone there is a true metamorphosis of the individual; the former, on the contrary, is called INCOMPLETE (*m. incompleta*), since in it there is, properly speaking, no change of form, but merely a repeated casting off of the exterior skin.

Although these terms are strictly derived from the condition of change, other writers, Fabricius for instance, have had different views.

The names he proposed for the, according to him, several kinds of metamorphoses are the following:—

COMPLETE (*m. completa*) is, according to him, that species of change wherein the larva is formed exactly like the perfect insect. It is found only among such as are destitute of wings in their perfect state (e. g. *Pediculus, Cimex*).

SEMI-COMPLETE (*m. semi-completa*), when the young resembles the parent with respect to form, but is as yet deficient in the wings peculiar to the latter.

INCOMPLETE (*m. incompleta*), when the young creeps from the egg as a maggot, and the pupa has free, distinct limbs, although quiescent (*Hymenoptera, Coleoptera*).

OBTECTED (*m. obtecta*), is the change only distinguished from the latter by the limbs, as well as the body, being enclosed in a hard corneous case, upon which their form and position are strongly indicated (*Lepidoptera*).

COARCTATE (*m. coarctata*) he calls, lastly, that change wherein the larva is a maggot without legs, and the pupa is enclosed within a round, almost egg-shaped, corneous case, upon which there is not the least indication of the parts of the perfect insect.

In opposition to this apparently very precise distinction of the different kinds of metamorphoses, we may object that many cases occur which will not admit of being arranged under any of those heads; for example, the larva of *Xylophagus* is without feet, and yet the limbs of the perfect insect are perceptible upon the pupa case; it is the same with the genus *Stratiomys*; and again, a footless maggot is transformed into a pupa with free limbs, as in *Ichneumon*. Exclusive of these considerations the idea of a complete change is most strictly applicable to what Fabricius terms incomplete, and his most complete, on the contrary, being evidently the most incomplete. It consequently appears to us preferable to adopt but two chief kinds of metamorphoses, as, as we have seen, between the several subdivisions, very many connective and alternative conditions exist.

§ 52.

The larvæ of insects with an imperfect metamorphosis, are to be recognised in general by their want of wings and scutellum (§ 76) with the exception of the few instances wherein the perfect insect has no wings. In such cases certainty can be derived only from their relative size in knonw species, as the larvæ are invariably smaller than the imago. In other respects, they wholly agree with their parents as regards their conformation; the same orismology consequently applies to them as to the latter, and with which we shall become acquainted in the description of the perfect insect.

§ 53.

All larvæ with a perfect metamorphosis have a long, generally cylindrical body, composed of thirteen more or less distinct rings or segments[*]. Many, which have neither a distinct head, nor feet, are called MAGGOTS (Pl. II. f. 1); in others the head is clearly distinguished, but the feet are wanting (Pl. II. f. 3); others again, in addition to the head, have six feet, which are placed upon the three first segments of the body following the head—these are called LARVÆ (Pl. II. f. 4. 6); others, lastly which are called CATERPILLARS (*Erucæ*), possess, besides the six horny legs of the three first segments, several membranous legs, called PROLEGS, upon the ventral and anal segments (Pl. II. f. 5, 7—12).

The portions of the body of larvæ, consequently, which chiefly merit our attention are, the HEAD, the BODY, with its various clothing, and the LEGS.

The HEAD (*caput*) always occupies the first of the thirteen segments of the body. In many cases it does not at all differ from the other divisions of the body, and is, like them, covered with a soft skin, and equally flexible and changeable in its form. This conformation

[*] With respect to the number of the segments, the text might create a little confusion; for Burmeister says, at § 57, in rather an obscure passage, as it does not clearly define whether he includes or excludes the head, that it consists of twelve segments; thus contradicting what he has previously said above; and Ratzeburg[*], in a paper upon the apodal larvæ of the *Hymenoptera*, figures them generally as consisting of thirteen segments, which is their true number,—the first and second of which become the head, the third, fourth, and fifth, the thorax, the sixth the pedicle, seventh to thirteenth the abdomen; but, at fig. 43, he represents the larva of *Apis Mellifica* with fourteen segments. Whether this arise from his having figured the larva of the male of that insect, I do not know, for the text does not elucidate it; but the accompanying figure (44) appears to be the pupa of the male, as it has seven segments to the abdomen. I am not aware that it has been before observed, that the larvæ of the males of the aculeato *Hymenoptera* will necessarily have an additional segment. Ratzeburg seems to take great merit to himself for having discovered that the larva of the *Hymenoptera* are headless, as he says, and seems to insinuate a censure upon Swammerdam, Reaumur, De Geer, Kirby and Spence, Latreille, &c., for not having noticed as much. It is evident that these writers considered the two first segments as the head, and justly; for although as yet destitute of the usual organs, they were in fact the head, only requiring further development.—TR.

[*] Nov. Act. Med. Phys. Acad. Cæs. Leop. Carol. Nat. Curios. t. VIII., pl. i. p. 145.

of the head occurs only in the maggots, which are destitute of all the organs observable in the heads of caterpillars, such as antennæ, eyes, &c.; but there are to be seen, in the anterior opening which forms the mouth, two horny bristles, which seem to represent the mandibles, which serve for the destruction of its prey, when, for instance, the maggot feeds upon other insects. In larvæ and caterpillars, however, the whole head is covered by a peculiar corneous case, which is divided into two by a perpendicular suture descending from the vertex, and separating in a fork just above the mouth. The general form of this covering is more or less round, resembling a hemisphere; in many instances it has a triangular, and often a complete heart-shaped figure (*Sphinx Ligustri, Smerinthus Populi*, and many others); sometimes each half is produced at the vertex into a pyramidal process (*Apatura Iris*, Pl. II. f. 16), or the whole superior part of the head is completely covered with thorns and spines (*Limenitis Amphinome*, Pl. II. f. 15).

As peculiar organs of the head of larvæ, we must notice the oral apparatus, the antennæ, and the eyes. All true caterpillars have mouths adapted to manducation, as have also all larvæ with horny legs, and, indeed, many without legs. The mouth is discoverable at the anterior or inferior contracted portion of the head; it is formed by the flat, longitudinally quadrate (sometimes taking the shape of a segment of a circle) corneous upper-lip, or LABRUM (*labrum*, Pl. II. f. 13, *a*); the equally strong corneous, horizontally-moving upper-jaws, or MANDIBLES (*mandibulæ*, Pl. II. f. 13, *b, b*); the weaker, but very similar, under-jaws, or MAXILLÆ (*maxillæ, c, c*), with their feelers, or PALPI (*palpi*), and the likewise flat, more or less triangular, horny under-lip, or LABIUM (*labium, d*), which also is very generally furnished with short FEELERS, or *palpi;* and this under-lip, or *labium*, closes the mouth from below, as the *labrum* does from above, whilst the closed mandibles completely shut the orifice in front. All these organs are also found in the perfect insect, and we shall consequently describe them more in detail when we arrive at that stage of its existence.

The ANTENNÆ (*antennæ, f, f*) are placed near the mouth, at the base of the mandibles and maxillæ. In larvæ they consist of but few, generally but three joints, or short narrow corneous cylinders, united together by a delicate skin. They are always of a bristly or filiform shape, even when the antennæ of the perfect insect are very differently constructed; for in caterpillars they present themselves as very short conical processes, while in the butterflies, which proceed from them, the antennæ are very long, and many-jointed.

Many larvæ are destitute of eyes, namely, all maggots with an undeveloped head, as well as many larvæ with a distinct corneous head-plate. The eyes of larvæ are always simple, and perfectly agree in form with those eyes of the perfect insect, with which we shall become acquainted as *ocelli*. They are also placed in the vicinity of the mouth, close behind the antennæ (*g, g*); they vary in number from one to six on each side; but the caterpillars of butterflies appear invariably to possess the latter number.

§ 54.

These, as well as the larvæ of the saw-flies (*Tenthredonodea* and *Urocerata*,) and those of the May-flies (*Phryganeodea*), possess, attached to their maxillæ, a peculiar organ, which Kirby and Spence very aptly call a SPINNERET (*fusulus*, Pl. II. f. 14), which is of great importance to them for the preparation of their cocoon. It originates from the anterior portion of the labium, and is a slight tube, obliquely truncated at its apex, and composed of several alternately corneous and membranous slips. It is through this tube that the clammy liquid passes, which has been secreted by two glandular organs for the preparation of the silk, and which can be spun into thicker or thinner filaments at the will of the caterpillar, by the power it possesses of distending or contracting the cavity of the tube. The larvæ of some *Coleoptera* and *Dictyoloptera*, which also spin cocoons, do not, however, possess this organ; but the silk is produced by an apparatus at the anus: a very different construction must consequently obtain in them.

§ 55.

The head is immediately succeeded by three segments, which ultimately, in the perfect insect, form the thorax. They are recognised in many larvæ by the short, corneous, articulated and conical feet, which are observed only upon these segments. In general they are constructed like the rest; but in the larvæ of many *Coleoptera*, particularly of the superior families, they are distinguished by a peculiar conformation; their exterior integument is corneous, like that of the head, whilst that of the abdomen is enclosed by a soft skin. Among the case or caddis-worms also (*Phycis, Phryganea*), which, as larvæ, dwell in a case made by themselves of sand and bits of stick, and wherein also they transform themselves into pupa, a similar construction is perceptible (pl. III. f. 1).

§ 56.

The LEGS (*pedes*) of larvæ take a different form, according to their position

The true LEGS, THORACIC LEGS (*pedes* merely, or *pedes veri*, Pl. II. f. 17), are affixed to the three first segments of the abdomen, and consist of several joints, like those of the perfect insect. Each of these joints is inclosed in its peculiar corneous cylinder; and it is only where these joints are connected, that a flexible membrane completes their union. By means of this arrangement we are enabled distinctly to recognise the joints analogous to those of the perfect insect, so that the leg of a caterpillar may be considered, as truly as that of the butterfly, to consist of the hip (*coxa*), trochanter (*trochanter*), thigh (*femur*), shank (*tibia*), and foot (*tarsus*). It is, indeed, true that these joints, particularly in caterpillars, follow so closely upon each other, from their shortness, that the whole leg has the appearance of a small conical process; but in many other orders, for example, in the larvæ of the *Carabodea*, the individual joints closely approach in form to those of the perfect beetle.

In general, all larvæ provided with legs possess the true legs, or thoracic legs; indeed, in most of the larvæ of the *Coleoptera* and *Dictyotoptera*, these alone are to be found.

The VENTRAL and ANAL LEGS, or PROLEGS (*propedes, pedes spurii*, Pl. II. f. 18), are short, thick, muscular, unarticulated processes upon the ventral and anal segments of many larvæ; they are exclusively peculiar to this second stage of existence, and entirely disappear upon its transition to the pupa state. In form, they are sometimes short cones, with an obtuse apex; sometimes longer thin pedicles, distended at their extremity into a flat SOLE (*planta*); sometimes indistinct, very moveable knobs or tubercles, which are protruded or withdrawn at the will of the larva. In these cases, the sole is very generally either half or entirely surrounded by a double or single row of short CLAWS, or crotchets, by the aid of which the caterpillar is enabled to attach itself firmly in climbing; the tubercles, on the contrary, are mostly unprovided with them; and, indeed, many of the prolegs of the first adduced form do not possess these claws. In many, particularly those whose sole is much distended, it is clapper-shaped, that is to say, composed of an exterior and interior flap, which move in opposition to each other like a pair of tongs, and thus form a claw. Kirby and Spence have constructed a tabular division of larvæ from these differences, which we shall here introduce for the purpose of giving a general view of them.

I. Larvæ without feet.

    1. With a membranaceous head of indeterminate shape (*Diptera*, Pl. II. f. 1).

2. With a corneous head of determinate shape. (many *Coleoptera*, the *Rhynchophora*, many *Hymenoptera*, *Culicina*, *Tipularia*), Pl. II. f. 3.

II. Larvæ with feet.
1. With legs only, and with or without an anal proleg.
    a. Joints short and conical (*Elaterodea*, *Cerambycina*), Pl. II. f. 4.
    b. Joints longer (*Cicindelacea*, *Carabodea*, *Hydrocantharides*, *Brachyptera*, *Lamellicornia*, *Coccinellacea*, *Neuroptera*), Pl. II. f. 6.
2. Prolegs only (*Tipularia*, and other *Diptera*, *Œcophora*), Pl. II. f. 2.
3. Both legs and prolegs (*Lepidoptera*, *Tenthredonodea*).
    a. Without claws (*Tenthredonodea*), Pl. II. f. 5 and 7.
    b. With claws (*Lepidoptera*), Pl. II. f. 9 and 11*.

Prolegs, in some instances, occur upon all the segments of the abdomen, and even upon the thoracic segments there are found legs resembling the prolegs in form, in those cases where true thoracic legs are wanting (*Rhynchophora*). But in the majority of cases, the first abdominal segment, or fourth segment of the body, has no prolegs, but they are sometimes observable upon this segment (*Œcophora*

---

* Burmeister, in this table, does not exactly follow that given in the Introduction to Entomology, vol. iii. p. 144. But why, after quoting it as that of Kirby and Spence, he should make alterations in it, it is difficult to say, particularly as these alterations are not material. But he refers to the German translation of their work; and, from not knowing that book, I am unable to determine how far it was the cause of the difference : but, to do justice to these authors, I give the table in their own words :—

I. Larvæ without legs.
  i. With a corneous head of determinate shape (coleopterous and hymenopterous *Apods*—*Culicidæ*, some *Tipulariæ*, &c. amongst the *Diptera*).
  ii. With a membranaceous head of indeterminate shape (*Muscidæ*, *Syrphidæ*, and other *Diptera*).

II. Larvæ with legs.
  i. With legs only, and with or without an anal proleg (*Neuroptera*, and many *Coleoptera*).
    1. Joints short and conical (*Elater*, *Cerambycidæ*, &c.).
    2. Joints long and subfiliform (*Staphylinus*, *Coccinella*, *Cicindela*, &c.).
  ii. Prolegs only (many *Tipulariæ*, and some subcutaneous lepidopterous larvæ, &c.).
  iii. Both legs and prolegs (*Lepidoptera*, *Serrifera*, and some *Coleoptera*).
    1. Without claws (*Serrifera*, &c.).
    2. With claws (*Lepidoptera*, &c.).—Tr.

Rajella*), and in the rat-tailed maggot (the larva of *Eristalis tenax*), which has no thoracic legs, but only prolegs upon the segments of its body. The following table presents an arrangement of larvæ, grouped according to the position of their prolegs.

1. Prolegs upon all the segments of the abdomen except the first (eight pairs).

The genus *Cimbex*, Pl. II. f.7.

2. Prolegs upon all the ventral segments, excepting the first and penultimate (seven pairs).

The genus *Tenthredo*.

3. Prolegs are wanting upon the first, antepenultimate, and penultimate segments (six pairs).

The genus *Hylotoma*, Pl. II. f. 5.

4. Prolegs upon the anal and four ventral segments, viz. the sixth, seventh, eighth, and ninth, Pl. II. f.9.

The majority of caterpillars, namely all the hawk moths (*Sphingodea*), butterflies (*Papilionacea*), bombyces (*Bombycodea*), as well as the majority of owlets (*Noctuacea*).

5. Prolegs upon the anal, and three ventral segments, viz.

   a. The sixth, seventh, and eighth.

   The caterpillars of many owlets.

   b. Upon the seventh, eighth, and ninth.

   Many caterpillars of the *Pyralodea, Hypenarostralis*.

6. Prolegs upon the anal and two ventral segments (*Larvæ geometriformes*), Pl. II. f. 10.

The genera *Plusia, Ophuisa, Acontia, Metrocampus,* Lat.; *Ellopia,* Tr.

7. Prolegs upon the anal, and one ventral segment (the last but three), *Larvæ geometræ*, Pl. II. f. 11.

The majority of the *Phalænodea*.

8. Prolegs upon the anal segment only.

Some moths (*Tineodea*), the genus *Lyda*, and many coleopterous larvæ.

9. No prolegs upon the anal segment, but upon four of the ventral segments (the seventh to the ninth), Pl. II. f. 12†.

The larvæ of many moths (for ex. *Harpya, Platypteryx*).

---

* Naturforsch. St. IV. p. 37, &c.

† This is a similar arrangement to that of Reaumur, in his second Memoir in the first volume, only somewhat modified and enlarged.—Tr.

Besides these, the larvæ of several *Diptera* have been described by different writers, as having, some, prolegs upon all their segments, and others only upon their first and last. Much irregularity appears to prevail in this Order with respect to the feet of the larvæ, which is clearly evinced from the descriptions of those of the different families of the Order. The preceding sketch of their distribution must, consequently, suffice for the present, until we proceed to their detailed description. A precise, and, at the same time, natural division of them, is scarcely possible, from their multitudinous differences; but what we have remarked above, we hope will serve, in some measure, as a guide.

§ 57.

We now proceed to the consideration of what still remains to be observed upon the construction of the body of the larvæ.

It has already been remarked, that it properly consists of twelve segments, which are separated from each other by slight constrictions. Beyond this, there are but few generalities to notice in it. For the most part, each of the segments, with the exception of the second, third, and last, has, on each side, a small longitudinal aperture, which is surrounded by a broad callous margin, and is called SPIRACLE, or STIGMA (*spiracula, stigma*), and by means of it the air is accessible to the respiratory organs distributed throughout the body. Many of the larvæ which live in water, have, instead of spiracles, membranous laminæ, or plates, throughout which the *tracheæ*, or AIR TUBES, are distributed, and which thus supply the function of gills, and may, therefore, be very properly called gill plates (*branchiæ,—aëriductus*, of Kirby and Spence). They are distinctly observable in the larvæ of many May-flies (*Ephemeræ Phryganea*). A similar respiratory apparatus is observable in the larvæ of many *Diptera*, although seated at a different part. Some bear, like the larva of *Stratiomys* and gnats (*Culex*), a coronet of a plumose form at their anus, by means of which they more easily sustain themselves at the surface of the water. In the middle of this coronet, or close to very similar appendages, are found the orifices of the tracheæ (compare the larva of *Dytiscus*); in others (*Eristalis*, Pl. II. f.8) a pair of thin tracheæ run parallely the whole length of the body, and their orifice remains at the surface of the water, while the larvæ themselves repose at the bottom of the puddles and pools.

§ 58.

Different from these peculiar appendages, which we may consistently consider as particular organs, is the spinose and hairy clothing of the majority of caterpillars. We may, indeed, admit that the majority of larvæ are quite naked; but this assertion does not admit of extension to the order of the *Lepidoptera*, for very many caterpillars move about enveloped in fur. The SPINOSE caterpillars (*larvæ aculeatæ*), are almost peculiar to the butterflies (*Papilionacea*), but the larvæ also of the tortoise beetles (*Cassida*), are armed nearly all over with longer or shorter spines, but particularly so upon the abdomen. In some we observe, upon each segment, four, five, six, seven, or eight simple, and indeed, not unfrequently, branched spines (*Vanessa polychloros*), which gives the creature a wild and forbidding appearance, and which may contribute much to the fear with which the common man in general views these innocent and harmless caterpillars. Much more terror is frequently evinced at the indeed larger, but quite naked caterpillars, of the hawk moths, which are furnished, upon their last segment, with a straight or bent horn (*Sphingodea*, *larvæ cornutæ*), of which it is fabled that it supplies the place of a poisonous and severely wounding sting. A few have, instead of this, a furcate process (*Harpya*, Ochs, *Cerura*), the branches of which are pierced, so that the caterpillar possesses the faculty of protruding slender threads through these tubes, for the purpose, as is supposed, of scaring inimical ichneumons (*Larvæ furciferæ*). But, with respect to their powers of injury, greater attention is claimed by the HIRSUTE CATERPILLARS (*Larvæ ursinæ*), which are completely clothed with long hairs and bristles, and which, from their stiffness and sharp points, will often cause an unpleasant inflammation upon a delicate skin; for, when rudely seized, the handling will cause it to lose its dense hair, which, by piercing the skin, causes an itching sensation, that induces the wounded person to rub the spot, and thereby produces a swelling.

To go into greater detail upon the forms of larvæ, appears unnecessary, as, in the natural history of each Order, a characteristic arrangement of their larvæ will be at the same time given, and to which we therefore refer.

III.—THE PUPA STATE.

§ 59.

We have now arrived at the third and last stage of development, viz., the PUPA STATE.

The pupæ of insects, with an incomplete metamorphosis, perfectly agree with their larvæ in form and structure; but those whose imago is provided with wings, have, at this period of their existence, the rudiments of these organs, as an evident mark of distinction. They may, accordingly, be distributed into two divisions—

1. Pupæ without alary appendages, which, according to the Fabrician definition of the metamorphoses, must be called COMPLETE PUPÆ, but which, according to us, are necessarily incomplete pupæ. To these belong the lice (*Pediculus*), the bed bugs (*Cimex lectularius*), many species of the genus *Phasma**, and some other wingless *Hemiptera* and *Orthoptera*.

2. Pupæ with the rudiments of wings, according to the former definition, *Semi-complete Pupæ*, but by us they are called *Sub-incomplete*. These comprise all the pupæ of the winged genera of the Orders, *Hemiptera*, *Dictyotoptera*, and *Orthoptera*.

Lamarck calls *nymphæ* all pupæ with an incomplete metamorphosis.

§ 60.

In insects with a complete metamorphosis, the pupa state is a very peculiar and characteristic period of their existence. Exteriorly a perfect stand-still appears in the process of development, for the pupa, in the majority of cases, is quiescent, and does not take the least nourishment to itself; but, internally, the greater changes are in progress. In a subsequent division of this work, we shall treat in detail of these changes, for we must restrict ourselves here to the consideration of the exterior form alone of these pupæ. We divide them into the two following groups.

---

* Or rather of the family *Phasmidæ*. They are all contained in the sub-family *Apterophasmina*, which comprises twelve genera in Mr. G. R. Gray's valuable "Synopsis of the Species of Insects belonging to the family of Phasmidæ," just published by Longman and Co., and to which we call the attention of Entomologists, as containing an elaborate distribution of all the known species of this singular and interesting tribe.—TR.

I. Pupæ which freely lie, hang, or are in any way fastened or attached in their particular element, NAKED PUPÆ (*Pupæ nudæ*). This mode of change is not particular to any individual Order, but it occurs, as well as the following, throughout all the Orders.

II. Pupæ which repose in cases artificially prepared by the larvæ; INCASED PUPÆ (*Pupæ folliculatæ*), which case is called COCOON (*incunabulum, folliculus*).

But these differences do not at all apply to the shape of the pupa itself. The following are the terms thence given by former writers.

COARCTATE and OBTECTED pupæ (*Pupæ obtectæ, coarctatæ*), are those which are inclosed in a firm, egg-shaped, corneus case, and which do not in the least indicate the parts of the perfect insect (Pl. II. f. 21). This transformation is peculiar to many families of flies (*Syrphodea, Œstracea, Muscaria*). The surrounding case is the dried skin of the larva, and, strictly considered, it is analogous to the cases of many insects with a *pupa folliculata*—for the true pupa, with its clearly distinguishable limbs, lies inclosed beneath this case. This kind of pupa is probably peculiar to all such insects whose larvæ do not moult.

MASKED PUPÆ (*pupæ larvatæ*), are those whose general inclosure is likewise a horny case, but upon which the different parts of the future insect are traced in lines (Pl. II. f. 19). Lamarck calls both these kinds of pupæ *chrysalis*, the former *chry. dolioloides*, the latter *chry. signata* (*Lepidoptera*, many *Diptera*).

EXARATE or sculptured pupæ (*pupæ exaratæ*), are such in which the limbs of the perfect insect are observed to lie free, although still closely attached to the body (Pl. II. f. 24). These Lamarck calls *mumia*, and particularly *mumia coarctata* (*Coleoptera, Hymenoptera*), whilst the pupæ of the *Phryganea*, which, in the last stage of their pupa existence possess some degree of motion, he calls *mumiæ pseudonymphæ*.

A naked pupa is called SUBTERRANEOUS (*pupa subterranea*), when, during this period of its life, it lies buried in damp earth. But if it hangs perpendicularly with its head downwards, as in many butterflies (*Hipparchia Egeria*), Pl. II. f. 20, it is called an ADHERENT pupa (*pupa adhærens*), but if placed upright against a vertical object, and supported by a delicate filament passed transversely across its thorax (Pl. II. f. 26), it is called a BOUND pupa. This kind is also only found among the butterflies (*Pontia Cratægi*). An incased pupa, whose cocoon remains partially open (*Saturnia, Phryganea*), is usually called a GUARDED pupa (*pupa custodiata*).

§ 61.

With respect to the construction of the body of the pupa, we find much more distinctly in it, than in that of the larva, the indication of the division of the body into three chief parts, the head, thorax and abdomen. This division of the body is shown by a constriction in the pupa case, as we observed, also, to be in the larva. If we, with Kirby and Spence, perhaps not quite appropriately, call this exterior sheath the CASE (*theca*) of the pupa, we may then divide it into the following parts, from its now more distinctly apparent exterior organs.

HEAD-CASE (*cephalotheca*) is the anterior hemispherical division, which incloses the head of the future perfect insect. In it we must again distinguish the EYE-CASE (*opthalmotheca*), the MOUTH-CASE (*stomatotheca*), which, in the *Coleoptera*, incloses the mandibles and palpi; or, as in many *Lepidoptera*, covers the protruding proboscis; and, in this latter case, is called by Kirby and Spence TONGUE-CASE (*glossotheca*). In front of the mouth-case lie the LEG-CASES (*podothecæ*), inclined towards each other at acute angles; very near to them, but directed outwards towards the back, the either long, pointed, or shorter thicker ANTENNÆ CASES (*Ceratothecæ*)*. Next to the head-case follows the TRUNK-CASE (*thoracotheca*,—*cytotheca* of Kirby and Spence), which is covered below by the WING-CASES (*pterothecæ*), which originating at its sides, embrace it in the direction of the abdomen. The form of the trunk-case is influenced by the different conformations of the thorax in the several orders, so that the three segments of the thorax are sometimes more distinctly discriminated; and, when so we may apply the terms PROTHORACIC-CASE (*prothoracotheca*), MESOTHORACIC-CASE (*mesothoracotheca*), and METATHORACIC-CASE (*metathoracotheca*), (*Coleoptera* and *Hymenoptera*); but sometimes, from the preponderating size of the middle portion, we observe all the three divisions unite in one (*Diptera, Lepidoptera*). Immediately upon the trunk-case follows the ABDOMEN-CASE (*gasterotheca*), which consists of nine (more or less) distinctly separated segments; and at its apex we observe the future anal orifice indicated; and on both sides of each segment the easily recognisable SPIRACLES (*stigmæ, spiraculæ*) are perceptible.

The apex of the last segment (*apex abdominis*,—*cremaster* of Kirby and Spence) it is still important to notice, from its truly innumerable differences. Very generally it terminates in a conical, either acute or

---

* Not *Cerathecæ*, according to Kirby and Spence.

obtuse process (*Sph. ligustri*), or there are two close together (*Noct. amethystina*), which sometimes, as in *Hydroph-piceus, Noct. lucipara*, hang downwards as long bent hooks. Sometimes we observe many little crotchets or points; and, also, as in *Harpya Fagi*, an indented pectinated process (P. II. f. 25, and other forms in f. 22 and 23).

If the abdomen terminate in a protruding ovipositor (*Sirex, Pimpla, Cryptus*), this, also, has its peculiar case (*acidotheca*); which, when the ovipositor is short, stands forth free (*Sirex*); but when much longer, as in *Pimpla*, it is turned round upon the venter, or the back of the pupa.

§ 62.

The superficies of pupæ is still more generally naked than that of larvæ. But few instances have been hitherto observed, in which they are covered with isolated bristles (*Hydroph. piceus*), or fasciculate (several *Bombyces*, for example, *Orgyia pudibunda, Pygera bucephala**), or covered with wreaths of hair. The processes, and angular or produced parts of the pupa itself, which arise from the form of the included insect, must be clearly distinguished from such clothing. With these processes may be classed the already described apical spines, and the also before indicated protruding proboscis of many *Lepidoptera* (*glossotheca*). In the hawk moths (*Sphinx Convolvuli, Ligustri*), it presents itself in an obtuse club, bent towards the body between the two first pair of legs; in the owlets (*Cucullia Tanaceti, Plusia consona*, and others of these genera), it protrudes as a clavate process beyond the legs, and then lies free opposite the first ventral segments of the abdomen. The tracheæ, also, of many dipterous pupæ which live in water, for example, of the gnats (*Culex*), in which they project from the sides of the thorax as two clavate processes, well deserve to be mentioned here.

Shorter processes, such as spines and wrinkles, arise from several portions of the body of the pupa, and exclusively belong to its case. Thus the pupa of the stag-beetle (*Lucanus cervus*) has, upon the sides of its first abdominal segment, several spines united in a bundle, resembling those of the *Hydroph. piceus*, in front of its thorax, or the pupa of an *Asilus*, figured by De Geer, with spines upon its head, and abdominal segments †. The pupa of the goat moth (*Cossus ligniperda*)

---

* Burmeister has evidently made a mistake here; for the pupa of *Pygera bucephala* is perfectly smooth The pupa of *Leucoma Salicis* would have been a better example.—Tr.

† Memoirs, 76, pl. 14, fig. 8.

has, upon the sides of each abdominal segment, a row of slight crotchets, as have, also, many other lepidopterous pupæ; in many they present themselves as elevated, somewhat notched, or indented stripes (*adminicula* of Kirby and Spence).

§ 63.

Many pupæ have other protuberances, which, from their shortness and thickness, can neither be considered as processes nor as spines, but are merely prominent angles, which equally proceed from the form of the inclosed insect, and are exclusively peculiar to the pupæ of some *Lepidoptera*, and *Diptera*. These forms are found only among the butterflies of the former order; of which they are, however, the characteristics of the majority. In general, two conical processes rise in front of the eyes; these appear to enclose the palpi of the butterfly, and are then called PALPI-CASES (*pselaphothecæ*); then the trunk-case expands in several lateral angles; but chief of all is the process upon the back, in the form of a long pyramid, or resembling a man's nose, so much so, that a pupa of this description, upon the first glimpse of it, looks like a human face, particularly when, as is often the case, there are dark spots within the impressions above the pyramid, which, consequently, have all the appearance of eyes. Pupæ, thus formed, are called ANGULAR (*p. angulares*); the rest, in contradistinction, are styled CONICAL (*p. conicæ*).

§ 64.

Before we conclude our consideration of the pupæ, we will add a few words upon their different colours.

All pupæ which are placed in shady, dark situations; for example, in the earth, or in water, or in perfectly obscure dwellings (as the obtected pupæ) are of a yellowish white, but which become darker upon exposure to the light; the rest, particularly the pupæ of the nocturnal and crepuscular *Lepidoptera*, and of the minute moths, &c. are of a bright brown when their place of concealment is within the earth, but they are darker when they are inclosed in transparent webs. The majority of the pupæ of the diurnal *Lepidoptera* have a greenish, or yellowish grey brown colour, many are speckled (*Pontia Cratægi*), others have large spots of a glittering gold colour upon the thorax and abdomen, and they alone thence obtain the name of *chrysalis, aurelia*, which names have been applied in general, but chiefly by early writers, to the pupæ of all the butterflies.

IV.—The Insect in its perfect State (*Imago*).

§ 65.

An insect, when it quits its pupa case, is called PERFECT (*imago, insectum declaratum, perfectum*). Upon observing it more closely, we immediately detect several divisions of the body, which have become now more distinctly separated than they were in the earlier stages of its existence. Henceforward we always observe three chief divisions, which are called HEAD (*caput*), THORAX (*thorax*), and ABDOMEN (*abdomen*). We will now take these parts consecutively, but prievously insert an observation or two upon the name of these creatures.

It is from this division of the insect body that the various names which have been applied by naturalists for the designation of the class, are deduced. Aristotle, the most ancient of all, called insects Ἔντομα, which word is derived from ἐντεμνειν, to cut in. His name, therefore, very evidently refers to the divided body of these creatures. The Roman writers followed the example of this great man, and called our favourites *Insecta*, derived from *insecare*, which likewise signifies, to cut in. This name was adopted by all authors, and Linné introduced it among the systematic names of animals, whence it has passed into almost all the living languages. The Germans have also long used the word, insect; but Oken, latterly, when he sketched his German nomenclature for all natural bodies, called insects *Kerfe*, a word which has doubtlessly the same signification, he having derived it as we surmise, we conceive correctly, from *Kerben*, to notch, or indent. Other German writers, as Carus, Wagler, Burmeister, &c. have adopted Oken's term, as having in fact the great merit of being of genuine German extraction, and which at the same time equally well preserves the advantage of a designation expressive of the predominant character of the class.*

---

* We retain this latter paragraph, which has rather a German than an English interest, in deference to the opinion of a very distinguished man. But it may be of use, from the German language having now become so prevalent and important a study, to explain a term which has not yet found its way into the dictionaries, and which, possibly, every writer may not think it necessary to illustrate when employing it.—TR.

I.—THE HEAD (*Caput*).

§ 66.

The HEAD*, the first of the three divisions of the insect body, displays considerable variety in its form. In general it approaches to the globose, or semi-globose, and is surrounded by a plain corneous case, and contains the different organs of the senses. From its simplicity, it is evident that we cannot so readily distinguish by peculiar terms particular divisions in it, as we can certain regions, and these must agree with the analagous portions of the head of the higher animals.

With respect to the most usual forms of the head, modifications of the globose seem to prevail, with the occasional predominance of either its longitudinal or transverse diameter. Thence proceed the egg-shaped, longitudinal, obtuse-triangular, heart-shaped forms, &c., which we meet with in so many groups of insects. It is very frequently produced into notches and prominences which are called HORNS (*cornua*); these are always integral portions of the corneous case, and are never articulated and moveable.

§ 67.

The following are the portions of the head most usual to note.

We must first distinguish the true SKULL (*cranium*, *calva* according to others), and thence proceed to the generally moveable organs attached to it; it therefore comprises the whole of the head, excluding the antennæ, eyes, and oral apparatus. If we wish to notice the upper part, from the front across the vertex to the posterior cavity, we call it UPPER-HEAD, SKULL-CAP (*calva*, *epicranium*, Straus†), Pl. III. f. 11, A. It is limited in front by the CLYPEUS (*clypeus*), called LOWER FACE (*hypostoma*, in the *Diptera* by Meigen and Bouché, the *epistomis* of Latreille), or that portion which lies above the organs of the mouth; it is bordered laterally by the sides of the head, and extends as far as

---

* In explanation of our occasionally differing from other writers in the nomenclature of the parts of the insect body, we refer to what we have said at § 9, II. and the note.

† Considérations Générales sur l'Anatomie comparée des Animaux articulés. Par Herc. Straus-Dürckheim. Paris, 1828. 4to. av. 10 fig. (p. 52, &c).

the eyes (Pl. III. f. 11, c). Kirby and Spence call this part the NOSE (*nasus*), and distinguish the anterior part as *rhinarium*, and the more lateral ones as *post-nasus*; certainly without foundation, for although many naturalists have supposed the organs of smell to exist here, none have yet been able to prove they do so, and we must therefore decidedly reject a name founded upon such a supposition. The FRONT, FOREHEAD, or BROW (*frons*), is that portion which intervenes between the posterior margin of the clypeus between the eyes, to where the head commences to be flattened above (Pl. III. f. 11, B). Nitzsch distinguishes that portion of it which lies between the eyes as MIDDLE HEAD (*sinciput*). VERTEX (*vertex*) is the upper flattened portion of the head upon which very generally the simple eyes or OCELLI (*ocelli*) are found (Pl. III. f. 11, a). In many insects, particularly *Coleoptera*, the vertex is not apparent, as they bear their head withdrawn into the thorax. FACE (*facies*) is the anterior portion of the head above the mouth, and includes the clypeus, the front, and the parts bordering upon the eyes. It is chiefly from the front and the vertex that the above-mentioned prominences originate, called HORNS (*cornua*), from their frequently not inapt resemblance to the horns of the ruminants. These parts are often covered with hair, which is then called HEAD HAIR (*capilli*); a fringe of hair seated upon the clypeus, over the mouth, is called WHISKER (*mystax*), and is found chiefly among the *Diptera* in the families of the flies of prey (*Asilica*) and the true flies (*Muscaria*).

The lower part of the head is divided into the following portions.

The GULA (*gula*, Pl. III. f. 12, D), or THROAT (*jugulum*) extends, according to Kirby and Spence, from the anterior portion, where the chin (see below, § 68) is attached, or from the orifice of the mouth in general to the commencement of the neck, and comprises consequently the whole middle portion of the lower head, and which Straus calls, from its being the support of the whole, the basal part (*basilaire, pars basalis*). In many of the *Coleoptera*, for example in *Geotrupes nasicornis*, it is produced into a smooth boss; in other instances (*Carabus*), this part is sloped, and its anterior raised margin, to which the chin is attached, is swollen into a thick callosity (Pl. III. f. 12 and 13, d.). When it assumes this form, some entomologists are inclined to call it, but very injudiciously (consult § 9, ii. and note) head-breast-bone (*sternum capitale*). Straus correctly considers this swelling as belonging to the basal part, and which he calls prebasal part (*prebasilaire*).

The sides of the head, from the eyes downwards to the mouth, are called CHEEKS (*genæ*, Pl. III. f. 14, E), particularly when they considerably protrude, as in some of the *Diptera* (*Myopa*). We again distinguish in them the anterior portion, extending as far as the articulation of the mandibles and maxillæ, or the commencement of the mouth, by the name of reins or LORA (*lora*, Pl. III. f. 13, E), and the posterior portion lying proximate to the eyes, as the TEMPLES (*tempora*, Pl. III. f. 13, F).

The back of the head around the commencement of the neck is the OCCIPUT (*occiput*, Pl. III. f. 12—14, G). In many instances, chiefly among the *Coleoptera* and *Orthoptera*, in which the longitudinally formed head is deeply withdrawn within the thorax, this portion is not at all visible, but it is prominently perceptible in the *Diptera* and *Hymenoptera*, which carry their heads free. The aperture behind the head, through which the internal organs are continued, is called the OCCIPITAL FORAMEN (*foramen occipitale*).

In many insects the commencement of the neck is likewise an integral portion of the head. The NECK (*collum*) is that part which unites the head with the thorax. In the majority it is merely a membranous tube, and it is among a few of the *Coleoptera* only (*Staphylinus, Leptura*) that the back of the head is constructed into a short corneous cylinder, to which the membrane of the neck is attached. Some entomologists call this part the COLLAR (*collare*), a name which is applied by others (for example, Klug, Kirby and Spence,) to the prothorax of the *Hymenoptera*.

THE MOUTH (*Os*).

§ 68.

From this consideration of the different parts of the head we pass on to the investigation of the several organs attached to it. These are the PARTS OF THE MOUTH, the ANTENNÆ, and the EYES.

The ORAL ORGANS, or parts of the mouth (*partes oris, instrumenta cibaria, trophi*) lie at the anterior, or inferior part of the head, and surround the MOUTH (*os*). When attached to a long corneous and generally cylindrical prolongation of the head, this part is called the snout or ROSTRUM (*rostrum*), which, however, must be well distinguished from the proboscidal prolongation of the oral organs themselves; the rostrum being merely a continuation of the corneous covering of the head, and not a distinct organ.

PARTIAL ORISMOLOGY.

The exact description and knowledge of the oral organs is of great importance in Systematic Entomology, as these parts supply the characters of many genera, and not rarely of entire families: we must, consequently, here give a very precise definition of their forms.

In the first place we must distinguish the BITING organs (*instr. cib. mordentia, s. libera*) from the SUCKING ones (*instr. cib. suctoria*); and the former are also specially called MASTICATING organs (*instr. masticandi*); these stand freely beside each other, and display much uniformity in their structure as well as great regularity of shape *, whereby they announce a superior degree of development, so much so, that insects with a masticating mouth, notwithstanding its very similar conformation, take the precedence of those with suctorial organs. The latter are more or less united together, and assume very different shapes in the several orders, of which we shall particularly treat below.

The masticating mouth (as found in the *Coleoptera, Dictyotoptera, Neuroptera,* and many *Hymenoptera*) consists of the following organs: —

The upper lip, LABRUM, (*labrum, labium superius,* Pl. III. f. 11. i), is very generally of the form of a segment of the circle, or a triangular, or quadrangular, somewhat convex corneous plate, which is united posteriorly by a membranous hinge with the clypeus. Fabricius † originally called this organ *clypeus*, in which he was followed by Illiger ‡. This latter writer applied the name of *labrum* to the narrow anterior appendage of the true labrum, which is very seldom present, but is found in some of the *Hymenoptera* (*Hylæus* §), and is called by Kirby and Spence the APPENDICLE (*appendicula*).

The upper jaws or MANDIBLES (*mandibulæ*, Pl. III. f. 11—13. o, o), which are two strong, corneous, somewhat bent hooks, their inner margin being more or less dentate; and which articulate with the cheeks at their broad basis, and move by ginglymus, opposed to each other like the blades of scissors.

The under jaws or MAXILLÆ (*maxillæ*, Pl. III. f. 12 and 13, P, P), are also a pair of organs which in many respects resemble the mandibles, although smaller and more delicately constructed. They are not simple, but distinctly consist of four pieces. The two first hang attached to

---

* See what Kirby and Spence say upon their variety, Introduction to Entomology, vol. iii. p. 473; what Burmeister says above must be taken comparatively.—TR.

† Philosoph. Entom., p. 37.   ‡ Terminologie, p. 220.

§ Burmeister says it is the genus *Hylæus*, without indicating that he means of Fabricius. I know it only in the females of the genus *Halictus*, which are comprised in the above genus of Fabricius.—TR.

each other as well as to the head and labium by means of soft ligaments; the lowest, the HINGE, (*cardo*, Pl. III. f. 16 and 17, 1, 1, or the BASE, *pars basalis;*—according to Straus, *branche transversale,*) is narrow, thin and transverse, and articulates with the throat, forming a right angle with the one that follows it, which is the STALK (*stipes*, *pièce dorsale* of Straus, 2, 2 of the same figure), and is thicker, stronger, and larger, and above somewhat horny, but beneath softer and membranaceous. Closely attached to this is the third piece, which is a corneous scale, at the anterior margin of which the palpus is inserted (thence called *squamæ palpiferæ*, by Straus), and which forms beneath the case or covering of the maxilla. The fourth piece (the same plate and figure, 4, 4) borders upon the two preceding, and is completely horny, hooked, its interior margin concave, or, as well as the stalk, covered with short stiff bristles. It is called the MAXILLARY LOBE (*lobus maxillæ,—intermaxillaire* of Straus), from its more generally taking the appearance of a superior appendage of the stalk. In many insects, particularly the *Hymenoptera* and coprophagous *Petalocera* among the beetles (for example, *Copris, Aphodius*), it is a simple, variously formed, flat, coriaceous scale, with its margin beset with short hair; in others, as among the Capricorn beetles (*Lamia, Cerambyx*), it is thicker, and more solid and compact, and is divided into a harder, INTERNAL (*lobus internus*), and more membranaceous, EXTERNAL LOBE (*lobus externus*). This exterior lobe is the same organ which in the *Orthoptera* covers the internal lobe like a cap, and then takes the name of HELMET (*galea*—Pl. III. f. 17, 5 of *Cychrus*, Pl. IV. f. 2, 5 of *Copris*). In many insects it is wanting; in other instances it occurs as a two-jointed filiform appendage, and this is then the second internal maxillary palpus, as already Illiger * very correctly indicated. It is exactly where the lobes border upon the stalk that the maxillary palpi are also inserted.

The underlip, or LABIUM (plainly *labium*, or *labium inferius*), which is that organ that assists to close the orifice of the mouth from below (Pl. III. f. 12 and 13, Q). It consists of two chief parts, each of which may be considered as a separate organ;—these are,

The CHIN (*mentum*, Pl. IV. f. 3 and 4, A, A), a thin, sometimes triangular, sometimes of the shape of a segment of a circle, or trapezoidal corneous plate, deeply emarginated upon its anterior side, and connected, like the upper lip, to the clypeus, by means of a membrane,

* See Kæfer Preussens, 1 Vorrede, p. xxxvi. note 15.

with the margin of the throat (the *sternum capitale* of some entomologists), and forms from beneath the inferior covering of the mouth.

The TONGUE (*ligula*, Fab.; *lingua*, Kirby and Spence, Pl. IV. f. 4, B) reposes internally upon the chin. It is, in general, a membranaceous or more or less fleshy organ, which frequently protrudes beyond the anterior margin of the chin, in which case its exterior inferior side is horny; this horny part is then called TONGUE-BONE (*os hyoideum*), or FULCRUM (*fulcrum*). The LABIAL PALPI (*palpi labiales*) are close to this, and indeed frequently inserted upon it. The upper fleshy part, the true tongue, is frequently simple, and visibly separated from the chin (Pl. IV. f. 5), as in the *Orthoptera* and *Neuroptera*; in other cases it is divided, and very closely connected with that organ (*Coleoptera*). In the wasps it is separated into several (three or four) lobes. In the bees it projects as a long cylindrical, frequently pubescent, retractile filament: in some of the fossores (*Scolia*) this filament is divided into three.

Illiger and Latreille call the tongues of insects with a masticating mouth the *labium*; in Fabricius, on the contrary, the *labium* is sometimes our *mentum*, and sometimes, when the chin and tongue are not distinctly separated, the whole inferior flap of the mouth.

The already frequently mentioned FEELERS (*palpi*) are the auxiliary organs of a masticating mouth; they are many-jointed and but seldom simple appendages, inserted upon the maxillæ and labium. Those upon the maxillæ, the MAXILLARY FEELERS (*palpi maxillares*, Pl. III. f. 16, A), generally originate from where the scale is connected with the external lobe, and are united to it by a very supple hinge. The LABIAL FEELERS (*palpi labiales*, Pl. IV. f. 3. c, c) are placed laterally upon the labium, close to the tongue, more or less approximate to the part where it projects beyond the chin (*Cerambycina, Carabodea*); in other instances they are decidedly inserted in the margin of the chin (*Libellula, Lamellicornia*). The number of the joints of these organs, whose length, form, and relation to each other, is very various, never exceeds SIX; and, in general, the labial palpi have fewer joints than the maxillary. We have already spoken of a third two-jointed pair of feelers—the INTERNAL MAXILLARY PALPI (*palpi maxillares interni*, Pl. III. f. 17, 5, and Pl. IV. f. 10, 5), which are found only in the tiger beetles (*Cicindelacea*), the *Carabodea*, and the water beetles, and which are analogous to the HELMET (*galea*) of the *Orthoptera*.

§ 69.

Before we pass on to our general consideration of the organs of the suctorial mouth, we must give the most remarkable differences of the above-named masticating organs; but we will first notice the relations of the head to the thorax, as well as the proportions of its own parts.

We observe in the head the direction in which its longitudinal diameter stands to the axis of the body. If they form one plane, it is called PROMINENT (*prominens, Elater*); PORRECT when it projects, likewise horizontally, far from the thorax (*Agra*); NUTANT (*nutans*) when its longitudinal diameter forms an obtuse angle with the axis of the body (*Feronia, Amara, Harpalus*; PERPENDICULAR (*perpendiculare*) is when its longitudinal diameter forms a right angle with the axis of the body (*Saperda, Diptera, Hymenoptera*).

We must next observe the manner of its connection with the thorax.

FREE (*exsertum* or *liberum*) is a distinctly visible head, never covered by the thorax (*Agra, Anthia, Hymenoptera, Diptera*).

INSERTED (*insertum*), when it is partly, particularly the occiput, concealed within the thorax.

RETRACTED (*retractum*), when it is concealed as far as the brow within the thorax (*Buprestis*).

CONCEALED (*absconditum*), when it is entirely withdrawn within the thorax, or is covered above by the thoracic plate (*Cassida*).

RETRACTILE (*retractile*) when a thus concealed head can be pushed forwards at the will of the insect (*Hister*).

VERSATILE (*versatile*), when it can be freely moved every way (*Hymenoptera, Diptera*).

From its anterior margin it is distinguished into CLYPEATE HEAD (*c. clypeatum*, Pl. IV. f. 6), when tolerably flat, and the margin of the clypeus and the front are produced into a broad border (*Copris, Onthophagus, Ateuchus*); TURRETED (*c. turritum*, Pl. IV. f. 7), when it is produced anteriorly and above into a pyramidal point (*Truxalis*). We have already mentioned HORNED (*c. cornutum*) and ROSTRATE (*c. rostratum*) heads. A head furnished with swollen cheeks is called BUCCATE (*c. buccatum*, Pl. IV. f. 1, *Myopa*).

With respect to the differences of the masticating organs themselves, we shall proceed as we did in their description, by taking them consecutively.

The upper lip, or labrum, differs as to its figure, surface, margin, and relation to the other organs of the mouth; there are, however, no differences exclusively peculiar to it, and we may consequently refer to General Orismology for the notification of its discrepancies, without the necessity of repeating them here.

In explaining the construction of the upper jaws (*mandibulæ*, Pl. IV. f. 8), Kirby and Spence have, and we think very happily, instituted a comparison with those of the superior animals. They consequently distinguish the PROSTHECA (*prostheca*) in the mandibles, which is a cartilaginous process, near the base within, and is found very generally among the *Brachyptera;* for example, in *Staphylinus maxillosus*. They call TEETH (*dentes*) the pointed processes on the inner side, and very skilfully distinguish the superior, compressed, sharp edge as CUTTING TEETH (*dentes incisivi*, the same figure, *a*); or they call them CANINE TEETH (*dentes laniarii, s. canini*), when they are very sharp and conical. GRINDING TEETH (*dentes molares*) are the inferior thicker teeth, provided with a broad grinding surface (*Melolontha*). The MOLA, or grinding surface (*mola*, the same fig. *b*), they call the broad, flat, and often, like the teeth of the elephant, ridged space of the molares of many insects (for example, of the *Bombi*, *Melolontha*, &c.). In the *Coleoptera*, this molar tooth is clothed laterally with short stiff hair, which Straus calls the BRUSH (*brosse*). The processes at the base are also important, from their supplying the articulation of the mandible with the head; they are three in number, and are placed at the ends of the edges, beneath which the three surfaces of the mandibles join. The lower one, viewing the mandible in its natural position, is shaped like a ball, and corresponds with a cavity, or socket, in the head. The upper one, on the contrary, is concave, and consequently forms a socket corresponding with the ball upon the head-case (the same fig. *d*). The third is less observable, and lies within towards the orifice of the mouth, at the end of the masticating edge of the mandible (the same fig. *e*). The *musc. adductor mandibulæ* is attached to it; its antagonist, the *musc. abductor*, is inserted in the exterior margin, between the two articulating processes. The upper jaws very generally consist of a firm corneous substance (*mandib. corneæ*); in other instances they are membranaceous (*m. membranaceæ*), as in the *Lamellicornia coprophaga:* in these also they have in general a hooked shape. In the *Hemiptera*, and many *Diptera*, they are SETACEOUS (*m. setaceæ, setæ rostri*); but in other families of the latter order (*Tabanica*) they are LANCEOLATE (*m. lanceolatæ*).

Very similar forms are observable in the under jaws (*maxillæ*). The teeth upon the inner margin of the maxillæ, when present, are more uniform, finer, and more delicate; they are frequently, however, wholly deficient, and in lieu of them there are short bristles. In other instances the whole superior process of the under jaw is clothed with short hair, and such maxillæ are called PENICILLATE (*max. penicillatæ*, Pl. IV. f. 9); for example, in *Lucanus*. But this superior lobe presents itself much more generally as a pergameneous, variously-shaped plate (*max. membranaceæ*, Pl. IV. f. 2). They are SETOSE (*max. setosæ, s. setæ rostri inferiores*) in the *Hemiptera* and many *Diptera*; in some of the latter (*Tabanica*) also LANCEOLATE (*max. lanceolatæ*). They are UNGUICULATE (*m. unguiculatæ*), when the terminal tooth is moveable, and can be moved to, and withdrawn from, the internal margin of the superior lobe at the will of the insect (Pl. IV. f. 10). This superior development of the lower jaw has hitherto been detected only in the tiger beetles (*Cicindelacea*).

We shall find the differences of the labium much more various than any of the yet examined organs, probably by reason of its being more compact than either of the others.

We will first observe the chin, upon which we may almost repeat what we said above of the labrum; the differences of form are also found in many other organs, and thus, as GENERAL, have been already described in the first chapter. One peculiarity is its being more or less deeply divided into two or three lobes, as well as its globose convexity in the dragon-flies (*Libellulina*, Pl. IV. f. 11). The tongue also has but few exclusive peculiarities, and these we have already mentioned; consequently nothing further remains to be said upon it. The under-lip of the larvæ of the dragon-flies is of a very singular nature. The chin is a thin stalk, which, in its pliable articulation, can be withdrawn to the prothorax. Attached to it in front, and similarly articulated, is the flattened, nearly longitudinal, heart-shaped tongue, which, in repose, closes the orifice of the mouth, but which can also be distended as a prehensile instrument. In front of the tongue there are two claws, which, like the nippers of a pair of tongs, move in opposition to each other, and thus capture objects between them. With these the larva seizes its food, which consists of small water-insects, and then withdraws its chin and tongue, so that its prey is brought directly in front of the orifice of the mouth, when it very quietly sucks the insect dry. The claws are analogous to the labial palpi.

Much more various is the construction of the palpi. With respect to the number of their joints they are subject to great variety; but the maxillary palpi have never more than SIX, and the labial palpi but seldom so many as FOUR joints. In every order a certain relation between their numbers appears to be followed, to which, however, there are a few exceptions. In the *Coleoptera*, for example, the maxillary palpi have very generally four joints—the labial palpi three; in the *Orthoptera*, the former five—the latter three; in the *Hymenoptera*, the former six—the latter four, but with very many exceptions, particularly in the maxillary palpi; for example, *Sirex* has but one joint. Among the *Neuroptera* these numbers are five and three; among the *Lepidoptera*, two, or more rarely three joints in both; the *Diptera* have one, two, or four joints. The *Hemiptera* are destitute of palpi; but if the jointed sheath of the promuscis may be considered to represent them, we shall also here very generally find three or five joints.

The most usual shape of the feelers is FILIFORM (*palpi filiformes*, Pl. IV. f. 12, *a*); that is to say, such which have all their joints of an equal cylindrical shape; MONILIFORM (*p. moniliformes*), when the joints are globose, like beads; SETACEOUS (*p. setacei*), when tolerably long palpi become gradually thinner, and the last is pointed. On the contrary, they are CONICAL (*p. conici*, Pl. IV. f. 13, *a*), when the joints are very short, and each successive one is smaller than the preceding (the *Curculionodea*). The greatest differences, nevertheless, proceed from the form of the terminal joint, for the first ones are almost invariably cylindrical or ovate, and the last only differs in its form. We have thence the following designations:—

SECURIFORM (*p. securiformes*, Pl. IV. f. 14), when the last joint is broadly triangular, and hangs by a point to the preceding (*Securi palpata*).

LUNATE (*p. lunati*, Pl. IV. f. 15), when the same joint has the form of a half-moon (*Oxyporus*).

FASCICULATE (*p. fasciculati*, Pl. IV. f. 16), when it is split into many threads and processes (*Lymexylon*).

LAMELLATE (*p. lamellati*, Pl. IV. f. 17), when they are divided longitudinally or transversely into several leaves (*Atractocerus*).

SUBULATE (*p. subulati*, Pl. IV. f. 19), when the last joint forms with the preceding a fine and delicate termination (*Trechus*).

CLAVATE (*p. clavati*, Pl. IV. f. 20), when the whole organ becomes thicker towards its apex (*Trox*).

WEDGE-SHAPED (*p. cuneiformes*), when the last joint has the form of a wedge, which is attached by its sharp end to the preceding joint (*Carabus, Calosoma, Cychrus*, Pl. III. f. 16, *c*).

TURGID (*p. turgidi*, Pl. IV. f. 22), when the last joint has the appearance of a distended bladder (*Gryllotalpa*).

EXCAVATED (*p. excavati*, Pl. IV. f. 23), when the same joint is concave at its extremity. (Compare below in the Anatomy of the Organs of the Senses, § 198).

TRUNCATED (*p. truncati*), when the last joint appears to terminate abruptly (*Prionus*).

DIVIDED (*p. fissi*), when the last joint is divided longitudinally.

·PILOSE (*p. pilosi*), when the joints are covered with sharp stiff bristles (*Cicindela*, Pl. IV. f. 10).

SQUAMOSE (*p. squamosi*), covered with broad scales (*Lepidoptera*, Pl. IV. f. 24 and 25).

ELONGATE (*p. elongati*), are those palpi which stand freely from the mouth (*Carabus*).

SHORT (*p. brevissimi*), when, in looking at the mouth, they are not perceived (*Curculionodea, Libellulina*).

VERY LONG (*p. longissimi*), when they are longer than the head, or even than the antennæ (*Hydrophilus*).

UNEQUAL (*p. inæquales*), when single joints take a different form (*Banchus, Ichneumon*, Pl. IV. f. 26).

EQUAL (*p. æquales*), on the contrary, when this is not the case.

SUCTORIAL ORGANS OF THE MOUTH.

§ 70.

The suctorial organs (*instrumenta suctoria*) are, fundamentally, merely the masticating ones transformed, or rather those stopped upon a lower stage of development, for a precise investigation clearly rediscovers the same identical organs. We however find no general uniformity among them, excepting in their function—that of taking nourishment by suction; for every order of insects with suctorial organs has a peculiar and then throughout all the families which compose it, a very uniform structure.

We thence distinguish the following principal forms:—the PROBOSCIS (*proboscis*), or HAUSTELLUM (*haustellum*), we find in the *Diptera* only. It consists of a membranaceous or more or less fleshy organ, which descends in a perpendicular direction from the orifice of the mouth, and which in general shortly from its origin is geniculated forward, and terminates in a flapper-shaped suctorial surface. Upon the superficies of this membranaceous sheath, and generally at the angle of the knee, is found the mouth, covered by a small horny flap, and surrounded by several bristly or lanceolate organs. Frequently, indeed, this muscular sheath consists merely of a corneous channel, in which the bristles lie (for example, *Culex*); and when thus formed, Fabricius calls it *haustellum;* but the muscular sheath itself, *proboscis*—styled by Kirby and Spence the *theca*.

The following, however, is the definition of these parts:—The SHEATH (Pl. V. f. 1. A), whether it be muscular or horny, represents the under lip, and is thence called *labium*, and the upper portion of the knée the STALK (*stipes*): when horny posteriorly, it is the CHIN (*mentum*). The anterior terminal flap is merely a feeler, and represents the labial palpi, which also only serve to supply the place of a muscular lip; it is called the KNOB (*capitulum*, Pl. V. f. 1, A). Upon the stalk, close to where the bristles, or setæ of the mouth are found, are placed the, from one to four-jointed, palpi (Pl. V. f. 1—7. c, c). The setæ themselves are concealed by the superior, broader, somewhat convex, upper lip (Pl. V. f. 2 *a*, 3 *a*, and fig. 5, SHEATH, *vagina*, Fab., *valvula*, Kirby and Spence); beneath it lie from one to five setæ, the two upper ones of which represent the MANDIBLES (the same, *b. b.* the KNIVES, *cultelli*, of Kirby and Spence); the two lower ones, the MAXILLÆ (the same, *c, c,* the LANCETS, *scalpella*, of Kirby and Spence); the middle one, the TONGUE (the same *d*, here called *glossarium*); between them lies the MOUTH (the same, fig. 5, *e*). When there is but one seta, it is the tongue: it is also the true piercing instrument, which is pushed down into the upper channel of the under lip; and thus embraced by the terminal flaps, pierces into the aliment; the jaws move up and down by its side, and form, while the suctorial ventricle distends, a decided pump, in explanation of which we shall go into greater detail further on.

The PROMUSCIS (*rostrum,—promuscis* of Kirby and Spence, Pl. V. f. 8) is peculiar to the *Hemiptera*. It is much more uniform in its construction than the proboscis, although it generally consists of the same identical parts. We must distinguish in it the small triangular plano-convex UPPER LIP, (*labrum*, fig. 8, 9, and 11, *a*, from above, fig. 14 from beneath), which incases the commencement of the promuscis from above, and is attached to the clypeus; and the, from three to five-jointed, sheath (fig. 8. *b*), which consists of two equal lateral flaps, which may represent the maxillæ and their palpi, and four fine setæ (fig. 10, *c, c,* and *d, d*), which, as in the flies, are analogous to the upper and under jaw. Between them is found the orifice of the mouth, at the apex of a small lanceolate tongue, concealed within the sheath (fig. 10, *e*, and fig. 13, *e*), which is enclosed by the setæ of the jaws. The jointed sheath of the promuscis is called *vagina*; the setæ of the jaws, *setæ superiores et inferiores*; the central tongue, *ligula*.

The SPIRAL TONGUE (*lingua spiralis*, Fab.; *antlia*, Kirby and Spence; *spiritrompe*, Lat.), or sucker of the *Lepidoptera*, is the third form of a suctorial mouth. It equally consists of all the organs of a masticating apparatus, which, however, here, adopt the following configuration. A small triangular piece attached to the clypeus, and which extends downwards towards the mouth, is the LABRUM (fig. 15, *a*, and fig. 16); near to it are placed the short, conical, slightly-bent MANDIBLES (fig. 15, *b, b*, and fig. 17). They are both covered by the large forwardly-bent labial palpi (Pl. VI. f. 3, *d*), and can be discovered only by a very laborious research. The MAXILLÆ have the same form they are described to take above in the masticating apparatus; but the superior lobe is stretched into a long, cylindrical, transversely-wrinkled filament (Pl. VI. f. 1, *a*); at the inner margin of which, two narrow bands are found (fig. 2, *a, a*), which symmetrically agree with those of the other maxilla, and by means of which, therefore, the space occurring between the two maxillæ is formed into a tube (fig. 2, o). The filiform maxillæ are also hollow (fig. 2, *p, p*), and by these cavities they are connected with the furcate commencement of the æsophagus, so that the Lepidoptera have, as it were, two mouths, or rather two separated suctorial tubes. Where the upper filament of the maxilla is attached to the stalk, a small two-jointed FEELER (fig. 1, *b*) is inserted. The LABIUM (Pl. V. f.18, *e*, and Pl.VI, f. 4, *e*), is tolerably large, generally triangular, and frequently divided at its apex. Each lobe bears a large, three-jointed, very hairy FEELER (Pl. V. f. 18, *d, d*, Pl. VI. f. 3 and 4, *d, d*), which falls forward, and forms the sheath of the sucker, when it is drawn up spirally in repose.

The suctorial organ of the bees (Pl. VI. f. 2—9, see description of the plates), and of the other suctorial Hymenoptera, is but a more or less prolonged transformation of the masticating apparatus, the same as that of the May flies (*Phryganeodea*), and we shall therefore treat of them in detail in our systematic description of their families. The mouth of the flea (*Pulex*), to which Kirby and Spence ascribe a peculiar suctorial organ, does not essentially differ from the structure of those of the *Diptera*, which have no fleshy lip; and which we shall also treat of in its proper place. The same observation refers likewise to the lice (*Pediculi*).

THE EYES.

§ 71.

Having now concluded this detailed description of the oral apparatus, we can pass on to the consideration of the other organs, and the eyes occur as the most immediate objects to proceed with.

The EYES plainly (*oculi*, Pl. III. f. 11, 12, 13, *a. a.*, Pl. V. f. 15, A., Pl. VI, 3 and 8, A. A.) also called COMPOUND EYES (*oculi compositi*), are placed at the sides of the head, above the mouth, and generally present themselves as large hemispheres, the superficies of which, at least upon close investigation, appear to consist of numerous regular hexagonal surfaces. They are generally circular in circumference, but many other figures (as OVAL or KIDNEY-SHAPED) are observable in them. Each of the above hexagons is itself an eye (as we shall more explicitly illustrate below in the Anatomy of the Eye), their surfaces consequently are so many slightly convex horny cases, whence the quick sight of these creatures is readily explained. Their margins of separation are often thickly set with hair (*oculi pilosi*), in other instances they are naked (*oculi nudi*). The number of these lenses or facets has been calculated by several authors, and their almost incredible multitude has very justly excited astonishment. Hooke counted 7,000 in the eye of a house fly; Leuwenhoek more than 12,000 in the eye of a dragon fly; 4,000 in the eye of a domestic fly; and Geoffroy cites a calculation, according to which there are 34,650 of such facets in the eye of a butterfly. They must also necessarily be very numerous in the eye of the *Lamellicornia*, in which, even under a tolerably strong lens, the divisions are not perceptible, whence Fabricius * called them simple eyes.

The general rule is for the eyes to be separated by the brow (*oculi distantes*), but they frequently join closely together in male insects (*oculi approximati*, for ex., in the dragon flies, the male *Syrphi*, the Drones). There are, in general, but two of these compound eyes, but a few exceptions are found to the universality of its application in the whirlwigs (*Gyrinus*), and some *Ephemera*, which have absolutely four

---

* Philosoph. Ent. p. xix, § 4.

eyes. In some of the *Coleoptera*, a corneous process originating at the clypeus (*canthus* of Kirby and Spence), either completely or partially divides the eyes, and these beetles, (*Ateuchus, Geotrupes,* Fabricius, &c. &c.) then appear to have four eyes. The genus *Tetraopes*, also, among the Capricorn beetles (*Cerambycina*), has apparently four eyes, from the antennæ being inserted exactly in the middle of the long ovate eyes, and which thence seem divided into an upper and lower half.

The SIMPLE EYES or auxiliary eyes (*ocelli, oculi simplices,* Pl. VI, f. 8, B, *stemmata,* Kirby and Spence), are generally THREE in number, and more rarely we find but TWO. They are placed upon the vertex or upon the brow, most frequently in a triangular position; they are much smaller than the true eyes, and consist of but one very convex case. They are found in all the orders of insects; among the *Coleoptera*, indeed, only as exceptions *, in others, the *Diptera*, for example, very universally. The larvæ of insects with a perfect metamorphosis are destitute of compound eyes, and instead of them have mostly simple eyes; in many instances they have none.

THE ANTENNÆ (*Antennæ*).

§ 72.

The ANTENNÆ must be distinguished as the third most important group of the organs of the head. They are two jointed organs, one of which is placed upon each side of the head between the angle of the mouth and the eyes. They appear never to be wanting, and there are never more than a single pair present. In some parasites only (*Philopterus, Docophorus*), there is close to and in front of each of them a small moveable stalk, which Nitzsch has called the little BEAM (*trabeculus*). It is different in the classes nearest to that of insects, the *Crustacea, Myriapoda,* and *Arachneodea;* in which we find sometimes none, sometimes only two, and even four, or six antennæ.

As the differences of antennæ are very great, we must divide our consideration of them under several heads. These are their *situation, relation to the body,* their *general construction, construction of the individual joints, and their clothing.*

---

* Germar discovered them in *Omalium*; they were afterwards discovered in *Anthophagus* and *Paussus*. A very particular observer, on the contrary, Straus-Durckheim, denies their being eyes, although he does not dispute the existence of the points, page 58.

1. *Situation of the Antennæ.*

FRONTAL (*ant. frontales*), they are called when they are inserted directly upon the brow (*Bees*, Pl. VI. f. 8, c, c).

PREOCULAR (*ant. præoculares*), are such as are inserted close to the front of the eyes (*Carabus*, Pl. III. f. 11 and 13, γ, γ, γ).

INTEROCULAR (*a. interoculares*), when they are placed between both the eyes.

EXTRA-OCULAR (*a. extra-oculares*), when placed very distant from the eyes.

INOCULAR (*a. inoculares*), when the eye surrounds the base of the antennæ (*Cerambyx*).

INFRA-OCULAR (*a. infra-oculares*), when inserted beneath the eyes.

When they are placed, as is usual, upon the upper part of the head, they are called SUPERIOR (*a. superiores*); but when beneath, INFERIOR (*a. inferiores*).

When their basal joints are inserted very closely together, they are called APPROXIMATE (*a. approximatæ*); but when they are wide apart they are styled DISTANT (*a. distantes*).

2. *Relation of the Antennæ to the Body.*

ELONGATE (*elongatæ*), when of the same length as the body (*Leptura*).

LONGER (*longiores*), when longer than the body (*Saperda*).

VERY LONG (*longissimæ*), when they are considerably longer than the body (*Lamia ædilis*), Fab.).

SHORT (*breves*), when about the length of the head.

SHORTER (*breviores*), when they are longer than the head, but shorter than the body.

VERY SHORT (*brevissimæ*), when not so long as the head.

3. *Forms of entire Antennæ.*

Antennæ which entirely consist of equal joints are called EQUAL (*equales*), whereas those whose joints are dissimilar receive the name of UNEQUAL (*inequales*). Both kinds are subjected to various differences, which we will now proceed to consider.

a. Equal Antennæ.

Setaceous (*setaceæ*, Pl. VII. f. 1), are such which very gradually decrease, becoming pointed at the apex (*Locusta*, Fab.).

Setiform (*setiformes*, Pl. VII. f. 2), when it resembles a slender, short bristle which springs from a thicker basal joint (*Libellula*). This form is distinguished from the subulate (*subulata*, Pl. VII. f. 3), by the latter being shorter, thicker, and slightly bent (*Leptis*).

Filiform (*filiformes*, Pl. VII. f. 4), when of the same thickness throughout, and composed of cylindrical joints (*Carabus*).

Moniliform (*moniliformes*, Pl. VII. f. 5), is when the joints are globose (*Tenebrio*).

Ensiform (*ensiformes*, Pl. VII. f. 6), when the joints are compressed, and have a sharp edge on each side (*Truxalis*).

Falciform (*falciformes*, Pl. VII. f. 7), when arched like a sickle.

Dentate (*dentatæ*, Pl. VII. f. 8), when their joints are armed with slight, pointed spines (*Stenochorus*).

Serrate (*serratæ*, Pl. VII. f. 9), when the joints are triangular, and are so arranged that the prominent angle is placed anteriorly, and inclines downwards (*Elater*). Biserrate (*biserratæ*), when a similar angle is also placed upwards, and, when so, the point of insertion of the joints is not at the superior angle, but at the centre of the base of the triangle. In the latter case, the joints of the antennæ form an isosceles triangle, whereas in the former they are more or less rectangular.

Imbricate (*imbricatæ*, Pl. VII. f. 10), is when the joints are conical, but deeply excavated, so that one joint is inserted half way within the other (*Prionus*).

Pectinate (*pectinatæ*, Pl. VII. f. 11), when the joints have long processes on one side, like the teeth of a comb. Bipectinate (*bipectinatæ*), when such a process issues from each side of the joint (*Lophyrus*); or doubly pectinated (*duplicato-pectinatæ*, Pl. VII. f. 12), when there are two processes on each side of the joints (*Ctenophora*). Cirrate (*cirratæ*, Pl. VII. f. 13), when the branches of such doubly or singly pectinated antennæ are very long and curled, and sometimes, but not always, fringed with hair. Distichous (*distichæ*), when the processes originate from the apex of the joint, and do not incline at right angles towards the sides, but bend forward at acute angles. Flabellate (*flabellatæ*, Pl. VII. f. 14), are pectinated antennæ, whose joints are very short, but the processes are very long and flat, and consequently lie close together. BIFLABELLATE (*biflabellatæ*), when both sides of the joints send forth such processes.

BRANCHED (*ramosæ*), when some of the joints only send forth processes upwards (Pl. VII. f. 15). This form should, by rights, be placed under the following head; but as they are in general filiform antenuæ which are furnished with such appendages, and they consequently bear great resemblance to the preceding forms, we have preferred introducing them here, among those they were most like.

FORKED (*furcatæ*, Pl. VII. f. 16), is when throughout its whole length it is separated into two branches or prongs (*Schizocerus*, Lat.).

b. Unequal Antennæ.

THE inequality of antennæ proceeds chiefly from the differing form of their second and last joint, on which account they demand especial notice. Very generally the first or second joint is much longer than the following, and is also not placed in the same direction with them, but the third joint is inserted laterally upon the second at a right angle. Such antennæ are called BROKEN (*fractæ*), or GENICULATE (*geniculatæ*, Pl. VII. f. 17); and the long joint is distinguished as the SCAPE (*scapus*, the same, *a*), and the following as the BRANCH (*flagellum*, the same, *b*).

The branch of such geniculated antennæ is frequently merely cylindrical or filiform (*Apiaria*, fig. 17); in other instances, on the contrary, the joints of the branch differ again from each other. We thence distinguish many forms which are also found in not geniculated but merely unequal antennæ. The following are of this description:—

CLAVATE (*clavatæ*, Pl. VII. f. 18), when the joints become gradually broader, so that the whole organ assumes the form of a club (*Silpha*).

CAPITATE (*capitatæ*), or such whose terminal joint forms a large round knob. If the knob is formed by but one joint, it is called SIMPLE (*capitulum solidum*); but when composed of several, it is called, in contradistinction, COMPOUND (*capitulum compositum*, Pl. VII. f. 19, *Necrophorus*). PERFOLIATE (*cap. perfoliatum*), when the joints of the knob slightly stand off from each other all round (*Hydrophilus*,

Pl. VII. f. 20); LAMELLATE (*cap. lamellatum*), when the joints of the knob extend on one side into broad leaves (Pl. VII. f. 21, *Melolontha*); TUNICATE (*cap. tunicatum*), when each successive joint is buried in the preceding funnel-shaped one (Pl. VIII. f. 1, *Lethrus*); INFLATED (*cap. inflatum*), when the knob has the form of a broad bladder (Pl. VIII. f. 2, *Paussus*); SPLIT (*cap. fissum*), when the joints upon one side are divided as by incisures (Pl. VIII. f. 3, *Lucanus*).

HOOKED (*uncinatæ*), when the last joint bends back upon the preceding (Pl. VIII. f. 4, the male of *Odynerus*).

NODOSE (*nodosæ*, Pl. VIII. f. 5), are those antennæ which have their intermediate and terminal joints thicker than the remainder (many *Curculios*).

ANGUSTATE (*angustatæ*), on the contrary, when the middle joints are thinner than at the beginning or the end (Pl. VIII. f. 6, *Asilus*).

SÈTIGEROUS (*setigeræ*), are such whose terminal joint has upon its upper side a fine BRISTLE (*seta*). The bristle is either SIMPLE (*simplex*, Pl. VIII. f. 7), or PLUMOSE (*plumosa*, Pl. VIII. f. 8, *Volucella*), when upon each side it sends forth fine and delicate branches. These forms are in general only found in the three-jointed antennæ of the *Diptera*, the very various forms of which are shown in the figures 6 to 17 of the eighth plate.

MUCRONATE (*mucronatæ*), are those whose last thick joint suddenly terminates in a sharp point (Pl. VIII. f. 18, *Empis*).

AURICULATE (*auriculatæ*), are those antennæ whose inferior joint is distended into a concave plate, not unlike the shell of an ear, and which partially covers the rest (Pl. VIII. f. 20, *Gyrinus;* f. 19, *Parnus*).

IRREGULAR (*irregulares*), lastly, are all such antennæ, all or several of the joints of which are dissimilar in form to each other (Pl. VIII. f. 22, *Cerocoma;* f. 30, *Agaon*).

4. *Number of the Joints.*

Antennæ which consist of but ONE joint are called EXARTICULATE (*exarticulatæ*); others, which have but few joints, are named from their number, as *biarticulate*, with TWO; *triarticulate*, with THREE joints, &c. But those whose joints are very numerous are called MULTIARTICULATE (*multiarticulatæ*).

The number of the joints of the antennæ is tolerably regular, and only varies in the different orders and families of insects; but a few only, as the *Diptera pupipara*, have exarticulate, or one-jointed antennæ; the majority of the rest of the *Diptera*, such as the true flies (*Muscaria*), and *Syrphi*, have THREE joints (see Pl. VIII. f. 6 and 8—14, and 16 and 17). Just so is it in the genera *Nepa* and *Ranatra* (Pl. VIII. f. 21), in the family of water-bugs (*Hydrocorides*); while the remaining genera of these, as also of the field-bugs (*Geocorides*), have FOUR joints, with the exception of the five-jointed genera, *Pentatoma*, *Tetyra*, and *Reduvius*. All the *Cicadaria* have THREE joints, with the exception of *Cicada*, Lat. (*Tettigonia*, Fab.), which has FIVE. The genera *Asilus*, *Dioctria*, *Dasypogon*, *Hilara*, *Empis*, and *Sargus*, among the *Diptera*, have FIVE joints (Pl. VIII. f. 7 and 18). It is the same in the apterous flea (*Pulex*), the lice (*Pediculi*), and the genus *Philopterus*, among the equally apterous parasitic skin-destroyers (*Dictyotoptera mallophaga*). Two other genera of this family, viz. *Liotheum* and *Gyropus*, have but FOUR joints; the fourth genus, *Trichodectes*, has but THREE. Six-jointed antennæ are rarely found, the genus *Perga*, and some species of the genus *Cimbex*, among the *Hymenoptera*, display this number; and among the *Diptera*, the genera *Hæmatopoda*, *Hexatoma*, Meig. (*Heptatoma*, Latr.), and *Nematocera*, Meig. (*Hexatoma*, Lat.). From SEVEN to EIGHT-jointed antennæ are found in other *Diptera*, in the genera *Stratiomys*, *Oxycera*, *Tabanus*, *Pangonia*, *Chrysops*; but the last five or six are so closely attached together, that they appear to form but one joint. NINE joints are found in the hymenopterous genus *Tenthredo*; TEN in the approximate genus *Athalia*. ELEVEN-jointed antennæ are possessed by the *Coleoptera*, with a few exceptions; for example, TEN in *Melolontha*, *Oryctes*; NINE in *Copris*, *Oniticellus*, *Ateuchus*, *Aphodius*, *Geniates*, Kirby; *Phanæus*, Leach (*Lonchophorus*, Germar), and many of their affinities; EIGHT, *Dorcatoma* and *Calandra*; FIVE, *Platypus* and *Claviger*; TWO, *Paussus*. More than ELEVEN joints are found in some species; for example, TWELVE in *Cebrio gigas*, *Chrysomela stolida*, some *Saperda*, and the males of the genera *Stenochorus* and *Trachyderes*. In *Prionus imbricornis* the female has NINETEEN, and the male TWENTY joints; *Rhipicera marginata*, Latr. (*Polytomus*, Dalm.) has THIRTY-TWO joints; *Rh. femorata*, TWENTY-THREE; *Rh. mysticina*, even FORTY. Among the bees, wasps, and the other families of the *Hymenoptera aculeata*, the female has TWELVE, and the male THIRTEEN joints. The *Diptera*, with uniform and multi-articulate antennæ, possess a varying number; *Bibio*, Latr. (*Hirtæa*, Fab.), has NINE; ELEVEN, *Dilophus*, *Scatopse*, and *Simulia;* the *Tipularia*, from THIRTEEN to SEVENTEEN; and all the *Tipulariæ fungivoræ* have SIXTEEN. Multiarticulate (20—50) antennæ are found among the *Lepidoptera;* the most of the *Ichneumonodea* and *Urocerata;* all the *Neuroptera*, and the most of the *Orthoptera;* but in many species of the genus *Locusta*, Leach, there are found FOURTEEN or SIXTEEN; in *Gryllus*, Fab., not many more than TWENTY; in *Forficula*, sometimes only TWELVE or FOURTEEN, but even as many as THIRTY.

5. *Forms of the individual Joints.*

They are in general CYLINDRICAL (*teres, s. cylindricus*), but the joints become very frequently thicker towards their end, and consequently not unusually adopt an obconic form (*a. obconici*). Bell-shaped, or CAMPANULATE (*a. campanulati*), are those which are concave at their broadest end (Pl. VII. f. 10). TORULOSE (*a. torulosi*), such as have greater or smaller tumours upon them. Those which are produced laterally into lobes or processes (*art. lobati, s. producti*), have been previously mentioned. Moon-shaped, or LUNATE joints (*art. lunati*), are found in the male individuals of the genera *Nephrotoma* and *Eucera* (Pl. VIII. f. 29). The first conical joint upon which the antenna turns like a ball within a socket, is called by Kirby and Spence the TORULUS (*torulus*).

6. *Clothing of the Antennæ.*

The great majority of antennæ are completely naked; others, on the contrary, have a clothing consisting of shorter or longer hair, in which case the terms explained above (§ 25) may be applied to them. Some peculiar terms, however, may here find a place.

VERTICILLATE (*verticillatæ*), are those antennæ, the joints of which are surrounded, at equal distances, with stiff hair (*Erioptera, Psychoda*, Pl. VIII. f. 23).

FIMBRICATE (*fimbricatæ*), on the contrary, when the long parallel hair is placed only upon one side of the joint; or *pectinato-fimbricatæ*, when the antennæ are at the same time pectinated (*Phalæna*, Pl. VIII. f. 24).

BEARDED (*barbatæ*), when the short and thickly-set hair covers the antennæ completely upon one side.

FASCICULATE (*fasciculatæ*), when every joint has a distinct pencil (*Callichroma alpinum*, Pl. VIII. f. 25).

SCOPIFEROUS (*scopiferæ*), when a thick brush of hair is placed upon one part of the antennæ (many species of *Lamia*, Pl. VIII. f. 26).

PLUMOSE (*plumosæ*), when the hair clothing the antennæ is long, and is so far apart that each may be distinctly discerned (*Chironomus*, Pl. VIII. f. 27, f. 28).

II.—THE THORAX.

§ 73.

THE second chief division of the body of an insect, and which succeeds to the head, and is connected with it by the neck, and precedes the abdomen, is the THORAX (*thorax, stethidium**). In calling this portion of the body the thorax, we differ from other writers, who apply this name to parts only of this division of the body; but why we do so is readily explained to those who remember the note to § 9, II, and who agree with us in the rule we there lay down †.

Fabricius divided the body of an insect into *caput, truncus, abdomen,* and *artus*. That this subdivision is inadmissible, is sufficiently explained at the above-cited place. How this, his *truncus*, our thorax, again consists of several divisions, will be more fully shown below. These segments, or divisions, he named in the following words:—*truncus inter caput et abdomen constat thorace, scutello, pectore, sterno* ‡. He called the upper part of the trunk *thorax* (§ 8); *pectus* was the part beneath, corresponding with the thorax (§ 10, page 25); *sternum*, lastly, the central longitudinal line of the breast (§ 11). The term thorax, which Fabricius used sometimes for the dorsal superficies of the anterior segment of the trunk, as in the *Coleoptera, Orthoptera,* and sometimes for the whole superior surface of the trunk, as in the *Hymenoptera* and *Diptera*, was afterwards applied to that whole division of the body whose superior surface it was intended only to indicate; and thence sometimes meant the entire anterior segment, and sometimes the whole trunk. Illiger sought to put a stop to this

---

* This term, used by Illiger, Bouché, and others, is less applicable than *thorax*, because it is borrowed from the Greek (derived from στῆθος), whilst *caput* and *abdomen* are Latin. It is true, indeed, that thorax also originates from the Greek, but was long used by the Latin writers of the best period.

† Passing over other authorities, we will merely cite in support of our opinion, Ch. L. Nitzsch. See Germar, Magaz. der Ent. iii. band, p. 275, note, who there explains himself upon the subject.

‡ Philos. Entom., p. 22, § 7.

confusion, by applying the terms in general use to signify the parts of the superior animal, and he therefore called that entire division the thorax; and he distinguished its upper surface as the thorax superior, and its lower one as thorax inferior *. Thus all difficulties were at once removed. But Kirby and Spence re-adopted the obsolete, incorrect nomenclature, endeavouring to justify their course by its priority; and in addition to which they named every possible part with such excessive and painful precision, and even every direction or position of the body, that the multitude of terms which their imagination has conceived, and, it must be admitted, not always very happily, is sufficient to excite astonishment. Before them, Knoch had essayed an orismological detail of the thorax †, but which also does not suffice for every requisition; but, that we may be as complete as possible, we will give a summary of his, as well as of Kirby and Spence's prolix nomenclature.

According to Knoch, the body of a beetle—for it is only to the *Coleoptera* that his names apply—exclusive of its head, consists of the trunk (*truncus*), which comprises the neck (*collum*), the breast (*pectus*), the abdomen, the scutellum, and the wing-cases (*elytra*).

The neck (*collum*, our *prothorax*) is divided into the upper side (*thorax*), and the under side (*jugulum*). In the centre of the under side is found a prominent narrow portion, the collar-bone (*sternum collare, cartilago ensiformis*, Lin.). That portion of the trunk which lies between the neck and abdomen, but which above is covered by the elytra, he calls breast (*pectus*). This is divided into several portions: the anterior part placed in the middle, limited posteriorly by the sockets of the intermediate legs, he calls *peristethium*; close to which, on each side exteriorly, are the *scapulæ*, which sometimes (*Cychrus*) are soldered to the *peristethium*. Next to the *peristethium*, and behind the sockets of the intermediate legs, follows the large central *acetabulum*; close to which, on each side, limited anteriorly by the *scapulæ*, are the *parapleura*, or side-pieces, which, in many genera (*Cychrus*), are divided into two. Behind the *acetabulum* and *parapleura* is placed the *mericæum*, which forms the anterior surface of the sockets of the posterior legs. The breast has frequently, as well as the neck, a central prominent carina (*Hydrophilus*); this is called breast-bone (*sternum pectorale*). The whole upper surface of the breast is called

* Magas. Vol. V., p. 11, No. 1578.
† Neue Beitrage, Book I., p. 41.

the back (*dorsum*), with the exception of the *scutellum* lying between the elytra.

The following Orismology of Kirby and Spence is much more diffuse:—

The trunk (*truncus*) is divided into two chief parts—the anterior bearing the anterior legs, called *manitruncus*, and the posterior, *alitruncus*, upon which are placed the four posterior legs and the wings.

The upper side of the *manitruncus* is distinguished as the *prothorax*, and its broad lateral margin as border (*ora*); the *patagia*, two corneous scales densely covered with hair in the *Lepidoptera*; the *umbones*, two moveable thorns on the sides in *Acrocinus longimanus*; and the *phragma*, the posterior margin descending in front of the alitrunk. The under side is called *antepectus*, the central prominent ridge of which is called *prosternum*, and the *antefurca*, which is an internal process for the insertion of the muscles.

The *alitruncus* has the following divisions and parts:—the first division upon which the anterior wings are placed is called above the *mesothorax*, or is divided into the *collare*, particularly visible in the *Hymenoptera*, it appears to be wanting in insects with a distinct manitrunk, the *prophragma*, a thin partition which descends from the anterior margin of the *mesothorax* into the cavity of the trunk, and separates the anterior segment from the intermediate one. The *dorsolum* is that portion of the superior surface which lies between the *collare* and *scutellum*, upon which are found the wing-sockets (*pteropega*). These cavities are, in the *Hymenoptera*, covered by two small scales (*tegulæ*). The *scutellum*, a triangular corneous piece placed behind the dorsolum, and between the superior wings, serves as a point of insertion of the elytra. The under side of the anterior division of the alitrunk is called *medipectus*, in which is again distinguished the *peristethium*, or anterior central part lying in front of the sockets of the intermediate legs (the same part of Knoch); the *scapularia*, placed exteriorly next to the *peristethium*; the *mesosternum*, the prominent central ridge of the *medipectus*; and the *medifurca*, a forked process of the interior surface of the *medipectus*. The superior surface of the posterior division of the trunk is called *metathorax*. Upon this is found the *mesophragma*, a separating partition running parallel with the *prophragma*, and descending from the anterior margin of the *metathorax*; the *post-dorsolum*, the intermediate piece between the *mesophragma* and *post-scutellum*; the *post-scutellum*, that piece which follows the middle piece, and which extends to the end of the *metathorax*; *pleuræ* (the sides), the space between the *scapularia* and the insertion of the wings. The under side of the posterior division of the alitruncus they call the *post-pectus*; it is divided into the *mesostethium*, the central piece between the intermediate and posterior legs (Knoch's *acetabulum*); the *parapleuræ*, the lateral pieces on each side of the *mesostethium*; the *metasternum*, the elevated central ridge of the *mesostethium*; the *post-furca*, the internal descending process of the *metathorax* and the *opercula*, which cover the spiracles of the *metathorax*.

To whom is not the elaborately strained nature of these definitions apparent? To call the anterior legs, hands, and that portion of the body upon which they are placed, the manitrunk, is certainly a very forced endeavour to find analogies. The upper surface also cannot be called *thorax*, and the under side *pectus*; for *pectus* universally means the anterior portion of the thorax, and its posterior or upper surface is called *dorsum*, or back. It is also erroneous to consider the *collare* as a distinct part, as it is evidently what they call thorax in the *Coleoptera*. Notwithstanding their assertions to the contrary, they will never be able to convince us of it. Wheresoever a part is not immediately recognised, it displays no art to give it a peculiar name; but, on the contrary, it shows much to prove, by a careful study, the relations of the several parts in the different orders, and the variations they are subjected to. This has been the problem which the following sections, containing a description of the thorax, seek to solve.

§ 74.

The thorax of insects consists of three corneous segments, from each of which a pair of legs originate; and the two posterior, or only the intermediate one, always bear besides a pair of wings. We distinguish these segments as the PROTHORAX, MESOTHORAX, and METATHORAX [*]. In its most simple conformation, each of these segments is wholly

---

[*] Ch. L. Nitzsch, who first proposed these three names for the three segments of the thorax, wrote *protothorax*; but as he himself called the third segment *metathorax*, forming it consequently of a preposition and a substantive, the analogously compounded name of the first segment proposed by Kirby and Spence is, therefore, better than the former. Had Nitzsch compounded all the three names of ordinal numerals, his would have had the preference, as being the first; in consequence, therefore, those proposed by Kirby and and Spence take precedence.

uniform, without further composition, as in all insects deficient in wings, *Pediculus*, the *Mallophaga*, *Pulex*, &c.) In such no distinct parts are to be noticed, they are consequently named only according to their position, the upper part being called the BACK (*dorsum*), the under the BREAST (*pectus*) and the SIDES, where they are distinct or prominent, (*pleuræ*). As portions of the whole superficies they are distinguished by the name of the segment upon which they are situated; for example, the upper side of the prothorax is called the BACK OF THE PROTHORAX (*dorsum prothoraces*). But this most simple construction of the thorax passes through a great variety of conformation in the different orders, whereby the undivided segments, here seen, become separated into parts of which sometimes one, and sometimes the other, is most strongly developed; but the three great divisions are always distinctly determined, although in some cases the second and third, and in others all three, are so closely united that they appear to form but one undivided whole.

The orders in which we observe the first segment to be most freely united to the second are the *Coleoptera*, *Orthoptera*, *Neuroptera*, and *Hemiptera;* the other four display a tolerably close union of all the three segments into one entire undivided thorax. Although this more distinct separation of the prothorax is evidently conditional upon a not unimportant transformation of organic relations, we shall nevertheless observe no new parts in these orders, but be able to show an analogical structure in all the rest. The greater freedom of union does not seem to imply a higher grade of organisation, for we observe the same structure in the apparently highest and lowest orders; but in the higher orders each thoracic segment is composed of several parts, which in the lower ones unite into one, although we even then find the indication of such separations.

When most fully developed, the thorax consists of four corneous plates. The superior, which we call PRONOTUM*(Pl. IX. and XII. A, A, A, *Prothorax* of Kirby and Spence), takes very different figures. In general it is more or less quadrate, but so that the sides seldom form straight lines, but either bow out or undulate. The anterior margin is generally emarginate, the posterior straighter; the lateral margins frequently dentate, and sometimes armed with strong spines or with smaller teeth. The centre of the superficies very generally exhibits a narrow longitudinal impression, which beneath and within projects as a sharp

---

* This name is compounded of πρo, anterior, and νότος, the back.

corneous ridge. The prothoracic case is thereby divided into two lateral halves (for example, in *Gryllotalpa*, Pl. XI. No. 1, f. 3, c). Sometimes the upper surface projects in a similar central pectinated ridge, as in many of the genus *Gryllus*, Fabr. (*Acridium*, Latr.) Besides its DISC (*discus*) and MARGIN (*margines*), we distinguish upon it the surrounding BORDER (*limbus*). Between this *pronotum* and the anterior sternal plate we find on each side in the cursorial (*Carabici*) and natatorial beetles (*Hydrocanthari*), a distinct corneous scale, which, as the muscles of the coxæ originate at them, should be called shoulder-blades; and, that we may distinguish them from the larger shoulder-blades of the intermediate legs (which have been long called *scapulæ*), may be called the smaller or anterior shoulder-blade (*omium**). It is a flat, more or less heart-shaped plate (Pl. IX. No. 1 fig. 4, of *Carabus*, No. 2, fig. 4, *Dytiscus*), and which forms the posterior portion of the sides of the prothoracic segment, and is contiguous in front to the wings of the *prosternum*, which extend upwards to the *pronotum*. Its superior margin turns inwards (the same b*), and forms a broad, bowed corneous ledge, thus presenting a still wider surface to the muscles of the coxæ, upon which they may spread themselves. In *Buprestis*, which has this margin very broad (No. 3, fig. 1, A, A), I found upon its posterior edge a small round corneous plate, which was distinct from it (the same *b, b*), which upon the opposite side was contiguous to the prosternum, and is doubtlessly the analogue of the anterior shoulder. I have not observed it in other families of the beetles, in which the turned margin of the *pronotum* takes its place (Pl. X. No. 3, fig. 1.)

The inferior plate, the PROSTERNUM (Pl. IX. &c. B, B), has much more limited dimensions than the superior. It is less flat, rather inclining beneath to an angle, the edge of which is frequently prominent, or not rarely prolonged into a mucro posteriorly (*Elater*). Close to the central ridge the SOCKETS (*acetabula*) of the anterior legs are seated, one on each side; in front the articulating membrane is affixed, and posteriorly the membrane which connects it with the mesothorax. The SPIRACLE of the prothoracic segment is found here; it is a longitudinal gap surrounded by a callous margin, into which the tracheæ of the anterior part of the body open themselves (Pl. XI. No. 1, fig. 2, *a, a*). In all those families to which this division of the prothoracic case is not

---

* The Latin language has no diminutive of *scapula*, we have therefore derived it from the Greek, in which language ὤμιον signifies a small shoulder.

peculiar (for example, the *Cerambycina*), the superior plate is united to the inferior without the indication of any separation, so that the parts distinguished in the former can be regarded in these only as regions. The prothoracic case has, besides the feet, no other limbs or peculiar appendages, with the exception of two instances. In the one, we observe a moveable spine on each side of the prothorax, (*Acrocinus longimanus*); the second instance is found in the family of the *Rhiphidoptera**, on each side of the prothorax of which a contorted and twisted corneous appendage is attached. All other prominences of the prothoracic case are integral portions of it, and are to be considered only as processes. There is a multiplicity of them and of the most distinct forms, the families of the *Lamellicornia* and *Cicadaria* display the most remarkable. The PATAGIA (*patagia*) of the Lepidoptera, which Kirby and Spence consider as appendages of the prothorax, are not seated upon this, but upon the mesothorax.

§ 75.

In those orders in which the prothorax is in closer connection with the mesothorax, we often find analogous parts; but it just as often forms, as well as the whole thorax, one entire piece, upon the superficies of which the different parts are indicated by means of deep impressions and furrows. This is the case in the *Diptera* and the *Neuroptera*; for, notwithstanding the distinctness with which the different thoracic plates are marked out, for example, in the *Libellulina* (Pl. XI. No. 3, f. 1—3), they are, nevertheless, firmly attached together, and require considerable force and art to separate them. In the *Hymenoptera*, this separation is not merely indicated, but it actually takes place. A small corneous plate with two sockets, and seated quite in front of the prothorax, represents in this order the prosternum (Pl. XII. No. 1 and 2, B, B, B.); a larger plate, which has a narrow margin, and which, descending perpendicularly, bows round and extends on each side to the origin of the wings (the *collar* of Kirby), takes the place of the *pronotum* (Pl. XII. No. 1 and 2, A, A.). Kirby and Spence consider this plate as an integral portion of the second segment, and confirm themselves in this view of it by its generally remaining attached to the mesothoracic segment when the first pair of legs are separated from the prothorax. They, consequently, think they have observed

* *Strepsiptera*, Kirby.

that some insects (*Vespa, Cimbex*) possess both a *collar* and a *pronotum;* and that in others (*Xylocopa*), the collar forms a complete ring. Their first observation is perfectly correct, but not convincing; it frequently happens that the first segment of the thorax is more strongly affixed to the thorax than to the abdomen, and remains attached to the former when we wish to separate the latter (*Hister, Gryllus, Gryllotalpa,* &c. &c.); the same remark may be made with respect to the *coxæ*, and with still greater latitude, but which are, notwithstanding, joints of the legs: why should not, therefore, the *pronotum* occasionally be affixed more firmly to the second segment of the thorax than to the *prosternum?* The second observation is absolutely erroneous; for what Kirby and Spence consider as their *prothorax*, (our *pronotum*), is sometimes the extended membrane of the neck (*Vespa, Cimbex*), sometimes a plate, as in the *Libellulina*, representing the anterior part of the *mesonotum;* and which, in the *Coleoptera*, is covered by the *pronotum*. The third observation is also imaginary, for proportions of that kind are always the peculiarities of entire families; and this conformation of the prothoracic segment is found as little among the rest of the bees as in *Xylocopa*. Whereas, on the contrary, the following reasons clearly prove this part to be the *pronotum* :—

1st. In all those orders which possess a *collar*, the *pronotum* would necessarily be deficient, as they possess no part excepting this which responds to it. On the other side these orders would have a corneous part more upon the mesothoracic segment than any of those provided with a distinct and free *prothorax*, in which we in vain seek upon the mesothoracic segment for a part analogous to the *collar*.

2ndly. That Kirby and Spence's *collare* is our *pronotum*, is proved incontestibly by the circumstance, that, upon its separation from the second segment, there is a spiracle. We observe this spiracle very distinctly in the *Diptera* (Pl. XIV. No. 1, f. 2, *a*), which shows us very evidently the limits of the *prothorax*, for which, without this indication, we might look in vain, as the entire order is deficient in a clear separation of the plates of the thorax. (See also Pl. XIV. No. 2, f. 2, *a.*) In the *Hymenoptera* and *Lepidoptera*, this spiracle lies beneath the *patagium*, and, in the former (*Vespa, Scolia,* &c.), appears as a distinct opening beneath the superior wing. This process, which forms a sort of flap, may be called TILE (*tegula*), for the organ which Kirby and Spence have so called is the same with their *patagium*

(Pl. XII. No. 1 and 2, *d, d*; see § 77). The first spiracle is constantly the property of the prothorax throughout all the orders which have this part free, and in a very flexible articulation with the second; consequently, in all the remaining orders, the first spiracle of the thorax must necessarily belong to its first segment, and not, as would be the case were the collar a portion of the mesothorax, to the second thoracic segment.

3rdly. We may even adopt, as proofs in our favour, the reasons cited by Kirby and Spence, in opposition to their own views. In the first place, they say the collar lies directly over the *prosternum* (*Chlorion*), and then moves freely with it (*Pompilus, Chrysis*), when the *collar* has no *prophragma* (see lower down); but which is found upon the dorsal piece lying behind it. Kirby and Spence have not refuted all these reasons, but have considered them as rendered ineffective by their contrary reasons, which we have entirely refuted. It clearly appears to us, therefore, that the term COLLAR will, in future, be useless, and instead of it, this part must be called by its more appropriate name of *pronotum*.

In the order of the *Lepidoptera*, this pronotum approaches to the shape of a collar, for in them it leans against the second segment, in the form of a thin plate, and thus forms its commencement (Pl. XII. No. 1, f. 1, *a*). Besides which, it is here called *collare* by the describers of *Lepidoptera*, particularly wherever it is covered with differently coloured hair, or small scales. But even here it is the true representative of the *pronotum*.

§ 76.

The intermediate ring of the thorax, the MESOTHORAX consists, in its most developed state, of seven pieces, the three pairs of which are so closely united, that each appears to form but one piece; thence, consequently, we have four chief pieces, which we distinguish as MESONOTUM, MESOSTERNUM, and the SCAPULÆ.

The MESONOTUM (Pl. IX. &c. c, c, c. Kirby and Spence's *dorsolum and scutellum*), forms superiorly the corneous covering of the *mesothorax*. It is generally of a quadrate shape; it is convex on the exterior and concave within, bent down laterally, and is here, chiefly, in direct union with the remaining corneous plates. It is divided into two parts, which are never distinctly separated, but merely indicated upon the superficies. The anterior piece or true back (*dorsolum* of

Kirby and Spence), generally exceeds the posterior piece in size. In the orders with a free prothorax, this covers it, and it is only visible upon the removal of the latter ; in the rest it occupies the whole central surface of the back. In front, at its exterior angles, the corneous ribs of the superior wings articulate, and two corneous ridges, originating at this point and proceeding into the cavity of the thorax, serve for the insertion of the muscles which move the wings. In the *Hydrocanthari*, the mesonotum is very small, and indicated only by a delicate corneous transverse line (Pl. IX. No. 2, f. 7, c.); it is very large in the *Mellifera* and *Lepidoptera*, as well as in the *Diptera ;* in the dragon flies, (Pl. XI. No. 3, f. 1, 2, c, c.), it forms as an obliquely descending bent plate, the anterior portion of the thorax in front of the wings, and therefore does not represent the collar of the *Hymenoptera* and *Diptera* (our *pronotum*), as Kirby and Spence maintain. The posterior division, the SCUTELLUM (*scutellum*), is here seated, as in all, between the wings. This SCUTELLUM (Pl. XI. &c. c, c.), is, properly, no separated part; but, as we have already seen, a mere process of the *mesonotum*. It is to be observed very distinctly in the *Coleoptera*, in which it presents itself as a small triangular plate seated between the *elytra* and the *pronotum*. In some genera (*Macraspis*), it attains considerable size; indeed in *Tetyra* and *Chelyphus*, it almost covers the whole abdomen *. It always extends far backwards, between the posterior wings ; and in many families, it completely covers the third thoracic segment (Pl. XIII. No. 4 and 5, c, c. ; Pl. XIV. No. 1 and 2, c, c.) ; not unfrequently a strong membrane or even a peculiar corneous ridge (*Cicada*, P. XIII. No. 5, f. 1, d, d.) proceeds from the side of the scutellum to the base of the superior wings, and thereby strengthens their connection with the dorsal piece (Pl. XIII. No. 4, f. 1, d, d). This ridge or membrane, Kirby and Spence call the *frenum*. In many *Coleoptera* the scutellum appears to be deficient, from its not displaying itself upon the superior surface between the *elytra* (as in *Copris*) ; but it is, nevertheless, present, although covered by the *elytra* and *pronotum*. These have been called *Escutellati*, wanting a scutellum.

It is not unusual to find other processes upon the scutellum, as spines and teeth, and which are occasionally found in almost all the orders (*Psilus Boscii*, *Stratiomys*, *Sargus*, *Reduvius*). But we more rarely observe

---

* Compare Dalman, Analecta Entomol. p. 32, p. 2, B.

such excrescences upon the mesonotum (*Clitellaria*). The prominences upon the surface of the mesonotum (for example, in *Cimbex, Sirex, Tabanus, Asilus*, &c.) arise from the insertion of the muscles; the furrows which separate them correspond with similar ridges upon the interior, which the bundles of muscles embrace. A great partition, of a horny substance, separates superiorly the cavity of the second thoracic segment from the first; it descends from the upper side of the dorsal piece, in greater or less distension, and likewise serves for the insertion of the muscles of the back. Kirby and Spence call it PROPHRAGMA. At its superior edge the membrane is affixed, which unites the first and second segments.

§ 77.

The SCAPULÆ are contiguous to the mesonotum (Pl. IX., &c., D, D). On each side, in front, close to the mesonotum, they assist to form the articulating socket of the superior wings (*pteropega*, Kirby and Spence), and they here contract themselves, that they may pass into the cavities of the prothorax in those orders which have a distinctly separated prothorax, and with their opposite wing they pass down the sides of the mesothoracic segment. They consequently fall into two divisions, which may be distinguished as the anterior and posterior wings of the scapulæ (*ala scapulæ anterior et posterior*). Beneath and beyond the posterior wings of the scapulæ, in the *Coleoptera*, is found the spiracle of the second thoracic segment; it is entirely covered by it, which explains why it has been hitherto overlooked. Straus-Durckheim discovered it, and has distinctly shown its situation*. My attention being thus drawn to it, I have fully convinced myself of its constant presence in the *Coleoptera*, by numerous investigations. In the orders with an unseparated prothorax, this part appears to diminish in compass as well as in importance; at least we never clearly discern a distinctly separated scapula, but peculiar pieces, analogous by their situation, doubtlessly represent them, although with an altered function. As such we consider the *patagia* and *tegulæ* of the *Lepidoptera* and *Hymenoptera*; they are both decidedly the same part, and are also seated precisely at the same place, but differ in their mode of attachment, the *tegula* of the *Hymenoptera* being affixed to the mesonotum above the wing, and the *patagium* of the *Lepidoptera* beneath it, to that part which we

---

* Consid. Gen., Pl. VII. fig. 6, II.

consider as the analogue of the posterior wing of the scapula (see Pl. XII. No. 1, f. 1 and 2, *d*; No. 2, f. 2, *d*). In the *Diptera*, this scale appears as a mere protuberance (Pl. XIV. No. 1, *d*) in front of the base of the wings; thus also, by reason of its smallness in many of the *Hymenoptera* (*punctum callosum ante alas* of Fabricius); but in these it is always a separate piece. That which has been called the SHOULDERS (*humeri*) in other *Diptera*, for example, in *Myopa*, is certainly erroneous, for it is the analogue of the *collare* of the *Hymenoptera*, and the same as our *pronotum* (Pl. XIV. No. 2, A). In all the apterous genera, as well as in all those orders which display a closer union of the several pieces of the thorax, the scapulæ are not either to be recognised as distinct pieces. In the *Coleoptera* and *Orthoptera* they are never wanting; but their separation into two parts, which we have called their wings, is not always apparent.

The third piece, the MESOSTERNUM (*peristethium* of Kirby and Spence), is, as well as the scapulæ, divided into two parts; but here they are equal. It is directly opposite to the *mesonotum*, upon the underside of the thoracic case, and includes one-half of the acetabula of the intermediate legs. It is distinctly observed in all the orders; in many (*Diptera*, *Hemiptera*) it is not separated from the other pieces by clearly defined limits, but merely indicated by furrows; in others (the *Hymenoptera*), it attains considerable size (Pl. XII. No. 2, f. 2 and 3, E, E), and in these extends upwards upon the sides of the thoracic case, as high as the articulation of the superior wings. In the *Coleoptera* and *Orthoptera*, which display considerable resemblance in the conformation of their thorax, it is small, and frequently appears but as a small prominent ridge between the intermediate legs (*Hydrophilus*, *Gryllotalpa*, Pl. IX. No. 1, f. 8, E); in the former it is sometimes even excavated for the reception of the dagger-shaped process of the prosternum (*Elater*, *Buprestis*, Pl. IX. No. 3, f. 5, E; *Dyticus*, Pl. IX. No. 2, f. 8). This sternum is separated into two equal halves by a central longitudinal division, which, however, is but little apparent upon its superficies, and can be discovered only upon a close inspection (*Buprestis*, *Dyticus*, &c.).

§ 78.

The third and last segment of the thorax, the METATHORAX, resembles the second, in being of a more united structure than the first, which is to be ascribed chiefly to the circumstance of their having both wings and legs attached to them, whereas the first has but legs alone; consequently greater compass was required for the reception of the muscles of the wings, and which explains the reason of their much more artificial construction. We likewise observe the fullest development in the number and situation of the parts to occur here, also, in the *Coleoptera*, as was to be expected in the highest order. The third segment, likewise, consists of seven pieces, which are similar to those of the second. The superior central piece, the METANOTUM (Pl. IX., &c. F, F), occupies the whole superior part of the metathorax; it is generally an oblong quadrangle, with the anterior angles advanced: it is frequently hollowed in front. A somewhat arched partition (*mesophragma* of Kirby and Spence), which descends into the cavity of the thorax, separates the cavity of the meso- from that of the metathorax, and serves for the insertion of the muscles of the back, as well as of the legs. The membrane which connects this segment with the preceding passes over this partition, but which is, however, no longer apparent in the *Hymenoptera*, and in all those orders wherein the corneous plates are attached together. In general, the posterior edge of the SCUTELLUM projects somewhat over the anterior margin of the metathorax; it often (*Diptera* and *Cicadaria*) conceals its centre—though rarely its entire surface (*Tabanus*, Pl. XIV. No. 1. *c*; *Chelyphus*, *Tetyra*). Sometimes a straight furrow, which, however, occasionally runs concentrically with the scutellum, separates from the remainder an anterior portion of the metathorax, which has been called POSTSCUTELLUM. In the saw-flies (*Tenthredonodea*) this portion, particularly laterally, very strongly projects, and displays two small, very generally white, points, which are called CENCHRI.

The posterior wings are placed at the anterior angles, and often occupy the whole sides of the metathorax. This occurs through the medium of a peculiar organisation, the description of which belongs to the anatomical division; thus much may stand here—the strong corneous nervures are attached to the metathorax by articulation, and the membrane is formally affixed to it, and is supported, upon the expansion of the wing, by the horny plates contained within it.

A pergamenteous partition at the posterior margin, and called the METAPHRAGMA, and which descends in a perpendicular direction, bowing in its middle towards the abdomen, separates the latter from the thorax (Pl. XIV. No. 1, f. 2, H); there remains only a small space below for the passage of the intestines, the organs of the nervous and respiratory systems, and of the vessels, &c. In all insects with a pedunculated abdomen (*abdomine petiolate*), this partition is exposed, and thus forms the covering of the truncated posterior portion of the metathoracic segment; it even seems to distend itself towards the superior surface, and to terminate only at the above indicated furrow of the metathorax, whereby this becomes a positive suture (Pl. XII. No. 2, f. 1 and 2, *Scolia* and other *Hymenoptera*).

Directly opposite to the metanotum, and precisely in the centre of the under surface, we find the METASTERNUM (Pl. IX., &c. G, G); likewise very generally a quadrate, corneous plate, but which more rarely takes the shape of a triangle, hexagon or octagon (*Hister*, Pl. IX. No. 3, f. 12, G), and which helps to form anteriorly the acetabula of the intermediate legs, and, posteriorly, those of the posterior legs. It is sometimes perfectly flat, sometimes slightly convex, and sometimes distinctly ridged, and occasionally prolonged posteriorly into a point (*Xiphus metasterni*); and when thus, it projects over the abdomen (*Hydrophilus*). It differs considerably in extent in *Oryctes* (Pl. X. No. 2, f. 4, G) and *Cetonia* (the same, No. 1, f. 2, G); it occupies nearly the whole pectus; sometimes, as in *Hister* (Pl. IX. No. 3, f. 12, G), only the centre; sometimes it is compressed into a comparatively small compass by the *coxæ* of the posterior legs; it is thus formed in *Dyticus* (Pl. IX. No. 2, f. 8, G). In many *Coleoptera*, for example, in the *Lamellicornia*, the meso-and meta-sternum are so closely united, that it requires violence to effect a separation. In others (for example, *Buprestis*, Pl. IX. No. 3, f. 5, G), the metasternum consists of two halves, which are separated by a central longitudinal suture, which internally forms a ridge.

The construction in the other orders differs materially from this description of it in the beetles; but in the *Orthoptera* very slightly. In these, likewise, the metasternum is a clearly distinguishable, but undivided plate, placed between the acetabula of the four posterior legs (Pl. XI. No. 2, f. 5, G). In the apterous genera, we do not observe the meso- and meta-sternum to be divided into several pieces, and they adhere tolerably closely to the original annular form of the segments (see Pl. XIII. No. 1 and 2, the thorax of the female *Tengyra* and *Myrmosa*). In the *Hymenoptera*, the construction of the metasternum closely approximates to the above description of that of the beetles; it is likewise seated between the acetabula of the posterior legs, and appears as a distinct, but undivided plate, as in *Scolia* (Pl. X. No. 2, f. 2 and 3, G). In the *Lepidoptera* it takes the figure of a semicircle, which lies in front of the coxæ of the posterior legs, separates them from those of the intermediate legs, and between them it projects, with its obtuse ends, at the sides of the thorax (Pl. XIII. No. 4, f. 2, G). It appears indicated in the same situation in the *Diptera*, but is not separated, for in them all the parts of the thoracic segments are firmly united. In the *Hymenoptera*, the metasternum merits particular attention, from its deviating from the structure of the other orders by possessing a spiracle peculiar to it, which is placed anteriorly upon its superior lateral margin (see Pl. XII. No. 1 and 2, f. 1 and 2, β). In the *Lepidoptera* and *Diptera*, it is placed as in the other orders, between the meso- and meta-thorax. Latreille, therefore, considers this portion of the thorax as belonging to the abdomen, maintaining that no spiracles are to be found upon those segments of the thorax which are provided with wings; which assertion is, however, unfounded, as we have seen. He thence concludes that the *halteres* (see the end of this section) of the *Diptera* cannot represent the posterior wings of the other orders, because a spiracle is found upon the segment where they are placed. But that this circumstance proves nothing will have become self-evident.

Between the metanotum and the metasternum, two other horny pieces are found on each side, which we, with Kirby and Spence, distinguish as the PLEURA and PARAPLEURA. Straus calls them ISCHIA, and distinguishes the former as the *ischium primum;* the latter as *ischium secundum.*

The PLEURA (Pl. IX. No. 2, J, J) is contiguous to the metanotum, and is united to it by a delicate membrane; the membrane of the wing proceeds from it, and this is attached in the same manner to the pleura beneath, as it is affixed above to the metanotum. It is a small, longitudinal, scarcely observable plate, which, in repose, is covered by the elytra, and is not perceptible until they are removed. In the *Orthoptera* (for example, *Gryllotalpa*, Pl. XI. No. 1, f. 8, J), the pleura is much extended, and posteriorly it is drawn somewhat downwards, so that it extends to the acetabula of the posterior coxæ. In the *Libellulina*, it is almost supplanted by the very large parapleuræ, and in these insects, from the two pieces being united posteriorly, it appears as a small triangle* beneath the cavity where the abdomen is affixed (Pl. XI. No. 3, f. 3, J). In the *Hymenoptera, Lepidoptera, Diptera,* and *Hemiptera,* the pleuræ and parapleuræ are not distinctly separated, but form a single, undivided pleura, which often, besides, is strictly united with either the metanotum or metasternum, or indeed with both together.

The PARAPLEURÆ (Pl. IX., &c. H, H) of the *Coleoptera,* as well as of the other orders in which it is distinctly found, lies between the metasternum and the pleura. In general, they are larger than the latter, lie nearer the under side of the body, and adapt themselves in shape to the space left by the other plates. They are very frequently quadrate (Pl. XI. No. 1, f. 6, H; No. 2, f. 10), with sometimes parallel, and sometimes diverging sides (Pl. IX. No. 3, f. 6, H); in other cases, three-sided (Pl. IX. No. 2, f. 8, H); and very large and trapezoida lin *Gryllotalpa* (Pl. XI. No. 1, f. 8, H), as well as in *Libellula* (No. 3, f. 2, H). In these they are prolonged posteriorly, make a bend at the angle of the thorax, and in the centre of the metasternum they unite in one piece (Pl. XI. No. 3, f. 2 and 3, H). In the other orders, the pleuræ and parapleuræ are not separated, but form one single plate. In the *Diptera* peculiar interest attaches to it, from the remarkable *halteres* being seated there. They originate frequently in a stalk (*stipes*), as fine as a hair, from the anterior margin of the pleuræ, and shortly terminate in sometimes a round, and at others a compressed knob (*capitulum*). They frequently stand quite free, and are then called NAKED (*halteres nudi*), or else they are covered by one or two delicate SCALES (*squamæ*), which are attached to the mesothorax, and extend from its margin upwards to the scutellum, and are doubtlessly analogous to the previously described *frenum* of the other orders. We have not yet attained any very distinct idea of the import of the halteres; but this is not the place to introduce an investigation of the subject; we refer to the proper place, in the second and third divisions, for much that applies to it.

---

* Without this somewhat forced view, it would be scarcely possible to explain the construction of the thorax in the *Libellula.* We must imagine the feet to be drawn forwards, whilst the back and the wings project posteriorly, whereby the parapleuræ are advanced in front of the pleuræ, and these united posteriorly into one piece.

§ 78 a.

After having thus explained the construction of the thorax in the different orders of insects, it remains for us now to notice the works of other naturalists upon the same subject, and to indicate the difference of the results of their investigations.

The earliest work of this kind is that of Chabrier; it appeared as the introduction to his treatise upon the flight of insects *, which was presented to the academy of Paris on the 28th of February, 1820. He here, with Latreille, divides the thorax into *prothorax, mesothorax,* and *metathorax*, but unites the two last divisions as *tronc alifère*. Each of these segments is subdivided into the upper, or DORSAL, and under, or PECTORAL, part; called also *conque pectorale*, from which processes, the *entosternum*, spring inwards. Between both, upon the metathorax, are found the *clavicules thoraciques;* and upon the mesothorax, the *plaques fulcrales*. The partitions, or phragmæ, he describes as *præ-* and *post-dorsum;* and he calls the scutellum, *bascule*. He consequently adopts as many pieces as we have described: the annexed table will show more distinctly their conformity.

Chabrier was succeeded by Audouin in a similar investigation, in which, however, the chief object was the particular description of the sternum. This was also presented to the academy, and a report of it was given by Cuvier, in the Annales Générales de Physique, tom. vii. (1821 †). He has here adopted, in general, the same parts; but each single one is divided into several pieces, with particular names, although such pieces are never found separated from each other. It may also be objected to Audouin's performance, that he has not distinguished the several dorsal and pectoral plates of the three segments by distinct names, but has merely called them *terga* and *pectora*. We cannot, therefore, retain his nomenclature. But Audouin admits of three segments, which he calls *pro-, meso-,* and *meta-thorax;* each consists of *tergum, episternum, sternum,* and *entothorax;* to which are added, in the prothorax, the *trochantinus* and the *peritrema;* in the mesothorax, the *peritrema* and *paraptera;* and in the metathorax, the *parapterum* only. Each *tergum* consists of the *præscutum*, or the anterior deflexed margin, which, in the mesonotum, becomes the pro-

* Essay sur le Vol. des Insectes. Paris, 1832, 4to.
† Audouin himself published the paper in the Annales des Sciences Naturelles, tom. i. p. 97, and p. 416.

phragma, and, in the metanotum, the mesophragma; the *scutum*, the disc of each dorsal plate; the *scutellum*, or the posterior margin; and the *postscutellum*, the posterior deflexed margin, which, in the mesonotum, becomes sometimes the mesophragma, or, upon the metanotum, it forms itself into the metaphragma. Upon the prothorax, the *episternum* and the *epimerum* form our omium: the former is the exterior surface; the latter the interior surface, directed towards the acetabula. Where the shoulder-piece is not free, they then belong to the pronotum, and form the lateral parts. The *trochantinus* by no means belongs to the thoracic case, but to the coxæ (§ 168, II. 4); the same applies to the *peritrema*, which forms the corneous ring of the spiracle. The *entothorax* is what we shall describe below (§ 165) as the *processus internus sterni*; it is in strict union with the sternal plate, and is never free or separated from it. I do not distinctly know what the *parapterum* is; probably a lateral process of the dorsal plate. I have never found a free portion in that situation. In the mesothorax, the *episternum* and *epimerum* are our scapulæ: but upon the metathorax, the parapleuræ.

After Audouin, Straus-Durckheim * and Macleay † both produced, nearly about the same time, a work upon the thorax of insects: the description of the latter adheres very closely to that of Audouin. He uses the same names and adopts the same parts; but in his sub-division of them, he goes still further, without there being a sufficient reason for it. For example, the sternal plates of the meso- and metathorax, he says, consist each of eight pieces, although in no insect with which I am acquainted is there the least indication of any other separation than the above-adduced division into two halves.

Straus-Durckheim pursues in his description of the thorax, as well as throughout his work, a peculiar path, without troubling himself in the least about the labours of his predecessors. He divides the whole thorax into *corselet* and *thorax*, the latter comprising that portion which bears the wings; this is again divided into *prothorax* (our mesothorax) and *metathorax*. The *corselet* consists of the *bouclier*, our pronotum; the two *pubis*, the *rotule*, Audouin's trochantinus, and the *sternum antérieure*. He distinguishes in his *prothorax* the *ecusson*, our mesonotum, the *clavicule antérieure*, Audouin's para-

---

* Consid. Gen. sur l'Anat. comp. des Ani. Articul. Par. 1828, 4to. p. 76, &c.
† Zoological Journal, Vol. v, (1830), No. 18, p. 145.

pterum, a part unknown to me; the *iles* or *ilialiques*, our scapula, and the *sternum moyen*, our mesosternum. His *metathorax* consists of the *clipeus*, our metanotum; the *clavicule postérieure*, a part which I also could not find, and which I consider to be either a mere process of the metanotum, or one of the joint pieces at the root of the wing; the two *ischion*, our pleura and parapleura; and lastly, the *sternum postérieure*, our *metasternum*. He also takes notice of the corneous rings of the spiracles, as parts of the thorax, and which are seated in the articulatory membrane of it: he calls them *cadres*.

The description is good and praiseworthy, like all the works of the skilful Straus; but the French names which he adopts must give place to the partially older Greek ones.

In a comparative view of the number of the thoracic pieces named by different authors, we find that Knoch has twelve, Kirby and Spence, twenty, Chabrier and myself, eighteen, Audouin, thirty-six, of which Macleay makes fifty-two, by the separation of each dorsal plate into four pieces; and Straus-Durckheim, twenty-two, because, besides the eighteen described ones, he adopts a *clavicule* to both the meso- and meta-notum.

The annexed table gives a precise comparative view of the nomenclature of the several writers.

COMPARATIVE VIEW OF THE NOMENCLATURE OF THE SEVERAL AUTHORS, FOR THE PARTS OF THE THORAX AND THEIR PROCESSES.

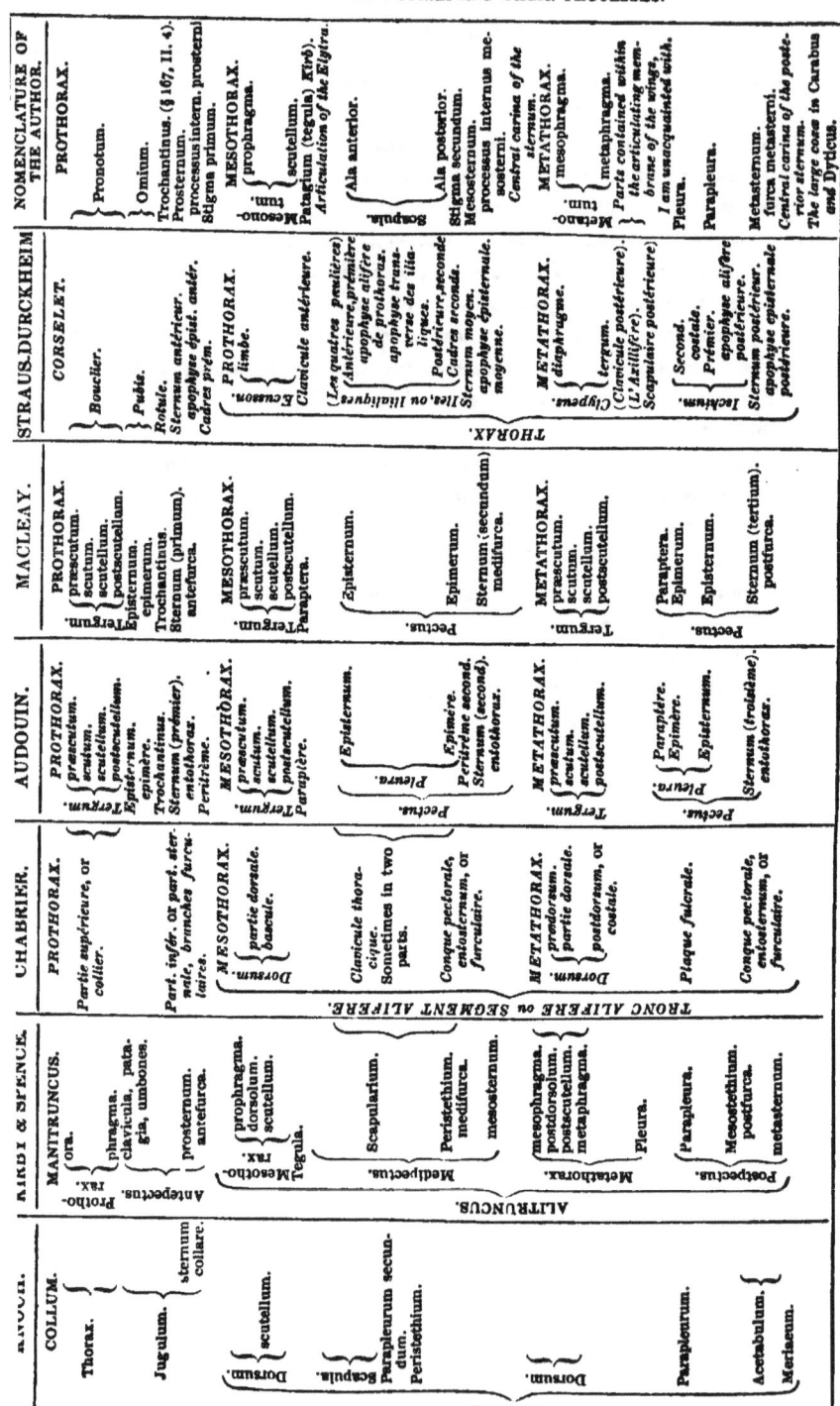

Note.—The names in capitals show the segment; those in capital initials indicate peculiar distinct parts; those entirely in small letters are mere processes, which stand in immediate connexion with the parts in front of them.

Organs of Motion upon the Thorax.

A. *The Wings.*

§ 79.

The organs of motion are of two kinds, either WINGS (*alæ*), or LEGS (*pedes*).

The wings, generally four in number, are placed, as we have already seen, upon the second and third segments of the thorax, and united to it by means of joints or an articulatory membrane. They always consist of a double membrane, which is traversed by corneous VEINS or RIBS (*neuræ, venæ, costæ*), and by means of which they are held expanded. This, their general structure, suffers a variety of modifications in the different orders, which may be comprehensively represented in the following table:—

I. Four wings.
  1. All of similar structure and membranous:
      A. Of equal size. *Neuroptera* (with the exception of the families of the May-flies), as well as the families of the *Libellulina* and *Termitina.*
      B. Of unequal size. *Hymenoptera, Lepidoptera, Phryganeodea,* the remaining *Dictyoloptera,* and many *Hemiptera homoptera.*
  2. The anterior corneous or pergamentaceous, the posterior membranous:
      A. The anterior corneous.
          a. Entirely corneous, *Coleoptera.*
          b. Half corneous, half membranous, *Hemiptera heteroptera.*
      B. The anterior pergamentaceous. *Orthoptera,* and some *Hemiptera homoptera.*

II. Two membranous wings. *Diptera.*

The general observations which we purpose here introducing upon the wings, will merely refer to their number, situation, form, and clothing. The inquiries into their structure, import, and purpose, belong to other divisions of this work, and will, consequently, remain untouched upon here.

Very little is to be said upon their number; sometimes, and indeed, in certain genera and species of almost every order, they are wholly deficient, more frequently only the posterior pair: thus, in all the *Diptera*, some *Cimices* and many *Coleoptera*, but in the majority of cases there are four distinct wings present. The deficiency of the first pair has never been observed.

Their situation is more certain than their number, for wherever we find wings, they are attached to the second and third segments of the thorax, and, indeed, at its superior exterior dorsal edges, close to where the dorsal and lateral plates adjoin. If we find no wings here, we can speedily convince ourselves whether the insect does not possess them, or whether it has lost them by some casualty, which is not of unfrequent occurrence. We speedily detect such a mutilation by the presence of the joint sockets and a portion of the wings. Apterous insects entirely want the sockets.

Before we proceed to the consideration of the form of the wings, we must remind ourselves of the differences indicated in the preceding table, as they exercise an important influence upon the form of the wing. The horny or pergamentaceous anterior wings, namely, differ so considerably in their whole structure from the membranous posterior wings, that they have been very justly considered as different organs, and have been called the WING CASES (*Elytra*). The whilst the beetle, or any other insect which possesses elytra, reposes, they lie parallel beside each other upon the back and abdomen, and thus conceal not only the posterior wings, but also very generally the whole abdodem. It is from this function that they derive their name.

We distinguish in the *elytra* their BASE (*basis*), the part by which they are attached to the thorax, and the opposite extremity, the APEX: then the MARGINS and the inner ones, which lie contiguous, and which we call the suture. Should the posterior wings be wanting, the union of the elytra is generally so strict, that it requires great force to separate them; such elytra are called CONNATE (*Elytra connata*). The angles are thus distinguished, the superior exterior one, as shoulder angle (*angulus humeralis*), the interior one, as the *angulus scutellaris*.

The most usual form of the elytra is the longitudinal extended, we might almost say oblong, did not the exterior bowed margin very generally join the sutural margin, a ta pointed angle, or by its rounding very gradually pass into it. The upper surface is convex, the under concave; the exterior margin is very generally deflexed, and often forms on the exterior a sharp edge.

The following are the chief differences of the elytra:—

TRUNCATED (*truncata*), are such elytra which are a little shorter than the abdomen.

ABBREVIATED (*abbreviata*), when they cover but a little more than its half.

DIMIDIATE (*dimidiata*), when exactly half as long as the abdomen.

SHORT (*brevissima*), when they are not half the length of the abdomen.

MUTILATED (*mutilata*), are those which cover only a portion of the abdomen, yet more than the half, but less than the apex; they are, consequently, longer than the SHORT and shorter than the TRUNCATED elytra (*Aptinus*).

FASTIGIATE (*fastigiata*), are such which extend a little beyond the apex of the abdomen.

ENTIRE (*integra*), when they are exactly the length of the abdomen, and display no distinguishing peculiarity of form.

AURICULATE (*auriculata*), are those which have at their humeral angle a peculiar, free appendage (*Lycus, Cassida.*)

SUBULATE (*subulata*), are those which gradually decrease towards their apex, and which leave, both upon the sutural and exterior margins, a portion of the abdomen uncovered (*Necydalis*, Fabr.)

ELONGATE (*elongata*), are those which are much longer than the abdomen.

DEHISCENT (*dehiscentia*), when the suture is somewhat divergent at the apex.

AMPLIATE (*ampliata, s. amplificata*), when the edge of the exterior margin is very high and prominent (*Dyticus latissimus.*)

COMPLICANT (*complicantia*), when one elytra extends over the other, and partially covers it (*Meloë*).

According to their inclination we distinguish

EVEN (*plana*) elytra, the whole superficies of which is upon one plane.

DEFLEXED (*deflexa*), when the vicinity of the suture lies higher than the exterior margin; sometimes they rise into a pyramid, called

TURRETED (*turrita*), or they are very convex in the centre, viz. GIBBOUS (*gibba*).

Both the elytra together are called the sheath or covering (*coleoptera*), and each single one a wing case (*elytrum*).

The differences of surface have been already sufficiently described at section 19, for almost all the differences of form there named are to be found in elytra. The same applies to the differences of margin, but with greater limitation.

Their clothing, also, is so variously different, that scarcely any description of it is found upon the insect body, which does not also occur upon the elytra; we, therefore, here again refer to the General Orismology.

The hemelytra, or half corneous wing-cases of the *Hemiptera heteroptera*, have most qualities in common with the entirely horny elytra. In the majority we can distinguish four divisions separated by furrows, the first three of which are horny, but the fourth forms the membranous portion. The first, the NAIL, (*Clavus*, Pl. XV. f. 1. *a*), is a longitudinal almost parallelly sided piece, situated at the interior margin, contiguous to the scutellum, and, in repose, partially passing its sharp edge beneath it; close to this, upon the exterior, lies the HEM-ELYTRUM (Pl. XV. f. 1, *b*), which is the largest of all the divisions, and forms a triangular horny piece, which enters the mesothorax with its anterior acute angle. The APPENDIX (Pl. XV. f. 1. *c*), which is frequently wanting, follows the HEMELYTRUM; it is likewise a triangular, but much smaller, and often right angular horny plate, the right angle of which is contiguous to the exterior margin of the hemelytra, so that the hypothenuse is turned towards the inner margin. The fourth and last division is attached to this, and which is called the MEMBRANE (*membrana*, Pl. XV. f. 1. *d*), from its membranous quality. It is generally of a rhomboidal form, with obtuse angles, or it is ovate, but more rarely forming a somewhat reversed half moon. It likewise consists, like all wings and wing-cases, of a superior and inferior layer, between which horny ribs pass, and distend it.

The pergamentaceous cases, called TEGMINA, differ from the true elytra, by being less firm in their substance, and from the true wings, by their greater strength. They are situated at the same place with the elytra and hemelytra, and they approach nearer to the latter in their structure, but most closely to the true membranous wing. For, although in the hemelytra the ribs and veins are more apparent, yet in the tegmina they are so clearly developed, that they are no longer subject to doubt. Lower, in the anatomy, we shall find that the elytra also possess such veins, but which, from the thickness of their substance, do not become prominent.

In form, the tegmina are subject to greater differences than the elytra or hemelytra; for sometimes they are shorter than the body, broad, ovate (*Gryllotalpa*); sometimes as long, with parallel sides, rounded (*Blatta*); sometimes longer, very slender, acute, and narrowed at the base (*Gryllus*, Fabr.); and sometimes very wide, large, and elliptical (*Mantis*). By means of the veins originating from a main stem, which furcate from the very base, they are divided into three principal areas; the first of which, seated upon the exterior margin (Pl. XV. f. 2, A), is in general the narrowest, and towards the apex of the tegmina contracts gradually to a point; it is also usually of a harder substance than the following. This second piece (Pl. XV. f. 2, B) lies contiguous to the former, and is separated from it by the beforementioned chief vein; it is the largest of the three areas, embraces the majority of the ramifications of the veins, becomes gradually wider towards the apex of the wing, and consists of a softer membrane than the marginal area. The third, or sutural area (Pl. XV. f. 2, c), lies inwardly beyond the second, and it is also harder than the central area; in many families it forms the superior dorsal covering, while the two other areas fall down upon the sides of the body (*Gryllodea, Locustaria*). It varies considerably in figure; it, like the marginal area, is sometimes a very pointed isosceles triangle (*Gryllodea*); sometimes, as in the hemelytra, a space surrounding the scutellum (*Achetaria*); it also sometimes appears to be wanting, or not distinctly separated from the central area (*Mantodea*).

There seems likewise to be some difference in the ramification of the horny veins throughout these three areas; in the marginal one they are small, broad, multitudinously divided veins, which appear to spread from two or three radiating main branches. In the central area, the large stems spread more parallelly from the inner side of the chief stem, which separates them; the transverse veins also run parallel, and thus divide the whole area into small squares. In the inner area, lastly, the veins are most delicate, and ramify variously on all sides, whereby an irregular reticulation is formed.

§ 80.

The mere membranous wings (*alæ*) distinctly differ from the preceding organs by their transparency, and purely membranous nature. In respect to their situation and general function, they perfectly agree with the former; but the wings are exclusively organs of flight, while the different kinds of elytra have the additional purpose of covering the soft upper part of the abdomen. Therefore all insects provided with wings only are entirely inclosed in a hard case, and, although they possess wings, are equally unprovided with a protection against exterior influences, as those genera and species which have no wings.

The observations we are about to make upon the wings will refer to their exterior perceptible construction, and their different forms and clothing. The investigation into their progressive conformation, their internal coherence, their functions, &c., belong to other divisions, and will be treated upon in the proper place.

In outward appearance, the wings present themselves as flexible, but firm, dry membranes, which are traversed by various horny ribs. These RIBS (*costæ*), or more properly VEINS (*nervæ*), as they are, in fact, vessels, but incorrectly called NERVES (*nervæ*), arise all from the roots of the wing, and through their main branches, of which we usually observe two or three, they are connected with the thorax by articulation. The first and most exterior of these veins is called the MARGINAL RIB (*costa marginalis*, Pl. XV. *a, a*), or, by pre-eminence, the RIB (*costa*), which forms its anterior margin when expanded, and extends from the base to the apex. Jurine, who made use of particular names to indicate the veins of the wings of the Hymenoptera, calls it *radius;* and a horny expansion of it in its course, which is particularly distinct in this order, but which is also observable in others, he calls the POINT of the wing (*punctum*, or *carpus*) ; but Latreille, and Kirby and Spence call it STIGMA (Pl. XV. f. 4, β). The second vein originates close to the first, and distinguishes itself from the rest, like the former, by its superior robustness. Its course also is in a direct line towards the apex, but it gradually diverges from the marginal vein; so that the portion of the wing enclosed by it, takes the form of a triangle. Kirby and Spence call this the *postcosta* (Pl. XV. f. *b, b, b*); Jurine, *cubitus;* and Latreille, *nervus internus*. It also ultimately attains the apex of the wing. It is seldom simple; in the majority of cases it divides itself into branches, so that the main stem ceases before it attains the disc of the wing; but the branches extend from the separation, either continuing simply to the end of the wing, or again ramifying. By means of these ramifications, a varied net-work is produced upon the disc of the wing, the reticulations of which are tolerably constant in the several orders, families and genera, and is therefore of importance for the determination and distinction of the groups. The spaces enclosed by these veins are called AREOLETS (*areolæ*), or CELLS (*cellulæ*, Jurine); and those lying close to the marginal rib are called MARGINAL AREOLETS (*areolæ marginales*, Pl. XV. *d, d*); Jurine's, *cellulæ radiales;* those succeeding to them, and formed by the postcosta and its branches, SUBMARGINAL AREOLETS (*areolæ submarginales*, Pl. XV. *e, e*); *cellulæ cubitales* of Jurine. The transverse veins which branch from the longitudinal nervures of the main stems, are called the CONNECTING VEINS (*venæ anastomosis*), or *nervi recurrentes* of Jurine. The areolets seated at the end of the wing, and, sometimes not quite closed, are called IMPERFECT (*areolæ imperfectæ*, Pl. XV. *f, f*), or *cellulæ incompletæ* of Jurine. The APPENDED CELL (*cellula appendicea*) of the same author is a small, almost triangular areolet, situated at the apex of the wing, which is formed by the furcate division of the vein springing from the stigma (in many genera of the *Tenthredonodea;* for example, *Perga*, &c.).

The space behind the second principal vein of the wing is its third and last chief areolet, which, in many cases (*Hymenoptera*), is anteriorly limited by a peculiar, slight vein, originating near the second principal one; and this areolet extends to about the middle of the margin of the posterior wing. Several other veins and areolets (*nervi et cellulæ brachiales*, Jurine) are found within this space, which, as they do not vary much in large groups, are consequently of less importance for the determination of genera.

In the membranous wings we also find the same distribution into three chief areolets which we have already indicated in the tegmina, and we here distinguish them, with Kirby, as the MARGINAL AREOLET (*area costalis sive marginalis*), CENTRAL AREOLET (*area discoidalis s. intermedia*), and POSTERIOR AREOLET (*area analis s. posterior*). In repose, during which the wings lie parallely upon the body, the posterior areolet passes beneath the central one, turning upon its limitary vein, like a door upon its hinge. In those orders, however, in which we meet with elytra, or an analogous structure, the inferior wings are folded in several directions. Thus, in the beetles, the whole apex of the wing is very generally folded from the stigma back towards the base, or the whole wing, from this point, folds itself like a fan (*Forficula*), or this plication originates from the base of the wing, according to the direction of the radiating veins (*Orthoptera*).

The preceding general description treats chiefly of the anterior wings;

but it will equally apply to the posterior ones, when they are of the same size and quality as the former (see the table, § 79). Where the posterior wings differ in form from the anterior, they are in general smaller —often, however, broader, if not longer. It is chiefly in the *Orthoptera* that we observe this more significant size of the posterior wings; in these they are sometimes even longer than the anterior, and extend beyond them (*Gryllotalpa*); it is the same in some beetles with short elytra (*Necydalis, Atractocerus*). In general, however, the true wings of an Order are perfectly uniform in structure, although their veins ramify differently, and, this also applies more generally to the posterior wings, which less distinctly show the above-described separation into three principal areolets, although, upon a careful inspection, these would not be found deficient in them.

The following are the most important orismological definitions of the wings:—

The ANTERIOR WINGS (*alæ anteriores*) are those attached to the second thoracic segment; they are also called SUPERIOR (*al. superiores*) from their covering the posterior ones in repose; or, the FIRST (*primariæ*) from their preceding the others in flight. The posterior wings have had, from opposite reasons, opposite names applied to them, as *al. posteriores, al. inferiores,* and *al. secundariæ*. In each wing we distinguish, as the ANTERIOR MARGIN (*margo anterior*), or EXTERIOR MARGIN (*margo externus*), that margin which, in flight, lies in the direction of the head; that opposed to it as the INNER MARGIN (*m. internus*); the third, generally taking the direction of an obtuse angle, with regard to its situation as to the others, is called the POSTERIOR MARGIN (*m. posterior*). The angles formed by these margins at their point of contact, receive the following names:—the ANTERIOR ANGLE (*angulus anterior*) is that at the apex of the wing, formed by the anterior and posterior margins; the POSTERIOR ANGLE is that formed by the contact of the posterior and interior margins. We have already made mention of the humeral and scutellar angles.

The general outline of the wings is distinguished according to its form; the following terms are used to express them:—FALCATE (*falcatæ*, Pl. XV. f. 12) are wings whose anterior margin forms a circle bending outwards, and their posterior margin is also directed forwards (many *Lepidoptera*).

TAILED (*caudatæ*, Pl. XV. f. 13) are those which have a long and narrow appendage extending from the internal margin. This form is found chiefly in the posterior wings of the butterflies (*Pap. Machaon, Podalirius,* &c.).

DIGITATE (*digitata*, Pl. XV. f. 14) is a wing, which has its otherwise undivided surface indented with deep incisions between the ribs or veins (*Orneodes*).

Besides these outlines, which are peculiar to the wings, we likewise find in them the majority of the differences mentioned in § 18.

The same applies to the differences of margin; we therefore refer to § 20.

The surface of the true wings is subjected to but few changes; in general it is a smooth skin, with here and there some hair spread over it (in many *Diptera,* for example, *Psychoda*). In one order, however, (the *Lepidoptera*), the general law prevails for their being clothed with flattened scales (*alæ squamosæ*).

The situation of the wings in repose is much more various in peculiarities. We proceed to the consideration of these differences, and thereby form a conclusion to the investigation we have here made upon these organs.

EVEN (*alæ planæ*), are those wings which, in a state of repose, preserve the same extension as when in motion.

Opposed to them are the FOLDED wings (*plicatæ*). By this term we understand such as are longitudinally folded in repose, like a fan, and expand only during flight into a uniform surface (*Orthoptera*). We consider such wings as RE-FOLDED (*replicatæ*), when their apex falls back upon the base.

CONVOLUTED wings (*al. convolutæ*), are such which embrace the body from above downwards, and enclose it as in a tube (*Crambus*).

INCUMBENT (*incumbentes*), when, lying parallely upon each other, they cover the abdomen above (*Tenthredo*).

CROSSED (*cruciatæ*), are those incumbent wings which pass over each other only at their apex (many Bees, the hemelytra of the *Hemiptera heteroptera*).

HORIZONTAL (*horizontales*), whose direction is in the same plane with that of the body. The reverse of these are the ERECT wings (*erectæ*), whose line of direction is perpendicular to the plane of the body (*Papilio*).

EXTENDED (*extensæ*), form also in their direction a right angle with the body, but lie in the same plane with it; from these we must distinguish the OPEN wings (*patentes*) by the angle which they form with the axis of the body, being at least of 45° (*Tabanus, Musca*, &c.). The ERECT-OPEN wings (*erectæ patentes*) do not lie in the same plane with the body, but cut it at an angle of less than 45° (some *Lepidoptera*, for example, *Hesperia*).

CONNIVENT (*conniventes*), are such wings which, in repose, perfectly unite with each other at their corresponding margins (*Papilio*); DIVARICATED (*divaricatæ*), are such which only partially cover each other (*Agrion*).

DEFLEXED (*deflexæ*), are such which, with their internal margin, meet at an acute angle, and so cover the body (many *Noctuæ*); from them must be distinguished the REVERSED wings (*reversæ*) by this, that the anterior margin of the posterior wing projects beyond the same part of the anterior wing (*Gastrophaga alnifolia*); this is also often the case in the open wings.

B. THE LEGS.

§ 81.

The other chief organs of motion, the LEGS (*pedes*), are distinguished from the wings in a multitude of ways, in form and number, as well as in their function.

In number, they exceed that of the wings by one-half; for although we never observe more than four wings, we constantly find, in perfect insects, six legs. These six legs are placed in pairs upon the lower part of each of the three segments of the thorax, and consist of many joints, to the observation of which we now pass.

We have already become acquainted with the ACETABULA (*acetabula*) upon the segments or plates of the breast, for the reception of the legs.

I. These cavities receive pieces formed exactly to their dimensions, frequently conical, or more longitudinal and rounded, called the HIPS (*coxæ*, Pl. XVI. f. 1, *a*). Surrounded and enclosed by a corneous substance, it has, only at each of its opposed ends, an opening for the passage of the muscles which unite it to the surrounding parts. This typical form of structure is somewhat modified by the closer or looser union of the coxæ with the thorax; so that it appears sometimes as a cone truncated at its apex, and then attached to the thorax by the whole of its basal surface (*Diptera, Lepidoptera, Hymenoptera*, &c.); and sometimes moves itself freely in a proportionate cavity of the thorax, to which it is affixed by a single small spot (many *Coleoptera*); and sometimes, lastly, it displays itself more flattened, in which case it is affixed to the thorax by a firmer and closer union, which admits of no free motion (for example, the posterior coxæ of *Dyticus*, *Buprestis*, &c.). In this last case, frequently also in the first, the coxæ appear to belong more strictly to the thorax than to the legs, as they stand in much more intimate connection with the former than with the latter; but their very general free motion speaks strongly against the adoption of this opinion.

II. A much smaller corneous piece, the TROCHANTER (Pl. XVI. f. 1, *b*), stands in moveable connection with the coxa. The form of this part is subject to many changes; we sometimes find it quite annular, with surrounding, equally high sides; sometimes compressed and obliquely truncated, or prolonged into a lateral point (*Carabus*, *Dyticus*). This form is found chiefly among the beetles; in other orders (the *Diptera*, for example) it has very generally the annular form. In these orders, the articulation of the coxæ consists only of a firm membrane; but in the former, ball-joints appear to be fitted to corresponding sockets, whereby the strength of the union is very much increased.

III. The trochanter is succeeded by the THIGH (*femur*, Pl. XVI. f. 1, *c*), which is the largest joint of the leg. It is generally of a cylindrical, but not always equally thick, frequently knobby or clavate, form. It is very often much longer than the two first joints together; in general also longer than the following, but always thicker and more robust. Besides this roundish form, we also observe angular, prismatic, parallelopipedal, flat, very much compressed, and provided with a longitudinal furrow, or even globose and elliptical forms. Its union with the trochanter is sometimes very close, at others looser. We meet with its firm conjunction in the *Coleoptera*. In these the motion of the thigh appears to be very limited, and in general the trochanter moves in the articulation upon the coxæ, when the thigh is touched; it is different in the *Diptera*, in which the freer union of both admits of greater motion. The upper surface of the thigh is like that of the coxa and trochanter, generally smooth; but its margins are not rarely armed, sometimes with solitary spines, sometimes with hair, or with long cilia. Some have broad lobate appendages (*Trachusa lobata*, *Mantis oratoria*). We do not usually observe such processes upon the two first joints, for coxæ armed with a spine belong to the rarer exceptions; these we observe among some of the *Ichneumons* (*Ich. melanogonus*, Grav.; *Pimpla mesocentra*, Grav.)

IV. The fourth joint of the leg is the SHIN (*tibia*, Pl. XVI. f. 1, *d*.) But in the same way as the thigh is united to the hip through the medium of the trochanter, so is the shin connected with the thigh, viz. by ginglymus, but in a reversed direction, for whilst in the former articulation the shanks are directed upwards, in the latter it is the apex. With respect to its form, it is very generally as long as the thigh, and it is equally often thinner and more slightly framed. Notwithstanding which, we observe more differences in the tibia than in the thigh; it is found conical, tubular, triangular, quadrangular, compressed either partially or entirely, leaf-shaped, uneven and rough. It is not unfrequently that we perceive them armed or clothed with spines, either solitary or placed in rows, with very long hair, teeth, fringe (*tib. fimbriatæ*), and setæ. Indeed they occur more frequently upon the shank than upon the thigh. In form, however, it is very much regulated by that of the thigh, and its structure appears to agree as intimately as is compatible with the preformed figure of that joint. For example, should the thigh be conical, the shank forms a bow, which fits closely to the cone (*Chalcis*), or if the thigh be convex, the shank then forms a corresponding inflection. The same is the case in raptorious legs (*Mantis*). At the end of the shin, and around the cavities, wherein the following joint articulates, in general we observe some spines, which are usually called SPURS or TERMINAL SPINES (*Calcaria, Spicula*, Pl. XVI. f. 1. δ, δ.) They are indeed most frequently mere processes of the horny substance, but they are sometimes articulated, and have a free motion at the will of the insect (*Mantis*). In this case they form a species of pincers (*Hylobius Abietis*), which assists the insect in climbing.

V. It is to the shin that the last division of the leg, the FOOT (*tarsus*, Pl. XVI. f. 1, *e*.) is attached. It consists of a series of consecutive joints, the first of which is generally the largest, and the following gradually decrease until the last, which is again longer than the one by which it is preceded. The last is armed with claws and appendages at its termination. The connection of the first with the shin is also by ginglymus, and indeed the fork of its two shanks point upwards, whereas the joints of the foot itself are connected so together that they form but one surface in their union. The cavity of each joint is placed near the upper surface, often in its very centre, and its anterior margin is produced beyond it. By means of this arrangement, the joints can only bend upwards, but they are allowed in many cases a slight inflection downwards.

The number of the foot-joints varies from 1 to 5. As these numbers are tolerably uniform in the several families, and as many insects closely allied to them possess the same number of foot-joints, they have been used in forming divisions in the several orders, which are thus distinguished.

PENTAMEROUS (*pentamera*), when all the feet have FIVE joints.
CRYPTO-PENTAMEROUS (*crypto-pentamera*), are those which truly possess FIVE joints, but in which the penultimate is so small that it can be perceived only upon the most rigid inspection, and by means of a lens (*Cerambyx*). Kirby and Spence call this joint the ARTHRIUM.

HETEROMEROUS (*heteromera*), when the four anterior legs have, FIVE, but the two posterior ones only FOUR joints.

TETRAMEROUS (*tetramera*), when there are FOUR joints to all the feet. The CRYPTO-TETRAMEROUS appear to have but THREE joints, the penultimate being very small (*Coccinella*).

TRIMEROUS (*trimera*), feet with three joints.

DIMEROUS (*dimera*), feet with two joints. And lastly,

MONOMEROUS (*monomera*), when the foot has but one joint.

The different forms of the whole foot as well as of the individual joints are shown at § 83.

§ 82.

Forms of the Legs.

The most simple form of the legs, in which all the joints have the usual construction, and no peculiar qualities are displayed even by the feet, is distinguished by the name of CURSORIOUS LEGS (*pedes cursorii*), even in those cases where the insect is anything but a runner, and but slowly moves about. The *Carabi* are the chief representatives of this form.

AMBULATORY (*ambulatorii*), are those whose feet have a broad hairy sole (*Lamia*).

GRESSORIOUS (*gressorii*), are those whose anterior pair is imperfectly developed, whilst the rest are formed upon the type of the cursorious legs. Sometimes the foot is wholly wanting (*Ateuchus, Lonchophorus*, Pl. XVI. f. 2); sometimes all its joints are small and imperfect (*Vanessa, Hipparchia*, Pl. XVI. f. 3).

NATATORIOUS (*natatorii*), are the legs of insects which live entirely, or partially, in the water; their shins and feet are broad, compressed, and fringed on each side with long hair (*Dyticus, Naucoris, Notonecta*)

SALTATORIOUS (*Saltatorii*, Pl. XVI. f. 5), are those which have very thick posterior thighs, by means of which the insect is enabled to make wide leaps (*Haltica, Orchestes*).

RAPTORIUS (*raptorii*, Pl. XVI. f. 6), are those whose shins and feet in repose turn back upon the thigh, and often pass, into it like a knife within its handle (*Mantis, Syrtis, Nepa, Ranatra*). This structure is found only in the anterior legs, and somewhat justifies their being called hands, which Kirby and Spence proposed, from the raptorious legs serving to seize the prey with.

FOSSORIOUS (*fossorii*, Pl. XVI. f. 7), are those legs whose tibiæ, and frequently feet, are very broad, and resemble a hand, serving the insect to dig holes and passages in the earth (*Clivina, Heterocerus, Gryllotalpa*.

§ 83.

Forms of the Joints.

We must here, at the conclusion of our notice of the legs, observe the differences of the structure of their joints, although we have touched upon many of their forms in the preceding descriptions.

1. HIP.—Besides the above noticed difference, we must distinguish immoveable hips, which are affixed to the thorax (for example those of *Dyticus*, Pl. IX. No. 2, f. 8), as FIXED (*fixæ*), and the moveable ones, which turn in the socket, as FREE (*liberæ*, Pl. XII. No. 5, f. 2 and 3). These last might, particularly in reference to their form, be called JOINT BALLS (*capita femorum*), as the whole hip can in fact be nothing else than a moveable thigh ball. Hips, beneath which there is a curled lock of hair, are called FLOCCULATE (*floccatæ*, for example *Andrena*, Pl. XVI. f. 8).

2. TROCHANTER.—Kirby and Spence call it FULCRANT (*fulcrans*) when it is continued for a space along the thigh, thereby strengthening its union (*Carabus*, Pl. XVI. f. 9). This joint occasionally consists of two rings (for example, *Pimpla*, Pl. XVI. f. 10), and it is then called DIMEROUS (*dimerus*), but it is most usually MONOMEROUS (*monomerus*), having but one joint.

3. THIGH.—We have fully distinguished its differences above.

4. SHIN.—We add the following differences to those in § 81. IV.

POLICATE (*policata*) is when it is produced inside into a short bent spine.

PALMATE (*palmata*, Pl. XVI. f. 2), when the whole shin is compressed, and upon its exterior margin there are short but strong teeth (*Hister, Ateuchus*).

FOLIACEOUS (*foliacea*, Pl. XVI. f. 11), when, instead of its usual tubular form, the shin is entirely or partially extended into a thin horny plate (*Lygæus, Coreus*); or CLYPEATE (*clypeata*, Pl. XVI. f. 12), when the enlargement is only upon one side, and is slightly convex (the males of some *Crabro's*).

SCOPATE (*scopacea*, Pl. XVI. f. 13), is a broad shin, densely covered with short hair (many bees). This, considered as a distinct organ, Kirby and Spence call a brush (*sarothrum*).

5. FOOT.—Of all the divisions of the leg, the joints of the feet are subjected to the greatest varieties of form. Most frequently cylindrical, by the narrowing of the base they gradually pass into the conical shape, but even these feet are somewhat flattened beneath, and thus form a kind of sole (for example in *Carabus*). This kind of narrow sole has no other distinction than that it is limited by two small ridges, which in front are produced into two small spines (Pl. XVI. f. 14). These kind of feet are peculiar to those insects which run upon rough and especially horizontal surfaces (the *Carabidea*); others, which move upon perpendicular and moving objects, have flat broad joints, which are provided with a peculiar clasping apparatus. Such flattened joints are sometimes, cordate (Pl. XVI. f. 15), triangular (f. 16), quadrate (f. 17), simple, or emarginate in front (f. 15), sometimes more deeply divided and bilobate (Pl. XVI. f. 18). This last form is in the majority of cases peculiar to the penultimate joint only (for example in the *Cerambycina*, as *Callidium violaceum*); in other cases several are divided, for example, the three first in *Brachycerus*, the third and fourth in *Lycus*, &c. The individual joints are nearly equally long and broad, but it is not unusual for the first to be longer than the following, and it is then called, particularly when in its general structure it diverges from the following (as in the bees), *metatarsus*. The remaining equal joints then form the TOE (*digitus*) or the FINGER (*dactylus*); they are individually called the PHALANGES, and not, as some writers presume, fingers and toes. All insects are consequently one-toed (*monodactyla*), the genus Xya. Ill. (*Tridactylus*, Latr.*) only having actually two equally long toes (Pl. XVI. f. 19).

---

* See Charpentier, Horæ Entomologicæ. *Vrat.* 1825. 4to. p. 84 Tab.

If the foot-joints are broader than long, and assume a lunate form, and are so closely attached together that the first large one embraces all the following within its deep concavity, and the whole foot appears to form but one disc, it is called PATELLA. The males of the genus *Dyticus* display this structure (Pl. XVI. f. 23. a, b), the underside is then thickly beset with compact hair, and between which several unequal cups, PATELLULÆ, are placed which serve as organs of attachment. We pass to this structure by the ENLARGED FEET (*tarsi amplificati*); these consist of heart-shaped joints, which are also clothed beneath with brushes and feathers. But in these we distinctly discern each individual joint; indeed sometimes they are not all so, but only some upon some pairs of legs, for example the first three joints in the anterior pair of the male *Cicindelæ*, (Pl. XVI. f. 20); the four first in *Carabus* (f. 21); and but seldom only one joint is dilated (in *Hydrophilus*). Modern entomologists (Zimmerman, for instance *), call a thus widened foot *palma*, and the single joints *patellæ*, which is scarcely admissible from the above indicated definition of these words.

COMPRESSED FEET (*tarsi compressi*) stand in direct opposition to the DEPRESSED or flattened feet (*tarsi depressi*). We find them most fully formed among the bees. In these, namely, the first joint is most closely affixed to the shin, and appears to be but a division of it, whereas it properly belongs to the foot. The cause of this structure is to be found in their economy; for covered with hair, as is also the shin in this case, it serves to carry the pollen of flowers. Such a hairy shin, in conjunction with the first joint of the foot, is called BRUSH (*sarothrum*) as we mentioned above. The second kind of compressed feet is peculiar to the water beetles (Pl. XVI. f. 4), but here its superficies is smooth, and the margin only occupied with a fringe of stiff setæ.

The last joint of the foot is particularly distinguished from the rest by having at its end two slightly bent moveable hooks, which with it form a CLAW (*unguis*), by help of which insects move upon smooth surfaces, and indeed are enabled to creep up perpendicular walls. The HOOKS (*unguiculi*) of these claws are either equal (*Carabus*, f. 24), unequal (*Anisoplia fructicola*, f. 25), or round, compressed, and in this case of immense size (*Rutela*, f. 26) very generally they are SIMPLE (*ung. simplices*), but also BIFID (*ung. bifidi* or *fissi*, *Meloë*, *Tetraonyx*, Pl. XVI. f. 27), sometimes armed beneath with one (*Melolontha*,

---

* See his Monographie der Zabroiden. Berlin, 1831. 8vo.

Pl. XVI. f. 29), or several (*Hippobosca*, Pl. XVI. f. 29), teeth (*unguic. dentati*), and at others, the under-edge is toothed like a saw (*unguic. serrati*, or *denticulate. Calathus, Cistela*, &c. Pl. XVI. f. 30).

Between these two hooks of the terminal joint, we perceive in some insects a second smaller claw, called the SPURIOUS CLAW (*pseudonychia*), but by Nitzsch *empodium*. Among the beetles, we find this structure in *Lucanus* (Pl. XVI. f. 31). This claw perfectly agrees with the larger one in its conformation, and consists, therefore similarly to this, of a stalk-like basal-joint, at the end of which there are two little hooks. In the *Hymenoptera, Diptera,* and some families of other orders, we find instead of them, soft, gently convex, oblong, membranous cushions, the SOLES (*plantuæ*) or CLIMBING CUSHIONS (*arolia*, Nitzsch, Pl. XVI. f. 32). These attach like sucking-cups, and therefore the insects provided with them (for example the *Diptera*) can run lightly and securely upon vacillating objects. We seldom observe spurious claws and cushions together (*Laphria*, Pl. XVI. f. 33); still, more seldom, are both wanting as well as the larger claws (*Xenos*, Pl. XVI. f. 34).

The underside of the foot, or SOLE (*planta*) has, when very narrow, nothing to distinguish it. But if the foot is depressed, the sole has a peculiar clothing, which has been called FOOT-CUSHION (*pulvillus*). It consists very generally of short and stiff hair (*Lamia*, Pl. XVI. f. 35), more rarely of radiating plumes (*Zabrus*, Pl. XVI. f. 36), occasionally of true fleshy cushions (*Xenos*, Pl. XVI. f. 34). Some genera (*Timarcha*) display minute cup-shaped hollows in the sole, which is then called SPONGY (*pl. spongiosa*, Pl. XVI. f. 37). In the majority of the first adduced instances, the margin also is covered with short hair.

III.—The Abdomen.

§ 84.

The third and last chief division of the body of an insect bears the general name of abdomen. Notwithstanding its being very variable in form, it does not exhibit an equal difference of structure, but consists of several consecutive horny rings or segments, in some cases merely following upon, in others, retractile within each other. These rings vary much in number, but never exceed nine. Upon consideration, we shall remember that the body of all caterpillars and undeveloped insects consists of thirteen segments (§ 53). Of these, one constitutes the head, three the thorax, and, consequently, nine remain for the abdomen. These, however, are not always present; frequently, several appear united in one; and, more frequently, the last are so completely covered by the preceding, as wholly to escape observation upon a superficial examination. Sometimes, also, the back presents more divisions than the belly; indeed, in *Carabus* we observe nine distinct dorsal divisions, whereas, we can distinguish in the venter but five. The belly very generally presents one less than the back. We observe, also, a difference of number in the sexes; for, in many *Hymenoptera**, the males have seven and the females but six segments. These segments are either simple horny rings, or else each consists of a superior and inferior half ring, which are connected together at the sides by means of a delicate membrane; sometimes a longer or shorter free process of the superior half segment projects over this point of union, thus covering this delicate part from all exterior injury. In the *Coleoptera*, and, in general, in such insects as are provided with hard superior wings, this structure is not to be perceived, but the soft uniting membrane lies exposed, and even the horny substance of the superior half segment is very small and soft, from the very natural cause of the hard elytra supplying the place of all other modes of protection. In these orders, therefore, the ventral portion of the segments acquire

---

* All the *Aculeate Hymenoptera.*—Tr.

additional and proportional consistency and firmness. This part is called the BELLY (*venter*) in contradistinction to the upper superficies corresponding with the breast, which is named the BACK (*dorsum*).

The union between the several superior and inferior segments is effected in precisely the same way as between the upper and under half segments, by means of a soft membrane. This connecting membrane is perceptible only upon the back, and only in those instances where the back is protected by hard superior wings or wing-cases; in all the rest, the posterior margin of each segment laps over the commencement of the succeeding one, thus covering and protecting the soft uniting membrane. If we observe the abdomen in its most distended state, for example, in a gravid female, it appears as a large membranous bag, covered above and beneath with equally broad parallel, transversely round and convex horny plates; or, if the horny substance be considered as its fundamental material, it may be compared to a horny bladder divided by parallel membranous girdles, and which are also separated laterally by similar membranous stripes running at right angles with the transverse parallels.

Precisely at the points of intersection of the membranous longitudinal and transverse stripes, there is placed on each side a small opening surrounded by a callous margin, and which is called the air-hole, STIGMA, or SPIRACLE (*stigma, spiracula*), which is the opening to the respiratory organs ramifying throughout the body. In the usually contracted state of the abdomen, the natural situation of these spiracles is beneath the horny processes of the superior half segment; but in the *Coleoptera* with corneous elytra, they lie upon the upper surface of the abdomen close to the sides, and are equally protected by those organs. These spiracles, consequently, are in every instance most carefully protected from external injuries.

Other openings which lead to the intestines and the organs of generation we shall notice lower down.

The uniting membrane of the horny plates Kirby and Spence call *pulmonarium*, from the circumstance of its containing the commencement of the respiratory organs; but its chief purpose being evidently the union of the several horny rings, it must also justly thence be called UNITING skin (*conjunctiva*). In descriptive entomology, however, it is of but little importance, as it is never visible, being always covered either by the processes of the horny segments or by the wing-cases.

With respect to the general form of the abdomen, it varies so extremely, that we can scarcely suggest a universal type of construction. It is sometimes ovate, longitudinal or cylindrical, sometimes compressed and angular or broad and flat; but its transverse section may always be readily reduced to the form of a rectangular triangle, the base of which lies above, the apex pointing downwards. It is not possible to give a more definite determination to this triangle, for its sides are sometimes straight, sometimes, chiefly the upper one, convex, sometimes the opposite sides form an apparent semicircle, occasionally they bend inwards or outwards, &c. &c.

The form of the abdomen depends much upon the mode of its attachment to the thorax. In the majority of cases, for instance, in the *Coleoptera, Orthoptera, Dictyoptera, Hemiptera*, and in many families of the other orders, the abdomen is conical, that is to say, it commences with a broad base and gradually decreases towards its apex; when this broad base is united by its whole circumference to the metathorax, the abdomen is called SESSILE. But even a perfectly conical abdomen, the base of which is sharply truncated, is sometimes connected with the metathorax by means only of a small portion of its margin (*Vespa*). This mode of union between both parts of the body is most perceptible in those insects whose first abdominal segment has the form of a thin tube, which, towards its apex, distends more or less trumpet-shaped. The succeeding broader and larger segments are united to the first in the same way as among themselves, and by this means the either ovate, conical, compressed, falcate, flat, or longitudinal abdomen appears as if, like the leaf of a tree, it was supported by a distinct stalk, whence it has been called by entomologists PETIOLATED (*ab. petiolatum*). The tubular first segment itself is called the PEDICLE (*petiolus*). It is not always a direct tube, but occasionally swollen into knots (*pet. nodosus*), or distended upwards into a thin scale (*pet. squamatus*). If the second abdominal segment be of greater compass than the following, so that its margin stands freely out, and the succeeding segment completely received within it, the abdomen is then called CAMPANULATE (*ab. campanulatum*, for example *Zethus*). But if, on the contrary, the abdomen be constricted at its commencement, and not perfectly petiolated, as in the Butterflies and most *Diptera*, it is called COARCTATE (*ab. coarctatum*).

In many instances, all or individual segments of the abdomen have peculiar processes, which are found sometimes at their sides, and which project as lappets (*ab. lobatum*), or rise in thorns or spines from the surface of the plates. If a solitary large horn be placed upon the centre of the venter, it is called HASTATE (*ab. hastatum*); HORNED (*ab. cornutum*), on the contrary, when it proceeds from the back; MARGINATE (*ab. marginatum*), when its sides project in sharp ridges, (*Coreus marginatus*); or winged (*ab. alatum*), when the projection of the margin is very considerable (*Coreus quadratus*, many *Tingis*). These differences of margin are generally found only in such insects whose superior wings form horny wing-cases; consequently only among the *Coleoptera*, although among these but rarely, *Orthoptera* and *Hemiptera*, and among the latter most frequently.

§ 85.

We must now turn our attention to the abdominal appendages.

The appendages of the abdomen may be classed into three large groups, according to whether they belong to the anus or the sexual organs, or to neither one nor the other.

The ANUS is a round opening near the upper side of the last abdominal segment, and is in but few instances provided with peculiar appendages, but lies within the last abdominal segment which closes the rectum with its two halves. In these cases, the sexual organs open into the cavity formed by the last segment, and are similarly covered by it. It might not, therefore, be inappropriate to call this cavity with its opening by the name applied to the analogous construction in Birds, the CLOACA. Kirby and Spence propose *podex* as the name for the superior flap, and for the lower one, *hypopygium*. In those instances in which the anus is not closed by the flaps of the last segment of the abdomen, we observe peculiar thick processes which close its aperture like the prongs of tongs; they are sometimes hooked, and are then called UNCI (*Locusta, Gryllus*).

The appendages attached to the sexual organs are more remarkable both in shape and function.

With respect to those upon the anal segment of male insects, they are generally less peculiar than those of females. Both sexes are deficient in these appendages when the last segment forms a *cloaca*; on the contrary, we find in those which have a free sexual opening a sort of tongs close to the male organ, between the prongs of which the penis is found, either lying freely exserted, or else retracted within the abdomen. The hooks of such tongs are of very different construction. In *Dolichopus*** they are lamellate, and armed with hooks at their end; lanceolate with an obtuse apex in the *Libellulæ*, narrow, round, and spinose upon their inner margin in many *Noctuæ*; simple, almost straight, but suddenly curved at their extremity in *Locusta*; short, thick, cylindrical, with lobate appendages in *Laphria* and *Asilus*. The last segment frequently takes a very different shape in consequence of these appendages, in *Tipula* it is clavate, in *Myopa*, conical, cheliform in *Panorpa*, &c.

The appendages of the sexual organs of female insects consist almost exclusively of more or less prominent ovipositors, by the aid of which they more easily deposit their eggs in appropriate places. We distinguish their following chief varieties.

1. The STING (*aculeus*, Pl. XXIII. f. 5—18) is a thin, delicate, finely-pointed tube, consisting of several valves, and which sometimes projects from (*Sirex*) and is sometimes withdrawn within the abdomen (*Vespa*). This sting is never a simple horny spine, but always consists of two or three pieces, the largest of which is barbed at its extremity, and is longitudinally channelled (Pl. XXIII. f. 7, *c*, and f. 12) to receive the rest (the same, f. 7, *d*, *d*). It possesses, besides, two lateral VALVES (*valvulæ*, the same, f. 6, *a*, *a*), between which the sting lies like a sword in its case. If the sting project beyond the abdomen, they accompany it, but only in those insects in which it lies freely exserted. In the bees and wasps, which use it also as an offensive weapon, the valves remain within the abdomen during its use.

Latreille calls the freely projecting ovipositor the BORER (*terebra*).

2. The TUBE (*tubulus*, Pl. XXIV. f. 15) is a mere continuation of the abdomen, which occurs in *Chrysis* and many *Diptera*, viz. the house-fly. It consists of several cylindrical joints, which are united by a soft membrane, and are retractile within each other, like the joints of a telescope. This kind of ovipositor is found only in insects which have but few abdominal segments, whence it is not improbable that the joints of the tube are nothing else than segments of the abdomen itself.

3. The SHEATH (*vagina*, Pl. XXIV. f. 10) consist of two long, convex continuations of the abdomen, generally inclining upwards, which, when

---

* Meigen. Zweif., Vol. iv. Pl. XXXVI. f. 21

placed together, exactly correspond, and form a single organ—the ovipositor. Between them lies the female sexual aperture, and the eggs are laid encompassed by them. (*Locusta*.)

Besides the above-named organs, several other forms are observed at the apex of the abdomen, which neither belong to the anus, nor can be considered as standing in connection with the sexual organs. They bear the general name of TAIL (*cauda*) or CAUDAL APPENDAGES (*Appendices caudales*): as such we may consider

The FORCEPS (*forcipes*, Pl. XIV. f. 8), two toothed cheliform hooks, which move in opposition to each other, in the earwig. (*Forficula*.)

The FORK (*furca*, Pl. XIV. f. 9) a continuation of the lower portion of the terminal segment, which is directed forwards, and is furcate, by means of which the insect springs upwards. (*Podura, Smynthurus.*)

The STYLES (*styli*, Pl. XIV. f. 10), two short exarticulate processes, close to the anus in *Staphylinus*.

The CERCI (*cerci*, Pl. XIV. f. 11), likewise short, lanceolate, and generally flattened and articulate appendages at the sides of the anus. (*Blatta*.)

The THREADS (*fila*, Pl. XIV. f. 12), longer or shorter articulate cylindrical processes of the last segment, which grow gradually thinner. (*Acheta, Ephemera, Lepisma*.)

The BRISTLES (*setæ*, Pl. XIV. f. 13) are such appendages when exarticulate and simple. (*Machilis*.)

The SIPHONETS (*siphunculi*, Pl. XIV. f. 14) are the hollow processes upon the upper side of the penultimate segment in the plant-lice (*Aphis*), whence the sweet juice exudes which the ants seek so eagerly.

SECOND SECTION.

ANATOMY.

§ 86.

The examination of the exterior form of the body is succeeded by the investigation of its internal construction. This branch of natural science is distinguished by the name of Anatomy (derived from ἀνατέμνειν, *to cut up*); but the portion of it which treats of the interior structure of insects might be appropriately called Entomotomy (derived from ἔντομον, *insect*, and τέμνειν, *to cut*).

As it was not our object in the preceding chapter to explain the mode whereby the different parts of the body stand mutually connected, but which combination and connection is of importance to the formation of the complex organism we have already examined externally, it is therefore incumbent upon us, in this section, to display the fundamental parts, or, as it were, the keys of this entire organism, and what the different materials are which must necessarily unite to constitute the organic body we have just treated of. The information which will be conveyed in this section will consequently be richer in its results towards a knowledge of the life of insects in general, as it will materially tend to show how far the differences of form are influenced by differences of structure, and what their mutual relations are. We shall nevertheless restrict ourselves, even in this section, to a mere description of forms, but principally of the internal parts, and consequently of their structure, reserving the reply to all questions upon the importance of each individual organ, its function, and sphere of action, to the next ensuing section.

But, before we pass on to the contemplation of these new objects, a few general remarks will not be inapposite to determine the natural succession of the investigations we are about to institute.

§ 87.

Experience has instructed us that every organism is not only transitory in its duration, but that it also requires the assimilation of fresh matter, if it is to be preserved from perishing immediately after its appearance. To meet this necessity nature has furnished every organic body with two different sets of organs, which are called systems, the one of which provides for the preservation of the individual by means of nutriment, and is thence called the NUTRIMENTAL SYSTEM, and the other for the continuance of its resemblance, or kind, and which is called the RE-PRODUCTIVE SYSTEM. Both systems, therefore, are the essential peculiarity of every organic body, and without them no organism can be imagined.

§ 88.

Indeed, the very lowest organic bodies, plants, display no other organs than such as belong to these two systems; but the animal destined to a higher grade of organisation adds to the phenomena of vegetable life two new proofs of its vitality, and which must be treated as the results of a greater freedom of nature. This liberty displays itself at once in its independence of its original place of abode, by the power it possesses of constantly changing it; in fact, the power of LOCOMOTION is the first and principal peculiarity of the animal, and this power also qualifies the second phenomenon peculiar to animal life. If, namely, the animal is to make an advantageous use of the freedom it derives from its power of locomotion, and if it be to be secured against all the disadvantages consequent upon this power, it must necessarily possess faculties which apprise it of the nature of its situation, and these it has received in the organs of SENSATION. Both, consequently, the organs of locomotion and sensation, are peculiar to the animal, and wholly wanting to the plant, whilst the organs of nutriment and re-production are common to both.

§ 89.

And as the organs of nutriment and re-production are first observed in the plant, and as the whole vegetable kingdom displays no higher development of life, they are distinguished as VEGETATIVE ORGANS, and their circle of action the VEGETATIVE SPHERE. Whereas the organs of locomotion and sensation, as the exclusive peculiarities of the animal, have received the name of ANIMAL ORGANS, and their compass of action the ANIMAL SPHERE.

§ 90.

The greater development or separation into several distinct organs, and the more complex structure of each, are the phenomena gradually displayed in the progressive ennoblement of the animal kingdom, commencing at the most simple conditions of animal existence. Insects maintain in every respect a central situation in this series; their organs, therefore, will not display to us a very artificial structure, nor will their combination be very complex. But we shall find the above indicated four chief differences, which are dependent upon the vital phenomena of the organism, sufficiently distinctly exhibited in them. Now, as the several organs of each individual system not only aim at one object in their functions, but also display considerable conformity in their structure, it will be suitable to regulate the arrangement of our present investigation by their differences, whence we derive the following themes:—

I. Investigation of the vegetative system and its organs. These are,
   A. The organs of nutriment, consisting of—
      The general integument. As this in insects is a horny case, to which the organs of locomotion are attached, its description must be classed with the consideration of the animal organs, it being but the passive agent of motion. Therefore of
        a. The INTESTINAL CANAL with its appendages, as digestive organs;
        b. The HEART and BLOOD VESSELS, as organs of circulation;
        c. The AIR VESSELS, as respiratory organs.
   B. The organs of re-production; consisting of—
        a. The FEMALE organs of re-production, and
        b. The MALE organs.

II. Investigation of the animal system and its organs.
   A. Organs of locomotion:—
        a. Passive organs of motion; here the EXTERIOR INTEGUMENT as analogous to the osseous system.
        b. Active organs, the MUSCLES.
   B. Organs of sensation:—
        a. The BRAIN;
        b. The NERVOUS SYSTEM in general;

c. The NERVOUS SYSTEM OF THE DIGESTIVE ORGANS;
d. The ORGANS OF THE SENSES.

We consequently commence our description with the vegetative organs, as being the inferior; and thence proceed to the survey of the animal organs, as the superior ones. But we do not wish by this arrangement to imply that the lowest insects have no organs of locomotion and sensation, but that in them both these organs, and also partially the vegetative ones, are not quite so perfectly developed and completely combined as in the higher orders, and *from* the circumstance of this difference the latter stand HIGHER and the former LOWER in the system. And by these expressions, as well as by the synonymous ones, of MORE or LESS PERFECT, we would indicate that the structure of the former is more complex, artificial, and various than the groups characterised as standing lower and less perfect. But each group is perfect in its kind.

FIRST SUBSECTION.

VEGETATIVE ORGANS.

§ 91.

THE organs of the vegetative sphere are, as it were, transmitted from the plant to the animal; it will therefore be not unimportant if we can prove that their fundamental texture displays a vegetable origin.

The plant commences its existence in the form of a cell; cell is added to cell, and the entire vegetable is but a congeries of small cells, with here and there long delicate tubes interspersed, forming, as it were, free passages between them. All the organs of vegetables consist of these two forms, consequently the nutrimental and re-productive organs must display a similar, or at least an analogous, structure, if they are to prove themselves of vegetable origin. Nothing, in fact, is more astonishing than the confirmation of this law; for cells, which in animals become small vesicles or larger bladders, and tubes, constitute the various forms of the vegetative organs. A vesicle, the egg, is the origin of animal existence; vesicles distend themselves, and become cases; they link themselves in a series, and form vessels; and thus, by degrees, each vegetative organ is formed from the vegetable original.

We will examine this more closely in the individual organs.

§ 92.

The INTESTINAL CANAL is a tube which originated from the elongation of one or the connection of several bladders. This is proved not only by its form in the lower animals, but also from its being in many, likewise in the larvæ of insects, a mere blind sack, consequently a bladder open only in front. In animals of a higher grade, in which it consists of several divisions separated by constrictions, it is very easily imagined as consisting of the union of several bladders.

The same holds good of the vessels: for example, the chief vessel of insects, namely, the large dorsal vessel, so evidently displays a cellular construction that we may not consistently doubt its original growth from bladders.

The very name of the air-tubes announces their form. It must, however, strike as important that the air-vessels of insects have so deceptive a resemblance to those of plants that everybody must immediately admit of their analogous structure.

The vegetable origin of the nutrimental organs is thus evidently proved.

§ 93.

It is not more difficult to show the same in the organs of reproduction. These, namely, very much more distinctly display their vesicular origin. The OVARY of the female is a large bladder, containing many smaller ones, the eggs. The OVIDUCT is an elongation of this large bladder; the UTERUS is another distension of it, and the VAGINA another elongation: other incidental appendages of the above parts display more or less distinctly a vesicular form.

It is the same in the male organs. The testes have not uncommonly the shape of a bladder (*Lamellicornia*), or else they are long convoluted tubes, which we know to be but modifications of bladders; the VASA DEFERENTIA are elongations of these bladders; the VESICA SEMINALIS another distension of it, and the DUCTUS EJACULATORIUS another and its final constriction.

Thus the sexual organs are a still more evident repetition of the vesicular form, they being always closed at one end at least.

§ 94.

We shall show in full detail, at its proper place, that the character of the organs of the animal sphere differs wholly from the vesicular character of the vegetative organs by the integral solidity of each individual part.

FIRST CHAPTER.

OF THE ORGANS OF NUTRITION.

1. THE INTESTINAL CANAL AND ITS APPENDAGES.

§ 95.

The intestinal canal (*tractus intestinorum*) is the internal tube, extending from the MOUTH, appropriated to the reception and transformation of the nutriment. It has in general a second aperture opposed to the first, the ANUS, through which the indigestible unassimilating remains of the food are rejected. The instances in which such an anal aperture is deficient are very rare among insects, and occur only among larvæ and maggots, but never in the imago.

This tubular structure of the intestinal canal is subject to considerable modification from distension and constriction, by means of which it is separated into several divisions, which have very justly received different names, from their functions being dissimilar. Besides these separations of the intestinal canal itself, we observe peculiar processes and appendages, which originate from it, or which, as perfectly independent parts, merely open into it. Their variety and modifications produce relations which yield multifarious differences in form and structure, and which link certain groups of insects more closely together by their complete uniformity, whereas they separate others, in which such a similarity of arrangement is not observed, more distinctly from each other, and thus more fully corroborate the dissimilitude expressed in their exterior conformation by this difference of their internal structure.

§ 96.

The entire intestinal canal consists of three skins, or layers of membrane.

The innermost membrane (Pl. XVII. f. 1), which may be considered as a continuation of the exterior epidermis, is very smooth and textureless, and only sometimes longitudinally folded, and armed above with horny lines, ridges, or teeth (Pl. XVII. f. 2. 5—7). It is particularly distinct in the pharynx, crop, and proventriculus, the horny teeth of the latter being formed by it. This internal membrane is most apparent in insects with hard cases, as the *Coleoptera* and *Orthoptera*, whereas it is not so evident in the haustellate *Diptera* and *Lepidoptera*. From the proventriculus it forms a very delicate perfectly uniform covering, and generally occupies less compass than the other intestinal membranes. We here call it the epidermis, it being its analogue, or properly, the mucous membrane, as it corresponds with the tunica mucosa of the superior animals.

The second layer, which we call with Straus the PROPER skin (*membrana propria*), is white and smooth, and usually thin, but sometimes thicker and spongy, most frequently without any texture, but occasionally figured (*Hydrophilus*, Pl. XVII. f. 2.). This membrane, which Ramdohr treats as a layer formed of transuded chyle, is peculiar to the intestinal canal, and is not found in the other internal organs; it may therefore be considered as a continuation of the second layer of the exterior integument, of which we shall treat below. Indeed, the space between the mucous membrane and this peculiar skin, which is very considerable in the stomach, and particularly in caterpillars, is often occupied by a flocky web, formed of transuded chyme, and this may have misled Ramdohr in his idea of it. According to Straus, horny prominences are sometimes observed in this intermediate skin, particularly in the vicinity of the stomach, which might be considered as absorbing pores, but which Straus, perhaps more correctly, treats as glands, and they are therefore called gastral glands (*glandulæ gastricæ*). I have observed these organs only upon the inner surface of the muscular membrane, but particularly distinct in *Hydrophilus*, in which insect the long cylindrical stomach is completely and regularly covered with such glands, which consist of a transparent case inclosing a darker kernel (Pl. XVII. f. 3.).

The third layer (Pl. XVII. f. 3 and 4.) is a compact, firm, fleshy muscular membrane (*tunica muscularis*), in which distinct longitudinal and transverse vessels can be discerned, and it lies closely upon the preceding. These vessels, which are sometimes completely reticulated, sometimes furcate separately and rejoin in the same manner *, are generally of a uniform size, but occasionally the transverse ones are stouter, the others more delicate and slender, but also more numerous and closer together, so much so that their distinct threads may be considered as the separated bundles of muscles †. This muscular membrane is not equally observable in all parts of the intestinal canal: it is very obvious in the pharynx, stomach, and colon; but it vanishes almost entirely in the crop or craw.

§ 97.

The situation of the intestinal canal is the same in all insects. It always commences as a cylindrical, and chiefly narrow tube at the somewhat wider cavity of the mouth, and proceeds in a direct line through the head and thorax. It takes the same direction in all insects which have a long and at the same time thin body (e.g. *Pimpla, Tipula, Agrion*). In these cases, however, the intestinal canal is of the same length as the body, and only in some of the broadbellied ones, for example, the long bugs (*Gerris, Emesa, Ranatra*), it makes a small curve before its termination, so that it becomes about half as long again as the body. But if the creature be thick bodied, and the cavity of the abdomen is distended on all sides, the intestinal canal becomes longer than the body, and makes convolutions within the cavity of the abdomen; but it always passes in a direct line through the head and thorax.

These convolutions of the intestinal canal are kept in their proper situation by the multitudinous branches of the air-vessels which spread about them; indeed, this reticulation of the air-vessels is so delicate and firm that it not only makes it difficult to represent the intestinal canal with all its appendages (which besides is closely enveloped in the fatty mass) in its full extension, but makes a perfect separation of all these air-vessels absolutely impossible. We never find in insects a peritoneum, which in the higher animals retains the intestines in their place, but its purpose is supplied by these air-vessels.

* Ramdohr, Ueber die Verdanungswerkzeuge der Insecten Halle, 1811. Pl. XIV. f. 4, from *Pompilus Viaticus*.

† The same Pl. XVII. f. 2., from the fauces of the larva of the Ant-lion.

§ 98.

The length of the intestinal canal increases with its convolutions; or these rather are but the consequences of its extension. We very frequently find the intestinal canal twice the length of the body; indeed so often is this the case that it may be considered as the most usual structure. A nutrimental canal of this extent is called MODERATELY long; such an intestine makes from one to three convolutions, according to their size. The LONG intestine (*Chrysomela, Cimex*) makes also two or three, but larger convolutions, and is from three to five times the length of the body. The intestine is, lastly, very long in the *Lamellicornia*, in which it is from seven to eight times as long as the body, and makes many folds in the cavity of the abdomen.

But these proportions refer only to the perfect insect, for the majority of larvæ, namely those with a perfect metamorphosis, have a nutrimental canal of the same length, or at most of twice the length of the body. This short intestine increases in length in every distinct period of its life; but some instances occur in which this gut becomes shorter during the metamorphoses, namely, in the *Diptera*, the larvæ of which have a very long and much convoluted intestine [*].

§ 99.

No general law regulating the various length of the intestinal canal has yet been discovered; in insects, in particular, it appears exposed to much irregularity. It is not however improbable, from all hitherto instituted investigations, that herbivorous insects have a longer and more distended intestine, and that those which feed upon animal matter have it shorter and narrower. We, however, find a decided exception in the vegetable devouring *Orthoptera* (e. g. *Gryllus, Locusta*), their intestine being not much longer than their body, but at the same time very broad. We perceive greater uniformity, if not in length yet in structure, in the different orders of insects, and this law we shall observe to prevail still more forcibly in the still smaller groups.

§ 100.

We will now pass from this general description of the entire intestinal canal to the examination of its different divisions. We can there-

---

[*] Ramdohr, Pl. XIX. f. 1 and 2.

fore make a primary separation of it into its SEVERAL DIVISIONS and its APPENDAGES.

The divisions of the intestinal canal are, the PHARYNX, the ŒSOPHAGUS, the CRAW, the PROVENTRICULUS, the STOMACH or VENTRICULUS, the DUODENUM, the ILIUM, the CŒCUM, and the COLON.

The peculiar appendages of the intestinal canal are, the SALIVARY, BILIARY, and ANAL VESSELS.

These parts are never all present together; sometimes one is wanting, and sometimes the other. For example: insects with a suctorial mouth never possess apparent pharynx, but the œsophagus originates immediately at the base of the sucking tube; they also want the proventriculus, instead of which they possess a bladdered crop, which however does not occur in mandibulated insects. The part most frequently deficient is the duodenum, which has hitherto been observed only in some of the pentamerous *Coleoptera*, after which the cœcum is least frequently present, for it appears to be peculiar to those families only the genera of which feed upon animal matter.

With respect to the appendages, the biliary vessels are seldom wanting (*Chermes, Aphis*), the salivary ones frequently, but the anal vessels very generally.

THE PHARYNX.

§ 101.

The pharynx is the distended commencement of the œsophagus, bordering upon the cavity of the mouth, and is found, as we have recently remarked, only in the mandibulata, consequently in the *Coleoptera, Orthoptera, Neuroptera,* and *Hymenoptera*. In these it is nothing else than the almost trumpet-shaped commencement of the œsophagus, and in the majority of cases is not separated from it by any evident difference of texture or construction. In some of the grasshoppers and cockroaches, in which, in consequence of their large mandibles, the cavity of their mouth is very expansive, their pharynx is very much distended, and more clearly separated from the much narrower œsophagus *. Its membrane is more dense and compact than that of the latter, excepting which it displays no other difference. The mucous and muscular membranes lie close together, and it is scarcely possible to

* Ramdohr, ib. Pl. I. f. 9.

THE ŒSOPHAGUS.

§ 102.

The œsophagus (Pl. XVII. 22, A, A,) extends from the pharynx to the stomach; it is distinguished from the former by its smaller capacity, and from the latter by a variation in structure. The most remarkable form of the œsophagus is doubtlessly its very general furcate division in the *Lepidoptera*, and that from each of the two spiral sucking tubes it originates by a distinct branch, which branches then unite into one channel. In general the branches of the fork are very short, but in the swallow-tail butterfly (*Pieris Machaon*, O.) their union into one tube commences only at the thorax *. In the other orders of insects the œsophagus passes through the entire cavity of the thorax as a simple tube, and either terminates where the cavity of the abdomen commences, or before this, within the thorax itself; for example, in its centre in those insects the cavity of whose thorax is broad, and which consequently admits of a greater expansion of the organs which traverse it. The length of the œsophagus therefore depends upon the length and dimensions of the thorax. Insects with a thin and narrow, and in particular with a petiolated abdomen, have a long œsophagus, when the thorax also is long (*Pimpla, Fœnus*); and it is the longer in proportion to the entire intestinal canal, the shorter, narrower, and smaller we find the abdomen. The most remarkable proportions must occur in this respect in the genus *Evania*, but which has never yet been anatomically investigated. The longest œsophagus yet observed consisted of more than half of the entire intestinal canal†; and among the shortest is that of the cockchafer, which occupies scarcely one-sixtieth of the entire length of that canal ‡.

We are already acquainted with the texture of the œsophagus; its central layer however is very slight, whence the two other membranes lie closer together, which, as Ramdohr assures us, makes their separation very difficult. The inner membrane is generally here quite uniform, much more rarely thicker in parts, almost like parchment, or, as in *Carabus*,

---

* See Treviranus, Vermischte Schriften, vol. ii. p. 200.
† In *Pimpla Enervator* and *Pompilus viaticus*, Ramdohr, Pl. III. f. 2 and 3.
‡ Ramdohr, Pl. III. f. 1.

Meloë, Chrysomela, Blatta, and the grasshoppers (Pl. XXI. f. 2 and 3), internally covered with short stiff setæ and teeth; the muscular fibres of the exterior membrane generally lie regularly above each other, but they sometimes form a loose confused net-work from open spaces remaining here and there between them.

The separation of the œsophagus from the stomach is effected sometimes by a positive constriction (*Diptera,* Pl. XVIII. f. 3.); it occasionally passes insensibly into it, and sometimes the crop intervenes between them, as the organ of transition; in this case the œsophagus expands by degrees into a sack-shaped CROP (*ingluvies,* Pl. XVIII. f. 1. B, B,) which takes the place of a first stomach, and prepares the swallowed food for digestion. In *Gryllotalpa* it occurs as a perfectly sack-shaped appendage of the œsophagus * (Pl. XXI. f. 7.). To facilitate this the inner surface of the crop is covered with glands (for example, in *Dyticus, Blatta,* &c.), the secretion of which has the function of a preparing juice. Such an expansion of the œsophagus before the proventriculus might readily be considered as analogous to the crop of the higher animals, of the birds, for example; an opinion which Ch. L. Nitzsch has already propounded †. The expansion, however, without a contemporaneous proventriculus, is of a different and peculiar kind, namely, the sucking stomach, indicated by G. R. Treviranus, and which we proceed to describe.

THE SUCKING STOMACH.

§ 103.

The *Hymenoptera, Lepidoptera,* and *Diptera* are the orders in which the proventriculus is deficient, but they possess, nevertheless, a bladder-shaped distension of the œsophagus (Pl. XVII. and XVIII. c, c,), which in the first lies directly in front of the cardia; in the second it forms a distinct bag, which opens into the œsophagus, contiguous to the cardia; and in the third it hangs appended to the œsophagus by means of a long thin duct, frequently far in front of the opening of the stomach. This organ is the before-named sucking stomach. Its function does not consist in being a receptacle for nutriment, but in promoting the suction of food, by distending, at the will of the insect, and thus, by the rarefaction of the air contained within it, facilitating the rise of

---

* See Suckow, in Heusing. Zeitschrift. f. d. Org. Phys. vol. 3. p. 53. Pl. II. f. 134.

† Gattungen der Thier-Inseckten, Germar's Magaz. iii. p. 280.

fluids in the proboscis and œsophagus. Insects which chew are naturally deficient in this apparatus, or at least in this function of it; in them it is a true crop.

In the *Hymenoptera* (Pl. XVII. f. 10, c,) the sucking stomach is a distension of the œsophagus in front of the cardia, and consequently perfectly resembles a true crop. Indeed, in those families of this order, which possess more a mandibulate apparatus than a suctorial, this sucking stomach must gradually become superfluous; and it is, consequently, so little distinct from the œsophagus that it was formerly always described with it, and as nodose *. It exists however as a distinctly defined organ in the families of the bees and wasps, which possess a true suctorial apparatus; and here it is a large bag, which hangs below the œsophagus, in front of the mouth of the stomach †. If it be empty it lies folded longitudinally; when filled with air it is distended as a transparent bladder, and embraces the long funnel-shaped mouth of the stomach, which is furnished at its aperture with valves.

In the *Lepidoptera* (Pl. XVIII. f. 5.) we find the sucking stomach still more distinctly separated from the œsophagus. In these it projects with a short neck at right angles from the end of the œsophagus, and when simple it lies as a folded bladder contiguous to and over the stomach, or upon each side of it when, as in *Zygæna* ‡, it consists of two equal halves. This division is sometimes unequal, when a smaller bladder hangs beneath the large one §. It is always proportionate in compass to the length of the proboscis, so that it completely vanishes when the proboscis dwindles to a short cone, as in *Gastrophaga pini* and *Cossus ligniperda* ‖.

Many *Neuroptera*, for example, the genera *Hemerobius* and *Phryganea*, have apparently similar bags, which are likewise inactively folded, but which also admit, like those of the *Lepidoptera*, of being distended into tight bladders. These organs may possibly be sucking stomachs, particularly as these insects, although provided with a mandibulate apparatus, take food more by suction (this is the case especially in *Phryganea*) than by mastication.

* For example, in the *Tenthredos* and *Ichneumons*, Ramdohr, Pl. XIII. f. 2 and 3. and Pl. XIV. f. 2.

† Ramdohr, Pl. XII. f. 6. Pl. XIII. f. 1. Pl. XIV. f. 3. Treviranus, Pl. XIV. f. 3. and Pl. XVI. f. 3.

‡ Ramdohr, Pl. XVIII. f. 1.

§ Treviranus, Pl. IX. v, v. ‖ Ib. p. 109.

In the *Diptera*, lastly, (Pl. XVIII. f. 2 and 3, c, c,) the sucking stomach is still more distinctly divided from the œsophagus, and is a single mouthed bag, having one or several ends, and furnished with a solitary evacuating duct. When empty it is small and wrinkled, but when distended it is of large dimensions. In its natural situation it lies contiguous to and over the stomach, at the very commencement of the abdomen, whence its delicate evacuating duct, rising anteriorly, accompanies the stomach as far as the œsophagus, of the size of which it generally is, and opens into it more or less closely to the cardia *. According to Ramdohr this organ is the food bag (*speisesack*), as it serves for the reception of food. Meckel calls it, from the same cause, the honey vessel (*honigbehälter*), and he found in it a peculiar, coloured liquid. But Treviranus' representation is much too illustrative, and his investigations in insects opened alive much too conclusive to admit of the least doubt being entertained of the function of this organ.

The *Hemiptera*, which likewise live upon imbibed juices, have no sucking stomach, nor any analogous apparatus; this is the case also in the *Pupipara* and the flea, although they must necessarily be classed among the *Diptera* †.

THE PROVENTRICULUS.

§ 104.

The PROVENTRICULUS (Pl. XVII. f. 8 & p. 21, f. 8—10) is the third division of the intestinal canal, if we may consider the crop or sucking stomach as nothing but a distension of the œsophagus. It is a small narrow and tubular cavity, much folded within, and furnished with teeth, spines, or projecting horny ridges. It lies directly in front of the mouth of the stomach, and as which it may properly be considered. It is found in all mandibulate insects which feed upon hard substances, or require the comminution of their food previous to digestion; consequently in all the carnivorous tribes (*Carabodea, Hydrocantharides, Brachyptera*), the wood-beetles (*Cerambycina,* but here somewhat altered), many *Rhinchophora*, the *Orthoptera*, (with the exception of the *Phasmæ* and the *Grylli*, whose whole crop is furnished with spines which serve to triturate the food), and the *Neuroptera*. Exteriorly it has always a round somewhat ovate appear-

* See Ramdohr, Pl. XVIII.—XXI., and Trevir. Pl. XVII.
† See Ramdohr, Pl. XXI. f. 6., and Pl. XXIII. f. 2.

ance, and is compact, opaque, and more distinctly muscular than the rest of the intestinal canal. It consequently answers to the gizzard of the gallinaceous birds, an analogy which still 'more strongly confirms the general analogy of organisation existing between insects and birds.

A closer anatomical investigation of this organ displays two very distinctly-separated membranes, the exterior of which is tight and muscular, and the interior folded, smooth, and partially horny. The folds of the inner membrane are by no means accidental, but perfectly regular and differently formed in the several families. In the predaceous beetles (*Cicindelacea* and *Carabodea*, Pl. XVII. f. 8), four is the prevalent number. Four large arched folds, densely covered with short horny spines, bend inwardly in the cavity of the organ, and between these lie four smaller ones, which are sharply ridged in front. Within the large folds there are four robust bundles of muscles, which unite above and below, and thus form a closing muscle at each opening. The similarly constructed mouth of the stomach in *Staphylinus* has five large folds and as many small ones. In *Cryptorhynchus Lapathi* there are nine equal prismatic folds, from the inner ridges of which originate two rows of diverging horny processes, which meeting from fold to fold, separate a central star-shaped space from the entire cavity *. In the capricorn beetles (*Cerambycina*) there is no cavity at all, but at the inner margin of the cardia there are four large and four smaller horny plates (Pl. XXII. f. 1, *Lamia ædilis*). The *Orthoptera* (for example, *Acheta*,) have six chief plates, which are covered with scale-shaped horny plates. In the *Termites* (Pl. XXI. f. 8—10.) I discovered a proventriculus, which consisted of a ring of twelve equal broad folds, between which again twelve finer and sharp edged ones lay. Around this ring, which formed the central girdle of the cavity of the organ, there were six strong fasciculi of muscles, which united above and below like the ribs of a gothic arch, and thus formed closing muscles. In *Blatta*, instead of folds we find hooked horny teeth, which spring from a broad base at the sides of the stomach, and project into its cavity. In *Gryllus migratorius* (Pl. XXI. f. 1—6.) I found no proventriculus, but the entire pharynx and crop were armed with rows of small but differently sized teeth, which, running longitudinally, formed in the centre transverse waved lines, but towards the cardia again stand in twos and threes upon elevated mus-

* Ramdohr, Pl. X. f. 1—4.

cular ridges. The cardia itself was armed with six Y-shaped horny teeth (Pl. XXI. f. 6. a, a). In Müller's representation of the intestinal canal of *Phasma* no proventriculus is visible*, I consequently surmise they would present a similar structure.

The exterior skin of this organ is tense, not folded, and it closely incloses the interior one as a similarly shaped distended bag. It agrees in structure with the muscular membrane of the intestinal canal. The space between both is occupied by fasciculi of muscles, and the spongy layer or middle membrane must necessarily be deficient here as well as in the crop, it being the produce of digestion, and therefore can only be present where this has commenced.

The larvæ of all the above-named insects whose metamorphosis is complete, entirely want this organ, and in them the pharynx passes immediately into the considerably wider stomach. We do not either observe in the very voracious caterpillars of the *Lepidoptera* any further comminuting stomach.

§ 105.

THE STOMACH.

The stomach (*ventriculus*, Pl. XVII.—XXII. D, D), according to most entomologists, is that portion of the intestinal canal which extends from the end of the œsophagus, or of the crop, to the opening of the evacuating ducts of the biliary vessels. Straus, Treviranus, and Joh. Müller † call it the duodenum, as digestion commences in it, in those orders which have the proventriculus, and perhaps this interpretation may be more correct than that hitherto used.

Upon examining the form of this portion of the intestine it soon becomes apparent that it is subject to many changes; it always approaches more or less to the tubular, but it at the same time distinguishes itself from the following divisions of the canal by its greater compass. The shorter the stomach is the further does it recede from the tubular form, and approaches to the ovate, conical, or bladder-shaped.

The *Lepidoptera* (Pl. XVIII. f. 5. D) have the smallest stomachs of all insects. In these it takes the shape of an egg, the ends of which contract into narrow tubes, and its upper surface is folded in irregular

---

* Nova acta Phys. Med. n. cur. T. 12. B. Pl. L. f. 2.
† Joh. Müller de Glandul. Secern. Struct. Pen. p. 68. Lips. 1831, fol.

constrictions. Generally, upon both upper and under surface, a narrow sinewy or muscular stripe runs longitudinally, for the purpose of strengthening the there more delicate envelope. Meckel informs us * that this stomach in *Acherontia Atropos* is shaggy externally, a solitary instance of this structure in the *Lepidoptera*.

The longitudinal, more tubular, and regularly transversely folded stomach of the *Hymenoptera* (Pl. XVII. f. 10. D) approaches very closely in structure to that of the *Lepidoptera*. It commences with a funnel-shaped orifice, which is evidently analogous to the before-described proventriculus, and as such projects into the cavity of the sucking stomach, which can be closed by valves that open inwardly †. This funnel-shaped orifice facilitates the passage of the food from the œsophagus into the stomach, its aperture being thereby brought nearer to the former, indeed, during suction, rising quite up to it; the valves however preventing the return of the chyme into the sucking stomach. This structure of the stomach is found in all the *Hymenoptera*, but it varies much in compass; in some (*Sirex*) it is short, broad, and straight, the crop, on the contrary, is very long and nodose; in others (*Chrysis*) it is distended in the middle and recurvate at the extremity; in the bees and wasps it is of tolerably equal breadth, but not straight, for it bends inwardly at both ends, so that it is partially inclined towards the axis of the body.

In the larvæ of these insects the whole intestinal canal (Pl. XVII. f. 9. D) consists but of this transversely folded stomach, and all the following divisions, including also the anus, are deficient: this stomach, consequently, is more compactly constructed in them than in any other insect, it being composed of five skins, whereas the others have but three. It is probable that both the mucous and muscular membranes have separated into two layers ‡.

In the *Diptera* (Pl. XVIII. f. 3. D) the stomach is a long tube, which frequently distends at the two extremities, and is narrowest in the centre (*Musca*); a callous ring is found at the cardia, which is the remains of a small bladder existing there in the larva state; the vicinity of the cardia is granulated, that is, uneven, arising from transverse and longitudinal striæ. Some of the large group (perhaps all), which Latreille calls the *Diptera Athericera*, have peculiar, glandular,

* Verglei. Anatomie, vol. iv. p. 87.
† Compare Treviranus, Vermischte Schriften, vol. ii. Pl. XV. f. 2.
‡ Compare Suckow, in Heusinger Zeitschr. f. d. Org. Phys. vol. iii. p. 18. Pl. VI. f. 131.

secretory organs which evacuate themselves at the very commencement of the stomach, closely behind the cardia *. They are doubtlessly the same forms we shall more fully describe below in the *Orthoptera*, and which have been considered as the analogues of the pyloric cæcum of the pancreas, or liver.

The *Neuroptera* have a short, sometimes smooth, sometimes transversely striated cylindrical or conical stomach, in front of which, at least in *Myrmecoleon* and *Panorpa*, there is a distinct proventriculus. This is wanting in the *Libellulæ* and *Ephemeræ*: their stomach is long, cylindrical, and separated from the pharynx by a slight constriction only. *Lepisma*, which genus, as well as the two families of *Termites* and the mandibulate parasites, I unite in the order *Dictyotoptera*, has a very small stomach, and in front of it a proventriculus armed with six teeth, contiguous to which lies a broader and larger crop. The same is the case in the *Termites*, but their stomach is longer. The *Mallophaga* † have also a tolerably large crop, but the true stomach is small, and is provided beyond the cardia with two considerable points; perhaps they, as well as the genus *Psocus*, for both devour hard materials (the former, for example, feathers), are also furnished with a proventriculus.

The three remaining orders display stomachs of a much more complex form than the preceding.

In the *Coleoptera* we find a considerable variety in the structure of the stomach, we observe the most simple in those *Lamellicornia* which feed upon feculent substances, or upon the juices of flowers (for ex., *Scarabæus*, Pl. XX. f. 2., *Melolontha, Trichius*). In these the short and narrow œsophagus passes, without any distinct indication of its termination, gradually into a very long, cylindrical, and equally wide stomach. The object of this great length of the stomach is evidently to prepare the food more fully for assimilation, for in the larvæ of these insects it is much shorter, but in compensation it is supplied at both ends with blind, pointed appendages (organs of secretion), of which, in some cases (for example, *Hister*, a genus closely approximate to the *Lamellicornia*,) traces still remain in the perfect insect. Next to these, the tribes which feed upon fresh vegetable matter, and particularly the juices of flowers, the *Chrysomelina* and *Cerambycina*, have

* *Bombylius, Leptis, Chrysotoxum*, see Ramdohr, Pl. XX. and XXI.
† Ch. L. Nitzsch, in Germar's Magaz. der Entomol., vol. iii. p. 280. and vol. iv. p. 277.

the most simple stomachs; in these also it is a long, tolerably broad, smooth tube, which rarely (for ex., in *Chrysomela*,) is beset with short flocks. These flocks are portions of the internal mucous membrane which pass through the muscular membrane, but are not covered by it. In some genera (for ex., *Lema, Callichroma moschatum,*) portions of this tubular stomach are broader, others again narrower, but in the majority it gradually decreases in size.

The structure is more anomalous in other families, which, although chiefly feeding upon vegetable matter, consume it in a more crude and unprepared state, viz , as fresh leaves or harder fruits. The majority of these have also a long, cylindrical stomach, but the œsophagus is divided from it by a distinct muscular ring, and it is more tense, and occasionally, as in the *Hymenoptera*, transversely ringed. Among these are the *Rhynchophora*, many of which even possess the proventriculus and the before-mentioned flocks, (for ex., *Cryptorhynchus Lapathi*), the *Vesicifica* (as *Lytta, Mylabris, Meloë*), the tortoise-beetles '*Cassidaria*), &c.

But the *Buprestidea*, of all the vegetable feeders, exhibit the most remarkable structure of the stomach: in these, at its very commencement, it distends on each side into a long blind appendage, equal indeed in length to the stomach itself; and this appendage, as well as the commencement of the stomach, is furnished throughout three parts of its extent with short, blind processes, like that of the flesh feeders. The remainder of the cylindrical stomach is smooth *. The *Elaterodea* form a transition to this remarkable arrangement, for in them the commencement of the stomach has on the two opposite sides a short folded pocket, it then continues, as a narrow, cylindrical, transversely folded tube, and distends widely at its termination †.

The *Carnivora* display the most complex structure of this organ among the *Coleoptera* (Pl. XIX. f. 4. D, D). Here the before-described proventriculus lies in front of the stomach, from which it is separated by a distinct constriction; the stomach itself is not very long, at least considerably shorter than in the vegetable feeders, and it is covered upon the whole or major part of the upper surface with long, thin, and blind flocks. These flocks originate, as was already observed in *Chrysomela*, from the inner mucous membrane of the stomach, and

* Compare H. M. Gäde, in the Nova Acta Phys. Med., vol. xi. part ii. p. 329.; and J. F. Meckel's Beiträge zur Vergl. Anat., vol. i. part ii. p. 129.

† Ramdohr, Pl. XI. f. 1.

, ...e exterior muscular membrane, the filaments of which it pushes on one side. They doubtlessly consist of secerning organs, whose secretion makes more soluble the heavily digestible animal matter. These flocks are found in the *Cicindelacea*, the *Carabodea*, the *Hydrocantharides*, the *Brachyptera*, the *Peltodea*, the *Melanosomata*, and the *Helopodea*.

The stomach of the majority of the *Orthoptera* is still more artificially constructed, although in many respects not dissimilar to that just described. They equally have a crop and proventriculus, the stomach itself is not very long, but tolerably broad and most frequently transversely ringed above; at its mouth there are broad, sack-shaped, blind appendages, which are not mere processes of the mucous membrane, but are also covered by the layer of muscular membrane. There are two such appendages in *Acheta* and *Gryllotalpa*, and as many in *Locusta*, but here shorter, and more vesicular. In *Gryllus migratorius* I found six tubular ones (Pl. XXI. f. 6.) lengthened above and below, each of which opened into the stomach by an oval aperture (the same A, A, A,) and thin tubes, which lay convoluted in the tubular appendages passed into these openings from the internal membrane of the stomach (the same fig. 5.); consequently these apertures do not merely open into the stomach itself, but also between the innermost and central membranes of the stomach (see fig. 2. at the *). In *Blatta* there are eight such appendages, four short and four long; these are also, without doubt, organs of secretion, which have been not inappropriately compared to the blind appendages in the pylorus of fishes. They would thus be analogous to a gastral salivary gland, or pancreas.

We have yet to examine the stomach of the *Hemiptera*, which is the most composite of all (Pl. XX. f. 3). The narrow, and generally long œsophagus suddenly distends itself upon its entrance into the abdomen into a broad, bladder-shaped, generally long, and often irregularly folded stomach (D), which is, without doubt, analogous to the crop of the other orders. The *Hemiptera* which imbibe raw juices, either animal or vegetable, require several successive stomachs for the gradual transformation of these substances. The first of these stomachs serves as a preparatory receptacle, wherein the materials accumulate, and where they are slightly changed, that they may be more effectively elaborated in the following divisions. This first stomach is consequently the widest of all, and thus corresponds to the crop of the *Coleoptera* and *Orthoptera*. With respect to its precise form, it is smooth and cylindrical in *Nepa*, somewhat wider and transversely ringed in *Lygæus*, shorter but wider, with irregular longitudinal folds, which form apparent large pockets, in *Cimex*. In *Cimex rufipes* two compact, round, transversely ringed bodies lie above, contiguous to the cardia, one upon each side of it. In *Cicada* the first stomach is short, but also very broad and bladder-shaped. The second stomach (D *) is in general the narrowest, but always the longest; it has the appearance of a compact muscular tube, whose function can be no other than the further preparation of the imbibed juices; it is consequently of a more solid structure, and indeed in *Nepa* * it is internally covered with elevated ridges, which form a reticulation of hexagonal cells. Its function and even structure therefore correspond with the proventriculus; it more triturates the food than extracts it. It is separated from the following stomach by a perfect sphincter, and sometimes is distended in front of this into a large bladder (D**, *Cimex rufipes*, *C. baccarum*), which must not be considered as a proper stomach but as a second receptacle for the triturated matter, as a second crop before the third stomach. This distension, in greater or less compass, appears peculiar to all the bugs, but is wanting in the rest of the *Hemiptera*. In the *Cicada* the second stomach is nodose, very wide in front, growing gradually narrower behind. The third and last stomach (D***) is in the bugs wider than the second, but narrower than the crop lying in front of it. In form it resembles the transversely striped stomach of the bees, its cavity being formed by four half cylindrical tubes (*Cimex baccarum* and *C. prasinus*), and these half tubes completely separate in *C. rufipes*, so that their third stomach properly consists of four contiguous stomachs †. In many water bugs, *Hydrocorides* (for ex., *Nepa*, *Naucoris*), this stomach is wanting, but in compensation the second, as well as the following portion of the intestine, are longer, as in the land bugs (*Geocorides*). In the *Cicadaria* (Pl. XVIII. f. 1. D**) it is of the same length as the second, but of less breadth, while the second (D*) is granulated upon its exterior surface. Separated from the former by a distinct sphincter, it, like it, gradually decreases and turns upwards into the first stomach, indicated as the crop (D), so that the transmission of the food describes a complete circle in the three

* Ramdohr, Pl. XXII. f. 8.
† Compare G. R. Treviranus, in the Annalen der Wetterausch. Gesellsch. sur die Naturgesch, vol. i. No. ii.

stomachs. The remainder of the intestine is continued at the opposite side of the stomach, and it is there also that the biliary vessels empty themselves.

Thus much upon the form of the stomach in the several orders of insects; with respect to its structure, almost all that can be said upon it has been mentioned above, in treating of the nutrimental canal. The three membranes described there are found also in the stomach, and here particularly distinct. They are here more loosely united than in any other portion of the intestinal canal, and their exhibition is consequently attended with no difficulty. The middle membrane is attached more closely to the innermost, and the granules are found in it which Straus (see above, § 96.) indicated as gastral glands; between this and the inner mucous membrane the chyle collects, and then transuding through the latter, it enters the abdominal cavity, undulating about all the organs.

But little also can be said of the situation of the stomach, as it is not subject to much deviation; it is always found in the abdomen, whilst the œsophagus, and very generally the crop, are seated in the thorax. As soon, therefore, as the intestinal canal enters the abdomen it becomes the stomach, and frequently, indeed, even in the thorax (*Melolontha* and many others). If the intestinal canal be only as long as the body, the stomach then lies directly in its axis, but if it be longer, it then makes windings, which are the larger and more numerous the longer and more extended it happens to be. These convolutions generally lie in the anterior portion of the abdomen, encompassed and retained in their place by the ramifying branches of the air vessels, the hinder portion being chiefly occupied by the sexual organs; the stomach and intestine also approaches closer to the back, the internal sexual organs filling the ventral portion, or the space beneath the nutrimental canal.

§ 106.

THE DUODENUM.

The divisions of the nutrimental canal which follow the stomach are generally more simple than the preceding, and also subject to fewer changes of form. In breadth they do not generally, with the exception of the last, or colon, equal that of the stomach; they are mostly narrower, and also more delicately constructed. This entire intestine also consists of the three membranes, which, however, often lie more closely attached to each other, but frequently in the ilium, particularly when the muscular membrane is very delicate (*Lamia ædilis*)*, they leave a considerable space between them. Here and there also the muscular membrane is thicker than in the stomach, which may possibly be explained by the distribution of similar fasciculi of fibres over a narrower space, whereas in those cases in which this intestine is as distended as the stomach (for example, *Lamia ædilis*,) the muscular membrane of both is uniform in its consistency.

The passage of the stomach into the duodenum is formed by a distinct constriction, which supplants a sphincter, or is possibly one; the ring thus projecting internally is called *pylorus*, immediately beyond which the mouth of the gall vessels pierce the intestinal membranes.

This intestine is also separated into different divisions by means of constrictions, which have different functions, and have consequently received different names.

The first of these divisions is called the DUODENUM according to Ramdohr, but it is scarcely analogous to the similarly named portion of the intestinal canal in the superior animals, but it more probably entirely belongs to the following ilium. In the few beetles in which it has been hitherto observed (*Silpha, Necrophorus, Melolontha, Lampyris*) it generally appears as a short, smooth tube, of equal width, or narrower (*Melolontha*) than the ilium, from which it is distinguished exteriorly by the ringed constrictions of the latter (*Necrophorus*†, *Silpha*‡). A stronger ringed constriction separates it from the following portion of the small intestines.

§ 107.

THE ILIUM.

Wherever the duodenum is wanting the ILIUM (Pl. XVII.—XXII. E, E,) follows immediately upon the stomach, from which it is separated by the above described pylorus. This portion of the intestine is likewise sometimes wanting, so that the stomach lies immediately contiguous to the colon (*Libellula* §, *Reduvius* ||). This appears to be the general rule of structure in the bugs; and when even occasionally a small portion of the intestine is found beyond the stomach in which the biliary vessels bury themselves, it is nevertheless so inconsiderable

---

* Ramdohr, Pl. IX. f. 6.   † Ib., Pl. V. f. 1.   ‡ Ib., Pl. IV. f. 2.
§ Ib., Pl. XV. f. 4. || Ib., Pl. XXV. f. 5.

that it may consistently be considered as deficient. This deficiency in them may be accounted for by the number of their stomachs, for that transmutation of the food which is properly the function of the ilium takes place in their third stomach, and which consequently renders the ilium unnecessary.

With respect to its structure, we have already indicated some of its peculiarities in treating upon the membranes of the stomach. Those of the ilium are generally tenser than the latter; it is invariably equally distended, and, as it were, inflated, whereas the stomach is not unusually folded up. We have already mentioned that the ilium, as well as the stomach, is frequently transversely ridged, and by this means is distinguished from the duodenum.

The length and situation of the ilium varies considerably; it is rarely so long or longer than the body (*Necrophorus*), in general shorter, and even shorter than the stomach. The latter proportions are found especially in the *Chrysomelina*, and in many others which feed upon vegetable matter it is the general rule. In many of the carnivora, for example, the water-beetles (*Hydrocantharides*), the ilium on the contrary, is longer than the stomach, particularly in their larvæ, in which it is twice as long; but this is not the case in the ground-beetles (*Cicindelacea* and *Carabodea*), the ilium in them being not so long as the stomach. The butterflies have the longest ilium, in proportion to the stomach of all insects, for in them it is not merely twice as long, but even three or four times the length of the stomach, which is the more extraordinary as in the caterpillar it is excessively short, scarcely extending to one-eighth of the length of that organ. In the *Diptera* also it is shorter than the stomach; in the bugs alone is it sometimes wholly deficient. It is regularly wanting in the *Libellulæ* and *Ephemeræ*. There are no fixed laws which regulate the length of the ilium, but Ramdöhr has endeavoured to show its most prevalent proportions to the stomach and the other parts; they are as follows:—the most usual relation to the stomach is as 1 : 1, or 1 : 3; to the whole intestine 1 : 5, or likewise 1 : 3. Some of the proportions are extraordinary, as in *Necrophorus*, viz., the ilium to the intestinal canal as 2 : 3, to the stomach as 9 : 4; indeed, this beetle has the longest ilium of any yet investigated. In *Tenthredo nigra* it is very short, viz., in proportion to the entire nutrimental canal it is as 1 : 17. In the caterpillars of the butterflies it is always very short, and in general it is short in all larvæ, and it is the shorter in proportion to the extension of the stomach.

The situation of the ilium is so far determined that it is always found beneath and contiguous to, and never above the stomach, but its situation in itself varies considerably. In perfect insects it is seldom straight, but always so in those whose intestine is not longer than the body (*Gryllus*, *Phasma*, the larvæ of butterflies). In the opposite cases it makes convolutions of different size and form, which are the more numerous and larger the more extended the ilium itself is.

§ 108.

In some instances the ilium appears under a different form, namely, gradually distended, and thus becoming clavate, which is however peculiar to a few beetles only. According to Ramdohr, who considers a thus distended ilium as a distinct portion of the intestine, it is called the CLAVATE intestine. In the *Chrysomelina* the short ilium is thus frequently distended. In many of the capricorn beetles a somewhat distended portion of the intestine is separated by a constriction from the very narrow ilium, and this represents the clavate intestine.

In the *Lamellicornia* (*Melolontha*, for ex.) the clavate intestine appears likewise as a distended sack-shaped ilium, and is therefore called by Ramdohr the THICK intestine. It is particularly distinct and large in the larvæ of these beetles (Pl. XX. f. 1. P); here, namely, it appears as a broad bag here and there constricted, which, in its natural situation, turns back upon the stomach from its commencement, and extends as far as the length of the narrow ilium will admit, consequently to the end of the stomach. The bag here contracts, and the again narrow colon originates beneath it, in a bow of it, taking its course in a contrary direction towards the anus. In the perfect beetle (the same fig. 2.) this bag is to be distinguished exteriorly only as a bellied distension of the ilium, which, at least in *Melolontha*, has five slight impressions. But if this portion be opened five elevated ridges are observed, which are divided by incisions at regular distances, so that each band appears to consist of short, contiguous, three-sided prisms [*].

If the name of this portion of the intestine is to be determined according to its divisional distance from the stomach it must be considered as

---

[*] Suckow in Heusinger, vol. iii. Pl. . f. 94. Straus Durckheim, Pl. V. f. 8.

the true ilium, which is however contradicted by its function, which, like that of the cæcum of the glires of the mammalia, subjects the food to a second digestion and extraction before it is rejected. We are convinced of this by the comparison of its state in the stomach, and in this portion of the canal, for we find it here much more pappy than there, but yet not so viscous as in the colon.

§ 109.

THE COLON.

The last division of the intestinal canal is called the COLON (Pl. XVII.—XXII. H, H,). It is divided from the preceding portion of the intestine by a valve which can completely shut its aperture. G. R. Treviranus was the first to describe and figure it *. Its internal surface, particularly near the mouth of the ilium, is thickly beset with glandular warts or flocks, which are not found in the ilium itself. We have observed glands only in the crop, and as their function there was evidently the secretion of the first menstruum of the food, they may here possibly produce a secretion to assist the rejection of the fæces.

The COLON generally exceeds the ilium in size, but when the conical or thick gut precedes it it is narrower; but it then is even longer than the ilium, which is not usually the case. The form of the COLON varies, sometimes cylindrical, or clavate, or distended above (bees); sometimes sack-shaped (*Carabodea*), or longitudinally folded within (caterpillars and the larvæ of *Calosoma*). These folds are produced by the internal intestinal membrane, and are either straight or waved, and supported by horny ridges. The muscular membrane does not assist to form these folds, but it is more compact and firmer than in the preceding portions of the intestine, yet the above described thick gut or occasional analogue (by situation) of the ilium is frequently much more fibrous. The colon is also occasionally fenestrate, that is to say, there are six ovate transparent spots in it which are surrounded by a horny margin or edge, and form either one or two rows, varying in situation, so that the spot in the lower row lies where in the upper one is found the intervening space. This structure Suckow first observed in the bees †. I found in *Harpalus ruficornis* a perfectly similar structure of the colon, these fenestral spots were in the internal

* Vermischte Schriften, vol. ii. p. 105. Pl. XII. f. 3.
† In Heusinger Zeitschr. f. d. Org. Ph., vol. iii. Pl. VI.

membrane, and were very bright and transparent. According to Ramdohr's observations, the width of the colon is in proportion to that of the pharynx (crop), for where the latter is broad so is also the colon, and *vice versâ*.

The situation of the colon is always determinate, for it is always found at the apex of the abdomen, surrounded by its last segments. The evacuating opening, or ANUS, is found in the last segment itself; it is covered above by a peculiar valve, and beneath this the anal vessels, which we shall describe lower down, open themselves. The corresponding lower valve conceals the sexual aperture, so that both the anal and sexual apertures open into one cavity, which might be called the CLOACA, and which are separated only by a fold if no other organ, for example, an ovipositor, be present. The anus, as well as the ilium and its correspondent the thick gut, are wanting in the larvæ of the bees, wasps (Pl. XVII. f. 9.), the *Formicaleo*, and of perhaps all the internal parasites, for example, the *Ichneumons*; their intestinal canal consisting of the pharynx and stomach, and a small bag beyond it, into which the biliary vessels open themselves; it is here that the fæces collect, which are evacuated upon the perfect insect quitting the pupa state, when it is provided with an anus.

§ 110.

THE CÆCUM.

In many insects we find, in connection with the colon, a blind, sack-shaped appendage, or rather similarly shaped superior distension of it which we call cæcum (Pl. XIX. f. 3 and 4 G, G). It originates at the very commencement of the colon, contiguous to its connection with the ilium, and extends anteriorly towards the stomach, in either larger or smaller distension; it is consequently not separated from the colon by any constriction or valve, but both cavities are in immediate connection with each other. This, as well as their uniformity of structure, proves that it must only be considered as a distension of the colon. In form this cæcum is sometimes nodose (*Silpha*) and directed forwards, sometimes laterally distended (*Necrophorus*), sometimes it is a long tubular point (*Dyticus*), sometimes a shorter cylindrical process of equal width with the colon (*Nepa*), similar to this, but sometimes slightly constricted at its commencement, we find it in the butterflies. It thence appears that this portion of the intestine is more peculiar to the carnivorous tribes, as Ramdohr, somewhat justly, remarks; yet its structure in the nectar-sucking butterflies modifies this assertion. The cæcum might also here, as in the *Mammalia*, have the function of a second stomach, and thus, therefore, be more serviceable to the carnivora, which consume coarser materials than the vegetable feeders, which are besides provided sometimes (*Melolontha*, &c.) with analogous organs, as the clavate and thick intestine. The cæcum is represented in the *Carabodea* by the broad sack-shaped colon. The long cæcum of the water-beetles has, according to Leon Dufour, the function of a swimming bladder, which is much to be doubted in the *Coleoptera*, they being provided with so many air vessels: we cannot either well imagine how air can be introduced into it, certainly not through the anus; for it is not for this purpose that water-beetles raise their anal ends to the surface of the water, but to take air beneath their elytra, as has been long well known.

§ 111.

THE BILIARY VESSELS.

The BILIARY VESSELS (*vasa bilifera*, (Pl. XVII.—XXII. K, K,) occupy the first place among those organs which, although distinct, stand however in direct connection with the intestinal canal. They are narrow filiform tubes, which open at one end into the duodenum, and where this is wanting into the ilium close behind the pylorus, and at the other end are either free and closed, or pass into each other and thus apparently form one vessel, which pierces the intestinal membranes with both its ends. The biliary vessels also, at least according to Ramdohr, sometimes empty themselves into the end of the stomach, sometimes (for example, in *Meloë*,) upon the limits of both, that it is difficult to say whether it is the stomach or intestine. According to Ramdohr, the mouth of the biliary vessels does not pierce the internal intestinal membrane, but only the exterior muscular one, which assertion, however, is contradicted by Meckel's observation, for, by pressing these vessels, he forced their contents into the intestine. In fact, the biliary vessels always enter the cavity of the intestine, and their mouths lie at the same height, forming a circle around it; more rarely upon one side only, for example, in a vesicular distension of the ilium in *Lygæus apterus*. Other differences in the mode of their evacuating themselves are not rare. In the flies (*Muscaria*) the four biliary vessels unite into two short stems, which open into the intestine at its opposite sides, or all four form but one, as in *Cimex baccarum*. Occasionally, also, the openings of the gall vessels do not lie by the side of but above each other, for example, in some of the *Neuroptera*, in which four of the eight biliary vessels enter upon the one side and the other four upon the other side of the intestine (*Myrmecoleon*). If many biliary vessels exist their mouths lie contiguously, above and below each other, or although more rarely, all upon one side (*Acheta*), or else they unite into a tolerably long evacuating duct, (for example, *Gryllotalpa*).

In form these vessels are generally narrow, cylindrical, filiform, and twisted, but they are not always of the same dimensions throughout: many commence narrowly and afterwards double in size; some, by means of a spiral furrow, resemble a turned slip; others have alternately small vesicular distensions (*Musca*); a few have long rectangular processes, which are occasionally furcate (*Melolontha vulgaris*).

There are generally FOUR in number, never fewer, unless entirely wanting (*Chermes, Aphis*), sometimes there are six or eight, and they are even, occasionally, innumerable. These differences in number are regulated by the order to which the insect belongs as well as by its food, whether it be vegetable or animal, as is shown in the following table:—

I. No biliary vessels, *Chermes, Aphis*.
II. Few (4—8) biliary vessels.
  1. Four biliary vessels.
    a. Free at the end; most *Diptera*, as well as the families *Termitina, Psocina*, and *Mallophaga*, of the order *Dictyotoptera*.
    b. Anastomosing; many *Coleoptera, Hemiptera*, and *Diptera*.
  2. Six biliary vessels.
    a. Anastomosing; many *Coleoptera*, for example, *Cerambycina* and *Chrysomelina*.
    b. Free at the end, *Lepidoptera*.
  3. Eight free biliary vessels, *Neuroptera*.
III. Many biliary vessels, *Hymenoptera, Orthoptera*, and the *Dictyotoptera subulicornia*.

Occasionally the biliary vessels join the intestinal canal at a second place, but this union takes place only with the exterior muscular membrane, for it is attached by means of solitary fibres, but a second opening into the intestine does not occur. This union is found chiefly in those insects furnished with a clavate intestine (the analogue of the ilium), for example, the *Cerambycina*, most of the *Neuroptera*, and the *Cicadaria*.

The length of the biliary vessels is in direct proportion to their number, for when there are but few they are very long, indeed the longest of all (for example, *Melolontha*); but they are short, on the contrary, where they are numerous, for example, in *Gryllotalpa, Libellula*, &c. The long biliary vessels lie generally around the intestine; they first ascend parallel to the stomach as far as the pharynx, they then return and form a thick knot of vessels around the ilium; where there are many, some return upwards along the stomach, and the rest below along the ilium. The length also of the single biliary vessels sometimes varies, for example, in the *Cerambycina*, in which they form concentric circles, but the two opposite sides are always of the same length.

The biliary vessels are also always more simply constructed than the intestinal canal, for they appear to consist of but a single skin, which, besides, is very delicate and transparent, so that their contents can be distinctly recognised as a finely granulated mass. The delicacy of the smooth shining case is proved by the difficulty of removing the biliary vessels from the enveloping fatty substance, and by their being very easily torn, even when the greatest precaution is used.

In colour they generally resemble the yellowish white of the intestinal canal; in some beetles (for example, *Carabus, Dyticus,*) they are of a dark brown, but which becomes paler as it approaches the opening. In many caterpillars, while parallel with the stomach they are whitish, but at the intestine of a saffron yellow; Swammerdam thence applied the name of saffron vessels to them.

It may be here remarked, at the close of our observations upon the biliary vessels, that some insects in which they are numerous, for example, the bees and wasps, have in their larvæ state but few (4—6) long and thick ones, which, by degrees, whilst during the pupa state the remaining gall vessels are forming, shrink up, and become shorter until they contract to the same length as the rest *. Do they not perhaps entirely disappear, and are replaced by the shorter ones? Perhaps they are very different vessels possessing a different function, which probably disappears when the intestine and anus become formed in the insect.

* See Ramdohr, Pl. XII.

§ 112.

THE SALIVARY VESSELS.

Cuvier says, in his " Comparative Anatomy," that the secretory organs of insects always assume a tubular form, and that consequently conglomerate glands are wholly wanting in them. This assertion is strictly true with respect to the biliary vessels, which have been considered as analogous to the liver, but in the salivary vessels we find exceptions, and which are most strongly exemplified in the testes, some of which (the *epidydimis* in *Hyrdophilus*) possessing many accumulated acini. Nevertheless, the form considered by Cuvier as universal is certainly the most general.

Under the name of salivary vessels we comprehend those glandular appendages of the nutrimental canal which evacuate themselves either into the mouth or into the commencement of the intestine in front of the stomach, and by their secretion promote the digestion of the food. The following are their chief differences:—

A. Salivary vessels which open into the mouth, generally beneath the tongue, and more seldom at the base of the mandibles. They take the following forms:—

1. As simple, long, undivided, twisted tubes; thus in the majority of insects, viz., all butterflies, many beetles and flies.
2. As a narrow vessel which empties itself into one or two bladders, whence the salivary duct originates (*Nepa*, Pl. XXII. f. 1; *Cimex*, Pl. XX. f. 3. A, A; *Sarcophaga*).
3. As a ramose vessel with blind branches, (*Blaps*, Pl. XXII. f. 3).
4. As two long, cylindrical pipes, which unite into one evacuating duct (*Reduvius*, Pl. XXI. f. 15).
5. As four small, round bladders, each pair of which have a common duct (*Pulex*, Pl. XXI. f. 16; *Lygæus*, *Cimex*).
6. As a multitude of such vesicles in *Nepa* (Pl. XXII. f. 2).
7. As capitate tubes, in the free ends of which many very fine vessels empty themselves (*Tabanus*, Pl. XXII. f. 4).
8. As tubes which at intervals are surrounded by twirling blind bags (*Cicada*, Pl. XXII. f. 5).
9. As granulated glands which on each side unite into a salivary duct, both of which join into a single evacuating duct (*Gryl-*

lus, Pl. XXI. f. 12.). J. Müller observed such granulated salivary glands in *Phasma;* Treviranus in *Apis*; and I have found them in *Locusta, Gryllus,* and *Termes.*

B. The salivary vessels which do not empty themselves into the mouth, but into the commencement of the stomach. These we have already partially described, in treating of the stomach (§ 105), as short or long bags, which were either simple or furnished with processes (*Buprestis*); other forms, as well as those just cited, are found chiefly among the *Diptera.*

1. As two capitate tubes, in the free ends of which many delicate vessels open, we perceive them in *Hemerobius perla* (Pl. XXII. f. 4).
2. As two short processes of the same width as the stomach, in *Leptis* (Pl. XXII. f. 6. *a, a,*) and *Acheta.*
3. As two bags covered entirely with short blind processes in *Bombylius* (Pl. XXII. f. 7.) and *Buprestis* (§ 105).
4. As triangular processes, each edge of which is occupied by a row of vesicles in *Chrysotoxum* (Pl. XXII. f. 8).
5. As six narrow tubes, which surround the commencement of the stomach in *Gryllus* (Pl. XXI. f. 1 and 6).
6. We also consider the blind processes which clothe the stomach in the predaceous beetles among the salivary vessels.

Salivary vessels which open into the mouth are found in all the haustellate and in many mandibulate insects which feed upon hard substances. Ramdohr was the first to observe them amongst the beetles in *Cryptorhynchus Lapathi.* In this insect he found a long twisted vessel, which opened into the mouth, which is indeed contrary to all analogy, for the salivary vessels are elsewhere found in pairs. Leon Dufour subsequently discovered salivary vessels in many *Heteromera,* viz., *Œdemera, Mycterus, Mordella,* &c. I have found them of the above form among the *Orthoptera,* in *Locusta,* and *Gryllus,* and among the *Dictyotoptera* in *Termes.* Among the *Neuroptera, Hemerobius* and *Phryganea* exhibit salivary organs.

The salivary organs which empty themselves into the stomach are found among the beetles, especially in those which devour flesh and wood; and in those *Orthoptera* also which feed upon hard vegetable matter, and in the *Diptera,* among the *Syrphodea,* which consume the nectar of flowers, and probably also their pollen. Among the grasshoppers we occasionally find both kinds of salivary organs.

Where we meet with salivary vessels we generally find two; some insects have, on the contrary, four, each pair of which unite into one evacuating duct (*Apis, Cimex, Pulex*); *Nepa* has even six salivary vessels, three on each side, all of which open into the cavity of the mouth; two unite on each side into one stem, the third, which has been considered as a poison-secreting organ, remains separated as far as the mouth.

Many larvæ, particularly the caterpillars of the *Lepidoptera*, have also four salivary vessels of different structure; two are slender, very long (*Cossus*), and filiform; two broader, sometimes bag-shaped (for example, *Cossus ligniperda*, O.), and considerably shorter. The first secrete a viscous liquid, from which the caterpillar spins its silk. The evacuating ducts of both unite into one, and open into the under lip, namely, into the canal of the above (§ 54) described spinneret. This pipe would therefore be more correctly called spinning vessel. Such spinning vessels are naturally found only in those larvæ which prepare a web for their pupa change, such as the caterpillars of the nocturnal *Lepidoptera*, the larvæ of the saw-flies, and of the *Phryganodea*. It distinguishes itself chiefly by its length and size from the true salivary vessels, which are often very small and insignificant. The true salivary vessels, according to Suckow [*], open at the base of the upper mandible with a small warty protuberance (Pl. XXI. f. 13), and remain even in the perfected moth; whereas the spinning vessels totally disappear during the pupa state [†].

In *Myrmecoleon* the spinning vessels lie at the anal end of the abdomen, and true salivary vessels have not yet been observed in it [‡].

The structure of this organ appears, according to all investigations hitherto instituted, to be very variable, for sometimes there are two membranes (the muscular and mucous) and sometimes but one. The former vary in consistency, but occasionally are uniform with those of the intestine; in the latter case they are transparent and delicate, and occasionally granulated or irregular.

The length also of the salivary vessels differs much: in some caterpillars they are two or three times as long as the intestine; in perfect insects, on the contrary, they are generally shorter, and do not usually

---

[*] Suckow's Physiol. Unternich. uber Insecten und Krustenthiere, p. 28. Pl. VII. f. 32. *a*.
[†] Ib. p. 29. Pl. II. f. 1—10. h. h.
[‡] Ramdohr, Pl. XVII. f. 1—4.

extend beyond the thorax. It is thence that we detect the salivary vessels, with the exception of the very long ones of caterpillars, only in the thorax. They here lie around the pharynx, crop, or stomach, generally low down in the breast between the coxæ of the legs, whilst their meandering evacuating duct, rising from beneath the nutrimental canal, ascends to the cavity of the mouth, and here, after having united with its companion, opens beneath the tongue. *Locusta* displays this aperture very distinctly. In the bees, in which the salivary organ consists of four granulated valves, the anterior one lies in the head, directly beneath the forehead, before the eyes, and was originally described by Ramdohr as the organ of smell, but subsequently recognised as the salivary gland. The evacuating duct empties itself into the tube of the proboscideal tongue, and is a spiral vessel resembling the trachea, as Treviranus has described and figured it*; in *Locusta* I found it simple, thin, and transparent, but accompanied by a delicate trachea, which followed it throughout all its ramifications and divisions.

§ 113.

THE URINARY VESSELS.

As the last distinct organ, but which is doubtlessly in strict connection with the digestive apparatus, we must take some notice of the variously formed urinary vessels, which empty themselves above the anus. These, like the salivary vessels, are sometimes mere vascular canals, at others glandular bodies which in the latter case unite into one duct, to which not rarely there is attached a vesicular distension— the URINARY BLADDER. The duct of the latter is always separated, and never unites to those of the opposite side, and empties itself laterally contiguous to and above the anus, but strictly separated from it by the anal valve.

These vessels are found in all the *Carabodea* and the *Hydrocantharides*, in many *Heteromera* (*Blaps*), and again in *Bombylius* and *Leptis*, among the *Diptera*. Ramdohr, who first observed them, drew them to the intestine, and called them anal vessels; but Leon Dufour subsequently described many of their forms in detail †.

In their most simple form (in *Harpalus*) the urinary vessels appear as reniform bodies contiguous to the colon, whence a short evacuating

---

* Vermischte Schrif., vol. ii. p. 123. Pl. XV. f. 1.

† Annales des Sciences Natur., t. 8. p. 6. Pl. XIX. and XX.

duct extends to the orifice. In *Carabus auratus* this body is a bunch of small round vesicles; in *Car. cancellatus* it is divided into two equal halves, the two short ducts of which speedily unite into one. The urinary bladder, which is wanting in *Harpalus*, is present in *Carabus*, has the shape of a fig, and stands almost at right angles with the evacuating duct. It is much the same in *Cymindis humeralis;* in *Aptinus* three equal ducts open into the bladder, each of which originates from five granulated glands with five branches. In *Brachinus* the glands are convolutions of shorter or longer, and sometimes furcate filaments. In *Chlænius* and *Sphodrus* there are many solitary granules, each of which has a small duct, they all unite into one stem, which then opens into the bladder.

In the water beetles (Pl. XXI. f. 11.) the portion lying above, and over the urinary bladder, is but a simple, twisted, but tolerably long, although delicate vessel; the bladder, on the contrary, is round, but not petiolated. It is the same in *Bombylius*.

With respect to the structure of these organs, two membranes are distinctly discerned in the evacuating duct, the interior of which is much less than the exterior; this is constricted by parallel transverse rings. The glands also have occasionally (*Chlænius velutinus*) similar transverse rings, particularly when they are somewhat larger.

§ 114.

CHANGES IN THE INTESTINAL CANAL OCCASIONED BY THE METAMORPHOSES.

In the preceding description of the nutrimental canal in insects, we have restricted ourselves chiefly to their form and structure in the perfect creature. As, nevertheless, the differences which are produced in the nutrimental canal by their metamorphoses are by no means unimportant, for the intestinal canal in larvæ assumes very generally a very different form, and its changes are subject to peculiar laws, partially influenced by the order to which it belongs, we must not omit taking notice of them as far as is possible in a general sketch, and must therefore make room here for a description of these transformations.

Insects with an imperfect metamorphosis, viz. the *Hemiptera, Orthoptera*, and *Dictyotoptera*, have in all their stages a very uniform nutrimental canal. We find in them the same divisions in the same proportions, and even the appendages, such as the salivary and biliary vessels, agree with those of the perfect insect. The whole change, therefore, which the nutrimental canal undergoes in these orders consists in its lengthening in proportion to the increasing size of the insect, and at the time of moulting it covers itself internally with a new mucous membrane, the old one being rejected by the anus, or probably absorbed. This changing of the skin in the intestine is certainly remarkable, and proves, as well as the similar phenomenon in cutaneous affections in man, in which the epidermis peels off (for example, after scarlet fever), the perfect uniformity of the intestinal mucous membrane with the exterior epidermis. The larvæ of the *Libellulæ* alone appear to make a slight exception to the rule of the intestinal canal remaining the same, their's being somewhat larger, particularly broader, than in the perfect insect, and in the latter the respiration of the colon disappearing, which was peculiar to the former.

Insects with a perfect metamorphosis, on the contrary, undergo in the intestinal canal, as well as exteriorly, important changes, which, however, refer only to the form, the structure remaining constantly the same. It is true the membranes are originally much more delicate, looser, and admit of being more readily separated, particularly in the stomach, but this difference gradually vanishes. During their larva state the intestine assumes a new skin at every moulting †; towards the end of this period, and still more during their pupa state, the intestine shrinks, particularly the stomach, and acquires thereby a more compact appearance. It is the divisions of the nutrimental canal and their relative lengths which chiefly vary, but these are regulated by very different laws in the several orders, and consequently demand of us an especial notice.

The maggots of the *Diptera* (Pl. XVIII. f. 2. maggot; f. 3. fly) have a longer intestine than the flies, but it is the stomach chiefly which occasions this greater length. The sucking stomach is present, but larger, more shortly pediculated, and, besides, there are large cylindrical salivary bags, which in the course of their change transform themselves into filiform salivary vessels. The biliary vessels remain uniform both in number and shape. During the larva state the intestinal canal remains unchanged, but it alters the more quickly in the pupa state;

---

* Compare Suckow in Heusing. Zeitschr. f. d. Org. Phy. vol. ii. p. 24, &c.

† In the larvæ without an anus (*Myrmecoleon, Vespas, Apis*) the old skin remains in the bag behind the stomach (compare §. 105.), and is evacuated only after the pupa state through the new-formed anus.

but it is still the stomach only which shortens, until it decreases to scarcely one half of its former extent.

In the *Lepidoptera*, on the contrary (Pl. XVIII. f. 4. caterpillar; 5. imago), the intestinal canal lengthens, but so that here also the stomach becomes shorter but the ilium longer. In the caterpillar the broad, cylindrical, folded, and transversely ringed stomach occupies more than two-thirds of the entire intestinal canal, and this is succeeded by a shorter, scarcely narrower ilium; the preceding pharynx is short, and so short that it is observed only in the head. Contiguous to the stomach lie the long twisted spinnerets, and attached to it are the six united biliary vessels. In the imago the pharynx is long, and beneath it lies the sucking stomach, of which we observe no trace in the caterpillar; the stomach, on the contrary, is small, short, ovate, folded, and narrow; the ilium, again, long, filiform, twisted; the colon broader, elongated above into a short cæcum, which is likewise deficient in the caterpillar. The spinnerets disappear, but the salivary vessels, which are very small in the caterpillar, become more distinct, larger, and longer.

We have already noticed the very interesting metamorphosis of the intestinal canal in the wasp and the bee. In the order of the *Hymenoptera* also the law prevails of the stomach becoming smaller and narrower whilst the pharynx and ilium become longer. This will also apply to *Myrmecoleon*, in whose larva the colon becomes the spinneret.

But of all the orders the *Coleoptera* display the greatest changes of the intestinal canal. The larvæ of the carnivora wholly want the folded horny orifice of the stomach (Pl. XIX. f. 1 and 3). Their stomach is broad, but smooth, and not beset with filamentary processes; the ilium is also broad, but short, and much shorter than after the metamorphosis. This consists in the crop distending, the proventriculus forming itself, and the stomach sending forth filamentary processes. In the *Carabodea* the ilium becomes much longer; but in the water beetles, where it is already very long, it appears to become somewhat shorter, at least in *Dyticus marginalis*, according to Dutrochet, whose investigations I have repeated, and can now confirm (see Pl. XIX. f. 3. the larva; f. 4. the beetle). In the vegetable feeders, namely, in the *Lamellicornia*, the intestinal canal in the larvæ is triflingly longer than the body, whereas in the perfect insect it is three or four times as long. The larvæ have a long, broad, cylindrical stomach beset with filaments at its commencement and end; a short, narrow ilium; a broad, sack-shaped thick-intestine; and a tolerably long but not broad colon: the beetles have a very long but narrower cylindrical stomach, an ilium resembling that of the larvæ, a much narrower, gradually distending, thick-intestine, and a longer cylindrical colon, which distends very widely close to the anus. In both cases, consequently, the intestinal canal is longer in the perfect state than in the larva, but in the vegetable feeders more considerably so than in the carnivora, in which it, namely in *Dyticus*, is shorter. Whereas the beetle has a much more complex intestine, and more organs to effect the change and transformation of the food than the larva, which is the more remarkable, as both, at least generally, take the same food, which is not always the case in the other orders, for example, in the *Lepidoptera* and flies.

§ 115.

II. THE FATTY MASS, OR RETE.

The fatty mass of insects is a web of generally white or yellow ragged or stringy substance interwoven in every possible way, enveloping the intestinal canal and the organs connected with it, as well as all the other internal parts, but it is never in direct immediate connection with any organ. It receives its name from its undeniable resemblance to the fat of the higher animals, and which is expressed in the above peculiarity, and even more strongly in other circumstances. It thence appears that it forms no portion of the intestinal canal, being nowhere in connection with it, but as it is the produce of digestion and as it is increased or decreased by the perfection or imperfection of the function of digestion, it must therefore, as standing in relation to the organs of nutriment, be treated of and described when treating of them. We are the more strongly impelled to this by the opinion expressed by Oken, and which Treviranus has recently supported by analogies, that the fatty mass of insects must be considered as their liver. Indeed in the scorpion a substance similar to the fatty mass stands in connection with the nutrimental canal by means of vessels, but they possess besides two twisted biliary vessels, which likewise here and there quit that substance. In all true insects, however, we find no such close connection of both organs, and if it cannot be denied that the fatty mass is of importance to digestion, and that much nutrimental matter is derived from it, yet this admission proves by no means its analogy to the liver. In fact, it is neither absolutely liver nor gland, but nutrimental matter, which, during the metamorphosis, particularly during the pupa sleep, is absorbed like the fat of the lethargic mammalia during their hybernation. But the degree of reference the function of the liver has to the preparation of the fat is sufficiently well known from the example of the lethargic mammalia, therefore the above opinion, when we consider the small size of the biliary vessels supplanting the liver, or the treatment of these vessels as kidneys, a view also recently promulgated, may possibly have many supporters.

The nature of this fatty body is in so far uniform that it consists of shreds, which upon microscopic investigation are found to be constituted of small globules of animal aboriginal matter. This is the only character this fatty mass presents upon the closest investigation; exteriorly it is surrounded by delicate membranes, which consequently may be compared to the membranes of the cellular texture, but the lens does not show it very distinctly, from its transparency, delicacy, and texturelessness. Ramdohr, who considered the fatty mass as plastic lymph, obtained from experiments upon that of the *Gastrophaga quercus* the following result:—it melted in boiling water, effervesced with sulphuric acid, at the same time smelling like burnt horn, and in cold water was precipitated in white flocks; heated over a lamp it hardened into a white firm mass, swelled up upon the application of greater heat, and then burnt away, dispersing a stinking vapour. According to my experiments, made with the large flabby fatty mass of *Cossus ligniperda*, it melted in a spoon over a lamp into a perfectly clear transparent yellow liquid, which paper instantly absorbed, and was rendered transparent by it like fat; it had a peculiar smell, like that of freshly opened caterpillars; its taste was fatty and insipid. Upon increased heat it boiled up in bladders but did not become firm, or else it consumed to ashes. Laid fresh in hot water it became softer, more transparent, and particles of it floated on the top like oil.

These very contradictory results tend at least to prove that the fatty substance in different insects consists of very different constituents, which is the more striking as both experiments were made from insects of the same order, in which they even approach very near each other. Probably Ramdohr's caterpillar had been long immersed in spirits of wine, thus consequently, and by the additional influence of heat, the fat parts had separated, and only the cellular portion of the enveloping membranes remained.

The entire fatty mass forms a reticulated meshy web, which envelops the interior organs and completely fills all portions of the cavity not occupied by them. In larvæ the threads and laces of this net are larger and more ragged, particularly in the fat larvæ of the crepuscular and night moths. The nearer it approaches the pupa state the larger are the proportions of this substance; but as soon as the insect becomes fully developed this material loses its size, and it becomes a broad, delicate, laced web. It is consequently during the pupa state that the greater portion of this substance becomes absorbed, whereby the shreds shrink up, the delicate membrane becomes narrower, and thus the preceding coarse shreds become delicate and fine laces. In this shape the fatty mass not merely represents the rete of the vertebrata, but actually becomes it, for it is the envelope of the intestines, and in conjunction with the air vessels it supports and fixes them. Thence is it that earlier (Malpighi) and more modern (Cuvier) anatomists have called it the net of insects. It is scarcely necessary, after such facts, to adduce other reasons in opposition to the above disputed opinion that this net is the liver of insects; whoever has but watched the development of a single butterfly, indeed, whoever shall but have compared an opened caterpillar with an opened moth, to him it will be evident that the fatty mass cannot be the liver.

Chemical analysis has as yet contributed nothing towards the removal of the difficulties which still involve the different views upon this subject, although a careful investigation would most certainly settle the dispute. In ants[*] and the cochineal insect fat has actually been found, and this consequently may certainly contribute to support the adoption of the opinion of this substance being found in all other insects.

§ 116.

III. THE BLOOD VESSELS.

We shall find the vascular system just as simple and uniform in insects as we have found their digestive apparatus complex. A vessel which passes along the back from the head to the anus constitutes the only blood vessel to be discovered in insects. That this canal is a true blood vessel, and indeed an artery, is proved by its regular contraction and expansion, which is very easily perceived exteriorly in transparent thin-skinned larvæ. Malpighi, its discoverer, considered it as such,

---

[*] Compare Gmelin, Handb. d. Theor. Chemie, vol. ii. Div. i. p. 469, No. 24, and p. 508. No. 1; 2nd Div. p. 1473, &c.

and has described it as a great pulsating * vein. Subsequently to him, the other great entomotomists, Reaumur, Swammerdam, Bonnet, De Geer, have recognised the same organ, and concur with him in representing it as a simple and wholly closed vessel. Even the very cautious Lyonnet can consider it as nothing else; but he described the lobes of the dorsal vessel in greater detail, and has figured them more accurately than any of his predecessors. In recent times Cuvier, in his " Comparative Anatomy," has repeated the descriptions of earlier anatomists, and even after this organ had been subjected to the most painfully patient investigations by Herold and Müller, its true structure has not yet been ascertained. Carus † at last discovered the motion of a fluid not only in the dorsal vessel but also in other parts of the body, and shortly after him Straus—Durckheim recognised a structure of the dorsal vessel, which had been previously overlooked, which so entirely agrees with the insect type of organisation, that no doubt can be entertained of the correctness of his observation. My attention being drawn to it by Straus' communications, I made investigations upon the structure of the heart in several insects (for example, in the larva of *Calosoma sycophanta, Lamia ædilis, Termes fatalis*, &c.), and I have distinctly seen the valves and apertures mentioned by him.

§ 117.

According, therefore, to these most recent observations, the dorsal vessel (Pl. XXII. f. 8 and 9.) is a thin canal composed of a delicate membrane, it is largest in the abdomen, and gradually decreases towards the head. In the abdomen it has on each side several apertures, as well as lateral muscular lobes, whereby it is attached to the back; where it enters the thorax it bends downwards (the same, f. 8. B.) that it may pass through the narrow, more deeply situated opening into its cavity, and then pursues its course above the œsophagus to the head, where it terminates with a small orifice. The number of the lateral apertures appears to vary (the same, a, a, a). Straus found eight in *Melolontha*, I could observe but four on each side in the larva of *Calosoma*. According to Müller's description of the heart there appears to

* Compare his Dissert. Bombyce. Lond. 1669, 4to. or his Collective Works, Lugd. Bat. 1687, 4to., vol. ii. p. 20.

† Entdeckung eines einfachen, vom Herzen aus bleschleunigten Kreislaufes in den Larven netzflüglicher Insekten. Leipz. 1827. 4to.

be but one aperture in *Phasma*, which also has but one pair of lateral muscles. By means of these apertures the heart is divided into so many chambers, for behind each opening there are valves which separate the preceding space from that behind the opening, so that in *Melolontha* there are eight (Pl. XXI. f. 1—8.) such consecutive chambers. The first, which lies close to the dorsal sheath of the last abdominal segment, is the smallest, and consists of one heart-shaped bag, which in front, towards the head, has an opening like a slit. The lips of this aperture consequently form the anterior side of the bag and close it, if blood, pressing forward from within, does not part them. The blood enters it through two small apertures, which likewise lie in front upon each side of the bag, but it cannot flow back through the same openings, for a half-moon-shaped valve which is affixed within the cavity of the bag beneath the aperture closes upon it, and thus, when the heart contracts, the blood must necessarily pass through the anterior opening. This first and most posterior chamber of the heart is succeeded by another in front, formed very similarly, but longer and more cylindrical, and which has also an aperture behind, viz. the anterior one of the first chamber. It is through this that the blood passes from the first chamber to the second when the heart contracts, and upon its dilatation blood pours into the chambers through the two lateral anterior openings. Thus, therefore, each chamber is always provided with blood, for the blood streams from one chamber to the other, beginning at the posterior, when that which has been received through the lateral openings from the cavity of the abdomen passes on by their successive contractions. We will explain how this contraction (systole) and dilatation (diastole) of the heart take place after we have said a few words upon its structure.

§ 118.

According to Straus, two membranes are observed in the heart, the exterior of which is smooth, dense, and longitudinally fibrous, consequently muscular. It is this which forms the above-described valves, for at the two margins of each lateral aperture it bends inwards. The posterior return forms the inner valve of that opening, and the anterior return the partition of the chamber, or both the anterior ones form the lips of the anterior opening. Both valves, as well as the entire internal lining of the heart, are covered with a transversely folded and looser layer of muscle, which is still thicker and stronger in the middle of each chamber. Perhaps both membranes are but the different layers of one muscular membrane, and then we might, by the analogy of all blood-vessels, entertain the idea of the presence of an innermost structureless mucous membrane, which escapes observation by its delicacy.

It is from the presence of these muscular layers that it is possible for the heart to contract and dilate. By both membranes simultaneously contracting the heart becomes straitened, and this distends again as soon as the membranes become flaccid after the contraction, when the muscles of the lobes contract themselves.

§ 119.

To the posterior portion of the dorsal vessel which we find provided with apertures and valves, and which we must consider as the true heart, several triangular, flat, membranous muscles are affixed, the points of which pass on to a dorsal plate of the abdomen, and there attach themselves (Pl. XXII. f. 9). If these wings (flügel) of the heart, as they are called, are short, or consequently of the shape of an equilateral triangle, other muscles of the form of a band originate at the apex of this triangle, and pass in a diverging direction from each other, and insert themselves upon the abdominal plate, where this becomes membranous (*Lamia ædilis*). Generally, however, the wings are so long as not to require the muscles of attachment (*Melolontha*, &c.), and they then take the shape of a very acute triangle. The conjunction of these muscular wings with the heart, which they merely retain in its place, is very intimate, without its being possible to say where; whether it be by fibres passing from these wings into those of the heart, or whether the membrane of the heart sends forth lateral folds it is impossible to say. They lie in a row upon the two opposite sides of the heart, precisely where the anterior aperture of each chamber is found. They pass over these apertures, the fibres attaching themselves to a small membranous arch which crosses these orifices transversely; consequently, in front of each orifice, there is a small semicircular hole in these wings, which are thus prevented from interrupting the flow of blood.

These wings are wanting to the dorsal vessel of the *Libellula*, and *Phasma* has but one pair in the sixth abdominal segment. Besides this we find a pair of muscles passing from the posterior margin of the heart, their apex being attached to the last abdominal segment and the colon, which has not yet been observed in other insects *.

§ 120.

The anterior portion of the dorsal vessel which passes through the thorax to the head, and which is not furnished with apertures and muscles (Pl. XXII. f. 8. c), may be called the aorta if we call the posterior portion the heart. The part which may be considered as such commences where the dorsal vessel bends near the thorax to pass into its cavity, for from here the apertures and muscles are wanting. This bend is greater or smaller, according to the size of the posterior partition of the thorax, largest doubtlessly in the petiolated *Hymenoptera* or the *Diptera*, whose thoracic cavity is entirely separated from the abdominal cavity by the metaphragma. When the aorta arrives in the cavity of the thorax its course becomes then direct as far as the head, constantly keeping the central line, and accompanying the here straight œsophagus or stomach, and frequently united to it by a cellular membrane or the fatty substance. When there is a free and moveable prothorax it passes likewise into this through the common opening, or more rarely (as in *Gryllotalpa* †) through a small aperture in the mesophragma (Pl. XI. No. I. f. 7. *a*), and here still accompanies the œsophagus as far as the head. Here, close to where the œsophagus bends down to the mouth, consequently behind the cerebrum, the aorta suddenly ceases with a somewhat distended orifice, without previously sending forth any smaller vessel; in other instances it divides in a fork, each branch of which bends laterally, and terminates after a very short course likewise with a free orifice; or, lastly, we find three short, equal, radiating branches, each open at the extremity (for example, in *Gryllus hieroglyphicus*, Klug. ‡).

§ 121.

We thus conclude the description of the blood-vessels of insects. The most laborious and patient endeavours of Entomotomists to discover other vessels remained unrewarded, until Joh. Müller discovered a union of the ovaries with the aorta §. We shall treat in greater detail of this

---

* Comp. J. Müller, über das Rückengefäss, in Nova Acta. Med. Nat. Cur. vol. xii. pars ii. pp. 576 and 586.

† Ibid. p. 596.   ‡ Joh. Müller, ib. p. 613.   § Ib. p. 613.

connection lower down, in the Chapter where we speak of the sexual organs; but we must defer hinting at their hypothetical use, as well as of the doctrine of a circulating system in insects, until the following division, to which we consequently refer.

§ 122.

IV. OF THE ORGANS OF RESPIRATION.

We shall find the respiratory organs of insects as complex and perfectly developed, as we have found their blood-vessels simple and imperfect. The relations between these systems appear to be in them completely reversed, for the air-vessels intersect the insect body as multitudinously as we find the blood-vessels do in the superior animals. We cannot here show whence this transposition of the usual relations proceeds, nor how an entirely different structure can produce a similar result, this belongs to Physiology; we are here required merely to explain the structure and distribution of the air-vessels, and their external orifices. Our subject thence divides itself into two portions; the first of which treats of the exterior organs attached to the respiratory organs; and in the second, we shall describe the internal air-vessels themselves.

§ 123.

A. Exterior Organs of Respiration.

The exterior organs of respiration which are found upon the surface of the body, are of a triple character, namely, SPIRACLES, AIR TUBES, and BRANCHIÆ. The first are easily distinguished from the last, by the presence of an orifice that opens directly into the tracheæ, whereas the branchiæ are membranous leaves, throughout which tracheæ are dispersed, without opening anywhere.

I. The SPIRACLES (*spiracula, stigmata*), which are the most frequently found of all the exterior organs of respiration, appear as incisions or small round openings at the sides of the segments of the body, which are sometimes surrounded by a peculiar oval horny ring; or are encircled by merely the usual integument of the body, without any apparent distinction. Both kinds of structure are supplied with a muscular apparatus which opens and closes the aperture, so that the insect can either open it to receive air, or close it against it. We shall proceed with a description of their various forms, after this short indication of their differences.

Some which are never free, but lie concealed beneath portions of the horny integument, have no exterior horny ring, but a double-lipped incision, the lips of which are formed by a thickened margin fringed with short hair. This structure is very apparent in the large spiracle which lies in the uniting membrane of the pro- and mesothorax, and particularly in *Gryllotalpa* (Pl. XI., No. 1, f. 2, *a. a.*), where, by reason of its length, it is very distinct. The horny lips are connected at their corners by a kind of joint, but in *Gryllotalpa* the lower corner of this incision, which lies near the anterior coxæ, is broader and more prominent; and the corner of the exterior lip projects beyond the opposite interior one, forming a kind of covering, thus preventing the influx of improper substances. The entire spiracle is closed by means of a small muscle, which, originating from an inner horny projection of the lower corner of the lip, inserts itself in two horny half-rings, which surround the commencement of the tracheæ. The orifice is opened or shut by the contraction or dilatation of this muscle.

Other spiracles, which besides the lips possess an oval horny margin, present a somewhat more complicated structure. The horny ridge (Pl. XXIII, f. 1—3,*a*,) is no distinct part, but merely the raised edge of the integument surrounding the spiracle; it thus forms an exterior ring, to which the lips of the incision are attached. These lips (the same *b. b.*) stand at the base of the ring, and are frequently covered upon their external surface like it upon its internal circumference, with sculptured horny scales (*Oryctes nasicornis*). Where they meet they again form a small projecting margin which, as in the former kind of structure, is surrounded by a fringe of fine hair. The corners of the lips lie close to the inner margin of the exterior ring, so that the true opening, upon the lips being closed, appears as the diameter of the oval ring. The closing apparatus of these spiracles is very complicated. The ends of the incisions, namely, or the corners of both lips, are prolonged inwardly into a point (the same, *c. c.*), to which two triangular horny plates are so attached, that one angle of the triangle with the projecting point, and the second with the opposite one of the other horny plate, form a joint, but the third remains free. From the last, as well from the sides of the triangle which are applied to each other, a flat muscle originates (the same, *e.*) which, when it contracts, brings the free points of both triangles together, but those which stand in connection with the inner points of the corners of the lips, it separates from each other; thus is the incision closed: but when the muscle again relaxes, it re-opens. We must observe, at the same time, that a bag-shaped expansion of the tracheæ originates from the circumference of the spiracle, and narrows towards the latter, in a funnel shape. By means of the tracheæ arising from the point of the funnel, the whole expansion is drawn backwards, so that the axis of the funnel stands obliquely to the axis of the tracheæ; upon the inner side of this funnel, or that part next to the ventral cavity, the just described apparatus for the closing of the spiracle lies (see Pl. XXIII, f. 1—3). Such spiracles are found only upon free or slightly covered parts of the body, for example, under the elytra of many beetles.

A third form of the spiracles is distinguished from the preceding by the want of lips. In very small and round spiracles, the opening is free (for example, in the *Lamellicornia*), or at most covered with short hair upon their inner margin, and the entrance into the tracheæ is only rendered difficult by the obliquity of its axis to that of the spiracle. In larger oval spiracles, the margins are occupied with stronger plumose spines, or hairy tufts (Pl. XXII. f. 10), and these resist extraneous substances still more forcibly. The air is purified through these as through a sieve, and all prejudicial substances are caught there. This structure is very distinct in the large spiracle of the first abdominal segment of the male *Cicada*, as well as in the dorsal spiracles of the water beetles [*].

The fourth and last form of the spiracles is that observed in the larvæ of the *Lamellicornia*. In these the very minute spiracle appears at first view to take a circular shape, and upon closer inspection it is found to consist of a broad margin and a concentric middle space, which beneath breaks through the margin and connects itself with the surrounding integument. This margin, which is often ornamented with distinct sculpture (Pl. XXIII. f. 4. *a, a,*) Sprengel considered as a half moon-shaped opening, occasionally closed by a sieve, when the sculpture of the margin was cribriform, or by toothed processes, when the sculpture took that figure, opposite which the inner round plate lay and assisted to close it. Treviranus [†] opposes this view of it, and asserts that the spiracle is entirely closed, but that minute ramifications of tracheæ are spread upon its internal superficies, and imbibe the air,

---

[*] See Carus, Analekten zur Naturwissensch. Dresden, 1829. 8vo. P. 187. Pl. I, f. 18. And Sprengel, Commentar. &c. Plate II, fig. 23; and Plate III, fig. 29.

[†] Das Organische Leben, neu dargestellt. Bremen, 1831. 8vo. Vol. I. p. 258.

as in the branchiæ, through the plate of the spiracle. Both were mistaken, for these spiracles have likewise a central aperture, which leads directly into the stem of the tracheæ. This orifice, which is a small transverse incision, lies in the central round plate (Pl. XXIII. f. 4. *c*), and is very small in proportion to the entire spiracle, and may therefore be easily overlooked; but Kaulfuss, in his drawings to Sprengel's Treatise, has everywhere indicated them. The exterior margin is, however, by no means perforated, but merely covered with sculpture, just like the exterior oval horny ring. I consider this margin therefore as the pre-formation of the subsequent oval horny ring, the central plate, however, as the two lips of the here still smaller incision. Internally the main stem of the trachea is observed to originate from the circumference of the aperture, a distinct proof that the incision is its orifice (Pl. XXIII. f. 4., *d. d.*).

§ 124.

After noticing the form of the spiracles, the next most important subject is their situation in the body, which is tolerably uniform in the several orders, but there are a few divarications from it, which we may here briefly indicate.

In the *Coleoptera* each segment of the body has a spiracle, or, to speak more correctly, upon the boundaries of every two segments we find one. The first, and generally the largest spiracle, is seated in the uniting membrane of the pro- and meso-thorax, more closely approaching the exterior and lower margin of the former, where it generally remains when those two portions of the body are separated. The second spiracle lies in a very similar situation, namely, between the meso- and meta-thorax, but it is so concealed by the elytra, that it can be discerned only upon very close investigation. It is then observed between the two horny plates which we called above (page 81) the anterior and posterior wings of the scapulæ. In a state of repose the two plates lie closely together, and thereby completely cover this spiracle; but upon the expansion of the wings during flight, when the body filled with air distends, this spiracle also quits its concealment, that it may, like the rest, allow air to flow in and out. The concealed situation of this spiracle explains how it has been overlooked, particularly as we observe none in the similarly named segment of the larvæ. Straus first observed it, and has exhibited it in the cockchafer and in others. The third spiracle lies between the meta-thorax and the first abdominal segment; it is frequently minute and indistinct, but occasionally, as, for example, in the Capricorn beetles, it is very large, indeed larger than the first. The following spiracles, six or seven in number, lie always between every two of the successive abdominal segments, so that the two last segments alone have no spiracles; we thus obtain ten spiracles upon each side, twenty together, a typical number which is never exceeded, but often also not attained.

In the *Orthoptera* the spiracles are not differently situated. The first which is in the connecting membrane between the pro and meso-thorax is very large, particularly so in *Gryllotalpa* (Pl. XI. No. I. f. 2. *a, a*); the second, between the lower wing of the scapula and the dorsal piece is here quite free and uncovered (the same, fig. 8. β). The third spiracle, which properly should lie between the meta-thorax and the first segment of the abdomen, approaches more closely to the latter, and lies in *Gryllus*, F. (*Acrydium*, Lat.) in a half moon-shaped hollow, which upon one side is partly closed by the projecting cover-shaped margin. All the succeeding ones are placed in a similar situation, namely, at the lower margin of each dorsal plate of the abdomen. In the *Blattaria*, on the contrary, the spiracles are always placed in the connecting membrane between two segments, and precisely where the dorsal and ventral plates meet; the same is the case in *Forficula*; in these also the third spiracle lies at the anterior edge of the dorsal plate of the first segment of the abdomen, where it is very distinct although but small.

In the *Hemiptera*, which, by the structure of their thorax, approach closely to the *Orthoptera*, the first spiracle likewise lies in the connecting membrane between the pro- and meso-thorax; it is tolerably large, and narrow, and is only apparent upon the removal of the pro-thorax. A second spiracle is found between the meso- and meta-thorax, and resembles the former in being a rather long, half moon-shaped, or straight incision, and is covered by a posterior projection of the margin of the meso-sternum. This spiracle consequently cannot be seen from the exterior from the preceding projection (Pl. XIII. No. 5. fig. 2. β) lying over it, and above it is concealed by the elytra. The succeeding spiracles are in these insects, as in the *Orthoptera*, more approximate to the ventral segments, a spiracle being placed in each abdominal segment, whereas by analogy it should lie between every two segments. In the male *Cicada* the first is very large, free, and always beset with strong setæ at the margin, the following are smaller and indistinct.

Kirby and Spence describe large lateral spiracles in the bugs, lying between the meso- and meta-thorax, but I could perceive in our bugs (*Pentatoma rufipes* and *P. hæmorrhoidalis*) depressions only at these parts; but if the acute posterior margin of the prosternum, which lies precisely in this cavity, be removed, the spiracle is observed very distinctly beneath it. In *Belostoma* a very distinct spiracle is found at the posterior margin of the pleura, consequently between the meta-thorax and the abdomen, which, however, appears to belong to the first abdominal segment, because in the bugs the spiracles lie always in the ventral segments themselves, and, indeed, at the exterior margin of the ventral plates, and not, as in the beetles, beneath the wings and the elytra.

The *Neuroptera* alone, of the remaining orders, have a distinctly separated pro-thorax; it is here therefore that we must notice them. *Semblis* displays two distinct pairs (Pl. XIV. No. 3. f. 2. 4. a and β,) of spiracles in the thorax, the first between the pro- and meso-thorax, and the second between the meso- and meta-thorax. Whether there be a third pair between the meta-thorax and the abdomen I could not clearly perceive either here or in *Myrmecoleon*, but in the dry specimens examined by me there appeared to be incisions. The two first pairs lie, also in the ant-lion, exactly in the same place. *Panorpa* displays two pairs of spiracles in the thorax and five pairs in the abdomen; the two first lie between the pro- and meso-thorax, and between the latter and the meta-thorax, and display themselves as small brown points. In the abdomen they are placed, as in all *Neuroptera*, in the connecting membrane of each pair of segments, closely in front of that to which they belong.

In the *Dictyotoptera*, as those most closely allied to the preceding order, with the exception of the *Libellulæ* and *Termites*, they are, from their minuteness, difficult to investigate. The *Libellulæ* have two pairs of spiracles in the thorax, one pair being between the pro- and meso-thorax, each of which, however, is covered by a small scale originating at the posterior margin of the pronotum; the second pair is seated between the meso- and meta-thorax, at the sides of the thorax. The former are long, somewhat bent incisions; the latter very small, ovate, two-lipped spiracles. I have observed none between the meta-thorax and the abdomen. It has also been said that they have no abdominal spiracles. But Reaumur and Sprengel admitted their existence in those larvæ which live constantly in water, but Kirby and Spence * again denied it, their attention being probably drawn to it by Roesel's † observation of their respiration through the anus. This intestinal respiration Suckow ‡ has confirmed by showing branchiæ in the colon, and thus proved the entire inutility of spiracles. But in the perfect insect there are seven pairs of spiracles upon the central abdominal segments, which are covered however by the margins of the dorsal plates lapping over them as they lie in the soft connecting membrane.

In the *Termites* the spiracles are found in analogous situations, but those of the abdomen are so small that they are seen with difficulty.

The remaining three orders very closely agree both in the structure of the thorax as well as in the situation of the spiracles. All possess our in the thorax, two of which are upon the limits of the pro-thorax, between it and the meso-thorax, and the other two lie between the meso- and meta-thorax. In the *Hymenoptera*, in which the thorax consists of a hard horny case, and the segments are closely united together, the posterior pair of spiracles lie upon the meta-thorax itself, whereby they distinguish themselves from all the other orders; besides which the anterior pair of spiracles are covered by a small scale-shaped projection of the posterior margin of the pronotum, which scale (*tegula*, comp. § 77.) lies precisely beneath the anterior wing, and is very readily recognisable in the wasps. In Pl. XII. No. I. f. 1., wherein the thorax of *Cimbex* is represented, the letters α and β point out the situation of the spiracles, as also in the same plate, No. II. f. 2. in the thorax of a *Scolia*. The spiracles of the *Lepidoptera* are distinguished only by possessing a narrow, scarcely perceptible, horny ring, which lies concealed beneath the hair (Pl. XIII. No. IV. f. 2. shows at α and β, where they are placed.) In the *Diptera* they appear as short, somewhat compressed tubes, particularly the first, between the pro- and meso-thorax, as is shown in Pl. XIV. No. I. f. 2. in *Tabanus*, and No. II. f. 2. in *Myopa*. A similar uniformity exists in the situation of the spiracles of the abdomen, for they always lie in the connecting membrane of the segments, and are covered by the projecting margins of the dorsal plates.

The numbers of the spiracles are thus shown in their situation. If

---

* Introduction to Entomol., vol. iv. letter xxxviii.

† Insectenbelustigungen, 2 band. Wasserinsecten der 2 classe, Taf. II. and III.

‡ Heusing. Zeitschr. für die Org. Physick. 2 band. 2 hft. S. 36, &c. Pl. I. and II.

we call to mind also the general law which makes the insect body to consist of thirteen segments, whereof one forms the head, three the thorax, and nine belong to the abdomen, the number of the spiracles is readily ascertained. The thirteen segments have namely twelve connecting membranes, of which the first only (between the head and pro-thorax) and the last are never supplied with spiracles, consequently there cannot be more than ten on each side at most. But as the number of the abdominal segments considerably varies, it consequently frequently happens that there are fewer spiracles. I have observed twenty in the water-beetles (*Dyticus*). According to Degeer and Latreille*, the locusts and *Lepidoptera* display as many: the *Lamellicornia* and *Cerambycina* possess eighteen. Many *Orthoptera*, the *Termites*, and *Libellulæ* possess the same number. The *Hymenoptera* have but seven distinct abdominal segments, the last of which, according to the general rule, bears no spiracle; in general they possess sixteen: *Panorpa* has fourteen; many *Diptera* still fewer, as but five or six distinct abdominal segments are perceived in them.

§ 125.

II. The AIR TUBES are absolutely nothing but elongated spiracles, although they are not always found, where the spiracles are placed. They are only observed in insects which live in the water, namely, in the larvæ of many *Diptera* and some water-bugs (*Nepa, Ranatra*), and are placed either at the first or the last abdominal segment. They here appear as either long or short horny tubes, which pass directly from the general integument of the body, being open at the end, and within the orifice they are surrounded by simple or plumose setæ, or else entirely unprovided with them.

The larva of the common gnat (*Culex*, Pl. III. f. 3) is very generally known as possessing this organ, which is placed obliquely at the last abdominal segment. Simple branches of the tracheæ pass into this tube, opening where it terminates. The end of the tube is surrounded by setæ, and these support the animal upon the surface of the water when it places itself there to breathe. In the pupa state the tube at the end of the abdomen disappears, and instead of it two bent tubes project from the thorax between the pro- and meso-

---

* P. A. Latreille sur quelques Appendices du Thorax des divers Insectes. In Mém. du Muséum d'Hist. Naturelle, tom. vii.

thorax (Pl. III. f. 4). The majority of the larvæ of the genera most closely allied to this gnat possess no such air tube, but true branchiæ or gills, yet the larvæ of *Chironomus** have likewise two conical air tubes upon the anal segment (Pl. III. f. 5); besides which they are easily distinguished by a more elongate vermiform shape †, as well as by their blood red colour, from the true larvæ of the *Culicidæ*. A similar structure is found in the larvæ of *Stratiomys*; in them the entire last segment of the abdomen is elongated into a tube, and at the aperture of the tube it is provided with a wreath of plumose hairs placed in the form of a star. This coronet, which is much larger than that of the larva of *Culex*, likewise supports the much larger creature upon the surface of the water when it goes thither for fresh air; and it likewise takes air bubbles, which are inclosed by the setæ, down with it to the bottom of the stagnant pools which it inhabits, as a provision for its next inspiration ‡. The larvæ of the genus *Eristalis* display a considerably longer anal air tube; in these also the last joint is extended into a membranous tube, in which a second narrower and corneous one is contained, which at its open end is provided with a similar crown of hair. It is into this tube that the two branches of the tracheæ pass after having united into one. The thick, white, cylindrical larva which lives in the mud of pools, in sewers, and in excrement, directs this tube to the surface of the water, which hangs there by means of the above-mentioned setæ, while it itself lies tranquilly at the bottom, or else continues feeding. If the water should rise, for example, after rain, it lengthens this tail by pushing the inner tube as far out as is requisite. This elongation can be extended to several inches, whereby the length of the tail exceeds several times that of the body. For the expiration of the air thus received two other very short air tubes are placed upon the first segment of the body, directly behind the head; the anterior ends of the above described main stem of the tracheæ pass into these after having previously, as well as the posterior ends, become united by means of a transverse branch.

We also observe anal air tubes in the genera *Nepa* and *Ranatra*, but which are distinguished from those above described in the first place by

---

* The larvæ have gills (branchiæ), as I have recently observed (Author, MS. Note).

† These larvæ were formerly considered as a genus of annelides, and were called *Branchiurus*. See Oken's Zoologie, 1 band. s. 383. Taf. 9., and Viviani Phosphor. Maris, 3. 13, 14.

‡ See Swammerdamm, Biblia Naturæ, Pl. XXXIX. f. 1—3.

their number, two always being present, and secondly by their form, they being simple horny tubes unprovided with setæ at their end. In *Ranatra* they are as long as the body, and in *Nepa* half its length.

It seems to be a very general law, that the situation of the spiracles should be at the posterior end of the body, not only in the *Diptera*, but also in all larvæ which live in water and are unprovided with branchiæ. With respect to the larvæ of the *Diptera*, those yet investigated have their spiracles in that situation: for example, the flies and *Œstridæ*. The larvæ of the water-beetles likewise (for example, *Dyticus* and *Hydrophilus*) have their spiracles at the anal end, contiguous to the anus, and have none at their sides, although Sprengel describes and even figures them there *.

§ 126.

III. GILLS, or BRANCHIÆ.—This third description of the organs of respiration is particularly distinguished from both the others by its want of apertures to admit the air into the tracheæ. The gills are processes of the epidermis in the form of hair or leaves, in which delicate tracheæ ramify in every direction. These vessels imbibe the air mixed up mechanically with the water, and conduct it to the main stems concealed in the body, by means of the branches of which it passes to all the internal organs. Through this arrangement insects provided with gills do not require atmospheric air, they consequently do not rise to the surface of the water, but live constantly in it concealed among water plants.

The branchiæ may be separated into two divisions, by their forms; the one being delicate and slender, resembling hair, while the other is broad, thin, and lamelliform.

The hair-shaped branchiæ seldom appear singly, but generally in approximate fasciculi, which are formed by either the ramifications of one or of several main stems (Pl. III. f. 6.), or by filaments radiating from one point (the same, f. 10). The epidermis of these processes is exceedingly delicate, as well as the small silvery tracheæ enclosed by it. This kind of branchiæ is the most usual and general; it is found particularly in the larvæ and pupæ of the gnats.

The lamellate branchiæ are found only in the *Dictyotoptera* and the *Neuroptera*, and appear as broad or pointed lanceolate leaves, and are found on each side of each abdominal segment, or only at its end.

* Commentar., p. 37. No. xx. Pl. II. f. 20.

Several, or at least two leaves, are found at each place, so that each segment of the body has never less than four branchial leaves. They are generally uniform, but an instance is known (*Ephemera fusco-grisea*, De Geer *,) in which one of the branchiæ is lamellate and the other is a fasciculus of filiform ones.

If we look to the orders in which branchiæ are found, we shall speedily see that they are not rare, and, indeed, that the majority of larvæ which live in water breathe by means of gills.

The following are the genera whose larvæ thus respire:—

Among the *Coleoptera* we find hairy branchiæ in the larvæ of the whirlwigs (*Gyrinus* †), which rise from the sides of each segment, and clothe the body as simple, tolerably stiff, hairy processes. The closely allied *Dyticus* have no gills, but spiracles, which lie contiguous to the anus; the larva of *Hydrophilus piceus* likewise breathes through spiracles thus placed, but the larva of *Hydrophilus Caraboides*, has, according to Roesel's figure ‡, ramose branchial fasciculi on each abdominal segment.

The *Orthoptera* never live in water either as larvæ or as perfect insects, they have consequently only spiracles as the exterior organs of respiration.

Many of the *Hemiptera*, both in their larva and perfect state, live in water, but branchiæ have never yet been observed in them. Both young and old, when they wish to breathe, come to the surface of the water, and receive air through the spiracles. *Nepa* and *Ranatra* have air tubes, which we have mentioned above.

Whereas in the orders of the *Dictyotoptera* and *Neuroptera* the branchial apparatus is very general. In the first of these orders, the larvæ of the *Ephemeræ* and *Libellulæ* live constantly in the water, and have branchiæ. In the larvæ of the *Ephemeræ* they lie at the sides of the body, four upon each segment, and they consist of small leaves of various forms. In *Ep. fusco-grisea* one branchia is a leaf, and the other a fasciculus; in *Ep. vulgata* § both are leaves, very narrow, and clothed at the margin with long fine hairs. The branchiæ of the larvæ of the *Libellulæ* are not placed at the sides of the abdominal segments, but upon or within the last segment; and in *Agrion* they form three large

---

* De Geer, Mémoires sur les Insectes, vol. ii, part ii. p. 29. Pl. XVIII. f. 3.
† Ib., vol. iv. Pl. XIII. f. 16—19.
‡ Insectenbelustigungen, vol. ii. Wasser-Insecten d. Erst. Klasse. p. 32. Pl. IV.
§ De Geer, ib. Pl. XVI. f. 3.

clavate leaves fringed at the margin. The larvæ of *Æschna* and *Libellula* breathe through fasciculated branchiæ, which lie in the colon. Thither proceed the terminal ends of the four main stems of the tracheæ; they transpierce the membrane of the colon, and hang as thick fasciculi within the cavity of this organ *. As the creature imbibes water by means of it, and thus again rejects it, it helps to assist it in swimming, which, without this auxiliary aid, it would find it difficult to effect, from its deficiency of other swimming leaves. Other larvæ swim by means of the branchial leaves, which move with an incessant alternating vibration.

Among the *Neuroptera* we are acquainted with the families of the *Phryganodea* and the *Semblodea*, whose larvæ inhabit water. Both breathe during this state only through branchiæ, which in the former consist of two leaves placed on each side of each abdominal segment, but varying in form according to the genera, but in the latter they appear as simple or plumose, tolerably long processes, which consist of several joints, becoming gradually acuminate, upon the under surface of which the tracheæ ramify, protected by two rows of setæ †.

Branchiæ seem very general in the family of the gnats, among the *Diptera*, as they are found not only in the larvæ but also in the pupæ. This is the case in the genus *Chironomus*, whose larvæ described above breathe through exterior tubes, but whose pupæ are furnished with two radiating fasciculi of branchiæ at the thorax (Pl. III. f. 6.). These branchial fasciculi are seated close to the spot where later the first spiracle of the thorax is found, namely, between the pro- and meso-thorax. The same is the case in the genus *Simulia ;* the former has air tubes at the anal end as well as at the thorax, the latter two large branchial fasciculi between the pro- and meso-thorax (Pl. III. f. 9 and 10 ‡). The reversed relations obtain in the genus *Anopheles*, whose larva, described as a remarkable water animal, first by Goeze §, and afterwards by Lichtenstein ||, but which G. Fischer ¶ ascertained to be the larva of this gnat, bears hairy branchiæ at its anal end, but whose pupa is provided

---

* Suckow in Heusing., vol. ii. part i. p. 55, &c. Pl. I. and II.
† Ib., p. 27. Pl. III. f. 24.
‡ Compare Thon's Archiv. der Entomologie, vol. ii. no. ii. Pl. II.
§ Beschäftigungen der Berliner Gesellsch. Naturfors. Freunde, vol. i. p. 359. Pl. VIII.
|| Wiledemann's Archiv. für Zoologie und Zootomie, vol. i. No. i. p. 168. Pl. III.
¶ G. Fischer, Sur quelques Diptères de Russic. Pl. I. f. 1—16.

with two curved air tubes between the pro- and mesc-thorax (Pl. III. f. 7 and 8.)

Among the *Lepidoptera* but one caterpillar, that of *Botys stratiotalis* has been observed to possess branchiæ*. In this they consist of delicate small hairs which clothe the whole body, but particularly laterally, in the vicinity of the future spiracles, they stand in fasciculi. The tracheæ are observed in them as glittering silver-white threads. The caterpillar lives constantly in the water upon the leaves of *Stratiotes aloides*. I have myself observed a very similar caterpillar of a moth upon *Ceratophyllum demersum*, but I was not successful in breeding it. Doubtlessly others also exist among the allied genera and species, but which have hitherto escaped detection. It must strike as remarkable, that among the *Lepidoptera*, which apparently, from the great development of their organs of flight, are destined to dwell in the air, larvæ should be found which select a place of residence of such a very opposite nature, whereas among the *Hymenoptera*, which appear more adapted to dwell in a variety of media, no single instance should occur of one having been observed, either in its larva or perfect state, to live in water. It is indeed true that some of their larvæ live in moist places, such as the parasitic larvæ of the *Ichneumons*, but branchiæ have never yet been detected in them.

§ 127.

B. INTERNAL ORGANS OF RESPIRATION.

The internal organs of respiration are the most simple and most uniform parts found in the insect body; for they universally present themselves as ramose tubes originating from the spiracle, the exterior air tube, or from the root of a branchia, and thence spread to all the other organs. Malpighi, who by his dissection of the silk-worm was the first to obtain a correct insight into the internal structure of insects, was also the first discoverer of these internal organs; previously it was thought that insects did not breathe, an opinion which was originally propounded by Aristotle, and subsequently generally received.

As to the structure of these tubes serving for the function of respiration, and which have been called AIR TUBES or TRACHEÆ, we shall find

---

* De Geer, vol. i. part iii. Pl. XXXVII. f. 5 and 6.

that they consist of three distinct layers, which, taking them from the exterior, appear in the following form :—

The outermost membrane (Pl. XXII. f. 11.) is transparent, very smooth, without being perceptibly fibrous, but hard, and generally colourless. Coloured tracheæ, which we now and then observe, for example, brown in *Locusta viridissima*, red in *Phasma gigas*, or black, as in the larvæ of *Dyticus* and *Hydrophilus*, derive their colour from this exterior skin, whereas both the others, especially the second, are constantly of a silvery white, and shining. A dark colour facilitates very much the detection and unravelment of the extremely delicate tracheæ, particularly when they run upon the clear ground of other organs. But in those cases where the tracheæ are not coloured their investigation is not very difficult when freshly killed individuals are selected for the purpose, for in them the tracheæ are still filled with air: they then display themselves as silvery white, glittering threads, which here and there appeardull and transparent, from moisture having at those parts already penetrated them. In general, the last and most delicate ends are still filled with air, which, however, is forced out when the creature has been long immersed in spirits of wine, and it then becomes difficult to obtain a satisfactory view of their distribution. The exterior membrane of the tracheæ consequently is structureless, nor is it in very close connexion with the second, but loosely surrounds it, leaving everywhere a free space between them, which is quickly perceived upon a microscopic investigation, and thereby readily convinces us of the presence of at least two layers.

The second layer consists of a single, tense, elastic, and very delicate filament, which twines spirally around the innermost membrane, so that its windings are everywhere, or at least very generally contiguous. This thread appears to be simple and round, but which is occasionally difficult to ascertain from its delicacy, but the microscope displays how it distributes itself about the circumference of the vessel, and that it scarcely leaves the smallest space between its successive windings, and which is filled only by membrane. In some instances, for example, in *Locusta viridissima*, and indeed in all insects provided with large tracheal stems, the filament becomes broader, resembling a band, and can be distinctly distinguished as such. Sprengel * detected in such larger tracheæ ramose filaments, or perfectly closed rings, which were

---

* Commentar. de Parl., &c Pl. II. f. 14.

separated by broader membranous spaces, these he has figured as round in *Cetonia aurata* *: in *Lamia textor* he even saw small spots between the windings, whereby the vessels of this insect appeared punctate. When an air-vessel sends off a branch the space between the two successive convolutions then widens, and the branch commences with its own spiral filament (Pl. XXII. f. 11), whereas that of the stem continues uninterruptedly; but if a trachea divides into two equal branches, each begins with its own new spiral filament, and that of the stem terminates at the point of division. These spiral filaments of the tracheæ may be considered as analogous to the cartilaginous rings in the windpipe of the superior animals, although these are separated from each other, and connected only by their softer parts. But this fibrous layer of the muscular membrane in the vessels has the same function, for the contraction of the spiral filament straitens the tracheæ, and thus helps to promote expiration, whilst its succeeding expansion facilitates the inspiration by opening a larger space in the vessel for the admission of air. The cartilaginous rings of the windpipes of the superior animals fully accomplish this last purpose, and they thereby distinguish themselves from the tracheæ of insects.

The innermost third membrane, which Lyonnet, Marcel de Serres, and Straus-Durckheim admit, but Sprengel denies, is, according to the investigations of the former, a smooth, transparent, delicate, mucous membrane, and, as it were, a continuation of the exterior epidermis, with which it also stands in connexion at the orifice of the spiracles. The spiral filament lies closely adhesive to it, so that upon a rupture of the vessel its remains hang affixed to the detached spiral thread, whence Sprengel prefers considering it as a connecting membrane between the spiral fibres rather than as a distinct layer. But the fact of this innermost membrane peeling off when caterpillars moult, or pass from the larva to the pupa state, and that in place of it a new one is formed beneath, speaks distinctly in favour of its being considered as a peculiar and a separate one.

This anatomical structure of the air-vessels is found precisely the same in all the orders, and although their form is subject to many variations, yet their structure but very seldom participates in this difference. This participation of the structure in the difference of form is maintained by Straus and Marcel de Serres to be found in the air bags of the

* Commentar. de Parl. Pl. 11. f. 19.

Lamellicornia, in which, according to these entomotomists, the spiral filament is deficient, whereas others, particularly Suckow and Sprengel, assert that they exist, of which we shall speak in detail below.

§ 128.

With respect to the differences of form in the tracheæ, according to Marcel de Serres they may be divided into three main groups, which that writer thus distinguishes:—

1. ARTERIAL AIR-VESSELS.—They originate directly from the spiracle, and ramify with the most delicate branches from this simple stem to all the internal organs.

2. TUBULAR or PULMONARY AIR-VESSELS.—They do not receive the air directly, but stand in connexion with the spiracle by means of the former. They are larger than the arterial air-vessels, their course is more regular and straight, their diameter broader, and their branches, on the contrary, smaller.

3. VESICULAR AIR-VESSELS.—They are of two kinds, either large bladders, in which the air collects, and whence the branches spring, or small bladders in the branches themselves, and frequently the terminal distended ends of the branches; both forms are never found together.

Upon inspecting first the arterial air-vessels, as those most generally found, but little that is extraordinary is to be remarked in them; each main stem originates from the internal margin of each spiracle with a broader base, which narrows somewhat after a short course. Here also is the point of division of the main stem; next a branch spreads forwards and backwards, which passes to the anterior and posterior spiracles to unite with each main stem originating from them. By means of these arches all the stems of the tracheæ stand in close connexion together. Between these two communicating tracheæ the remaining ramose branches originate, and each spreads more particularly to those organs which lie most approximate to it. These branches frequently open into each other, and form stems running contiguously to the intestinal canal, the muscles, and the sexual organs, and whence the delicate branches for these organs originate.

The number of the branches originating from a main stem, with the exception of the two connecting tubes, is indeed very variable, but we may assume that more branches spread from the tracheæ of the thorax than from those of the abdomen. This arises from the greater number of organs existing in the thorax, particularly the number of muscles, whereas in the abdomen there are many spiracles, but proportionally fewer internal parts. The vessels of the thorax consequently belong more to the organs of motion, and those of the abdomen to the intestinal canal and the sexual organs.

Two of the many branches which the main stem of the first thoracic spiracle sends off always go to the head. One runs superficially over and contiguous to the mandibulary muscles, and also unites to its opponent upon the opposite side (*Melolontha*), and distributes itself with its branches to all the superior internal portions of the head. From it the ring encompassing the eye proceeds, or, where this is wanting, the branches which spread in the pigment of the eye. The inferior branch accompanies the nervous cord and the œsophagus into the head, and distributes itself to the lower lying muscles, the maxillæ, and the labium. A third branch, which descends downwards anteriorly, or as in the *Mantodea*, two equal branches spreading in this direction pass into each anterior leg, and each distributes itself with innumerable ramifications to its very point. The extreme posterior branch is the one connecting it with the second thoracic spiracle, the remainder originating between this and the beforementioned one, distribute themselves to the muscles, and several pass into the meso-thorax. The spiracle between the meso- and meta-thorax, generally the smallest, has also the fewest branches, namely, besides the connecting ones which unite it to the first and third spiracle, it has a main branch for the middle leg, and several ramifications for muscles. From the third spiracle between the meta-thorax and the abdomen it is generally that the greatest number of branches originate, namely, the two connecting branches, the branches for the third pair of legs, and several large ones to the muscles. The spiracles of the abdomen have each their two connecting branches, and besides which several ramifications for the internal organs. The number of these branches differs much in the genera and families, but they are about the same from the several spiracles. In the *Mantodea* they unite to a second, more internal, common duct, and from which the branches for the internal organs originate*.

In all caterpillars, maggots, and in the larvæ of the *Hymenoptera* we observe only arterial vessels, the same in all the predaceous and swimming beetles, and in the *Heteromera* and *Tetramera*. In all other

---

* Marcel de Serres, Mém. du Muséum, vol. iv. Pl. XVI. f. 1.

insects we find them in conjunction with pulmonary and vesicular vessels, but the terminal ramifications, as well as the secondary ones, are of the arterial description.

§ 129.

Tubular air vessels are chiefly peculiar to such larvæ as are provided either only at one end or at both ends of the body with spiracles; besides which the communicating tubes of the stems of the spiracles are tubular. Under the name of TUBULAR we understand such air-vessels which proceed uninterruptedly from one end of the body to the other, and which only send forth here and there small accessory branches; or else the simple communicating vessels between two approximate spiracles, and which are without any accessory ramifications. Both have this in common, that they preeminently extend according to the longitudinal axis of the body, whereas the arterial air-vessels take their course in an opposite direction to this longitudinal course. Whence it becomes apparent that the tubular air-vessels are never insulated, but can only exist in conjunction with the arterial; the former are, as it were, the main stems and the latter their twigs.

We will now describe in greater detail some of the chief tubular air-vessels.

With respect to their first form we may assume that all larvæ which live in water possess more or less developed tubular main stems. Among the *Coleoptera* this is the case in the larvæ of *Dyticus* and *Hydrophilus*. The yellowish green larvæ, figured by Roesel * of the large water-beetles (*Dyticus marginalis, dimidiatus*, &c.), have two large spiracles at the apex of the last abdominal segment, exteriorly contiguous to the short, plumose, anal apex. Two large, broad, black tracheæ originate from them, which ascend undivided as far as the first thoracic segment, the future prothorax. There each furcates, and then both branches run to the head, one spreading over the muscle of the mandible and the other beneath it. Two small accessory branches of these two main stems spring from it at the commencement of each abdominal segment, but the inner one of these two is considerably the largest in the fourth, tenth, and eleventh segments, for these three pass to the intestinal canal, the anterior one to the stomach, the posterior ones to the ilium and thick

---

* Insectenbelustigungen, tom. ii. Wasserinsekten der Ersten Klasse, p. 8. Pl. 1. f. 2—7.

gut, whereas all the rest are branches which run off to the muscles. But, on the contrary, the two exterior branches in the second segment exceed the inner ones in size, turn upwards to the back of the segment, and here anastomose, whereby is formed one transverse communicating passage between the two main stems. All the transverse accessory branches are here arterial, but the large main canal which runs longitudinally in the insect is tubular. We find a similar disposition and structure, in all the essential portions, in the tracheal system of the larva of *Hydrophilus piceus*, as is evident from Suckow's figures[*].

Tubular air-vessels are very general among the *Orthoptera*, where likewise, as is always the case, they are connected with arterial branches, or even with vesicular vessels. The tracheal system of *Mantis oratoria* described and figured by Marcel de Serres may serve us for an example [†]. Two narrow vessels originate from each of the seven abdominal segments, the shorter exterior ones of which unite in a direct tubular vessel, which runs beneath the margin of the abdomen, and passes on to the third spiracle of the thorax. The inner somewhat longer vessels unite in arches, forming a second longitudinal tube, which proceeds in an undulating line close to the superior wall of the intestinal canal, and also passes into the thorax. A third tubular vessel comes out of the thorax, running very closely to the intestinal canal: it also takes an undulating course, but beneath that organ, and sends forth branches laterally, which again unite in a fourth direct tubular vessel, and which is connected at its anterior and posterior extremities with the first named one, which runs at the edge of the abdomen. All these tubular vessels give off but few branches, and it is only from the central lower longitudinal tube that some delicate branches are given off to the intestine, and it is from the central inner small vessel, originating at the spiracle, that the air tubes come for the sexual organs.

The air-vessels of the larvæ of the *Libellulæ* are also tubular, and are very uniform in their distribution with those of the larvæ of the beetles which live in water. Two large main stems, serpentine at the dorsal portion of the intestinal canal, which, after being bound by the

---

[*] In Heusinger Zeitschr. vol. ii. No. i. Pl. IV. f. 26. See a detailed description in H. M. Gaede Dissert. Sistens. Observation. quesd. de Insector. Vermumque Structura. Chilon, 1817. 4to.

[†] Mém. du Muséum. tom. iv. Pl. XVI. f. 1.

colon, from which they originate in a tuft, take their course to the head, where they again furcate. On each side of the ventral portion two smaller vessels lie, which are united to the dorsal vessels by means of transverse branches. The upper one of these runs also to the head, the lower one, taking its course nearly in the centre of the body, terminates on the contrary in delicate ramifications * at the stomach. We find also in the perfect insect both the ventral and dorsal stems, the latter communicating by means of delicate canals with the seven spiracles of the abdomen.

The tubular vessels, lastly, are found very generally in the larvæ of the *Diptera*. The larva of the common gnat (*Culex*) has two large dorsal stems, which originate, already divided, from the above described posterior air tube, and give off their fine branches to the internal organs †. In the larva of *Eristalis tenax*, Meig., which has been called the rat-tailed maggot, from its long air tube (Pl. II. f. 8.), both the two great tracheal stems unite, previously to their passing into the inner tube of the air tube, by means of a transverse branch, and remain for a small space separated, lying convoluted in front of the internal aperture of the tube, but it is only where they pass into the inner tube that they are truly united together. In the body itself they are never again united, but in the first segment in the membranous head there is another connecting tube which proceeds directly behind the cerebrum. In front of this connection they become considerably narrower, but behind it each stem proceeds out of the head as a fine tube passing into a small air tube placed at each side of the head, which were necessary for the expiration of the previously inspired air. It is probable that such anterior air tubes are found also in the larvæ of other *Diptera*. A similar structure is found in the larvæ of all the flies; but they want the tail, and both the tracheal stems separately vent themselves at the posterior obtuse surface of the body (Pl. II. f. 1.).

The larvæ of the *Hymenoptera* have also tubular main stems, but which, as they are formed of small tubes that proceed from the spiracles, are never so large and developed. Two main stems consequently proceed on each side of the body, united in each segment by means of a transverse connecting vessel, but there orginate from them, at those places where the tubes of the spiracles pass into them, innumerable

---

* Suckow in Heusinger, f. 7. & 9.
† Swammerdam Bib. Naturæ, Pl. XXXVII. f. 5. *h*.

ramose or arterial vessels, so that the tubular main stem is less insulated [*]. Precisely the same structure is exhibited in the larvæ of the *Lepidoptera*, but the peculiar tubular structure is still more indistinct, for in general the transverse connecting tubes are also wanting.

§ 130.

The vesicular air vessels are properly only distended tubes, or the distended ends of accessory branches, it is thence that they are never found alone, but they are always in conjunction with arterial or tubular air vessels. They also appear under two chief forms, for they are either very large bladders, lying chiefly in the abdomen, whence arterial air vessels originate, or they are the vesicular distensions of the branches of arterial air vessels themselves.

The first form of the vesicular air vessels is found in the *Hymenoptera, Diptera, Cicada,* and in a somewhat altered figure in many grasshoppers.

In the *Diptera*, at least in the true flies (*Muscidæ*) the *Syrphodea* and the *Œstridæ*, two large air bladders have been observed at the base of the abdomen, contiguous to the intestinal canal, which are tolerably uniform in structure with the large tubular vessels, but the twistings of the thickish spiral filament are wider apart, the filament itself divides here and there, and is interrupted at other parts, whence the entire surface does not appear so regularly transversely striated as in the tubular vessels (Pl. XXII. f. 12., membrane of the air bladder of *Musca vomitoria*). Their form is regulated by that of the abdomen, so that they are often ovate or very generally vertically compressed, and are here and there angular, in consequence of constrictions. A large trachea originates from their under surface; it runs forward and backward to the head and anus, and gives off lateral tracheæ to the spiracles of the thorax and abdomen. Other finer vessels run over the superior surface of the bladder, and ramify to the internal organs. Whether they originate from the bladder itself or from the connecting vessels lying beneath it I could not perceive distinctly in flies, but it is the case in *Scolia* and in *Apis* according to Leon Dufour. But this whole air bladder is nothing else than the tubular vessel of the larva, which during the pupa state has shortened and distended, and of which we took notice in the preceding paragraph; this air bladder must

---

[*] Compare Swammerdam Biblia Naturæ, Pl. XXIV. f. 1. in *Apis Mellifica*.

consequently be found in all flies whose larvæ breathed through the tail itself, or through spiracles seated there. The presence of this air bladder explains the cause of the glassy perfectly transparent abdomen of so many *Diptera*, for example, of *Volucella pellucens*, Meig. The *Asili*, which have a longer, narrower, more extended abdomen, possess, according to Marcel de Serres*, several small and successive vesicles, for example, *Asilus barbarus* has sixty on each side.

Many *Hymenoptera* display a similar structure. In some species of *Bombus* I have found precisely the same air bladders at the commencement of the abdomen, as has also Leon Dufour in *Scolia* †.

Carus ‡ has described them in the large *Cicada*. The air bladder originates within the circumference of the large spiracle which lies between the thorax and abdomen, it distends a little anteriorly, but spreads especially backwards, where it extends to the sixth or seventh segment; before impregnation, whilst the ovaria and testes are still filled with their contents, they are limited to a smaller space, but after copulation they occupy almost the whole abdomen, particularly in the males, in which they are generally larger in compass, doubtlessly in connection with the vocal organ, which in the females is merely indicated. Hence is explained the opinion of the ancients, who held that the males were empty.

In the grasshoppers the bladders have a somewhat different connection with the rest of the respiratory system; and they also vary considerably in form from the former, for in these they consist of bags of a somewhat longish oval shape, very pointed at both ends. In *Locusta viridissima* two such bags originate at each spiracle, they thence ascend close to the inner side of the general integument up to the back, where they attach themselves to a flat horny arch, which originates from each ventral plate projecting into the cavity of the abdomen, and which is affixed to the ventral plate only at its commencement. Each of these arches supports two air bladders, which, however, do not proceed from one but from two separate spiracles, so that they altogether form a zigzag line. But they are connected also above and below by a narrow longitudinal tube, and from the lower ones there are vessels connecting them with the opposite ones of the other side, and from the upper ones originate the branches which are distributed to the internal

---

* Mém. de Mus., as above, p. 362.   † Journal de Physique, Sept. 1830.

‡ Analekten zur Naturwissenschaft und Heilkunde. Dresden, 1828. page 158. fig. 15—17, 9.

organs. Thus, therefore, the air bladders of the abdomen form a compact net-work, which is, as it were, spread out between the spiracles and the horny arches. If the abdomen be drawn together by muscular contraction the horny arches rise, extend the tracheæ longitudinally, and consequently the air contained within them is forced out; but upon its expansion the air again streams in, when every bladder, through the elasticity of its filament, is again shortened and distended. The respiratory system of *Truxalis nasutus*, of which Marcel de Serres has given a figure*, is still more complicated, for in it the bladders do not originate immediately from the spiracles, but, by means of long tubes, from the common tubular vessels which connect all the spiracles, and at the opposite end unite in a second but more delicate longitudinal tube. Also the two opposite bladders are held in connection together by undivided tolerably narrow tubes. In the abdomen there are twenty bladders, ten on each side; in the thorax six larger ones, four in the meso- and metathorax, one very large pear-shaped one above, at the dorsal portion of the pro-thorax, close to the crop, and besides many vesicular distensions of the arterial vessels; in the head there are six large bladders, two laterally, contiguous to the muscles of the mandibles, two above, at the vertex over the eyes, two in the forehead before the eyes, and between these several smaller vesicles.

The second chief form of the vesicular air vessels is found among the *Coleoptera* in the family of the *Lamellicornia*, among the *Lepidoptera* in the *Crepuscularia*, particularly in the males, and then in the dragon flies.

In the *Lamellicornia* the chief distribution of the air vessels, as throughout the *Coleoptera*, is arterial, for fascicles of air vessels originate from each spiracle; but each finer branch distends, prior to its ultimate and finest ramification, into an oval bladder, which is of a more delicate structure than the rest of the branch, whence Marcel de Serres and Straus deny the presence of the spiral fibre in these vessels, which Suckow maintains to be the case. It is true that these bladders are more transparent than the tubes, but they exhibit a peculiar punctured structure, as was even perceived and figured by Swammerdam †, and also by Sprengel ‡; and thence I would assume

---

* As above, Pl. XV.

† Biblia Naturæ, Pl. XXIX. f. 10. ‡ Commentar., Pl. I. f. 11—13.

that in these bladders, as in the larger ones of the flies, the spiral filament has torn from the distension, and only the rudiments of it are present in the darker places. These bladders accompany all the intestines, pass everywhere between the muscles, and are particularly accumulated superficially beneath the integument. A precise description is consequently impossible, from the manifold reticulation of the branches, and a single glance at the masterly representation of it in Straus will explain it better than any words unaccompanied by figures could possibly do, we therefore refer to his anatomy of *Melolontha*.

The vesicular distensions in the tracheæ of the *Libellulæ* are found chiefly in the thorax, and in it they lie exteriorly, contiguous to and between the muscles. They are generally pyriform, whereas those of the *Lamellicornia* and *Lepidoptera* are perfectly oval; the bags also appear to me to be connected by tracheæ and to form distinct lacings.

Among the *Lepidoptera* we find the bladders chiefly in the male *Sphinges* and *Phalenæ*, and are sometimes small and sometimes large, as in *Acherontia Atropos*, Ochs. They are of a coarser structure than those of the beetles, so that the presence of the spiral fibre is here subject to no doubt. According to a figure in Sprengel the membrane of the bladder has sometimes a cellular appearance, and this might then be considered as an approximation to the structure in the *Lamellicornia*.

SECOND CHAPTER.

OF THE ORGANS OF GENERATION.

§ 131.

The second chief system of the vegetative organs comprises the sexual organs destined to the propagation of the species. Under this name we understand both the vesicular and the tubular parts which lie in the abdomen generally affixed at one end, which, in a variety of forms and connections are united together in main stems, and open in one evacuating duct at the end of the abdomen beneath the anus. This last definition is subject to no exception in true insects, for what has

* Commentar., Pl. III. fig. 24.

been considered as exterior sexual organs and sexual apertures at the base of the abdomen in the male *Libellula* are by no means such parts, as we shall have an opportunity of proving below; in them also that aperture is found at the end of the abdomen, in the vicinity of the anus.

These vesicular and tubular organs consist, like the intestinal canal, of several divisions, which, as the general character and function of the sexual organs consist in the secretion of fluids, may be distinguished as proper secreting organs (testes and ovaria), conducting organs for the secreted fluids (vasa deferentia and oviductus), repositories for the secreted fluids (vesica seminalis and uterus), and as evacuating organs of the secreted material (ductus ejaculatorius and vagina). These main divisions are found in function, although frequently but little distinguished in form and figure from each other, in all the internal sexual organs, as will be shown in the course of our investigation. This sketch consequently comprises the most general structure of these organs, and it will therefore be merely the individual, generic, family, and ordinal differences which will occupy us in the course of our investigation; but we will previously say something about their anatomical structure.

§ 132.

The determination of the structural relations of the membranes of the sexual organs is subject to many difficulties, in consequence of the delicacy and minuteness of these parts. It is only in those divisions which possess a greater extension that it has been possible to distinguish the presence of two layers of membrane. The exterior of these two membranes is coarser, firmer, and of a muscular consistency; the internal one, on the contrary, is more delicate, transparent, simple, and corresponds with the internal mucous tunic of the intestinal canal or the exterior epidermis. The presence of both the membranes in the large vesicles is subject to no doubt; they can there be readily and securely exhibited; even in the more delicate evacuating ducts of the secerning organs they are distinguished by the difference of their consistence, which in the internal one is considerably less than in the external one. It is more difficult to prove their presence in the secerning organs themselves, but J. Müller * has shown them, at least in the

---

* Nova Acta Phys. Med. XII. 2. Pl. LV.

ovaries: but it still remains doubtful whether the glandular testes consist of these two layers, which, however, may be assumed, from the similar structure of analogous parts.

§ 133.

The preceding observations apply with equal force to all sexual organs. But if we contemplate their general form we shall immediately meet with varieties which do not admit of any further generalisation, and this circumstance compels us in this place to examine more closely the differences of form which the sexual organs severally present.

Propagation is, like life in general, the result of two agents acting reciprocally upon each other. In the lowest forms of organisation, where such a separation of the animating activities shows itself less perceptibly, the propagating agents themselves cannot either appear separately, we consequently there find simple germs susceptible of development. By degrees an ACTIVE and a PASSIVE agent are produced, both of which are found at first in the same individual (snails), but they soon separate into two distinct individuals, and thereby constitute the essential character of such individuals. In the former, luxuriant energy, universal momentum, and a continual impulse towards the appeasement of internal urgent desires; in the latter, patient sufferance, quiet reserve, a tarrying for excitement, and an ultimate satisfaction in the discovery, of the deficient unknown something. The former character is called the MALE, and the latter the FEMALE. But where shall we find the differences of these two characters more distinctly expressed than in the multiform insect world? The above cited distinction is here found so strongly marked that its high significance can no longer be subjected to doubt. We shall return to this subject in our physiological chapter, and it is there only that it will find its true place; we can merely indicate it here to enable us to arrive at the primary difference of the sexual organs. This we have now found, we have thus become acquainted with two kinds, and have distinguished them as MALE and FEMALE.

§ 134.

The differences of the organs of generation of both therefore lie based deeply in the conditions of life. We necessarily ask, how does it become evident to us? Anatomically investigated, the character of the female is the formation of the germs, that of the male secretion of sperm;

all organs, therefore, which display germs (eggs) are female, and all which prepare spermatic moisture must be called male. The female sexual organs of insects consequently display bags full of eggs, ovaria; the male, sperm-secreting vessels or glands; from both originate the above characterised closer or more distant evacuating ducts, which are pretty uniform in both sexes. We may consequently distinguish in both female and male organs different divisions, which are, however, connected together, and which must necessarily constitute the different divisions of our description of the sexual organs.

§ 135.

I. OF THE FEMALE ORGANS OF GENERATION.

The female sexual organs (*genitalia feminina*) of insects consist of internal and external ones; the internal ones of OVARIES, the OVIDUCT, the UTERUS, other peculiar appendages, and the VAGINA; the exterior ones of the ORIFICE OF THE VAGINA, and its appendages, as the ACULEUS, the VAGINA TUBIFORMIS, and the VAGINA BIVALVIS.

It is not always that all the above named parts are present together, either one or several are wanting, the ovaries are deficient only in barren, undeveloped females (the neuter bees, &c.), but the evacuating ducts never; all other appendages may, on the contrary, disappear.

A. INTERNAL SEXUAL ORGANS.

§ 136.

THE OVARIES.

The ovaries are tubes or bags in which the eggs are secreted from the formative substance of the creature, and where they remain until their impregnation. We always find in insects two such organs of similar structure in the same individual; they are so placed that one lies on each side of the intestinal canal, generally filling the lateral space in the abdomen. In colour they are generally yellow, but in form they are subject to many varieties, which, however, may be classed under the following divisions:—

I. The ovaries are simple bags, in which the germs of the eggs ar contained. This primary form, which is the most simple of all, is subjected to no subordinate differences[*].

---

[*] The ovarium saccatum described by J. Müller in Nova Acta Phys. Med., tom. xii. p. 612. does not belong here, but will be classed below, with the ovarium furcatum.

Such ovaries are found in *Ephemera* and *Stratiomys*. Müller calls this form bunches of ovaries (*ovaria racemosa* *), and supposes that the exterior tunic of the bag, or properly the bag itself, is wanting, the eggs being connected together by means of air-vessels; but Swammerdam's figure misled him †. In a female of *Ephemera marginata*, Fab., De Geer, which I dissected, I clearly observed the exterior tunic, the ova were contained within it, egg being linked to egg by a delicate filament. In *Stratiomys* also Swammerdam has distinctly represented the bag ‡.

II. The short ovaries, which contain but few germs, are placed longitudinally upon a large, bag-shaped, common ovarium.

There are many subordinate differences of this peculiar form, which we will briefly indicate.

1. OVARIA PECTINATA (Pl. XXVII. f. 2.) are short egg tubes, which contain but few germs, and are placed in a row upon the upper side of a common duct (*Mantodea*).

2. OVARIA ECHINATA, common egg ducts, long, broad, wider anteriorly and suddenly pointed, having beneath many very small scale-shaped egg tubes, which lie over each other (dragon flies).

3. OVARIA IMBRICATA (Pl. XXVII. f. 8.). The whole upper surface, with the exception of a narrow edge upon the lower margin, is covered with short tile-shaped egg-tubes, which lie upon each other, and embrace the intestine like a roof. Each tube contains a large developed egg and behind it the minute germs of two or three others (grasshoppers, crickets, *Phryganea, Sialis, Tipula, Sirex*, &c.).

4. OVARIA BACCATA. The common ovarium is a bladder or tube upon the entire upper surface of which are placed the short egg-tubes, generally containing but few eggs, (*Coleoptera vesicifica*, each tube with from one to four eggs; *Semblis*, each with six to nine eggs).

5. OVARIA DICHOTOMA (Pl. XXVII. f. 5. *ovaria furcata*, Müller). The common ovarium is forked, and upon each prong, and particularly upon their opposite sides, there are many tubes, containing but few (3) egg germs (*Gryllotalpa*).

6. OVARIA RAMOSA (Pl. XXVII. f. 6.). The common egg duct does not simply furcate, but several branches are given off one after the other, each of which contains some egg germs (*Lepisma*).

---

* Nova Acta Phys. Med. p. 601. 11. † Bib. Naturæ, Pl. XXV. f. 1.
‡ Ib. Pl. XLVIII. f. 1.

III. Long tubular ovaries, which contain many egg germs, are collected together at one part of the common duct. These tubes are either entirely free, and distinctly separated from each other throughout their whole course, or else united together by a loose cellular tissue (for example, in *Harpalus ruficornis*).

1. Ovarium spirale (Pl. XXVII. f. 10). There is but one egg-tube to each ovarium, but which is very long, and it is twisted spirally from its apex to its base; a rare form, which has been observed only in *Sarcophaga carnaria* and some other kinds of flies.

2. Ovaria furcata (Pl. XXVII. f. 7. *Ovaria saccata*, Müll.). There are but two short ovaria, containing indistinct egg germs, and which unite with the common duct by means of a fork; at the point of union there is a bag (uterus) in which the egg germs pass through their changes until the pupa state (*Diptera pupipara* *). In *Polistes* also there are but two egg-tubes, each of which however contains several eggs.

3. Ovaria digitata (Pl. XXVII. f. 8 and 9). A few, from three to five, such egg-tubes hang at one spot of the common duct. Many *Lepidoptera* (for example, *Liparis Mori*, with four tubes, each of which contains about sixty eggs), particularly the smaller ones (for example, *Tinea*, likewise with four tubes, each of which contains about twenty-five eggs; and *Pterophorus*, with three tubes, each containing about twelve eggs); and the *Hymenoptera*, (for example, *Chrysis*, with three tubes, each with three eggs; the same in *Xylocopa*; in *Anthidium*, also three tubes, each with about eight eggs). In *Nepa, Pediculus,* and *Psocus* there are five tubes, each in the latter genera containing five eggs.

4. Ovaria verticillata (Pl. XXVII. f. 11). Many very long tubes originate at one spot, upon the very short common egg duct. They run upwards in a long filiform point.

Such ovaria are found in the majority of female insects, namely, in most *Lepidoptera*, many *Hymenoptera*, and almost all *Coleoptera*. Müller's ovaria conjuncta are but a trifling variety of this form, the superior filament hanging more closely together, and forming an intertwisted cord. The fertility of the species regulates the number of the egg-tubes and their turgidity. *Oryctes nasicornis, Melolontha, Cetonia,*

---

* Leon Dufour in the Annales des Scienc. Nat. tom. vi. p. 299, &c. According to him the ovaria contain merely a whitish mass, but no distinct egg germs.

and *Notonecta* have six tubes, each with from five to six eggs; *Vespa vulgaris* and *Silpha atrata* seven tubes; *Tenebrio, Leptura, Saperda, Blatta, Ascalaphus, Bombus terrestris*, from seven to ten tubes, each with from four to six eggs; *Cicindela, Carabus, Dyticus, Staphylinus, Hydrophilus, Cerambyx, Lamia tristis* from ten to fifteen tubes; *Buprestis mariana* twenty; *Blaps mortisaga* thirty, each with four eggs; *Apis mellifica* above a hundred, each with seventeen eggs.

5. OVARIA CAPITATA (Pl. XXVII. f. 12). They merely differ from the preceding in their short tubes not running upwards in a point, but which distend into a large knob, whence the point proceeds as a thin filament (*Lucanus*).

§ 137.

The situation of these very various ovaria is nearly the same in all insects, for they always lie laterally in the abdomen contiguous to the intestinal canal, and fill the whole remaining space of the abdominal cavity not occupied by that organ. They often lie free and separated from each other, but sometimes fold over from both sides towards each other, and thus form a covering over the nutrimental canal, containing it between them. The latter then forces itself into the anterior portion of the thus formed longitudinal canal, runs within it, and posteriorly it again presents itself, passing over the common duct, which the colon always covers above. Such approximate ovaria are connected by the tracheæ, which approach them with their large stems, and then accompany each of their individual tubes by delicate accessory branches to their very extremity. There is still another means for retaining the ovaria in their place, which is their communicating duct with the dorsal vessel, discovered and described by Joh. Müller*. Each individual egg-tube, or occasionally the common egg bag, extends in a thin, very delicate, but tolerably firm filament, which ascends anteriorly and above to the dorsal vessel to discharge itself therein. This connexion invariably takes place at that portion of the organ which we have described as the aorta, sometimes at a great distance from the ovarium, for example, in the thorax. This kind of connexion is peculiar to the ovaries of the third chief division, for the connecting filaments of each egg-tube unite in a cord, or frequently, prior to their connexion with the dorsal vessel, they meet and form a single short tube, for example,

---

* Nova Acta Phys. Med. n. c. vol. xii. part ii. page 555, &c.

in *Carabus**. The connecting filaments of the egg-tubes of the second class remain, at least frequently, separated, and discharge themselves singly into the aorta †. It yet remains undiscovered how the connexion is formed with the vesicular ovaries, but it is probable that a single duct passes from the end of the bag to the artery.

We shall treat of the use of this connecting duct, which Müller has so admirably represented, in our physiological division, where we speak of the development of the eggs.

§. 138.

THE OVIDUCT.

The OVIDUCTUS, or *tuba ovarii*, is that portion of the evacuating duct of eggs which extends from the ovarium to the connexion of the two ovaries in the common evacuating duct. It is a delicate long or short tube, sometimes thin and filiform, or broader and vesicular, and when so it has a thicker muscular structure (*Semblis*). It is rarely that each oviduct is supplied with peculiar glandular appendages which secrete a gluten to spread over the eggs, by means of which they are glued together. In *Hydrophilus*, which has four such appendages attached to each side of the oviduct, they are filamentary, gradually decreasing, blind canals, and have a granulated glandular appearance, and are doubtlessly glands, and most probably secrete the material from which the female prepares the glutinous mass enclosing the eggs; but where such appendages are wanting this takes place in the vagina, or in the duct common to both ovaries, which is then supplied with peculiar appendages for this purpose.

In general the oviduct is longer in small ovaries which contain but few egg germs, shorter, on the contrary, in larger ones rich in germs; but their dimensions are regulated by the age of the insect; long ducts are found in young individuals, and they become shorter in older ones which are ready for impregnation, or already impregnated.

§ 139.

That portion of the duct of the ovaries which extends from the union of the tubes to the orifice of the spermatheca is called the egg-canal. It is generally of greater compass than the oviduct, and distends into a belly in the middle, forming a convenient cavity for the reception of the eggs. But no other object attends this reception

---

* Nova Acta Phys. Med. n. c. Pl. LI. f. 3. † Ib. Pl. L. f. 2.

than their mere passage, for the impregnation of the egg, as we shall see below (§ 208), does not take place here, but probably at the end of the egg-tube, at least its development commences there. In those instances only in which this portion of the female organs is provided with appendages which secrete a gluten do the eggs remain somewhat longer in this common duct to be covered by the secretion of those glands, that they may be thereby fixed as with a gum to the leaves of plants and other objects. Consequently this portion of the sexual organ is nothing more than a canal, and we must ascribe as well to insects as to many other inferior animals a uterus bicornis; indeed in the majority of cases, particularly those which possess ovaries having many egg-tubes, a uterus multicornis, for at the end of the egg-tube the development of the egg commences, and here consequently also its impregnation by the semen ensues.

§ 140.

APPENDAGES TO THE EGG-CANAL.

The egg-duct is most rarely a simple organ unprovided with vesicular or vascular auxiliary cavities, as, for example, in *Donacia, Eristalis tenax, Musca, Tipula, Ephemera* (Pl. XXVII. f. 13); in the majority of insects, on the contrary, it exhibits various appendages which take a variety of forms, and exercise different functions.

These appendages vary in number from one to five. If one only be present it is always a vesicular or purse-shaped distension of the duct, which appears destined to the reception of the male semen during copulation, and is thence called the SPERMATHECA. This organ is always situated at the superior parietes of the duct, and opens into it with a small orifice surrounded by a callous margin. This margin is properly the sphincter of the neck of the bag, which prevents the escape of the semen. When it opens the semen flows immediately into the duct from the mere situation of the bag. According to Audouin, the male organ during copulation passes into the orifice of this bag, and thus pours the semen directly into this receptacle. We find this kind of simple vesicular appendage in *Acheta, Blatta, Anthidium* (Pl. XXVII. f. 14.), *Ascalaphus, Sialis, Semblis, Psocus,* and *Nepa;* the same in *Hydrophilus, Tenebrio, Lytta,* and *Chrysis,* but in the latter it has a superior or lateral vascular apex (Pl. XXVII. f. 15.), which is evidently the organ we shall presently describe as the gluten gland. In general, namely, this vessel discharges itself into the duct contiguously to the spermatheca, yet in the instances named above not, but into the spermatheca itself. It is somewhat similar in *Psocus*, for here the gluten vessel does not merely discharge itself into the spermatheca, but lies entirely in it. For thus I interpret the purse-shaped appendage found by Nitzsch * in *Ps. pulsatorius*, in which from one to four pediculated knobs are enclosed which unite into one duct, which runs into the excretory duct of the spermatheca.

If TWO appendages are found at the duct it must be carefully observed whether they are symmetrical in situation and form or not. Two dissimilar appendages are found in most insects, (namely, the genera *Carabus, Harpalus, Melolontha, Lucanus, Meloë, Spondyla, Sirex, Apis, Xylocopa, Tinea, Pterophorus*, and *Cercopis*). The one is larger and broader than the other, purse-shaped, and corresponds both in situation and function with the just described spermatheca. In *Melolontha* (Pl. XXVII. f. 16. *a*), *Lucanus, Spondyla*, and *Cercopis* it is a short-necked pear-shaped bladder; in *Pterophorus* the same, but a short blind bag springs from it laterally; in *Xylocopa* (Pl. XXVII. f. 17. *a*), *Apis*, and *Tinea* it has a longer very narrow neck; in *Trichius* a superior vascular appendage; in *Sirex* (Pl. XXVII. f. 18. *a*), in which it is very large, at the part where the bladder contracts into a neck, two tolerably long, pointed appendages are found; in *Meloë* it is constricted near the middle, and the lower smaller half has a round auxiliary bladder, which discharges itself into it by a narrow canal.

The second appendage (Pl. XXVII. f. 16—18. *b*.) is in general much longer, but also thinner and vascular. This form itself, which is common to all the secreting organs of insects, bespeaks its glandular function. Observation has also taught us that a white glutinous liquid is secreted in this organ, which, after the eggs are laid, disappears. This gluten likewise covers the impregnated eggs, and it is very probably what fastens them together, as well as to other objects; consequently all appendages which are not spermathecæ are called gluten glands or vessels. With respect to their form, besides the simple, tubular, and vascular form which are found in *Trichius, Tinea,* and *Cercopis*, there is a clavate one found in *Melolontha*, and a vesicular one furnished with a short neck in *Meloë*. In *Xylocopa* it is a long gradually decreasing bag, which discharges itself by a very

---

* Compare Germar's Magaz. vol. iv. p. 281. Pl. II. f. 3. e. f. fig. 4 and 5.

narrow tubular pedicle into the uterus; in *Harpalus* and *Spondyla*, on the contrary, it is a round bladder, which has a very long, twisted, fine duct, and which in *Spondyla* contains a hard horny interior; in *Pterophorus* the vessel distends before its orifice into an ovate bladder; and in *Lucanus* (Pl. XXVIII. f. 1. *b, b*) there are two such bladders, which unite by means of two short ducts into a common one, and originate from very fine, short, twisted vessels, by their distension. The form of these organs, lastly, is very peculiar in *Elater murinus*, in which, according to Leon Dufour, they are vessels successively furcating, which at the base of each fork distend into a triangular bag. The symmetrical appendages in *Hippobosca* resemble these, but the bag-shaped distensions are wanting.

Where the duct has two symmetrical appendages, as in *Lepisma* (Pl. XXVIII. f. 3.), *Musca*, and *Pediculus* they are always gluten depositories; in *Lepisma* they are large and bag-shaped, and upon the upper surface here and there constricted; in *Musca* longer and clavate; but in *Pediculus*, on the contrary, they are two short blind bags, provided with accessory points.

We find three appendages in *Gryllotalpa, Calosoma*, and *Stratiomys*. In the first instances two of them are equal, namely, clavate or vesicular gluten vessels, which empty themselves into the duct by means of narrow canals; the third, on the contrary, is the bag-shaped spermatheca, which in *Gryllotalpa* has another superior, long, vascular appendage. In *Stratiomys* Swammerdamm * found three long, vascular, gluten ducts, which originated from round glandular bodies.

Four appendages are seen in some *Lepidoptera*, for example, *Pontia Brassicæ*. The most anterior one is a simple, tolerably long, twisted vessel, which in others (*Gastrophaga Pini*, see further below) consists of two furcate branches; the second is the spermatheca; the following are again long twisted vessels, which unite in a short duct after they have previously distended in two oval bladders. In *Cicada*, Latr. (*Tettigonia*, Fab.), in which there are also four appendages, two symmetrical vessels are found in front of the spermatheca, but the vessel behind it is simple but much longer than the two first.

Five appendages, lastly, are found in several, particularly the *Noctuæ*. A bladder-shaped, one-sided, sometimes long and clavate, or distended

* Bib. Naturæ, Pl. XLII. f. 8.

and egg or pear-shaped one, which discharges itself into the duct by a narrow canal, is the spermatheca; the other four are vascular gluten glands. In *Vanessa Urticæ* they are short, the anterior one broader than the posterior, both discharge themselves into the duct at one part but at opposite sides, before the spermatheca; in *Gastrophaga Pini* (Pl. XXVIII. f. 4.) they are very long, and the anterior as well as the posterior unite into a simple but very short canal. The anterior one, which discharges itself close in front of the spermatheca, is distended in the middle into a bladder; in the posterior ones, which discharge themselves into the vagina, this vesicular distension takes place at the end of each single tube before they unite into a common duct.

The poison vessels of the *Hymenoptera aculeata* are appendages of a peculiar description. In them a round, perfectly ovate bladder (Pl. XXVIII. f. 5, 6. *b*, *b*), with a narrow duct, discharges itself into the sting, which we shall describe below (§ 145). This bladder lies quite at the end of the abdomen close to the orifice of the sexual organs. It contains a bright clear fluid which is secreted by two either long very fine, much twisted vessels, or of shorter ones, originating from a fasciculus of furcate vessels (*Pompilus* *), which opposite the orifice sink into the bladder, and either separated as far as their orifice, as in *Vespa crebro* (Pl. XXVIII. f. 6. *a*, *a*), or as in *Apis mellifica* (f. 5. *a*, *a*), are united into one vessel, a little distance before the connexion with the bladder. May not the posterior vessels of the *Lepidoptera*, which we have just described, be analogous to these, and both be properly considered as organs secreting urine?

§ 141.

THE VAGINA.

The last portion of the common evacuating duct lying behind the egg-evacuating duct is called the VAGINA. It is a short direct tube, narrower than the egg canal but wider than the oviduct. Its function being to receive the penis of the male and to assist in depositing the eggs, it is, like all the other organs of insects which require constant distension, held in this state by horny leaves and ridges. There are generally three such horny plates, one above, one lateral, and one beneath. In *Harpalus* the superior plate is a thin bone, which towards the exterior distends in the shape of a shovel, and is there armed with

---

* Ramdohr, Verdauungsorgane, Pl. XIV. f. 5.

strong thorns; in the capricorn beetles (*Cerambycina*) it is elongated into a horny, many-jointed ovipositor. In *Hydrophilus* it runs out on each side into a horny point, which Suckow* considers as the analogue of the clitoris. In *Melolontha* the vagina has on each side a small pocket, into which the lateral wings of the penis pass during copulation, which explains the cause of the protracted union of this insect.

In all insects provided with an aculeus or an ovipositor, the vagina opens at its base, so that its canal passes directly into that of the ovipositor. The valves and spines of this apparatus are consequently nothing more than the horny bone which lies within the vagina, and which is then prolonged beyond it.

B. EXTERNAL SEXUAL ORGANS.

§ 142.

The external sexual organs of insects do not always project beyond the apex of the abdomen, but usually lie in the cavity into which the orifice of the anus and of the vagina open. This cavity, common to both, is formed of two valves, the one larger, lying upon the dorsal side, and the other smaller, upon the ventral side, and beyond which the former projects all round. These two valves, which are not visible exteriorly, but are enclosed by the dorsal and ventral plates of the last abdominal segment, are evidently nothing but the last segment itself, those called the last being the last but one. It is only thus that we can explain the disappearance of the segments of the larva in the perfect insect, in which we shall also generally discover nine segments if we include the last concealed one. But where there are nine visible segments the last is not then concealed, but free. It is within this last abdominal segment, whether it be concealed or free, that the orifice of the vagina is found, and indeed, beneath the anus, divided from it only by a projecting plate. The entrance itself is opened, mostly by horny substances, which have partly been described in the preceding paragraph in the description of the vagina. The lateral horny ridges, namely, become more elongate, so that they project as far as the limits of the valves, gradually separating, and thus forming a spacious entrance. The length of the vagina depends upon that of these horny ridges; they are short in the *Carabodea*, and often armed at their apex with a strong hook (*Har-*

* Heusing. Zeitschr. vol. ii. p. 254.

palus ruficornis), which doubtlessly retains the penis during copulation. In the capricorn beetles unprovided with an ovipositor (the *Prionodea*) they are long, superiorly broader, pointed towards the apex, and gently bending from each other. There are other forms in other insects. In the orders possessing an ovipositor they appear as its valves, or as its wings in those which possess only a vagina bivalvis, this leads us to the investigation of the free sexual organs which project beyond the apex of the abdomen.

§ 143.

The free, exteriorly visible, sexual organs of female insects are of a threefold description, at least three chief forms entomologists have distinguished by peculiar names, namely, the LAYING TUBE (*vagina tubiformis*), the LAYING SHEATH (*vagina bivalvis*), and the ACULEUS, called also the TEREBRA, but which is one and the same organ with the preceding.

The LAYING TUBE (*vagina tubiformis*, Pl. XXIV. f. 14.) is a mere continuation of the abdomen, and consists, like it, of rings which gradually decrease in compass, so that the largest and first, exactly as is the case in the telescope, receives within it all the rest, when this organ is withdrawn within the abdomen, wherein it lies concealed. These rings are nothing else than segments of the abdomen itself, which have adopted this altered shape and function in the course of the progressive alteration of the relations of organisation. The proof that this opinion is correct is shown in their number, for in the majority of cases (for example, in the flies,) there are nine abdominal segments, when these rings of the vagina are added to the visible ones of the abdomen. The anal aperture also lies in this tube, which could not be the case if it were merely an ovipositor. Thence, therefore, the last of these tubes only can interest us here, from its containing the female organs. In *Cerambyx* it is a leathery canal, of which that side nearest the venter is supported by two horny ridges; at the end of each bone there is a short two-jointed process, the first joint of which is large, thick, bulbous, and armed on the exterior with short spines; the second, however, is small and round, and has two stiff setæ at its extremity. In the flies, which all possess a tubiform vagina, its last joint has above a horny plate, to which also two short single-jointed, hook-shaped, crooked processes hang attached. The tubiform vagina of the ruby tails (*Chrysis*) appears, as far as I have been able to ascertain from dry specimens, to have precisely the same structure, only that in these, as well as in the flies, each ring has its horny covering, which are connected together by membranous parts.

§ 144.

The VAGINA BIVALVIS is most closely related to the *vagina tubiformis*. It is found in the *Orthoptera*, some *Neuroptera* (*Raphidia*), and the *Tipularia*. In its most complete development it is a sabre-shaped tube, which curves upwards, into which the vagina opens, and it is formed of two valves (*Locusta*, Pl. XXIV. f. 10—14.) I consider these two valves as the two lateral horny leaves mentioned above in the description of the orifice of the vagina, and which here are prolonged and now take the form of valves to that organ. The internal valves corresponding with the last abdominal segment become also visible, and here appear as the cover both above and below (f. 10. A, B,) at the base of the vagina bivalvis itself. All *Orthoptera*, consequently, have nine distinctly visible abdominal segments. In *Locusta* this vagina is long, sometimes indeed (*Locus. viridissima*) even longer than the body, each valve is gently sloped, and has a channel upon its exterior surface which projects internally as an elevated ridge. At the base it is covered beneath by the last deeply emarginate ventral segment, above it lies the anus, and contiguous to it two short, simple, spinous processes. Between the two larger valves there are two smaller ones (f. 12 and 14. *b, b,*) which are connected by a delicate membrane with the internal elevated ridge, and sometimes lose themselves in this or remain separated from it. Frequently the apex of the exterior vagina is split at the channel, when the exterior sheath appears, at least at its end, to consist of four pieces *. In *Gryllus*, instead of this projecting vagina we observe four short thick processes, the lower ones of which are moveable, and form one articulation with the superior ones that are closely attached to the abdominal cover. From the superior, stronger, thicker ones thus intimately connected two processes are continued within the abdomen, and to which are attached the muscles moving the lower ones; the orifice of the vagina lies between the lower ones, and the anus above the superior ones. We may make the following

---

* Kirby and Spence, Introd. to Ent., vol. iv. p. 152., mention six pieces, but I have never observed in our indigenous Locusta any but the structure described above, and never six divided pieces.

comparison between this organ and that of *Locusta*, the lower moveable processes are analogous to the two valves of the vagina bivalvis, the superior ones however to the spinous processes contiguous to the anus, but with this difference, that in *Locusta* these processes are articulated to the horny piece which bears them, and which lies between the orifice of the vagina and the anus; in *Gryllus*, on the contrary, the superior processes form an integral portion of that horny piece. *Acheta* agrees in structure with *Locusta*, but its vagina is more delicately constructed; the anal processes are longer, and at their apex apparently jointed.

The female *Tipula* have likewise a bivalve vagina which very much agrees in structure with that of *Gryllus*. In *Ctenophora atrata*, two pointed, long, and sabre-shaped processes originate above from the last dorsal plate, and bend from the sides towards each other, forming a bivalved vagina. They correspond to the superior immoveable processes of *Gryllus* or the moveable processes of *Locusta*. Beneath this last dorsal plate, and consequently between the valves, the anus is placed. A triangular fleshy process encompassed by a delicate horny margin separates it from the orifice of the vagina lying beneath it. It also has on each side two processes of the last ventral plate, which are above shorter, broader, inwardly arcuate, and gently bowed externally. These two valves form the true vagina, and therefore correspond to the inferior processes in *Gryllus* and the long vaginal valves in *Locusta*. In a state of repose they lie concealed between the superior or anal processes, and all four appear to form a bodkin-shaped process.

§ 145.

The TEREBRA, or ACULEUS, is found in all the *Hymenoptera* and in the *Cicadaria*.

With respect to the aculeus of the *Hymenoptera*, although it has been occasionally tolerably well explained by the earliest entomologists, it has not always been recognised by modern ones, and therefore frequently imperfectly described. This fact is the more striking as it has actually nearly the same structure in its essential parts in all the families, and is merely subject to slight differences of form. For the present we will pass these over, and proceed to examine its essential parts.

The chief character in which the terebra is distinguished from the vagina bivalvis is the presence of a second pointed boring organ lying between the valves. This fuller development of it is not found in the vagina bivalvis, but it is indicated in the shorter internal valves, which in *Locusta viridissima* are united to the larger ones by membrane, but in other instances they are found free and separate. The terebra of the *Tenthredos* is an intermediate form ; it, consequently, does not pierce firm substances, but merely guides the eggs into already existing cavities ; but the aculeus forms the cavity itself for the egg, pierces into bodies not firmer than itself, and as a defensive instrument it wounds very severely. We may therefore distinguish the EXTERIOR SHEATH (*vagina aculei*) and the inner STING (*aculeus, seu terebra*) as the chief parts of this kind of ovipositor; we will first turn our attention to the sheath.

We have but little to say of the exterior sheath, for its differences are unimportant. It always consists of two valves (Pl. XXIII. f. 6. *a, a*), which are united by articulation with the dorsal plate of the last abdominal segment, by which it is partially covered above ; the ventral plate then covers it from below. They are as long as the sting itself, and lying together form a tube, in which the latter is completely concealed. If the sting project beyond the apex of the abdomen they accompany it. A thus projecting sting (*aculeus exsertus*) Latreille calls a terebra. But when the sting lies concealed within the abdomen (as for example, in the bees,) the valves are there also, and they embrace the concealed sting (*aculeus absconditus*) precisely in the same way as the exserted one. The exterior upper surface of the sheath is generally rough and uneven, particularly in the projecting aculeus, and entirely covered with short hair; the edges are simple, smooth, and fit closely together.

The internal sting is differently formed according to the peculiarity of its function.

In the *Tenthredonodea* it diverges most in form. In these it should not properly be called a sting, but a saw, and indeed earlier entomologists have compared it with this tool. It consists (Pl. XXIV. f. 8.), like the sheath, of two valves (*a, a*, and *b, b*), between which at their base there lies a short triangular process (*c*). Each internal valve has the same form as the sheath enclosing it, but it is smaller, so that it can be entirely embraced by it. The inferior edge of the inner valve is finely toothed (Pl. XXIV. f. 9. *a*), very sharp and narrow, inwardly separated by a projecting line from the remaining very smooth surface of the valve. The exterior has likewise a corresponding projecting ridge (the same, *b, b*), which, like the ridge, is finely and sharply toothed ;

raised lines run over the whole of this surface from tooth to tooth, and from the elevated ridge to the superior edge, which makes the whole exterior surface even, and gives it the appearance of a fine file. With this saw-like apparatus the *Tenthredo* cuts the substance of leaves, letting an egg drop in, which is there developed that it may subsequently feed upon it. The short triangular process forms merely a key-stone to the margins, gaping at the base, and is of no importance to the function of the organ; but it is necessary to mention it, as it is of great consequence in the structure of the sting in the rest of the *Hymenoptera*.

If we examine the projecting sting of the *Ichneumons*, for example, *Pimpla* (Pl. XXIII. f. 12—14.), we first observe the two exterior valves, (f. 14. *a, a,*) and between them, a fine horny sting which is a little dilated at its extremity (f. 12.). This sting was long considered simple, and even Gravenhorst, in his monograph of the European Ichneumons, describes it so [*]. But it also is double; the upper part (f. 13. *a.* and 12. *a.*) is channelled beneath, completely smooth, and only at its broader point beset with small teeth; the lower (the same, *b,*) much finer portion is a hair-shaped very pointed bristle, which lies within the channel of the superior one; this also is broader in front and lancet-shaped, and fits into a cavity of the upper part of its own shape. There is thus truly a passage in the aculeus, but so narrow an one that no egg can pass down it, and in this cavity how should it move along? The egg merely slides down the superior channel, and is secured and pushed on by the inferior bristle pressing against the channel from the base towards the apex, pushing the egg above it. But, to refer this structure back to that described in the saw-flies, we must conceive the two internal valves as united in the superior simple half tube, and the bristle as the elongation of the central process at the base of the valves.

Its structure is still more artificial in *Sirex* and the Bees. In *Sirex* (Pl. XXIII. fig. 5—11), in which the sting projects, we find likewise the exterior valves (*a, a*) and the central aculeus (*b*). This again consists of the superior channel (*c, c,*) and the bristle lying within it, which is here double. (*d. d.*) All three are dilated at their end (f. 7), the channel is split, and that portion as well as the bristle upon its entire

---

[*] Ichneumonologia Europæa, tom. i. p. 89. "Hæc seta terebra est, et canali centrali longitudinali instructa esse dicitur, per quem ova poneruntur."

margin beset with short serrated teeth (f. 9 and 10). That the bee's sting is similarly formed, although it lies in the abdomen, is shown in Swammerdamm's figure *. Latreille cites the true aculeus in *Sirex* as double †, but personal investigation will readily convince of his error and the correctness of our representation. The spirally twisted aculeus of *Cynips* (Pl. XXIII. f. 15—18), according to the opinion of early entomologists, viz. of Roesel, differs in structure from that of the bee's only in that its apex, which is covered by valves beset with hair, projects above the abdomen. Its supposed spiral twisting consists in its base being somewhat bent; the point however somewhat sinks, so that it represents the figure of an 8. (f. 16. a section; *a, a*, the valves; *b, b*, the two exterior setæ lying in it; *c*, the central one).

The description of the aculeus of the *Cicada* still remains. Its form in *C. Fraxini* is as follows: the large triangular dorsal plate of the last abdominal segment (Pl. XXIV. f. 1. A.), which at its apex is bent down, covers from above the two double-jointed sheaths (the same, B. and C.). Both joints are connected together by a soft membrane; the basal joint (f. 2. B. B) is broader, shorter, and hollowed out; the last joint (the same, c. c.) is longer, narrower, towards its apex somewhat broader, triangular, within hollowed in a channel. This last joint is free, but the first is connected by a joint to the ventral plate. Between these lie the aculeus (the same, D.), a horny, round organ, a little dilated at its base, and near its apex compressed, where at the edge it is toothed; and this again consists of three horny ridges connected by soft membrane. A still larger one (f. 3, *a, a*, seen from beneath, f. 5 from above), broader in front, and there likewise toothed at the margin, lies above and forms the channel; two finer narrower ones, pointed at the apex (f. 3, *b, b*, from beneath, and f. 4 from above) lie in the preceding, and project beyond it at the end, forming its apex (the same, f. 2 D.). They all form combined a tube capable of distension, in which doubtlessly the eggs are pushed down by the valves themselves after the aculeus has pierced the vegetable substance, for which purpose evidently it is armed at its apex with the strong teeth.

This, therefore, is the structure of the ovipositor in the different groups of insects: in its investigation we have concluded our examination of the female sexual organs, and pass now on to the male organs.

---

* Biblia Naturæ, Pl. XVIII. f. 3.   † Gen. Crus. et Ins., vol. iii. p. 242.

II. OF THE MALE ORGANS OF GENERATION.

§ 146.

WE have already indicated that the male sexual organs consist essentially of the same parts as those of the female. They also are divided into interior and exterior; the former of which comprise the TESTES, VASA DEFERENTIA, VESICA SEMINALIS, and DUCTUS EJACULATORIUS SEMINIS; and the latter, the PENIS and the PREHENSILE ORGAN connected with it, and placed at the sexual orifice. We will therefore now proceed to the consideration of the internal male organs of generation.

A. INTERNAL ORGANS OF GENERATION.

§ 147.

THE TESTES.

The TESTES are glandular white bodies generally present in pairs, and which secrete the spermatic fluid. They regulate themselves in form and structure according to the differences presented by the glandular organs in insects in general, so that the majority are long convoluted vessels; some take the form of fasciculi of blind filaments, and a few lastly appear as round glandular bags. Their structure is regulated by their exterior appearance. Vascular testes have, like all the glands of insects, two tunics; the internal loose mucous one displaying a parenchymatous appearance, the exterior one smooth, but coarser in structure, and corresponding with the exterior muscular membrane of all internal organs. Round testes have likewise a smooth coating, which enclose a multitude of small vesicular bags in the cavities of which the sperm is secreted.

As the testes are analogous to the female ovaries, we should conceive that they as well as the latter should stand in connection with the dorsal vessel; but this has not yet been detected, although many forms of testes extend in delicate filaments upwards which may apparently be the indication of such a communicating thread, as is the case in the ovaries. The analogous importance of both organs, which is most strongly proved by the progressive metamorphoses of insects, to which we shall subsequently return, is evinced also by the situation of the testes in the abdomen, as they occupy precisely the same place possessed by the ovaries of the female, namely, the lateral spaces in the abdominal cavity contiguous to the intestinal canal, yet inclining more towards the venter. Those only which are united into one testis lie directly in the middle of the body immediately beneath the nutrimental canal.

With respect to their precise shape, having thus indicated their most general differences, and distinguished them as tubular or vesicular, they may be arranged under several chief forms with various subordinate differences, which the following classification endeavours to display.

I. SIMPLE TESTES. The long testes which, in the early stages, are divided, approach more closely together in the progress of development, and, lastly, in the pupa state, unite into one single globular testis, (Pl. XXIX. f. 1.) the earlier separation of which is indicated by a ring upon its surface. Each of the hemispheres divided by this ring has its own peculiar duct, which unite afterwards together.

This structure of the testes is peculiar to all the diurnal, crepuscular, and nocturnal *Lepidoptera*, as well as the *Pterophori;* other moths (the *Tineæ*) have them always separated. This testis consists, upon closer inspection, of a thick cellular mass, which is pierced everywhere by delicate ramifications of the tracheæ.

II. SEPARATED TESTES. The testes remain during the whole course of the insect's life separated from each other, and lie on each side of the intestinal canal.

A. SIMPLE VASCULAR TESTES. Each testis is a simple filiform or wider vessel, which lies either extended at full length, or makes convolutions, but it sometimes is entangled in a hank.

1. *Testiculi lineares* (Pl. XXIX. f. 2.). They lie stretched out, and are wider than the ductus ejaculatorius into which they pass by means of a sudden constriction, and run upwards in a conical point. (*Libellula.*)

2. *Testiculi clavati.* (Pl. XXIX. f. 3.). Each testis is an obtuse club, which gradually contracts itself into the ductus ejaculatorius, and thus imperceptibly passes into it. (*Cercopis, Tinea.*)

3. *Testiculi filiformes.* (Pl. XXIX. f. 4.). The testis is a twisted filament, which lies wound up in the abdomen, and, before it passes into the duct, distends into a longitudinal sperm bladder. (*b. Tipula.*)

4. *Testiculi spirales.* (Pl. XXIX. f. 5.). They distinguish themselves from the preceding merely by each filiform testis being twisted

spirally, and originating in a superior free and very fine filament. (*Ranatra.*)

5. *Testiculi furcati.* (Pl. XXIX. f. 6.). The testis here is also a twisted canal, which furcates at its extremity and extends into two short capitate ends *. (*Apis mellifica.*)

6. *Testiculi convoluti.* (Pl. XXIX. f. 7.). The filiform testis is very long, much longer than the abdomen, and convoluted into sometimes a round (*Dyticus*), sometimes ovate (*Calosoma*) ball. (*Carabodea Hydrocantharides.*)

B. COMPOUND VASCULAR TESTES. Each testis is a bundle of shorter or longer filiform or filamentary blind vessels, or bags, which all unite into one common duct.

1. *Testiculi scopacei.* (Pl. XXIX. f. 8.). The short blind processes which the testes form, are of equal length, and sit close together upon the upper side of a common duct. (*Hydrophilus.*)

2. *Testiculi fasciculati.* (Pl. XXIX. f. 9.). The somewhat longer blind processes are tolerably equal in size, and are seated contiguously at one spot, namely, at the end of the funnel-shaped distended sperm duct. (*Buprestis Trichodes, Clerus*, Epidydimis in *Locusta*, Pl. XXVIII. f. 5, a.).

3. *Testiculi stellati.* (Pl. XXIX. f. 14.). From the end of the simple sperm duct, short fine, star-shaped or radiating filaments originate. (*Apate.*)

4. *Testiculi flosculosi.* (Pl. XXIX. f. 15.). The filaments at the end of the sperm duct are here short, distended bags, which are placed around the distension of the sperm duct, like the petals of a flower of the class *Syngenesia*. (*Asida, Tenebrio, Œdemera.*)

5. *Testiculi imbricati.* (Pl. XXIX. f. 10.). Short purse-shaped, smooth pockets, which pass over each other like tiles, clothe a broad compressed bag, which runs out into a short, at first serpentine sperm duct. (*Locusta viridissima.*)

C. COMPOUND VESICULAR TESTES. Each testis consists of oval or round and large or small vesicles, which unite either by degrees together, or at one end of the there distended sperm duct.

1. *Testiculi racemosi.* (Pl. XXIX. f. 11.). The bladders are

---

* Sockow, in Heus. Zeitschr. f. d. Org. Physik. vol. ii. p. 234. Pl. XII. f. 30. According to Swammerdamm, Biblia Naturæ, the testes are kidney-shaped bodies.

tolerably large, pear-shaped, and open by degrees, sometimes several together, into the common sperm duct. The lower bladders are larger and longer stalked. (*Staphylinus.*)

2. *Testiculi granulati.* (Pl. XXIX. f. 12 and 16.). The end of the sperm duct is dilated into a bladder, which is entirely covered with round, button-shaped blisters. (*Blaps, Pimelia, Musca.*)

3. *Testiculi vesiculosi.* (Pl. XXIX. f. 13.). The long testis consists of several rows of little bladders, which are placed around the extremity of the sperm duct. In *Semblis* there are three rows of such bladders present.

4. *Testiculi vesiculoso-cirrati.* (Pl. XXIX. f. 7. b.). The reflected end of the sperm duct bears several petiolated, larger, capitate bladders, and between these there are fasciculi of smaller, ramose vessels, the extreme ends of which originate from four delicate glandular bodies. (*Silpha obscura*, according to Leon Dufour.)

D. CAPITATE TESTES. The testis consists of several sometimes round or long kidney-shaped glands, which lie at the end of the common sperm duct, or each duct bears but one such glandular body.

1. *Testiculi capitato-simplices.* (Pl. XXIX. f. 17.). Each testis consists of a single, differently formed glandular body. In *Lytta* and *Meloë*, this body is globose or uneven and granulated (f. 17.); in *Sialis, Phryganea,* and *Apis* (according to Swammerdamm), it is kidney-shaped, and the duct opens at the spot where the kidney is emarginate.

2. *Testiculi capitato-gemini.* (Pl. XXIX. f. 18.). The sperm duct is furcate, and each branch bears a similar round glandular testis. *Donacia* and *Callichroma* have equal branches: in *Lamia ædilis*, the superior one is longer (f. 18).

3. *Testiculi digitati.* (Pl. XXX. f. 1.). At the end of the sperm duct there are five conical glandular bodies, which extend in long serpentine fine vessels. (*Nepa.*) This form is as it were intermediate between the capitate and vascular testes.

4. *Testiculi capitato-compositi.* (Pl. XXIX. f. 19 and 20.). The sperm duct gradually divides into several branches, each of which sends off one (*Cetonia Prionus*) or several capitate testes. (*Lepisma Cicada.*)

5. *Testiculi capitato-verticillati.* (Pl. XXX. f. 2.). Each testis consists of several globose frequently-compressed glandular bodies,

concave in the centre, each of which has its peculiar duct. All the ducts are of equal length, and unite at one and the same spot to a common sperm duct. The number of glandular bodies varies: we find six in *Melolontha vulgaris* and *Oryctes nasicornis*, nine in *Trichius fasciatus*, and twelve in *Tr. nobilis*, on each side. This form appears to be the most complete of all, whence it is peculiar to the beetles only.

§ 148.

THE EPIDYDIMIS.

The epidydimis is likewise a glandular organ frequently formed upon the type of the true testes, and opens with a peculiar either narrower or wider duct into the common duct of the sexual organs. We find this organ in a few beetles only: its function also is not distinctly known; the few hitherto observed forms are the following.

We observe the epidydimis most distinctly in *Hydrophilus piceus* (Pl. XXX. f. 3). They are here two long oval pointed bodies, turned back about their centre, which contain within an exterior fine tense skin a second glandular one, forming many rather long and regularly successive little bags. Upon a first inspection, this body appears, from its narrow, contiguous and parallel bags, as a convoluted vessel, and as such Suckow erroneously explains it *. From this organ there originates a long broad bag, with at first a narrow but suddenly distending orifice, which appears to be formed like the tracheæ of a spiral filament, but, upon closer investigation, displays a structure similar to the epidydimis. It also consists of two membranes, of which the inner parenchymous mucous membrane likewise forms narrow, parallel bags, which I almost consider as the actual secreting cavities. In them we find a yellowish finely granulated liquid, the secretion of this epidydimis. Both these bags (Pl. XXX. f. 10. *aa.aa.*) open at the end of the common duct in front of the sperm bladder. (The same, *a*. a**.) They are somewhat longer, or certainly quite as long as the testes with the sperm duct, and extended they are of about the length of the abdomen, but they are usually rolled spirally. Similar appendages are found in *Lytta* and *Meloë*, but the epidydimis here is a serpentine, lace-shaped vessel, which, upon the ventral side, empties itself into the vesicular distended point of union of both the conical

* In Heusing., vol. ii. p. 232.

sperm ducts*. In *Trichodes*, the epidydimis is also a simple, very much convoluted vessel, without distension or appendages †.

In *Locusta* and *Gryllotalpa*, the epidydimis forms a convolution of vessels. In *Gryllotalpa*, each of the four thick testicular bodies appears to consist of one convoluted vessel. The superior one or epidydimis is smaller, conical, and provided at the end with a long free filament; the lower true testis is larger and kidney-shaped. Both display upon their surface evident windings of vessels, which are surrounded by a darker mass. Their ducts unite beneath the large testis into a small sperm bladder, into which also the thick convoluted gluten vessel empties itself ‡. In *Locusta*, each epidydimis consists of two divisions: the upper one (*a.*) is a fasciculus of long, snow-white convoluted vessels, which all unite by degrees into a tolerably large duct; the lower one (*b.*), on the contrary, is an oval bag, the superior surface of which sends off short round, tolerably narrow, filamentary processes. The sperm duct empties itself into the neck of the bag, but the duct of both bags, as well as the short one of the upper fasciculated epidydimis, form likewise two short tubes, which speedily unite with the broad, almost bag-shaped ductus ejaculatorius. At this point of union, we find on each side a small round little bladder, which is the vesica seminalis.

These are the different forms of the hitherto observed epidydimes: other vascular appendages of the male sexual organs we shall shortly investigate, and discern in them gluten organs.

§ 149.

THE VASA DEFERENTIA AND VESICA SEMINALIS.

The ducts which connect the testes with the common ductus ejaculatorius, are called vasa deferentia, or sperm ducts. They are fine tubes, originally of very small circumference, which either retain a uniform size, or distend in front of their orifice, and widen into an oval, long bladder. This distension is called the *vesica seminalis* or sperm bladder.

We can speak only of the number and length of the sperm ducts. With respect to their number, we observe where several testicular bodies are found. There are also at first several sperm ducts, all of which, either

---

* See Brandt and Ratzeburg Arzeneithiere, vol. ii. Pl. XIX. f. 12 and 13. *e. e.*
† Suckow, as above, Pl. X. f. 5—7. ‡ Ibid. Pl. XII. f. 20.

by degrees or at one spot, unite into one common duct. The first case is found only in the compound capitate testes (*T. cap. compositi*), but universally here. Thus the twelve ducts of the twelve glandular bodies of *Cetonia aurata* unite by degrees to a common sperm duct; indeed some of them previously unite together before they empty themselves into the common duct. In *Prionus* (Pl. XXIX. f. 19.) the single ducts empty themselves alternately into the end of the common sperm duct; the same in *Cicada*, Latr., in which each branch bears several glands. The second connection of the sperm duct is peculiar to the verticillate testes: here all the single sperm ducts unite at the end of the common duct, consequently at one spot. It is similar in the double testes (*T. cap. gemini*), where consequently the sperm duct furcates at its extremity; the same in *Blaps*, where two equal branches are found, each bearing a testis, and then a third, longer originating from the fork, which, however, bears no testis. The length of the sperm ducts is subject to no less variety. They are short in all those instances where they do not exceed the length of the abdomen, and, consequently, make no convolutions, as for example, in *Lucanus, Hydrophilus, Locusta, Callichroma, Libellula, Nepa,* and, in general, where there are large testes; moderately long, that is, from twice to three times the length of the abdomen, they are found in those instances in which the different appendages we are about to describe are wanting, for example, in *Semblis, Sialis, Phryganea,* and *Cercopis;* long or very long in those testes which are smaller and composed of several bodies, or in general of a convoluted canal, for example, in *Dyticus*, in which they are about five times as long as the body, and, like the testes, convolute themselves into a small knot (Pl. XXIX. f. 7. *b*.); then in *Necrophorus* and *Blaps* eight or ten times as long; in *Cicada*, Lat. fourteen times as long; and in *Cetonia aurata*, nearly thirty times as long. A short but very broad and indeed gradually distending sperm duct is found in *Meloë* and *Lytta* (Pl. XXIX. f. 17. *b*.), whilst in other cases it maintains a uniform compass.

The sperm bladder has generally a more muscular structure than the sperm duct. The size is proportionate to that of the testes, and is wholly wanting to the less compact sexual organs, where the narrow sperm duct passes into the common ductus ejaculatorius without any distension. It is wanting, for example, in the *Carabodea* and *Hydrocantharides*, in *Lucanus*, the Capricorn beetles, all *Lepidoptera*, *Libellula, Cercopis,* and several others; as a slight distension at the end of the sperm duct, it appears in the *Lamellicornia*, in *Semblis*, *Tipula;* as a large ovate distension, at the end of the sperm duct in *Hydrophilus* (Pl. XXX. f. 10.) and *Apis;* as a peculiar appendage to the sperm duct, in *Phryganea* (Pl. XXX. f. 6. *b.b.*). In *Lytta*, *Meloë*, and many others, we find but one sperm bladder, which has originated from the union of both the sperm ducts; into this the lace-shaped epidydimis then empties itself.

§ 150.

PECULIAR APPENDAGES.

We perceive appendages to the male organs similar to those glandular ones we noticed above in the female sexual organs. With respect to their peculiar purpose, we know certainly as little as of the true function of the vessels accessory to the female organs; but it is just as probable that here as there they are gluten secreting organs, and, consequently, glandular. That such appendages are not absolutely necessary, is proved by the circumstance, that, as in the female, so also in the male sexual organs, they are frequently entirely wanting, and that sometimes they correspond in both sexes, as in *Musca*, *Donacia*, *Semblis;* in other cases are found only in the female, as in *Tipula*, *Ephemera*, and *Nepa;* and in others again are found in the male alone, as in *Pterophorus* and *Cercopis*. This deficiency of them in one sex, when present in the other, speaks against the opinion of Suckow[*], according to whom they secrete urine; for this would necessarily be peculiar to both sexes, but which does not invalidate their being gluten secreting vessels of the sexual organs, which in general in male individuals are much more numerous, and are of a different form and situation to those found in the female. These appendages are also found where urinary organs show themselves, as in the *Carabodea* and *Hydrocantharides*. Comp. § 114.

If we more closely investigate the number and the form of these appendages, their first and most important character is their almost symmetrical situation and equal number. *Tipula* and *Blatta* only, as far as our knowledge extends, make an exception to this rule; as in *Tipula* (Pl. XXX. f. 14.), according to Suckow, an uneven clavate process is found at the point of union of both sperm ducts, which, according to all analogy, can be explained only as a gluten organ,

---

[*] Heusing., vol. ii. p. 248.

particularly as in many other insects the same part appears in a similar form. In *Blatta*, according to Gaede *, there is a large bladder at this precise spot.

The symmetrical gluten organs are, in the first place, double, and, indeed, short clavate processes, which, at the point of connection of the sperm duct, empty themselves into the ductus ejaculatorius. We thus find them in *Sialis, Ephemera, Lepisma, Nepa, Apis* (Pl. XXX. f. 8.), and *Piophila casei*, Meig., in which, however, the clavate bag has a lateral pocket. In the *Carabodea* and *Hydrocantharides*, it appears longer, indeed as long as the abdomen, proportionately narrower, and already making some windings. In the former, at least in *Calosoma sycophanta*, each bag is flat, somewhat depressed from its apex, spirally convoluted, and into it, shortly before its termination, the sperm duct empties itself (Pl. XXX. f. 13.); in *Dyticus*, on the contrary, it is round, irregular, twisted, and with its opponent, as well as with the sperm duct, it is bound together. Still longer, and, consequently, more twisted, but otherwise uniform, they appear in *Gryllotalpa*, where they are at least twice the length of the short testes; in *Stratiomys*, it is once and a half as long as the testes and the sperm duct; in *Tinea*, equally long, but narrow and filiform. In all these cases, they unite with the sperm duct at one spot, to form a common ductus ejaculatorius. Longer than the testes, but likewise thin, narrow, and filiform, we find them in the *Lepidoptera:* here, consequently, they make several turnings, and then empty themselves in the sperm duct itself, a short space before its union with the ductus ejaculatorius. (Pl. XXX. f. 12.) The *Lamellicornia* possess the longest. They here appear as two long narrow, much convoluted filiform vessels (Pl. XXX. f. 9. *b*.), which, towards their base, distend into a long oval occasionally broad bladder (*Melolontha*), which, together with the sperm duct, passes into the common duct at one spot. The length of this vessel is sometimes considerable; for example, in *Oryctes nasicornis*, about twenty times as long as the body, but in *Cicada*, Lat., where we observe similar vessels only five times as long.

The ramose is the last form of the single-paired gluten organs. We have already observed such in the female appendages in *Elater* and *Hippobosca*; among those of the males, we find them in the Capricorn beetles. In *Callichroma moschatum*, I found a thick tangle

---

* Beiträge zur Anatomie der Insekten, p. 20.

of very fine vessels, which, upon opening the insect, was covered by the dorsal portion of the posterior end of the intestinal canal. Upon closer inspection I found that all these vessels were merely the branches of a main stem that was furcated, which was the case also with each branch, and I thus found eight successive furcations. The terminal ends I could not distinctly perceive, but they are probably loose. In *Lamia ædilis*, at least, where only one furcated vessel is found on each side, the branches are free, but unequal, the exterior one being shorter, and the interior longer, the stem emptying itself into the sperm duct (Pl. XXX. f. 11.); and it is the same in *Callichroma moschatum*.

Where there are two pairs of appendages, they display the same forms. In *Ascalaphus Italicus* they are, according to Hegetschweiler, four unequal, pear-shaped bladders, which empty themselves into the sperm duct: the smaller ones have besides a superior vascular appendage. According to Posselt *, two pairs of vascular appendages are found in *Geotrupes stercorarius*; to Hegetschweiler, in *Clerus alvearius*; to Gäde, in *Tenebrio molitor;* and also in *Blaps mortisaga*, *Meloë* and *Lytta*, in which they are short, but of unequal length, and one pair empties itself upon the upper surface, and the other pair upon the under surface, into the sperm bladder †. In *Hydrophilus*, there are also two pairs of unequal appendages; the inner ones are shorter but broader, the exterior ones longer, and they furcate into two equal branches: both empty themselves between the sperm ducts, the testes, and the epidydimis, into the end of the common ductus ejaculatorius. (Pl. XXX. f. 10. *b. b.* and *bb. bb.*).

In *Notonecta glauca* there are even four pairs of equal vascular appendages; and in *Buprestis mariana*, according to Gäde ‡, there are two pairs of vesicular ones and two pairs of vascular ones together. One pair of the first is very small, the other longer, clavate, and bent: also one pair of the vessels is bag-shaped, and the other filiform and tolerably long. All unite at one spot in the ductus ejaculatorius, into which also the sperm ducts, but at some little distance further backwards, empty themselves.

* Beiträge zur Anatomie der Insekten, Pt. 1. f. 16.
† Brandt and Ratzeburg Arzeneithiere, vol. ii. 4 Pt. Pl. XIX. f. 13.
‡ Nova Acta Phys. Med., vol. xi. p. 331.

§ 151.

DUCTUS EJACULATORIUS.

The DUCTUS EJACULATORIUS SEMINIS is that tube which extends from the point of union of both sperm ducts or sperm bladders to the commencement of the penis. It displays in its structure coarser muscular fibres, and is of a more compact nature than the sperm duct. It is analogous to the egg canal of the female organs, and appears sometimes, like this, vesicular (*Hydrophilus*), and sometimes contracted by degrees, consequently clavate (*Lucanus, Lytta*), sometimes simple and of equal width. In length it varies much, sometimes short, scarcely visible, yet broad (*Locusta, Gryllotalpa*), sometimes longer, but yet, in proportion to the other internal sexual organs, still short (*Calosoma, Melolontha, Trichius*); moderately long when it attains about the same length as the sperm ducts (*Hydrophilus, Lytta, Meloë, Papilio*); long, lastly, when it is longer, indeed considerably so than the sperm ducts (*Lucanus, Lamia*). The most remarkable form of the ductus ejaculatorius I observed in *Lamia ædilis*. In this it is about eight times as long as each sperm duct, and geniculated. But to display this remarkable structure most justly, I must extend my description to that of the entire sexual apparatus.

If a male *Lamia ædilis* be opened from its back, we first observe in the centre the convoluted intestine, and contiguous to it, on each side, about the centre of the lateral space, two white testes. Both unite into a narrow sperm canal, which runs towards the anus, and there unites itself with the opposite one of the other side, after each has received a furcated gluten gland. After a short course in a direct line, the ductus ejaculatorius bends forward, runs in a serpentine direction up the central line as far as the abdominal nervous cord, but beneath the intestinal canal, as far as the thorax, and here again bends a second time, turning upon itself like a knot, it then runs back again in a gentle curve to the anus, there to pass into the penis. From its first bend, this duct is no longer free, but it is enclosed in a wider membranous tube, into which also pass eight delicate tracheæ, the fine ramifications of which spread upon the duct; and accompany it as far as the second bend, after they having one after the other previously dispersed themselves in fine branches. But from its second bend, the ductus ejaculatorius is accompanied by a strong horny ridge, which lies in the superior portion of the enclosing tube, retaining it tensely distended, and which terminates only where it passes into the penis. In the other capricorn beetles (for example, *Callichroma moschatum,*) the ductus ejaculatorius is indeed much shorter, but likewise twice geniculated. That portion from the point of connection to the first knee is wider, more vesicular, and transversely ridged, taking the place of the sperm bladder, which is wanting, to the equally wide sperm ducts; the other, double as long but much narrower portion, bends forwards as far as the commencement of the sperm bladder, re-bends back to the anus, and then passes into the penis, having reached the spot of its first geniculation. The penis, or rather its exterior case, is united to this first knee by means of a muscle.

We are as yet unacquainted with other remarkable or peculiar forms.

B. External Organs of Generation.

§ 152.

THE PENIS.

Having already perceived a great variety of form in the female external organs of generation, we might expect to find this still more extensively the case in the male organs, had their parts been as widely investigated and described. But that which does not invite close inspection by its exterior or the problematical nature of its form, but much rather withdraws itself from the eye of the inquirer, and is concealed upon a first superficial examination, does not so easily excite curiosity and stimulate the desire for instruction, because it is not supposed to exist. This is the reason why the structure of the penis has been made less frequently the subject of description than the female ovipositor, although possibly there is no other so variously formed an organ, nor one subjected to such characteristic and generic differences.

The PENIS of beetles consists essentially of two parts, namely, of the exterior horny case analogous to the bone in the penis of the dog, and the internal delicate membranous penis itself, which admits of being considered the free ductus ejaculatorius. The exterior sheath alone is visible upon a first examination, as it entirely covers the internal tube and allows it only at its apex, where it is divided a little, to project. This sheath is clothed, either entirely or partially, by a delicate membrane (the *præputium*), which may be considered as a continuation of the inner membrane forming the cloaca. This membrane has also sometimes horny ridges to support it. Thus much upon the penis in general; more will be derived from the following particular description of it in individual insects.

In *Carabus* (*C. glabratus*, Fabr., Pl. XXV. f. 1—4.), in which the withdrawn penis extends to the commencement of the thorax, the præputium extends only to the end of the fourth segment (the last connate one counted as two); it is wide, bag-shaped, truncated at its extremity, and is supported by two fine bones, which have the same shape as the bag. At the base both bones lie closely together, but they with their shanks so separate that the two shanks of the upper one pass to the upper valve of the cloaca, and those of the lower one to its lower valve. The basal portion of the penis projects beyond the upper portion of the bag, driving this before it, so that it is covered by a continuation of it. Besides, the sides of the bones stand in close connection with the exterior integument by means of muscles, which hold the prepuce back when the penis is pushed forward. Three horny pieces are also found in the case of the bag, one heart-shaped one beneath, exactly between the shanks of the bone, and the two others at the apex of the upper portion which clothes the free part of the penis. There are likewise bony processes which support the case of the produced part of the bag, and stand in flexible connection with the horny sheath of the penis. The apex of the produced portion of the bag is divided where the upper end of the penis lies, and through this aperture the ductus ejaculatorius seminis passes into the latter.

The penis itself is a gently bent, horny cylinder, above round, distended towards its end, and flattened with obliquely truncated extremities; upon its lower or ventral side it has a longitudinal aperture, which is surrounded by a callous margin, which indicates the outlet of the ductus ejaculatorius.

Dyticus (Pl. XXV. f. 5—10.) displays already important differences. The two valves which form the cloaca are much larger, the upper one is soft and ovate, the lower one harder, larger, and longitudinally divided into two lobes. Both lobes are placed upon a transverse horny piece, one wing of which encompasses the exterior margin of each lobe, and is bound to it as well as to the ventral plate by strong muscles. The prepuce of the penis lies between these two valves, which, as in *Carabus*, is a membranous bag, but the horny bones of which are differently formed, and display stronger muscular connections. The prepuce itself is held distended by two horny pieces. A broad horny arch, shaped to the bag, surrounds its whole circumference, but lies lower down, so that the withdrawn penis projects beyond it; the upper margin of this horny arch is somewhat reflected, and forms two processes, to which muscles are attached that assist to push the penis forward (Pl. XXV. f. 7. *a, a*). The second flat longitudinal horny piece lies in the lower part of the bag between the shanks of the arch (Pl. XXV. f. 6. *b*). If the prepuce be opened we first meet with the horny sheath of the penis, a bilobate organ gently bent from right to left, between the valves of which lies a similarly bent and pointed horny spine. Both valves are closely connected by membranes and muscles, and are themselves enclosed in a membranous sheath (Pl. XXV. f. 9. *a.*), which is withdrawn by means of a fine horny bone flattened at its end; it so lies between the prepuce and the penis that it retains the skin when the muscles push the penis forward. The valves of the penis are thickly beset, upon the bowed inner margin, with long setæ, which are placed in a close row, as is also the inner spine. This spine has, similarly to the above-described female ovipositor, an excavated channel, in which lies a fine lancet-shaped bristle; both are connected together by means of flexible skin and muscles, and between the bristle and the channel is the outlet of the ductus ejaculatorius. This spine therefore is the true penis, and the two valves are its case.

The penis of *Hydrophilus* (Pl. XXV. f. 11—14.) approaches very closely in many particulars to that of *Dyticus*. The prepuce here also is a truncated bag, from the upper surface of which the penis projects. In the lower part of the bag lies a broad, shovel-shaped, horny plate, from the margins of which on each side a bone originates, which form the lateral limits of the bag; upon the upper side, at the end, lies a triangular perforated valve, which forms also the superior valve of the anal aperture, and sends off two free lateral processes to the bone of the lower portion (*c, c*). The cloaca penetrates beneath this valve, and is separated from the penis merely by a fold of the prepuce. The penis itself consists of the bivalved sheath and the unequal spines lying between them. Upon the inferior side the valve borders upon a heart-shaped horny plate (G), which appears to form the support of the entire organ; its lateral margins turn upwards, and a coarse skin is attached to it, which closes the canal of the penis from above. The valves (E, E,) of the penis itself are pointed downwards, they are bent, concave, horny bones, which are internally filled by membrane and muscles, which unite to them the central spine of the penis. The most central spine (F. F,) is not bivalved, as in *Dyticus*, but a perfectly closed tube, at the under surface of which runs a narrow spatel-shaped horny bone, and there is a hair-shaped one at its superior surface; the aperture (x) is enclosed by two small horny arches.

In *Melolontha* the penis is only half covered by the prepuce; its case is posteriorly, particularly upon the upper surface, entirely horny, and distended like a bladder; two processes originate from it, which are nearly conical, somewhat sloping, and furnished anteriorly with a knob; these are contiguous beneath, and above they are united by a strong membrane: between them lies the membranous canal of the penis, which consists of several folds of the ductus ejaculatorius[*].

In *Callichroma moschatum* the prepuce is a thin cylindrical bag, which in front is obliquely truncated, and it terminates above with a triangular horny plate. At each of its lateral angles a bone originates, which inclining forwards proceeds beneath to unite itself there with the corresponding one of the other side, forming a perfectly horse-shoe-shaped arch. The case of the penis, which is similarly shaped, lies entirely enclosed within this prepuce; it is likewise more membranous, but terminates in front with two horny valves, the broader and lower one of which entirely embraces the narrower superior one upon the lateral margin, and sends forward two flat processes into the skin of the case. The membranous canal of the penis lies within this case, as a continuation of the ductus ejaculatorius (Pl. XXVI. f. 1 and 2.).

Among the *Orthoptera* we find in *Blatta* the penis perfectly unsymmetrical. The sexual organs are only visible upon the removal of the dorsal plate, for they lie concealed between the two last ventral plates, and are protected on each side by the short, jointed processes; we then observe a triangular irregular valve (Pl. XXVI. f. 17, 18. a), which covers the passage to the sexual aperture from above, and contiguously, two other, likewise unequal, bags (the same, b and c), which protect the sides, and lastly, beneath, a hook bent upwards obliquely over these parts (the same, d, d). Upon closer examination the superior valve displays itself as a triangular membranous lobe supported by several horny pieces, at the anterior apex of which there is placed a stiff horny hook, which is curved backwards (Pl. XXVI. f. 5). The inferior valve, standing opposite to this superior one, is a flat horny plate (f. 6. a), with which laterally the right dorsal valve which bends upwards (f. 6. b) is united by means of a flexible membrane. The yet remain-

---

[*] See Straus, as above, Pl. III. f. 5., Pl. V. f. 1—3., and Pl. VI. f. 1.

ing portion of the visible sexual organs is the penis (f. 7), consisting of a superior sheath formed by two horny pieces, which are united by a membrane (f. 7. *a*,) and the central unequal upwardly bent spine, which is furnished at its extremity with a barb (f. 7. *b*.).

The comparison of this organ with that described in the *Coleoptera* has therefore now no further difficulty; the superior and inferior valves are the case of the penis, here indeed entirely transformed, which is united by the withdrawn prepuce to the surrounding parts; the penis itself lies formed in it, at least in situation, just as we have described it in *Dyticus* and *Hydrophilus*.

In the *Hymenoptera* I shall first describe the penis of the saw-flies. When in a *Cimbex* the last ventral and dorsal plates are removed, upon the dorsal side we immediately meet with the flexible anal valve, beneath which the anus lies, and then with a fold of the prepuce, which separates the anus from the sexual organs. These are entirely enveloped in the membranous prepuce, and consist of two large hooked horny bodies, which are united at their base by a flexible membrane; between these likewise lie the bivalved flexible penis, in which, precisely as in the female saw-flies, the central bone is wanting. The particular form of each single joint is shown in the figures 8—10. of Plate XXVI. The exterior valve consists of two joints (f. 8 and 10. *a*, *b*), the upper one of which is small, triangular, somewhat arched, and membranous; the lower one is larger, and consists of strong horn. Between these lie the broad lobate valves surrounded by a horny ring (f. 8 and 10. *c*, *c*), from which the canal of the penis (f. 10. *d*.) is continued.

In *Vespa*, where we find almost the same parts, we immediately detect an important difference, which is, that the central unequal spine of the penis, or here rather the true penis itself, is present. Figures 11—13. of Pl. XXVI. show the male organs of *Vespa Germanica*. Two large round valves, to which above there is attached a small spinous process, form, as in *Cimbex*, the exterior case of the penis (f. 11. *a*, *a*). Between these exterior ones the inner ones lie (the same, *b*, *b*); these are smaller and more delicate organs, which embrace the penis, they are of the consistence of parchment, and distended at their end into a shovel shape. The penis itself is a delicate bent shovel, which, previous to its dilatation, is provided with two barbs (f. 13. *a*, *a*), and has upon its superior side a deep almost tubular channel, through which the semen is ejected.

The male organs of the *Lepidoptera* (for example, of *Deilephila Euphorbiæ*, Pl. XXVI. f. 14—17.) display two exterior horny valves densely covered with scales; these valves are attached to a projecting horny ridge upon the circumference of the sexual organs (f. 14. *a, a*). Beneath these exterior valves there are two interior finer, pergamentaceous, and delicately haired ones, which, as well as the exterior ones, correspond together at their internal margin, and on their external margin they stand free. Each runs upwards in a sharp fine hook, and has beneath also, contiguously to it, a membranous process, which partially covers the penis (fig. 15. displays this inner valve from the inside). The penis lies between these inner valves; it is a pergamentaceous somewhat bent tube, which is open and emarginate in front (f. 15 and 17.). Upon the upper side, opposite the valves, there is a strong, bent, conical hook, which has anteriorly two points, an exterior one which bends inwards, and an interior one which bends outwards, and between the points a conical membranous process projects, which is also perforated (f. 14. *c*), and forms the anal tube. Both organs, the former internal valves supplied with a hook, and these hooks standing opposed to it, serve, without doubt, to retain the female organs during copulation.

The male sexual organs of the *Diptera* have, in the majority of cases, been noticed and figured by Meigen in his monograph of this order*; we can therefore give a more comprehensive description of them than of the preceding ones.

We everywhere find exterior, and even often interior valves, and between these the penis. The chief difference of this order is, that the male sexual organs in most instances project beyond the apex of the abdomen, and lie there exposed, which was not observed in the former ones. We thence find the prepuce, or rather that membranous bag which contains the withdrawn organs to be wanting in the *Diptera*. The differences of the exterior valves is very great. In the family of the *Tipularia* I formerly described a new insect (*Nematocera nubeculosa*), which was distinguished by large projecting sexual organs †. Two thick, large, black, shining processes, each of which bears a small bright brown reflected appendage, form the exterior valves, and be-

---

* J. W. Meigen's Systematische Beschreibung der bekannten Europäischen, zweiflügligen Insekten, 6. B. mit Kupfern, 1818—32.

† Comp. Thon's Archiv. der Entomologie, vol. ii. p. 36. Pl. I. f. 13.

tween them lies the short tubular penis. A very similar structure is observed in the predacious flies, particularly *Laphria* and *Asilus*, yet the large cylinder is bound by membranes to the ventral side, in which shape it forms an actual bivalved sheath, and the exterior superior smaller appendage is wanting. The sexual organs are most striking in the *Empidodea* and *Dolichopodea*. In the former we observe at the last abdominal segment of the male two large orbicular sloping valves, which are fringed at their margin; between their lower edges there is a long, fine, upward bending bristle, which frequently lies completely concealed between the valves. This bristle, in which we detect above a fine channel, I consider as the penis, and the valves as its case. In the *Dolichopodea* the last segment of the abdomen, turned downwards towards the venter, forms the case, which is exteriorly convex but interiorly concave. The upper free space of this cavity is occupied by a horny bristle, which is so united by membrane to the case that it can open and shut its aperture. In the thus formed cavity of the capsule the penis lies. In front, attached to the capsule, there are two bent, thickly fringed lamellæ, completely resembling those of *Nematocera*. I am almost induced to consider them as the projecting inner valves, but they evidently serve as retaining organs. The anal aperture appears to lie at the base of these valves.

In the true flies (*Musca*, for example,) the sexual organs are placed at the ventral portion of the last abdominal segment, the ring of which is hook-shaped, and by this curve covers the organs in repose; contiguous to the apex of the hook there are two moveable, differently formed valves, the analogues of the exterior valves in *Dolichopus*, and in front lies the anal aperture; further towards the venter, about the middle of the hook, we find the sexual organs, likewise two either longer or shorter bent lobes, between which a simple, thicker, sometimes clavate process (the penis) is displayed. Occasionally we find, contiguously to the larger ones, two small triangular valves, which may be considered as the inner valves of the penis.

Among the *Hemiptera*, we discover in *Cercopis sanguinolenta*, both in the male and in the female, two valves at the apex of the abdomen, of which those of the male are considerably the smallest; when opened, we find at the base, between the exterior valves (Pl. XXVI. f. 18.), two smaller internal ones (f. 19. *a, a*), which are attached by articulation to two horny bones. Between these the penis rises, and is, like the ovipositor, a long, thin, setiform organ, which is not however, as in the female, bent from below upwards, but from above downwards, so that its apex is turned towards the venter. This point is broader than the upper part, and apparently armed with barbs; consequently, during copulation this spine of the penis must penetrate the ovipositor of the female if impregnation is to follow. This insertion, however, is only made possible by the hook-shaped bend of the penis, and much facilitated when the male sits upon the female. The *Cicada* actually thus copulate, but as their connection lasts long, and the constant weight of the male would be oppressive to the female, the male descends and sits by her side, when she reposes. In some genera of the *Cicada*, the pronotum of which is decorated with processes and excrescences, which project beyond the abdomen (*Combophora, Centrotus*), the first act of copulation can only take place in this position of both sexes by the side of each other, they have probably therefore a laterally bent penis for this purpose, thus adapted like the downward bent one of the preceding.

We must lastly notice the male sexual organs of the *Libellulæ*, as the erroneous opinion has long been held that they were not placed at the end of the abdomen, but at its base. This very naturally originated from the observation that the male flew about with the female, retaining her anal extremity by means of clasps affixed to the base of the abdomen, and at the same time held her in the neck by the valves of its tail, apparently occupied in copulation. But if we closely examine the economy of these insects we shall speedily observe that males fly at sitting females and rapidly copulate with them, like the flies. The preceding is merely an expression of mutual inclination which announces itself by the male suddenly seizing the female by the neck in the air, and thus flying off with her, whilst she, if willing to respond to this attention, bends up her anal end to the male, and allows herself to be there seized by the hooks lying at the base of the abdomen; but if not pleased with his caresses she does not bend her body up to him, but hangs it freely and unparticipant downwards, and remains like a prisoner attached to his chain.

The following is an accurate description of the male sexual organs, as well as of the prehensile organ at the base of the abdomen.

We observe in the ventral plate of the ninth abdominal segment an aperture closed by two valves (Pl. XI. No. 3. f. 9. *d*). If these valves are removed we detect a small, delicate, horny ring, which surrounds the aperture of a short membranous cylinder; this cylinder is the penis, and the anterior aperture the extremity of the ductus ejaculatorius. Hence the structure of the external sexual organ is as simple as that of the internal ones (comp. § 147. II. *a*. 1).

The prehensile organ which lies in the ventral plates of the second and third abdominal segments has, on the contrary, the following very complicated structure. In the first place it consists of three divisions (the same, 4 and 5. A, B, C), the two first of which are placed upon the second abdominal segment, which apparently, at least laterally, consists of two rings ; the third forms the ventral plate of the third abdominal segment. The foremost division (the same, f. 8.) consists of six horny pieces, two anterior triangular smaller ones (*a, a*), to which two broad, thin, sithe-shaped hooks, which are bent backwards, are attached (*c, c*), and the two posterior ones (*b, b*), which are harder and more horny, and distend about the middle of the upper edge into two dentate knobs. At *d* the anterior and posterior parts are jointed together (f. 5. represents them extended, f. 8. as bent), and in the centre, between the two pieces of the two sides, there remains a deep unoccupied cavity (f. 4). The second division (f. 4 and 5. B. and f. 7.) consists of two pieces. The larger basal piece, or the ventral plate of the second division of the second abdominal segment, is quadrate, provided at each angle with a small process, which unites it with the preceding and succeeding pieces. Its central surface is deeply excavated, but it rises on each side to a strong obtuse point directed forwards (f. 7. *a*), the posterior edge of which is thickly beset with bristles. Between the two points, consequently in the concave central groove, the second piece lies, which is a geniculated, strong, horny hook (f. 7. *b*) ; it is united to the first by a joint, and can, by means of muscles, be directed upwards or withdrawn within the groove. The third division (f. 4 and 5. c. f. 6.) is larger than the preceding, and appears as a bellied, anteriorly concave, horny knob (f. 6. *a*), which is entirely filled with muscles. These muscles serve to move the anterior hook-shaped appendage, which again consists of two parts, the large, bellied, double-pointed hook (f. 6. *b*), and the thin, cylindrical, double-jointed pedicle (f. 6. *c, c*) ; this hook, in repose, lies in the anterior excavation of the horny bladder (f. 6. *d*), but when raised it stands free upon the two-jointed pedicle. A long, thick, pointed, horny bone proceeds backwards from the horny bladder, and it is this which forms the ventral plate of the third abdominal segment (f. 4 and 5. c. *e, e*.).

But this entire prehensile organ is only seen when the reflected margins of the dorsal plate are bent backwards; it is therefore entirely covered in dry specimens by these margins. Males may be detected in dry specimens by their above thick and clavate abdomen and the larger anal fangs.

III. Development of the Sexual Organs during the Metamorphosis.

§. 153.

It is evident, from Herold's * admirable investigation, that even in the larva the germ of the future sexual organ exists, and indeed with the distinctions of male and female. The larvæ are born with these extremely small and almost invisible germs, which develope themselves in the course of its life, but most rapidly in its pupa state, until they attain their perfect development upon the full growth of the insect.

If a caterpillar be opened from the back we observe, after the removal of the fatty substance, upon the intestinal canal, at the posterior extremity of the large stomach, two small roundish or ovate bodies, from which posteriorly two filaments originate, which unite into one canal close to the anus, beneath the rectum. But these filaments are so fine, or become so in their progress, that they almost entirely disappear, and could not be followed to their termination by even the exact Lyonnet. If several larvæ, of different sizes and of different ages, be opened, we soon detect differences in these bodies, for some (in *Pontia brassicæ*) are more cylindrical, and are divided by constrictions into four successive vesicles; the others are flatter, subsequently ovate, and by constrictions from the apex to the base divided into four equal lobes. In the first instance they were small testes, and in the last the preformed egg-bags or ovaries. This form remains unchanged until the pupa state, merely increasing considerably in size.

In the pupa state the convoluted sperm ducts, and in the female the gluten glands and ovaries, gradually develope themselves. In *Pontia Brassicæ*, upon which insect Herold made his observations, the testes gradually approach each other until they lie contiguously. From this common situation a closer connection is formed, the sides press each other flat, and by degrees intimately join together. Thus, from the earlier separate four-chambered testes a simple globose testis is formed,

---

* Entwickelungsgeschichte der Schmetterlinge. Kapel and Marburg, 1815, 4to. with plates.

which, however, probably still consists of two divisions. From the two hemispheres two delicate canals originate, which, after many convolutions, unite into a thicker but frequently twisted duct; closely in front of this point of union there hangs attached to the sperm duct a simple, long, twisted vessel, the gluten gland. The development of the female organs displays itself most conspicuously in the enlargement of the ovaries. They increase at the expense of the egg canal, which by degrees disappears, whereas the egg bags become continually longer, and twist themselves up spirally from the apex. The point of union of the very short oviducts distends, and sends off on one side a pointed bag, the spermatheca; opposite this a smaller vesicle is formed with a longer, vascular, much twisted appendage: farther below, near the vagina, there hang also vascular, long, and much convoluted gluten glands. Both distend prior to their emptying themselves, and perforate the vagina at one spot close to each other.

This is an abbreviation of the description of all the changes made during the pupa state. In the caterpillar there were simple bodies with simple delicate canals, these pass over unchanged in form into the pupa, and undergo by degrees changes the results of which are the lastly completed structure which we have here briefly indicated.

It is to be regretted that similar observations have not been made in several insects, and although they would probably present the same results, many attractive details worthy of observation might be produced. This refers particularly to insects with an imperfect metamorphosis. We may ask does the transformation of the sexual organs take the same course, and the bodies present at the birth of the larva merely enlarge, and only when the pupa displays the rudiments of wings undergo a general change of form? If we refer to the development of the intestinal canal, which has, from the commencement, its perfect form, we might feel inclined to adopt the same view of the sexual organs: we must confess that this view appears the most natural, because in insects with an imperfect metamorphosis the pupa state appears to be of infinitely less importance, and that consequently the changes in structure cannot be so great as there where the pupa sleep steps in so abruptly between the preceding and succeeding active periods. And may not possibly the lesser degree of importance which the pupa state possesses in insects with an imperfect metamorphosis be the consequence of their smaller change in the form and structure of their organs? Could not, therefore, as the change of the internal organs is significantly less, and is indeed limited almost to the mere enlargement of the parts with their retained relative proportions, the change also of the exterior form almost entirely disappear, and the whole metamorphosis be restricted to a mere increase of size? Truly both phenomena are dependent upon the same law, neither eventually conditionates the other, but must proceed from the similar results of one cause, which evidently lies deeply concealed in the mode of development of the *Articulata* in general, so that where the one displays itself the other must also be present and both synchronical, neither the latter before the former nor the former before the latter.

IV. CONFORMITY OF THE FEMALE AND MALE SEXUAL ORGANS.

§ 154.

At their origin both kinds of sexual organs, as we have seen above, appear under the same form. This same conformity, displayed at the origin of the internal parts, is also subsequently verified in their fully developed state. This law we laid down at first (§ 131), for both systems have the same object, viz. the elaboration of the productive fluid. In the female it is the OVARIES where this fluid is prepared, and in the male we call the same organ the TESTES. Very similar ducts originate from these organs, and afterwards unite and conduct by a single narrower canal their contents outwards. This conformity of importance in the internal parts is still more strongly proved by their forms frequently agreeing. Long cylindrical testes correspond with long ovaries filled with the germs of eggs (*Libellulæ*); ramose bunched testes with similarly formed fasciculated ovaries (*Locusta, Gryllotalpa*); compound, radiating, and united testes with similar radiating or twirling ovaries (*Lamellicornia*); indeed, sometimes the number of the single bodies in the testes agrees with the number of the egg tubes (*Melolontha, Trichius*). It is very natural that the appendages should be differently formed, for their function is different; for example, the spermatheca of the female organs must necessarily be wanting in the male, for they receive no sperm, but only impart it: consequently the reciprocal conformity of the internal organs is so evident, that it is difficult to doubt it; but this is not the case with the exterior organs. In these no endeavour has yet been made to trace the parts of the one in the other sex. But if the descriptions be compared which we have given of the male and female external organs, it will escape no one that this analogy is not to be overlooked even here. The female vagina in every case consists as well as the male penis of horny bones and ridges, which are united together by a flexible membrane. If these horny bones project beyond the abdomen they form the aculeus, or ovipositor, which has in its entire structure the most striking resemblance to the penis. Exterior valves enclose in both organs an internal compound instrument, which is, as in the grasshoppers, where we observe the ovipositor, either connate with the exterior valve, or it remains separated, as in the bees, wasps, and other *Hymenoptera*. If the structure of such a sting be compared, for example, with the penis of *Dyticus*, we observe, even to their smallest parts, the greatest conformity; indeed, even the male sexual organs of the wasp agree both in number and situation of the individual parts wholly with the sting of the female. Henceforward, therefore, it may not appear hazardous to assert that the ovipositor, by its conformity in structure with the penis, is analogous to the clitoris of the superior animals. This view, which as far as I know is here propounded for the first time, may be liable to many objections, particularly by those who do not pass beyond forms, nor elevate themselves to general simplifying and retrogressive ideas; but they who study natural bodies in conjunction with others furnished merely as orismological auxiliaries, and who are not merely acquainted with ten thousand species, but endeavour also to discover the general results of their various vital phenomena, will here discover a not wholly unimportant contribution to the solution of this great problem.

We have above shown that the jointed ovipositor is no peculiar organ belonging only to the sexual ones, but rather the mere apex of the abdomen; its divaricating in form therefore cannot be cited as a proof against the opinion that the ovipositor is a transformed clitoris.

SECOND SUBSECTION.

THE ANIMAL ORGANS.

§ 155.

The animal organs forming the systems of sensation and of motion no longer display a vegetable, but strictly a peculiar, purely animal character. We have before seen (§ 91.) that the intestinal canal, the vessels, and the sexual organs are mere repetitions of vegetable structure, in as far as they consist, like plants, of cells, tubes, and thin membranes. But we will now show that these aboriginal forms of structure are not found in the animal organs.

§ 156.

The characteristic of the animal organs is rigidity and solidity. The entire organ is throughout of one structure, and consists of one substance, which, indeed, still frequently is encircled and enveloped by vegetable forms, as for example, the nerves by thin membranes, but these constitute no essential component of the peculiar mass, but serve only as its exterior case or covering.

If we examine the muscular system with this view we detect solid fibres, which lie closely contiguous to each other, forming by degrees larger bundles, that unite into an entire muscle. Even the nicest microscopal investigation detects no cavity in the individual fibres, but a solid uniform mass throughout. Each solitary fibre therefore is entire in itself, which, indeed, upon close examination, appears divided by transverse partitions, and thus seems composed of cells, but in fact it is not so. But we therein see the difference between the vegetable and animal organs, the former growing into an individual organ from the aggregation of consecutive vesicles or cells, and the latter from the union of solid globules. The animal organs, therefore, originate in the following manner; it is not cells added to cells, but globules, animal atoms, as some naturalists express themselves, to globules; a row of such globules form a solid fibre, several fibres the bundle, and several of these a muscle or nervous cord.

§ 157.

The nerves consist of filaments formed of consecutive globules, which are enclosed by delicate membranes, the nervous sheath (*neurilema*). These globules are originally very loosely connected, and the nervous filament then appears as a delicate tube, which encloses a finely granulated pappy mass. The first commencement of the nerves is found thus formed, as well in the embryo of the superior animals, as also in all the inferior ones; and whilst the latter constantly retain this original grade of organisation, the nervous cord in the former works itself on in the progress of development to a firm filament. Several of such little filaments form the thicker nervous thread, and several of these the nervous cord. Where such threads or cords anastomose, meet, or cross each other, the nervous mass distends and forms knots or ganglions. That which we call the brain (*cerebrum*), which lies in the head, is the largest and most perfect of these ganglia, and indeed composed of various other smaller ones, and in its most perfect state of organisation it is even furnished with internal cavities. It is there first found where a head is first distinctly separated from the body. In all animals without a head there is no brain, but their nerves originate from a nervous ring encompassing the pharynx, which here represents the central organ of the nervous system, whilst the brain, where it is developed, gradually draws this ring to it.

THIRD CHAPTER.

OF THE ORGANS OF MOTION.

§ 158.

THE organs of motion fall into two different sub-systems, namely, the ACTIVE or muscles, and the PASSIVE. The passive organs of motion are, according to the different groups, subject to great changes, and only in the higher grades of animal development do they become a distinct system, namely, as bones, whereas beneath the grade of the *Vertebrata*, they by degrees disappear, and only here and there, for example, in the *Sepia*, the *Echinus*, and some of the *Mollusca*, viz. the *Terebratula*, we observe more or less important precursory formations. In general, in the *Invertebrata*, the exterior integument supplies the place of the passive organs of motion, and this is especially the case in the *Articulata*. In the *Crustacea* and *Insecta*, by their solidity in the latter, and their quantity of calcareous matter in the former, they imitate the structure of the true bones, and send off processes into the cavities they form, which serve for the insertion of muscles, and in every respect appear as a skeleton removed to the exterior. As such we shall also consider and describe them. But it must nevertheless not be overlooked, that the integument, as a continuation of the intestinal canal, and, as it were, a re-fold of it, belongs properly to the vegetative organs, and will in its structure present us with many accordances with it.

I. OF THE HORNY SKELETON.

§ 159.

The exterior of insects displays itself to us as a horny case, which is sometimes firm and brittle, and sometimes soft and flexible, and in this last consistence it takes the appearance of a leathery skin. This case acquires its greatest consistency and strength in the beetles, especially in their elytra, which wholly consist of it: we find it very soft and thoroughly membranous in many of the *Diptera*, in most of the parasitic insects, and in almost all larvæ, particularly in the orders with an imperfect metamorphosis. Also at first, when the developed head quits the pupa case, the horny integument is in all equally soft, flexible, thicker and more fleshy, and even colourless; but after a few hours it attains firmness, and gradually hardens in the course of a few days to a rigid coat of mail, in which the insect is clothed. This change of the integument takes place chiefly under the influence of the solar light; the colours particularly are brought out by its impulse. For as plants which grow in the dark take a pale or light yellow colour, insects also retain this their original colour as long as they are withheld from the effects of the light of the sun. Thence also is it that the majority of larvæ which live in the earth, or in dark shady places to which the light of day cannot approach, are generally pale or colourless, and it is thence also that even perfect insects remain paler if they cannot, immediately after quitting the pupa case, get into the light. From the same cause the many pale yellow and particularly red-legged varieties proceeds which we find in vast numbers of truly black or dark brown insects. We must not, however, wholly attribute the darker colouring solely to the effect of light; the increase of the pigment during the development contributes much to it; indeed in some, namely, such insects whose legs remain of a bright red whilst the remainder of their body is entirely coloured, it may be caused by the original deficiency of the pigment. The effect, nevertheless, of the solar light is incontestable, particularly in the colouring of larvæ, for they are always variegated, when from the very commencement of their life they have been exposed to the influence of light, as is the case, for example, in the caterpillars of the *Lepidoptera*. Also, from variegated or coloured larvæ, beautiful insects appear to proceed, whereas, from dull-coloured ones, or pale or brown, and more or less uniform coloured ones, brown or black insects. But the influence of climate is great upon colour, and, as is the case in birds, we find the most beautiful and gayest colours in tropical climates, whereas, the farther they recede from the equator, the darker or blacker they become.

§ 160.

In structure, the horny case displays considerable conformity with the skin in general, as it, like the latter, consists of three layers.

The exterior and finest layer, the epidermis, is smooth, shining, and without any traces of texture. It admits of being pretty easily separated from the coloured mucous rete lying beneath it, particularly in recently developed insects which have been preserved in spirits of wine, and is, in the majority of cases, colourless, sometimes, too, even brown, and but rarely black, if the mucous layer be black. Uncoloured, as it is in general, it is transparent and perforated all over with small holes, through which hairs rise when the surface is hirsute.

Beneath this delicate epidermis we find the soft rete mucosum. According to Straus it consists of two layers, of which the superior smooth one is closely attached to the epidermis, and this alone appears coloured. It is here we find the cause of the glittering, brilliant colours with which many insects are so beautifully decorated. In the butterflies and many others, namely, those with membranous wings, it is brown or black, as also in all black insects. The variegated colours of these do not therefore proceed from the rete mucosum, but from the hairs clothing the surface. In spirits of wine it readily dissolves, and thereby distinguishes itself from the second layer, which is not affected by this fluid, and is uniformly black or brown*. This second layer is always covered by the first, and participates no otherwise in the colouring than by its darkness or depth adding to the intensity of the colour above it. In bright yellow, red, or white-coloured spots, it passes over naturally into this lighter colour.

The third and thickest layer of the general integument, the true leathery tunic (*corium*), betrays itself by its want of colour and peculiar structure. It consists, namely, of several layers of crossing fibres, which form a light web, which, upon a careful investigation, again admit of separating into several stratifications. Straus sometimes distinguished three, at others five, such strata. In the elytra of beetles (for example, *Dyticus, Hydrophilus*), there are delicate canals between these layers, in which the formative juice seems to flow, when the still small and short elytra of a just-developed beetle distend themselves; it is also in this leathery skin that the bulbs lie which surround the roots of the hair. It is from this skin that the roots of the hair derive their nutriment. A perforated point, many of which are displayed upon the surface of a multitude of insects, is a partial deficiency of this leathery skin. The epidermis and mucous rete consequently sink down, and thus a hollow is formed upon the surface. At the same time, the sinking of the harder epidermis forms a point to which the layers of the corium are attached; thence is it that the points stand generally in rows between two fibres of the corium, for example, the three rows of punctures in the large water beetles. (*Dyticus marginalis*, &c.)

§ 161.

We must consider the spines, hairs, and scales which cover the surface of many insects, as portions of the integument, and, as it were, partially separated parts. All three are like the horny substances of the higher animals, for example, the claws and nails, not processes of

---

* According to Straus, p. 16. But if the brightly-coloured layer dissolves in spirits of wine, how is it that so many insects, namely, the blue metallic or æneous ones, retain their colour in this fluid, and only some red or yellow ones lose it?

all three layers of the integument, but merely of the epidermis: they are thickenings, and also often folds of this cuticle, between which a coloured mucous has inserted itself. The corium is wholly wanting in these excrescences. They are divided according to their form, and the mode of their connection with the integument, into three different groups.

1. SPINES differ from the following kinds by their wanting a true root. They are therefore nothing else than pointed, spinous, conical or hair-shaped processes, which rise from the surface, and correspond with it in colour and clothing. As a clear proof that they are mere processes of the epidermis, or, when they appear more bossed (as in the great horns of the *Lamellicornia*), that they are true elevations of the entire integument, is evinced by the circumstance that they produce a hole in the horny substance exactly of their own dimensions when broken off. These spines are not always simple, they are frequently ramose, furcated, &c., as is observed in many of the caterpillars of the butterflies.

2. HAIRS are distinguished from spines in the first place by their greater fineness and lesser compass, in combination with their proportionately greater length, and again by the root by which they are attached to the true skin. The hairs themselves are fine horny cylinders, which frequently split and divide themselves like feathers, and send off branches, thus acquiring a resemblance to the feathers of birds. In general, they are largest in compass at their centre, and become narrower towards both ends: the lower one is somewhat puffed out, and has a small knob which sticks in the corium like a bulb in the earth, and this is surrounded by a thin shell, exactly as is the case in the large beard bristles of the mammalia.

3. The SCALES are properly flattened hairs: this is shown not only by their gradual transition from linear to lanceolate and spatulate forms, but also their exactly similar connection with the integument. Each scale, namely, has a small pedicle, at the end of which the knobby root is placed, and this with its sheath is inserted in the skin. The scale itself is either round, pointed, forked, toothed like a saw in front, and provided with longitudinal furrows upon its superficies. Even this delicate and sometimes extremely fine membranous excrescence consists of two layers of the epidermis, between which the pigment has inserted itself. In the iridescent butterflies (*Apatura Iris, A. Ilia, Papilio Adonis, Menelaus, &c.*), the scales of the wings

play into a multitude of shades of colour, which proceeds, according to Roesel*, from their peculiar structure. For whilst the surface of the scales in the majority is flat, there are in these sharp parallel ridges just as if small prisms were affixed to their surface. These prisms are all upon one side of a metallic blue, and on the other side brown, and thus according to the position of the butterfly or of the observer, either the brown or blue side is seen †.

§ 162.

With respect to the chemical composition of the common integument, it agrees in general with that of horn, but nevertheless distinguishes itself by some peculiarities of proportion, which may probably arise from its being formed, by not merely the epidermis alone, but by the entire cutis.

All true horny substances consist essentially of azote (10. 2—12. 3), carbon (43. 0—53. 7), hydrogen (7. 3—2. 8), and oxygen (29. 3—31. 2). In nitric acid it is dissolved, as also in a heated solution of potass or natron; muriatic acid, on the contrary, is coloured only by degrees. Boiling water somewhat distends horn, but a continued boiling in closed vessels (Papin's digester) will nearly entirely dissolve it. Dry distillation developes ammonia in combination with carbonic acid, as well as other hydrocarbonates, and a peculiar stinking oil, besides which other burnt matter remains which is no further changeable.

The horny case of insects has as externally, a uniform consistency, so also internally, the same constituents; but it nevertheless distinguishes itself by the admixture of a peculiar substance, viz. chitine or entomeilin, as well as by small portions of phosphate of lime and magnesia. The peculiar character of chitine is its insolubility in caustic potass. Exhibited separately, which is very easy by means of treating horny parts in a solution of potass, it appears as an almost colourless transparent substance, which becomes brown in nitric acid, and in the dry distillation produces no carbonate of ammonia, and therefore appears to contain no azote, and it burns in fire

* Insektenbelustigungen, vol. iii. p. 254. Pl. XLIV. f. 5—8.

† This supposition of Roesel's is erroneous; the change of colour arises from the reflection of the light, the same as in the buds of the Iris. The scales are merely longitudinally striated.—*Author's MS. Note.*

without previously melting, but it is soluble in boiling or heated sulphuric acid.

Besides the above, small portions of albumen, a peculiar brown colouring matter which dissolves in caustic potass, but not in boiling alcohol, as well as traces of phosphate of iron, have been found in the horny integument of insects, upon different analyses. The albumen belongs doubtlessly to the third tunic, as does the brown colouring matter to the mucous rete: to this also we attribute the chitine, whereby the true horny skin, namely, the epidermis, will be found to agree entirely with the horns of the higher animals[*].

§ 163.

After this general inspection of the horny skeleton, we arrive at the different parts of which it is composed. As we have already, in the first section, in stating the orismological definitions of the insect body, sufficiently exhibited its structure and explained its composition of different pieces, we may here proceed more briefly, and merely add the description of those parts which escape the observer upon an exterior orismological examination. It will suffice then to repeat that the entire body of the insect consists of HEAD, THORAX, ABDOMEN, and the limbs, namely, SIX FEET and TWO or FOUR WINGS.

The HEAD exhibits itself as a single horny bladder with an anterior and posterior aperture. The anterior one is closed by the cibarial organs, and by the posterior one it stands in connection with that of the thorax.

The THORAX consists of three divisions. The first or PROTHORAX has two or four horny plates; the DORSAL PLATE (*pronotum*); the BREAST PLATE (*prosternum*), and the SHOULDER PLATES (*omia*).

The second or MESOTHORAX exhibits four, six, or seven plates. The simple DORSAL PLATE (*mesonotum*); the sometimes simple, sometimes divided BREAST PLATE (*mesosternum*), and the two, also sometimes simple, or likewise divided SHOULDER PLATES (*scapulæ*). In many orders (*Diptera*, *Hymenoptera*), the three or six last are connate, and form ONE ring.

The third or METATHORAX has, like the middle one, either two,

[*] Compare Aug. Odier Mém. sur la Composition Chemique des parties Cornées des Insectes, in Mém. de la Soc. d' Hist. Natur. de Paris. Par. 1823. T. i. p. 29, Straus Durckheim, p. 32, and Mr. Children in Zoological Journal, vol. i. 111—115.

four, six, or seven different plates. Above, in the centre, is the third DORSAL PLATE (*metanotum*); opposite to it on the breast, the simple or divided third BREAST PLATE (*metasternum*); between the two, the SIDE PLATES (*pleuræ*), and AUXILIARY SIDE PLATES (*parapleuræ*), sometimes separated, or either united together, or with the pectoral plates.

This is the result of the investigations there instituted upon the thorax: it now remains for us to inspect the cavities formed by these plates, from the interior; perhaps, also, from this point of view we may discover some peculiarities.

§ 164.

INTERNAL SKELETON OF THE HEAD.

In the *Hemiptera* and *Diptera*, the head is a mere horny bladder without any internal processes or bones for the insertion of muscles. The same is the case in the head of the *Lepidoptera*, but the occipital aperture is divided by a transverse bar into two holes, the under one of which is the smallest, and admits only the nervous cord through it; through the upper one pass the pharynx, vessels, tracheæ, and muscles. These parts are not found in the *Hymenoptera*, but, on the contrary, a broad ridge springing upwards from the lower margin of the occipital aperture, which is prolonged towards the frons in two points, and divides the upper portion of the head from the under. The *Libellulæ* among the *Neuroptera* exhibit the former division of the occipital aperture into an upper and under one; they have also several ledges in the head, which spring from the anterior margins of the eyes, and divide the large eyes from the brain, and this again from the frons. In the *Orthoptera*, we again find the separation of the aperture into an upper and under one. On each side, contiguous to that cavity, there springs a process; both unite in an arch, forming a narrow cover, which is attached in front to the frons by means of two other processes. I call this cover the *tentorium*, because, as in the higher animals, for example, *Felis*, beneath it lies the cerebellum of insects, or the second ganglion of the nervous system, from which the mandibular and labial nerves originate. Over it runs the pharynx, and above it lies the first ganglion or the cerebrum. In the cavity of the head of beetles we do not find the tentorium in the shape just described, but as two high ledges originating from the throat and the lower margin of the occipital aperture, between which lies the cerebellum, and it is covered only by the pharynx. Sometimes (*Dyticus*) the pharynx rests upon a bar, connecting both ledges, and then the cerebellum lies beneath it, and further forward, but the nervous cord runs between the ledges. Contiguous to the occipital aperture two small hooks spring from the ledge, which encompass the nervous cord, and other longer fine branches of them project forwards towards the front, which they do not reach, but bend upwards, and serve for the insertion of small muscles, which retain the pharynx, running between these branches. This frame-work is larger or smaller according to the development of the cibarial apparatus, consequently most distinct in the predaceous beetles with large oral organs.

§ 165.

INTERNAL SKELETON OF THE THORAX.

In the structure of the thorax, the *Hemiptera*, *Orthoptera*, *Neuroptera*, and *Coleoptera* accord better together, from their prothorax being more distinctly separated than in the other orders, in which the entire thorax forms but one whole. This last structure is certainly the most simple, and we will therefore commence with its inspection.

Upon paying some attention in the examination of the thorax of a fly, bee, or butterfly, the important preponderance of the mesothorax cannot escape immediate observation. The central dorsal plate occupies the entire dorsal surface, whereas the anterior one forms but a ring (collar), and the posterior one also is not much more developed, and, indeed, in flies and butterflies is entirely covered by the scutellum, (compare Pl. XIV. No. 1. f. 2. and No. 2. f. 2.).

The internal skeleton of this simple thorax is very unimportant in the *Diptera*. Where we observe furrows on the exterior there are internal ridges which correspond, and which surround the muscles at their insertion, and separate them from each other. Audouin calls those projecting ridges, which are also generally found where two separate parts join together, *Apodemes*, APODEMATA, and those to which muscles are attached *Apodemata insertionis*. The largest of all these ridges is Kirby and Spence's METAPHRAGMA, a thin, pergamentaceous partition, which, descending from the superior margin of the metathorax, arches itself convexly outwards towards the abdomen, and thus separates the entire cavity of the thorax from that of the abdomen. Beneath this partition, namely, at the pectoral side, a lunate space remains free, through which the internal organs pass from the thorax into the abdomen. Besides this most important position of the internal skeleton of flies, we find, in the neighbourhood of where the wings are attached, other horny arches, which serve for the insertion of the alary muscles. In front also of the larger partition the scutellum sends into the cavity of the thorax a small ridge, which is however as unimportant as the other is important. The dorsal muscles ascend obliquely through the thorax from the great partition to the mesonotum, and thus hold the whole structure together.

In the *Lepidoptera*, which in the structure of their thorax have most resemblance to the *Diptera*, the conformation is already somewhat more complicated. In this both agree that everywhere where there are exterior furrows we find corresponding interior ridges which separate the points of insertion of the muscles, and thus increase their firm adhesion. Such a ridge rises from the centre of the mesonotum, which passes to the scutellum, and there unites with the ridge that separates the scutellum from the mesonotum. From the posterior margin of the scutellum a broad partition (the mesophragma of Kirby and Spence) descends, it bends first backwards and then forwards, and thus forms a hook, to which the large dorsal muscles are attached. This partition is analogous to the ridge of the scutellum in the *Diptera*. The third very narrow thoracic segment leans against it, forming also a posterior partition, which, however, is much more delicate and fine than the first; consequently the relations of both the partitions, in comparison with those described in the *Diptera*, are changed, here the first is the largest, and there the second. The pectoral side of the thorax exhibits a central projecting ridge as the line of separation between the coxæ and other smaller ones corresponding with the exterior furrows.

The *Hymenoptera* make the direct passage from the forms already described to those in which the prothorax is separated. The exterior furrows of their thorax are true sutures, in which their parts are joined. This has been already sufficiently explained above (§ 74—78.), and it is there shown that the collare is the true prothorax of the *Hymenoptera*; we will therefore here proceed with the internal processes. In the prothorax there are two strong pointed processes (Pl. XII. No. I. f. 4. *a, a*), each of which has a double root; one exterior one comes from the margin of the prosternum, and an interior one from the central ridge of the same part; between these roots the muscles of the coxæ pass, and between the processes themselves run the pharynx and the nervous cord, and it is to these processes that the connecting muscles of the pronotum and prosternum are attached. In the mesothorax we first find the prophragma (the same, 3. *a*), a small, not very high, horny partition, which descends from the anterior margin of the mesonotum, and we next find a delicate ridge which encompasses the whole distinctly separated mesonotum. The mesosternum and scapulæ are closely joined in a half ring, and from the central carina of this ring springs a broad strong ledge, which at its upper margin is furnished on each side with a strong process (the same, 6. *a, a*); they form with the ledge a rectangular cross, and serve as points of insertion for the muscles of the coxæ of the middle legs, lying on each side contiguously to the central ridge. In *Cimbex* the cross is very distinct, in *Scolia* it is merely a ridge, somewhat distended above. The metathorax of the *Hymenoptera* is more complicated than in the *Diptera* and *Lepidoptera*, because in them the abdomen is attached by only one small spot, namely, by the circumference of the aperture beneath the metaphragma, consequently there the metathorax encloses more powerful muscles than in the preceding orders. The metaphragma is therefore exposed, and appears, for example, in *Scolia*, as an equilateral triangle above the articulation with the abdomen, upon the very smooth apex of which the abdomen turns (Pl. XII. No. 2. f. 1). The apex itself is perforated, and admits a strong band through it, which retains the abdomen (Pl. XII. No. 2. f. 3*). In front of this triangle is placed the very narrow metanotum (the same, f. 1 and 2. F, F), and at its posterior margin a triangular process runs inwards (the same, f. 4* and 5*), to which the muscles retaining the abdomen are affixed. Between the metanotum and metaphragma the two large side pieces and their auxiliaries lie, separated from each other by furrows, from which internally strong ridges spring, and to which the muscles of the posterior legs are attached. In the saw-flies, which do not possess a petiolated abdomen, the pleuræ join together behind the metanotum (the same, No. 1. f. 1 and 2. H, H), and the metaphragma lies internally as a narrow margin of the metanotum, but the band is a semicircular tense membrane, which is distended by the pleuræ, and is very distinct in *Cimbex*.

Among the orders with a free prothorax the *Hemiptera* occupy the lowest place. The entire prothorax is a single, above very broad, beneath narrower ring, from the centre of the pectoral plate of which two horny arches spring, which pass over the cavities of the coxæ, and attach themselves to the sides of the pronotum. These arches serve for the insertion of the muscles of the coxæ. Two other spinous processes originate from the upper half of the ring yet more laterally, and bend down to the beforementioned arch, proceeding gradually further from the exterior case. In the very large mesothorax, anteriorly there is no prophragma, whereas posteriorly, beneath the scutellum, a very large mesophragma, which is longitudinally divided, the lower points of which unite with the arch, which, as in the prothorax, span themselves over the cavity of the intermediate coxæ. Other lateral ridges correspond with exterior furrows. The metathorax is again very narrow; it has no metaphragma, and no arch spanning the cavities of the coxæ, the muscles of which are attached to the mesophragma. This description is sketched from *Cicada fraxini*, Latr. In the bugs, which possess a much smaller, at least flatter, thorax, I found (namely, in *Pentatoma hæmorrhoidalis*,) traces of the horny arch, and a distinct metaphragma, which likewise, like the mesophragma of the *Cicada*, is divided, but at its centre diverges much more considerably, and is in intimate connection with the pleuræ.

The skeleton is much more perfect in the *Orthoptera*. Among them the grasshoppers occupy the lowest place. In the prothorax, the saddle-shaped pronotum of which encloses the entire part, we observe two bent, flat, but high processes, which originate from the exterior margin of the prosternum and rise to the pronotum. Two other processes spring from the middle between the cavities of the coxæ, and form in removing from each other two arches, which span those cavities. On the interior of each bow there is also frequently a smaller process, which bends to its opponent, and thus covers the nervous cord (Pl. XI. No. 2. f. 2. *a, a*). Both processes serve for the attachment of muscles, and the larger bow for those of the coxæ; from the smaller ones two narrow muscles spring, which ascend to the back and affix themselves to the margin of the dorsal piece. The same processes are found also in the second and third thoracic segments, which likewise form small arches, beneath which the nervous cord runs. Instead of the first named exterior ones from each pleura a strong hook-shaped carina runs, which separates the muscles of the legs and wings (the same, 6. *b, b*). The superior partitions, the meso- and metaphragma are small, and do not lie vertically but obliquely, whence the cavity of the thorax acquires much compass and wide avenues. The most perfect skeleton amongst the *Orthoptera* is found in the mole cricket (*Gryllotalpa vulgaris*). In the prothorax (Pl. XI. No. 1. f. 1—3), which is formed of a very large, hard, bellied pronotum (A) and a very narrow, small, keel-shaped prosternum (B), we observe a large horny partition (c), which descends from the central line of the pronotum and spreads forward in two furcating processes (E, E); to these processes two others attach themselves, which originate from the upper margin of the aperture of the neck, distend themselves in an arch downwards, and posteriorly, and thus encounter the fork of the central ridge. And thence where these processes join the furcate process the prosternum, which anteriorly is formed like a T, unites itself to them with its two branches, and thus closes the anterior aperture of the prothorax. Posteriorly two other processes originate from the central line (F, F), which descend downwards, bend there towards each other, and join the posterior extremity of the prosternum (*); at the same time each gives off a hook which is directed upwards and backwards, and between these a single horny bone lies (H), which stands in connection with them by means of muscles (* *), and upon which the large pharynx rests. Beneath this bone runs the nervous cord, encompassed by the posterior shanks of the central ridge. The skeleton of the meso- and metathorax is much smaller. Two processes descend from the scapulæ (Pl. XI. No. 1. f. 4 and 8. D, D.) and unite together beneath, at the central line of the mesosternum (the same, E). From the point of union there arises a short dagger-shaped process (the same, 5), which is barbed on each side at its base, and proceeds nearly to the end of the metasternum. This point is, as it were, the true breast-bone, to which the muscles are attached, and upon it the intestinal canal rests. From the anterior margin of the metanotum the small mesophragma originates, and which is perforated by a hole (the same, 7. *a*), through which the aorta passes, and besides there comes from the suture of the metasternum and the pleura a clavate ridge, prolonged internally at its anterior end into a pointed spine.

Some of the *Neuroptera* are very similar in structure to the grasshoppers, at least I found in the *Termites* just such horny arches upon each of the three thoracic segments as covers for the nervous cord, and horny ridges which separate the muscles from each other on the inner surface of the pleuræ.

The most perfect internal skeleton of all however is found in the

Coleoptera, although some portions of the thorax, namely, the prothorax, do not form so complex a frame as in *Gryllotalpa*.

The prothorax consists in the majority of beetles of two separated pieces, which, only in some capricorns (*Callichroma, Saperda,*) and all the *Rhynchophora*, are connate*. In *Carabus, Dyticus, Buprestis* there lies between both two other free pieces, which I have called omia, and which must be considered as the free lateral walls of the dorsal plate. The moveable spines in *Acrocinus longimanus* (Kirby and Spence's *Umbones*) are probably these same pieces, at least we can give no other explanation of these otherwise perplexing organs. The internal skeleton of the prothorax consists in a process originating from the prosternum between the cavities of the coxæ, which divides itself into two when those cavities are distant from each other (*Oryctes*). Above, this process has a tooth on each side, which bends towards the side of the prothorax, and sometimes unites with it (in *Hydrophilus*, Pl. X. No. 3. f. 6 and 7. *a*, *a*). It has frequently more or less the appearance of a fork, or the letter Y, and Kirby and Spence thence call it antefurca, a name which, notwithstanding its bad construction, does not suit, because this process does not always furcate, and is indeed wanting in many beetles, namely, in those with a simple prothorax. In such cases a partition between the cavities of the coxæ occupies its place. I call it, when present and of importance, the *processus internus prosterni*. The nervous cord passes between its branches.

In the mesothorax the partition or prophragma descends from the anterior margin of the mesonotum, and is directed somewhat forward. It is in general but very short, and rather a small ridge, to which the connecting muscles of the meso- and metathorax are attached. We again find the internal process upon the mesosternum, but here it originates with more widely divided shanks, each of which shanks forms an arch, which, as in *Cicada*, spans the aperture of the cavities of the coxæ, and ascends as high as the suture of the scapulæ, to unite itself with the surrounding margin of that part. In the *Lamellicornia* this arch does not reach the suture, but projects freely into the cavity, serving as a point of attachment for the muscles. In this shape the entire

---

* Meckel erroneously says this of all. See his Vergleich. Anatomie, vol. ii. Part i. p. 76.

process is called by Kirby and Spence the medifurca; I call it, to correspond with the first, the *processus internus mesosterni*, or *arcus sternales interni*.

The metathorax has the most developed skeleton, and is in general in the beetles the largest of the thoracic segments, whereas it was the central one in the flies, butterflies, *Hymenoptera*, and *Cicada*. We observe, at the metanotum, the meso- and metaphragma, two partitions descending perpendicularly from the anterior and posterior limits of this plate; they are not very high, but to them the large dorsal muscles are attached. In apterous genera (*Carabus*) the entire metanotum, and with it both partitions are very small. We find, besides these two partitions, no other elevated process at the metanotum, whereas there is a very large one at the metasternum. This originates as a thin, frequently merely pergamentaceous, triangular partition from its central line, and projects freely into the cavity of the thorax, but with its apex more directed towards the abdomen. The thither directed edge of the triangle is thicker, like a ridge; it is placed upon its posterior margin, and originates from the spot where both the cavities of the posterior coxæ are united. When this ridge reaches the upper point of the triangle it sends off on each side a strong process, which together form a direct cross with the ridge itself. A third process, which is, as it were, the continuation of this ridge, originates between both, and runs in a direct line parallel with the carina of the sternum as far as the mesothoracic segment, gradually decreasing to a point. This central process is excavated above, and thus forms a small channel, in which the intestinal canal rests. In *Dyticus* it even furcates, and with both prongs of the fork it encloses the intestine, and lower down the nervous cord. In *Oryctes*, however, all three processes, the two transverse ones and the central one, equal both in form and size, thus construct a three-rayed star; in *Hydrophilus* the central process is wanting, as well as in *Carabus* and *Callichroma*, where the whole frame is much smaller, and is placed between the cavities of the coxæ, whereas in others, at least in *Dyticus* and *Oryctes*, it projects as far as the base of the abdomen. To this skeleton numerous muscles are attached; posteriorly the muscles of the coxæ; at its lateral points delicate muscles, which rise to the limits of the back; to its anterior points likewise two delicate muscles, which pass through the cavities of the meso- and prothorax, and affix themselves to the horny plates of the membrane of the neck (see § 167. 4). Besides this large process, which Kirby and Spence call the postfurca, Audouin, on the contrary, styles it, in connection with the preceding ones of the pro- and mesothorax, the entothorax *, we find but a few other ridges produced by the sutural connection of the pleuræ with the sternum; these are Audouin's apodemata, which vary in their course according to the varying forms of the parts, and are of much less importance.

§ 166.

INTERNAL SKELETON OF THE ABDOMEN.

The abdomen has no internal skeleton, but consists of horny rings connected together by a flexible membrane, and each of which is divided into a dorsal and a ventral plate. In the grasshoppers, at least *Gryllus* and *Locusta*, horny half circles arise from the lateral edges of each dorsal plate, which are about one-third of its width, and extend as high as the dorsal depression. It is to these arches that the long air bags are attached, which form a zigzag, and which we have fully described above. Marcel de Serres †, who first discovered and described them, called them ribs, a comparison which in so far is not inappropriate, from their encompassing and protecting the air bags of these creatures. But they are properly elastic processes, which are in a directly opposite action to that of the oval air bags, which they distend by springing back, when the contraction of the spiral fibre has shortened them, and has thereby removed the process to which the bag is attached from the abdominal plate. They consequently belong to the respiratory system, and were considered under it by their first discoverer.

§ 167.

SKELETON OF THE LIMBS—MODE OF ARTICULATION.

The skeleton of the limbs is merely external, and as such it has been sufficiently described above (§ 79) in a preceding division; we have also there indicated the way in which the different parts of a limb are connected together, it therefore remains merely necessary here to give a special description of all the different kinds of articulation both of the limbs as well as the other portions of the skeleton.

I. CONNECTION WITHOUT MOTION (*synarthrosis*).—This kind of

---

* See Meckel's Deutsche Archiv., &c. tom. vii. p. 440.

† Mem. de Musée, tom. iv. (1819).

connexion of the parts of the skeleton we find chiefly in the thorax, in the sutures by which the several plates are united together. We may distinguish two descriptions of it:—

1. The SUTURE is the connexion of two plates of the skeleton by insertion, a projecting ridge of the one corresponding with a channel in the other, and the connexion is thus made without the intervention of membranes. This mode of connexion is found between the several plates of the thorax. Where both join they bend inwards, and thus form an even suture. All sutures in insects are therefore simple, smooth, without teeth, or interchanging processes.

2. SYMPHYSIS is a connexion upon the whole resembling a suture, but which is produced chiefly by the intervention of a soft membrane. This admits of a slight separation of the connected parts, which is increased in proportion to the elasticity of that membrane. It is by means of this that the posterior wing of the scapula is connected with the parapleura. This sort of connexion, thus admitting some degree of separation, was the more necessary here, as the second spiracle of the thorax lies between the two plates, and therefore a firm union would have prevented a free respiration.

A mere variation of this form, which, however, admits of a greater motion of the connected parts, is called by Straus a scaly joint (*articulation écailleuse*). It is distinguished chiefly by the lip of the one plate passing over the connecting membrane, and thus covering the lip of the other plate like a scale. This mode of articulation is found in the plates of the abdomen, in which each successive plate is covered by that preceding it. The mobility of parts thus connected is but passive, whereby an extension of the body on all sides, but chiefly longitudinally, is made possible, for example, when its contents swell, as is frequently the case in the female after impregnation.

II. CONNEXION WITH MOTION (*Diarthrosis*).—All connexions classed under this head are generally called JOINTS. They are found chiefly in the limbs, in the connexion of their several parts. In insects we distinguish the following different forms of articulation:—

1. The FLAP JOINT (*syndesis*).—When two parts meet at a suture, and are connected together by membranes at the inner side, but so that they may move in the suture to and from each other. This mode of articulation is found, for example, in the under lip, where the mentum joins the gula.

2. GYNGLIMUS.—When two parts are so connected that the one is inserted within the other at its origin, and stands in intimate connexion with it only at two opposite points. The part turns upon these two points as upon its axis. This therefore admits of but one kind of motion, viz. that of its approaching to or receding from the other part. It is thus that the coxæ and trochanter, femora and tibia are connected, and the mandible with the head. A more detailed description will more clearly explain the peculiarity of this articulation. Upon examining the upper extremity of the tibia, which has been removed out of its socket, we shall observe upon the exterior as well as interior a precise semicircular furrow, behind it a concentrical but smaller ridge, and beyond this a circular fossulet. The inner surface of the femora displays on each side a ridge accurately corresponding with the furrow, beyond this a furrow corresponding with the preceding ridge, and in the centre a minute elevation, from which a small but very firm band passes into the central fossulet of the tibia. This band appears to pierce transversely through the hole in the tibia, and passing through the opposite side to be affixed to the corresponding central elevation of the femora. Thus, therefore, a very firm connexion and a secure joint is produced. The articulation of the mandible is very similar, but which is distinguished from it by the upper side of the mandible having a semicircular ridge, and upon its under side merely a spherical ball joint.

3. ROTATION (*rotatio*).—Is that kind of articulation when a cylindrical, ovate, or conical part is sunk into a cavity adapted to its convexity. Both the inserted body and the cavity are drilled at one spot, and are united around the aperture by means of a membrane: besides which there are balls at both poles of the axis of rotation adapted to corresponding sockets of the other part; whereby a rotation of the encompassed part upon its axis is made possible within the corresponding cavity. This mode of articulation is found in the coxæ of the *Coleoptera*, *Hymenoptera*, *Hemiptera*, or more or less evident in the hip-joints of all insects.

4. A FREE ARTICULATION (*arthrodia*).—Is when a conical part is inserted in a corresponding cavity, both being pierced at one spot, and united by membranes around the circumference of the cavity. This mode of union, which is the most common of all, admits of the freest motion upon all sides; and, indeed, what is still more, the exsertion

of the ball out of the socket, as far as the membrane admits of extension. We find thus united the joints of the antennæ, palpi, and tarsi, the head with the thorax, and the prothorax with the mesothorax, in those insects which have a moveable prothorax. At the neck, or the connecting membrane of the head with the thorax, we find, besides, in the *Coleoptera*, two bean-shaped horny plates (*pièces jugulaires* of Straus), upon which the occiput moves. These plates, which might be called throat plates (*jugularia*), lie transversely in the posterior portion of the membrane which spans the large aperture of the prothorax like a drum-head, and serve for the insertion of several small thin muscles, and, among others, to the two which originate from the central point of the internal metathoracic process which passes through the cavity of the thorax. Their true function is doubtlessly to retain the membrane of the neck distended, and to offer to the occiput a smooth surface, upon which it may turn with facility. In black or dark beetles it is of the colour of the exterior integument (*Hydrophilus piceus, Oryctes nasicornis*), and is therefore very perceptible when the head has been removed from its articulating cavity. In *Dyticus* I likewise found similar plates between the meso- and meta-notum. A small horny piece, similar in function, lies also in the membrane between the coxæ and the sternum in the four anterior legs. It is properly a process of the joint become free, and which, in the intermediate legs, in which the motion is less, stands in closer connection with the coxæ. Audouin calls it *trochantinus*. I have been able to find this piece only in *Dyticus*; it exists also in *Melolontha*, according to Straus, who calls it *rotule*.

§ 168.

STRUCTURE OF THE WINGS.

We have already, in a preceding division, sufficiently described the formal differences of the WINGS and ELYTRA, as well as of the legs, to complete which we have but to give here a detailed explanation of their peculiar structure. In the description above, we have already mentioned that they are bags formed of a simple membrane, in which horny ribs are distributed. This simple membrane is nothing else than the epidermis, which, proceeding from both sides of the thorax, forms the wings. This is most distinctly seen in those wings which have a broad base, as in the *Coleoptera, Orthoptera*, &c., in which we even observe at the base a much greater thickness of the wing, which is caused by the two layers of the epidermis not having closely joined together. Upon the margin of the wing the two layers pass into each other, and thus the bag is formed. This bag admits of being distinctly represented as such, if just-developed insects be placed in spirits of wine; the fluid then passes between the still fresh and soft membranes of the wing, and filling their internal space, distends them like a bag. Heusinger* observed this in fresh specimens of butterflies, and I have myself detected it in a young individual of *Anthophagus plagiatus*, Grav.

Howsoever smooth, fine, and transparent the membrane of the wing appears to the naked eye, an investigation with the microscope reverses this, and exhibits it as covered with innumerable small hairs, which rise from bulbous roots upon the wing, and densely cover its whole surface. In some insects, for example, the common gnat, they are longer, broader, and lanceolate, and pass over into the scales of butterflies, which are absolutely nothing else than transformations of the hair peculiar to almost all insects.

The ribs of the wings are hollow, horny tubes, by which the two plates of the wings are supported. Their situation and reciprocal relation, as well as the cells formed by their connection, we have become acquainted with above: we will merely add here, that each rib is filled internally with a soft parenchyma, in which I have detected a vessel very large in compass, and by the side of it a fine nerve. The vessel appeared to come from the cavity of the thorax, and the nerve entered from the same part, coming probably direct from the approximate ganglion; therefore, close to the posterior wings in beetles, upon which I made the observation, and from the third ganglion of the thorax. In the vessel itself I could detect no structure, and, least of all, the spiral fibre observable in the tracheæ, even upon an enlargement of three hundred times†. I thence conclude that it is a blood-vessel, which is supported by Carus' observation of the motion of a fluid in the ribs of *Lampyris*. How else could the wings be distended, were not the liquid flowing into these vessels the cause of it? But it is not necessary that we should thence conclude upon a

---

* System der Hystologie, 2 Heft.

† I have since detected the spiral fibre in these vessels, and observed that they are genuine tracheæ.—*Author's MS. Note.*

connection of these vessels with the heart, it being well known that blood is found in the entire cavity of the body of insects, and, by each contraction, can be injected into the open ribs of the wings. Chabrier * describes, besides, a bag in the posterior wings of beetles, which lies at their point of flexure, and which is filled with a fluid during flight. The equilibrium is thereby thus supported. He considers in the other orders the stigma analogous in function to this bag. The clammy fluid contained in this stigma is probably merely parenchyma, but even in insects which had been immersed in spirits of wine, I have found a moisture in the bag, but which, without doubt, was introduced from without.

The connection of the wings with the thorax varies according to the different orders. Broad wings, attached by their entire bases, are found in the *Coleoptera, Orthoptera, Dictyoptera, Neuroptera, Hemiptera,* and *Lepidoptera,* consequently in the majority; wings with pedicles, and attached to the thorax by a narrow base, are found in the *Hymenoptera,* some of the *Neuroptera,* and the *Diptera.*

The superior wings, or elytra, of the beetles have at their base two short processes, the one of which originates at the inner margin, and the other at the outer margin. Both articulate with two processes at the mesonotum, which originate from it at the anterior part of the lateral margin, and are united to those of the elytra by means of a flexible membrane. In this membrane several free horny pieces are placed, to which the muscles are attached which move the wings. Straus found in *Melolontha* four such plates, and called them shoulder pieces (1. *pré-épaulière,* and 3. *épaulières*). From the posterior margin of the internal process of the joint of the superior wing, a delicate semicircular membrane springs (*frenum* of Kirby and Spence), which passes over to the similar process upon the mesonotum, and which retains the expanded wing. In *Dyticus* it is narrower, fringed upon its margin, very broad in *Hydrophilus,* and in apterous beetles (*Carabus*) it is wanting. This membrane, which is present in the majority of insects, and which, for example, in *Libellula,* is the coloured triangle at the posterior margin of the wing, and appears very similarly in the wings of the grasshopper, is so far of importance, that from it the scale behind the wings of the *Diptera* derive their significance. They are, namely, the frena of the superior wings, which cannot longer

---

* Sur le Vol des Insectes. Mem. du Musée, tom. vi.—viii.

remain in immediate connection with the base of the wings, from this being contracted and narrowed, whereby the scale is separated from the wing. We nevertheless still find in many *Diptera* a connection. It is remarkable, and confirmatory of this opinion, that those *Diptera* which want this scale, are such whose wings stand off in a state of repose, as, for example, in *Tipula*. But this frenum passes always from the superior wing to the lateral margin of the scutellum, and the scale of the *Diptera* is always found in this situation. The *Lepidoptera* are not deficient in this membrane; in the *Hemiptera* (for example, *Cicada*, Plate XIII. No. 5. 1.), it is partially horny; in the *Hymenoptera* it has but small compass, but in these it is not either ever wanting.

The connexion of the posterior wings is still more intimate than that of the anterior pair, whenever they are larger than the latter. The *Coleoptera* exhibit towards the base of the wing several plates, which lie free in the membrane, and which, like those of the elytra, promote and support their motion. Straus distinguishes five in *Melolontha*, and calls them axillary pieces (1. *préaxillaire*, and 4. *axillaires*). Neither is the connecting membrane which runs from the last portion of the joint to the margin of the metathorax wanting here. This is likewise the case in the large posterior wings of the *Orthoptera* as well as of the *Dictyotoptera* and *Neuroptera*, in which the plates and membrane are also found, and in the latter frequently very much developed. Nor is it wanting in the other orders.

The *Diptera* are remarkable from having no posterior wings, but instead of them they are provided with two pediculated knobs, which are called halteres. Latreille and other French naturalists will not allow these organs to be considered as the rudiments of the posterior wings, whereas the majority of the earlier entomologists, and many modern ones, particularly the Germans, consider them as such. If we look to the situation of these organs, it speaks incontestibly in favour of this opinion, for they are exactly situated where the posterior wings of other insects are found. Besides, they stand in the same connection with the metathorax; and, indeed, in the larger flies, for example, *Tabanus bovinus*, we detect the analogue of the connecting membrane. The knob is also sometimes (*Tipula gigantea, lutescens*) broad, flat, and provided with ribs like the wings, these are all facts which cannot be disputed, and which corroborate the correctness of this opinion. Latreille's decision, therefore, that the last segment of the thorax in the *Diptera* belongs to the abdomen, because a spiracle is found upon it, requires no refutation after the description given above of the general situation of the spiracles.

We must still make an observation upon the connection of the wings together. I know but of two of all the orders of insects which exhibit an apparatus for the connection of both the wings together, these are the *Hymenoptera* and the *Lepidoptera*.

In the *Hymenoptera* it consists of a row of minute hooklets, which are bent backwards, and are placed upon the anterior margin of the posterior wing, and which fit to a small groove along the posterior margin of the superior wing.

In the *Lepidoptera* this apparatus is somewhat more complicated. Giorna, who appropriates to himself the priority of this discovery, although it was made thirty-seven years before him by De Geer*, has, however, given the most detailed account of it †. There is found, namely, at the base of the posterior wings of many of the crepuscular and night moths, a spine projecting from the anterior marginal rib, which is sometimes divided into several radiating branches. This spine is enclosed by a hook placed upon the central main rib of the superior wing, which surrounds the whole circumference of the spine, which passes through it as through the eye of the needle, but which can freely move itself to and fro within it. If the superior wing expands by means of the spine, it draws the inferior wing with it, and both remain in immediate connexion; a provision of nature which is rendered the more necessary, as we shall see below, from the mesothorax being furnished with large muscles of connexion and motion, which are entirely wanting in the metathorax, so that the muscles which distend the superior wings must act likewise upon the inferior ones. We find a similar adaptation in the muscles of the *Hymenoptera*.

II. THE MUSCULAR SYSTEM.

§ 169.

The muscles of insects, like those of the higher animals, consist of two parts, viz. the tendon and the muscle. Under the name tendon we understand the in general more compact, firmer, and uncontractile

---

* Mém. pour servir à l'Hist. des Insectes, t. i. p. 173.
† Trans. of Linnæan Society, vol. i. No. 7. Lond. 1791.

ends of the muscles, by which they are attached to the parts to be moved: the muscle itself is the contractile fleshy portion lying between these tendons. If the tendon be wanting, the entire generally very broad end of the muscle is affixed to the horny skeleton, and such muscles appear applied more to the strengthening of all the parts than to the motion of individual ones.

The tendons vary much in shape according to the structure of the muscle, but they always consist of a horny mass, distinguished from that of the skeleton by its wanting the epidermis, and the coloured layer of the mucous tunic, and therefore Straus considers them as an elongation of the internal layer of the horny skeleton, to which the epidermis cannot assist, as it lies externally, and this view appears to be correct. The horny tendons, consequently, cannot participate in the external colour of the exterior integument, but they are, like its internal layer, of one uniform black or brown hue, so that they are easily distinguished from the flesh of the muscle. In form they are longer or shorter bones, which, at the side turned to the muscle, gradually distend into a flat surface, to which the muscle is attached. The form of these surfaces varies according to what is required by the muscle, for it is broad and plate-shaped for short thick ones, and for long thin ones we find it also long and resembling a scale.

The muscle itself is a union of delicate white, or yellow and red parallel fibres, which frequently, particularly if the insect has been preserved in spirits of wine, are readily separated from each other. If these fibres be examined under the microscope, we distinguish partitions at short distances, which appear to separate it in equal parts; but upon a careful examination, we find that the fibre consists of small laminæ lying one upon the other, and which at one spot are depressed into an angle, and are thereby attached to each other, which consolidates their union. This discovery, for which we are indebted to the careful Straus[*], is the more important, as thereby we detect a uniformity of structure of the animal organs in their most minute parts, as the fibres of the nerves likewise consist of consecutive globules. In the muscular fibres these globules have become plates from their firmer connexion together, and their consequent mutual pressure. Straus found this union in all the muscles, but in the larger ones the individual fibres first formed bundles, whereas, in the smaller ones, they lie

---

[*] Consid. Général. p. 143.

regularly together. In the *Mammalia* (the ox) he did not find this structure, whereas he saw it in the eagle, a fact, which, if shown to be the case in all birds, would still increase the evident parallelism of both classes*.

With respect to the general form of the muscles, we may in the first place separate those without tendons from those with. Those unprovided with tendons have the peculiarity of retaining throughout their whole course parallel sides, and always take the form of flat bands or thick prisms. Such flat band-shaped muscles we find between the several segments of the abdomen, and which serve to unite them together: the prismatic muscles without tendons we find between the phragmata, and indeed the dorsal ones in general are of this form.

The muscles with tendons, Straus arranges under the following five divisions:—

1. CONICAL MUSCLES. The belly of the muscle has the form of a cone, originating from a broad flat base, and proceeding to a smaller point of insertion. From the apex of the cone the long tendon springs, and distends itself in the belly of the muscle, in the direction of its axis, here spreading into a flat surface, to which the individual fasciculi are attached. Sometimes this surface is divided into several lobes.

2. PYRAMIDAL MUSCLES. The belly of the muscle is shorter, as is likewise the entire tendon surrounded by it. This is broad and divided into several leaves (for example, the mandibulary muscles).

3. PSEUDO-PENNIFORM MUSCLES. Flat triangular muscles, the fibres of which originate all in a row, and attach themselves sometimes at one, and sometimes upon both sides of the long tendon (the muscles of the femoræ in *Locusta*).

4. PENNIFORM MUSCLES differ, from the margin of their tendon being fibrous. These fibres originate sometimes at one side and sometimes at both sides of the long tendon.

5. COMPOUND MUSCLES are those which consist of simple bellies, all the tendons of which unite into one band, or in which one tendon after the other takes up several bundles of muscles.

To these five forms we may add, as a sixth, CYLINDRICAL MUSCLES, the tendon of which is a flat round plate, to which the fibres are

* Compare Nitzsch in Meckel's Archiv. 1826.

attached. From the centre of this plate a longer or shorter straight process springs, which unites itself with the part requiring motion. The great muscles of the wings are formed in this manner. Audouin considers these horny tendons as processes of the thorax, and he calls them *Epidèmes*.

Double-bellied muscles, or such, namely, where two bellies lie behind each other, and are united together by a central tendon, as they are found in the superior animals, are not discoverable in insects.

Besides this division of the muscles, according to their variations of form, we may likewise separate them into three groups, according to their functions.

The first, which we will call connecting muscles, pass within the cavity of a part from one portion of the skeleton to the other, and thus consolidate the connexion of the several plates together. These are in general the largest of all the muscles, and they have no tendons: when they contract, the cavity in which they are found contracts likewise, but when they become flaccid, it again distends. To these belong the large muscles of the back, which are spread between the phragmata, and likewise the large muscles of the sides, which pass from the back to the breast, and then those which lie between the plates of the abdomen.

The others, which may be called distinctively the muscles of motion, pass from a portion of the horny skeleton to the limbs, or from one joint of the latter to the other. They originate with a broad base from a part of the skeleton, and pass on by a thinner apex, terminating in a tendon, to a part of the limb. Their character also divides them into two groups. The first, which are called FLEXORS (*adductores seu flexores*), lie on the inside of the limb, and draw it to its base, to which it is affixed; the others, or EXTENSORS (*abductores seu extensores*), work in an opposite direction, distending the limb again as soon as they get in action. They lie on the exterior of the limb, and attach themselves to the exterior angle or edge of the parts to be moved.

These are the various general qualities of the muscles; we come now to the investigation of the individual ones, which we will examine in the order of their situation, examining first the muscles of the head and its joints, then those of the thorax and the limbs attached to it, and lastly those of the abdomen.

A. Muscles of the Head.

§ 170.

The muscles of the head may be divided into those appropriated to the motion of the whole head and the muscles of the oral organs and antennæ. The head has the freest motion of all the moveable parts of the body; it has thence the most numerous muscles of motion, namely, such which raise it (extensors), such which sink it (flexors), and such which turn it to the right and left (the rotatory muscles).

The extensors, or raisers of the head (*elevatores capitis*), are two-fold; two bellies originate close together from the central line of the pronotum, they somewhat separate in their course, and attach themselves laterally to the margin of the occipital aperture (thence called external extensors, *elevator externi*). They are shorter and broader than the two other bellies, which come from the prophragma, proceed contiguously over the pharynx and through the prothorax, and passing between the preceding affix themselves to the central part of the superior margin of the occipital aperture. All four raise the head up, one acting alone draws it somewhat on one side.

The flexors, or depressors (*depressores capitis*), are two small muscles which lie at the under side of the neck, and originate from the neck-plate, or, where this is wanting, from the inner margin of the prosternum, and affix themselves to the lower margin of the occipital aperture.

Contiguously to them two other small muscles originate, which turn outwardly and attach themselves to the lower part of the lateral margin of the occipital aperture; they correspond with the anterior bellies of the extensors, and might consequently be called external flexors (*depressores externi*).

The rotatory muscles of the head (*rotatores capitis*), are two broad flat muscles, which, coming from the lateral margin of the prosternum, affix themselves to the corresponding margin of the occipital aperture, and bend the head outwardly if one only be in action, but in conjunction they assist to draw the head into the cavity of the thorax.

In all insects with a free head, (*Diptera, Lepidoptera, Neuroptera, Dictyotoptera,* and *Hymenoptera,*) all these muscles are very small, flat, and like a band; the following, on the contrary, which belong to the plates of the throat, are, as well as these plates, entirely wanting.

The muscles which run to the plates of the throat may properly be classed with the flexors of the head, for, as the true flexors are attached to these plates, a contraction of these plates likewise draws the head downwards and backwards. There are three on each side:—

One, the flexor of the throat-plate, originates from the inner process of the prosternum, and affixes itself in the centre of the plate of the throat.

The second, or straight extensor, affixes itself internally, contiguously to the other, and passes diagonally from the prophragma through the cavity of the prothorax.

The third, or oblique extensor, comes from the exterior margin of the pronotum, and affixes itself to the plate of the throat, between the former and the flexors of the head. The two last retain the plates of the throat in their place, which naturally, from the situation of the flexors of the head, is exposed to greater force; the first assists the head inwards, and also to draw the plate of the throat down, acting in opposition to the two extensors.

§ 171.

MUSCLES OF THE MANDIBLES.

Of the muscles of the joints of the head we will first examine those of the mandibles; we find two, namely, a flexor and an extensor.

The flexor of the mandible originates from the entire posterior and upper side of the skull; it becomes pyramidal and affixes itself, after passing the lateral portion of the brain, by means of a strong and frequently divided tendon to the inner margin of the mandible. In many insects, for example, the grasshopper, the entire muscle consists of two contiguous bellies.

The extensor of the mandible originates beneath the former from the posterior and lower portion of the skull; it is smaller and weaker, it has a long thin tendon, and affixes itself to the exterior margin of the mandible between the two above-described joint balls.

The maxillæ, which are of a much more complicated structure, have several motive muscles, which may be divided into four groups, according to the part of the maxillæ to which they pass.

There are three muscles which move the entire maxillæ.

The first, the flexor of the maxillæ, is the largest; it originates from the inner side of the throat, closely in front of the occipital aperture, and is sometimes conical, and affixes itself to the innermost process of the transverse basal portion (*p. basilaris s. cardo*).

The extensor of the maxillæ originates from the inner side of each temple, beneath the eyes; it is the smallest of the three, and affixes itself to the most external process of the base.

The third muscle, which may be called the first contractor of the maxillæ, originates from the lower margin of the occipital aperture, passes transversely over the flexor, and inserts itself between the flexor and extensor at the base. Both contractors acting in conjunction draw the maxillæ together.

Two other muscles, which likewise move the entire maxillæ, are inserted in the piece described as the stem.

The one, which may be called the second contractor, originates likewise from the margin of the occipital aperture, but in the centre, in front of the first, and inserts itself in the lowest most internal angle of the base; the other, or second flexor, originates from the inner wall of the occiput, lies above all the others, and inserts itself with a long thin tendon, likewise at the lower inner angle of the stem, closely contiguous to the second contractor. It is the longest and largest of all the muscles of the maxillæ.

The galeæ, which are, as they have been called, the internal maxillary palpi, receive each two muscles, which lie in the maxillæ themselves.

The flexor of the galea is the largest; it originates from the inner side of the stem, and affixes itself to the inner margin of the galea.

The extensor of the galea, which is longer but smaller, originates from the inner side of the exterior wall of the stem, and inserts itself at the exterior margin of the galea. The exterior one gives off also numerous fasciculi to that portion of the maxillæ which bears the palpi, and it is thereby united intimately with the stem.

The last muscles of the maxillæ, which, like the preceding, lie wholly in it, move the maxillary palpi. Their flexor originates from the inner margin of the palpal plate belonging to the maxillæ, and inserts itself at the inner margin of the first joint of the palpus; their extensor comes from the inner side of the exterior wall of the stem, and inserts itself at the exterior margin of the first joint of the palpus.

The joints of the palpi themselves have each two muscles, a flexor and an extensor. The former springs from the inner margin of the preceding joint, the latter from the exterior, and both insert themselves at the corresponding parts of the basal aperture of the joint which they move.

§ 172.

MUSCLES OF THE LIPS.

The upper lip, or labrum, has in *Melolontha* but one kind of muscle, namely, the flexor or bender, which originates on each side from the brow, close to the eyes, and runs down to the extreme angle of the labrum. In *Locusta*, I have distinctly observed two different muscles; both were flat, resembling bands, and originated from the forehead, the anterior one, or abductor of the labrum, originated between the eyes, and inserted itself upon the inner surface of the exterior wall of the labrum; the second, or adductor of the labrum, originated above the former, at the boundary between the forehead and vertex, and ran separated from it as far as the apex of the labrum, leaning against the membrane of the soft palate, and supporting it.

The labium, like the maxillæ, being of a more complicated structure, receives several muscles.

The adductor of the labium originates from the most anterior edge of the skeleton of the head; it has a broad basis, and runs pyramidally to the mentum, joining it in front of the articulation of the palpi. In the *Coleoptera* there are two adductors, one on each side of the mentum; in *Locusta* I found but one central one.

In front of it, or between them when there are two adductors to the labium, the muscles of the tongue originate, which are two, likewise short, pyramidal muscles inserted at the lower side of the tongue, and connect this with the labium: I call them the reins of the tongue. In *Locusta* I found but one muscle of the tongue, resembling that of the labium in its broad flat form, which originated in front of the latter, from the tentorium, and passed to the posterior wall of the tongue. To the anterior wall, or the soft membrane clothing the tongue, on the contrary, another muscle passed, which I call the flexor of the tongue, and which, running likewise closely to the membrane of the tongue and of the palate, originated with a broad base from the anterior boundary of the tentorium.

The first joint of the labial palpus has its flexor and extensor; the former originates from the centre of the mentum, and passes to its inner margin, and inserts itself at the exterior margin of the joint. The succeeding joints have a similar structure to those of the maxillary palpi.

§ 173.

The antennæ have three muscles which move them—an extensor, which originates from the forehead in front of the eyes, and affixes itself to the exterior margin of the basal joint; a flexor, which originates from the anterior apex of the inside of the skull, and affixes itself to the inner margin of the basal joint; and an elevator, which originates exteriorly contiguous to the extensor from the margin of the eye, and inserts itself at the lower margin of the basal joint.

The individual joints have each two muscles, namely, those known from their situation as extensor and flexor.

Besides the above-named muscles there are other smaller ones, which retain the pharynx and palate in their proper place. In *Locusta* the muscles of the lips and tongue participate in this; in the *Coleoptera* they originate from the inside of the skull, and insert themselves at the pharynx, or from the forehead itself when the processes of the head do not advance so far. In *Dyticus*, from the skull of which two long, bent, horny processes originate, which extend as far as the forehead, and enclose the pharynx between them, they originate from the inner margin of these processes. In *Melolontha*, in which this internal frame of the head is smaller, two come from the forehead itself, and two others, smaller, on each side, from the *clypeus*: it is the same in *Locusta* and *Gryllus*.

§ 174.

In insects with haustellate oral organs the muscles of the mouth are much smaller. The *Hymenoptera* display the greatest conformity, particularly as they have large mandibles, and we can even recognise in their maxillæ analogous muscles. The entire suctorial apparatus, namely, the proboscis, with the maxillæ, palpi, and labium, has a moveable basis, formed of several united bony pieces, which, by means of a soft but tense membrane, stand in connection with the margin of the large oral aperture of the head. According to Treviranus[*] there lie in this membrane one simple and four double horny bones. The

---

[*] Vermischte Schriften, vol. ii. p. 117, Pl. XIII. f. 1.

two first (Pl. VI. f. 5. 1.) lie in the anterior margin of this membrane, in a transverse direction to the proboscis, but linearly with respect to each other, directly behind the mentum. From the exterior ends of each of these two pieces there originates a similar (2) bone, which extends posteriorly upwards, the point of which touches a third (3) bone, which furcates and descends from here to the posterior end of the membrane. Both the prongs of the fork join at their ends a fourth (4) uneven main bone, which lies transversely at the end of the membrane, and opposite to the two first, which lie immediately behind the mentum; the fifth paired main bone (5) originates likewise at each end of this fourth unpaired bone, and runs at the margin of the membrane close to the horny aperture of the head. All nine thus construct one valve, the anterior lobes of which are formed by the two first transverse and anterior lateral bones, and the posterior lobes by the second lateral bones, the fourth transverse and the two marginal bones originating from its end. The articulation takes place at the point of connexion of the two second and third bones. If the mentum (the same, *a*.) be withdrawn, the membrane and bones lie like a valve together, but if, on the contrary, the suctorial apparatus be distended, the membrane is stretched out by means of the bones, and these push the chin forward before it. The motive apparatus of the butterflies is much more simple; in them a double band-shaped muscle runs along each half of the proboscis, which clothes the entire cavity, leaving merely a narrow central canal. Both these muscles roll up and distend the proboscis, and also unite it with the head, inserting themselves partially upon the horny wall, and partly upon the, indeed very small, internal frame-work of the head. The smallness of their head arises from the disappearance of the muscles of the mandibles. The same may be maintained of the *Hemiptera*; they also have but delicate muscles, which elevate and withdraw the sheath, as well as still smaller ones, which rein the setæ. The *Diptera*, although they have in general a large head, derive it from the preponderance of their eyes, for the muscles which pass to their mouth are likewise abortive; the fleshy proboscis alone, which we consider as the labium, receives two large and tolerably broad band-shaped muscles, which originate from two ridges placed internally over the aperture of the mouth, and arched from the cheeks to the clypeus, and which extend also to the apex of the proboscis. They withdraw the proboscis within its cavity, and are therefore called the extensors of the haustellum.

§ 175.

B. Muscles of the Thorax.

The muscles of the thorax must be considered under several points of view, which proceeds from the differences of structure displayed in this portion of the body. The muscular system differs in insects with a free prothorax from that of those with an immoveable connate one; to which we may add the muscles of the limbs, which likewise all lie in the thorax, and a portion of which pass to the wings and the rest to the legs. We have thus four main divisions into which the muscular system of the thorax may be separated: we will therefore commence with the system observed in insects with a free prothorax.

§ 176.

MUSCLES OF INSECTS WITH A FREE PROTHORAX.

The prothorax exhibits on each side four muscles, whereby it is held connected with the meso- and metathorax.

The largest or superior retractor (*retractor prothoracis superior*) originates from the centre of the mesonotum with a broad basis, and runs pyramidally to the prophragma or the anterior partition of the mesonotum.

Opposite to it there lies a smaller lower retractor (*retractor prothoracis inferior*), which unites the internal furcate process of the pro- and mesosternum.

The elevator (*elevator prothoracis*) is a small pyramidal muscle, which originates on each side from the exterior margin of the prophragma, and affixes itself to the corresponding fork of the prosternum.

The fourth and largest of all, the rotator (*rotator prothoracis*), comes from the posterior margin of the pronotum, passes beneath the prophagma, and affixes itself to the exterior edge of the mesophragma or the anterior portion of the metathorax.

The mesothorax, which, in the beetles, is the smallest portion of the thorax, has but few muscles which unite it with the metathorax.

One, the holder of the mesonotum, is a flat, thin but broad muscle, which passes from the posterior wall of the prophagma to the mesophragma. Another, which may be called the withdrawer, goes from the lower margin of the prophragma to the wings; passing in its course closely to the exterior margin of the mesophragma, it assists to expand the wings, and at the same time draws the mesothorax closer to the metathorax. Another holder of the mesosternum, corresponding with that of the mesonotum, originates from the posterior wall of the furcate process, and passes to its anterior portion upon the metasternum. (*Le prétracteur de l'apophyse épisternale postérieure* of Straus.)

The muscles of the metathorax are considerably larger. They may be considered as the stem of the entire trunk of the beetle, to which the other parts are all attached. It is thence that the true muscles of the metathorax serve only for its own consolidation and strength, and not for its connexion with other parts.

The largest and strongest of all is the dorsal muscle (*musculus metanoti, l'abaisseur de l'aile* of Straus), a thick powerful fleshy bundle, which passes from the entire mesophragma to the metaphragma. It falls properly into two halves, one of which belongs to each side of the thorax, but both join together at the central line.

The lateral dorsal muscles (*musculi laterales metanoti, les prétracteurs de l'aile* of Straus) do not much yield in size. These originate from the lateral portion of the metanotum, descend obliquely to the metaphragma, and thus consolidate the dorsal plates.

The third connecting muscles of the metathorax run from the sides of the metanotum to the side of the metasternum, but so that they originate at the anterior margin of the metanotum, in front of the last-named muscle, and pass obliquely to the posterior lateral part of the sternum, and, consequently, to the cavity of the posterior legs. They are divided into several bellies lying contiguously, all of which closely unite the dorsal plate and sternum together, and, by their contraction, they appear very much to promote respiration. I call them the lateral muscles of the metathorax. They are what Straus calls *les elevateurs de l'aile.*

We have already mentioned one muscle connecting the meta- with the mesothorax. Besides which, we find thin prismatical muscles, which, originating at the furcate branches of the internal process of the sternum, pass transversely to the sides of the dorsal plates, and thereby unite it still more strongly with the sternum. They encompass below the intestinal canal and above the straight dorsal muscles, and insert themselves contiguously to them at the mesothorax. They are most distinct in the grasshoppers and *Termites*. In the *Coleoptera* several are found upon each side, some of which come from the front and others from behind from the back. I call them furcate dorsal muscles (*musculi furci-dorsales.*) They are the *flèchisseur latèral de l'apophyse épisternale postérieure, l'abaisseur du tergum, et l'abaisseur du diaphragme,* of Straus.

§ 177.

THE MUSCULAR SYSTEM OF INSECTS WITH A CONNATE THORAX.

While in insects with a free prothorax the greatest portion of the entire thorax is occupied by the metathorax, in those orders in which the thoracic case is closely united together, the mesothorax preponderates in a like manner. The *Cicada* make the transit to this conformation, for in these insects, although they possess a free and moveable prothorax, still the greatest space is occupied by the mesothorax. The large muscles of attachment and muscles of connection consequently lie in the mesothorax in insects of this structure and in the *Hymenoptera*, and indeed between the prophragma and the mesophragma, or, when the former is very small, between the mesonotum and the mesosternal plate. In the first case, it is the dorsal muscles which are chiefly developed, and, in the latter case, the lateral muscles of the back. We thus find it in *Cicada*, whose enormous lateral muscles of the back nearly entirely supplant the true muscles of the sides. In the *Lepidoptera*, on the contrary, the true dorsal muscles are the largest, although the prophragma is but small: they consequently originate from the anterior portion of the mesonotum, and so increase that they occupy two-thirds of the thoracic cavity. In the *Diptera*, lastly, the lateral muscles are very large. They originate, as is always the case, from the lateral ridges of the mesonotum, and pass on to the mesosternum in front of the cavities of the coxæ. In *Eristalis tenax* I have distinguished two separated lateral muscles on each side, the most posterior of which inserts itself between the cavities of the intermediate and posterior coxæ. But this is possible in the *Diptera* only, for in them the mesophragma is wanting, or, rather, is so small, that it may be considered as deficient. The dorsal muscles, therefore, are also distended between the mesonotum and the metaphragma, but do not run parallely with the former, but incline more obliquely downwards.

The connecting muscles of the sternal processes exhibit no other differences than that the smaller these processes become, the more they also decrease in size. In general, these processes are very small in the above orders, and it is thence, probably, that I could never discover in them the furcate dorsal muscles, if these positively exist, which I feel much inclined to doubt from the course of my observations.

§ 178.

MUSCLES OF THE WINGS.

The true muscles of the wings originate, like the lateral muscles, from the lateral parts of the sternum, and pass on with pointed tendons to the ribs of the wings. We find their extensor the most developed, and their flexor the least so.

The large extensor of the wing (*extensor alæ magnus*) originates inwardly from the lateral portion of the sternum, closely contiguous to its internal process, and proceeds transversely to the large marginal rib of the wing, inserting itself at a plate-shaped tendon, which hangs in immediate connection with the base of this marginal rib. (Pl. XI. No. 3. f. 8. *a.*) If the anterior wings be the largest, as in the *Hymenoptera* and *Lepidoptera*, the dorsal muscle of the anterior wing is likewise the largest; but if the posterior wings are wanting, as in the *Diptera*, their extensor is also wanting; and if both are of equal size, as in the *Libellulæ* and the majority of the *Neuroptera*, their extensors also are of equal size; but if the posterior wings are the largest, as in the *Coleoptera* and *Orthoptera*, this is likewise the case with their extensors. The extensor of the elytra is, for instance, very small, whereas the extensor of the wing is of great size.

The small extensor (*extensor alæ parvus*) originates behind the larger one from the lateral part of the sternum, or, frequently, from its inflexion, formed by the cavity of the coxæ, it runs contiguously and parallel with the larger one as far as the articulation of the wing, and likewise inserts itself, by means of a plate-shaped but smaller tendon, to the second or posterior chief rib of the wing.

The flexors of the wing (*flexores alæ*) are much smaller: they originate from the parapleura, or, where this is not separated, from the superior part of the lateral process of the sternum, and insert themselves at the posterior margin, or upon the horny plates lying at the base of the wing. In the *Coleoptera*, the flexor of the posterior wing consists of three bellies, which pass like three rays from the pleura, and insert themselves at the most posterior horny piece lying at the base of the wing (the *axillaire troisième* of Straus).

Besides which, small muscles support the bending back of the wing, and which originate from the plate-shaped tendon of the large extensor, inserting themselves at other horny plates at the base of the wing: when in action they cause the relaxation of the extensors, and are thence called *relaxatores extensorum*.

§ 179.

MUSCLES OF THE LEGS.

The motive apparatus of the legs is much more complicated, both from their being so much more moveable, and from their consisting of several consecutive joints.

The coxæ or hips receive the majority of muscles, but which are adapted to the variations of their connection with the sternum.

If they, as in the *Coleoptera*, consist of a cylinder revolving upon its axis, the flexor of the fore legs are placed at the posterior margin of their inner aperture, and the extensors at the anterior margin; but in the posterior pair, the latter are placed at the posterior margin, and the former at their anterior. Both come from the lateral parts of the notum, or from the internal processes of the sternum. In *Melolontha*, Straus found in the fore legs, which, in all beetles, have the freest motion, four extensors, which differed in size, and all came from the posterior part of the pronotum, and but one flexor; in the intermediate pair, three flexors and two extensors, the longest of which came from the margin of the prophragma, and the shortest from the internal process of the sternum: the posterior coxæ had, again, four extensors and three flexors, some of which originated from the internal process of the sternum, and the others from the dorsal and lateral plates. In the water beetles, the very large posterior coxæ are intimately connected with the metasternum, and not articulated, from its receiving the enormous muscles which move the remaining portion of the leg. The muscles of the coxæ are compressed by them, and the muscles which move the leg pass from the internal process direct to the trochanter.

Such coxæ as are free do not differ in structure from those which are received within a cavity of the sternum, with the exception, that their aperture exactly corresponds with the aperture of the sternum.

Their motion is rendered thereby indeed somewhat greater, but it consists chiefly in revolving about the axis of the superior aperture of the coxa; and in such coxæ we find likewise flexors which are inserted at the posterior, and extensors at the anterior margin of the aperture, or reversed, the latter behind and the former before; and between both, the articulating balls are found. But the muscles of motion appear merely to proceed from the inner processes of the sternum.

The muscles which move the trochanters lie in the coxæ, the extensors on the exterior, and the flexors at the interior. In *Melolontha*, Straus found in the first pair of legs three extensors and one flexor; in the two posterior pairs, however, but one flexor and one extensor. The *Dytici* possess the largest muscles to the trochanters. In these insects I found the extensor originate not from the coxa, but from the lateral branch of the large furcate process, whereas, the weaker flexors sprung from the inner surface of the coxæ.

In the trochanter there is but one muscle the tendon of which is inserted upon the head of the femur protruding into the cavity of the trochanter, and it thereby lifts the thigh when it contracts, but lets it fall again when lax.

In the thigh itself there are two muscles, one extensor, which lies at the upper margin of the thigh, and which is attached to the superior head of the tibia, by means of a long tendon, that lies within the muscle, and one flexor, which lies opposed to it at the lower margin, and which is correspondingly attached to a lower ball of the tibia. In *Locusta* these muscles are very large, and have large bellies at their base, varying according to the form of the thigh; the thin membrane lies quite free for about one-third of the length of the femur, but it receives above, close to its connexion with the tibia, where the thigh is somewhat broader, a narrow flat auxiliary muscle, which springs obliquely from the case of the thigh, and attaches itself to the tendon.

In the tibia there are also two muscles, which move the whole foot. The extensor of the foot is the smallest; it originates from the lower half of the posterior and lower margin with a broad basal surface, it becomes pyramidal, and attaches itself to the superior margin of the first joint of the tarsus. The flexor of the foot originates above it at the same spot; it soon becomes more slender, and with its free tendon it passes into the cavity of the first joint of the tarsus, it sends its tendon on through this as through all the consecutive joints, and inserts itself at an arch in the last joint, where the two claws are internally connected; it consequently bends the whole foot, whereas the extensor, by drawing the first joint, again extends it.

In the last tarsal joint we again find peculiar muscles, viz., one which originates from the base of the claw, and affixes itself to the tendon of the tarsal flexor. It helps to bend the claws, and is thence called *flexor unguium*. The other originates with a broad base from the inner wall of the superior surface of the claw-joint, and runs, becoming pyramidal, to an arch connecting the two claws. It raises the claw, and is therefore styled *extensor unguium*.

§ 180.

C. MUSCLES OF THE ABDOMEN.

The collective muscles of the abdomen serve partly to connect it with the thorax and partly to unite the internal organs with it, and they are thence divided into three groups.

The muscles which unite the abdomen with the thorax are, when the abdomen is sessile, like all the abdominal muscles, flat, and like bands, and originate from the posterior and lateral margins of the thorax, affixing themselves to the first segment of the abdomen.

Those situated at the dorsal surface, which we call the superior connecting muscles of the abdomen (*musc. conjungentes superiores, s. dorsales*), are divided into several contiguous bellies, which run flatly from the metanotum and metaphragma to the first dorsal plate. The lower connecting muscles, which lie upon the ventral surface (*musc. conjung. inferiores, s. ventrales*), come from below, from the posterior margin of the metasternum, and pass between the femoral cavities to the first ventral plate.

Between both lie the lateral connecting muscles (*m. conjung. laterales*), which come from the lateral margin of the metasternum and the lateral plates, and, passing into the cavity of the abdomen, uniting themselves to the lateral wings of the first or second ventral plate.

In insects with a petiolated abdomen all these muscles, it is evident, cannot be present, but instead of the dorsal muscles we find a single large band (*funiculus* of Kirby and Spence), which originates from the inside of the metaphragma as a pyramidal muscle, passing with its point through the hole at the end of the metaphragma, and affixing itself to a short tooth which lies at the anterior margin of the first dorsal plate (Pl. XII. No. 2. f. 9. *a.*). The dorsal and ventral plates of the first abdominal segment are prolonged into a broad upwardly bent and gradually widening process, which is provided on each side with a longitudinal groove (the same, *b.*), to which a corresponding process of the inner margin of the metaphragma fits. Besides the abdomen and thorax are still more intimately bound by means of a flexible membrane surrounding the large aperture (the same, fig. 7 and 8. A, A.). I have also plainly distinguished two flat lateral muscles, which pass from one part to the other.

The connecting muscles of the abdominal plates may be divided into the dorsal and ventral muscles.

The dorsal muscles are two large, broad, but flat band-shaped muscles, which run from the first to the last abdominal segment, and are throughout intimately united with the connecting membrane of every pair of plates.

The ventral muscles are smaller, and do not pass in one line, but only between every two contiguous ventral plates, taking an inward oblique direction, so that their exterior boundary forms a zig-zag line.

I also found in *Locusta* transverse ventral muscles, which originating from the descending ends of the dorsal plates, run transversely across the ventral plates. They contract the cavity of the abdomen, and thereby especially promote expiration. The abdominal muscles in general seem less to connect the segments than to promote the freer expiration of the air.

The remaining muscles of the abdomen, which raise and sink the last plate, and at the same time unite the cloaca with the surrounding parts, are subjected, like that organ itself, to so many differences, that a general description will be possible only when a tolerable number of insects of all orders and families shall have been examined. From all observations hitherto made it appears that both the dorsal and ventral plates receive an extensor and a flexor, which originates from the penultimate plate, and affixes itself to the terminal one, the former more exteriorly and anteriorly, and the latter more interiorly between the preceding, and extending further to the apex.

The muscles of the cloaca and of the colon originate from the circumference of those organs, and pass as broad and flat bands to the dorsal and ventral plates, surrounding them. Both only serve to retain the cloaca and colon in their places when the fæces are voided from the latter, or when the vagina or penis are protruded from the former.

The muscles peculiar to the penis and the vagina, lastly, differ as much in form as those organs themselves. We have already taken a general notice of them in our description of those organs. Different layers are detected in them, the exterior of which retains and turns back the prepuce; the inner ones, which lie between the valves themselves or pass on to them, open and shut them. Straus, in his anatomy of the cockchafer, has given a very elaborate description of all these muscles as they are found in that insect, and which is the less desirable to be repeated here, as from the (indeed but limited) investigations made by myself in other insects, they are subjected to very considerable differences. The more comprehensive representations of all the modifications of the external as well as internal sexual organs, which I purpose one day undertaking, will then serve to fill this gap, and until then these indications may suffice.

§ 181.

THE MUSCULAR SYSTEM OF LARVÆ.

The muscular system of the larvæ of those orders of insects having an imperfect metamorphosis agrees with that of the perfected creature, with the exception of the mere indication of the presence of the muscles of the wings; we have therefore nothing further to say of them than that these muscles of the wings, during the several moultings, and particularly during the pupa state, acquire the size they are intended to retain during the imago state of the insect.

But the muscular system of the other orders, particularly of the *Lepidoptera* and *Hymenoptera*, is very different; the larvæ of the *Coleoptera* display much more conformity with that of the developed beetle, for they are of all the most perfect larvæ, and in the structure of their feet agree very much with their perfected state.

The most conformable muscular distribution in all larvæ is found in the abdomen, in which two straight, broad, band-shaped muscles descend both the ventral and dorsal sides and connect every two segments together, the muscle itself being intimately united with the connecting membrane of the several segments.

Beneath these two large muscles, which may be called the longitudinal muscles of the back and belly, lie smaller ones, which pass obliquely from the connecting membrane at the anterior margin of a joint to the corresponding part of the posterior margin of the same joint, which may be therefore called the oblique dorsal and ventral muscles. They strengthen the connexion of the joints together, and contract the body during expiration. They appear to be wanting in smaller coleopterous larvæ, which are enveloped in a horny case; in the robust fleshy caterpillars there lies beneath them a third layer of muscles, which take the same direction as the preceding, but differ from them by their shortness and their separation into several parallel fasciculi. They may be called the smaller oblique dorsal and ventral muscles, and those above described as the larger superficial ones, and the smaller ones as the deeper.

We observe, besides these ventral muscles which run parallely in the longitudinal axis of the body, others which connect the dorsal plate of each segment with the ventral plate. They originate contiguously to the deep oblique ventral muscles with a broad basis, contract pyramidally by degrees, come then outwards, close to the direct ventral muscles, and ascend on the outside of the straight dorsal muscles to the dorsal plates, inserting themselves contiguously to the deep oblique dorsal muscles upon the dorsal plate. I call them *musculi ventri-dorsales*. In larger caterpillars, for example, the *Cossus ligniperda* [*], we can distinguish several layers and bundles of these muscles, and it consequently is not difficult to make the number of the muscles of a caterpillar amount to 4061 if, as Lyonet maintains of the goat-moth caterpillar, each particular fasciculus be a distinct muscle [†].

Exteriorly, contiguous to these muscles, there lie beneath each other, and close to the lateral wall of each segment, several fasciculi of oblique and crossing muscles, which strengthen still more the connexion, and which, from their situation, may be called the lateral muscles. With their diverging ends they embrace the spiracles of the caterpillar, and they appear to assist chiefly in closing them after expiration.

The muscles of the three first segments, which subsequently form the thorax, are more numerous, for besides the usual connecting muscles we here also find those of the legs, as well as the commencement of the future muscles of the wings.

The longitudinal dorsal and ventral muscles are here in general narrower, that they may make room for the other muscles, yet they so

---

[*] Consult Lyonet, Traité Anatomique, &c. à la Haye, 1760, 4to. Pl. vi. vii. & viii.

[†] According to Lyonet, the number of muscles found in the head amount to 228, those of the body to 1647, and those of the internal organs to 2186, making an aggregate of 4061. Traité Anal. p. 584.

develope themselves, at least the dorsal ones, and particularly during the pupa state, that they subsequently present themselves as the large dorsal muscles, distended between the phragmata. The straight ventral muscles, on the contrary, so contract together, that they transform themselves into the small connecting muscles of the internal sternal process. The lateral muscles again enlarge, and then exhibit themselves as the large lateral muscles of the thorax.

The crossing pectoral muscles are peculiar to the thoracic segment. They are the small band-shaped muscular strips on the pectoral side, originating from the posterior margin of the first thoracic segment, and running obliquely to the lateral parts of the following thoracic segment. With their lower shanks they embrace the nervous cord, and cross each other precisely over it, that coming from the left passing over to the right and those from the right to the left; each passes directly through the straight ventral muscle, and affixes itself to the exterior wall of the segment. In the perfect insect they exhibit themselves as the above described furcate dorsal muscles. In the larvæ of *Coleoptera* I found besides transverse pectoral muscles, which originating at one side of each of the three thoracic segments passed over to the opposite side, and in the first and third segments covered the nervous cord, but in the second were covered by it. I have not detected its development and conformable appearance in the perfected insect.

The muscles of the legs correspond evidently with those of the perfect insect. The profoundest, or muscles of the coxæ, come from the lateral parts of each segment, and insert themselves at the inner margin of the ring of the coxa. In larvæ with long and large legs there is found at the inner lateral part of each thoracic segment a projecting horny ridge, which passes over the cavity of the coxæ, whence spring all, or at least the more deeply seated, muscles of the coxæ, whereas the superior ones pass over this ridge, coming from higher situated parts of the thoracic case. The muscles which move the thighs lie in the ring of the coxæ, and form three or four narrow fasciculi; thus also in each successive joint is found the muscles of the third in advance. The last joint, or claw, the preformation of the subsequent tarsus, receives two muscles, which originate with several heads from the several rings of the foot, both from their superior and inferior sides, and all are attached to two tendons which are again attached to the inferior margin of the claw. Their common contraction bends the claw with great force, and retains it in this situation. We find no extensors of the claw joints.

The ventral feet of caterpillars receive, according to Meckel, three muscles, an anterior and a posterior one, which spring from the corresponding membrane of the ring, and attach themselves to the inner wall of the tube of the foot. The central one is larger than both the others, and originates from a higher spot of the lateral part of the segment of the body. It here originates with a broad basal surface, and runs down, contracting gradually as far as the centre of the foot sole. It admits of being divided into two halves, and has consequently been described by Lyonet and Cuvier as double.

The rudiments of the muscles of the wings are upon the whole very indistinct, and very difficult to discover with certainty among the many muscular strips of the thoracic segment. In the caterpillar of the *Cossus* I consider those muscular strips which pass obliquely from the posterior lateral margin, and anteriorly ascending upwards, as such incipient muscles of the wings*, particularly as in the following ventral segments no corresponding muscles are found. I found similar strips in other larvæ which I investigated, for example, in that of *Calosoma sycophanta*.

The muscles, lastly, which bend the head to the thoracic segment, and which move it, may, as in the perfect insect, be divided into an extensor, a flexor, and a rotator of the head.

The extensors of the head form several layers over each other, the most profound of which is nothing else than a continuation of the dorsal muscle, and which attach themselves to the superior margin of the large occipital aperture. Above these lies a narrower one, which distends posteriorly, being attached at the occipital aperture between the preceding, and originating at the anterior margin of the second thoracic segment †. Other small strips, which lie above it, originate from the centre of the pronotum, and pass over it to the corresponding margin of the occipital aperture.

The flexors form three similar layers. The innermost layer is a continuation of the longitudinal ventral muscle; the second, which runs obliquely, comes from the anterior margin of the second thoracic segment, and affixes itself between and beneath the former, at the

---

* Lyonet, Pl. VIII. f. 4. † Ibid. Pl. VI. D, D.

inferior margin of the occipital aperture. The third is formed by small muscular strips, which originate from the pectoral plate of the first segment of the body, and affix themselves beneath the former at the large occipital aperture.

The rotators are divided on each side into two fasciculi, the superior one of which springs more from the dorsal side, and the inferior one from the pectoral side of the first segment of the body, and insert themselves in the skull, closely contiguous to the margin of the occipital aperture. The inferior ones are in general the shortest bundles, and the superior ones the weakest. They both appear to me to be merely modifications of the oblique lateral muscles, as those profounder extensors and flexors may possibly be merely transformations of the oblique dorsal and pectoral muscles.

The muscles lying in the head itself, which move the oral organs and the antennæ, agree so much in form, situation, and insertion with those above described belonging to the perfect insect, that their small divarications, which proceed from the less developed state of the skeleton of the head, require no further notice, particularly as they stand in precise connexion with the various forms of the head, and their special description consequently exceeds the boundaries of our object. We must here, however, notice of the apparently headless larvæ of the *Diptera*, that the most anterior membranous segment of the body takes the place of the head, and that its anterior orifice is the mouth, which is armed with several, generally four, frequently bent setæ, which receive their peculiar extending and withdrawing muscles. They lie withdrawn in the bag-shaped oral cavity, and appear, from their darker colour, through the pointed anterior end of the larva as a black body.

FOURTH CHAPTER.

OF THE ORGANS OF SENSATION.

§ 182.

THE organs of sensation are the last portions of the bodies of insects that we have to examine, and at the same time also the most simple; for the commerce of insects with the external world, although considerably more multifarious than in any other invertebrate animal; yet it does not unfold itself to that universal intercourse found in the superior animals. But they are nevertheless sensible to every possible external impression, and indeed for many more sensibly so than the class of fish immediately above them, which, however, and this supports the above assertion, are provided with distinct organs of hearing and of smell, which are wanting in insects, although they require them much more in the so considerably more tenuous element they inhabit, than the fish, which pass their lives as it were concealed.

It is thence evident what we understand by organs of sensation, namely, all forms which may be considered either as direct conductors of immediate feelings, or as the recipients of higher and more distant perceptions. To the first we may class the nerves, to the last the organs of the senses, and in insects especially, the eye.

The nerves, which are the foundation of all the organs of sensation, consist of fine fibres, which appear to be composed of the consecutive disposition of solid globules. These atoms, from which all nerves appear to be originally formed, preponderate so much in insects, that we never detect in the ganglia and in the nervous cords but rarely a fibrous formation, which would admit of the conclusion of its being formed of a concourse of individual threads. The nervous mass is contained within a very delicate structureless and perfectly transparent membrane, the nervous sheath (*neurilema*), which appears to be the mould of the entire nervous system, at least in insects. In it the nervous mass is enclosed, which is a soft pulpy substance which flows out when the sheath is opened. Upon a first superficial examination, the chief nervous cords of insects, at least both the large ventral cords, appear to be formed of several contiguous fibres, parallel stripes being observable in them; but these disappear upon a closer inspection, and each nervous cord is found to be nothing else than a tube formed of the nervous sheath filled with the nervous mass. The apparent striature proceeds from the globules not being irregularly placed, but disposed in longitudinal rows. Thus individual nervous cords appear, and they even become so when, as in the superior animals, the mass thickens, and thereby presses the globules together, and the neurilema falls down between the striæ.

The nervous mass itself consists of two different substances, namely, the firmer, white central mass, and the softer, darker-coloured cortical substance, and which is sometimes of a beautiful carmine, according to my observations in the caterpillar of *Noctua Verbasci* *. But they can be clearly distinguished only in recently opened insects: in those which have been long immersed in spirits of wine, the former darkens by degrees, and the latter becomes discoloured, so that neither exhibit any longer a difference. The cortical substance appears to be deficient in the filaments, and merely the white milk-coloured core appears to be present: these, therefore, are in general brighter, and do not at all participate in the colouring of the ganglia.

With respect to the general form of the nervous system of insects, it presents itself as a double cord running along the ventral side, which from segment to segment is re-united by ganglia. Two of these ganglia lie in the head, one above the pharynx, the other beneath it, and together form the brain, whence pass the nerves of the senses to the eyes, antennæ and oral organs. In the same way there spring from each of the successive ganglia a number of lateral branches, which are subjected to manifold differences, the three first of which pass to the legs, wings, and muscles of the thorax; those of the following ganglia to the muscles of the abdomen, to the posterior end of the intestinal canal, and to the organs of generation. The anterior portion of the canal, namely, the crop and the stomach, has its peculiar nervous system, which is formed by several auxiliary ganglia lying in the head.

Our investigation of the nervous system will thence fall into the following subdivisions.

1. The brain with the nerves of the senses originating from it.
2. The ganglionic ventral cord with its branches.
3. The nervous system of the œsophagus and stomach.

To this we may add the organs of the senses themselves, of which the eye alone will require a particular description; as for the majority of the remaining senses, no determinate organs have yet been fully ascertained.

---

* This reminds us of the red nervous points in many of the lower animals, namely, the Infusoria, especially the Rotatoria. Ehrenberg, in his admirable work upon these beginnings of organisation, considers these red points as eyes, but they are evidently nothing but a mass of the nervous substance.

I. The Brain.

§ 183.

The brain (*encephalum*) of insects consists of two ganglia, one of which passes over the pharynx and the other beneath it [*]; both are connected by means of nervous cords, which run from the upper to the under, and which embrace the œsophagus. I consider that which lies above as the cerebrum of the higher animals; the lower one, on the contrary, as the cerebellum: and, indeed, because, as in the higher animals, the nerves of the superior organs of the senses, namely, of the eye, spring from the upper ganglion; and from the lower one, on the contrary, the nerves of the mandibles, lips, and tongue proceed. It must not appear strange that the nutrimental canal passes through the brain, particularly as the entire spinal cord lies beneath the intestinal canal, and that the entire dorsal side of the higher animals is transferred to the ventral side of insects. We are convinced of this by the situation of the limbs and their connexion with the thorax, which also takes place at the ventral side, whereas, in the superior animals, they pass from the back, and, besides, the structure of the plates of the breast, which so completely imitate the spine of the superior animals that no doubt can be fairly entertained of their analogy, and of which we shall speak more fully below. But whosoever should think the assertion absurd that the œsophagus passes through the brain, we will merely remind him of the certainly still more striking circumstance in the mollusca, in which the colon passes through the heart, an assertion which has found no contradiction, although both organs in the higher animals are far more distant from each other than the brain and œsophagus.

§ 184.

The Cerebrum.

The cerebrum (Pl. XXXI. and XXXII. A, A, A,) is a nervous cord of a yellowish white colour, lying transversely across the œsophagus,

---

[*] J. Müller asserts of *Phasma gigas*, that the brain lies beneath the œsophagus (Novæ Actæ, T. xii. Pt. 2. page 568), which I much doubt, notwithstanding my conviction of the general perfect accuracy of his investigations. He distinctly describes the cerebellum, and he has overlooked the cerebrum, which lies over the œsophagus.

generally forming two ganglia. This cord sends off a branch on the opposite sides to each eye, which is the optic nerve. Its entire circumference is covered by a thin transparent membrane, which loosely surrounds it, and which in many cases, as for example, in *Dyticus*, is beset with small darker knots, placed in regular squares (Pl. XXXI. f. 1). The large muscles of the upper jaw spread above it, extending upwards to the skull, so that it is entirely covered by soft parts. The general form of the brain varies in as far as the two hemispheres are more or less separated. In the *Coleoptera* they approach closely together, and indeed so closely that they form but one stripe, which is merely swollen on each side near the middle; in other instances, as for example in *Gryllus migratorius*, the two hemispheres are nearly entirely separated, and are attached together by a central thin nervous cord only, analogous to the corpus callosum of the superior animals. The nerves which pass from the cerebrum are:—

1. The nerve of the antennæ (*nervus antennalis*). It originates from the anterior margin of each hemisphere, but more exteriorly when the antennæ are lateral, and centrically when those organs are inserted in the face. It runs as a simple undivided filament, which in the first case passes over the tendon of the mandibles, and in the last proceeds contiguously to the great flexor of the mandibles, to the root of the antennæ, immediately beneath the membrane which connects it with the clypeus, but yet without sending off branches. In many cases it is equally thick throughout, in others, for example in the bees and the cockchafer, it is more or less swollen at its base. When arrived at the antennæ the main stem still runs in this direction, and very distinctly to the apex of the organ, and between the muscles, but it gives off on all sides delicate auxiliary branches to the muscles themselves. It is accompanied by a single branch of the trachea, which originates on each side from the superior stem of the head, running between the flexors of the mandibles, and branching off according to the ramifications of the nerve itself.

2. The optic nerve which originates from the lateral margin of each hemisphere, with either a thicker or a thinner base, and extends to the orbit, becoming gradually clavate. It varies much in form, but it always retains the general characteristic of gradually distending. In *Dyticus* it originates with a thin base, then suddenly distends, and afterwards runs as a straight cylinder to the orbit; in *Melolontha* it is not perceptibly distinguished from the hemisphere of the brain, nor is its dis-

tension towards the orbit very distinct; in *Locusta* the cerebrum is smaller than the optic nerve, which springs from it with a very narrow base, but which then very suddenly widens into a cone; this is precisely the case also in the *Libellulæ* and flies which possess large eyes and a small skull, and in which the optic nerve of one eye is generally much larger than the entire cerebral ganglion. When arrived in the orbit it radiates into many branches, as we shall describe more fully below, in the detailed description of the eye. The auxiliary optic nerves (*nervi optici secundarii*), which are peculiar to such insects only that possess stemmata, originate from the central portion of the cerebrum, and extend as simple and very thin filaments to the spot where the stemmata are situated, and gradually diverge from each other. Thus each eye receives a distinct nerve, but which with its colleagues originate from one portion of the brain. It is well known that all the larvæ of insects with an imperfect metamorphosis possess merely stemmata, which are placed where subsequently in the perfect insect the large reticulated eyes are found. The nerves of these stemmata spring from the lappet-shaped distension of the cerebrum, sometimes separated (*Calosoma*, Pl. XXXII. f. 1), sometimes united at the base (caterpillars of the *Lepidoptera*), and run, each singly, to an eye. In *Vespa* the nerves of the stemmata have a common stem (Pl. XXXII. f. 7.); in the bees they sit upon short clavate projections of the cerebrum, and a distinct nerve does not seem to originate from these knobs *. In the neuter bees we find close to these large knobs two other small ones on each side, but which do not rise to the stemmata.

Besides these two main branches no other true nerves of the senses originate from the cerebrum; we observe merely smaller ramifications, which give off branches partly to the muscles and partly form filaments connected with the nerves of the cerebrum, and lastly, they may be partly considered as the commencement of the nervus sympathicus. But as below we shall devote our attention to this last system we will reserve our investigation of its origin from the nerves of the cerebrum until then.

The cords which connect the cerebrum with the cerebellum originate from the lower or deeper portion of the ganglion, as the nerves of the antennæ do from the anterior or superior portion, and after the optic

---

* Trevirnnus, Biologie, vol. v. Pl. II. f 1—3. *r, r.*

nerve the former are the thickest of all the nerves it gives off. Their direction as well as origin depends upon the situation of the head, for upon its horizontal position they spring further below from the cerebrum, but upon its vertical position we find them originate from its lower surface. Their length also stands in direct proportion to the form of the œsophagus; they are long in broad and expansive ones, and shorter in narrower ones. This is peculiar to haustellate insects, and in them therefore both the ganglia lie closely together. We observe this approximation of the two very distinctly in the bees, in which the connecting cord is nearly deficient, so that the cerebrum and cerebellum are quite contiguous, and there only remains in the middle between both a small aperture for the œsophagus. These connecting cords of the two brains very rarely give off auxiliary branches. I have observed the only instance of this kind in *Gryllus migratorius*, in which a smaller auxiliary branch originates at a little beyond half its length upon the inner side, which is united with its opponent beneath the œsophagus, running closely to that organ itself. Immediately in front of their point of connexion each again gives off a smaller branch, which runs back to the main connecting nerve of the two ganglia (Pl. XXXI. f. 7. *d, d.* and *d*, d*.*).

§ 185.

THE CEREBELLUM.

The cerebellum (Pl. XXXI. and XXXII. B, B,) is generally a cordiform or longitudinal ganglion; it lies at the base of the cavity of the skull, between the two projecting ridges of the previously described internal skeleton of the head, and is entirely covered by the tentorium. At the anterior portion of its lateral margin two strong nervous cords originate from it, which rise to the cerebrum, running contiguously to the tentorium, and enclose the œsophagus between them, forming the nervous loop described above as encircling it. At its posterior end, however, it again runs in two equal and very approximate filaments, which pass through the occipital aperture, beneath the transverse bone which divides it when present, out of the head into the thorax; they lie consequently very low in the neck, closely above the membrane of the neck and the flexor muscles of the head. They are the origin of the ganglionic nervous cord which runs along the pectoral and ventral sides of the body.

Between these two connecting nerves of the cerebellum with the portions of the nervous system lying before and behind it there originate from it on each side from two to four nervous stems, which pass to the mouth and the muscles of the head, and terminate in the various organs constituting the mouth; they are:—

1. The nerves of the mandibles (Pl. XXXI. and XXXII. *e, e*), which pass out of the anterior portion of the cerebellum, sometimes between the branches of the loop of the œsophagus (*Melolontha*, Pl. XXXI. f. 5.), sometimes from the exterior margin, contiguously to them (*Calosoma*, Pl. XXXII. f. 1.), and sometimes closer to the posterior margin, beyond them (*Gryllus*, Pl. XXXI. f. 7.). They give off several delicate auxiliary branches to the flexor and extensor muscles of the mandibles; and lastly, accompanied by branches of the tracheæ, they pass into the cavity of the mandibles themselves, between the tendons of both muscles. In the caterpillar of *Cossus*, according to Lyonet, the nerve of the mandible comes in a remarkable manner as a branch from the labium, and this receives four main stems (Pl. XXXI. f. 2. *e, e*.).

2. The nerves of the maxillæ (Pl. XXXI. and XXXII. *f, f.* and *f*, f*.*) originate sometimes in front (*Calosoma*, Pl. XXXII. f. 1.), sometimes behind (*Melolontha* and *Gryllus*, Pl. XXXI. f. 4. and 7.), the nerves of the mandibles from the cerebellum, and run closely to these to the maxillæ, taking their course between the muscles, and passing into the maxillæ themselves. Here each divides, one branch going to the palpus and extending to its apex, the other remaining in the maxillæ, spreading itself between its muscles. Sometimes (as in *Calosoma*, Pl. XXXII. f. 1. *f, f.* and *f*, f*.*) these branches are divided at their origin, and then the anterior one belongs to the maxillæ and the posterior one to the palpi; both give off, even in the cavity of the head, several branches, which pass to the neighbouring muscles.

3. The nerve of the labium (Pl. XXXI. and XXXII. *g, g.*) comes, when separated from those of the maxillæ, from the centre of the anterior margin of the cerebellum, and runs from here, very closely to its opponent, direct to the labium, and here divides itself into several, generally two, main branches, the inner one of which goes into the tongue and the outer one to the labial palpus. Where this nerve is wanting (*Melolontha*, Pl. XXXI. f. 5.) branches of the nerves of the maxillæ supply its place, and this is precisely the case where the tongue is small, hard, and cartilaginous. But it struck me as more singular in the *Locusta* (the same, f. 7.), which, notwithstanding that

it is furnished with a large fleshy tongue, I could find neither lingual nor labial nerves. In the caterpillar of *Cossus ligniperda* Lyonet observed a connexion of the two labial nerves before they passed into the labium; from this point of connexion other branches originated, which spread to the labium. Besides these the labium receives another nerve (the same, f. 2. *g, g.*), which originates quite posteriorly, close to the nerves of the maxillæ, and gives off in front of the labium an auxiliary branch for the muscles lying in the head.

§ 186.

II. THE VENTRAL CORD.

The ventral cord (*medulla spinalis, s. ventralis*) presents itself as a consecutive series of ganglia, every approximate two of which are united by one or two equal nervous cords. In the last case, consequently, this ventral cord consists of two equal nervous threads, which from spot to spot are connected together, and form a common ganglion. We have already spoken above of the structure of these ganglia and threads, we will here merely add that I have never detected a crossing of the two threads in the ganglion; they seem rather, upon their entrance into it, to terminate, and the ganglion itself appears to consist of a soft, uniform, granulated, nervous mass, which is enveloped within a softer, frequently darker (for example, of a carmine colour in the caterpillar of *Noctua verbasci*,) cortical substance.

The numbers of the ganglia differ in the several orders and families, but we may consider that there is properly one to every segment; hence their number would amount at most to thirteen, and we find, in fact, this number in many larvæ, namely, in all the larvæ of the *Lepidoptera*. Two of these ganglia lie in the head, and form the brain, the three following in the thorax, and the last eight in the abdomen. Each of them sends off two or three radiating nervous filaments, which originate at both its anterior and posterior extremities, diverge from each other throughout their whole course, and distribute themselves to the muscles, limbs, and several of the internal organs.

Besides the main cords which the ganglia form in conjunction, we find between those which are chiefly seated in the segments of the thorax other connecting filaments, as, for example, I have observed in the larva of *Calosoma sycophanta*, and shall therefore particularly describe. The first pair of these auxiliary connecting filaments originates from the posterior portion of the cerebellum (Pl. XXXII. f. 1. B, *h, h.*), closely contiguous to both the main stems; each diverges from the main stem in its course to about half its length, and then approaches it again as far as the spot where the main stem passes into the first thoracic ganglion, and then rejoins it. A delicate auxiliary branch of this exterior connecting nerve originates from it closely beyond its middle, passing to the first radiating nerve of the first thoracic ganglion, which it joins. The second connecting nerve (the same, $i, i.$) originates in the same manner from the first ganglion of the thorax as the first does from the cerebellum, and unites itself at a right angle with the first radiating nerve of the second thoracic ganglion. At their point of union a small ganglion is formed, from which two new radiating branches proceed, distributing themselves between the thoracic muscles. The third auxiliary connecting nerve (the same, $k, k.$) springs from the posterior end of the second thoracic ganglion, and passes into the third ganglion, forming an arch near the main stem, from which from two to three small nerves originate, and distribute themselves to the muscles. An auxiliary nerve connecting the third thoracic ganglion with the first abdominal one is not to be detected.

§ 187.

If we turn back from this general inspection of the auxiliary connecting nerves of these ganglia, which, as far as I know, have not hitherto been observed in any other insect, and certainly do not exist in many, particularly the larvæ of *Lepidoptera*, as may be adduced from Lyonet's accurate anatomy of the caterpillar of the great willow moth, to the differences of the chief form of the nervous system, we may adopt the following as a very general law :—

The ventral cord has as many ganglia as there are freely moveable divisions of the body.

This law is everywhere confirmed. The caterpillars of the *Lepidoptera*, whose similar segments have an equal motion, have as many ganglia as segments. In the *Diptera*, in which the three segments of the thorax are united into one, we find but a single large ganglion; lastly, in the larvæ whose thick fat bodies exhibit no distinct segments, the ganglia entirely disappear, and instead of a ganglionic we here find a simple thoracic cord, from which the fine nerves pass off on each side. We will inspect this in greater detail in the several forms of the nervous system and their transformation during the metamorphosis.

A simple short ventral cord, destitute of ganglia, is found in many larvæ of the *Diptera, Hymenoptera,* and *Coleoptera.* Among the larvæ of the *Diptera* I have found it in the rat-tailed maggot, and have represented it in Pl. XXXII. f. 3. It commences with two branches, which spring from the large cerebral ganglion lying over the œsophagus. These branches, which embrace the œsophagus, unite beneath it into one flat, tolerably broad, nervous cord, which extends to about the third pair of feet on the pectoral side, within the thoracic cavity, and here obtusely terminates. On each side of this cord there are from eight to nine small ganglia, whence the nervous filaments, as also at the obtuse apex of the cord, radiate posteriorly. The last, proceeding from the end of the cord, are the thickest; they extend downwards to the end of the abdominal cavity, and here distribute themselves with their terminal branches to the colon and the convoluted tracheæ lying at the end of the abdomen.

We should doubtlessly find a similar structure of the nervous system in the maggots of all the *Diptera* whose body is not divided into distinct segments. Upon the same principle, I think, I may conclude that the fat and irregularly-jointed larvæ of the *Hymenoptera,* namely, of the bees and of the wasps, have a similar nervous system without ganglia, and thence it would be explained how Swammerdam could discover no nervous cord in the honey-bee [*]. In the larvæ of *Stratiomys Chamæleon* the nervous cord is likewise indeed considerably shorter than the body, but it exhibits distinct ganglia, which, however, follow immediately upon each other, and display no long connecting cords, which we observe in the fly itself. According to Swammerdam's figure [†], we find besides the cerebrum and cerebellum ten consecutive and contiguous ganglia, and each sends off radiating lateral nerves.

Among the *Coleoptera* we perceive a similar nervous system without ganglia among the larvæ of the *Lamellicornia.* Swammerdam [‡] and Rösel observed it in the larva of the rhinoceros-beetle (*Oryctes nasicornis*); in these also it is a very short ventral cord, which extends as far as the proximity of the third pair of legs, and from the lateral margins of which innumerable delicate nervous filaments proceed. In this larva also the body is not separated into distinct segments and joints, it exhibits rather irregular folds and constrictions, which are

---

[*] Biblia Naturæ, p. 166. *a.*   [†] Ibid. Pl. XL. f. 5.
[‡] Ibid. Pl. XXVIII. f. 1.

very evident anteriorly, but nearly obliterated posteriorly. In the larvæ of the *Dytici* I likewise found a short nervous cord with closely contiguous ganglia, whence the auxiliary nerves proceed, and yet their bodies exhibit twelve distinct segments without the head. Perhaps this imperfect development of their nervous system is in relation to their constantly dwelling in water; at least the same structure in the equally distinctly jointed larva of *Stratiomys*, which likewise constantly lives in the water, points to one and the same cause of an analogous imperfection.

The positive opposition to this abortion of the nervous cord is found in the caterpillars of the *Lepidoptera* and the larvæ of many beetles. All these exhibit a ventral cord, which has as many ganglia as the body has segments, and in which, like the segments of the body, all the ganglia are of equal size. We must, however, here remark that a ganglion is not found in each segment, but that they gradually approximate together, so that the last ganglion, which follows immediately upon the preceding one without any connecting cord, is found as far advanced as the anterior margin of the penultimate segment. Each ganglion sends off four nervous filaments, the first pair of which extend more anteriorly, and the posterior pair furnish the parts lying behind the ganglion with their nerves. But the nerves of the ventral cord are almost exclusively destined to the organs of motion, and they consequently distribute themselves with their branches between the upper and lower layers of the muscles. In some cases the most internal muscles, particularly those lying about the cavity of the abdomen, receive a peculiar nervous branch, and which is found in the larva of *Cossus ligniperda*, and which here does not originate from the ganglion itself, but closely in front of it, from the there simple undivided connecting cord; it commences with a small root, which speedily divides into two equal branches, which take an opposite direction[*]. In the larva of *Calosoma sycophanta* I found six nervous filaments proceed from each ganglion, the middle pair of which likewise remained above the ventral muscles, whereas the anterior and posterior pairs passed beneath. The nerves for the anterior portion of the intestinal canal come from the cerebrum, and form a peculiar system, which descends that canal; the nerves of the sexual organs proceed indeed from the ventral cord, but merely from the branches of the

---

[*] Lyonet, Pl. IX. f. 1. 2, 2, 2.

much-radiated terminal ganglion. We observe a nervous system composed of thirteen ganglia not only in the caterpillars of the *Lepidoptera*, but also in the larva of the *Carabodea*, the predacious beetles, the majority of the *Heteromera* (*Meloë*, *Lytta*), the capricorns, and probably also in the *Chrysomela;* in the fat footless larvæ of the *Curculios* I surmise there is only a short ventral cord destitute of ganglia.

§ 188.

We find every variety of number between these extremes of ganglionic structure. The law which regulates the number of these ganglia is still undiscovered; for that adduced by Straus, of its being regulated by the relative greater or smaller mobility of the segments, appears not to suffice: he maintains, namely, in general, that the immobility of the segments together causes the disappearance of all the ganglia; and as a proof he cites the families of the *Dytici* and *Lamellicornia*, whose abdomen has no ganglia; but is motion less in them than in the very approximate *Carabodea* and in the genus *Lucanus?* Certainly not! This less degree of motion might be ascribed to the ventral plates, and yet we find in the abdomen distinct ganglia. The number of active organs found in a segment would seem rather to influence it; at least we observe the ganglia of the thorax of perfect insects always larger when they are furnished with perfect organs of flight, but smaller than those of the abdomen when the wings and the muscles which move them are wanting, for example, *Meloë* *. It therefore appears preferable to describe the different forms of the nervous cord of perfect insects in the series of their orders and families, for within those boundaries we seldom observe variations.

The greatest number of ganglia is found in the nervous system of the *Orthoptera, Termites, Libellulæ,* and many families of the *Coleoptera*, viz. the *Carabodea, Staphylini, Elaters, Buprestis,* and the *Capricorns*. In these the ventral cord exhibits immediately three ganglia, which lie in the three segments of the thorax. These differ in size, *inter se*, and indeed the smallest is found in the prothorax, the largest in the metathorax, and the intermediate size in the mesothorax. The ganglion of the prothorax lies immediately in front of the internal furcate branches of the sternum, at the very base of the horny plate, covered by the muscles which run from here partly to the head

---

* Brandt and Ratzeburg, Arzneithiere, vol. ii. part iv. Pl. XVII. f. 2.

and partly to the coxæ. Between the branches of this process, or when it is distinctly furcate between the fork, the nervous cords pass, proceeding over the connecting membrane of the pro- and mesothorax, running closely to it, and thus proceed into the mesothorax, again forming the second ganglion in front of the internal process of its sternum. If the branches of the first sternal process be united in an arch the nervous cord runs beneath this arch, and above, the muscles affix themselves to the process of the arch (*Locusta viridissima, Termes fatalis, Callichroma moschatum*). The branches of the second sternal process are not in general closed, the ganglion and cord consequently lie here freely, which is the case also in the third process. This, however, is higher than the preceding, often as it were pediculated, so that the ventral cord must raise itself that it may pass over this process into the abdomen. In front of this elevation the third ganglion then lies, immediately upon the surface of the sternum: it is the largest, and sends off the thickest nerves, and the second ganglion lies nearer to it than it does to the first, and thus, even in the nervous system, the more intimate connexion of the two posterior thoracic segments is clearly shown.

The nerves which originate from this ganglion vary in number; the first thoracic ganglion sometimes sends off two and sometimes three branches on each side. In the first case the first branch runs to the legs, the second to the muscles in the prothorax; in the second case both the first and third on each side are nerves of muscles, whereas the central one is the leg-nerve. Three branches are also found on each side of the second ganglion, the central one of which is a nerve of a leg, and the first and third pass on to muscles. It is probable that the anterior one gives off fine nerves for those contained within the hollow cavities of the ribs of the wings. The third thoracic ganglion also sends off three branches, which distribute themselves in a like manner. Of these the central or leg nerve is always the thickest, and most deeply seated, in as far as the direct muscles of the thorax, or the connecting muscles of the thoracic processes, pass over it; the others, on the contrary, raise themselves over these muscles.

The number of the abdominal ganglia varies considerably in the different groups. Insects with an imperfect metamorphosis, as the *Locustæ, Termites*, and *Libellulæ*, exhibit as many ganglia as segments, viz., from seven to eight, the two last of which, however, are so closely contiguous that they form one ganglion of a figure of eight. In the coleopterous families with abdominal ganglia we find in general not merely fewer than the first named instances, but also fewer than in their larvæ. During their metamorphosis, namely, either two ganglia appear to grow together, or else some wholly disappear; that may be the reason why the ganglia of the thorax are larger than those of the abdomen, at least the growing together of the third and fourth ganglia of the larvæ of the *Coleoptera* is very probable, particularly as this union is proved to take place in the *Lepidoptera* during their metamorphosis by Herold's history of that state of them. We therefore find in general in the perfected beetle only five ganglia, the two last of which are drawn so closely together that they form an eight-shaped ganglion. From each of these ganglia two undivided pairs of nerves proceed, which are rarely ramose at their extremity, and which, as well as the cord lying on the ventral plates, distribute themselves among all the viscera of the abdominal cavity near the surface of the plates. The radiating nerves of the last ganglion alone, which forms the analogue of the *cauda equina* of the superior animals, distribute themselves to the internal sexual organs and to the colon. In *Carabus, Hydrophilus, Cerambyx, Lytta,* and *Meloë* there are but these five ganglia, and never more.

Having observed in all these insects three distinct thoracic ganglia, one for each thoracic segment, we now come to those orders and families which have but two separated ganglia in the thorax. In the *Coleoptera* the large family of the *Lamellicornia* belong here. The accurate representation of the nervous system in *Melolontha vulgaris* in Straus * exhibits a heart-shaped ganglion lying in the prothorax, from which a robust nerve originates on each side, which speedily divides into several branches, the central thickest of which passes to the anterior leg, whereas the smaller ones distribute themselves between the muscles of the prothorax. The second ganglion, lying in front of the mesothorax, appears to consist properly of two closely contiguous ones, at least the aperture perceived in its centre evidently indicates an original separation. From the anterior division proceed the nerve of the intermediate foot and several branches for the muscles, as well as a nerve originating completely in front, which passes to the elytra; from the posterior division springs the nerve of the wing, which gives off branches to the muscles and the nerve of the posterior leg, which like-

* Straus, Pl. IX.

wise sends off many branches to the muscles. A third, also cordiform ganglion, lies closely to the posterior division of the second, and is seated, as well as that, in front of the tridentiform process of the metasternum; from it, as well as from the posterior margin of the preceding ganglion, fine radiating branches extend, all of which pass over the sternal process into the abdomen, and proceed to its ventral plates; two central thicker ones, the *cauda equina*, proceed to the sexual organs and the colon, distributing themselves there with many fine branches. The structure of the nervous system is similar in *Dyticus marginalis*: the prothorax has its own ganglion, which, by means of two thick and tolerably long nervous cords, is united to the cerebellum (Pl. XXXII. f. 2.). This ganglion lies always in front of the internal sternal process, and runs with its posterior cords through both its branches. The second ganglion, still larger than the first, lies precisely upon the mesosternum, in front of the commencement of its internal process; from it originate, as well as from the anterior, several nerves among which we distinguish at the first ganglion two large ones for the anterior legs (*a, a*), and at the second four thicker ones for the posterior legs (*b, b.* and *c, c.*). The nervous cord rises from this ganglion, runs between the branches of the sternal process, and lies here between the coxæ as a short nervous cord with four ganglia, which somewhat increase in size, whereas the first is scarcely one quarter so large as the second thoracic ganglion. From the circumference of these four ganglia numerous nerves originate, particularly from the last, which, radiating, proceed to the apex of the abdomen, and especially distribute themselves about the sexual organs. These last four ganglia consequently belong, as well as the third in *Melolontha*, to the abdomen, but they, however, rise as high as the coxæ, for here the most important muscles are found, whereas in the abdomen but few large ones are to be met with; on which account also in both cases the ganglia are wholly wanting in the abdomen.

This is not the case in the *Lepidoptera* and *Hymenoptera*, which likewise have but two ganglia in the thorax, but in them the abdomen also exhibits ganglia, namely, five in both orders, of which, however, the two last are also very approximate; and indeed in some cases, for example in *Philanthus pictus*, they are grown into one, so that in it we can detect but four distinct ganglia. The decrease of the ganglia in the thorax arises in the *Lepidoptera* from the growing together of most approximate ones, which takes place by degrees during the pupa state. Thus, from the first and second ganglia of the caterpillar the ganglion of the prothorax originates, from the third and fourth the common very large ganglion for the connate meso- and metathorax; the fifth ganglion of the caterpillar, as well as the sixth, entirely disappear; the seventh to the eleventh are found likewise in the imago. The ganglion of the prothorax lies in both orders between the branches of the internal sternal process, and gives off, besides the thick nerve for the anterior legs, finer branches for the muscles; the ganglion of the meso- and metathorax lies upon the central surface of the sternum, it is very large, and somewhat long; many nerves spring from it, eight of which are particularly distinguished. Two and two form an equal pair; the first and third pairs go to the wings, the second and fourth to the feet, the remaining finer ones distribute themselves among the muscles; the last pair, lying closely to the connecting cord, passes with this into the abdomen, and distributes itself in its first segment by means of several filaments. In *Bombus muscorum*, according to Treviranus' figure *, the second thoracic ganglion consists of an anterior larger and a posterior smaller half; but in many of the *Hymenoptera* inspected by me, for example, in *Vespa Germanica*, I could not distinguish them, there was but a single large ganglion visible.

Lastly, there are insects in which but one ganglion is found in the thorax, these are the *Diptera*. In them it is known that the thorax is formed of but one undivided piece, which consists especially of the mesothorax, to which the very small pro- and metathorax are but appended. In the mesothorax also we find the chief muscles, namely, the large direct dorsal and alary muscles, and accordingly a single large ganglion, which lies upon the centre of the sternum, between the intermediate and posterior legs. It takes the form of a long ganglion (Pl. XXXII. f. 4.), from which spring six main nerves for the legs. I have not yet detected nerves for the wings proceeding directly from the ganglion; perhaps they may be branches of the nerves of the feet. From the posterior margin of the ganglion a simple strong nervous filament passes, which, running between the apertures of the coxæ, proceed into the abdomen; closely before its entrance it gives off on each side a fine nerve, but in the abdomen itself it has no branch as far as the middle of its course. Here it first distends into a small ganglion, from which on each side a fine furcate nerve originates. A

---

* Biologie, vol. v. Pl. I. II. and III.

second somewhat larger ganglion lies some little distance beyond the first, exactly between the sexual organs, and gives off branches to this as well as to the colon. This description has been sketched from the *Eristalis tenax* of Meigen; in *Musca vomitoria* I found precisely the same structure.

§ 189.

III. THE SYMPATHIC SYSTEM.

A peculiar nervous system, which hung connected with the cerebrum by means of fine branches, and in its course spread itself about the anterior portion of the intestinal canal, was formerly discovered by Swammerdam in the larvæ of the rhinoceros-beetle (*Oryctes nasicornis* *), and by Lyonet in the larva of the large *Cossus* †. Subsequent anatomists took no further heed of this discovery; and until Cuvier, who described some of the forms of these nerves, it was not again thought of. Since then J. F. Meckel, Treviranus, and Marcel de Serres have described this system in individual insects; but Joh. Müller claims the greatest merit for giving the details of this system in a distinct treatise ‡, having proved these nerves to be peculiar to many insects, and for having represented them in several orders. J. Brandt § has likewise completed the observations of Müller, and has given a well-executed representation of the various relations of the nerves in the caterpillar and imago of the silkworm. From these earlier contributions, and from my own individual observations, I deduce the following results :—

§ 190.

The sympathic system is peculiar to all insects, but in the several orders it takes a different form: we may distinguish in it two main divisions. A single cord, which runs upon the surface of the œsophagus and stomach, giving off delicate branches on all sides, and where the œsophagus passes through the brain running with the œsophagus beneath the cerebrum: and a double nervous web, consisting of ganglia,

---

* Biblia Naturæ, Pl. XXVIII. f. 2 and 3.

† Lyonet, Pl. XII. f. 1. *h*.

‡ Nova Acta Phys. Med. Soc., tom. xiv. part i. p. 73, &c.

§ J. J. Brandt, Beobachtungen über die Systeme der Eingeweidenerven. Isis. 1831, p. 2003.

which originates on each side by one branch from the posterior portion of the cerebrum running down the œsophagus, and giving off here and there fine auxiliary branches to the single nervous cord. Both stand in a certain reciprocal relation to each other, in so far as where the double system preponderates the former diminishes, and where the single cord is considerably developed the double ganglia with their branches shrink up.

The single nervous cord is considerably most developed in the *Coleoptera, Lepidoptera,* and *Libellulæ*. It here originates with two branches arched towards each other, springing from the anterior portion of the cerebrum, contiguous to the nerves of the antennæ. Both branches unite at the centre, and form a small ganglion (*ganglium frontale*), and from this the single nerve proceeds beneath the brain (Pl. XXXII. f. 6—8. *a, a.*). This, from its bending form, Swammerdam and Cuvier called the *nervus recurrens*. The arch is sometimes double, as in the silkworm (Pl. XXXII. f. 6 and 7.). In the *Coleoptera*, on the contrary, always simple (the same, f. 8.); but yet in both finer branches originate from this arch, which sink to the anterior wall of the œsophagus, and pass even into the labrum. In some *Coleoptera*, for example, *Melolontha*, these arching branches are so fine that they even escaped the accurate Straus; he detected but two delicate filaments to arise from the frontal ganglion, lying in front of the cerebrum, which appeared to bend about the œsophagus. I also have not been able distinctly to perceive in several beetles this connexion of the frontal ganglion with the cerebrum. When the filament has passed behind the brain it runs along the œsophagus as a simple cord, which nevertheless gives off everywhere very delicate auxiliary branches to the tunics of the œsophagus, as far as the stomach, and here divides itself into two equal branches, forming at the point of division a small ganglion, from which, besides the two main stems, many other smaller filaments proceed. Where the stomach commences in the craw, consequently in the predaceous insects, and at the anterior half of the large simple stomach in the vegetable feeders, its last very delicate branches terminate, for they sink between the tunics of the stomach, and there lose themselves; indeed, in the cases in which the œsophagus is tolerably long, they but just reach the stomach itself, without spreading themselves over it. This description of the distribution of the single nervous cord will suit also the *Lepidoptera*, for in them also it never extends beyond the commencement of the stomach, but furcates shortly before this spot, and ramifies into the finest threads.

The double nervous system in these orders consists of four small ganglia, which lie directly behind the brain upon the œsophagus. The anterior generally somewhat larger ganglion (f. 6—8. *b. b.*) arises with one (*Coleoptera*) or two (*Lepidoptera*) branches from one half of the cerebrum, and sends outwards delicate branches about the œsophagus, but inwards a branch which unites itself with the single nervous cord lying between the two ganglia. The second smaller ganglion (the same, $b^*. b^*.$) stands in connexion with the first by means of a nerve of communication; it also sends off fine branches, which run along the œsophagus: indeed, in the *Lepidoptera*, it also unites itself again with the unequal cord. This last ganglion of the double system was discovered at the same time by Straus Durkheim, and Brandt: the first was discovered by Lyonet in the *Cossus* caterpillar, but its connexion with the single cord escaped him.

§ 191.

The double nervous system attains its most complete development in the *Orthoptera*, namely, in *Locusta* and *Gryllus*. In *Gryllus migratorius* (Pl. XXXI. f. 6.), there are found immediately behind the brain, upon the superior surface of the œsophagus, five different ganglia. The central and smallest (*b.*) lies nearest the brain, in which its two halves make considerable constrictions, being united on each side by means of a fine branch within each hemisphere. Between these two connecting branches this ganglion meets the single cord, which, coming from the frontal ganglion beneath the brain, originates likewise with two arched branches from the anterior side of the brain, and from the frontal ganglion itself sends off delicate branches forwards. Posteriorly this single nerve does not quit the central ganglion, but wholly terminates in it. Two other ganglia, which lie closely to the central one (*c. c.*), are the largest of all, and have the form of a figure of eight, and stand in connexion with the central one by means of one, and with the brain by means of two branches. At its posterior end two other branches originate from it, the exterior of which is the longest; both furcate, the latter after it has first swollen at the point of separation into a small ganglion (*e.*). Close to these two ganglia, we find at the lateral margins of the œsophagus two other oval but somewhat smaller ones (*d. d.*), which are connected with the central one by means of two, and with the brain by one only, but tolerably robust nerves. Two branches originate posteriorly from them, but which speedily reunite in a smaller ganglion ($d^* d^*$), which then sends off a long, rather strong filament. This filament runs down by the side of the œsophagus, and passes with it into the prothorax. The œsophagus here distends into the crop, and about the centre of which, each nerve forms a small ganglion ($f.f.$), from which two furcate branches, which embrace the œsophagus, proceed: the nerve then runs undivided on until it attains the end of the crop. Here it forms the second ganglion ($g. g.$), which again sends off three double branches, each of which furcates. The branches of these furcate nerves, six in number, or twelve on both sides, pass between the six cæca lying at the orifice of the stomach, and distribute themselves over them in the most delicate threads. In *Gryllus hieroglyphicus*, according to Müller[*], the upper ganglion is again found, but its relative proportion is not very evident from his representation; the nerve running down the œsophagus has no ganglia, but many fine branches are given off along its whole course. In *Acheta Gryllotalpa*[†], the downward running nerves are very distinct: both give off auxiliary branches, particularly to the sack-shaped distended crop. In the proventriculus, they again unite to form a tolerably considerable ganglion, whence many branches originate, which distribute themselves over it. *Blatta* and *Mantis* have but a central single nervous cord, which appears, however, to proceed from the ganglion lying behind the brain.

IV. The Organs of the Senses.

§ 192.

Of all the several organs of the senses, the eye alone possesses a superior development: nose and ear are not yet proved to exist, and taste likewise can be present only in a few, at least to a degree worthy of investigation; but touch, which never properly possesses a distinct and constant organ, but, according to the differences of animal organisation, is sometimes imparted to one and sometimes to another organ, has, in the majority of the orders, peculiar organs varying in their grade of development.

Of these senses, we will first examine that of sight, as the most perfect.

[*] Pl. IX. f. 5.   [†] Ib. f. 2.

The form, situation, number, and external differences of the eyes of insects, have been already sufficiently described in the first division of our present inquiry; we can therefore presume that all these points are known, and proceed at once to its internal structure. Upon turning a preliminary glance to the history of the progress of these observations, we shall find all the earlier investigations unsatisfactory. The facets in the eyes of different insects were numbered, the optic nerve and its radial branches were also known, and a distinction was made between compound and simple eyes, without the peculiar structure of the latter being detected. After such, upon the whole unsatisfactory, preludatory labours*, Marcel de Serres † undertook a more comprehensive investigation of the eyes of insects, in which he, indeed, discovered much that was new, but was far from exhausting the subject, which is evident from the subsequent labours of Joh. Müller ‡. It was reserved to this indefatigable inquirer to give a comprehensible explanation of the eyes of insects, and to lay the foundation of the correct doctrine of the sight of insects with both compound and simple eyes. The following is the result of his admirable investigation, confirmed by Dügès §, in opposition to Straus-Durkheim ||.

The simple eyes of insects agree entirely in structure with the eyes of the superior animals, particularly of the fish. It is found in all the larvæ of insects with a perfect metamorphosis, and in many families of perfect insects of all orders. The following Table will give a more precise survey.

I. Insects with merely simple eyes.
   a. The larvæ of *Coleoptera, Lepidoptera, Hymenoptera, Neuroptera,* and *Diptera* (with the exception of *Culex* and the approximate water larvæ, which possess compound eyes).
   b. The *Dictyotoptera, Thysanoura* (with the exception of *Machilis* and *Mallophaga*).
II. Insects with simple and compound eyes.
   a. The majority of insects with an imperfect metamorphosis,— consequently.

---

* Consult Schelver Versuch einer Naturgeschichte der Sinneswerkzeuge bei den Insekten. Gotting. 1798. 8vo.

† Mém. sur les Yeux composés, et les Yeux lissés des Insectes. Montp. 1813. 8vo.

‡ Zur Vergleichende Physiologie des Gesichtssinnes. Leip. 1826. 8vo., and Suppt. to it, in Meckel's Archiv. 1828.

§ Annales des Sc. Nat. xx. 341. 6. || Ib. tom. xviii. p. 463.

1. *Orthoptera* collectively, without *Forficula*.
2. *Dictyoptera, Libellula,* and *Ephemera*, have three simple eyes, *Termes* but two.
3. *Hemiptera*. The majority of bugs have two simple eyes; some, for example, *Lygœus apterus*, none. The majority of *Cicada* have three simple eyes; some, for example, *Membracis, Flata*, but two. The water bugs, as *Nepa, Ranatra, Naucoris, Notonecta, Sigara*, display no simple eyes.

b. Of insects with a perfect metamorphosis:
1. The *Diptera*. Generally three, seldom two (*Mycetophila*) simple eyes. The *Tipularia, Culicina,* and *Gallifica*, are excepted, as they possess no simple eyes.
2. The *Lepidoptera*. Two simple eyes in the crepuscular moths and *Noctuæ* (perhaps in all?)
3. All *Hymenoptera* have three simple eyes upon the vertex (some neuter ants are blind, as well as the majority of larvæ).
4. *Neuroptera*. Three simple eyes as well as compound ones in *Phryganea, Semblis, Raphidia, Panorpa, Osmylus*.
5. *Coleoptera*. Two simple eyes in *Onthophagus, Omalium,* and *Paussus*.

III. Insects with merely compound eyes.
a. All *Coleoptera*, with the exception of the above-named genera, *Anthophagus, Omalium,* and *Paussus*, the two points upon whose vertex are supposed to be simple eyes.
b. Besides, several already-named genera and families of other orders, as, *Machilis, Forficula, Hydrocorides, Tipularia, Culicina, Gallifica, Hemerobius, Myrmecoleon, Ascalaphus,* &c.
c. The larvæ of insects with an imperfect metamorphosis. In the larvæ of the *Cicada* and *Gryllus*, the simple eyes are indicated by spots, and the compound ones have fewer facets than in the imago.

With respect to the internal structure of the simple eye, there is found beneath the very smooth hemispherical, or, at least, convex transparent horny integument, a small globular transparent lens, which lies closely attached to the horny integument, and fits into a corresponding cavity in the inner surface of that integument. Behind the lens lies a truly lens-shaped glassy body, larger in compass than the lens, corresponding with the entire circumference of the eye, but proportionately less convex. Both hemispherical divisions of the glassy body are of a different convexity, and, indeed, the upper is the flatter, and the lower the most convex side. The rete or superior bowl-shaped distended end of the optic nerve spreads itself at the posterior margin of the glassy body. It closely embraces this body, which lies in it as in a shell. It is again exteriorly covered by the pigment. This bends itself in the entire circumference of the eye, up to the horny tunic, and forms around the lens a small iris beneath that tunic. Where the optic nerve spreads into the rete, the pigment covers it, but thus far it comes entirely free from the cerebrum, as was shown above. The pigment varies much in colour: in the majority of cases it is of a brown red or dark cherry brown, sometimes black, or of a bright blood red. In this case, or, rather, in general, the margin lying next to the horny integument shines through it, and thus forms in the circumference of the lens a beautifully coloured iris. It is more evident in the large eyes of the scorpions and of the *Solpugæ*, but even the small eyes of insects exhibit an annular iris.

§ 194.

The presence of compound eyes is shown by the above Table. Regarding their structure, the horny integument consists of many small hexagonal surfaces, which correspond exactly with each other, and cause the hemispherical, or, at least, convex figure of the superior surface of the eye. Each of these hexagonal facets, the number of which varies, and is sometimes very considerable, as the following list of them shows,

Mordella	25,088
Libellula	12,544
Papilio	17,355
Sphinx Convolvulus	1,300
Cossus ligniperda	11,300
Œstrus	7,000
Liparis Mori	6,236
Musca Domestica	4,000
Formica	50

forms a distinct lens, convex on both sides, varying in thickness. The proportion of its thickness to its transverse diameter is, for example, in a sphinx, 1 : 2 ; in others, this lens is still thicker, which is especially the case in all insects with an imperfect metamorphosis. Nevertheless, each lens is flatter in them than in other insects, and we must here consequently regard every individual lens as cut at its margin, so that merely the central most elevated portion remains. Were this not the case in thick and flattish lenses, objects would necessarily appear indistinct. In *Gryllus hieroglyphicus*, Joh. Müller * detected the proportion of the breadth to the thickness to be 1 : 7. The space at the circumference of the facets is covered by the pigment collected between the filaments of the optic nerve, so that each individual facet is surrounded with a ring of pigment or kind of iris; the disk, however, remains free and transparent. Upon the superior surface we occasionally observe, particularly in the bees and flies, fine hairs projecting, which may be considered as analogous to the eye-lashes, as they doubtlessly prevent the approach of external bodies, but at the same time limit the visual circle of each facet to the space itself occupies.

Upon the inner surface of each individual lens we find a transparent crystalline cone, the convex surface of which touches merely the centre of each facet, but leaves a small space around the circumference free for the ring of pigment. The circumference of each of these cones is for a certain space not inclined but perpendicular, thus giving the crystalline body a more cylindrical form, which, however, gradually diminishes, and they internally run to a point, to which a delicate filament of the radiating optic nerve passes. The pigment or peculiar colouring matter, which occupies the whole inner space of the eye, passes between these cones, enveloping the filaments of the optic nerve as far as the facets forming the iris around the circumference of the base of the cone. In this manner each individual facet with its crystalline body is separated from the other, and may therefore be considered as a distinct eye. The length of these cones varies not only in different insects, but often in the same, from its position being either marginal or central. We may consider, in general, that, in such eyes which form no segment of a circle, those cones which are found at the flattest part of the eye are the longest, and the others situated at the more convex parts, the shortest, but the basal surface of the cone does not vary, but is always regulated by the form of the facet. Their length cannot be precisely determined, but, in such eyes which form the

* Where cited above, p. 241.

segment of a circle, or which are hemispherical, it is regulated by the size of the entire sphere : larger and consequently flatter spheres, receive longer ones, and smaller, and, therefore, more convex ones, receive shorter cones. In one of the *Noctuæ*, Joh. Müller found the proportions of length to the breadth of the base to be as 5 to 1. In *Œschna*, these relations, according to Dügès' figure, are as 10 to 1 ; the base itself also rises so much, that it even appears conical.

As we have mentioned above, a filament of the optic nerve stands in connexion with the apex of each cone. These filaments are thin, extremely delicate nerves, which, like the rays of a sphere, originate from the exterior surface of the optic nerve, and spread themselves to the circumference, one passing to each cone. Nothing further can be remarked of them ; a separation or radiating division of them has never been observed. They bring the external portion of the eye into connexion with the cerebrum, and may be therefore considered as the most important conductors of the sense of sight. According to the figure of Straus, this nerve somewhat distends where it joins the crystalline body, and encompasses its apex, there forming a kind of retina ; but Müller and Dügès never detected this distension of the filaments of the optic nerve.

The dark pigment spreads all over the entire eye between the filaments of the optic nerve. It is a variously coloured, generally a dark purple red, sometimes brighter (*Mantis*), thickish fluid, which is transpierced throughout by fine tracheal branches, which proceed from a trachea surrounding the inner circumference of the eye like a ring. This layer of colour consequently corresponds with the *choroidea* of the higher animals, which is both colouring matter and a vascular tunic. The pigment in the majority of insects admits of being divided into two layers, from its difference of colour. The external brighter pigment displays very various colours, as is proved by the mere appearance of the eyes. All bright, glittering metallic eyes, or such as are ornamented with stripes and spots, derive their painting and markings from this superficial pigment. I will cite here merely the green yellow eyes of the butterflies of the genus *Pontia* and the banded metallic eyes of the *Tabani*, the brassy coloured ones of the *Hemerobia*, and the beautifully coloured eyes of so many other insects. The internal pigment is uniformly dark, but, likewise, it is not entirely similar in all insects, but varies according to the families and genera. *Mantis* exhibits it bright red, the moths violet, many butterflies of a blue violet, and other butterflies, the *Hymenoptera* and *Coleoptera*, of a dark blue or entirely black. Even in insects which possess but one pigment, the colour is not entirely the same, but darker nearer the centre, brighter at its circumference in the vicinity of the glass cone and lens. In some cases we discover more than two layers of pigment, as, for example, in *Gryllus hieroglyphicus*, an exterior pale orange colour, a central bright red, and a dark violet. The first and second were very thin, each thinner than the lenses; the innermost entirely filled the remaining portion of the eye[*].

Thus much upon the structure of the eye. We may here once more repeat that this entire description is but an extract of Joh. Müller's admirable treatise upon this subject, and that here merely the most interesting portion of his results are stated. The subsequent labours of Straus Durkheim[†] and Düges do not equal those of the above distinguished entomotomist, nor have they been able to add many new discoveries or corrections of his.

§ 195.

Much obscurity still invests our knowledge of the hearing of insects. G. R. Treviranus[‡] has, indeed, discovered and described the organ of hearing of the moths; it consists of a simple thin drum, which is seated at the forehead in front of the base of each antenna, and to which the nerves of hearing, which are branches of the nerves of the antennæ, spread themselves without the intermedium of a hearing bladder filled with water; but this admirable discovery of his has not been confirmed in insects of other orders, for a similar organ has not yet been detected in them. After him, Joh. Müller[§] described the peculiar organ of the grasshopper, which is seated on each side at the base of the abdomen; he considered it the organ of hearing, but incorrectly, as will be shown below: it is more likely to be an organ of sound. Other earlier opinions, for example, those of Ramdohr[||], who considered the anterior salivary glands of the bees as organs of hearing, are partly, as this latter, recalled, or else, as unsatisfactory, require no further notice. To these may be classed Comparetti's observations of bags and passages in the heads of

---

[*] Müller, p. 855.   [†] Considérations Général, &c., p. 409
[‡] Annalen du Wetterau. Gesell. f. d. Ges. Naturk. Vol. i. Pt. 2. 1809.
[§] Consult his Phys. du Gesischtssinnes. p. 438.
[||] Mag. du Ges. Naturf. Berlin. 1811. 389.

individual insects, to which cavities nervous filaments were said to be distributed*. It is evident that some misconception was here at work, for no entomotomist, either before him or since, has seen any thing of the kind. But as insects doubtlessly hear, as some, for example, the *Cicada*, grasshoppers, many beetles, &c., produce a peculiar sound, which serves to attract the attention of the female, they must evidently be provided with an organ of hearing, which is either very recondite, or referred to organs whose form does not evince their function. The antennæ are doubtlessly of this class, and, indeed, Sulzer, Scarpa, Schneider, Borkhausen, Reaumur, and Bonnsdorf, considered them as organs of hearing. That they are not organs of touch, is proved anatomically by their horny hard upper surface, and physiologically by the observation that insects never use them as such, this function being exercised by other organs, namely, the *palpi*. Besides, the analogy of the crabs, in which it is well known that the organ of hearing lies at the base of the large antennæ, speaks in favour of the adoption of the opinion of their being in general organs of hearing. If after this hint we look to the insertion of the antennæ, we likewise detect here a soft articulating membrane, which lies exposed, and which is rendered tense by the motion of the antennæ. This membrane, beneath which the nerve of the antennæ runs, might, without much inconsistency, be explained as the drum of the ear, and thus would the antennæ be transformed pelices, which, as very moveable parts, would receive the vibrations of the air, caused by sound, and act as a conductor to it. Whoever has observed a tranquilly proceeding capricorn beetle, which is suddenly surprised by a loud sound, will have seen how immoveably outwards it spreads its antennæ, and holds them porrect as it were with the greatest attention as long as it listens, and how carelessly the insect proceeds in its course when it conceives that no danger threatens it from the unusual noise. Carus ‡, Straus Durkheim §, and Oken ||, are of the same opinion, and which I have entertained for years, and endeavoured to confirm myself in by numerous experiments.

---

* Schelver, as above, p. 51. † Ib. p. 24. ‡ Zootomie, p. 65.
§ Consid. Générales, p. 415, &c.
|| It was not unpleasing to me to find in the recent edition of Oken's Naturphilosophie, my opinion stated in almost the same words in which I wrote them down. Consult that work, p. 421, No. 3355. The earlier edition of this work did not contain the idea. See Vol. iii. p. 274, No. 3100.

§ 196.

Much more doubt and uncertainty attends the observations and opinions upon the organ of smell of insects. Reaumur, Lyonet, and several modern French naturalists, consider the antennæ as such, but I would ask with what right? A hard, horny organ, displaying no nerve upon its surface, cannot possibly be the instrument of smell, for we always find in the olfactory organ a soft, moist, mucous membrane, furnished with numerous nerves. No such tunic is to be found in insects, at least in their head, or upon the surface of their bodies. Marcel de Serres *, and before him, Bonnsdorf †, endeavoured to prove the *palpi* organs of smell, he described pores at their extremities, namely, in the *Orthoptera*, which passed through its soft apex into the interior, and here distributed nervous branches ; he also considered that the tracheæ of the *palpi* opened into the mouth, and that thereby a constant stream of air was kept through them ; but it is all fanciful without any satisfactory foundation. The *palpi* have no pores at their extremity, and their tracheæ have no external orifice. Comparetti ‡ found cavities and cells beneath the frons, which nobody ever saw, either since or before, and these he considers organs of smell. More recently, F. Rosenthal § described a folded skin at the forehead, beneath the antennæ, to which two fine nerves passed, and which he considers as the organs of smell of *Musca domestica* and *vomitoria;* and he observed, after the destruction of the part, a deficiency of the function which had previously strongly exhibited itself. But it is with this as with the discovery of the organ of hearing in *Blatta;* we cannot reason from it, as similar structures have not been observed in other insects, and precisely in the dung beetles, which have the sense so acute, the forehead is covered with a horny shield, that it is wholly impossible odours should pass through it. Indeed, in the burying beetles (*Necrophori*), which decidedly possess the most acute smell of all the *Coleoptera*, have above the mouth, upon the clypeus, a triangular yellow somewhat deep spot, having the appearance of a membrane stretched over it, and this might be considered the analogue of the organ of smell discovered by Rosenthal ; but, upon closer inspection, this spot appears to consist also of a horny material, and we therefore cannot conceive it possible

---

* Annal. du Mus. T. xviii. pp. 426—441.
† De fabrica et usu Palporum in Insectis. Aboæ, 1792.   ‡ Schelver, p. 46.
§ Reil's Archiv. Vol. x. p. 427.

for scents to pass through it. This difficulty was endeavoured to be obviated by imagining that they passed through the mucous membrane of the mouth to that smelling membrane, in which case it might be common to all insects, but which is not the case. For this explanation of it appears to me forced, as well as a second advanced by Treviranus*, who wishes to persuade us that the entire mucous membrane of the mouth is the organ of smell, but then especially ascribes this sense to haustellate insects.

A different opinion is that formerly advanced by Baster, Dumeril, and, latterly, by Straus Durkheim †, namely, that the margins of the stigmata are smelling organs. We have, it is true, in favour of it, the analogy of the organ of smell in the superior animals being seated at the orifice of the respiratory organs, but that is absolutely all. The mucous membrane, the nervous rete, and the nerves of smell, are all wanting, or, at least, are not shown to exist. Perhaps, however, the tracheæ may possibly be organs of smell, if not at their aperture, yet in their terminal ramifications, as they conduct air to all the organs, and particularly likewise to the brain. Hence would follow the deficiency of a peculiar organ of smell, which, however, must strike as singular when we reflect upon the lower situated crab. But water organs and organs of humidity, and such the organ of smell evidently is ‡, for it is only with a moist nose that we can smell, more easily attain a certain degree of perfection than in those which live in a rarer medium. I will merely refer to the difference of the organs of smell in water and land birds, as well as to the observation that the organs of smell in birds are proportionably less perfect than in the amphibia and fishes, which evidently helps to confirm the law, and serves to explain the deficiency of these organs in insects. Thus insects, according to my opinion, would smell with the internal superior surface, if I may so call it, which is provided all over with ramifications and nets of nerves, since this is always retained moist by the blood distributed through the body and by the transpired chyle, the same as is surmised of the superior *mollusca*, namely, the *Pulmobranchia* and *Cephalopoda*, that their sense of smell is seated in their exterior integument and thus in a universally distributed smelling tunic.

---

* Vermischte Schriften. Vol. ii. p. 146. † Considérations, p. 421.

‡ The whales want the auxiliary cavities of the nose, which secrete the fluid, because, living in water, they do not require them. See Rudolphi Physiol. Vol. ii. Pl. I., p. 118.

§ 197.

The tongue is always the organ of taste where present. We have seen above that many insects, namely, the *Orthoptera, Libellulæ*, the majority of beetles, many *Hymenoptera*, and, indeed, all mandibulate insects, possess a more or less distinct tongue; we have but to ask, may we consider this tongue as the organ of taste?—Taste can be of importance only to such animals as feed upon a variety of substances and masticate them. In haustellate insects this is not the case; they always subsist upon one and the same food, and generally inhabit what they feed on, and consequently less require this sense. Indeed, they are wholly deficient in a fleshy tongue, which can alone taste, and when present as stiff setæ, taste cannot be spoken of. But that the fleshy tongue which we find in the *Libellulæ* and grasshoppers is certainly an organ of taste, is corroborated by its delicate and soft superior surface, its greater abundance of nerves, and, lastly, the various nature of their food, which is visibly slowly masticated, and furnished with saliva from the mouths of the ducts of the glands lying beneath the tongue. To these we may add the wasps and bees, which suck the honey of various flowers by means of their tongue, which is provided at its apex with distinct glandular points, that, besides the business of ingestion, serve doubtlessly to taste and distinguish the various kinds of honey. This may also doubtlessly be maintained of the in general soft membranous tongue of the *Staphylini*. Some physiologists, for example, Rudolphi, deny the sense of taste to insects; others seat it in the *palpi*, where it certainly does not belong; and others, again, Straus, for instance, discover it in the tongue, where it is doubtlessly to be sought, and frequently sufficiently distinctly exhibited. The abortion of the tongue in many mandibulate insects ought not to surprise us; its cause, as well as the abortion of the organ of smell, is the preponderance of the function of respiration, as the tongue is likewise a humid organ, for, in insects, every organ, by reason of the universal distribution of air in them, has a tendency to become dry and horny. In this they again find their parallelism in the birds, whose tongue is small, imperfect, almost cartilaginous, indeed frequently (*Pteroglossus*) perfectly horny, and resembling a feather, exactly like the tongue of many beetles, for example, the *Capricorns*, in the internal organs of which there is a strong disposition to become horny.

§ 198.

Everybody will admit that insects, more than many other animals, require a peculiar organ of touch, from their being encased in a hard insensible integument. It is true the antennæ have long had this function ascribed to them, but incorrectly; the hard horny antennæ may possibly well detect the presence of objects, but certainly arrive at no other precise perception, for this requires a soft organ clothed with a very delicate covering. Straus Durkheim * therefore justly wonders how this function could have been ascribed to the antennæ; but he astonishes us still more by considering the still harder feet as organs of touch. By far the majority of insects have hard, horny, perfectly closed foot-joints, and the few which are furnished with setæ, feathers, or pulvilli at their plantæ or apex of their tarsi do not use them as organs of touch, but merely to assist in climbing; indeed, there are some genera whose feet have soft fleshy balls (*Xenos, Thrips, Gryllus, Locusta*), but these instances cannot prove it throughout an entire class. For the rest, his opinion loses still more probability, when, instead of his tarsal joints other organs can be shown as instruments of touch. These organs are the palpi, already indicated by their name. If we inspect the palpi of the larger insects, for example, of the predatory beetles, the grasshoppers, humble-bees, and many others, we observe at its apex a white, transparent, distended bladder, which, after the death of the creature, dries into a concavity seated at the apex of the palpus. This bladder is the true organ of touch, the main nerve of the maxillæ and of the tongue spreads to it, and distributes itself upon its superior surface with the finest branches. Straus †, who carefully observed this bladder, explains it as a sense of a peculiar description, analogous to the taste-smell sense (*Geruchsgeschmackssinn*) of the *Ruminantia*, discovered by Jacobson, but just as little as a union of the senses of smell and taste conditionates the presence of a peculiar sense may we explain the palpi as sensual organs of a peculiar description: they are, whence they were named, namely, purely organs of touch. The deficiency of palpi in haustellate insects may be objected to here; but have not these in their long proboscis a better organ of touch, and do not we find everywhere in nature in all the organs an evident adaptation to

---

* Considérations, p. 425.   † Ibid., p. 427.

their object? Where the palpi are the sheaths of the proboscis, as in the *Lepidoptera* and *Hemiptera*, they could no longer remain true organs of touch; and where they have grown into a fleshy proboscideal sheath, as in the flies, this sheath is the organ of touch, and properly, also, the palpus itself is considered as contained in it. If, however, living insects have been observed, no further objection will be taken to the exclusive function of touch exercised by the palpi; who still doubts who has observed the play of the palpi of the spiders previous to copulation, or seen predatory insects fall upon an unexpected prey, and feeling it upon all sides? The common, well-known, domestic fly, lastly, can daily convince us, when we perceive it moving from spot to spot, and detect every drop of liquid and every atom of sugar with the sheath of its proboscis formed of the labial palpi. It first feels them, and then ravenously swallows them; but this touch is never exercised by its tarsi, but invariably by the sheath of its proboscis.

THIRD SECTION.

PHYSIOLOGY.

§ 199.

We have now, after the preceding description of the insect body, both external and internal, arrived at the point whence we can survey the life of insects in one large representation, and, as it were, overlooking form, shall only endeavour to seize their spiritual effects. This is, namely, the theme of Physiology, to exhibit to us in a simple but well-ordered description all the phenomena of the organic world, which befits it only as the abstract of living beings, and which must be considered consequently as the results of animation, and as the necessary attendants of life; and as general physiology undertakes to solve this problem with reference to the whole of animated nature, the physiology of a solitary group can be expected merely to occupy itself with the description of the vital relations of this group. Such a group is formed by the world of insects, and the task of our physiology found. Here, consequently, belongs all that does not refer to the description of form; and here belongs also every phenomenon which individuals or numbers of insects have betrayed to the observer, however insignificant and unimportant to the illustration of the whole they may originally appear to us; and it is its task to arrange these phenomena, and to reduce them to recognised laws, and where this will not succeed, thence to prove the possible falsity of a principle adopted as true. The OBSERVATION of insects is therefore the foundation of their physiology, and it will be only when all the various phenomena of all the families, genera, and species shall be fully known that a perfect solution may be expected to be given of the problem of physiology; until then our knowledge will be but fragmentary. But the difficulty of the fulfilment of this necessary requisition is evinced by the number of years that have already passed over the study of the insect world without more than one-hundredth of our native insects having been observed throughout all the conditions of their existence. But he who should wonder at this apparently small amount of observation will at least admit that observation is one of the most difficult occupations, and that to accomplish it as much earnestness, skill, and luck are required as patience, leisure, and industry, and that the former as well as the other requisitions are not found every day in everybody. We justly, therefore, admire and venerate men like Reaumur, De Geer, Swammerdamm, Rösel, Bonnet, Huber, Lyonet, Rengger, Carus, Treviranus, &c., whose multifarious endeavours and labours have acquired for us the knowledge which may be considered as forming the foundation of our conclusions and future deductions.

To observation, which is more subject to casual opportunity, we may append EXPERIMENT, as a second means of enlarging the compass of physiological knowledge. Experiment is an observation produced forcibly, and consequently not so fully to be depended upon as those derived from secretly watching nature; we must therefore be more cautious in experimenting, for nature constrained frequently adopts a form and figure which in a state of freedom she would despise. This is, namely, still more the case in the lower animals, from their possessing a greater power of adaptation to circumstances than the higher ones; I will merely refer to Trembley's well-known experiments upon the polypi, as well as to Spallanzani's history of the reviviscence of the wheel animal; which last, however, according to Ehrenberg's recent observations, are untrue. This has been also the case in insects; for who would not be incredulous upon being told that the larvæ of a fly (*Eristalis tenax*. Meig.) will admit of being pressed in a book-binder's press as broad and thin as a card without being killed, when freed from its confinement and returned to its usual dwelling-place?

§ 200.

Having learnt the way whereby physiological facts may be acquired, we must look for a method according to which these facts may be appropriately classed. If with this object we reflect upon all the phenomena relating to the life of insects, we shall find a portion of them refer particularly to the functions of the body, and another portion develope higher, and, as it were, intellectual tendencies in insects. To the first belong those observations which acquaint us with their generation, nutrition, motion, and sensation; to the other the care of the parent for the offspring, the construction of their habitations, the various localities of various groups, and the thence originating geographical distribution, and lastly, the influence insects exercise during their lives upon nature generally, and especially upon man, and which he, as if nature were created for him alone, distinguishes as the benefits and injuries of the insect world. Each of these main divisions has its several subdivisions. All observations, consequently, which belong to somatic physiology can refer merely to the functions of the organic system, and consequently they follow in the order of these four systems. The subdivision of the second, or psychological physiology, or their psychology, is more difficult, but a portion of their spiritual phenomena may be more or less accurately arranged according to those organic systems, and to which may be appended, lastly, the result of observations upon the influence of insects upon nature generally. This view presents the following arrangement:—

I. Somatic physiology.
    a. Origin and propagation of insects.
    b. Nutriment and development of insects.
    c. Motions of insects.
    d. Sensual phenomena.

II. Psychological physiology, or psychology.
    a. Sexual instinct.
    b. Nutrimental instinct.
    c. Dwelling-place—degrees of warmth and cold—geographical distribution.
    d. Benefits and injuries produced to man.

FIRST SUBSECTION.

SOMATIC PHYSIOLOGY.

§ 201.

The path pursued by somatic physiology in the development of its contents is the same as that followed by nature in the development of insects. We commence, therefore, with the first appearance of the insect in nature, with its generation, which properly precedes its existence, in fact producing it. If the generation be effective, its whole subsequent life is mere development, and its first appearance is its development in the egg. In the egg it first takes an independent existence, and it requires but the most universal agents in nature, light, air, and warmth, to raise its, as it were, preformed individuality to its perfect individuality, and thus its life in the egg characterises the first act of its existence as an insect. When the embryo period is closed, the larva, more independent than before, takes its place in nature. Its whole object is development, and this it attains by means of nutriment. Growth is the consequence of its then excessive voracity; its skin becomes too narrow, it strips it off, and acquires a new one. This moulting it repeats several times, until full grown, and it then first feels that it has, as it were, overfed itself; it therefore ceases, fasts some days, again moults, and in a tolerably long period of continual sleep it lives upon its own fat; the intestinal canal consequently shrinks up, and at its expense the organs of generation are developed. This period may be compared with the stage of puberty in man and animals. When, however, this last period of development is completed, the perfected insect makes its appearance in its full state of activity with preponderating irritable and sensible organs. Motion and sensation are its life, propagation its end, and to which its chief spiritual functions are directed. The male seeks the female with restless fervour, the latter allows itself to be found, and yields, and its spiritual life then commences in its care about the depositing its eggs, in the structure of its nest, and its anxiety for its young. The males do not at all participate in these occupations, but become, as in the bees, turned forth as unprofitable members of the community.

This therefore is the subject of our inquiry in the first subsection, and its transit to the second, and their connexion together is also thus exposed.

FIRST CHAPTER.

OF GENERATION.

§ 202.

Under generation, in its broadest sense, is understood the origin of organic beings. The full application of the principle, that "from nothing nothing can be produced," is here exemplified; a foundation must always pre-exist to produce a new organism. If this foundation be the universally distributed organisable matter whence absolutely lower organisms may be developed, it is called single generation (*generatio in æqualis*), or, also, equivocal generation (*generatio originaria s. æquivoca*). If, however, the foundation be another animated body whence the new individual is developed through the active agency of the old one, it is called double generation (*generatio æqualis*), or propagation (*generatio propagativa*). Propagation may be also of several descriptions; for either a portion of the old individual is separated, and becomes an independent being, which is called propagation by shoots; or else in the body of the old individual the commencement of a new one is developed, which germen having attained its maturity quits the maternal sphere, and thus acquires an independent existence, which is called propagation by germens; or lastly, the development of this germ can only succeed by the mother receiving, or even the germ itself made competent to it by the intromission of, a peculiar exciting fluid. This last and most limited mode of propagation is distinguished by the character of sexual, and the active individual or active portion is called male, and that upon which it acts, the passive part, or germ-forming individual, the female. If these two faculties be united in one individual, it is then called hermaphrodite.

These several relations are the abstract of all the phenomena characterised by the name of generation throughout nature. Indeed, some exhibit modifications in their form, but they remain absolutely the same: for example, the propagation by shoots, when, as in the *Infusoria*, it presents itself as a separation in halves. Here the stem forms a shoot, which costs it the half of its substance, whereas in the usual propagation by shoots in the polypi, but a very small portion separates from the stem. But we may first ask, do all these different modes of propagation present themselves in insects? or, are there generalised observations upon the origin of insects which exclude the one or the other kind of propagation? Are these observations sufficient to deduce thence a general law, or do they admit of extension to but a very few limited cases? The investigation of these several questions will constitute our first inquiry.

§ 203.

With respect to observations upon the equivocal generation of insects, we possess many credible authorities which confirm it. The best known phenomenon of this description is the Phthiriasis, or lousy disease, in which a particular species of louse (*Pediculus tabescentium*, Alt.*) originates upon the skin, and collects in great numbers at particular spots, chiefly upon the breast, the back, and the neck, between folds of the skin, making the skin uneven, so that scale-shaped lappets of the epidermis peel off, and beneath which the lice conceal themselves. We find in ancient, and here and there in modern authors, testimonies of their spontaneous origin, the true cause whereof may consist in a general corruption of the juices in old, weak, and enervated subjects. Pheretima, according to Herodotus, and Antiochus Epiphanes, both Herodians, Sylla, Alcmanus, the Emperor Maximian, the poet Eunius, the philosophers Pherecydes and Plato, Philip the Second, and the poet and actor Iffland, are said to have died of it; and very recently, at Bonn, at the clinical school there, a woman of seventy was found to be thus diseased, but was cured by the rubbing-in of the oil of turpentine. Fournier † relates another instance of it in a cleanly lying-in woman, who had much covered her head, and after suffering headache for a fortnight, which totally deprived her of sleep and the desire to eat, a great quantity of lice were found to have originated upon her. A very similar case was observed by my esteemed tutor, P. Krukenberg, of Halle, in a young girl, who had received a wound in the head, and which was communicated verbally to me. Also, where a predisposition exists, the lice appear to be able to originate in the internal cavities; at least, Fournier cites an observation of Marcheli's, upon a

---

* Alt., Dissertation de Phthiriasi. Bonn. 1824, fig. 4. 4to.
† Dict. Médicale, Art. Phthiriasis.

woman who frequently suffered from the menstrual flux, in whom the lice appeared in multitudes upon the skin, and indeed came out at her ears and anus, after she had combed herself, as she said, with a, probably, dirty comb; they were evacuated at the anus chiefly after clysters, which were applied in consequence of anxiety, pain, and colic. As in all these cases a decided transfer of lice probably did not take place, although in the last the patient herself surmised it, we may equally doubt it in children, the majority of whom, at a particular period of their lives, are furnished with them. We know many instances in which head lice are found in the cleanly children of opulent parents who associated merely with their equals, who were likewise kept very clean; and it appears that, as in childhood, the general constitution of the body favours the origin of lice, the same effect is produced in adults by uncleanliness. In Poland and Russia the body louse (*Pediculus vestimenti*, Fab.) is so common that the lower classes are seldom found there without them; to which we may add, the general distribution of lice among warm-blooded animals, almost each of which has its peculiar louse, indeed many harbour several species of parasites, which approach very closely to the true lice. But that these latter may be with facility conveyed from one individual to another is likewise certain, and it is thus that the distribution of lice takes place in many young animals and children; and in these they increase the more rapidly, from the predisposition already existing in young and juicy bodies. Whereas the true *Phthiriasis*, which presumes a very morbid state of the juices, is not contagious, as was proved by the case at Bonn, for the woman had, for a fortnight previously, slept in the same bed with her husband, who remained perfectly free from the lice. But the body louse, which is rather the parasite of healthy but dirty people, may be conveyed from one individual to another, yet with a little precaution it is easily removed. This, however, is not the case in the louse of the *Phthiriasis*, for in some of the preceding cases the greatest cleanliness effected nothing, new lice were produced, and their propagation did not cease until the sufferer dwindled to death.

Whether all the preceding cases were absolutely *Phthiriasis* remains uncertain, for in some indeed we are sure that it was not lice, but *Acari*, which were the destructive creatures. Thus Aristotle * relates of Alcmanus and Pherecydes, that the lice were formed in pustulous swell-

---

* Hist. Anim., Lib. v. cap. 31.

ings, out of which they came when opened. These creatures were doubtlessly no lice, but *Acarinæ*, for wherever insects have been found in pustules or vesicles beneath the epidermis, they belonged to this family, and not to the true lice. Many instances of this kind occur, and are generally known, at least to physicians; for such are the *Acari* of the itch (*Sarcoptis scabiei*, and *Acarus exulcerans*), which are found in the immature pustules of that disease, and which will produce it in healthy individuals when placed upon them. But as we exclude the *Acari* from the class of insects, we can take no further notice of those several cases nor of the species producing them; we consequently refer to the article *Acarina* and *Acarus* in the Allgem. Encyclopedie of Ersch and Gruber, tom i., which are written by Nitzsch, doubtlessly the best acquainted of anybody with parasitic insects and the *Arachnidæ*.

The *Acari* stand in the same degree of relation to the *Arachnidæ* that the lice do to insects, and consequently the similar mode of living of both families will not strike us as strange, but rather demonstratively; if the one originate spontaneously, so will the other: of the *Acari* it is certain, and consequently also of the lice, even although direct observations are wanting.

But we may ask, Whence originates the first louse in *Phthiriasis*? Does it proceed from the skin as a *deus ex machina*? or are certain parts of man developed to insects? or are they formed from substances merely deposited upon the skin?

With respect to the first opinion, it admits neither of being comprehended nor supported by argument, and must therefore be wholly rejected. For the transformation of lappets of the skin into lice, we might cite as analogous the supposed transformation of intestinal flocks into intestinal worms; but these have at least vessels, and participate in the vitality of the organism, which, in the dead lappets of the skin which peel off, is no longer the case, for it is impossible that such should be transformed to living beings; therefore the third is the only tenable opinion, and this we adopt. From the perspiration which accumulates chiefly at the above-named parts of the body, namely, at the head, neck, breast, along the back, beneath the arm-pits, and the softer parts, the germs of new organisms are developed in such individuals whose secretions have a strong tendency to corruption, and this is precisely the case in children and diseased individuals. These germs can produce only such organisms that are adapted to the organ upon which the germ has formed itself. For the skin these are parasitic insects, and consequently only such, viz. lice, can be produced; beneath the skin, however, the parasitic arachnidæ (*Acarinæ*) originate precisely in the same manner. In the pustules of the itch they are developed only so long as they themselves are forming, and therefore containing lymph. We may therefore consider that it is from this lymph that their germs are developed; subsequently, however, when the material producing the germ is exhausted, the lymph itself corrupts, and becomes pus. Precisely the same takes place in the *Endozoa*. Von Bär has observed this development in the remarkable *Bucephalus*, and it is as good as proved in many others; why should not therefore the skin, which has precisely the same structure as the mucous membrane of the intestinal canal, give rise also to parasites peculiar to it? I know nothing that satisfactorily opposes the adoption of it. Equivocal generation consequently takes place in the lowest insects: they can originate from it, and do so frequently.

§ 204.

The second kind of propagation, that by shoots, has not yet been observed in insects; it is also perfectly contradictory to the idea of creatures so highly organised they are. Some observations, however, seem to confirm the possible development of insects from germens or eggs laid by an unimpregnated female. We will here communicate these instances.

All observations hitherto made upon this subject may be divided into two groups, the one of which seems to prove that this mode of propagation constantly and regularly takes place in certain genera, and the other that it occurs but occasionally, and as exceptions. As a regular mode of propagation, it is ascribed to the *Aphides*, or plant lice. These produce throughout the whole summer living female young ones, which again, without any preceding impregnation, according to the observations of De Geer and Bonnet, also produce living female young ones. This spontaneous development is repeated to the tenth generation, and indeed still further, if, as Kyber has proved by experiment, the plant lice with the plants they inhabit be removed into heated rooms to pass the winter. Treated thus, Kyber observed a colony of *Aphis Dianthi* continue to propagate for four years without the single impregnation of a female by a male, but they continued to produce young ones which were all of the female sex*. But, according to Bonnet † and De Geer, male individuals appear in August, upon the decrease of the temperature, which then copulate with the females, whereupon the females lay eggs, from which, in the ensuing spring, young female *Aphides* are brought forth, which re-produce female individuals until the autumn, without they or their young having had any intercourse with the other sex. Bonnet ‡ even considered that the eggs of the females was but a procrastinated development of the young produced by cold, and this supposition is confirmed by Kyber's observations, who found them never to lay eggs when removed to warmed apartments.

These facts, which, after the repeated observations and experiments of Bonnet, De Geer, Reaumur, and Kyber, may be considered as incontrovertible, perfectly prove the possibility of a spontaneous development; at least the opinion of some naturalists, that the impregnation of the great grandmother extends to the tenth generation, is much more incomprehensible than the other. A second instance is furnished, according to former general assertion, by the genus *Psyche*, Latr., which contains the cased caterpillars. Reaumur § was probably the first who made the observation that the female, which he mistook for a caterpillar, because it was apterous, laid eggs without a male having been near her. Schiffermüller subsequently observed the same ||, as well as Pallas ¶, who described the species upon which he made his observations as *Phalæna xylophthorum*. Stimulated probably by these communications, Rossi undertook numerous experiments upon this obscure mode of propagation of the cased caterpillars, which, according to Ochsenheimer **, "were conducted with the greatest care," and yet produced the same results. Other witnesses were found in Bernoulli ††, who, among other instances of the kind, mentions one of a cased caterpillar, in Kühner ‡‡ and Schrank §§. Nevertheless Zinken, gen. Sommer has proved, by a long series of observations, that in these,

---

* Germar's Mag. der Entom., vol. i. part ii. p.14.   † Insectologie, tom. i.
‡ Contemplations de la Nature, tom. i.
§ Mémoires, edit. in 8vo, tom. iii. part i. p. 194.
|| Verzerchniss der Schmet. der Wiener Gegend.   4to, 1766, p. 288.
¶ Nova Acta, tom. iii. (1767) p. 430.
** Schmetterlinge von Europa, vol. iii. p. 178.
†† Mém. de l'Acad. Roy. de Berlin, 1772, p. 24.
‡‡ Naturforscher, St. VII. (1780), p. 171.
§§ Fauna Boica, vol. ii. part ii. (1802), pp. 94 and 97.

as well as in all the other genera of *Lepidoptera*, the copulation of the sexes and the impregnation of the female is regularly requisite to the development of the eggs, but that it probably takes place whilst the fully developed female still remains in the case spun for her pupa; at least he detected the escaped females in this situation, and saw them placing their heads and sometimes their anus at the aperture of the case.

But the other cases here and there observed as sporadical, and which consequently belong to the second group, are not thereby contradicted. That unimpregnated individuals lay eggs may be observed in the females of all the *Bombycidæ*, if, some days after their escape from the pupa case, they be impaled and allowed to die slowly. The females of the *Sphinges* do the same, but never the butterflies, according to Roesel's observations, nor likewise the unimpregnated females of the *Coleoptera*, as Suckow remarks[*]. Among the other orders I remember to have observed only some *Diptera*, particularly the *Tipulæ*, to lay eggs in the convulsion of death; for example, species of the genera *Rhyphus*, *Mycetophila*, and *Tachydromia*. But from these eggs it is but rarely that young are disclosed, and indeed only from some, and not from all that are laid. The earliest instance on record is probably that related by Albrecht [†], next to which is that related by Pallas, and observed by him in *Euprepia casta*, O. (*Bombyx casta*, Fab.). An instance is known of it in *Gastrophaga potatoria*, O. Bernoulli relates several instances, one in *Gastrophaga quercifolia*, O. (*papillon paquet de feuilles sèches*), which his friend, Professor Basler, had seen. He reared the caterpillar, it changed into a pupa, the imago came forth, which after a short time laid eggs, from which young caterpillars came. A second case Bernoulli himself observed in *Episema cæruleocephala*, Tr. Lastly, L. C. Treviranus [‡] has observed the same spontaneous development in *Sphinx Ligustri*, Suckow [§], in *Gastrophaga Pini*, O., and my friend, Dr. Al. V. Nordmann, recently in *Smerinthus Populi*. According to Lange [||] and Schirach [¶], the queen bee will sometimes lay unfruitful eggs without copulation with the drone, and indeed the females produced by such eggs will again lay productive eggs without having

---

[*] In Heusinger's Zeitschr., f. d. Org. Phys. vol. ii. p. 264.
[†] Miscell. Acad. Nat. Cur. an. 9 et 10. D. 3. obs. 11. p. 26.
[‡] Verm. Schrift, vol. iv. p. 106.   [§] In Heusinger, 263.
[||] Gemeinnutzige Arbeiten der Sächsis, Bieneugesellsch, vol. i. part i. p. 39.
[¶] Ib. p. 155.

copulated. Thus the *Aphis* has a companion in its great and highly remarkable fertility.

§ 205.

In the same way as a spontaneous generation is found as an exception among insects do we find imperfect hermaphroditism among them. Perfect hermaphrodites among animals are found only in the tape-worms, the *Trematodes*, many *Annulata* (for example, the leech and earth-worm), and the majority of the *Mollusca*. They possess male and female organs, but never impregnate themselves (perhaps with the exception of the tape-worms), but mutually. In insects, on the contrary, hermaphroditism is but one-sided, that is to say the one, generally left side, exhibits female forms and organs, and the opposite side male organs. Among the numerous instances of this kind the majority*, indeed almost all, are found amongst the *Lepidoptera*, and thus this order displays itself a second time as that which has the greatest tendency to diverge from the regular sexuality of insects.

The earliest observations upon this subject were made known by Schäffer in a separate treatise †. It was an hermaphrodite *Liparis dispar*, O., the right side of which was male and the left female. Then Scopoli ‡ described an instance in *Gastrophaga Pini :* according to his account, two caterpillars had enclosed themselves in one cocoon, and changed into one pupa, which produced an hermaphrodite imago, of which one larger side was female, and the other, smaller, had male wings and more strongly pectinated antennæ, at the anus there were both sexual organs, which copulated, after which the female side laid eggs, from which young caterpillars proceeded. Henceforward communications of this kind became more numerous. Esper § next described an hermaphrodite *Gastrophaga Cratægi*, in which the right side was male and the left was female; then Hettlinger ‖ a similar one of *Gastrophaga Quercus ;* Capieux ¶ saw an hermaphrodite of *Saturnia*

* Consult Rudolphi über Zwitterbildung in the Abhandlungen der Königl. Academie zu Berlin. Physkalischeiklasse, 1828, p. 50.

† Der wunderbare und vielleicht in der natur noch nie erschienene Eulenzwitter. Regensb. 1761, 4to.

‡ Introductio ad Hist. Nat. Prag, 1777, 8vo. p. 416.

§ Beobachtungen an einer neuentdeckten Zwitterphaläne (*Bombyx Cratægi*). Erlangen, 1778, 4to. Schmetterlinge, vol. iii. p. 233. Pl. XLV, f. 1—6.

‖ Rozier, Obs. de Phys. tom. xxvi. p. 270.

¶ Naturforscher St. xii. p. 72. Pl. II. f. 6

Carpini, the left wing and antenna of which was male, but the right, with the rest of the body, was female; Ernst * a reversed one, consequently right male and left female hermaphrodite of *Sphinx Convolvuli*; Schrank † one of *Vanessa Atalanta*, in which all the parts of the right side were smaller than those of the left.

After the preceding, Ochsenheimer sought ‡ to bring under one view all the hermaphrodites which were already described, or which he had himself seen, and partly possessed in his cabinet, and which we shall here add, with the addition of such as have been since made known.

He divides all hermaphrodites into two groups, namely, into perfect, in which one side is perfectly female and the other male; and into imperfect ones, where the habit of one sex prevails throughout the entire insect, and the forms of the other are perceptible in solitary parts.

A. Perfect Hermaphrodites.

Papilio Polycaon. Dixon, Secretary to the Linnæan Society, sent an hermaphrodite to MacLeay, which on the right side was male, and *P. Polycaon*, F. and the left female, and *P. Laodocus*, F. Thus the identity of this species is proved §.

Argynnis Paphia. Right male, left female, antennæ the same, the under side agreeing with both sexes, the abdomen having on the right side an anal tuft. Ochs.

Lycæna Alexis. Antennæ alike, wings on the right side female, with a faint blue iridescence within the inner margin of the posterior wings; left side male. The under side as in both sexes, abdomen female, above bluish. Ochs.

Lycæna Adonis. Left male, right female, male wings and antennæ larger, palpi also dissimilar, the left somewhat larger. The abdomen on the right side thicker, more bellied, the left dried up, bent inwards upon the right side, distended exteriorly. In the Royal Museum at Berlin.

Vanessa Atalanta. Left male, right female; abdomen chiefly female, but on the left male side more dried up (indicating the pre-

---

* Papillons d'Europe, tom. iii. p. 123. Pl. CXXII. n. 114.

† Fauna Boica, vol. ii. part i. p. 192.

‡ Naturgeschichte der Schmetterlinge von Europa, tom. iv. p. 185, &c.

§ Trans. of the Linnæan Soc., tom. xiv. p. 584.

sence of the right ovarium. Described by Germar, and caught near Dresden *.

Vanessa Antiopa. Right male, left female, the right antennæ considerably the shortest; abdomen as in the preceding. Bred from the caterpillar at Halle, and described by Germar †.

Deilephila Euphorbiæ, O. Left male, with smaller wings, right female; body distinctly divided in the centre, left green, as in the male, right reddish; palpi and legs white; abdomen female. Described by Germar ‡.

Saturnia Pyri. Right male, left female; abdomen more elegant than in the female, at its end, the organs of both sexes quite perfect, and distinctly close together. Ochsenheimer.

Saturnia Carpini. Left male, right female; abdomen female, with merely female organs. Ochsenheimer. Another instance in the Royal Museum at Berlin: smaller than usual, right antennæ and wings female, left male; body of the form of the male, but coloured like the female; a distinct separation not observable. Rudolphi, as above.

Endromis versicolora. Right male, left female; abdomen female, but upon the right side coloured as in the male. Ochs.

Liparis dispar. Right male, left female; back with a distinct central line of separation; abdomen smaller than in the female, but with female anal tufts and male organs. Rudolphi. Ochsenheimer describes a second instance, but the left side was male, the right female; abdomen smaller, particularly thinner than in the female, with large anal tufts.

Harpya vinula, O. Right male, left and the abdomen female; both sexual organs. Ochsenheimer.

Gastrophaga quercifolia. Left male, right female; distinct line of separation throughout the whole body, both sexual organs. Upon its anatomical inspection an ovarium was found upon its right side, the oviduct of which opened into the vasa deferentia about two inches before its termination, and that of the spermatheca, which hung attached to the common evacuating duct. Upon the left side there were two testes behind each other, which were connected by a thin vessel, one spermatic duct passed from the second testicle, and immediately received, as in all the *Lepidoptera,* the spiral vessel; further beyond, on the opposite side, was found a second vessel, which opened into it, probably the

---

* Meckel's Archiv. fur Physiologie, 1819, tom. v. p. 365—8.

† Ibid. ‡ Ahren's Fauna Insect. Europ., fasc. i. Pl. XX.

rudimental sperm duct of the second testicle, and the sperm duct now distended into a common evacuating duct, to which the spermatheca of the female was attached; it thence passed into the sheath of the penis. Rudolphi.

Gastrophaga medicaginis. Right male, left female; abdomen female, but more compact. The separation of the sexual organs merely indicated. Rudolphi.

Lucanus cervus. Left male, right female. Klug.*

Besides this remarkable hermaphrodite but one other instance of it is known in the *Coleoptera*, in *Melolontha vulgaris*, in which, according to Germar †, an individual has a male antenna on one side and female on the other.

B. Imperfect Hermaphrodites.

Melitæa Phœbe. Male: the right antenna and the wing of the same side larger, but agreeing with the left in colour and markings. Germar.

M. Dydimus, O. Male: the left eye, the left palpus, and antenna smaller; the latter annulated with white, yellow at the apex, the right of one colour; wings equal, male; abdomen male, but somewhat thick, the left sexual fang smaller. Upon its dissection the male sexual organs were found, and a free ovary upon the left side united to no other organ. Klug. ‡ and Rudolphi.

Pontia Daplidice. Female: the right anterior wing male, antennæ and palpi equal, sexual organs resembling the male. Rudolphi.

P. cardamines. Two instances: one a male, whose right superior wing has female markings; and a female with some male colours. Ochs.

Deilephila galii, O. Female; left antenna and palpus smaller, but agreeing with the right female one in colour and markings. Germar.

Saturnia Carpini, O. Female: antennæ male, superior wings formed as in the male, but coloured as in the female; posterior wings female, the left with a reddish brown spot. Ochs.

Liparis dispar, O. The males have frequently white colours; but there are two positive instances, 1st, a male, of which the abdomen and the right posterior wing is female; and 2nd, an individual in Mazzola's collection. The right antenna is male, the left female; the abdomen

---

* Schriften der Gesellsch Naturf. Freunde zu Berlin.
† Meckel's Archiv. vol. 5. p. 366.   ‡ In Froriep's Notizen, vol. x. p. 183.

narrow, but more feminine, of a yellow grey, with dark brown anal tuft; superior wings whitish, on each side dissimilarly mixed with brown; the right posterior wing coloured chiefly as in the male, the left as in the female. Ochs.

Gastrophaga quercus. Two individuals: 1st, body and antennæ female, as well as the left wings, the right male; 2nd, body and right side female, the left male; both antennæ brown, and pectinated. Ochsenh.

Gastrophaga castrensis, O. Male, but having all its parts tending to the female form; right a female, left a male antenna, also on the left side distinct female wings, whereas the right are entirely male, only somewhat larger than in male insects, and the colours brighter than in the female. In the Royal Museum at Berlin. Rudolphi.

If we now cast a critical glance at these instances of hermaphrodite structure we shall speedily recognise that all of them may be more correctly brought into the class of monstrosities. True natural hermaphroditism exhibits perfect female in conjunction with perfect male organs, and the external appearance of the animal is neither male nor female, but an intimate mixture of both, a really new form. But this in insects is never the case. One sex here is developed at the expense of the other, and the more equal their mutual development, the more heterogeneous is the appearance of the individual in its two halves. The perfectly equal development of both sexual organs may be supposed only in those cases in which the one half appears entirely male and the other wholly female; in all other instances one sex will predominate, to which the other is merely associated. This was the character of both those instances which were subjected to anatomical inspection; both were properly males, which, besides their testes, possessed an ovary. This is still more the case in the so-called imperfect hermaphrodites, for in them the preponderance of one sex is evinced externally. A question which still awaits an answer is—which side is in general male, the right or the left? and why is this male, and the other female? That we may answer this question we must group the observed instances, and we then find that in by far the majority of the true hermaphrodites (in fourteen of the cited instances) the right is male and the left female, and that seldomer far the right side is found to be females and the left male (in nine instances). Among the imperfect hermaphrodites, on the contrary, the majority (six) were female, and the minority (five) male with female characters: we may here remark, that the preponderating sex takes the right side, and that associated to it the left. This appears to harmonise with the preponderating plastic nature and energy of the right side in general, and to proceed from the same fundamental law.

Another question is—do such hermaphrodites suffice to themselves? The observation of Scopoli speaks in favour of it, but all other, and even regular hermaphrodite organisms speak against it. The hermaphrodite *Mollusca* never impregnate themselves, but mutually; consequently, how should imperfect hermaphrodites be able to impregnate themselves? Even this self-impregnation appears to be mechanically impossible, as the penis and the vulva are enclosed by valve-shaped organs, and by this means separated from each other. If, therefore, Scopoli's pine *Bombyx* really laid eggs, it did so like all the female *Bombyces*, namely, in the anguish of death; and if caterpillars were developed from these eggs, this development must have occurred as independently as the abovementioned instances of spontaneous development, an assertion which is rendered the more probable, as here, by the presence of the male organs to a certain extent, a subjective female sexuality already existed.

§ 206.

As we have now shown that the several kinds of generation, excepting the sexual by means of separate sexes, are irregular, and having proved that the observed instances are mere exceptions, it remains for us to notice this last mode of propagation, as that which is regular and general. We may therefore adopt that all insects are of separate sexes, and that they require the intermixture of both sexes to be fruitful. Experience confirms this doctrine. Indeed, in some families, as in the bees and ants, there are sexless individuals, which can operate neither masculinely nor femininely, and therefore never copulate; but observation proves that such individuals are merely abortive females, and that in these families the female functions are divided between two different beings, the one of which copulates and lays eggs, and the other attends to the nurture of the offspring. If we therefore more closely investigate sexual generation by means of separated sexes, as found among insects, our first object of inquiry will be the differences of both sexes; which is succeeded by their union for propagation or copulation, the consequence of which is impregnation, and thence follows the formation of the egg and the development of the embryo. A few divarications from the usual course will be appended, and we now proceed with the subject.

With respect to the differences of the sexes, their whole character may be thus distinguished, viz., that the male displays itself by the preponderance of evolution and the female by the predominance of involution. This difference is expressed as forcibly throughout the whole corporeal structure, as in the individual organs, so that in general the mere view of an individual will determine its sex; but it carries greater conviction to inspect the sexual organs, the differences of which we have fully shown above (§ 142 and 152). Independent of this character expressed in the structure of the entire body, we find in many insects, particularly those of the male sex, peculiar organs restricted to one sex only, and which likewise indicate the sexual character. Whence it is sometimes difficult, as well on account of the frequently vast discrepancy of form, and even more of colour, and chiefly in exotic insects, which we have not observed alive, to bring together the sexes of a species, and recently only, since the vast increase of species has proved the necessity of their reduction, greater attention has been paid to sexual differences; and von Malinowsky * and Klug † in particular have earned well-merited praise for separate treatises upon this subject.

If we more closely inspect these sexual differences in the several orders, we find, to begin with the *Coleoptera*, the above mentioned characteristic everywhere expressed. The body of the female is always thicker, larger, more succinct, frequently more convex; that of the male, on the contrary, more slender, smaller, more delicately formed, and furnished with longer limbs. Besides these general differences, the several families exhibit peculiar characters. In all male *Cicindelæ, Carabodea, Dytici*, the males have distended anterior tarsi. The number of these distended joints varies in the several families and genera. In *Cicindela* the three first joints only of the anterior legs are distended. In the *Carabodea* an increasing number is found in the distension of the tarsi; in many genera, for example, *Agra* and other exotic ones, the tarsi of all the six legs are distended; in others, for example, *Harpalus* and its affinities, the tarsi of the four anterior ones; in others again, for example, *Carabus* and its affinities, as well

---

* Neue Schriften der Hallisch. Naturf. Gesellsch. vol. i. Pl. VI.
† Magaz. der Gesellsch. Naturf. Freunde zu Berlin, 1807, p. 65, and 1808, p. 48.

as *Amara*, the *Zabrodea*, *Feroniæ*, and many others, merely those of the anterior pair. Each of these groups exhibit new differences, according to the number of the distended tarsal joints. We thus find in the third group, in which the anterior legs only have distended tarsi, sometimes four distended joints, as in *Elaphrus*, *Blethisa*, &c.; sometimes only the three first, as in *Chlænius*, *Amara*, *Feronia*, &c.; sometimes the two first, as in *Patrobus;* and lastly, the first alone, as in *Omophera*, Latr. In addition to these differences, we observe in the males of *Harpalus*, the *Amarodea*, *Pœcili*, and the entire genus *Feronia*, a brighter reflection upon the elytra; whereas those of the female are duller, sometimes indeed, for example, *Feronia* (*Abax*) *striola*, almost opaque. The same character is also found in the majority of the water beetles, and which has sometimes occasioned, as in *Hydroporus parallelogrammus*, Ahr., the separation of the male and female as two species; for Kunze described the male of this species, which Ahrens had described from a female specimen as *Hydroporus consobrinus* *. The same is the case with *Hydrop. picipes*, Kunz. †, and *Hydrop. alternaus*, Grav.; the former is the male, the latter the female, as specimens taken *in copulâ* prove. The differences of the structure of the tarsi is tolerably analogous in both families; thus the males of the true *Dytici* (for example, *D. latissimus, dimidiatus, punctulatus,* &c.) have three distended tarsal joints on the anterior leg; they are also distinguished from their females by having smooth elytra, whereas in the latter sex the upper half is in general deeply furrowed; in *Cybister* (*Dytici Roeselii*, Auctor.), on the contrary, the first pair only has distended platter-shaped joints, and the female has no furrows, but merely dull, scratched elytra. In *Colymbetes* the distended tarsal joints do not form, as in the two other instances, a round patella beset beneath with sucking cups, but they are long and extended, and

---

* Neue Schrift. d. Hallisch. Naturf. Gesellsch, vol. ii. part iv. p. 61, 2. We may here remark, *en passant*, that the following is the synonymy of this species :—

Hydroporus parallelogrammus. Ahr., Nov. Act. Nalens, vol. ii. fas. ii. p. 11. 1.

♂ *Hydr. consobrinus.* Kunz., ib. fas. iv. p. 61. 2.

Hyph. nigrolineatus. Schönh. Syn. Ins.

♀ *Hydr. nigrolineatus.* Kunz., ib. p. 61. 1.

Hyph. parallelogrammus. Gyll., Ins. Sues., tom. iv. p. 389. 13—14.

Hyph. nigrolineatus. Gyll. Ins. Sues., tom. iii. add. p. 688.

Dyticus lineatus. Marsh., Entom. Britt. i. 426. 35.

† Ibid, 61. 2.

more resemble the feet of the *Carabodea;* it is the same in the other genera, with the exception of *Cnemidotus,* the anterior tarsi of the male of which are not at all distended. In the predaceous beetles, or *Staphylini,* the distended feet are found only in one sex, yet in other instances the female also, as in *Aleochara,* has very broad feet. In many of the *Steni* also some of them only are distended. To these may be added other sexual differences, viz., an arched excision at the ventral plate of the last abdominal segment in the male, which is shown very distinctly in *Staph. laminatus.* The male of *Staph. hirtus,* on the contrary, has, according to Malinowsky, a strong shovel-shaped appendage at its thigh, which runs almost parallel with it. In *Tachyporus rufipes* the excision of the ventral plate is so deep that it has the appearance of being bilobate, and in *Lathrobium* that plate is thereby formed into a central carina, which is continued also in the preceding ones. Similar excisions are said to be found also in the males of the genus *Stenus.* The *Peltodea* exhibit but slight sexual differences; in *Silpha* four joints of the four anterior tarsi are distended; in *Necrophorus* the same joints, but only the anterior pair. Among the *Dermestodea* the male of *Dermestes* exhibits small hairy warts upon the ventral plates of the last abdominal segments; in *Attagenus* and *Megatoma* the last palpal joint of the male is long, thin, and conical, in the female smaller, thicker, shorter, and ovate. In the large family of the *Lamellicornia* sexual differences are very numerous, but all confirm the above law of the predominating evolution of the male. Thus, for example, the male *Lucani* have long mandibles, resembling the antlers of stags, and much longer anterior legs, a larger head surrounded by ridges, but a proportionately shorter body. In *Geotrupes, Dynastes, Oryctes,* and some true *Scarabæi* (for example, *Typhæus*), the males have large projecting horns, which proceed from the clypeus and pronotum, and which are but slightly indicated in the female; the same is exhibited in the scatophagous genera *Copris, Phanæus, Onthophagus,* and besides the males of *Phanæus* and *Ateuchus* want the anterior tarsi, instead of which they have a short hook, that retains the female during copulation. In *Cetonia* the females have convex ventral plates; the males, on the contrary, excised ones, and which are provided in the centre with a longitudinal impression. The *Melolonthodea* exhibit sexual differences in their antennæ: in *Melolontha* itself the lamellæ of the male are more numerous, and longer, and in the female shorter, and fewer. In *Rutela, Hoplia,* and *Anisoplia* the males have longer tarsi and stronger claws; in *Melolontha longi-*

Y

mana, Fab., the male has immensely long anterior legs, in the more robust female they are at least one-third shorter. In the genus *Goliath* the clypeus of the male projects beyond the mouth in two bent processes, which are wanting in the female. The male *Aphodii* have also small pointed teeth upon their vertex, which are merely indicated in the female, and among their affinities the *Palpicornia*, the male *Hydrophilus* displays the last joints of its anterior tarsus distended interiorly into a triangular lobe. In *Buprestis* the male has again an arched excision in its last ventral plate ; in the *Elaters* the more slender males have longer, strongly pectinated antennæ, particularly the genus *Ctenicera*, Latr. Similar differences are exhibited by many *Cantharides* (*Telephori*, Latr.), *Anobia*, as well as the genera *Ptilinus* and *Dorcatoma;* and very decided differences are exhibited in the male winged *Lampyri*, the remarkable genus *Symbius**, and some others (for example, *Drilus*), whose females have no wings. But the predominating evolution of the males is most distinctly displayed in the *Capricorns*, in which the constantly more slender males have much longer, frequently double as long, antennæ, which in the genera *Stenochorus* and *Trachyderes* have one joint more, viz., twelve joints, whereas the female has but eleven. In *Psygmatocerus*, Perty, (*Phœnicocerus*, Latr.), the male has fan-shaped antennæ, whereas those of the female are simple and filiform. Among the *Curculios* the males have frequently longer snouts and antennæ, as in *Anthribus*, *Brentus*, and *Balaninus*.

This law receives further confirmation in the other orders besides the *Coleoptera*, for example, in the *Hymenoptera*. In *Pteronus*, Jur. (*Lophyrus*, Latr.) the male has doubly pectinated antennæ, which in the female are serrate only upon one side. In the *Ichneumons* the antennæ of the males are longer, finer, and porrect, those of the female shorter, thicker, and, after death, spirally convoluted ; in many species also they have a white ring, whereas those of the male are uniformly black or brown. In all the aculeate *Hymenoptera* the male has thirteen joints to the antennæ, the female but twelve, and the former also seven abdominal segments, and the female but six. Besides which we find another important circumstance, namely, the deficiency of wings in the female, whereas the males are winged, for example, in *Tengyra*, Latr., the female of which is the apterous *Methoca;* the same is the case in *Myrmosa* and *Mutilla*. We find a similar difference in many

---

* Sundeval in Oken's Isis, 1830. No. 12.

Lepidoptera, for instance, in some of the *Geometers* (*brumata*, namely, and many others), and in the genus *Psyche*, Latr. The males of the *Bombyces* and *Geometers* have doubly pectinated antennæ, whereas those of the female are much less strongly so, or merely simple and setiform. The male *Sphinges* have longer narrower wings and thinner bodies, the females have shorter broader wings and thicker bodies.

Among the *Orthoptera*, in *Blatta* also we detect a deficiency of wings in the female, exclusive of which, in this order, the females are readily distinguished by their projecting ovipositor, and many males have differently formed wings, for example, the *Locustæ*, in which, at the base of the wing, there is a clear hyaline spot, which has been considered as the vocal organ.

The *Dictyotoptera* and *Neuroptera* exhibit in general no other differences but those derived from the sexual organs, in the *Libellulæ*, only, the males have stronger and larger anal fangs than the females; besides which, in the genus *Agrion*, the sexes differ considerably in colour, the brighter colours are peculiar to the males, and the darker bronzy ones to the females. In *Boreus*, Latr., a genus very nearly related to *Panorpa*, to which the *Panorpa hiemalis*, Lin., (*Gryllus proboscideus*, Pz. Faun. Germ. XXII. 18.) belongs, the male has small hook-shaped wings, but the female, which is furnished with an ovipositor, is apterous.

The sexual differences of the *Diptera* correspond in many instances with those of the preceding orders. In the *Culices* the males have long, very hairy, plumose antennæ, and sometimes, as in *Culex* and *Anopheles*, very long, clavate palpi, of the same length as the proboscis. Among the *Tipulæ* the genera *Erioptera* and *Ctenophora* exhibit in the male strongly pectinated ramose antennæ, and much longer and more delicate legs than the females. In *Nematocera*, Meig., (*Hexatoma*, Latr.) the male antennæ are twice as long as the female. Among the *Syrphodea* the larger approximate eyes form a distinct male character; and in some instances they have also, as in *Xylota* and *Helophilus*, thicker posterior femoræ than the female, a character peculiar also to some male *Empis*. Occasionally also, as in the genera *Hilara* and *Dolichopus*, the males have distended tarsi upon either their anterior or intermediate legs.

The *Hemiptera*, lastly, exhibit striking and sometimes peculiar sexual differences, among which the most remarkable is the vocal organ of the male *Cicada* (*Tettigonia*, Fab.). In other genera the male is horned, and the female is either wholly unarmed, or its horns are at least much smaller. But the most striking is the sexual difference in *Coccus*. In this genus the female has the appearance of either a thick conical or flat scale-shaped spot, upon which no external organs are perceived, or at most but the short stumps of feet upon the ventral side. The males, on the contrary, are winged; they have long distinct antennæ and visible legs, but their body is much smaller than that of the female, and in some cases, as in *Coccus Adonidis*, it is scarcely from the fourth to the eighth part of the size of that of the female. The females, from the abortion of their limbs, have scarcely any motion, whereas the males are exceedingly active, and consequently less frequently observed.

The differences of colour in the two sexes are in harmony also with, and corroborate the assertion of the predominant evolution and involution. The males have brighter, more beautiful, and glittering colours, whereas those of the females are darker, duller, and paler; or when the colours of the female are brighter than those of the male, for example, in the crepuscular moths and *Noctuæ*, at least the markings of the males are much more distinct, sharper, and clearer. Among the *Coleoptera*, *Harpalus*, *Amara*, and *Feronia* confirm these observations. Other instances are shown in *Tillus elongatus*, the prothorax of which is red, whereas the female, or *Tillus ambulans*, Fab., is entirely black. Some *Hymenoptera* however form an exception to this rule, for example, the genus *Lophyrus*, to whose black males we find associated variegated red and brown or yellow and black spotted females; just so in the genera *Tengyra* and *Myrmosa*, their males are uniformly black and the females partially red. Also in the *Scoliæ*, the females have generally brighter markings than the males, for example, *Scolia hortorum*, in which the head of the female is of a reddish yellow; Fabricius consequently considered it a distinct species, and called it *Sc. flavifrons*. In *Tiphia femorata* also the male is entirely black, whereas the female has red posterior femoræ. But among the butterflies this law receives full confirmation. Many exotic exceedingly splendidly marked males have dirty-coloured insignificant females, for example, the beautiful *Papilio Priamus*, the female of which is *Pap. Panthous;* as also *Pap. Helena* is the male and *Pap. Amphimedon* the female of one species; the same as *Pap. Amphrisius* is the male, and *Pap. Astenous* the female. The *Pap. Erechtheus* male, and *Pap. Ægeus* female, described by

Donovan, may be one species. In all these instances the male is darker coloured and more brightly marked, whereas the markings of the female are dirty and confused. In the extensive genus of blues (*Lycænæ*) the upper side of the males are almost all of a beautiful sky-blue, and the females brown; or the former are bright yellow-brown and the latter of a dark brown. In the large *Bombyces*, in the genus *Attacus*, for example, the markings of the male are much more decided, brighter, and distinct, whereas the colour and markings of the fe males are confluent. The same is the case in the *Geometers*. In the other orders we find a similar relation, particularly in the above mentioned *Coccus*, in which the small males have frequently beautiful markings upon their wings, whereas the females are uniformly brown-grey, or at least always darker. In all these sexual differences insects are paralleled by the birds. We here also in general find larger females, but the males are invariably more beautifully marked, have longer wings, longer crests, and spurs, which are wanting in the female. This, consequently, still further confirms the analogies of both classes pointed out above.

§ 207.

The act which precedes impregnation, and consists in the sexual union, is called copulation (*copula*). We shall consider it in the order of its time, place, duration, and particular relations.

As insects are preeminently animals of light, consequently the most important occupation of their lives (namely, copulation,) takes place in the light, that is, by day. This we find confirmed in all true diurnal insects. The butterflies copulate about noon, in the brightest sunshine. When the female has placed itself upon a flower or a leaf the male flies to her and flutters around her in a caressing manner; if agreeable to his caresses she indicates it by a gentle pulsation of her wings, and raising her abdomen upwards the male flies down, and copulation ensues. The common domestic fly copulates constantly in windows in the sun, the male ascending the body of the female, and instantly quitting it each flies off, resuming its preceding business. Bees, which live solitarily and in pairs, are frequently found copulating upon flowers which the female has visited in her industrious and laborious pursuit, and even without any cessation of her labours, and just as speedily as each accomplishes its amorous desires does their love cease; they then avoid each other as before, and the female continues, but perhaps more zealously, her preceding occupations. But females are not always so agreeable; many violently resist and maintain their independence in a severe contest, in which in general the males are subdued. The *Asili*, which alight upon leaves and the glowing sand to sun themselves, are frequently disturbed from this tranquillity by the arduous male, but they do not generally yield, for they defend their innocence as valiantly as successfully. The *Libellulæ* also do not copulate flying, but sitting (§ 152); the male, in these, attacks the reposing female, who yields not until the sexual instinct is fully developed, previously to which she takes wing and escapes; but their union in flight, on the contrary, although indeed an expression of love, and reciprocal, is certainly no copulation.

Other insects, which are more truly crepuscular and nocturnal, copulate merely at those times. The *Bombyces* sit immoveably during the whole day, and during even the brightest sunshine they do not yield to the developed sexual impulse. The males, however, are more impetuous; they swarm about the female even at improper times; for example, *Liparis dispar*, at noon, and when the sun is hottest, but yet without finding her propitious to their suit. But so soon as evening approaches, the female also arouses from her slumber, and twilight, which increases the susceptibility of all sensible beings, acts likewise influentially upon the *Noctuæ* and crepuscular moths. They are now urgent in their endeavours to approach the female, who does not, however, play the prude, but is regardful of the favourite, and yields to his solicitation. But, at this period, they are entirely absorbed in each other; all activity and motion cease during copulation. They sit apparently lifeless beside each other, with withdrawn antennæ, and limbs solely occupied with the business in hand, which, at least for the male, is the last he will pursue: they, therefore, enjoy it as long as possible; indeed, the latter frequently falls down lifeless when the female frees herself from him. This phenomenon can be observed daily, during the summer, in the common *Liparis dispar, Salicis*, and in others of the *Bombyces*. Towards evening their connexion commences, and it is still continued on the following morning, but it is not rarely that the male is already dead, or, at least, so exhausted, that it may be more classed with the dead than with the living.

The *Coleoptera* also appear to copulate more towards evening. This is well known in the cockchafer, which only about dusk acquires its full vivacity. The same is the case with the dung beetle and stag beetle. We, indeed, frequently find them thus occupied during the day, but, in general, it commences in the evening. Some, as, for example, the *Carabodea*, we seldom detect in this situation, whence I conclude, that they copulate in the evening, and that it is speedily over: some are certainly nocturnal animals, for example, *Calosoma sycophanta* and the large *Procerus scabrosus*.

The place they select for the purpose also greatly varies, but the majority seem to prefer the air to their other usual places of resort. Some copulate in flight, as the gnats, *Ephemeræ*, and ants; others select the moment that the female reposes: they then approach her, and fly off in connexion with her, and generally borne by her. Thus is it with *Sarcophaga carnaria* and the majority of the *Diptera*. Whereas, some *Hymenoptera*, whose females are apterous, *Methoca* and *Myrmosa*, for example, carry their females with them, and copulate in flight. Others, as the butterflies, copulate sitting, but separate immediately afterwards. The water-beetles unite themselves in the water, at least, individuals are found there thus circumstanced; and it appears to me not improbable that the males are, on this account, furnished with a perfect seizing apparatus, from a casual separation being so easy in that medium. The queen bee, which constantly stops in her hive, quits it at this period, that she may have connexion with the male outside, and, probably, in flight; the same is the case with the ants, who copulate whilst the males and females rise and fall in large columns, intermixed together, which, at a distance, appear like ascending smoke. We see them quit their dwellings in large troops for this purpose; they then climb to the top of the nearest plants, thence to take their amorous aerial expedition. The females of the *Termites* likewise quit their dwellings, at the time of copulation, to be impregnated by the males, and are then carried back by the workers, being left perfectly helpless by the act.

The situation of the sexes during copulation may also be referred to three chief positions, viz. upon each other, contiguous to each other, or opposite each other.

The first is by far the most general position; it varies only in that, as the general rule is for the male to be placed above the female, in rare instances it is reversed, as, for example, the flea, where the male carries the female. The participation of both sexes in the common motion in such positions, likewise varies. In some cases it is the female alone which moves, and the male merely adheres firmly to the female, for example, in the *Capricorns*. In other instances, this participation wholly ceases, and the male is carried along by the female as if lifeless; thus, in many of the *Chrysomelina*, the male contracts all its limbs, whereas the female endeavours to escape. Or both move at the same time, as among the *Diptera*, which fly about thus occupied, and also the swimming water-beetles; or, lastly, the male alone moves, as in *Methoca* (*Tengyra*) and *Myrmosa*, the females of which are apterous.

In their contiguous position, which we frequently observe in those *Cicadaria*, which are furnished with spiny processes upon their backs, and, consequently, cannot sit upon each other, all motion either entirely ceases, or else both sexes move at the same time; at least, I have frequently detected this in some of our native *Cicadaria*, for example, the species of the genera *Jassus* and *Aphrophora*.

The contiguous position is found chiefly in the crepuscular and nocturnal *Lepidoptera*. In these, generally, all motion ceases; both constantly remain in repose; or else the female alone moves, drawing the male with it, as in the cockchafer.

With respect to the duration of the act, we can say but little that applies generally. From what precedes, it will have been seen, that in some, for example, the butterflies, it quickly transpires. The same is the case in the *Hymenoptera*, viz. in the bees. Others remain for some hours in this situation, others again several days, as the cockchafer. These, consequently, do not repeat the connexion, one union being sufficient for impregnation: others, as the domestic fly, appear to copulate several times successively: it is also probable that the queen bee has intercourse with several males. Perhaps, also, the intercourse may be repeated in such insects in which it rapidly transpires, but many genera, for example, *Ephemera*, may make an exception to this rule.

Peculiar organs adapted to facilitate the duration of the connexion, are found in many insects. The *Carabodea*, according to Leon Dufour, have hooks at the penis, by which they retain the female, and the distended tarsi with their sucking cups in the male water-beetles, are also subservient to this purpose. In others, namely, *Panorpa, Laphria, Asilus, Dolichopus, Tipula*, the penis lies between fangs, which retain the pointed apex of the female's abdomen; in the males of many *Meloë* and wasps, the male antennæ are hooked; in the male *Crabros*, the anterior tibiæ are distended into lateral lobes, by means of which they cling to the thorax of the females; in the *Lepidoptera*, the sexual organs of both sexes have hooks, which retain each other during copulation. In *Melolontha*, knobs of the penis correspond with lateral pockets of the vagina, which promotes their firm adherence, or else the penis itself is provided with barbs, which so affix themselves to the vagina of the female, that the penis, after the completed intercourse, remains in the vagina, as Huber says he has observed in the bees. Audouin* also found the muscular portion of the penis completely torn off in the aperture of the spermatheca.

Some naturalists, namely, Oken, have suggested the question whether insects during copulation feel any voluptuousness, and the latter wishes to deny it, but incorrectly, as I imagine. Whoever has observed the ardour of the males before their intercourse, and their anxiety to attain their object by every possible means, and when, having attained it, their total abstraction in the delight of their ultimate success; and also how every other function visibly reposes, to admit of the entire energy of the body being devoted to this most important one, must speedily, I think, give up such an opinion. Is not, also, the ultimate gratification of an internal urgent passion, for which no sacrifice is avoided, the highest voluptuousness? and does not the observation of every individual copulation of insects most distinctly prove the presence of such an urging passion? The great multiplicity of nerves, likewise distributed throughout the internal organs of generation, their turgescence before and during copulation, and their exhaustion subsequently, admits of no other explanation: the so-much-enjoyed pleasure alone can exhaust and emaciate to the extent that we observe in male insects after its accomplishment, and not the mere satisfaction of the sexual instinct.

§ 208.

By means of the connexion between the male and female, the latter is impregnated, which produces the development of the germs of the eggs. Impregnation, consequently, is produced by the male by the sperm secreted by the testes, and which is a milkwhite clammy opaque substance of a peculiar smell, which chemical analysis finds to consist chiefly of water, and to which is added a peculiar slimy substance, as well as natron, phosphate of lime, and some nitrate of lime. Being continually secreted by the testes, the sperm descends the vasa deferentia

---

* See his Lettre sur la Génération des Insectes, in the Annales des Scienc. Natur. T. ii. p. 281.

into the vesica seminalis, and appears in both as a flocky matter, which alcohol renders crumbly, and which is animated by infusoria of the genus *Cercaria*, or others allied to it. According to Suckow*, they resemble *Volvox globator*, but are more ovate; but he probably overlooked the thin tail, or it was perhaps torn away, which is constantly the case, according to Nitzsch †, in the *Cercariæ* which inhabit fresh-water muscles, but, indeed, after these animalculæ have quitted the body of the muscle for the water. These animalculæ (*Spermatozoa*, according to De Bär) are developed by equivocal generation by the sperm, which surpasses all other organic fluids in its generative power, yet they must not consequently be considered as the truly animating and impregnating power in impregnation, but merely as a proof of the healthy and genuine quality of the sperm, as they are not found in that of old subjects, or of abortions or bastards.

During copulation, which the preceding paragraph has shown to take place in insects by an actual connexion of the two sexes, this liquid passes from the penis of the male into the vagina of the female, or, according to Audouin's repeated observation, into the spermatheca, into the neck of which the penis protrudes. This is probably the cause why the majority of insects, particularly the *Coleoptera*, possess such large organs of generation, and that the spermatheca is the last of all the appendages of the female organs. I also think that the frequently long duration of copulation in many insects may be explained by the spermatheca receiving the sperm. For example, the testicle cannot secrete at once as much sperm as is necessary to fill the spermatheca; it must, consequently, after the ejection of what is contained in the vesica seminalis, secrete an additional quantity, which secretion is promoted by the stimulus given to the whole body by the act of copulation, and is only terminated when the testes are exhausted in the production of semen. We may thence explain the entire enervation and frequently sudden death of the male after copulation (as for example, in *Ephemera*); the correlative size of the spermatheca with the duration of the connexion, speaks also in favour of the opinion of its being a place for the accumulation of the semen, which some physiologists are inclined to doubt. We invariably find in those insects which are long in copulation, large and broad spermathecæ, for example,

---

* Heusinger Zeitschr. f. d. Org. Phys. vol. ii. p. 261.
† Beitrag zur Infusorienkunde. Halle. 1817. 8vo.

in *Melolontha* and in *Meloë*, whereas in those which are rapidly connected (*Ephemera, Libellula, Musca*), it is wholly wanting.

But Hunter's * experiment proves that this appendage absolutely contains semen, for by the application of the fluid contained in it, he made the eggs of an unimpregnated female fruitful. Spallanzani † made the same experiment, but with sperm from the male vesica seminalis, and he also succeeded; but Malpighi ‡, who made a similar one, was unsuccessful, for he observed no development of the eggs. According to Meinecke §, this vesicle is empty prior to copulation, and after the laying of the eggs, but between these two periods, it is filled with a viscous fluid.

If the semen be really received in this reservoir, we may ask, how does impregnation ensue here as well as in those instances in which the vesicle is wholly wanting? We must have recourse to mere conjecture, for we have no positive observation upon the subject. It is the usual opinion that the egg is rendered fruitful when it glides past the aperture of the vesica seminalis, by the sperm suddenly falling upon it, but this is contradicted by the observation that the development of the egg commences even at the end of the oviduct, and that it has already acquired a hard horny shell when it passes the vesica seminalis. Nor does the conjecture explain the mode of fructification in those cases in which that appendage is wanting. Opinions which have been propounded to explain it in the higher animals, for example, the theory of absorption, whereby the sperm is conveyed through the blood to the ovaries, cannot be applied to insects, which are totally deficient in blood-vessels and absorbents. A third theory of generation maintains the passage of the semen into the oviducts, which Suckow ‖ states to have positively observed. This opinion is not contradicted by the distance of the oviducts, which, in many instances, is but trifling. Consequently these oviducts are not analogous to the ovaries of the superior animals, but to the tubes, the superior end of which only is the ovary, whereas its lower end is the uterus, for, as Müller has informed us, the development of the germen already commences there.

* Lectures on Comparative Anatomy, vol. iii. p. 370.
† Versuch über die Erzeugung. Pl. I. p. 245, &c.
‡ Opera Omnia. vol. ii. De Bombyce. p. 41. (Lugd. Batav. 1687. 4to.)
§ Naturforscher. 4 St. p. 115, &c.
‖ Heusinger Zeitschr. f. d. Org. Phys. vol. ii. p. 262.

If, therefore, an intermixture of the semen with the egg germ could take place, it must occur likewise in insects in the uterus and not in the ovary. But as much may be said against this intermixture in the superior animals, viz. from extra uterinal and tubular pregnancy, we find in insects also the successive development of several consecutive eggs in the same tube standing in the way of its reception, for the lowest egg only could come in contact with the spermen, and without the re-adoption of the already obsolete opinion of the aura seminalis, which Spallanzani has shown to be erroneous, we are left precisely in the same situation by adopting or rejecting it. We can consequently merely ascribe the incipient development of the germs to the formative energy imparted to the female body by the presence of the male semen, and to the stimulating excitement at the time of immission. These germs are proportionally larger and more perfect the closer they lie to the uterus, and, consequently, their development must be progressive, if a determinate time and proportion be given within which alone it can be effected, and this it appears absolutely necessary to adopt. Nevertheless, the semen may possibly pass from the oviducts to the tubes, and here come in contact with the lowest egg, which would thereby acquire its perfect development a certain time before the formation of the shell. Thus, both the dynamical and mechanical views have justice done them.

§ 209.

But before we pursue further the development of the egg, stimulated by impregnation, we must investigate the degree of participation the several appendages of the sexual organs have had in this impregnation as well as in the formation of the egg. We have already become acquainted with the function of one of the appendages of the female organs, viz. the spermatheca; the rest are, both in the female and in the male, according to what we have above indicated (§ 140 and § 150), organs which secrete a gluten. Their form, as we have there shown, proves this, from its resembling that of the majority of the glandular organs in insects, and also from the analogy of the superior animals, in which similar glands are found in connexion with the genitals. But if their secretion be positively a gluten, we may ask, what is the purpose of this gluten in relation to impregnation and the formation of the egg? That it is not absolutely necessary, is proved by the many instances in which those appendages are entirely wanting, as well as, *vice versâ*, their significant size necessarily contradicts the opinion that they are unimportant to the function of generation.

With regard to the appendages of the male organs, their analogy to Cowper's and the prostate gland bespeak in some degree their importance to impregnation. They contain a fluid which is thinner than the semen, sometimes perfectly hyaline, but yet of a viscous nature. This fluid pours itself out at the same time as the semen; consequently, after copulation, the gluten organs become lax and flaccid, whereas, previously, they were tense and turgid. Suckow therefore supposes that the gluten merely increases the quantity of the semen by rendering it more fluid, thereby giving it a general distribution, which promotes the impregnation of the eggs. Burdach * considers this also as the function of the prostate and Cowper's glands.

The secretion of the female appendages is not the same as that of those of the male; it consists of a thicker, more viscous, yellow liquid, which is not, as the former, poured out at the time of copulation, but subsequently upon the passage of the eggs through the vagina. It is here that the eggs are covered with this gluten, and are thereby affixed to their place of deposition, for example, to the leaves and twigs of plants. Many eggs derive their peculiar form from this coating, for example, the long pedicle of the egg of *Hemerobius* (Pl. I. f. 14.) is formed by this glutinous coat; it is also what connects together the eggs of *Gastrophaga Neustria*. The organs secreting this gluten are deficient in those insects which deposit their eggs immediately in or upon the food of the young, as for example, in the *Ichneumons*, many flies, the *Tenthredos* and *Cynipsodea*, and many others, although not yet proved by inspection.

A second function may consist in lubricating the vagina during copulation, or the tube of the oviduct upon the passage of the eggs, and thereby facilitating both processes; at least, in some instances, for example, in the *Lepidoptera*, we observe two different appendages, the smaller one of which may possibly fulfil this function, and the other larger one accomplish the first. By means of this gluten, thus generally distributed throughout the egg ducts, the passage of the male semen from the spermatheca to the egg tube may be facilitated and promoted.

* Physiologie, vol. i. p. 460. k.

§ 210.

After impregnation, by means of copulation with the male, the successive development of the egg germs, lying in the tubes, consecutively ensues, namely, one after the other. Joh. Müller * has instituted admirable observations relative to this development in *Phasma gigas*, and of which we shall here make an abridged extract.

If for this purpose we return back to the anatomical description of the ovaries, we shall there find an already indicated connexion of the egg tubes with the dorsal vessel. The mode of this connexion is thus: a delicate, but, by its structure, strong filament, passes from the superior extremity of each egg tube to the wall of the vessel, which is a continuation of the heart, and which we have described as the aorta, and it there unites itself to it. This connecting filament the discoverer Joh. Müller considers as a vessel which, passing from the aorta, transpierces the extremity of each of the egg tubes, and thence forms its internal coating. He further considers that the material which deposits the egg germs comes from the aorta through these connecting filaments, and that this connexion is of the greatest importance to their development. Howsoever apparently just these conclusions may appear, they have nevertheless an hypothetical origin. Nothing further is certainly evident from his representation, than that a continuation of the egg tubes in many, but not in all, cases, is attached to the dorsal vessel; but that these filaments are vessels which open into the dorsal vessel is not proved, for he did not see the contents of the dorsal vessel pass into these connecting filaments, which, indeed, in insects preserved in spirits of wine, would be very difficult to detect. To attach, therefore, less importance to this, the direct transformation of a blood-vessel into an egg tube, appears inadmissible, for then the egg germ must be developed in the blood-vessel, which merits certainly not the least attention. Indeed, the same skilful observer has regularly found in the common leech (*Hirudo vulgaris*) the nervous cord in the cavity of a central blood-vessel † ; but this certainly cannot be cited as an analogy to the transformation of a blood-vessel into an egg tube, which his earlier discovery endeavours to prove, and a more analogous case is much less to be found. I therefore consider this supposed connexion of the two organs as nothing else than a superficial attachment of the egg tube to

---

* Nova Acta Phys. Med. T. xii. Pl. II. page 620, &c.
† Meckel's Archiv. für Anat. und Physiol. 1828. pp. 26 and 27.

the aorta, but without admitting of the passage of the one into the other. What Joh. Müller considers as a continuation of the aorta, or as a blood-vessel, I conceive to be the inner coat or mucous tunic; his egg-tube tunic, on the contrary, as the exterior or muscular tunic. Nevertheless, the filament may be hollow as far as the heart, without, therefore, necessarily opening into the aorta. If such a passage existed, and it were of physiological importance to the development of the egg germs, it would be found in all female insects, but which, as Müller himself admits, is by no means the case. The contents of the hollow connecting filament is a white granulated mass, which extends in it as far as the heart, and can be even still detected where the filament has already dilated into the egg tube. From this point the mass becomes more and more consolidated together, and now assumes the appearance of a thick lump, which is found between every two egg germs. We first find the egg germs in the superior distended portion of the egg-tube, and indeed in their peculiar oval form, whereas the mass between two eggs is much smaller in compass, the egg-tube consequently between every two egg germs is somewhat contracted. The egg germs, however, increase in size the lower they are placed in the egg tube, so that the lowest is the largest of all, and the highest is the smallest. This highest egg germ is almost of the same size as the mass placed between it and the second one, which mass Müller calls the placentula, and the first egg germ also appears to have gradually formed itself from the white granulated substance lying above it.

The development of the last egg germ, lying at the base of the egg-tube, takes place thus: the placentula beneath it, in consequence of impregnation, enlarges, and gradually re-models itself until it takes the form of a cone, the apex of which is turned towards the egg germ. Its base, or broad basal surface, therefore, separates the internal membrane of the egg-tube until it comes into direct contact with the exterior or muscular tunic, and becomes organically connected with it by means of tracheæ, whereby a dark annular girdle is formed at the base of the egg tube, which Joh. Müller calls the ring of the vessel.

Hitherto the egg germ has no pellicle, or shell, but it consists of a thick, uniform, gelatinous mass. Now, after the placentula has distended itself, it is probable that the impregnation of the egg germ proceeds from it; and when this has taken place the shell commences to be formed from above downwards, so that it, as it were, grows over it, commencing at its upper end. Contemporaneously with it is the cicatrix formed; it is a horse-shoe-shaped, bent, but longer longitudinal projection, which lies upon one side of the egg, but which is yet observed only in a few eggs, for instance, in *Phasma*. Its purpose is not yet ascertained, although probably it is the analogue of the tread, and consequently thence the development of the embryo would originate. During this period the placentula retains tolerably long its former conical figure, but it loosens and becomes lighter as a distinct proof that it has lost something (the imbibed impregnating semen?), but henceforward it decreases with the increase of the shell and, pellicle beneath it, and, at last, entirely disappears when the development of the egg is completed. This, after the formation of the shell, is limited to involution, and yet, at least in *Phasma*, a new structure is added to it, namely, a crown-shaped appendage at the end of the egg, in direction from the egg duct. This crown, which is formed of a hard horny trellis-work, and which at its apex has a round aperture, rests upon a correspondingly large orbicular depression in the shell; at this spot also the pellicle appears more delicate than elsewhere. Beneath it is found a small vacant space, into which, the tracheæ which during the formation of the embryo, are forming in the vascular membrane, together with their main stem, open themselves. This delicate membrane may therefore justly be called the egg gill, for through it the air passes into the egg. In those eggs which have no crown, as is the case with the majority with which we are acquainted, the orbicular depression is very small, but it lies likewise at the end (Pl. I. f. 23.). The indicated involution of the egg has chiefly reference to the yolk, which has not yet completely filled the shell, it consequently appears, as well as the pellicle which closely envelopes it, folded upon the surface; but it acquires consistency, and exhibits cells in which, particularly towards its circumference in *Phasma*, a purple-coloured mass is deposited, whereas in other cases it is yellow or greenish. The more the yolk increases, the faster the folds disappear, and when the egg has acquired the maturity requisite for being laid, it entirely fills the shell, with the exception of the small vacant space beneath the germen. During this period of ripening the inner tunic of the egg-tube separates closely above the upper end of the egg, and dissolves into a pappy consistence, which is excluded together with the matured egg. The inner membrane with the next egg then descends to the base of the egg tube, and the development of the new, now lowest, egg germ proceeds in the same way.

If we take a retrospection of the whole process of the development of the germ to the egg we shall find that there are three distinct periods in its progress. The filiform superior appendage of the egg-tube is the first, for in it takes place the secretion of the formative matter, and from here it descends into the egg-tube as a germen. The remainder, probably albuminous portion, of the secretion, remains, as placentula, between every two egg germs. The second period is the loosening of the placentula by copulation. By means of it the internal tunic comes into close contact with the exterior vascular one, in consequence of which the ring is formed; and at the same time the impregnation of the germ takes place by the male semen imbibed from the placentula. The ring, lastly, is the third period; it promotes, by supplying the placentula with atmospheric air, its capacity of appearing as a new organic mass, so that it may be gradually imbibed by the growing egg. The yolk thus becomes perfectly formed, and envelopes itself with its second tunic, and then with its shell, which is hardened also by means of the air from the ring. The formation of the egg is then completed, and the period of laying comes, which takes place immediately, to make room for a still immature egg. It is from this circumstance that some insects, namely, those with many egg tubes, for example, the queen bee, require a long time to lay all their eggs, and only in those with bag and bladder-shaped ovaries, which are furnished upon their surface with short egg-tubes (as, for example, *Lytta* and *Meloë*,) can the eggs be almost all matured at the same time.

§ 211.

When, after all this procedure, the egg has quitted the maternal sphere, a distinct life, namely, that of the embryo, commences in it. If we first survey the structure of the laid egg we shall observe that it consists externally of a horny shell, which becomes tolerably hard in the air, and is in general transparent or colourless, but less frequently decorated with particular markings and colours. Beneath this external covering lies a second, finer, more delicate membrane, which forms the case of the fluid contained within the egg. This fluid is the yolk, (*vitellus*,) a yellow, whitish, or green, thick, granulated mass, which in *Phasma* is dotted with purple, and it chemically consists of albumen, some animal glue, a yellow fat oil and sulphate and phosphate of natron*.

---

* See John's Chemische Schrift, vol. ii. p. 112.

The separate albumen which is observed in the eggs of the *Mollusca, Arachnida, Crustacea*, many fish, and the *Amphibia*, and birds, is therefore wholly wanting in the eggs of insects, which consist solely of yolk.

We have as yet but little information of the progress of the formation of the embryo from this fluid; we only know from Suckow's * observation in *Gastrophaga pini* that a small dark spot is formed in the centre of the originally tolerably clear yolk, which he considers as the commencement of the embryo. From this point, which we prefer considering upon the surface of the yolk analogously to the development of other animals, and not as would appear from Suckow's observation in its middle, the formation of the embryo so proceeds that the ventral surface along which the nervous cord runs first presents itself. This ventral plate distends on all sides, gradually growing completely over the yolk, which is thereby enclosed completely within the ventral cavity. This mode of development has not yet indeed been observed in true insects, but the development of the *Crustacea* and of the *Arachnida* speaks in favour of it. After a short period the embryo appears distinctly as a half moon-shaped body, at the end of which the head is already perceived (Pl. I. f. 24. A.). The embryo swims in a bright green but clear fluid, the liquor amnii, and it is enclosed by two other membranes besides the shell. The innermost, the amnion, which contains the water, is spongy, and exhibits upon its inner surface small glands that are surrounded by a bright margin, and it is covered exteriorly by a cluster of webbed vessels (the same, *c, c, c*), which all proceed from a thicker main stem, which opens into the orbicular portion of the egg filled with air. These vessels, which doubtlessly convey air, consist, according to Suckow, of but a single transparent membrane, and therefore differ considerably in structure from true tracheæ. Michelotti's † experiments upon the eggs of *Liparis dispar* and *L. mori* have proved that the eggs, during their development, decompose air, viz., imbibe oxygen, and give out carbonic acid, but only in a temperature of from 15° to 20°, whereas beneath zero they leave the atmospheric air unaltered. This absorption of oxygen is necessary to their development, for the eggs speedily die in miasmatic gases, which are free from it. If now, as appears neces-

---

* See his Anatomisch. Physiologischen Untersuchungen der Insekten und Krustenthiere, vol. i. part i. Heidelb. 1818. 4to.

† See Pfaff and Friedländer französische Annalen, part iv. p. 48, &c.

sary, this oxygen be imbibed from the above-mentioned orbit of the egg germ, it can only be distributed by means of the vessels in the circumference of the entire yolk. The second external membrane lying over the amnion (the same, *b, b,*) is a transparent, colourless, simple, structureless tunic, which lies next to the egg shell, and clothes this throughout, with the exception of the above-named space containing air. It consequently corresponds with the membrane lying beneath the shell in birds, viz., the *chorion*, which is here also as deficient in vessels as among the birds. The resemblance to birds is very evident; a similar space containing air is also observable in birds' eggs, and, the same as here, the embryo imbibes the oxygen, which it requires for respiration, from the air contained in that space. The allantoid is wanting, and consequently the air vessels take their course upon the exterior surface of the amnion, the yolk bag however is contained within the ventral cavity. A canal to correspond with the navel cord is consequently likewise wanting; the entire yolk bag lies within the ventral cavity, and becomes the intestinal canal and stomach, and it is thence perhaps that the stomach of caterpillars is so monstrously large.

The larger the embryo becomes the more distinctly do the several organs display themselves. Interiorly Suckow first observed the intestinal canal, almost contemporaneously with the external formation, from the simple reason that so soon as the ventral plates had united at the back the yolk bag must necessarily present itself as the internal nutrimental canal. It is evident that the closing of the anus in many larvæ stands in close relation to this reception of the entire yolk bag. Suckow also observed, towards the close of the embryo life, constrictions upon this internal nutrimental canal, which separated the œsophagus and intestine from the stomach; until then it remained what it was, a longitudinally distended simple bag. Now appear the first traces of air vessels, in the form of tubes, one of which runs on each side of the body, and from division to division sends forth fasciculi of branches, which spread themselves to the intestinal canal. But during the embryo life the tracheæ do not enter into action, the stigmata are consequently closed, and their function commences only upon the exclusion from the egg. The dorsal vessel also developes itself and gradually commences action, at least distinct pulsations have been observed in embryos shortly prior to their quitting the egg shell. The sexual organs are also observed during the last few days of the embryo period, they present themselves in both sexes as small knobs with delicate ducts, which unite beneath the intestine into a short clavate evacuating duct. The commencement of the nervous system consists of two extremely delicate scarcely perceptible filaments into which the nervous matter by degrees accumulates; they then approach together, and connect themselves at different spots, thus forming the ganglia, and anteriorly the brain, which in the embryo is still very soft and almost fluid, and therefore very destructible. The muscular layers beneath the skin are also indicated, and particularly the head, with its mandibles, the legs and the anal horn become developed, as the most important external organs. In clothed caterpillars insulated hairs appear also upon the skin. We thus frequently see the matured embryo in its convoluted position through the thin egg shell (Pl. I. f. 22). After the termination of these evolutions the young larva strives for freedom and greater independency, it bores through the shell at its most delicate part, namely, at the orbit, and then comes forth from out its prison, and immediately commences its first appointed occupation, feeding voraciously. Producing this object many larvæ devour their own egg-shell immediately after quitting it.

§ 212.

In some few insects the exclusion from the egg takes place in the mother's body, and these therefore bear living young. Such insects are called ovoviviparous.

One of the most common instances of this kind is presented by the *Aphis*. In these the female bears through the summer living young ones, and in autumn it lays eggs. According to Bonnet, nevertheless, egg germs are found in the ovaries, as in all other insects; these develope themselves in the duct, here the young creeps forth, and is thus born living. Bonnet assures us that, upon an anatomical inspection, he discovered egg shells and young ones in the duct. According to other observers, viz., Kyber, upon *Aphis Dianthi*, eggs are never laid, but young ones constantly born, so long as the individual has not copulated; a copulated and consequently impregnated female lays only eggs; but Bonnet has nevertheless made it probable that the egg laying (as was remarked above, § 204,) is the consequence of the colder autumnal temperature, since the eggs more easily bear the intensity of winter than the young. Kyber's *Aphis* might therefore have continued producing living young ones in consequence of its being kept in a warmed apartment. De Geer, however, observed *Aphis Abietis* never to produce living young ones, but always eggs.

The flesh flies exhibit another instance of ovoviviparous production in insects. It is well known that these flies (*Sarcophagæ*) deposit their larvæ upon putrifying flesh, and the young immediately after their birth proceed with the removal of the substance upon which they were deposited. According to Reaumur*, who has described and figured the ovary, the larvæ may be found in the spirally twisted egg tube, and which, we may remark incidentally, according to him contains more than twenty thousand larvæ. According to De Geer †, the eggs first descend the egg duct after their development at the base of the egg tube is completed, and each ovary contains but from fifty to eighty germs. Their increase is nevertheless very rapid, for in from eight to ten days the larva is grown, and again after eighteen or twenty days the fly appears. If we admit merely the smallest number of eggs, and allow four weeks to the development of every individual, we find, upon supposing an equality of both sexes in each generation, in one summer (from June to October) a produce of more than five hundred millions, therefore about half as many individuals as there are human beings upon the whole earth, according to the received opinion. Meantime, how many are destroyed as larvæ by their multitudes of enemies? how many also as flies are there not consumed by birds?

Similar cases of an early exclusion from the egg within the body of the mother has been observed in other genera. Reaumur ‡ found the larvæ of a small *Tipula*, which, to judge from his figure, apparently belongs to Meigen's genus *Ceratopogon*, in one of his boxes, where also they changed into nymphæ. He obtained from these the fly which subsequently produced long worm-shaped larvæ; indeed, upon a slight pressure, he squeezed them fully developed from the body of the mother. According to Kirby and Spence § also many *Cocci* and bugs bring forth living young ones; the latter from the observation of Busch, upon which, however, I have not been able to obtain more detailed particulars.

But we have, more positive observation upon the development of the *Diptera pupipara*. The remarkable form of the ovary of the female is shortly indicated above (§ 136. III. 2.). The egg descends from the small ovary through the egg duct into the large, bag-shaped,

---

* Mémoires, &c., vol. iv. part ii. p. 153. Pl. XXIV. f. 1. Edit. in 12mo.
† Ib. vol. vi. p. 31. Pl. III. f. 5—18.
‡ Ib. vol. iv. part ii. p 168. Pl. XXIX. f. 10—15.
§ Introd. to Entom. vol. iii.

distended uterus, into the superior narrow aperture of which two ramose vessels, which terminate in blind filaments, open themselves, and which, according to Ramdohr*, are secreting vessels that convey nutriment to the larvæ, and in this uterus the egg changes into the larva, and subsequently into the pupa. As such the young is born, nearly of the size of the mother, and enclosed in a hard, simple, smooth shell, without any annular constrictions, and which shell is furnished at one extremity with a cover. This springs off so soon as the pupa has passed through this stage of its existence, and the perfect insect then issues from the pupa case. We therefore here observe a true development in the uterus similar to that of the mammalia, the larva receives within the body of the mother, and by means of her, its first nutriment, and in its state of puberty, consequently much later than the young mammal, it comes forth into the world. This period also quickly transpires, so that we may almost assert that the young one is capable of re-producing the very moment it is born; a solitary instance unparalleled throughout the whole organic world.

§ 213.

The number of the eggs laid by a female insect is generally very great. We have above very recently shown the possibility, at least, of a monstrous posterity in the flesh fly (*Sarcophaga carnaria*), and yet the female, according to De Geer, lays at the greatest number not more than 160 eggs. This number, which may be considered as a very general average, is in many instances exceeded; in fact, we must feel astounded at the incalculable multitudes which different authors give as the produce of a single individual, numbers which are exceeded only by the almost incredible productive powers of fishes. According to Smeathman, the female of a *Termites* lays in one minute sixty eggs, and therefore in one day more than 86,000, which, however, does not by far terminate her period of laying. A small insect, which is found in numbers upon the *Chelidonium majus*, Lin., namely, *Aleyrodes Chelidonii*, Latr., (*Tinea proletella*, Lin.), lays, according to Reaumur, 20,000 eggs (but the number of eggs is much exaggerated, it is only between twenty and thirty †); in the queen bee it varies from 5,000 to 6,000: the ant lays from 4,000 to 5,000, the common wasp (*Vespa*

---

* Magaz. der Gesellsch Naturf. Freunde zu Berlin, 6. B. s. 131.
† Author's MS. addition.

vulgaris) about 3,000, the *Coccus* from 2,000 to 4,000. If even these considerable multitudes are to be classed among the rare instances, yet a posterity of a thousand individuals in one generation is very common among insects. We find this number among the majority of *Noctuæ*; Lyonet considers this number as usual in *Cossus ligniperda*. *Euprepia caja* lays about 1,600. In the silkworm the average is about 500. Other orders are less fertile, for example, the *Coleoptera*; in these the average is fifty: many, as the *Chrysomelæ*, lay more (viz., *Chrysomelæ polygoni*); others, for example, *Meloë, Lytta*, which have baccate ovaries, also lay many eggs, namely, from 600 to 800. The burying beetle (*Necrophorus vespillo*) is said to lay only thirty eggs, and the flea, according to Roesel, only twelve; many *Diptera*, as the gnats, some dozens; others, particularly flies, very few, from six to eight: *Musca meridiana*, according to Reaumur, lays only two eggs, but certainly not in the whole, but at one time. The *Diptera pupipara*, the account of whose development we have given in the preceding paragraph, always lays but one egg, or rather brings forth but one at a time; and it is the same with the *Aphidæ*, who bring forth a numerous progeny, but only one at a time, at longer or shorter intervals, whereas insects which lay eggs continue to lay until their entire stock is exhausted. We may readily comprehend the incalculable number of insects from this multitude of eggs laid by a single one. Reaumur observed a *Phalena* from whose numerous eggs 350 living young ones were developed; many of them died as caterpillars, so that only sixty-five females were found among those that passed through their several metamorphoses; but even this number were calculated to produce the following year a posterity of 22,750, which in the succeeding one, by the same calculation, would give a succession of 1,492,750 young ones. A single *Aphis* likewise, by Reaumur's calculation, produces in the fifth generation a succession of 5,904,000,000, and it is well known that the great great grandmother still lays eggs when the ninth member of her descendants is capable of re-production.

SECOND CHAPTER.

OF NUTRITION.

§ 214.

Having now, in the preceding chapter, pursued the history of the formation and development of the insect embryo, proceeding from the most general phenomena of generation, and then directly applying them to the class of insects, I shall therefore now closely investigate the progressive advancement of the young, now rendered independent and excluded from the egg, and investigate the means whereby its development is attained. For this purpose we take the insect in its present stage, as it now exhibits itself, either as maggot, caterpillar, or larva, without asking why it assumes this or that peculiar form, reserving the answer to that question to the following chapter of "Somatic Physiology," where it will receive its reply, in connexion with the inquiry into the forms of perfect insects in general; and we therefore now direct our attention to the means appointed for the fuller development of the individual itself.

These are found to consist in its nutriment, namely, in the assimilation of the newly received organic substances. The young larva must feed upon fresh organic matter, either vegetable or animal, and transform it into its own substance if it is to live. An inquiry into the several kinds of food, and their modes of reception and assimilation, will constitute the subject of the ensuing chapter.

§ 215.

If we take a general survey of the process of nutrition in general, as we find it in the progressive development of animal organisation, we shall perceive that an internal cavity presents itself as its first organ. In this cavity, which is called the stomach, the food is received, transformed, and the unassimilating portions rejected either through the same orifice at which it was received (the mouth), or at another aperture placed at the opposite extremity of the cavity of the stomach (the anus). So long as the food remains in this sometimes simple or tubular cavity, which is occasionally furnished with auxiliary distensions and pockets like so many lateral purses, the digestible matter is imbibed by the parietes of the cavity, and so transformed into the substance of the body. We find this first and most simple mode of nutrition in the lowest animals, the *Infusoria*, the *Polypi*, the *Acalephæ*, and many of the intestinal worms.

The digestion of the food can only be perfectly accomplished when it has been previously adapted thereto by the secretions of peculiar organs, which, as it were, kill and decompose it. Where such auxiliary organs present themselves we find the cavity of the stomach more complex, longer, and tubular, and making several convolutions in the body. The first of the secreting organs that is added to the digesting cavity, which we may henceforth call the intestinal canal, is the liver, which is a glandular body that pours its secretion into the anterior half of the intestine beyond the stomach, and which thereby renders the chyme fit for absorption. The second secreting organs are the salivary glands: they first present themselves in such animals which take hard food, and by their secretion cause the transformation of the coarse materials into a uniformly fluid pap. We find upon this grade of the development of the digestive apparatus the muscles, snails, *Crustacea*, *Arachnidæ*, *Myriapodes*, and insects. Many of them want the salivary glands; many have a multilobed liver, as the snails; others have a small one, in the form of tubular canals. The deficiency of an anus is a rarity in this grade of organisation, but we however find it among insects.

Upon the third and last grade we observe not only the preceding secreting organs both more perfect and numerous, but other new ones present themselves, some of which pour fluids into the intestine, as the pancreas; and others rectify the absorbed chyle, as the milt and kidneys; of the last, however, we observe occasional prefigurations in the snails and insects. This most perfect development of the digestive apparatus is found in the *Vertebrata*.

§ 216.

It does not suffice that the digestive organ should thus become by degrees more perfect, thereby facilitating the separation of the nutritive matter, but the imbibed and decomposed chyle must be subjected to another change before it can be transformed into the organic mass. This change is produced by means of respiration, a function which consists in adding to the nutriment a new substance present in the atmosphere, viz., oxygen. This is, as it were, a second repeated killing of the nutriment, or, in its true sense, a real consuming of it. Where this consuming attains its culmination the blood and consequently the whole body becomes warm, and thence arises, at least chiefly, the uniform heat of birds and mammalia.

A distinct organ of respiration is entirely wanting in the lowest animals, viz., in the *Infusoria, Polypi, Acalephæ*, and many of the intestinal worms; and if they really breathe it can only be by means of the exterior integument, in the same way as the internal skin imbibes the nutrimental juices from the food. The first instance of a true respiratory apparatus speaks in favour of this opinion, for where found it is a continuation of the exterior integument, a sort of tufted or ramose fold of the skin, which projects into the medium, loaded with oxygen. Such respiratory organs, which are called branchiæ, we find in the muscles, the majority of snails, and in all the crustacea, and even among fishes and the naked amphibia, either throughout their whole lives or during the time they remain in the water. The respiratory organ being merely at one part of the body, a motion of the juices to this spot is requisite, and thus originate the vessels as new organs connecting the functions of the intestinal canal and branchiæ. Vessels must consequently be found in all animals with a partial respiratory apparatus, and they may therefore be deficient in such as have this apparatus universally distributed.

If the fold of skin which becomes developed to the respiratory organ pass inwardly, it is then called not gill, but lung (*pulmo*). The medium, which is generally the air that contains the oxygen, is received into the lung, wherein the oxygen becomes incorporated with the nutritive fluid. This also is in general merely partial, and then consists of membranous bags, which in its highest grade of organisation consists of a web of small cells, that by degrees unite into common ducts, the last and largest of which, the trachea, opens outwardly. Vessels convey the nutritive fluid (the blood) to the surface of these cells and bags, and by means of other vessels it is conducted hence to all the parts of the body. These organs of respiration are common to the majority of amphibia, all the birds, and mammalia; their first indication is found in the pulmonary *Mollusca* and in the *Arachnida*. A universally distributed lung, the analogue of the similar branchia, would require no vessels, as the oxydisation of the nutritive fluid would take place everywhere. We also absolutely find that animals whose body is traversed throughout by tracheæ, which may be considered as separated pulmonary passages, are deficient in a vascular system, and the fragment of it which is present more serves to promote a motion in the fluid that decomposition may be prevented by its stagnating during repose. Such animals are insects, as well as a portion of the *Arachnida* and *Myriapoda*.

We have thus become acquainted with the general mode of nutrition: we have seen that it requires two agents, viz., one to prepare the nutritive fluid (the intestinal canal), and another to make it organisable (branchiæ, or lungs), as well as frequently a third to conduct the fluid, and which acts as a connecting member between the two others. We will now investigate in detail the functions of these three agents in insects in the order in which we have above noticed them.

§ 217.

I. FUNCTION OF THE INTESTINAL CANAL, DIGESTION.

The activity of the digestive organs commences with the reception of food. This in insects takes place in a double manner, namely, by biting and chewing, or by the suction of fluids.

All the mandibulate orders, it is very natural to suppose, take their food by manducation; consequently the *Coleoptera, Orthoptera, Dictyotoptera, Neuroptera*, and a portion of the *Hymenoptera*. In them the horny mandibles, which move horizontally in opposition to each other, bite the portion off which it is the function of the labrum to retain, thus holding it between them; the same is done beneath by the maxillæ and labium. When the part is separated it passes between the maxillæ, where it is readily comminuted, during which operation it is held by the labium. It is then passed to the posterior parts of the cavity of the mouth, whence it glides down through the pharynx and œsophagus to the stomach. In many insects, namely, the *Coleoptera*, the mouth and pharynx are upon the same plane, so that it merely requires to be pushed forward to get into the stomach. Such beetles as the *Carabodea* and *Dytici* chew but little, perhaps from their possessing a proventriculus in which the food undergoes a second comminution. They also feed only upon flesh, which, as in the carnivora among the mammalia, requires no mastication previous to its being swallowed. In the herbivora, for example, the grasshoppers, particularly of the genus *Gryllus*, which possess no true proventriculus, but merely a crop provided with teeth, the food is longer chewed. The pharynx therefore lies higher than the cavity of the mouth, and the meal has to describe an arch, and to pass over the internal skeleton of the head before it can get into the crop. It is very easy to convince oneself of the continued chewing motion of the broad molar-shaped mandibles of these insects, and in which the maxillæ also take an active part. They are therefore analogous, both in this respect as well as in many others, to the graminivorous birds, particularly the *Gallinæ*, or, to indicate a higher parallelism, to the ruminants amongst the mammals, only that their rumination does not take place in the mouth, but as in the birds, in the proventriculus, or crop. In the *Lamellicornia, Pelodea,* and *Capricorns,* which all have complete oral organs, the power of mastication decreases in proportion to the decrease of the proventriculus. Their food also is partly more fluid and more decomposable, so that the hairy maxillæ laps it up, and it is thus readily taken into the mouth. A striking instance of this mode of feeding is exhibited by the stag-beetle, which, as is well known, laps up the exuding juices of the oak, and for this purpose is provided with very hairy maxillæ. In the *onthophagous Petalocera* the mandibles exhibit an analogous form adapted to their purpose, being flat, thin, lamellate, or rather shovel-shaped, to take up their thin food and convey it to the mouth. The *Chrysomelæ* either devour leaves, or as in the *Gallerucæ,* (*G. Alni, Viburni,* &c.), sweep off the pollen of flowers with their maxillæ. They want the proventriculus, and consequently their food requires to be masticated in the mouth; but as they bite off but small pieces the chewing is of shorter duration. This is the case also with the larvæ of the *Lepidoptera,* which, without exception, bite and chew, but they separate such small pieces that they can swallow them without their requiring much comminution; at least they continue biting off fresh pieces without stopping to masticate that already in their mouths. The masticating *Hymenoptera,* for example, the *Tenthredonodea* and *Ichneumons,* devour the pollen of flowers, and their honey, which they lap up with their flat, thin, shovel-shaped maxillæ, or else bite off in larger pieces by means of their dentate mandibles. They masticate certainly but slightly, and yet they want a proventriculus, which has always more or less relation to the duration of the mastication of the food. The *Dictyoloptera* and the *Libellulæ* masticate longer: but they are predaceous, and devour insects which they capture. For this purpose they are furnished with long hook-shaped mandibles and short but broad maxillæ armed with long teeth. It is distinctly seen how they masticate small insects with their maxillæ, swallowing them gradually, holding their bodies the while with their mandibles. The hard parts, namely, the wings and feet, they drop after they have devoured the soft body. They want the proventriculus, and therefore the maxillæ completely comminute all their food. The *Dictyoloptera mallophaga* likewise masticate, as, according to Nitzsch, they feed upon the down of feathers; they want the proventriculus, but they have a large crop, in which their swallowed food softens for a time and is prepared for digestion.

Upon reducing the different modes of mastication of insects to one general view we shall find it to present the following:—

Mandibulate insects devour,

1. Firm materials, which they bite off piecemeal, and which are masticated.
    a. Merely in the mouth. *Libellulæ*.
    b. Less in the mouth, but more in the proventriculus. *Carabodea*, water beetles, and *Staphylini*.
    c. Both in the mouth and proventriculus. *Grylli*.
    d. Neither in the mouth nor in the proventriculus, as the latter is wanting, whereas the creature bites off but small pieces, which can be swallowed entire. The caterpillars of the *Lepidoptera;* the *Chrysomelæ*.
2. Fluids or substances which easily dissolve.
    a. They are swallowed as separated by the mandibles. *Onthophagous Petalocera, Peltodea, Capricorns*.
    b. They are lapped up by the pencillate maxillæ and sucked out in the mouth. *Lucani, Tenthredonodea, Ichneumons*.

§ 218.

Many kinds of sucking approximate to this last mode of taking food. The *Phryganæ* make, as it were, the passage from the mandibulate to the haustellate insects, their oral organs being formed wholly upon the type of the mandibulates, although they only take their food by suction. Their mandibles are small, and entirely unadapted to biting, and have the appearance of two little knobs at the base of the labrum (Pl. VI. f. 9. *a, a*), whereas the upper lip, or labrum, is long, narrow, lancet-shaped, internally canaliculated (the same, f. 9.), the same as the still longer labium, which is distended at its extremity into a spoon-shape (the same, f. 10. *d.*); with it the two-jointed, flat, lobate maxillæ (the same, *c, c.*) stand in close connexion, as well as the four-jointed maxillary palpi (*e, e.*), at the base of these maxillæ, whereas the three-jointed labial palpi hang in front of the apex of the labium closely to the bone of the tongue (the same, f. 11. *f, f.*). We consequently find all the organs of mandibulate insects, and yet nothing is more certain than that the *Phryganea* do not bite, but only suck. Their food consists of the sweet juices of flowers, and we meet with the perfect insect only upon flowers, particularly upon the *umbelliferæ, syngenistæ, nympheæ*, and similar plants, which grow in the vicinity of water, whereas the larvæ live in water and have distinct and separate manducatory organs, and prey upon other minute water insects.

We now proceed with the general mode of taking food in haustellate insects. Their oral organs are thrust into the material which supplies them with food, and is sucked by means of the sucking stomach through the canal formed of the labrum and labium. The sucking stomach, according to Ramdohr's * representation, is a double bladder-shaped appendage at the lower end of the œsophagus. When distended the air within it, as in the œsophagus, is rarefied, which causes the ascent of the juices of flowers into the oral tube; it then comes into the œsophagus, which swallows it into the stomach, and this continues so long as the sucking bladder is distended, and only upon its contraction does it cease. This sucking stomach is found (see § 103) in almost all insects provided with haustellate organs, and by its distension the ascent of the liquid nutriment is occasioned. It appears to be peculiar to haustellate insects, and to present itself in this form in no other animals. The swimming bladder of fishes only has by its opening into the œsophagus some resemblance to the sucking stomach of the *Diptera*, and Treviranus † therefore compares it with that organ, a parallelism which, although not supported by the functions of the two organs, yet by their corresponding situation, form, and structure deserves consideration. The other *Dictyoloptera*, as *Hemerobius, Myrmecoleon, Ascalaphus*, and *Semblis*, have no sucking bladder, and therefore do not suck, but bite. They are in general carnivorous, and are therefore made to bite and manducate their food.

The wasps and the bees may be classed next to the *Phryganea*, from their mode of sucking their food. The conformity is greatest in the wasps. Their labium and maxillæ form a similar apparatus, but they are pro-

---

* Verdauungswerkz. Pl. XVI. f. 2.   † Vermischte Schriften, vol. ii. p. 156. &c.

portionally longer, and project beyond the anterior four-lobed portion called by entomologists the tongue. At the base of the labium lies the pharynx, covered by a triangular valve, which Treviranus * calls the second tongue; but it is impossible that this valve should be a tongue, as it lies over the orifice of the pharynx, and evidently serves to close that organ, comparable in form and function to the uvula of the mammalia. The sucking stomach is not so distinctly separated from the œsophagus, but rather an anterior crop-like distension of it (see § 103), and into this crop the funnel-shaped orifice of the mouth projects. When it distends itself this orifice of the stomach approaches closer to the upper thinner commencement of the œsophagus, and the passage of the food into the stomach is thereby promoted. This distension also causes the ascent of the honey into the oral tube, and when it has arrived at the pharynx deglutition passes it on. Treviranus has convinced himself of the correctness of considering this crop as a sucking stomach, as well as of its corresponding function, or at least of that of a similar appendage to the œsophagus of the majority of haustellate insects, by dissecting them alive; he always found this bladder empty, and it, as well as the pharynx, in a peristaltic motion, or interchanging distension and contraction, which was likewise observed before him by Malpighi † and Swammerdam ‡, who, however, did not detect its function. According to Meckel § the sucking bladder contains also, at least in the *Diptera*, fluids of different colours; Ramdohr || calls it a food bag, and ascribes it exclusively to the *Diptera*. But whosoever shall follow Treviranus in his description, without predilection or preconceived ideas, must, I am sure, be speedily convinced; it would be absolute obstinacy, after such clearness and such a distinct insight into the suctorial apparatus of insects, to require further proofs; an hypothesis which explains everything is no longer an hypothesis even if, as however is not the case here, it is not supported by observation.

Let us turn to the bees, in which, with a very similar form of the oral apparatus, it is however more difficult to comprehend their mode of sucking. Instead of a lobate tongue we find in the bees a long, filiform, hairy, hollow proboscis, which at its base has two membranous lobes (Latreille's *Paraglossæ*, Pl. VI. f. 7. *a, a.*); the aperture of the

* Vermischte Schriften, vol. ii. p. 134.
† Opera Omnia, Lugd. Bat. 1687, tom. ii. p. 44.
‡ Biblia Naturæ, p. 138. *a.* § Vergl. Anat. vol. iv. p. 92.
|| Abhand. über die Verdauungswerkz. p. 11.

mouth or pharynx likewise lies at the base of this proboscis covered by a valve, as in the wasps. From it the simple proboscis passes on to the stomach, distending in front of the latter into the sucking bladder. A peculiar vessel originates from the canal of the proboscis, the course of which indeed Treviranus could not completely follow, but which probably passes beneath the cerebellum and opens into the œsophagus; the ducts of the salivary glands also appear to open into the œsophagus. Treviranus therefore considers that this canal within the proboscis is the organ which imbibes the nectar, but he passes over in silence the function of the mouth, or orifice of the pharynx. If, however, I shall not undertake to question the justice of his remarks without adequate investigation, it yet strikes me as evident that the oral aperture or orifice of the pharynx must have some particular and important relation to the mechanism of nutrition, perhaps harder and larger particles of food, such as the grains of pollen, are swallowed by it, or, which is yet more probable, that the honey, which the neuter bees are known to cast up, is rejected through this aperture.

The suctorial apparatus of the *Lepidoptera* differs still more widely. Their oral organs consist of two spirally convoluted hollow probosces, which represent the maxillæ of other insects (see the detailed description of these organs at § 70). Into each of these sucking tubes a branch of the furcate œsophagus opens (§ 102). This itself is a narrow tube, which becomes the stomach at the commencement of the abdomen; and here, closely in front of this transition, it has a simple or double sucking bladder. The two probosces form, united, a central canal, into which the ducts of the salivary glands open. In these insects therefore the simple oral orifice has entirely disappeared, instead of which we find two proboscideal sucking mouths, through which the nectar, which is the universal food of the *Lepidoptera*, ascends, by the aid of the sucking bladder, and by means of the above described mechanism. Another corroboration of the correctly supposed function of the bladder, and of its connexion with the business of sucking the aliment, is found in its being very small in those *Lepidoptera* which have a short conical proboscis, as in *Euprepia caja* and *Cossus ligniperda*, whereas in the butterflies, which have a long proboscis, and also in the sphinges, it is of large compass.

The proboscis of the *Diptera* has been already above (§ 70) amply described; and we have also learnt from the anatomical description of the intestinal canal (§ 103) that they have a large sucking bladder, which opens into the œsophágus through a long narrow canal. Consequently they suck their fluid aliment in the same manner. The setæ, which lie in the sheath of the labium, are thrust into the substance which they suck, moving up and down like a pump during the operation, and thus the fluids ascend into the stomach by the alternating distension and contraction of the sucking bladder. If we attentively observe a gnat or fly thus occupied, the opposed motion of the setæ may be distinctly seen, and we also detect that the blood does not flow in a continued stream, but at distinct intervals; so that when the gnat has swallowed a drop a fresh drop follows it, but there is a momentary cessation of the operation between.

The flea and the *Diptera pupipara* do not possess this sucking bladder, and their proboscis differs by not possessing the lower fleshy sheath; they hereby approximate to the *Hemiptera*, whose rostrum is articulated, and they likewise have no sucking bladder. According to Treviranus * the setæ (see § 70), of which their rostrum is formed, are hollow, and vessels originate from their cavities which open into the first stomach by means of narrow canals (see Pl. XX. f. 3.); the œsophagus itself opens into or beneath the tongue, seated between the setæ, whither also the ducts of the salivary glands pass. He therefore assumes that the liquid ascends the hollow setæ, as in capillary tubes, and passes into the stomach through the vessels. I consider this opinion doubtful, as it appears to me too mechanical, for hereby the œsophagus would become superfluous, and particularly as the *Hemiptera* thus imbibe their food throughout their whole lives. I should prefer considering the lateral distension, which is found at the commencement of the stomach in many bugs, and the pyriform distension at the end of the œsophagus, into which the second stomach returns, as the analogue of the sucking bladder, and thus suppose in them a mechanism conformable to that found in the other orders. Ramdohr also, who has figured the intestines of many bugs, never found tubes conducting from the setæ to the stomach.

§ 219.

Their own variety conforms tolerably with the various modes of their taking food. Thus naturally fluid aliment can only be imbibed, and that which is of a firm consistency must be bitten off and masticated.

* Annalen der Wetterauschen Gesellsch. f. d. Ges. Nat. I. 2, p. 171.

But more important than these differences, derived from the external quality of their nutriment, are those which refer to their being either of vegetable or animal origin. Thus the food of insects may be divided into two groups, so that we can class it into four different kinds, each of which again admits of subdivision, according to whether it be fresh or whether putrefaction have already commenced, which we thus arrange:—

I. From substances requiring comminution. These are,
1. Of the ANIMAL KINGDOM, and are,
   a. Fresh and uncorrupted, and generally consisting of living individuals obtained by force.

   The predaceous beetles, viz., the *Cicindelæ, Carabodea, Hydrocanthari,* and *Staphylini,* support themselves by this kind of food. All devour other insects, chiefly larvæ, which they obtain by capture, or the flesh of dead and fresh vertebrata to which they can procure access. Some, as the *Dytici,* are said to attack living fish, and eat out their eyes; others, as *Hydrophili,* devour the spawn of fishes and frogs, and even such young frogs and tadpoles as they can master.

   b. Animal substances in which putrefaction has already commenced, particularly carrion.

   The large family of carrion beetles (*Peltodea*), especially feed upon such substances. Their larvæ live wholly in putrescent vertebrata, and devour their flesh, and the perfect insect also derives its nutriment from it. The burying beetle (*Necrophorus*) buries small vertebrata, depositing its eggs in their body; thus innumerable carcases are destroyed. Smaller beetles, for example, the *Aleochara,* many *Staphylini, Corynetes,* &c. assist them in this business. Others, again, consume only the dried skins of animals and their clothing, as the fur beetles (*Dermestodea*) and the clothes moths (*Tinea pellionella,* &c.).

   c. Excrementitial substances, animal excrements.

   The majority of onthophagous insects are extremely fond of the excrements of the herbivora. But this cannot be considered as distinctly animal or vegetable matter, but as an intimate mixture of both; therefore all beetles which devour such excrements are fed upon both animal and vegetable substances. To these belong all the onthophagous *Petalocera,* viz., *Copris, Onthophagus, Ateuchus, Gymnopleurus, Onitis, Aphodius,* and many others; then the *Histerodea,* many *Staphylini,* the genus *Spheridium,* as well as the larvæ of innumerable *Culices* and flies. But as these substances have considerable affinity with carrion, and the onthophagous insects with the *Peltodea,* many species of both kinds feed indiscriminately upon both substances.

2. From the VEGETABLE KINGDOM.
   a. Corrupt vegetable substances.

Many insects live upon the rotten portions of trees, as the larvæ of *Lucanus* and *Oryctes;* others devour the corrupt substances which are deposited beneath the bark of dead trees, for example, *Hypophleus, Engis, Ditoma, Colydium, Rhyzophagus,* and other genera of this family. The larvæ especially appear to derive their nutriment from such corrupting, fermenting, or decomposed portions of plants. Lastly, according to Reaumur[*], the larvæ of the *Tipula* feed upon earth only, but it is doubtlessly the vegetable extract which is mixed with the mould, and which is produced by annual plants that putrify yearly, and from the fallen leaves of others, that constitutes their nutriment, which during digestion is taken up from the earthy matter.

b. Fresh vegetable substances.

These yield doubtlessly the most nutriment. Some insects, as the larvæ of *Melolontha,* gnaw the roots of plants; others devour and bore into the hard stem; to those belong the *Ptini, Anobia,* and in general the entire family of *Deperditora,* the *Cerambycina,* and the bark beetles *Hylesinus, Bostrichus, Apate,* &c. Others again, and by far the majority, consume fresh leaves, for example, almost all the caterpillars of the *Lepidoptera,* the larvæ of the *Chrysomelina,* even the perfect beetles of this family, and the grasshoppers. Others again, the larva of *Noctua Tanaceti, Artemisia,* &c., feed only upon the petals of flowers, many upon pollen only and the internal parts of flowers; very many, lastly, feed exclusively upon ripe fruits, as the fruit moth (*Tinea* [*Carpocapsa,* Tr.] *pomana, Pyralis pomana,* Fab., or

---

[*] Mem. tom. v. p. 1. pages 14, 15, edit. in 12mo.

upon seeds. To these the larvæ of the *Curculios* especially have recourse. The *Apion frumentarum* and black *Calandra granaria* have acquired a fearful celebrity from this circumstance; the nut weevil also, *Balaninus nucum*, which bores the kernel of the hazel, and the cherry weevil, *Anthonomus druparum*, which devours the kernel of the sour cherry (*Prunus cerasus*), and which are frequently found fully developed in cherry-stones, are well enough known.

II. Fluid aliments which are taken up by suction or lapping. These are,

1. From the animal kingdom, and consist of,

    a. Fresh animal juices.

    These substances support the majority of toothless parasites which are distributed upon all the warm-blooded animals. They consist of all true lice and bed bugs, which imbibe only blood. Some are parasites only during certain portions of their lives, for example, the flea and the *Diptera pupipara* in their last stage; others, as *Œstrus* and the *Ichneumons*, only as larvæ. The remarkable *Rhipkidoptera* also are parasites chiefly as larvæ, for, inserted between the abdominal segments of many wasps and bees, they project into the abdominal cavities of these insects, but push their heads outwardly. It is still uncertain how they feed. The perfect winged insect appears not to be a parasite. The *Ichneumons* have a similar mode of life, for they live as larvæ in the larvæ of other insects, and are fed by their fat; but subsequently, when they are full grown, they attack the nobler organs, and thereby kill them. The perfect winged insect sucks the juices of flowers. Other genera, which are parasitic as larvæ upon insects and cold-blooded animals, are, in the *Coleoptera*, *Drilus*, which is parasitic upon snails, and *Symbius*, Sund., whose larva feeds upon cockroaches. The parasitic state of the larva of *Meloë* is still more remarkable, it lives upon bees only until its first moult, and in this state has been formed into the apterous genus *Triungulinus*, by Desmoulin; it is probable that it subsequently goes into the earth, and lives upon the roots of plants. There is a beauty in the almost constant law which makes the parasites of warm-blooded animals so during their whole lives, and they therefore always remain apterous, whereas those of insects and mollusca are parasitic only as larvæ, and acquire wings after quitting this mode of life. The former belong in general to orders with an imperfect metamorphosis, and the latter to those with a perfect transformation. The remarkable genus *Braula*, discovered by Nitzsch, which most probably belongs to the family of *Diptera pupipara*, and which is parasitic upon the honey bee, makes an exception; it is parasitic during its whole life upon cold-blooded creatures, but is also apterous, whereas the allied genera *Hippobosca* and *Ornithomya*, although dwelling upon warm-blooded ones, yet have wings. There are many other insects besides the parasites which feed upon animal juices, for example, the *Asilica*, which seize other insects, and by means of their long proboscis suck out all their juices; the *Tabanica*, which sting men and animals, and derive sustenance from their blood, besides many genera and species of the numerous family of gnats, for example, *Culex, Ceratopogon*, as well as the allied genus *Simulia;* lastly, the larvæ of the *Dytici*, which suck out insects, like spiders, by means of their large hollow mandibles, which are opened at their apex: the only analogy among perfect insects to this structure of the mandibles is to be found in the hollow proboscis of the *Lepidoptera*, whereas in the spiders it is the usual and most common form.

b. Corrupt animal juices.

These are the same as those mentioned under I. 1. *b.*, viz., the impure juices of carrion and dung; they are voraciously sucked up by many flies, for instance, *Musca Cæsar, Scatophaga putris, Scybalaria*, &c., and are even lapped up by the *Coleoptera*, whose oral organs are less adapted to manducation, as was fully shown in the preceding paragraph.

2. From the vegetable kingdom.

a. Fresh vegetable juices are sucked up by many insects, viz., the *Cicada*, bugs, and *Aphidæ*, as well as the species of *Chermes* and *Coccus*. The majority pierce young one-year shoots, and thereby so exhaust them that they die, particularly when, as in the *Aphides*, they are found in hosts upon one shoot. Almost each species selects a distinct plant, and it is frequently the case that they are to be found upon that alone. The same is the case with the parasites, particularly the constant ones, whereas those which are merely partially so, for instance, the gnats, the flea, &c., frequent all the warm-blooded mammalia of various families and orders. The partial parasites of insects and the *Mollusca* are also found tolerably limited to one species, or at least to but few, but two or three. Few animals are so much restricted to one and the same kind of food as insects. Thus the leaf-consuming caterpillars have generally each its distinct plant, and indeed some are so scrupulous that they reject all other plants, and will even starve to death rather than touch any but their usual food. Besides the crude unprepared juices which are found in the stem the more fully developed ones of the flower yield nutriment to many insects. All the *Lepidoptera*, without exception, suck the nectar of blossoms, the same with the wasps, bees, and many other *Hymenoptera*, and, lastly, among the *Diptera*, the *Bombylodea*, and *Syrphodea*, but they do not restrict themselves to certain plants, but frequent all, and those which are the richest in honey are the most agreeable to them. Some, as the wasps, lap also the fresh juices of ripe fleshy fruits, particularly those which are sweetened by the influence of the sun upon a wounded part.

We may also here briefly state that many beetles, for instance, the *Lepturæ*, *Coccinellæ*, &c., lap the honey of flowers, and that others prefer the crude juices of the stem, as *Lucanus*, &c. that of the oak.

b. Corrupt vegetable substances.

There are not many insects which resort to these. If we did not here include the juices produced by the rapid putrefaction of fungi, or the in general almost fermenting juices of mature fungi, upon which the larvæ and perfect insects of the numerous family of *Mycetophthires* feed, we should scarcely find genera that have recourse to such nutriment.

§ 220.

The first change of the food, and which is as it were a preparation for digestion, takes place during the mastication or sucking by the intermixture of the secretion of the salivary glands. These organs, as we find at § 112, are found in all haustellate and many mandibulate insects, particularly in those which feed upon vegetable substances, they secrete a peculiar white, frequently perfectly hyaline fluid, which appears to be of an alkaline nature, and becomes intermixed with the food in the mouth itself. This intermixture has a threefold purpose, namely,

1. The mechanical dilution of the nutriment. This attenuation is the more necessary, particularly in such insects which feed upon hard vegetable substances, from their containing very generally but little moisture, and their comminution in the mouth must necessarily be more difficult than when the food consists of soft animal substances. Thus by manducation, and being mixed with the saliva, it becomes changed into a thick pap, upon which the stomach can more easily act. The grasshoppers, *Grylli*, larvæ of the *Capricorns*, the wood borers, and the caterpillars of the *Cossus*, appear especially to require this mechanical attenuation of the food, from its generally consisting of hard wood.

2. The chemical effect of the saliva upon the nutriment is still more apparent. The saliva, by its very constitution, is a poison which as it were kills the food, depriving it of its natural living quality, and thereby transforming it into a scalded state. This is proved by the bite of poisonous serpents, whose poison is nothing else than the saliva secreted by peculiar glands. According to Humboldt * the saliva of serpents alone suffices to change the flesh of recently killed animals into a gelatinous substance, and they therefore lick their prey all over before they swallow it. The saliva of insects has a similar effect. Immediately after swallowing and the intermixture with the saliva in the mouth, the green leaves upon which caterpillars feed lose their bright colour and acquire by degrees a darker dirty colour, resembling that of boiled vegetables. The puncture also of blood-sucking insects convinces us, most distinctly, by the pain of the wound, of the corrosive effects of the saliva, and the inflammation attendant upon it, of its transforming power.

3. The dynamical effect of the saliva, under which we understand its faculty of changing the food into that state that the requisite nutrimental substances can be separated from it. It therefore requires no further proof, for it is evinced by too many experiments that the saliva does not always act in the same way, but that its effects are different according to the differences of individuals; consequently a variety of insects may feed upon the same materials and yet produce very different effects

* Ansicht der Natur. tom. i. p. 141.

from the action of the saliva and the other fluids which flow into the stomach: for example, the true *Cantharides* (*Lytta vesicatoria*) and *Sphinx Ligustri* feed upon the same plant, viz., *Ligustrum vulgare*, Lin., and yet in the *Sphinx* we do not find the least trace of the blistering principle which so greatly distinguishes the Spanish fly. And this is peculiar also to other species of Spanish flies, which however feed upon very different plants, and in the most distinct climates. With respect to the puncture of blood-sucking insects, everybody knows the difference of its effects from different insects. The puncture of the bed bug (*Acanthia lectularia*, Fab.) leaves behind it a small, whitish, projecting swelling; that of the flea a spot made red by the wound, but which is not painful. The puncture of our water bugs is painful; for example, the *Notonectæ*, *Naucoris*, and *Sigara*, the pain of which must especially be attributed to the saliva which is inserted in the wound. This is the case also in the puncture of the common gnat, for the mechanical injury is too trifling to produce such sensible pain. How very different however is the inflammation after the puncture of this creature than in the before named insects. The difference in tropical insects is still greater. St. Pierre, in his voyage to the Mauritius, relates an instance of a bug whose puncture produced a swelling of the size of a pigeon's egg, which lasted five days*. The large exotic *Tabani* also cause severe inflammation by their punctures, as Kirby and Spence have shown in an instance; with us also the species of the genera *Chrysops* and *Hæmatopota*, of the family of the *Tabani*, make painful punctures. The sting also of the smaller genera of *Culices* are sometimes very painful, as that for instance of the notorious *Simuliæ*, particularly when they attack man and animals in hosts; by the multitude of their stings they then set the skin in such an inflamed state that it produces severe illness, which frequently terminates in death. The same may be said of the mosquitos, which are small *Culices* that belong probably to the same genus, and which between the tropics are complete pests by reason of the intolerable itching produced by their punctures. The anthrax, or pustula maligna, which has been occasionally observed to arise after the puncture of an insect is scarcely to be considered as the consequence of its mere puncture, but of a poisonous lymph that has probably still adhered to the proboscis of such a fly, which immediately before may have punctured a diseased animal. The puncture therefore

---

* Kirby and Spence, Introduction, vol. i. p. 171.

of a particular species of fly cannot be considered as the cause of this malady.

These three different qualities of the saliva do not present themselves separately, but more or less contemporaneously. The vegetable fibres are by its admixture softened and loosened, then chemically changed and made tender, or, as it were, scalded, and, lastly, by its intimate incorporation it is rendered fit for assimilation and digestion. After this preliminary change a second comminution takes place in the crop when this organ exists. We consequently find among the mandibulate insects salivary glands only in such species, genera, and families, which are more or less strictly herbivorous, for example, the grasshoppers, *Grylli, Termites,* and they are entirely deficient in the carnivorous ones. In them the larger quantity of gastric juice that is secreted supplants the function of the saliva, whence it is that their intestine beyond the crop is beset with a multitude of blind, doubtlessly glandular, appendages; and even if such appendages are found in the herbivora, for example, in the grasshoppers and others, they are fewer in number and smaller in size. Where both salivary vessels and these appendages are wanting the long stomach is then entirely covered with glands, as in *Hydrophilus.* In haustellate insects the saliva attenuates the imbibed juices and becomes intermixed with it in the process of sucking. Thus in the bees the salivary duct opens into the same duct through which the honey is sucked; in the *Lepidoptera,* through the central canal which is formed by the union of the two probosces, and it drops down out of this channel whilst the insect is sucking. Reaumur and Treviranus have both seen it fall in drops. In the *Hemiptera* and flies it also opens into the proboscis, probably here also, as in general, beneath the tongue; by means of it the hard setæ are kept constantly lubricated, which facilitate their reciprocal motion. It is also intermixed with the imbibed nutriment in the mouth, it kills and scalds it, and thus prepares it for digestion, which then next takes place in the long or subdivided stomach. In the *Cicada* and bugs, the majority of which imbibe crude vegetable juices, this preparation for digestion is of considerable importance, and we therefore find in them very large salivary glands.

§ 221.

The remaining function of digestion, subsequent to manducation and the intermixture of the saliva, is exhibited less uniformly in insects than the functions just indicated. The most striking differences have already been exhibited in the remarkably divaricating form of the stomach. These divarications admit of being, as well as their functions, classed into the following three chief heads:—

> A. The digestion of FIRM, partly animal, partly vegetable substances. These take place,
> a. By the aid of a crop,
> b. Without a crop.
> B. The digestion of LIQUID substances always takes place without the assistance of a crop.

The form of the intestinal canal is thence adapted as far as the opening of the biliary vessels, and we therefore find

In the FIRST case a crop, a proventriculus, and a stomach, but which we shall call henceforth the duodenum, as it corresponds in function with that organ of the higher animals. In a thus formed intestine the hardest animal and vegetable substances are digested.

In the SECOND case, in which the proventriculus is wanting, the crop and duodenum are united in a single narrow and equally wide tube, which may be here properly called the stomach. We find this stomach in all insects which feed upon light vegetable, or even corrupt pappy animal substances. Sometimes this entire stomach, like the duodenum of the carnivora, is throughout shaggy.

In the THIRD case a true proventriculus is indeed wanting, but we sometimes observe an analogous form. These are wholly deficient in the *Lepidoptera;* their small oval food bag is both stomach and duodenum, and the crop is changed into the sucking bladder. In caterpillars the long, broad, cylindrical stomach is likewise stomach and duodenum, but the crop is wanting. The same is the case in the *Diptera,* but the stomach, together with that portion of the intestine forming the duodenum, is very long, round, and tubular. The *Hymenoptera* have a wide crop, which serves as a sucking stomach, a funnel-shaped orifice to the stomach, which represents the proventriculus, and a tolerably long transversely ridged duodenum. The *Hemiptera,* lastly, exhibit again all three divisions, but in these they are more widely separated: the crop is the first broad, purse-shaped stomach; the proventriculus we again find as a thin but compact muscular tubular second stomach; the duodenum is thus in the *Cicadaria* the narrow, but in the bugs wider, transversely ridged, third stomach, which is furnished with auxiliary ducts. If but two stomachs are present the middle one, or proventriculus, is wanting. Thus the chylifying portion of the intestine is formed in the several orders according to the differences of their food; for greater detail I refer to § 105.

If we now investigate the digestion of solid substances by the assistance of the proventriculus we shall find that those, when of the animal kingdom, are swallowed wholly unchanged but in pieces, but, when of the vegetable kingdom, they are already much comminuted and intimately mixed with the saliva. They consequently first arrive at the large crop placed in front of the proventriculus, which in some cases, as in the *Dytici*, is thickly beset internally with glands, and the superior surface of the internal tunic is occupied with wrinkles, horny lines, and teeth (Pl. XVII. f. 5—7.). The secretion of these glands, is a dark brown sharp corrosive fluid, which strongly smells like Russia leather, it supplies the place of saliva, envelopes the food, makes it soft, and thus prepares it for digestion. The food, after having thus remained a short time in the crop, advances by degrees into the infundibuliform orifice of the proventriculus, and thence into its narrow cylindrical or star-shaped cavity, where it is easily comminuted, and transformed into a uniform pap-like consistency. To produce this we observe in the crop, and particularly in the proventriculus, a peculiar motion, which consists of an alternating expansion and contraction. This contraction commences at its anterior extremity, and gradually advances to the end of the proventriculus, whilst the earlier contracted portion again expands. It thus greatly resembles the progressive advance of worms and footless larvæ; it is called the peristaltic motion. It is most distinctly observed in the proventriculus, which also, of all the parts of the intestine, is supplied with the largest fasciculi of muscles (§ 104), and it here appears as a contraction and distension of its internal cavity, produced by its rhythmical contraction and expansion. By means of this contraction the teeth and horny plates rub against each other, and thus grind the food into a simple uniform pap, which is called chyme. In this state we then find it in that portion of the intestine lying behind the proventriculus, which, as we have above seen, is supplied throughout or partially with short blind appendages. These appendages, according to Rengger [*], become shortened when the intestine is filled with food, and they then appear merely as lumps upon its surface. Its contents is

---

[*] Physiologische Untersuchungen uber den Thierischen Haushalt der Insekten. Tubing. 1817. 8vo.

a thick pappy mass, which melts by the addition of acid, and on the application of heat, it is found in the blind appendages as well as in the cavity of the canal. It is of a white colour, and is thereby distinguished from the brown nutriment found in the crop. Ramdohr and the earlier entomotomists call this division of the intestine, behind which the biliary vessels open themselves, the stomach; according to Treviranus, Joh. Müller, and Straus Durckheim*, on the contrary, it should be called duodenum †. This last opinion is doubtlessly the most correct, for the whole business of chymifaction is already over when the food arrives at this portion of the intestine, and the formation of chyle commences here. The resemblance of the crop to the anterior stomach, and the proventriculus to the muscular stomach of birds, is so striking, that the similar situation of that portion of the intestine behind the muscular stomach would oblige us to consider both as analogous forms, even were all other resemblances wanting. The chief difference however is, that the biliary ducts do not, as in the birds, open into this division, but behind it; but in lieu of which other secreting organs, which are the equivalents of the pancreas, namely, the blind appendages, are found around its entire circumference. Rengger does not consider these appendages as secretory organs, but as pockets, whence the lacteal juice is more readily passed into the ventral cavity, and because chyme is also found in them; but that is also found in the pyloric cæcum of fishes. Their abbreviation, however, upon the filling of the intestine, is not an objection, but it merely proceeds from the necessary distension of the intestine produced by the accumulation of more matter. Another reason, however, for not considering that division of the intestinal canal lying behind the proventriculus as the stomach, is the deficiency of a peculiar nerve in its vicinity. The nervus sympathicus descends, we know, from the brain to the pharynx, and distributes itself upon the surface of the crop, with several branches and ganglia, similar to the web of the superior animals. But if there be a proventriculus the branches of the nerves suddenly cease in its vicinity, and that portion of the intestine lying behind the proventriculus receives none; but where the proventriculus is wanting the nerves are distributed only at the anterior portion of the stomach, and the posterior part which corresponds with the duodenum receives none

---

* See above, § 105.

† The true duodenum of insects is the villose stomach, or, where this is wanting, the long tubular stomach itself.

either. These nerves, however, are a main condition of digestion, and they present themselves, especially, at the stomach and anterior stomach, because it is the most active portion of the intestine in exercising the function of digestion. Both comminute, especially the proventriculus, the remainder of the intestine absorbs; a considerable interruption of the function of digestion has consequently been observed in the superior animals upon the scission of this nerve.

In those insects which possess no proventriculus the digestion of the food is effected less by comminution than by the gastric juice found in the stomach. It also appears to be of an alkaline nature, at least Ramdohr observed a fermentation upon the application of acid, and according to Rengger it stains litmus paper of a brown red; and according to the former it also turns paper blue which has been previously stained red by an acid. Rengger's experiments upon the caterpillar of *Deilephila Euphorbiæ* most distinctly convince us of the purely chemical and dynamical transformation of the food in the stomach. The form of the small bitten pieces of the leaf remains unchanged, but they were somewhat loosened, and they appeared at the lower portion of the stomach to have lost substance. The fluid contained within the stomach was stained green by their extract. In other caterpillars, for example, that of *Pontia brassica*, the chyme appeared more comminuted and more pappy, doubtlessly because the substance of the leaf of the cabbage is more juicy, softer, and more decomposable than that of the *Euphorbia*. The separation and absorption of the chyme is promoted by the constant peristaltic motion of the stomach: this motion intimately intermixes the portions of the food, and gradually subjects them equally to the action of the gastric juice secreted by the glands of the stomach, and it partly helps to move the food from the anterior to the posterior extremity of the stomach. It is here that the elaboration of the food has attained its highest point, and it is therefore here that it least resembles its original quality; it has here become darker and browner, whereas it was originally of almost the same colour as that of the leaf of the plant. But the mechanical advance of the food is not however wholly owing to the peristaltic motion, but it also depends upon whether fresh food has been received. When this is not the case the whole process of digestion appears more slow; the food already in the stomach then remains there, but becomes gradually softer and looser, and loses its colour, and appears decomposing; at least, according to Rengger, it then smells very unpleasantly; it also gradually loses the fluid portion of the chyme. But if the period of fasting be too much prolonged the caterpillar dies, and the food is even then found in the stomach. In general voracious caterpillars, which usually consume daily three times their own weight of food, cannot fast very long, at least not more than eight or ten days; perfect insects, namely, some beetles, can do without food much longer. I myself have seen a *Blaps mortisaga* move about quite briskly after having fasted for three entire months. Other instances have been observed in capricorn beetles which have been enclosed in wood for years; they were in a torpid state, but revived upon being exposed a short time to the air. Predaceous beetles, such as the large *Carabi* and *Dytici*, cannot long fast, at most a few weeks. Caterpillars which are not fed after their last moult do not die, but change into pupæ, but the pupæ are easily killed, particularly if the caterpillar immediately after moulting has been deprived of food; but the voracity of caterpillars decreases with the increase of their age, and it is only during the first period of their existence that they exhibit a hunger which is almost without parallel.

Many beetles, viz., the *Carabi*, the grasshoppers, and the larvæ of the *Lepidoptera*, eject upon being touched a brown, corrosive, gastric juice, and cast it at their enemies. Whoever has collected insects, and especially the *Carabodea*, must be well acquainted with this mode of their defence, as also with the pain which the intrusion of it occasions when by accident, which is not rarely, it comes into the eye. This acute pain, which occasions a gush of tears, distinctly proves the sharp and caustic quality of the gastric juice. In some *Hymenoptera*, namely, in the bees and wasps *, the ejection of the food regularly takes place, for they cast up, farther elaborated, the imbibed nectar of flowers, and supply the young with it as food. The ejection of it is caused by the antiperistaltic motion of the stomach and proventriculus, and thus the gastric juice is passed into the mouth by a contorted motion of the animal, whence by another quick bending it is thrown from it. According to Rengger the muscles of the skin also contribute considerably to the retrograde motion of the stomach, at least the force was considerably diminished when he cut the caterpillar along the back, and then irritated it by pressing and tormenting, causing the ejection of its saliva. In many, the innermost tunic of the stomach, after great

---

* Spallanzani Versuche uber die Verdauungsgesch, p. 36. Reaumur, Mém. de l'Acad. des Sc. de Paris, A. 1752, p. 472.

efforts was thrown up, whereupon the caterpillar died. After this, air in the shape of bladders broke out. This air appears to be constantly found in the stomach during digestion, and is probably partially swallowed with the food, and is partly evolved from the food in the stomach. The first takes place, according to Rengger, that the gastric juice which is spirted forth as a defence may be the more easily ejected, yet the constant biting and swallowing small pieces of leaves necessarily occasions the passage of some air into the stomach. During the pupa state, the intestine contains only air, or even nothing: we also find in perfect insects, for example, in the *Ephemeræ, Libellulæ, Grylli*, &c., much air in the stomach and the whole intestinal canal.

The digestion of fluids which haustellate insects imbibe, takes place, doubtlessly, in the same manner as the firmer manducated nutriment, with the alterations only which arise from the difference of food. The more elaborated the juices are, the more simple is the structure of the intestinal canal, whence it follows that the digestion of the nectar of flowers takes place in the *Hymenoptera* in a single cylindrical, but compact, transversely ridged duodenum, whence the chyme, together with the addition of the secretion of the many biliary vessels, passes into the true ilium. In the bugs, this simple duodenum, as the above description of their digestive apparatus (§ 105) has shown, is separated into several intestinal divisions, the first of which corresponds with the crop, the second with the proventriculus, and the third with the true duodenum. In addition to this great perfection of the chymifying portion of the intestinal canal, we must include the long and multifarious salivary vessels as preparatory organs, which very much facilitate the progress of digestion by the contribution of their secretion. The juices are thereby made capable of assimilation, and the assimilating portion is absorbed by the parietes of the ilium. It arises thence, also, that that portion of the intestine which lies beyond the duodenum is, at least in the bugs, extraordinarily short, whereas in the *Hymenoptera* and in the flies it is of the same length, or, as in the *Lepidoptera*, even longer. The smallness of the stomach connected with the duodenum in the *Lepidoptera*, makes us surmise that they take but little, or, indeed, many of them in their perfect state no food at all, or that, as their food consists of the nectar of flowers, it requires but little change. Thence their small stomach and long narrow ilium; and, next to the saliva, the secretion of the biliary vessels may contribute considerably to the transformation of this honey. Among the *Coleoptera* we find a family which agrees entirely with the *Lepidoptera* in requiring but little food, viz. the capricorn beetles. They also, as beetles, probably eat but little; at least, in all those individuals that I have dissected, I found the intestine full of air; and their nutriment likewise consists of the delicate nectareous juices of flowers. But of all haustellate insects the *Diptera* are the most voracious: we observe them the whole day long lapping and tasting every possible substance which contains sweet juices, or such as are agreeable to their palate, and which are frequently nauseous and stinking. They have consequently the longest duodenum of all insects. In front, where it supplants the stomach, it is most compact and muscular; behind it is softer, more delicate and membranous. The food is received into this long intestine, and, as it is generally of a cruder nature than that of the *Lepidoptera*, it consequently requires several different elaborative fluids. We therefore find, besides the oral salivary glands, others which sink into the commencement of the duodenum.

§ 222.

The elaboration of chyle takes place even in the first portion of the intestine, which corresponds in situation with the stomach and ilium, or where a proventriculus is found only in the duodenum lying behind it. The chyle is a whitish or greenish or even brownish, thick liquid, which first presents itself as a flocky substance between the innermost and second tunics of the stomach, and, upon a microscopic inspection, appears to consist of minute globules. It is the produce of digestion and the object of all the functions of the intestinal canal, and it forms the foundation of all the other nutritive fluids. In the higher animals, the chyle is therefore absorbed by the lymphatic vessels placed along the intestine, and conducted into the venous blood, whence it passes into the lungs or gills, here becoming oxydised, and it is then poured forth by the heart as fresh arterial blood. But such a circulation of the juices is not found in insects, for they have neither absorbents nor veins, but merely a single arterial vessel placed along the back. If, therefore, the chyle or lymph is to pass into this vessel, it must be transmitted through the parietes of the intestine and pass through the cavity of the stomach, whence the heart receives it through the above-described valve. This passage of the chyle through the intestinal tunic observation has distinctly detected. Ramdohr saw the chyle which was contained between the mucous membrane and the true skin forced during the peristaltic motion of the stomach through the exterior muscular tunic, and the remainder, which was not thus passed through, was driven towards the end of the stomach, and here distended the exterior tunic in the circumference of the pylorus. In a cockchafer, whose longer ilium was filled only at certain parts with food, he observed, after the stomach was removed from the body, a continued distending of it at those parts where the food was found. Upon opening the external skin at those parts, the brownish green chyle streamed forth. Rengger also observed the transmission of the chyle through the intestine in larvæ, which he opened alive, for, having carefully dried the exposed stomach, he saw it speedily become again moist.

Upon the chemical inspection to which Rengger subjected the chyle, that he found between the tunics of the stomach, it did not exhibit the alkaline property of the saliva and the gastric juice. In weak acid it formed flocks, as also when exposed to heat, which was dissolved in concentrated sulphuric acid; but, upon the addition of water, it reformed flocks. He found similar flocks when he caused the caterpillar to vomit into diluted acid. Hence it appears that the chyle consists chiefly of albumen, which appears to be suspended in water. Rengger's experiment further confirms this opinion, for he injected water into the stomach of a caterpillar after he had tied up its end, and, upon opening it after a short time, he found the chyle at the anterior end much more full of water than that of the posterior, of which he convinced himself by the coagulation of the albumen by heat.

From the chyle being transmitted through the tunic at that part of the intestine usually called the stomach, is another reason for not considering it the stomach only, for the chyme alone is prepared in the stomach, from which the chyle is separated in the duodenum and ilium. We must, therefore, consider this portion, as in the lower animals, merely as the simple internal digestive cavity, whence gradually, by metamorphosis, different intestinal parts are produced, which present themselves as the crop, proventriculus and duodenum; or where such a division of the simple cylindrical nutrimental canal is not found, that that insect has remained stationary upon a lower grade of the organisation of the digestive apparatus. We should thus find within this single class a progressive succession of the perfection of the intestinal canal, for, commencing with the bag of the larvæ of the bees, which has no anal aperture, it terminates in the perfect structure of the predaceous beetles, and which corresponds distinctly with the development of the nutrimental canal throughout the animal kingdom. They thus represent in their crop and proventriculus the form of the canal of birds, and by means of the blind appendages of the duodenum they are likewise connected with the fishes.

§ 223.

In all the higher and in many of the lower animals, namely, the *Mollusca*, the formation of the chyle is produced by the addition of a peculiar fatty alkaline fluid, namely, the gall, which is secreted by a large lobate gland, called the liver, the duct of which empties itself into the duodenum, sometimes behind the pylorus, but in general in the vicinity of the opening of the ventral salivary glands. The object of this fluid appears to be to decrease the acidity of the chyme, and then by the intermixture of its component parts to prevent a prejudicial corrupt decomposition of the food upon passing through the intestinal canal; to transmit the fat in suspension, in which it is more readily absorbed; and to assimilate the nutriment by means of the gall and other animal matters it contains; and lastly to stimulate the peristaltic motion *. We may now ask if an analogue of these glands is to be found in insects, and whether its secretion when it exists is of such influential effect as the gall in general.

With respect to the existence in insects of such glandular secretory organs which empty themselves into the intestinal canal, we may observe, that but one kind of them is found, which is peculiar to all excepting *Chermes* and *Aphis*, and this is the above described (§ 111) biliary vessels. All other secreting organs which are found in the intestine of insects are peculiar to certain orders and families only. We have characterised them above as salivary organs, and given a detailed account of their form and presence (§ 112).

These gall vessels are actually gall-secreting organs, according to Cuvier, Posselt, Ramdohr, Carus, and the earlier opinions of Treviranus and Meckel. This opinion may be supported by

1. The general form of the secreting organs in insects.
2. By their situation, and by their insertion in the intestinal canal corresponding with that of the gall-secreting organs of other animals.

---

* Gmelin's Théor. Chimie, vol. ii. part ii. p. 1517. The result of the comprehensive experiments of Tiedemann and Gmelin upon digestion.

3. That at the spot where they empty themselves into the intestine there is frequently a bladder-shaped distension, a kind of gall bladder (for example, in *Lygæus apterus, Cimex baccarum*).
4. That sometimes, as in the secretory organs of other animals, stony concretions are found.
5. That they are very compact, and wholly surrounded by the fatty substance which is the formative matter whence all secreting organs derive the fundamental portion of their secretion.
6. That also the vena porta which conducts the blood to the liver in the higher animals takes its rise from such a fatty matter distributed within the ventral cavity, viz., from the mesenterium.
7. That the liver of the most closely allied animals, namely, of the crabs and many annelides (for example, *Aphrodites*), consists likewise of such blind vascular appendages which empty themselves into the intestine.

Whereas these opinions are contradicted by those of modern naturalists, namely, of Herold, Rengger, Straus Durckheim, Joh. Müller, and by the altered views of Meckel * and Treviranus † upon the following accounts:—

1. The biliary vessels empty themselves at a part of the intestine beyond where the chyle has been commenced to be absorbed, frequently closely before the colon, a short distance from the anus.
2. The chemical analysis of the biliary vessels, and of their contents, exhibits but little resemblance between it and the liver, for uric acid is its chief component. According to Chevreul's analysis ‡, the liquid obtained from the biliary vessels was alkaline, and vegetable colours, which had been turned red by acids, it stained blue; and upon the further addition of acids it precipitated uric acid, and smelt of ammonia when a weak solution of caustic potass was added to it. He thinks, therefore, that this liquid holds urate of potass and ammonia in solution. Wurzer § found also urate of ammonia, and both phosphate and carbonate of lime, which Brugnatelli ‖ and John equally found also in the excrement of *Lepidoptera* immediately after their exclusion from the pupa.
3. Besides these biliary vessels many insects have other secreting

---

* Archiv. fur Anat. u. Phys. Jahrg. 1826.
† Das organische Lebens neudargestellt, p. 335.   ‡ Straus Durk., p. 151.
§ Meckel's Archiv., iv. p. 213.   ‖ Ib., p. 629.

organs which empty themselves into the intestine, even indeed in front of the chylifying portion of it, namely, those blind appendages indicated as salivary glands behind the proventriculus.

4. In the spiders, secreting organs which resemble the biliary vessels empty themselves into the colon; and other vessels, which are in close connexion with the fatty matter, open into the ilium, and supplant the liver.

To harmonise if possible both views, which then would be the only true and correct one, we must in the first case ascertain if the liver, considering the organisation of insects, be absolutely necessary to their digestion. We find the liver large and of prominent development in all such animals in which the function of respiration is of diminished importance, especially those mollusca which breathe through branchiæ, and the fishes *. If we may thence conclude that animals which respire by means of lungs have a smaller liver, it is evident that insects, as those animals in which the respiration by means of lungs, or rather of pulmonary air-tubes, has attained its highest grade of perfection, must necessarily have the smallest liver of all. This may be caused by, as Carus † has remarked upon a similar occasion, the lungs and liver both separating the same substance, namely, such which contain carbon, by the former from an elastic fluid, and by the latter from a liquid. If, therefore, the lung is so predominant that it is found throughout the body, this separation takes place everywhere, and the liver, which by means of the veins receives the carbonated blood from the different parts of the body, where there is no lungs, is not required to act. The function of the liver as an excretory organ is therefore not requisite in insects, but yet as a secretory organ it is still of importance. Its chief object, viewed thus, is to reduce the acidity of the chyme, by means of the alkaline property of its secretion; but we have seen that the secretions of the salivary glands, and of the proventriculus, are both alkaline, and that the chyme beyond the proventriculus, or at the end of the duodenum, is perfectly neutral, and requires no addition of alkali to neutralise it; consequently even for this purpose the function of the liver is not necessary.

If we have thus shown that insects do not require a liver to promote

---

* This reciprocal relation appears to me as confirmed, and worthy of consideration, whereas the meritorious G. R. Treviranus denies it. Biologie, tom. iv. p. 420.

† Bootomie, p. 538.

digestion, it may be asked what is the function of the biliary vessels? Are they urinary organs or kidneys? Certainly not; for where shall we find, throughout the whole animal kingdom, an instance of the ureter emptying itself into the middle of the intestinal canal? And is not this the case with the biliary vessels in many, indeed the majority, of instances? The uric acid which chemists have found therein proves nothing, for many parts of the body of insects contain this acid, as Rudolphi * also correctly observes, it is likewise found in many other fluids besides urine †. Lastly, the resemblance of the biliary vessels to the urinary organs is too trifling, and the latter are always in closer connexion with the sexual organs than with the intestinal canal; besides, in some insects, namely, in the *Carabodea, Dytici,* and *Staphylini,* distinct urinary organs have been found (§ 113), the secretion of which indeed has not yet been proved by analysis to be urine, but which, both by their resemblance in form, and partly by their situation, have proved themselves urinary organs. Joh. Müller ‡, who has most strongly supported the consideration of the biliary vessels as kidneys, will not admit of these organs being considered as secreting urine, but explains them to be peculiar glands which secrete a sharp liquid, and compares them with the poison glands of the *Hymenoptera;* but even if we admit of this analogy we must yet oppose his assertion that the insects which are provided with these organs secreting a sharp liquid, for it is supported by no other observation than at most the explosion of the *Brachini.* As this exploding secretion is gaseous, it cannot necessarily be secreted by these organs, but may be merely be the air contained within the broad colon. Whereas the *Dytici,* upon being seized, as I have frequently observed, eject their hyaline livid urine, which has a peculiar pungent smell, very like feverish or corrupt human urine, but which never acts acutely or poisonously, and inflammatory. We may here justly ask why these few insects only have urinary organs, and the majority want them, which is absolutely a difficult problem to solve; but in some others, for example, *Bombylius, Leptis,* the same organs are again found, and in *Gryllus migratorius,* Fab., I observed a single serpentine vessel, which originated from a small kidney-shaped organ, and which opened at an analogous spot near the anus. It is therefore

* Physiologie, vol. ii. part ii. p. 145, note 1.
† Gmel. Handb. d. Théor. Chemie, vol. ii. part ii. p. 1473
‡ De Gland. secern. struct. pen., p. 68.

probable that in the other grasshoppers such vessels will be found, as well as in other voracious insects, which, as such, more require excretory organs; whereas in temperate insects, and such as feed upon highly elaborated finer substances, as well as haustellate insects from the greater preparation of their food, and its consequent perfect quality of assimilation, the excretory organs would be wholly superfluous. Wherefore then, it might be objected, have the voracious caterpillars and larvæ no urinary organs? To which we might reply, that it must not be forgotten that larvæ stand upon a much lower grade of animal development than perfect insects, and that they therefore do not display so great a separation and division of their organs; if the anus be wanting in some instances, how much more likely are the urinary organs to be deficient? and, besides, the majority of caterpillars have other excretory organs, viz., the spinning vessels, which take up from the body much useless matter. The unimportance of the urinary organs to the nutriment of larvæ explains their deficiency in those cases in which the beetle exhibits them; at least in the larva of *Calosoma sycophanta* I have not observed such organs.

If, then, the biliary vessels be neither exclusively liver nor exclusively kidneys, it remains to be determined what their function is. To arrive at this we look around us for analogous forms in other animals, and immediately discover the paired cæca of birds. These organs, which Carus* even wished to compare to biliary vessels, diverge in one respect by their frequently considerable shortness (for example, in all the diurnal birds of prey), and in a second respect by their contents differing so much from that of the biliary vessels of insects; they are also of a similar structure with the intestinal canal, which is not the case with the biliary vessels. But it is remarkable that the parallel orders of birds and insects exhibit some approximation in the length of these organs, for the biliary vessels are likewise very short in the carnivorous *Carabodea*, and if not exceedingly long yet they are very numerous in the herbivorous grasshoppers and *Grylli*, which I compare with the gallinaceous birds, into the detail of which I shall go below. We might therefore indicate, if not a strict analogy, at all events a certain approximate relation between these appendages of the intestinal canal.

Besides these paired cæca of birds we find no other appendages to

---

* Zootomie, p. 388.

the intestine in animals which admit of being compared with the biliary vessels, unless it be precisely the same forms in the *Annelides* and *Crustacea*. These have been, particularly in the *Crustacea*, explained as the liver, and therefore the biliary vessels must be considered as the analogues of these filaments, or at least, as the analogues of the liver. With respect to form, this is doubtlessly correct, the above cited reasons speak too clearly in favour of it; but in function they are not merely liver, indeed not purely secreting organs, but more justly excretory organs, which, however, do not separate urine alone, but also a kind of gall, and only in those instances where true urinary organs are wanting undertake as well the function of urinary organs. With respect to what may be objected from their opening higher into the intestinal canal, we may reply, that probably the whole remaining portion of the intestinal canal absorbs but little chyle, but instead, as Joh. Müller also considers, leads off the unassimilating remains. But in those instances where there are actual urinary organs the biliary vessels may be exclusively liver, at least their darker brown red colour in all these cases speaks in favour of it, particularly in the *Carabodea* and *Dytici*. In these then the tolerably long and especially broad and muscular ilium must also separate chyle.

I therefore positively consider the biliary vessels as analogues in form of the liver, but which do not exclusively exercise the function of the liver, but conjunctively, at least in many cases, the function of the kidneys, and of other secreting organs.

An opinion propounded by Oken explains the fatty substance as liver, but it is inapplicable, as has been shown by Meckel. Yet we cannot deny that the fatty substance has some relation to the liver, for the organisation of the *Arachnidæ* speaks distinctly in support of it. The biliary vessels may also, when they secrete bile, derive the foundation of their excretion from the fatty substance only, and we therefore find them everywhere closely enveloped by this fatty substance.

With respect to the direct observations of some physiologists, besides those already cited, upon the function of the biliary vessels, we find, according to Rengger, that they contain a clear fluid, in which the microscope detects a great number of globules. This fluid appeared more transparent and brighter when watery substances were received into the intestinal canal, and he therefore supposes that it is the water separated from the blood. He then observed the fluid, upon pressing the vessels, pour itself into the intestine, and Meckel remarked the same, whereby Ramdohr's opinion is contradicted of the frequent emptying of the biliary vessels into the space between the mucous membrane and the true skin. He further remarked, after this emptying, a refilling of the vessel and an advance of the fluid, without detecting the least motion in the vessel. The substance thus emptied he says he found again in the excrement, in the form of little globules upon its surface; also the reddish brown juice ejected by the *Lepidoptera* immediately after their exclusion from the pupa, consists chiefly of the excrement of the biliary vessels. That this fluid, as well as the excretion of the biliary vessels, contains much uric acid, has been proved by the analysis of Chevreul, Brugnatelli, and John, and which we have mentioned above. According to Rengger, the secretion of the biliary vessels dissolves neither in hot nor in cold water; it becomes firmer in alcohol, dissolves in concentrated acid, and is precipitated from this in a flocky form, upon the addition of water: upon proof paper it exhibits itself neither as acid nor alkaline, nor does it taste bitter, but insipid, like all the parts of a caterpillar. The excretion does not either re-act upon diluted chyme, and in the chyme from the intestinal canal beyond the biliary vessels, there was no fluid matter.

Straus Durckheim considers that there are in the cockchafer two different kinds of vessels which empty themselves into the intestines. The anterior ones which open beyond the stomach have ramose, transverse continuations, and are brownish; the posterior ones, whose orifices* he could not discover, are of a yellowish white and smooth, and without continuation. The anterior ones he considers as biliary organs, and the posterior ones as urinary organs. It is unimaginable how Straus, in so laborious and accurate an inquiry, should make such a mistake, particularly as two anatomists before him had described and figured the intestinal canal of the *Melolontha vulgaris*, namely, Ramdohr† and Leon Dufour‡. From both, as well as from Suckow's§ representation, it results, that in the cockchafer, likewise, there are but four very long biliary vessels, which pass into each other, and which at their anterior half send off ramose appendages, whereas posteriorly they have none. That the biliary vessels in many cases, for example,

* P. 270. † Abhand. uber die Verdauungsorgane, Pl. XVIII. f. 1.
‡ Annales des Sciences Natur. t. iii. p. 234, Pl. XIV. f. 4.
§ In Heusinger Zeitschrift. f. d. o. Phy. vol. iii. Pt. 1. Pl. III.

in the *Capricorns*, stand in connexion with the intestine at a second lower spot, but do not again open into it, has been shown above (§ 111). Joh. Müller has been misled by Straus to speak likewise of double vessels, which, he says, open at different parts of the intestine *, but such second vessels are not found in any insect.

§ 224.

The divisions of the intestinal canal which lie beyond the orifice of the biliary vessels, and which we have described above as the ilium, clavate intestine, cæcum, and colon, occupy a portion of the intestinal canal, which, in the majority of cases, is not half the length of that of the preceding part, and which is indeed often, namely, in the *Hemiptera*, so short, that it does not form one-tenth of the entire intestine. With respect to the law which regulates the proportions of the parts of the intestinal canal, we may consider that it is in general longer in carnivorous insects, but, on the contrary, shorter in the vegetable consumers, and that the larvæ have almost always, with the exception of the larvæ of the *Dytici*, as was remarked above, a very short portion of intestine beyond the orifice of the biliary vessels, whereas in the perfect insect it is longer.

If we inspect the contents as well as the function of this portion of the intestine in vegetable-feeding insects, for example, in the larvæ of the caterpillars, we shall find, according to Rengger's observation, that no further peristaltic motion is detected in it, and that the chyme contained within it separates no longer any chyle, nor, indeed, is any mixed with it. In the larvæ of the *Lamellicornia*, no food is observed in the ilium, but the great gut is closely filled with it. This nutriment is found here further comminuted and more pappy than in the stomach, differing in about the same proportion as the chyme of the stomach does from that of the cæcum in the *Rodentia*, and we must, therefore, at least in this instance, admit of a repeated separation of chyle, which is also confirmed by the dry, thick, excrementitious contents of the short colon. Ramdohr supposes that the biliary vessels, from their in general ascending and descending the duodenum, but subsequently spreading themselves about the greatest convolutions of the ilium, imbibe from it nutritive matter during the passage of the chyme, and that it is thence that the latter contains less moisture in the ilium : he ascribes the same

* De Glandul sec. Str. par. pp. 68, 69.

function likewise to the great gut, and, as the clavate gut is the same organ, it would necessarily also be attributable to this. Thus much is certain, that the chyme is further elaborated and extracted in the great gut of such larvæ before it is rejected from the body by the colon.

A function limited to the conveyance of the chyme cannot be attributed to the very long ilium of the carnivorous insects, namely, the *Dytici* and *Peltodea*, particularly as it is not only longer here than the duodenum, but even several times its length, for example in *Necrophorus*. In these, evidently, as in the higher animals, the ilium must throughout its whole course separate chyle; at least, a thin finely divided chyme is found throughout it. I am of the same opinion of the likewise very long ilium of the *Lepidoptera*, for the small egg-shaped stomach is too insignificant to separate all the chyle requisite for their support, although, as experience teaches us, the *Lepidoptera* are very temperate in the taking of food, and exhibit no trace of their previously voracious appetite as larvæ. All these insects with a long ilium have no distinct thick intestine, whereas in those with a short ilium, for example, the *Capricorns* and *Lamellicornia*, we find it described by Ramdohr as the clavate intestine. In the cockchafer and the other *Lamellicornia*, in their perfect state, instead of the broad sack-shaped thick intestine, we find an oval longitudinal thick gut, which is internally furnished with projecting longitudinal folds, which, as well as in the larvæ, subjects the chyme to a second elaboration, and also extracts it, for which purpose it appears to require the longitudinal folds. This second extraction can also, if it, which we may not doubt, likewise takes place in those insects which have a long ilium, occur only in the ilium. Indeed, such insects, namely, the *Dytici*, *Peltodea*, and *Lepidoptera*, have a longer or shorter cæcum, which, in *Dyticus*, is nearly half the length of the intestinal canal, and wherein the chyme may possibly be subjected to a second digestion. In favour of this opinion the multitude of glands upon its inner surface speak, as well as the viscous nature of all the nutriment contained within it. But we do not always find it filled with chyme, occasionally only in *Dyticus*; it sometimes only contains air, whence is explained Leon Dufour's opinion of its supplying the place of a swimming bladder. In the *Lepidoptera*, the brownish red fluid accumulates in it during the pupa state, which is rejected upon the exclusion of the perfect insect, and which, according to chemical analysis, consists chiefly of uric acid, and very much corresponds with the excretion of the biliary vessels. Treviranus, therefore, compares this cæcum of the *Lepidoptera* to the urinary bladder, and it would we were to institute an analogy with the birds, be analogous to the *bursa Fabricii* of those animals. Thus much is certain, that this cæcum cannot be of so much importance to digestion as, for example, the cæcum of the *Rodentia*, or the clavate and thick intestine of other insects which are analogous organs.

The true rejecting portion of the intestinal canal is therefore the colon. By its considerable size, in the majority of cases, it is adapted to the reception of much matter, and peculiarly adapted, by its strong muscular structure, to the compression of it into lumps of excrement. To promote this object, it has in many cases hard horny ridges and prominences, which assist it in its function. The shape of the excrement depends both upon the size of the colon and its folds. It is so various in the caterpillars of the *Lepidoptera*, that frequently, with a little attention, distinct genera and species may be distinguished by it, a skill which is not unimportant to those who have the care of plantations. In general, vegetable-feeding insects produce more excrement than the carnivorous ones. This is distinctly shown in the caterpillars and grasshoppers, the short but broad colon of which exclude at intervals of a few minutes considerable balls of excrement, which are shaped precisely according to its form. In general, the digestion of these insects is so rapid, that the just filled intestinal canal will have extracted all the chyle in the course of one hour, and the caterpillar recommence eating. Indeed, the food passes through the entire intestine merely to make room for constantly succeeding food, and a voracious caterpillar, therefore, will be continually evacuating excrement. In the perfect insect, the colon is wider than the rest of the intestine, but towards the anus it again contracts, and it consequently evacuates the excrement in smaller, at least thinner, portions, or in a more fluid, thick, pappy consistency; haustellate insects, such as the *Lepidoptera* and flies, reject it quite liquid. The colour of the excrement also depends upon the difference of food; for instance, that of the cockchafer is green, like the leaf of the plant upon which it feeds; that of the water beetle of a yellow white, like the flesh he has eaten; that of the flea red, like the blood it has imbibed; yet the colour always changes a little; it becomes, namely, darker, brownish or blackish, as in the flies, which lap so many different kinds of nutriment. No peculiar offensive or stinking smell is observed in the excrement of insects, and, indeed, their rapid digestion does not admit of so complete a decomposition as in the higher animals, particularly as the entire digestion of insects is almost limited to the imbibition of the juices contained in their food.

§ 225.

Lastly, we must here treat of some peculiar secretions which are the produce of digestion, or at least in their fundamental parts, but which exercise no influence upon it: among these we consider the secretion of the spinning vessels and other secerning organs, namely, those of the poison glands.

The spinning vessels (§ 112), which are found only in larvæ, are long twisted canals, which empty themselves into the spinning vessel found in the under lip, or in some rare instances, for example, in the larva of *Myrmecoleon*, present themselves in the shape of a pyriform bag, which, in the perfect insect, appears to be transformed into the colon: they lie at the anal extremity, and contain a viscous fluid, which, in the younger larvæ, is quite transparent, but, in more mature ones, it is more opaque and thicker. From this fluid the larva spins delicate filaments, which speedily harden in the air, and are then no longer soluble in water. The entire spinning vessel also, when dried in the air, likewise hardens to a firm fragile mass. Chemical analysis discovers the components of this fluid to consist of a substance like lime, a waxy portion, and a little coloured oil which smells like anise. Acids poured upon it harden it; in young caterpillars it precipitates a flocky substance (albumen); but in very concentrated acid it dissolves, as well as in a solution of pure potass: from the former it was precipitated by the addition of water, and from the latter by that of acid in a flocky shape. Hence it appears, that, besides animal albumen, a resinous and an oily substance form components of the spinning fluid, in favour of which the adhesiveness of the fresh material, its rapid drying, and fragility in a mass, speak greatly. It is, consequently, purely an excretion, and is made for the purpose of removing from the body the oily and resinous vegetable portions which are received into the blood by digestion, and again separated from it by the spinning vessels. In the spiders, which feed upon animal substances, and, therefore, doubtlessly, in the larvæ of the *Phryganeæ* and in the *Antlion*, &c., which also devour animal matter, it also contains ammonia* and a material allied to the horny

---

* Gmelin's Chemic, vol. ii. Pt. 2, p. 1475.

substance, the presence of which is to be deduced from the variety of their food.

True poison glands are less generally distributed: we have described them above (§ 140) among the appendages of the female sexual organs. They are found only in the *Hymenoptera*, viz. in the *Pompili, Spheges*, wasps and bees. The secretion of these organs is a sharp corrosive fluid, which is the principal cause of the violent pain that is experienced from the puncture of these insects. The form of the sting, which has also been described above (§ 145), enables them to insert this poison into the wound at the time of the puncture, as the sting is not simple, but consists of several setæ, which form a narrow canal. We find, likewise, in the *Lepidoptera*, appendages which, in structure and place of opening, appear to be analogous to these poison glands. This analogy is supported by the intelligence of some residents at the Cape of Good Hope, who inform us that there is a lepidopterous insect known there by the name of the bee-moth, which defends itself in stinging when captured, and the puncture is so painful, that a large swelling speedily arises which quickly produces inflammation [*]. The chemical composition of this poisonous fluid cannot be given without analysis: it perhaps contains a free acid allied to the formic acid, or is, probably, the very same thing, which supposition is supported by the similarity of the pain to that of a wound from an ant. These creatures, namely, have no sting, but yet they possess the poison organs, and project from their anus by raising their abdomen this sharp fluid against their enemies. Its acuteness is shown by the violent pain caused by being sprinkled with it. They also defend themselves by biting, but their bite is harmless. That these organs are analogous forms to the urinary organs of the *Carabodea* and *Dytici*, is on the one side supported by their similar situation at the extremity of the body, yet with this important difference, that these open above the intestinal

---

[*] Isis. 1831, p. 1917. From a letter received by Professor Reich from the Cape of Good Hope. It is the opinion of the entomologists cited there, that the projecting sting is the male organ, but it is contradicted by a Brazilian *Cossus* in the Royal Entomological Collection at Berlin, and which is a female: it has a long and very pointed sting, which is recurved, but I was not at liberty to inspect it more closely. According to analogy, this sting can be nothing else than an ovipositor formed by the projection of the horny ridges found in the vagina of all insects. It appears most to correspond with the sting of the *Hymenoptera*, yet it appeared to me that the exterior sheaths were wanting, if I may trust a very superficial glimpse which was all I could have of it.

canal, the former, however, beneath it, into the evacuating duct of the sexual organs; on the other side, by their similar form, they also forming serpentine or ramose canals, which terminate in a larger reservoir, or bladder. In both cases they are double, but the poison organs empty themselves into a bladder with a single duct, whereas the urinary bladders remain separated and have two distinct orifices.

We also discover frequently in insects peculiar secretions, which are found limited to certain families. They betray themselves especially by the smell which insects possessing them either constantly produce, or only upon certain occasions. Thus the large *Carabodea* smell like fresh Russia leather, which must be ascribed to a secretion that is emitted through one of the articulating membranes. This supposition is supported by the milky secretion which is poured forth in abundance through the articulating membrane between the head and prothorax and mesothorax, by recently captured *Dytici*, and which has an offensive stench like that of putrid urine. In *Meloë*, a different oily fluid is secreted in the articulating membranes of the legs. In neither of the two former instances could I discover a distinct secreting organ, and Brandt was equally unsuccessful in *Meloë**. The sharp secretion of the *Cantharides* is universally known, for which also no distinct secreting organ is to be found, but which seems to be deposited principally in the hard horny parts. Here the excretion exhibits itself as a peculiar substance, which chemists designate by the name of cantharis camphor †, and which alone possesses the property of blistering. It is also found in other genera and species of this family, for instance, in *Mylabris*, which is the true *Cantharis* of the ancients. Other volatile, ethereal, and peculiar secretions are observed in *Callichroma moschatum*, the spurious Spanish fly, which insect betrays itself at a considerable distance even, by its agreeable and peculiar smell; in the stinking burying beetle (*Necrophorus*), dung beetles (*Scarabeus*), and in some *Chrysomelæ* and *Coccinellæ*. The last especially, upon being touched, emit a yellow fluid through the segments of the abdomen, which smells strongly of opium. Perhaps it is from this that they have been applied in the toothach. The *Hemiptera* are distinguished among the other orders, and especially the bugs, by a very peculiar insufferable stench, which is, however, only to be detected

---

* Arzneithiere, vol. ii. Pt. 4, p. 104.
† Gmelin's Chemie, vol. ii. Pt. 1, p. 427.

upon touching or pressing the creature, and is probably produced by a peculiar secretion, which serves them as a defence against their enemies.

Among the *Hymenoptera* also many bees are distinguished by a peculiar very agreeable smell, which may in many instances however originate from the flowers they visit.

One genus of this large family, the domestic bee, produces a secretion of a distinct nature, which is not found in any other insect. This secretion, which distinguishes itself less by its smell than by its peculiar quality, is the wax of which the bees construct their cells. The secreting organ is found in the space between the ventral plates of the five intermediate abdominal segments, and exhibits itself as a delicate, soft, structureless membrane which passes from the superior half of each ventral segment, and, describing an arch, inserts itself in the preceding; hence it is the true articulating membrane itself, which has here transformed itself into a perfect secreting organ. But such a function of the articulating membrane is not without analogy in other insects, for in the *Dytici* the membrane between the head and thorax, in *Meloë* that between the femur and tibia, and in *Coccinella* that between the several ventral plates, is a true secretory organ. The form of the secreting surface presents itself as a long octagon, which is divided into two halves by a central horny ridge. This octagon lies at the anterior surface of each of the central five ventral plates, and stands in connexion with the posterior side of the preceding plate, by means of a process. Thus each bee has five secreting pockets in its abdomen. In these pockets the wax is prepared in the form of very thin, white, and very fragile plates, which are firmly attached to the secreting surface, and thence removed when the bee wishes to construct a cell. For this purpose it breaks the wax plates into small pieces, and by means of its saliva it prepares with it a soft pappy substance, which is stuck together in small pieces, and afterwards smoothed by the mouth with the assistance of the saliva*. The saliva, therefore, from possessing the property of dissolving the wax, must be of an alkaline nature, which is proved also by its organs becoming red when laid in vinegar. In the other families of the *Hymenoptera*, on the contrary, namely, in the ants, a superfluity of acid is found in the body, which

---

* See G. R. Treviranus, in the Zeitschrift für Physiologie, vol. iii. p. 62., upon these wax-preparing organs, and the mode in which the bees work it.

betrays itself not merely by its smell but more by a peculiar but not unpleasant taste. That this acid is found especially in the abdomen is well known, but we are unacquainted with the organ that secretes it; it is probable that the poison organs and the acid are both merely a very sharp urine.

Among the *Lepidoptera* peculiar secreting organs have been found in some larvæ, for instance, in the larva of *Harpya vinula*, which has a little bag at the ventral plate of the first abdominal segment, that, when filled, is of about the size of a pea, and the aperture to which is a transverse incision at the same spot. The fluid contained in it is a powerful acid, which produces pain and inflammation upon a delicate skin*. In the caterpillar of *Pieris Machaon* there is a similar furcate secreting organ in the neck, which is projected upon its being roughly handled. The getting greasy, as it is called in *Lepidoptera*, also indicates a great provision of secreted juices. In *Harpya vinula* it is frequently the case, and we might thence suppose it to be consequent upon the secretions of the caterpillar. The liquid, however, seems to be no oil, but rather an acid. Lastly, among the *Diptera* we find individual instances of a presence of peculiar secretions, for example, in *Cænomya ferruginea*, Meig. (*Sicus ferrug.*, *S. bilicor*, and *S. errans*, Fab.); some of the flies which belong to the division of those with a spiny scutellum (*Dipt. notacantha*), which Meigen called whey flies, from their penetrating smell, resembling that of green whey cheese. This smell, which proceeds from the whole body, and which cannot be ascribed to any local excretion, remains even a long time after death, whereas the majority of such odours then speedily evaporate.

§ 226.

II. FUNCTION OF THE AIR TUBES, RESPIRATION.

The chief object of respiration is to adapt the circulating fluid destined for assimilation with the organic mass to that purpose, by the addition of another substance, viz., atmospheric air or oxygen. To attain this we find in the majority of instances distinct respiratory organs, namely, a more or less distributed respiratory surface, which must be purely considered as either an internally or externally produced continuation of the epidermis, and in which the fluid circulates, and

---

*. Rengger's Physiolog. Untersuch., p. 427.

which thus stands in constant connexion with the air, whereas, when this continuation of the epidermis forms an internal cavity, the oxidised respiratory medium is received in it. These cavities, which are everywhere distributed throughout the bodies of insects, we have described above, according to their most general forms, as air tubes or tracheæ; they constitute the respiratory organ, which is consequently neither external nor partial, but is distributed throughout the entire compass of the cavity of the body in uniform perfection. The structure of the respiratory organ will, therefore, be fully known when we shall have proved that these air tubes and no other portion of the body actually constitute it. Commencing with this proof, the subsequent divisions of this chapter will be occupied with the mechanism of respiration, and its effects upon the corporeal functions.

§ 227.

With respect to the proofs that the tracheæ are the actual respiratory organs of insects, the most superficial anatomical inspection of an insect shows us that air is found in these tubes, and that we nowhere find internal apertures to these tracheæ, but constantly external ones. Besides, air is seen to pass through the external orifices, or spiracles, when living insects are cast into water, as air bladders rise from them to the surface of the water. But Treviranus's * experiment is the strongest proof; he placed the large green locust (*Locusta viridissima*) beneath a turned up glass filled with water, and then saw an air bubble rise from the spiracle between the meso- and meta-thorax, which regularly decreased with the respiratory motion of the creature, and again increased with its distension. Hausmann also observed an ascent and descent of the water in a glass tube closed above, the superior space of which contained air and a green locust, and this took place synchronally with the inspiration and expiration of the insect †. Other facts which prove the function of the air tubes as respiratory organs are, for instance, the speedy death of all insects whose spiracles are closed with oil or gum, so that no fresh air can enter the tracheæ, besides the ascending to the surface of all such water insects which have no branchiæ, and lastly, the projection to the surface of the air-tubes whilst the remainder of the creature is immersed in the water. In addition to these direct observations upon the respiratory function of

* Biologie, vol. iv. p. 158.   † De Animal. exsang. respirat., p. 8.

tracheæ we have other indirect proofs derived from their structure. These are their anatomical conformity with the tracheæ of the higher animals, their distension into bags and bladders, which correspond with the cells of the lungs and its bags; and, lastly, the deficiency of a peculiar respiratory organ, which would be the more necessary in insects, from their being covered with a hard integument, which could not exercise that function. All these facts confirm the tracheæ to be the true and sole respiratory organs of insects, and that air containing oxygen is received into them through the spiracles, air tubes, or branchiæ.

§ 228.

If we now return to the mechanism of respiration, we shall find that it presents itself throughout the animal world as a rhythmical motion of the body, whereby the medium containing the oxygen is brought into incessant contact with the respiratory organs. This motion in insects is consequently for the purpose of introducing atmospheric air within the tracheæ, which object is attained by the opening of the spiracles which close the apertures of the tracheæ. If the abdomen of the insect distends at the same time as the spiracles open, the air must necessarily pass into the tubes which are now opened, and when the abdomen contracts, the just inspired air will consequently be forced out again. Thus all respiratory motion presents itself as a rhythmical compression and expansion of the cavities of the body, and especially of the abdomen. The muscles which produce this motion are the same as those described above as connecting the several parts of the skeleton together, namely, the straight dorsal and ventral muscles of the abdomen. The thorax appears to participate less in the contraction of the cavities of the body, at least no contraction or dilatation of it is to be detected in insects quietly breathing; and also the intimate and firm connexion of the several parts of it together prevents such an alteration of its compass in repose. But whether the cavities of the tracheæ are also contracted upon the considerable compression of the abdomen, is uncertain. Nitzsch [*] has in many instances observed that there was no alteration during respiration, whereas he detected in the large air bladders of the *Diptera* and of the *Hymenoptera* a distinct compression upon the contraction of the abdomen, but which evidently appeared to proceed from the latter, and not from a contraction of the air bladder itself [†]. Hence,

---

[*] Comment. de Respirat. Animal. p. 38.   [†] Ibid. p. 39.

therefore, the rigid spiral filament which encircles all tracheæ is especially adapted to its constant distension, precisely as is the case with the cartilaginous tracheæ of the superior animals. Consequently, by means of the elasticity of this filament, the trachea spontaneously distends upon the distension of the abdomen, the compression of which had decreased its compass; and possibly it is as much distended beyond its natural size, by the introduction of air upon inspiration, as it had been previously contracted by the contraction of the abdomen, at least Comparetti's experiments * upon locusts opened alive appear to indicate as much, but it cannot be kept constantly contracted or distended beyond its usual size owing to this filament.

In general the respiratory motion is very unequal; it is either quicker or slower, according to the state of excitement or repose of the entire system. It appears also to vary considerably in the several orders. Sorg observed † in *Lucanus Cervus* from twenty to twenty-five contractions in a minute, whereas in *Locusta viridissima* ‡ there were from fifty to fifty-five, and in *Deilephila Euphorbiæ* § only twenty. In a cockchafer, whose elytra I had cut half off, I could detect no pulsation at all, even with the greatest attention, and by means of a lens, so long as it remained inactive and as it were asleep; but upon taking it into my hand, the warmth of which aroused it, pulsations were to be seen, at first, it is true, very irregular, both in intensity and the interval that elapsed between them, but it at last breathed regularly when preparing for flight, and there were now about twenty-five contractions in a minute; but the abdomen after each contraction gradually decreased, never subsequently distending so widely as at first, but likewise it compressed itself more and more, so that there was an equal ratio between the decrease of its dilatation and the increase of its contraction. Shortly before taking flight it moved its whole body as it were convulsively, the head was protruded and withdrawn, pro- and mesothorax were also loosened from each other and again brought together, and, lastly, the valve of the cloaca was widely opened, and it appeared to struggle during its violent respiration as if desirous of disencumbering itself of an oppressive load. But all its endeavours

---

* Obs. Anat. de Aurâ Internâ comp. p. 290, according to Treviranus's Biologie, vol. iv. p. 161.

† Disquisit. Physiol. circa Respirat. Insectorum et Vermium, p. 27.

‡ Ibid. p. 46. § Ibid. p. 66.

were in vain, for its clipped wings made flight impossible. *Libellulæ*, which are held by the wings behind, may be very well examined, and the pulsations of the abdomen are very distinct, but no motion is to be detected in the thorax. The number of these pulsations is greater than in the cockchafer, but not so great as in the green locust. I estimate them at from thirty to thirty-five in a minute. I consider, besides, that the pulsations increase when the voluntary motions, for instance, that of flight, are in exercise, which I conclude from the respiration of a *Libellula* held in the above manner, increasing upon its endeavours to free itself. During this, however, the spiracles of the abdomen did not appear to inspire, and the contractions of the abdomen recommenced only after the motion of the thorax. Treviranus[*] concluded, from similar observations, and, indeed, justly, that the spiracles of the abdomen respire during repose, whereas those of the thorax are especially in action during flight. He cites as a proof, that the same muscles which contract the cavity of the thorax, our straight dorsal and pectoral muscles as well as the oblique lateral and dorso-lateral muscles, effect the first expansion of the wings by the general contraction of the thorax, and, subsequently, in conjunction with the true alary muscles, produce the motion of flight by the alternating distension and contraction of the thorax. During this motion of the thorax, air must necessarily pour in and out, particularly as the expiration of the abdomen progressively increases, as is proved by my observations upon the cockchafer, and the deeper it becomes, the earlier do the spiracles of the thorax commence breathing, and this supposition is strongly supported by the motion of the head and prothorax. At the very moment, however, that the beetle flies off, it compresses its whole abdomen together, and this is continued during its whole flight, a clear proof that the whole function of respiration now is effected by the spiracles of the thorax. We may also note that the sudden breathing of the abdomen in insects upon their settling after flight, namely, in the flies, bees, and wasps, tends to support it. The longer the creature reposes, the slower and more regular the pulsations of the abdomen become. This opinion also of the respiration through the spiracles of the thorax gives a sufficient explanation of the humming noises produced by most insects during flight, as I shall prove in detail below, for it cannot be conceived that the mere flapping of the wing can produce it, but that it proceeds

---

[*] Das organische Leben, t. i. p. 262.

from the air streaming in and out of the thorax during flight. We find also the motion in the wings of insects even at rest during their chirping and crying, for instance, of the great grasshopper, to harmonise with this opinion, for without the air streaming out of the thorax upon the fluttering wings, not a tone could be produced. Therefore, the voice of all insects is no mechanical friction of portions of the skeleton, but in them, as elsewhere, it stands in immediate connexion with the respiratory apparatus and its outlets.

§ 229.

The spiracles themselves participate somewhat in the pulsations of the entire body, at least in the larger ones which lie exposed upon the surface of the body on opening and shutting of them, synchronal with the in- and ex-piration has been observed. We also know, from the preceding description of all the forms of these spiracles, that only those which lie exposed are supplied with a peculiar apparatus for the opening and closing of their lips, whereas those which are concealed beneath portions of the skeleton exhibit either none or only a partially closing margin. Such spiracles consequently do not appear to be able to be closed, but the air seems constantly to pass in and out with each breath. Other writers, on the contrary, maintain a complete closing of the spiracle in some insects by means of extraneous substances which lay in front of it. Reaumur was the first to observe this closing of the spiracles in a pupa by means of a viscous substance, and Sprengel * confirmed it. If now such a substance shall have been observed in insulated cases, which may not be doubted, from the positive assertion of Sprengel, it can occur only as an exception, perhaps, in consequence of the diseased state of the caterpillar; or it was perhaps a peculiar secretion which was separated around the spiracle, and at a moment of danger, for instance, upon being touched, flowed in front of the spiracle, to prevent the application of something prejudicial; subsequently, however, when the caterpillar no longer feared the presence of its enemy, was again absorbed, or mechanically removed; perhaps also the substance may have got there by accident. In all cases, however, free respiration would be impeded by it, and this stoppage could not last long without becoming prejudicial to the insect. It appears, therefore, probable to me, that all pupa in which such

* Comment. de Partib. § 4.

a stoppage of the spiracles has been observed, were either dead or upon the point of death. But that the function of respiration may be long interrupted in pupa, is attested by a number of experiments, and, therefore, it is not at all improbable that the pupa may have exhibited signs of life even when its spiracles were stopped up.

The earliest physiologists, viz. Malpighi and Reaumur, instituted experiments upon the effects of stopping the spiracles with oil or gum, and obtained the result, that if the stoppage were long continued, it would cause the death of the insect. More recently, Moldenhawer[*], in proof of his view that the spiracles were not the orifices of the respiratory organs, made many experiments by stopping them with oil, and the result obtained from his investigations was, that not merely stopping the spiracles, but even merely brushing it over with oil, was fatal to the insect system. But this is not the case. G. R. Treviranus[†], who repeated many of his experiments, observed death to ensue only upon the stoppage of all its spiracles, and not when the body or portions of it were brushed over with oil; and indeed upon the complete stoppage of all the spiracles, it was some hours before death was produced. This was the case with insects found under water. But the effects of the stoppage were very various: caterpillars lived longest; perfect insects were sooner killed; some, even upon a partial coating of oil, for instance, a wasp, the breast and venter of which was covered with oil of almonds, died in a few minutes. But as it is precisely upon the breast and ventral portions that the orifices of the spiracles are placed, we may presume that they were stopped in this experiment. That it does not prove fatal to cover some only of the spiracles, is proved by an experiment upon a *Meloë*, the ventral spiracles of which were closed. Its preceding activity remained almost unaltered, for the spiracles of the breast, which Treviranus does not indeed know in insects, remained free, and through these the beetle could breathe[‡].

Whereas it has been observed upon the covering of some of the spiracles only, namely, those lying upon the same segments, there ensued a partial laming of that portion of the body thus deprived of

---

[*] Beiträge zur Anatomie der Pflanzen, p. 309.

[†] Biologie, vol. iv. p. 151.

[‡] Das organische Leben, p. 257. The majority of observations here made upon the situation of the spiracles in the several orders is erroneous, as the description we have given above will prove.

air, Reaumur and Bonnet* among the earlier naturalists, and Treviranus among the moderns, have made experiments upon this point. According to Bonnet, the oil inserts itself within the spiracle, and by that means still more impedes respiration. Treviranus, who stopped only the posterior spiracles of the caterpillar of *Cossus ligniperda* with oil, observed a trembling, and raising of the last abdominal segment, but which, however, soon disappeared, after which the caterpillar exhibited no further morbid symptom. The same was the case with a green locust, the thoracic spiracles of which were stopped with oil: at first the legs appeared to become weaker and motionless, but it subsequently recovered. My opinion is that this phenomenon of a partial laming can present itself only immediately after the closing of the spiracle, for subsequently air will pass from other spiracles into those tracheæ whose orifices have been closed, particularly as all the tracheæ stand in immediate connexion together, at least in the majority of insects. It is only so long as the organisation is deprived of this auxiliary assistance, that symptoms of lameness can appear. But even without this assistance, it is scarcely advisable to seek in animals which stand only upon a central grade of organisation for the uniform phenomena observable in the more regulated conditions of life of the superior animals. How long a time cannot insects pass beneath water or in spirits of wine without respiring, and yet recover from their stupor! In the latter they indeed speedily die, but I know many instances of beetles having been immersed in spirits of wine for twelve hours, and, upon being removed from it, recover all their functions. But it is much more fatal for insects to inspire air impregnated with the fumes of evaporated spirits of wine; it is true that here they die more slowly, but at the latest in the course of half an hour, and when once thoroughly made torpid, they do not again recover.

§ 230.

The mechanism of respiration in insects which live in water is not in general different from that of those which live constantly in the air. But this observation refers especially to those only which breathe even in this medium through spiracles, whereas the process in those which breathe through gills is somewhat different.

Those water insects which breathe through spiracles must come to

---

* Contemplations de la Nature, t. ii.

the surface of the water when they wish for fresh air, and bring that portion of their body provided with these apertures in communication with the air above the surface. Among the beetles there are two families especially which live in the water, namely, the *Hydrocantharides* and *Hydrophilus*. The mechanism of respiration differs in both. The *Dytici*, when they wish to breathe, bring the posterior extremity of their body to the surface of the water, and they then separate the last segment of the abdomen from the elytra, and thus admit air beneath the elytra within the space between them and the abdomen; they then close it by pressing the last segment firmly to the abdomen, and return with their fresh supply to the bottom of the water. Here this air is so long inspired by the spiracles, which are situated also within this cavity between the elytra and the abdomen, as it is fit for respiration, after which the insect returns to the surface of the water, again to renew its supply. We thus observe in these insects the same process as we find in those which live in the air. The *Hydrophili* breathe differently. These, as Nitzsch * has observed and described in detail, do not bring the apex of the abdomen, but the head, to the surface of the water, and then project one of their clavate antennæ, the whole clava of which is covered with fine hair, until it comes into contact with the air. But they so twist the clava that its base is exposed to the air and the apex touches the breast, which, as well as the whole underside of the insect, is clothed with short silky pubescence. By this means a communication is made with the external air and that beneath the water covering both the clava of the antennæ and the whole under surface of the insect to which it adheres by means of the coating of down, and by means of this communication fresh air is transmitted to the venter of the insect, and by the same means the expired air is also removed, and the air is likewise transmitted from the ventral surface beneath the elytra, where it is in- and expired by the spiracles there situated. It is to the air thus adhering to the venter that the *Hydrophili* are indebted for their lightness. It is with difficulty that the majority can keep themselves at the bottom of the water by clinging to substances there, and, when once at the surface, only by the help of other bodies, for example, the stem of a plant, down which they creep, can they recover their situation beneath. The great *Hydrophilus piceus* alone, by means of its stronger muscular power,

* Reil's Archiv. für Physiologie, t. x. p. 440.

can work itself beneath the water, and swim about in it, although but slowly, if unassisted, whereas the *Dytici* swim with the greatest facility on all sides.—A third type of water beetles, the *Gyrinus* or whirlwig, also conveys an air bladder with it when it dives, which he can accomplish only with difficulty and the greatest exertion, or by means of other assistance; he, however, receives the air posteriorly between the abdomen and the elytra, which is the easier to him as he swims freely about in circles upon the surface. The larvæ of the *Dytici* and *Hydrophili* likewise breathe through spiracles which are situated at the anal extremity; they therefore only require to bring the end of the tail to the surface of the water when they wish to respire. They are, therefore, seen with a raised tail and pendent head hanging to the surface by means of their plumose anal leaves. As soon as an enemy approaches they hastily seek the bottom, but in the course of a few seconds resume their former position. The perfect insect, however, can remain longer beneath the water, as it conveys a supply of undecomposed atmospheric air with it.

The majority of the remaining insects which dwell in water breathe through tubes, with the exception of those which breathe by means of gills. The mechanism of this mode of respiration scarcely differs from that of the general mechanism of respiration. By raising the air tube to the surface of the water, the influx of fresh air is admitted to the tracheæ, and this ensues upon each expansion of the cavities of the body, whereas by means of each contraction the previously inspired air is again rejected. But it appears probable to me that expiration is effected not solely by the posterior tubes, but also through an aperture immediately behind the head in the first segment of the body. I have indicated these apertures in the description given above of the respiratory apparatus of the rat-tailed maggot; they are also found in the majority of the larvæ of the *Diptera* which do not live in water, for instance, in the maggots of the *Muscæ*, and also probably in the larvæ of the gnats, and in these they then develope themselves to the subsequent air tube in the thorax of the pupa. As now these anterior apertures remain constantly in the water, they cannot serve for inspiration, but being present they cannot be superfluous in the organisation of the larva; besides, nothing appears more probable than that the inspired air is again expired through these anterior apertures.

§ 231.

Respiration by means of gills is found only in such insects as live wholly in the water. The situation, form, and differences of these organs have been given above (§ 126) in sufficient detail: we will merely add here somewhat upon the mechanism of this mode of respiration. By their deficiency of external apertures the gills are chiefly distinguished from the other organs of respiration. The reception of atmospheric air within the tracheæ is thereby naturally rendered more difficult, for its imbibition through the tunic of the gills must proceed more slowly than its mechanical reception through numerous apertures. The gills, consequently, form large broad leaves or long bunches of hair, around which circulates the medium containing the oxygen. A second condition of the reception of this gas by means of gills is the constant motion of these organs, by means of which motion, fresh particles of water, saturated with this gas, are brought into contact with the gills. This motion of the branchiæ varies according to their situation and form.

Lamellate gills, situated at the sides of the abdomen, move like the fins of fishes from front backwards, so that throughout the whole series of these branchial leaves a constant undulating motion is perceived. The first lamellæ bend forwards, whilst the posterior ones strike backwards, and while the former strike backwards, the latter are bending forwards. Thus the motion of all the gills is not contemporaneous, but both progressive and alternating. By this means these larvæ do not swim in thrusts, but regularly, as by means of a portion of the leaves of their gills they are constantly propelled the while another portion reposes, and by this portion they are kept in motion when the preceding is again inactive. By this continued motion of the branchiæ, the larva is constantly changing place, and thereby an incessant influx of fresh air is promoted.

But if the lamellate or hair-shaped gills are placed at the anal extremity of the body, motion is produced by the serpentining of the abdomen, just in the same way as worms without swimming leaves move in water. Thus the larvæ of the *Agrions* swim and breathe at the same time. And, lastly, if the gills lie in the colon itself, as in the larvæ of *Æschna* and *Libellula*, by the opening of the anus and the distension of the colon, water is received in the cavity of this organ, and by its compression again rejected: and by the rejection of the water it is that these larvæ move.

Hair-shaped gills, which are situated upon the thorax, appear but rarely to move independently; in the majority of cases it is by means of the motion of the entire animal, which is effected by the serpentining abdomen, that these gills come in contact with fresh water. It is in this manner that the pupa of *Chironomus* swims, and its whole motion is consequently a respiratory motion, for these pupa take no nutriment. A variation from this is the serpentine motion of the anterior portion of the body when the animal has attached itself by its tail. This motion also, which Nitzsch * observed in the pupa of *Chironomus plumosus*, is a mere respiratory motion. Lastly, if the pupa dwells in an open case, the entire bunch of gills moves either within it or on its exterior: thus the pupa of *Simulia* appears to breathe. Whereas the contact of fresh water with the bunch of gills, which in the larvæ of *Phryganea* are situated within the case, is effected by the motion of the entire insect, in which fresh water is received anteriorly within the cylindrical cavity, and, when expired, is again rejected by the posterior aperture.

§ 232.

The question now arises, how do the insects breathe which dwell within the internal cavities of other animals whither little or no atmospheric air can reach?

To answer this question, we must first illustrate the cases in which insects are found in the interior of other animals. All these cases refer to two chief differences, for either these insects live in cavities to which atmospheric air can easily and does actually reach, and in which case their respiration has nothing problematical and wonderful; or else they live in cavities which are thoroughly closed from the admission of any air. The first case is found in the instance of the larvæ of the *Œstri*. These dwell either in the cavities of the nose or stomach, or beneath the skin, in tumours in horses and the ruminantia. The air can reach all these cavities, which also contain atmospheric air, and indeed those larvæ which live in tumours constantly protrude their anal end, where the two spiracles are placed, out of the tumour, and thus

* Comment. de respirat. Animalium, p. 40.

breathe like all others, or rather like the majority of the larvæ of the *Diptera*. The second instance, however, is found in the Ichneumons, which do not live in the intestine, but in the cavity of the body of other insects, between the intestine and the skin. That these creatures must breathe admits of no doubt; and indeed that they breathe precisely in the same way as the larvæ of the other *Hymenoptera*, namely, through spiracles, is as certain as that they do not at all differ in their organisation from those larvæ. We can, therefore, adopt no other supposition than that such larvæ participate in the respiration of the insect upon which they are parasitic, and that they breathe the air that passes through the tracheæ into the cavity of the body, or that they pierce a trachea, and, remaining in its vicinity, respire the air pouring from it. Such a wound to the respiratory apparatus would not produce death, for it has still sufficient unwounded tracheæ, and it would require only to be a small branch that would admit of the passage of sufficient air for the minute larva of an Ichneumon. Those caterpillars infested by parasites are always evidently ill, and this disease may proceed perhaps from the interruption in various parts of the function of respiration, and this interruption, together with the constant decrease of the fatty substance of the pupa, may deprive it of its remaining strength, and thus slowly kill it. After the death of the pupa, the remainder of its internal organs are consumed by the parasite, or else the numerous parasitic larvæ pierce the skin of the caterpillar, and thus kill it before it can change into the pupa state.

§ 233.

Having now shown the various kinds of mechanism by which atmospheric air is admitted to the internal organs of respiration, we further ask what is the object of this admission of atmospheric air, and what changes does it itself undergo? The reply is given in the result of the various experiments of Sorg, Hausmann, and others, upon the decomposition of air during the breathing of insects, and it is, "All breathing insects deprive the air of a considerable portion of its oxygen, and give off in lieu of it carbonic acid." The quantity of oxygen withdrawn by breathing varies according to the size of the creature, and the intensity of its respiration, and the quantity of carbonic acid given off varies just as much. But thus much appears confirmed, that considerably more oxygen is consumed by the creature than carbonic acid given off. And the more perfectly developed respiring animals are, the less are they enabled to deprive atmospheric air of its whole contents of oxygen: before its complete consumption they appear languid, and, as it were, apoplectic, and they die upon the continuance of this state, or if they have not a fresh supply of air. Whereas many insects, particularly butterflies, as animals upon a lower grade of organisation, so entirely consume the oxygen in the air, that in many experiments that have been made, not the hundredth portion of that gas has been found left in it*. But the loss which the air suffers by the withdrawal of the larger quantity of oxygen, in lieu of which but one half the quantity of carbonic acid is given back to it, appears to be replaced by a second excretion, consisting of azote. One portion of this azote is given off by the lungs or air tubes, and another portion, especially, by the perspiration of the skin. But as this perspiration can be but trifling through the hard integument of insects, if it be not indeed wholly deficient, they consequently must produce less azote but a proportionably greater quantity of carbonic acid.

These are the chief results of the experiments upon the respiration of insects. In proof of them we will give a tabular view of other experiments of Treviranus, without adding more recent ones of our own, occasioned by our less familiarity with such experiments, and from our deficiency in the necessary auxiliaries and instruments. And indeed the results of the experiments of so experienced and competent an observer may well suffice.

* Sorg, pp. 65, 67.

Proportions of Absorption in the same time (100 minutes) and quantity (100 grains).

Name of the Insect.	State of the Thermom. above °.	Quantity of Respired Air.	Excreted Carbonic Acid.	Absorbed Oxygen.	Excreted Azote.
Apis mellifica, neuter	11,5	27,2	0,82	1,33	0,53
Another with violent motion and in the sun	22	48,6	2,25	2,77	0,52
Bombus lapidarius A.	12,5	3,8	0,31	0,43	0,12
———— B.	15	23,7	1,70		
———— C.	16	10,0	0,72		
———— terrestris in the sun	14—23	11,0	1,74		
———— muscorum	17	46,2	0,64	0,82	0,18
Eristalis nemorum (*Meig.*)	16—16,5	7,4	0,50	0,80	0,30
Pontia Brassicæ (Caterpillar)	14—13	2,8	0,16	0,28	0,12
———— Rapæ A. after starving 28 hours	15	8,3	0,72	2,26	1,54
———— B. on dying	13,5—17	2,0	0,20	0,37	
Vanessa Atalanta A. after 3 days starving	13—28	27,0	2,65 (?)	2,85	
———— B. the same and weakened by the preceding experiment	15	105,0	1,50	2,35	
Libellula depressa A.	17—16,5	6,2	0,37	0,74	0,37
———— B.	16,5—14	7,5	0,33	0,93	0,60
Cetonia aurata (larva)	17	6,1	0,04	0,06	0,02
———— A.	16,5	2,9	0,21		
———— B. after 2 days starving	13,5—14,5	1,5	0,06	0,07	
Melolontha horticola	13—15	2,0	0,07	0,17	0,10
Feronia nigra	11—15	4,8	0,23	0,56	0,33

If we still draw further results from the above experiments, we shall find in these also a confirmation of the law deduced from the respiratory pulsations, namely, that in the sun and upon the general excitement of the body the respiration is more violent and intensive than in repose or in the shade. A working bee in the former situation inspired almost double the quantity of air, consumed once as much more oxygen, and gave off three times the quantity of carbonic acid, whereas the quantity of rejected azote remained the same. The same result was produced by several experiments made by Sorg. Hunger and the perfect satiation of the appetite likewise exercise great influence upon the function of respiration, and indeed hunger, as in general, acts also enervatingly upon respiration. Hungry insects breathe more slowly, but also longer, than well-fed ones inclosed in the same quantity of air. The latter, however, produce, proportionately, considerably more carbonic acid. A *Cetonia*, which was starved for three days, inspired less by half as much air and rejected only one quarter as much carbonic acid as a well-fed, healthy individual of the same species. The results are similar in butterflies experimented upon under the same circumstances.

That the developing egg respires precisely in the same manner, and under the same conditions, as the subsequent perfect insect, has been proved above by experiments in our description of the development of eggs.

§ 234.

Upon a careful investigation of respiration by means of gills, the same results are produced; the gills also imbibe oxygen, and give off carbonic acid. But the question suggests itself whether in insects which breathe by gills, these gills, as in the other animals with universally distributed blood-vessels, imbibe merely oxygen and expire carbonic acid, or whether they inspire perfect atmospheric air and expire the remainder, containing carbonic acid and azote, having separated the oxygen from it. We must first inquire, whence do the gills derive their oxygen?—Do they decompose the water, consisting of oxygen and hydrogen?—Or do they merely decompose the atmospheric air contained within the water? All experiments convince us that the air only which is contained in the water is changed, and not the water itself. Therefore, all animals die in distilled water deprived of air, and, what is still more, insects die even in well water, which contains more carbonic acid and in which less air is intermixed than in the water of rivers or ponds. This prejudicial effect of well water extends even to those insects which breathe through air tubes and spiracles, and which for this purpose ascend to the surface of the water: these also die quicker or slower in well water. But this does not answer the question whether insects imbibe oxygen or air through the gills. I think I must conclude that they extract the latter, from the following considerations.

In the first place, because the larvæ which breathe through gills exhibit the same internal apparatus as those which breathe through spiracles, and indeed generally possess larger internal air tubes than the rest. Did the gills merely imbibe oxygen, smaller narrower vessels would suffice.

Secondly, if pure oxygen were found in the tracheæ of insects that breathe through gills, they would be able to live a longer space of time even in such media as contain no oxygen, for instance, until the oxygen contained within their tracheæ was consumed. But this is not the case. Those larvæ which breathe through gills are deprived of life as quickly in spirits of wine as those which respire in the ordinary way.

Thirdly, did insects with gills inspire pure oxygen, so would all other insects, as the structure of their respiratory organs is the same, be enabled without inconvenience to breathe pure oxygen. But this is also not the case. Insects in pure oxygen breathe at first more violently than irregularly, and die in the course of a few hours, before near all the oxygen is consumed[*].

It hence appears necessary to adopt the conclusion, that even in insects breathing through gills there is a direct transmission of atmospheric air through the branchiæ into the tracheæ.

§ 235.

If we next ask the object of all respiration, and the effect it exercises upon the preservation and promotion of life, we shall find it to consist especially in the alteration of the blood. Observations upon the difference of the venous and arterial blood of the higher animals proves that oxygen intermixed with arterial blood colours it more brightly, and thus promotes its easier assimilation, although not by the mere colouring, yet by the other changes it produces in it, the testimony of which is its brighter colour. A similar alteration will necessarily take place in the juices circulating in the bodies of insects, but in proof of which we are the less enabled to give a striking instance, from, in the first place, the blood of these animals being wholly colourless, and, from the universal distribution of their respiratory organs, whence, consequently, this alteration of the blood is constantly everywhere taking place. In insects, therefore, arterial blood can alone be found, and the motion of the juices which has been detected in insects of different orders can consist merely in its general distribution, and not (as in animals with perfectly distinct arteries and veins) have likewise for

---

[*] Compare the Observations of Sorg, as above, pp. 19, 44, 98.

object a motion to and from the organs of respiration. This will be fully proved in the following division of this chapter.

But from the arterial blood all, and especially the animal, organs, derive that portion which is peculiarly theirs, and which is transformed in them. Hence respiration is the first and chief cause of the florid health as well as of the equal and uniform nourishment of all the organs of the animal. The muscles and nerves particularly appear to derive advantage from respiration, in consequence of the change thereby occasioned in the blood. Thence is it also that in animals with preponderant and highly developed organs of respiration muscular and nervous activity prevails. That this is the case in insects, at least with respect to their muscular power, requires no further proof; many experiments and observations, and, indeed, daily experience, convinces us of it. With what a monstrous expense of muscular power do not these little creatures labour! We have merely to reflect upon their rapid and continued flight, upon the migrations of locusts, upon the solid and compact woods which others destroy with their minute mandibles, upon the powerful pressure which they are enabled to make by their voluntary muscular force, when, for instance, a beetle is taken in the hand, and it endeavours to free itself from its restraint. With respect to their nervous activity, I will refer only to the subtlety and strength of their sense of smell, particularly as this more than any of the other senses stands in close connexion with respiration. But their hearing is also acute, and, above all, their sight. Where is there found such an accumulation of the organs of sight? Where such a relative size in any other class of animals? Where so much caution in the observation of their enemies, and patience in the completion of a once commenced undertaking? but which patience must be attributed to the acute perception of their senses and their great muscular strength.

Hence respiration is, as well as the reception and digestion of food, a chief cause of the undisturbed progress of all the animal functions; both go hand in hand, and the one is useless without the assistance of the other.

§ 236.

Another property which, if not produced by respiration alone, yet stands in an intimate connexion with it, is the peculiar warmth found in many animal bodies, especially in the mammalia and birds. Without entering here upon the several explanations of the causes of this equal temperature in both orders, in illustration of which we refer to the condensed and learned comparisons of G. R. Treviranus *, we will at once proceed to relate the observations that have been made upon the subject of this heat in some insects.

These insects are the bees and the ants. In the bees Swammerdam was the first to observe a peculiar warmth of the hive in winter, during a very low external temperature †. He supposed this warmth was partly to keep a portion of the honey fluid and partly to assist the eggs in hatching and to prevent the bees from freezing. Since Swammerdam similar observations have been made by Maraldi ‡, Reaumur, and Huber. Reaumur observed a thermometer standing at $-6\frac{3}{4}°$ external temperature rise in the hive to $+22\frac{1}{2}°$; according to Huber the average temperature of the hive in winter is 86° — 80 F. This warmth increased upon his causing a general motion among the bees by disturbing them, and so much so, that the small glass window in the hive soon became hot, whereas, when the bees were quiet and undisturbed, it felt almost cold; and indeed the wax of the combs melted several times and ran down. From this experiment especially it has been wished to conclude that the warmth in the hive is produced by the motion of the bees, particularly by their occasional general fluttering, which Maraldi considered to be the sole cause of the high temperature of the hive. According to Huber §, however, this occasionally repeated fluttering of the bees is produced by them merely to create a current of air, whereby fresh air is introduced, and that rendered noxious by continued respiration removed. In summer also, and not merely in winter, do they do this, and thereby even at that season produce an equally moderate temperature in the hive, which does not exceed that of the external air. The same has been observed in ant hills, in which the thermometer upon an external temperature of $+10°$ rose, according to Juch ||, to $+17°$. In the wasps and humble bees, also, which likewise live in society, we may with great probability infer a similar phenomenon.

If after such facts it is undeniable that insects under certain circumstances can produce a higher but equal temperature, nothing further

* Biologie, t. v. p. 64, &c. Das organische Leben, t. i. p. 413, &c.
† Biblia Naturæ, p. 161.
‡ Mém. de l' Acad. des Sc. de Paris, 1714, Ed. d' Amst., p. 420.
§ Nouvelles Observ. sur les Abeilles, t. ii. p. 338, &c.
|| Ideen zu einer Zoochemie, vol. i. p. 92.

may be thence concluded than that this warmth is produced only in their social assemblage. Mere mechanical motion is, however, not sufficient, for this produces in summer a lower temperature; the single insect, on the contrary, produces no warmth, but is exposed to the varieties of the external temperature, and dies when this sinks below zero. Hence it merely remains possible to suppose that warmth is developed by respiration.

We have learnt from a preceding paragraph that respiration increases upon motion, and especially on flight, and that consequently there must be a greater quantity of oxygen absorbed by the body. But the condensation which the oxygen necessarily undergoes upon intermixture with the blood, as well as the whole process of combustion, must evolve heat, and this heat upon expiration must pass from the body of the insect to the surrounding medium. If, therefore, many breathing insects are collected together in a small space, heat must be produced even during their quiet slow respiration, which the thermometer evinces; but if the swarm be put in motion, and if the bees flutter with their wings, they breathe, consequently, more strongly and more intensely, and, therefore, a greater quantity of earth is necessarily evolved. Hence even every individual breathing insect would develope some heat, which, however, from its rapid assimilation with the external temperature, is not perceived. But in small spaces, and where many individuals are inclosed together, this evolution of heat would certainly be detected in other insects*. But the reason why the temperature of the hive in summer is even less, or, at least, equal, upon the same motion, to that of the external atmosphere, is to be explained by the current of air produced by the motion by means of which fresh air is introduced and the warmed air removed, as well as that each draught, even upon the introduction of warm air, produces coolness.

§ 237.

III. FUNCTION OF THE DORSAL VESSEL. CIRCULATION OF THE BLOOD †.

THE most general physiological importance of the circulation of the juices has been stated in the introduction to this chapter, and indicated

* Compare Hausmann de Anim. Ex. Respirat., pp. 68, &c.

† It is quite impossible that we should here repeat all the different opinions of earlier anatomists and physiologists upon the function of the dorsal vessel: we hope it will suffice to assure our readers that all the most important treatises upon this subject have been resorted to, and their most useful facts inserted.

as a connecting link between digestion and respiration. The juices prepared by the intestinal canal require the addition of oxygen from the air before they can be assimilated with the corporeal mass, and for this purpose they pass through the vessels to the respiratory organ. Hence it appears that insects, from the universal distribution of their respiratory organ, require no conducting of the juices, and it was this consideration which, prior to a motion of the blood being observed in them, that was sought to explain their deficiency of blood-vessels, and the consequent deficiency of a circulation was thus illustrated as imperative. We nevertheless find in insects a regular motion of the juices, as was first discovered by the observations of Carus*, and subsequently confirmed by Wagner †. From the experiments of both these naturalists, the following general result of the mode of this motion of the juices has been found.

§ 238.

The juices prepared by digestion pass through the tunics of the intestine into the free cavity of the abdomen among all the organs there situated. It here presents itself as a clear and somewhat greenish fluid, in which oval or round globules swim, which are likewise transparent, and from $\frac{1}{503}$ to $\frac{1}{250}$ of a line in diameter. This fluid is received by the dorsal vessel, or rather by its posterior portion, which we have described as the heart, and which consists of a series of consecutive chambers furnished with apertures and valves (§ 117); through these apertures during its distension, and then by means of the contraction of the same organ, through which also the lateral apertures are closed by means of the valves lying in front of them, it is transmitted from one chamber to the other, and then from the last into the aorta ‡. The number of the contractions and expansions of the heart within a certain time varies according to the stage of development and the state of the temperature. The several chambers also do not simultaneously contract, but, commencing posteriorly, they proceed successively, so that the last and first frequently expand together, whilst the central

* Entdeckung eines Einfachen vom Herzen aus beschleunigten Blutlaufes in den Larven netzflüglicher Insekten. Leipz. 1827. 4to.

† Isis, 1832, p. 320.

‡ We must here remark, that this structure of the heart, ascertained to exist by the observations of Straus, was received and taught by even the earlier physiologists. See Bonnet's Contemplation de la Nature, t. i.

ones are still contracted. Thence proceeds the apparent undulating motion which is perceived in the heart through the integument of the body. From the anterior free aperture of the aorta the blood is driven by this motion into the lateral space of the body contiguous to the aorta, and it thence passes into all the vacant spaces of this cavity into the antennæ, feet, and wings, and thence, being continually driven on, it pursues its course at the sides of the body, until it has again reached the ventral cavity, where it then becomes mixed with the fluid there found, and which has been subsequently formed by the constant activity of the intestine, and upon the next expansion of the individual chambers it passes again upon its preceding course.

§ 239.

The motion of the heart itself was observed by the earliest anatomists. Malpighi even observed the contraction of the dorsal vessel progressing from behind forwards, and Swammerdamm as well as later anatomists have confirmed this observation. But as all considered the dorsal vessel as completely closed, it could lead to no insight into the circulating system of insects, and all the observations upon the manner of this motion of the dorsal vessel arrived at no important result. Herold * alone, who made the dorsal vessel especially the object of his investigations, recognised more distinctly its undulating motion. This undulating motion may be readily understood from the recently explained structure of the heart. Thus all the chambers do not simultaneously contract, but always one after the other, so that during the contraction the posterior one drives its contents into the one before it, and during its expansion again receives blood from the cavity of the body. As this alternating contraction and expansion passes from one chamber to the other, the motion of the entire heart, like the peristaltic motion of the intestinal canal, appears to progress in an undulating line, although the motion is not in the entire heart, but only in an individual chamber; but the motion of these chambers passes so quickly from one to the other, that the first and the last frequently expand at the same time, whilst those lying between still contract. With respect to the number of the contractions and expansions, differences have been observed in them, which partly, as in respiration, proceeded from the temperature, and were partly dependent upon the stage of development.

* Physiologische Untersuchungen über das Rückengefäsz der Insekten. Marb. 1823, 8vo.

According to Herold, the dorsal vessel of a full-grown caterpillar, in a temperature of from 16°—20° Reaum., made from 30 to 40 pulsations in a minute, but sank in a temperature of from 10°—12° down to from 6 to 8 pulsations in the same time. In younger caterpillars, the pulsations of the dorsal vessel, under similar circumstances, were quicker, namely, from 46 to 48 times in a minute, in a temperature of 18°, whereas in greater heat and with a quicker motion, in conjunction with great exertion, the rapidity of the pulsations still further increases, but they then appear so irregular and numerous, that no positive number can be given. According to Suckow*, the heart of the pine caterpillar (*Gastropacha pini*) beats 30 times in a minute, but sinks down during the pupa state to 18 pulses in the same space of time. In the just disclosed caterpillar the pulsation is slow and irregular, but subsequently its rapidity increases so much, that it then makes from 50 to 60 pulses in the minute. Herold says that the pulsations of the butterfly increase the moment it commences to strike with its wings, and purposes flying off, whereas he observed during copulation no alteration of its quickness.

§ 240.

The assertion of a motion of the juices is founded upon observations made upon the following insects.

Among the *Dictyoptera*, all such larvæ as live in water exhibit it very distinctly. In the larva of *Ephemera*, a motion of the globules of the blood has been observed in all the peripheric parts, which, according to Wagener, extend even to the last joints of the antennæ and of the feet. This motion was slower the more the water evaporated in which the larva was contained, but increased again upon the addition of fresh water. The stream of all the peripheric parts collect into two chief currents, which pass backwards on each side of the body, and send off other currents to the exterior margin of the segments, but which speedily return to the main branch after having passed through the branchiæ there situated †. Vessels inclosing these streams have never been observed, and, indeed, the frequently partial change of course distinctly proved the total deficiency of such organs. Individual currents have also been observed to extend even above and beneath the intestinal canal, and to bend over to the main stem of the opposite side

---

* Anatomisch-physiol. Unters. über Insekten und Krustenthiere, p. 37.
† Carus in the Nova Acta Phys. Med. vol. xv. Pt. 2, p. 8.

without being guided by a determinate canal, but, on the contrary, the globules of blood evidently passed between the fatty body and other internal parts. In the vicinity of each aperture of the heart portions of the stream of blood bent over to the heart itself, and upon each expansion passed into it, being received by those apertures. The blood poured forth immediately from parts that were cut off, namely, from the end of the tail, curdling into a thick greenish granulated mass.

In the larvæ of the *Agrions* there has been observed the motion of the dorsal vessel, the lateral returning main currents, a stream running upon the entire margin of the rudiments of the wings on the exterior taking its course inwardly and on the interior returning, from which here and there also globules passed in the contiguous passages between the parenchyma of the wings, a powerful current also passes through all the anal leaves, explained as gills, and flows inwardly upon the under side of the central tracheæ, but on the upper side again returns; and, lastly, a stream of blood is observed which advances in throbs, and which probably flows from the anterior aperture of the aorta, bending on each side to the eye, and thence proceeds beneath and back again posteriorly.

In all perfect insects of this order, namely, in the wings of just-disclosed *Libellula* (*L. depressa*) and *Ephemeræ* (*E. lutea* and *marginata*) Carus likewise saw a distinct motion of the blood.

Among the *Neuroptera*, those larvæ which live in water exhibited the same appearances. Distinct contractions were constantly seen in the heart of the caddis-fly larva, which is divided into seven or eight partitions and two lateral returning main streams, whence the globules of blood passed into the apertures between the several chambers. Several perfect insects also of this order, namely, *Hemerobius chrysops*, *Semblis bilineata*, and *Semblis viridis*, exhibited in their wings, and the latter also in their antennæ, a motion of the juices.

In those larvæ which live in water, of many of the *Diptera*, namely, of the gnats, Wagener observed a distinct pulsation in the dorsal vessel, in which its contraction was visible in several of the chambers of the posterior end. But even those very transparent larvæ he observed, on contrary, no motion of the globules of the blood. I myself, notwithstanding having made several experiments, it is true with not very perfect instruments, have been unable to detect such globules of blood. In one instance, and also in a second similar one, namely, in the larva of *Notonecta glauca*, Carus considers that the globules of blood are too small to be seen through the microscope, and that it is from this cause that the motion of the juices is not to be detected in the body.

Among the *Hemiptera*, Wagener observed through the transparent sides of the body of the young larva of *Nepa cinerea* distinct streams of moving globules passing from the front backwards; he could also observe the pulsating dorsal vessel contracting in its chambers. In the common bed bug (*Cimex lectularius*) I have perceived the pulsation of the dorsal vessel, and also an indistinct motion of fluids at the sides of the abdomen.

The remaining observations, chiefly compiled from Carus*, refer chiefly to the circulation of the blood in insects not living in water. Among the beetles, he observed it principally in the transparent elytra and wings of *Lampyris italica* and *splendidula*, *Melolontha solstitialis* and in a *Dyticus*; then in the prothorax of *Lampyris splendidula*. It here had the appearance of a strong current, which came from the abdomen, and which, towards the end of the pronotum, divided on each side into arms, that, upon each margin, turned backwards. In the *Orthoptera*, on the contrary, he vainly sought it in the wings, but Ehrenberg, according to the communication of A. v. Humboldt, has seen a motion of the juices in a *Mantis* †. The transparent wings of the *Dictyotoptera* and *Neuroptera* have likewise here and there exhibited a motion of the juices, as well as the wings of *Libellula depressa*, *Ephemera lutea*, *E. marginata*, *Hemerobius chrysops*, but most distinctly in *Semblis bilineata* and in the antennæ of *Semblis viridis*. In the former, he saw the streaming blood pass upon the anterior margin through the chief ribs, and distribute itself upon the whole margin to the apex; it returned back through the ribs lying nearest to the posterior margin. Through the central connecting transverse ribs, blood also passed from the proceeding to the returning current. In the *Hymenoptera*, no motion of the juices was perceived in the wings, and just as little in the *Diptera* ‡. In the *Lepidoptera*, also, it still remains doubtful; but Carus thinks he may

---

* Nova Acta Soc. n. c. C. L. vol. xv. Pt. 2, p. 1, &c.

† Bericht über die Natur historischen Reisen der H. H. Ehrenberg und Hemprich. Berlin. 1826. 4to. p. 22.

‡ In *Eristalis tenax*, Meig., and *E. nemorum*, M., I have recently observed blood pour out of the roots of the wings during their motion, when the wing itself was cut off.

adopt a motion of the juices in the germen of the wings in the pupa of some *Lepidoptera*, from the result of several of his experiments.

§ 241.

After such facts, I consider the asserted circulation of the juices as proved. Carus was formerly inclined * to limit the circulation to those insects still in their stages of development, and therefore concluded that it disappeared upon their transformation into the perfect state. This opinion he subsequently gave up †, upon being convinced of the contrary by his own experiments; and it also is positively contradictory to the generally adopted physiological significance of the circulation, for what in this respect is the case in young animals, must also be found in old ones. Indeed it is true that in many insects an alteration takes place in the reception of food, and its quantity becomes less, and that thence, consequently, there must be found in them a slower digestion as well as a smaller quantity of separated lymph, but it must not be forgotten, that, precisely at this last period, the compass of the body is smaller, whereas its internal organs are larger, and that these have already attained their perfect development, and require but a small addition to be retained in action; and that, lastly, the whole internal cavity of the body presents less free space in which the stream of blood can be distributed. These various causes appear to me to explain the decrease of the circulation; and indeed in the higher animals the pulse is lower in age than in youth; wherefore, then, should not the same relations be found in insects? But that a circulation is found in these creatures in their perfect state, is proved by direct observation; must these, then, be considered as exceptions to the rule, and that which is the rule in all other animals, form the exception in insects? I see no foundation for such a conclusion.

§ 242.

With respect to the physiological importance of the circulation in insects, I conceive it consists especially in preserving a general motion of the fluids, by means of which all the portions of it are subjected to an equal deposition of oxygen. If the lymph passed through the intestinal canal into the cavity of the abdomen, and remained there stationary, those parts of it which encompassed the tracheæ would

---

* Entdeckung, &c., p. 21.   † Nova Acta Phys. Med. vol. xv. Pt. 2, p. 14.

alone be oxidised; and, indeed, the fluid would not pass equally into the distant members, but that portion which once found itself in the cavity of such a member would there remain without being equally supplanted by fresh juices. But by this progressive motion of the whole body of juices this partial stagnation is prevented, and each organ furnished equally with fresh juice fitted for assimilation. Both the large streams of blood which run along and between the large lateral stems of the tracheæ, are constantly receiving fresh oxygen from the tracheæ, and carry with them the fresh lymph secreted by the intestine, and then give off the freshly-oxidised blood to the heart, which, by its rhythmical pulsation, conveys it on, and rejecting it by the free orifice of the aorta, drives it to all the parts of the body. The returning main streams, consequently, are comparable to the arteries of the lungs, or rather, as in the *Mollusca*, to those large veins which, collecting the blood from all parts of the body, return it through the lungs or bronchiæ to the heart. The passage of the oxidised blood into the heart is occasioned by its expansion and contraction, which takes place synchronally with the respiratory motion of the whole body, and particularly of the abdomen, and these individual motions of the heart are partially produced by its muscular tunic, and partially by the muscles of the wings which bind it to the dorsal plates. The muscular tunic of the heart contracts itself and makes the systole. The muscles of the wings, by their contraction, again expand the heart, and produce the diastole: when the blood streams in through the apertures and by the former, it is driven into the aorta. Hence throughout the whole body a constant oxidisation of the blood is taking place, as, even in the most remote members, tracheæ are distributed, and there oxidise the juices they found. But these juices also do not rest, but participate in the general motion. True venous blood is consequently deficient in insects, and if both the lateral streams have been called veins, this name is only so far tenable as there may be detected in it a returning motion of the blood to the heart.

§ 243.

But how can a motion of the blood be imagined without vessels? This question absolutely appears of great importance, particularly as Carus thought it necessary that there should be vessels in certain parts of the body. This opinion, however, will necessarily be limited to the vessels which are found in the ribs of the wings, and which we have mentioned above. I detected such vessels in many insects which I then examined, namely, in *Dyticus marginalis, Copris lunaris, Philanthus pictus,* &c., but I yet doubt, from more recent investigations that I have made in the bright and partially transparent pupæ of some capricorns, namely, *Prionus faber* and *coriarius,* the correctness of my above mentioned opinion. In the rudimentary wings of these pupæ I saw with unassisted eyes perfect tubes as silvery-white glittering filaments containing air. These tubes in the upper wing or elytron gave off no branches, but ran undivided in a direct line from the base to the apex. But at the extreme base they collected into two main stems, the one of which takes its course at the anterior margin, and the other upon the sutural margin, both originating at the thorax as a simple stem. The anterior one has two and the posterior one four straight radiating branches, which run parallely. The tubes of the inferior or true wing were divided, but likewise also only towards the apex. They also originated from two similarly disposed main stems, the anterior one of which likewise sent off two and the posterior one four branches. I could distinctly see this by means of a simple lens. Upon its inspection with the microscope, these tubes were observed filled with air, which was interrupted at certain parts, so that the tubes appeared to contain disconnected air-bladders. I could not even yet detect by means of the microscope the structure of the tubes, which was only visible upon removing the external tunic of the elytron, and the tube then lay distinctly in the parenchyma before me; an extremely fine filament was then seen, which wound itself spirally around the circumference of the tube, and left a tolerably wide space between it. On each side of these tubes there was a bright stripe, as if a channel lay free in the parenchyma contiguous to the trachea. I now repeated my investigation in other insects which had been immersed for some time in spirits of wine, but I found neither in the vessels of the elytra, nor in those of the wings, a spiral twisting, and just as little in dried specimens. Thence I might conclude that the spiral filament becomes invisible by immersion in alcohol as well as by drying in the air, at least under the microscopic power that was at my command, but that it nevertheless existed in all the vessels that take their course through the ribs of the wing; that consequently all these vessels must absolutely be considered as tracheæ, and that blood-vessels are not to be found even in the ribs of the wings.

Jurine's [*] and Chabrier's [†] observations upon the structure of the wings harmonise herewith; whereas, according to Carus, there is a threefold difference in the structure of the wings with respect to the vessels contained within their ribs. Some, as the elytra of the beetles, have blood and air-vessels; others contain only blood-vessels; the third, lastly, as the wings of the *Hymenoptera* and *Diptera*, exhibit air-vessels exclusively. But according to my opinion and observation, these differences do not exist, but all the ribs contain merely tracheæ or air-vessels, whereas within the rib around the trachea there remains a vacant space in which the juices can freely circulate, and it was in this free space that Carus saw, in all those instances where he perceived a motion of the blood in the wing, the globules pass and return.

Hence also is it that the wings derive their true significance. Oken even indicated that the wings of insects were no true members, but as mere continuations of the skin in which vessels were distributed, they were of analogous importance to the gills, and he thence called them air-gills (*luftkiemen*) [‡]. But if now, as I believe it is, proved that the blood actually flows through them, their function as gills is placed beyond a doubt. The partial interruptions of the ribs, Jurine's bullæ, are the places where the blood flows immediately beneath the thin membrane, and can there even imbibe oxygen from the air, which is, besides, presented to it everywhere by the tracheæ around which it circulates. Chabrier's observation, also, that a space filled with moisture is found in the under wings of the beetles §, is evidence that blood flows in the wings, and such a stream can only pass through the ribs contiguous to the tracheæ contained within it.

If the supposed presence of blood-vessels in certain parts of the body is thus contradicted, it may likewise be inferred of the whole body that it has no blood-vessel excepting the large dorsal vessel. Indeed Joh. Müller considers that he has detected vessels passing from the heart to the ovary; but these connecting filaments, as we have shown above, are no vessels. The proposition which I have just stated is therefore proved correct to its full extent. Yet this deficiency of blood-vessels in the bodies of insects is by no means so extraordinary, nor is it without parallel. In the membranes also of the developing

---

[*] Nouv. Méth. de Classer les Hymenop. Geneve, 1807. 4to. p. 48.
[†] Essai sur le Vol des Insectes. Par. 1822. 4to. p. 42.
[‡] Natur. Philosophie, 2nd Ed. p. 418. No. 3337.
[§] Essai sur le Vol, &c., p. 19.

embryo, the blood originally flows without vessels; and only after the stream has acquired some degree of regularity, do the vessels form themselves around it. The same appears to be the case in the motion of the juices in the lower animals. In these also the circulating fluid forms for itself a passage through the parenchyma of the body; it grooves as it were a course for itself, in which it afterwards constantly continues. This course is in insects attracted especially to the large tracheæ, because the vital air, that substance to which all blood must attain, is transmitted through them. Were the thick tunics of a vessel to be formed around it, the deposition of oxygen could not so easily take place; and indeed in insects it would have greater difficulties to contend with than in any other class, for in them the tracheæ, even to their extreme ends, retain their hard spiral filament, whereas in the vesicles and cells of the lungs and gills it disappears, whence the oxygen can more easily pass through the delicate membrane of the respiratory apparatus, and arrive at the likewise delicate tunic of the blood-vessels; but in insects it is more strongly retained, and would be even more so if the blood-vessel also had a thick membrane. It thence appears to me that the deficiency of blood-vessels is necessary to the undisturbed corporeal functions of insects; their organisation merely required a central organ whereby the motion of the juices is promoted, and by means of which it is regulated and guided; and this organ is their dorsal vessel. The course through it being originally traced, and the first impulse to the motion of the blood being given by the spontaneous motion of the dorsal vessel, the free stream of blood necessarily follows this direction until it again returns within the sphere of the activity of this organ, and is then again forcibly attracted to it, and, as before, involuntarily driven into its preceding course.

THIRD CHAPTER.

THE METAMORPHOSIS.*

§ 244.

In the preceding chapters we have explained how the insect originates, propagates, and subsists, without having noticed the several stages of life it has to pass through, from the first origin of its being until the time it is actively engaged for the preservation of its resemblance. We have indeed here and there drawn attention to the differences which exist with respect to the mode of taking food and its assimilation with the body between the undeveloped and the perfect insect, but we have not yet explained the several successive periods of development, nor shown their physiological character. This will be the subject of the present chapter. We must now look around us for the causes which determine the form of insects in general. We must endeavour to ascertain why insects take this form and no other, and exhibit a body thus composed of rings and limbs, and what necessary changes a thus formed body must be subjected to, in order to maintain its fundamental figure even through the several developments which every organic, or, at least, animal being, is obliged to pass through. But as an introduction to this investigation, we must prelude with some general observations, which refer to the differences of all animal forms, that we may be in a situation to discover from the differences of these forms, the shape of insects and the object of this shape from their opposition to the rest, and then only, when the cause of the articulated body of insects is discovered, can we proceed with the consideration of the several transformations peculiar to it.

§ 245.

The animal kingdom, like all organic matter, the essential character of which is expressed in the idea of becoming or having become, traverses a certain series of grades of development, upon which it

* In this chapter the §§ 245—248 and 251 have been entirely rewritten by the author, and the former §§ 248 and 249 have been changed into the present §§ 249 and 250.—Tr.

ascends from its first simple beginnings to its highest perfection. Nature attains these developments by antitheses. The immediate consequence of such an antithesis, and which is visible in the homogeneous mass of the body, is the antithesis between the interior and exterior, whereby the internal cavity of the body which prepares the nutrimental matter stands in opposition to its external surface, which conditionates its form; the further perfection of this first antithesis, developes the various organs which stand in connexion with those two organic systems. Thus from the originally simple digesting cavity of the body, by degrees the intestinal canal and its various appendages promoting digestion, viz. the glands, are formed; and from the originally uniform integument of the body, on the contrary, all those organs are produced which promote and effect motion. The correctness of these assertions is deduced from the history of the embryo forming in the egg. Thus there appears in the several grades of development of the animal kingdom, as it were a rivalry between the internal nutrimental organs and the external organs of motion, and it therefore may be readily imagined, in the varied direction Nature has pointed out for its creatures to pursue, that in some animals the perfection of the internal organs, and in others that of the external ones, has been especially promoted. We call all those animals in which the first is visible, namely, a prevailing development of the intestines, ventral animals (*Gastrozoa*), but those in which the external organs attain the greatest perfection, limb animals (*Arthrozoa*).

But the highest perfection of the animal kingdom is by no means attained by these two grades of development, for both as partial developments must still appear unperfected. There only is the highest perfection attained where the external as well as the internal organs are equally perfected, and both have acquired their highest grade of development. That this highest development appointed by nature for the animal kingdom may be attained, there must be a third chief group in the animal kingdom, the members of which make themselves apparent by this homogeneous perfection of the external and internal organs. We have long known this third group by the name of vertebrate animals (*Osteozoa* or *animalia vertebrata*).

The individuals of the animal kingdom which belong to these several chief groups, it is easy to discover from the above character of each group, and which the following Table exhibits :—

I. Group—GASTROZOA. The following classes belong here:
1. *Infusoria polygastrica.* Ehrenb. 2. *Polypina sive Corallina.* 3. *Medusina.* 4. *Echinodermata.* 5. *Mollusca.* Cuv.

II. Group—ARTHROZOA. Here belong the classes:
6. *Endozoa. Annulata.* 7. *Rotatoria. Crustacea.* 8. *Myriapoda. Arachnodea.* 9. *Insecta.*

III. Group—OSTEOZOA:
10. *Pisces.* 11. *Amphibia.* 12. *Aves.* 13. *Mammalia.*

§ 246.

The forms of the thus discovered three chief groups of the animal kingdom are adapted precisely to their internal organisation. The first group possess a figure conformable to its organisation, namely, that of a bag or sack, that it may receive in this sack its various organs. In the highest animals, also, the same organs which in animals of the first series are especially developed, also lie in large cavities and bags, that are formed almost exclusively of soft parts. The second group, which is constructed upon the predominant development of the organs of motion, exhibits an elongate form, generally divided into segments and limbs. Herein also they correspond in form with the same organs of the higher animals, which characterise the second series in the development of the animal kingdom, namely, the members, which, as well as them, are elongate, and consist of joints and consecutive divisions. The third group, consisting of the conjunct contents of both the others, has a form partaking of that of both; their bodies, consequently, appear as central bags and cavities, whence the periphrastic subdivided members proceed. They thus, therefore, repeat the forms of all the other animals; indeed, their form is, as it were, a compilation of all other animal forms.

§ 247.

Insects, consequently, by reason of the predominant development of their organs of motion, belong to the elongate animals, divided into segments and divisions. By means only of such a structure is free motion possible. One limb pushes itself forward, affixes itself, and draws the other after it; the alternating, affixing, and quitting is repeated then by every successive limb, and thus the general motion of the body is produced. In some worms, therefore, we can admit but of two limbs, namely, an anterior one, in which the mouth lies, and which, by the suction of the mouth, affixes itself, and a posterior one, which possesses the sucking cavity, and which, by the help of this organ, can attach itself. In the *Annulata*, which consist wholly of rings, for instance, the earth worm, small setæ supplant the sucking cup; in the higher *Annulata*, these setæ develope themselves into feet, which remain in the *Crustacea, Myriapoda, Arachnodea*, and insects; in the last, organs of flight are superadded. Thus insects maintain, in accordance with the law of successive development, the highest grade among all annulated animals or *Arthrozoa*.

§ 248.

It therefore appears that, in the further development of the three chief grades of the animal kingdom, the place of abode and the thence proceeding influence of the external world (the external medium) has a very peculiar effect upon the animal organism. There are, however, but three differences of abode, which are the water, the earth, and the air. But in these three chief groups of the animal kingdom, particularly in the second and in the third, we find three groups subordinate to these chief groups, which are determined by the places of abode. Amongst the *Vertebrata* these groups have long been known as classes; and are called fishes, as water-vertebrata; birds, as air-vertebrata; and mammalia, as earth-vertebrata. To these a fourth class is associated, that of the *Amphibia*, which apparently is not to be arranged with them, but which, however, presents itself as highly necessary. The living in water, air, and earth are, notwithstanding their great resemblance to each other, so strikingly different, that the animal organism cannot pass directly from one grade to the other, but it requires a connecting member, wherein the organisation is adapted to a residence in both elements. From this transition I have called all such classes—classes of transition.

The group of *Arthrozoa* admit of being separated in the same manner, if the division may be deduced from the mode of their development. We obtain thus, therefore, in their four classes:—

1. The WATER-ARTHROZOA. Comprising the intestinal worms (*Endozoa*) and the *Annulata*.
2. The CLASS OF TRANSITION. Here stand, as the direct links of transition, the wheel animals (*Infusoria rotatoria*,

Ehrenb.) and the crustaceous *Arthrozoa* (*Crustacea*, formerly called *Malacostraca* by me, not the *Malacostraca* of Leach).

3. The EARTH-ARTHROZOA. Here are arranged the *Myriapoda* and the *Arachnodea* (or *Arachnides*).

4. The AIR-ARTHROZOA. Which comprise the hexapod insects (*Insecta*).

Each of these groups has a peculiar organ whereby it is characterised, and as the general character of the *Arthrozoa* is expressed in the presence of organs of motion, we shall necessarily have to seek for the characters of the subordinate groups among those organs. The character of the WORMS or water-*Arthrozoa* is, that in them we first observe the presence of distinct organs of motion, but which yet are of no determinate type, and which, therefore, sometimes present themselves as sucking cups upon the head (*Cestodes*), or upon the head and belly (*Trematodes*), or upon the head and contiguous to the arms (*Hirudinei*), then as setæ (*Naidei, Lumbricini* sive *Chœtopodes*), and, lastly, as short pedal warts with hooklets (*Annelides antennati*, Lam.). In the following class they transform themselves partly to swimming organs (the rowing organs) and partly to jointed swimming and coursing feet, both of which forms are simultaneously common to the majority of *Crustacea*. In the earth-*Arthrozoa* the limbs are conformably shaped, feet adapted only to running; in the air-*Arthrozoa*, or INSECTS, we first find wings as the organs of motion for this element, they possess also legs for running and exercising other functions like the earlier ones.

§ 249.

Is the law indicated by the earlier physiologists, and applied by Oken, especially, to the natural system, correct, that the higher groups are repetitions of the lower ones in their development; or must we rather, with Von Bär[*], thus explain it, that the development of every class of animals admits of recognising the progressive perfection of the animal body as well by morphological as histological separation, as also by the progressive construction of a particular form from one more general? In either case it will necessarily be applicable to the development of insects. It is evident that both propositions tend to

---

[*] C. v. Bär über Entwickelungsgeschichte der Thiere. Königsb. 1828. 4to. vol. i. p. 231.

the same point. No one who speaks of the embryo of man passing through the lower grades of the animal kingdom can have imagined that man at any period was ever of his embryo life an infusorium, polypus, muscle, snail, worm, crab, spider, insect, fish, turtle, snake, lizard, and bird; but the assertion is nothing more than that man as man has once in the progress of his development been upon that grade upon which the several classes beneath him remain stationary in the progressive development of the entire animal kingdom; and Von Bär's proposition expresses precisely the same thing, for in the successive development of the animal kingdom there is found, just as in the development of each individual animal, a progressive morphological and histological separation as well as the gradual formation of a peculiar shape from a more general one. The most general form of the *Arthrozoon*, as which we have found the insect, is a body that is divided into rings and segments; and insects, therefore, must present us in their development both with a progressive formation of a particular shape from this more general one, as also with the morphological and histological gradual perfection of their individual organs. The series of *Gastrozoa*, as I succinctly call the first series, are, on the contrary, only so far repeated by insects in their development as they themselves in their own development have for object the progressive perfection of the nutritive and propagative organs. This repetition, however, does not extend to the external form, for this is the result of a new development not yet visible in the *Gastrozoa;* whereas the vertebrata which unite in themselves both forms, viz. that of the *Gastrozoa* as well as of the *Arthrozoa*, exhibit also formal approximations to the *Gastrozoa* in their development. Only so long as it remains in the egg-case is every insect a *Gastrozoon*, for it then has no other organs than the nutrimental; but upon quitting the egg-shell it becomes an *Arthrozoon*, and exhibits itself in its then appropriate jointed shape.

§ 250.

Hence, therefore, the essential character of the metamorphosis of insects is found in the repetition of the lower grades of the *Arthrozoa* by means of the development of the highest. No single class of animals, we might say, confirms this repetition more distinctly than insects. The maggot, caterpillar, or larva which creeps out of the egg is of the same form as the earth-worm. Some of these maggots are footless and headless, and move like the leech by affixing the first and last segments of their body, in which, indeed, no distinct sucking-cups are visible, but merely wart-shaped stumps of feet, at least upon the last. This form, which we observe in the larvæ of most of the *Diptera*, is consequently the lowest of all. And, indeed, what is still more, not merely in the organs of motion, but also in the mouth, do they resemble each other, the former, like the latter, possessing short hard-pointed puncturing instruments, with which they pierce their food and then imbibe it. The second grade of larvæ, namely, those maggots which are provided with a head, but are without feet, as, the larvæ of the *Hymenoptera*, and of many beetles, repeat another grade of the *Annulata*, in which, as in *Nais*, there is a distinct head, but the feet are wanting. The third grade of the *Annulata*, namely, those which reside in tubes, and are furnished with large bundles of gills, find, among insects, their representatives in those larvæ of the May and caddis-flies, which dwell in cases and breathe through gills. The fourth grade of *Annulata*, as *Nereis, Eumolpe, Aphrodite,* &c., has, besides a distinct head, many feet on the ventral side of the segments, and their analogies are, among insects, the caterpillars of the *Lepidoptera*, and those larvæ of the beetles which are furnished with feet.

In the pupa state, the insect advances into the class of the *Malacostraca*. Just as the pupa state is a mere transition in the life of the individual, so also is the class of *Malacostraca* a true transition group in the development of the *Arthrozoa*, for the *Arthrozoa* contained in it strive to detach themselves from the life in water to elevate themselves to the life in air. Thence arise the innumerable different forms, and, indeed, the greater difference between the individual organs found in them more strongly than elsewhere; with perhaps the exception of the amphibia, which stand in the same relation to the vertebrata: and the advance from the life in water to the life in air is nowhere observed more distinctly than in the order of the *Malacostraca*. The *Crustacea* are true water animals; they all live in this element, and quit it rarely and as an exception. The *Myriapoda* stand upon the confines between the water and earth-dwellers: some incline to the former and others to the latter. The *Arachnodea*, lastly, are true earth-dwellers, particularly the scorpions, but some true spiders seek the air as their medium, for they distend their web upon elevated sunny places, and, floating in it, seem to endeavour to revel in the purer air; and, indeed, a few raise themselves upwards in the air, for instance, *A. obtectrix*, which is raised by the wind upon its self-formed clouds, and swims in the fluid element. The majority are inimical to water: a few only seek it and dwell in it.

A very similar series of developments to those just observed in the *Malacostraca*, do we find in the pupa of insects with a perfect metamorphosis. The lowest, as the pupa of the gnats, some other *Diptera*, and the *Phryganeæ*, breathe like the *Crustacea* through gills, but their number is small compared with the large order of the *Crustacea*, which thence proceeds that they merely briefly indicate this order, and are not intended fully to repeat it. All other pupa breathe through spiracles. Some of them, as the pupæ of the flies, crepuscular moths, and beetles, lie in the earth; they represent the *Myriapoda*, of which many but rarely visit the light of day, but dwell beneath stones and in other shady places. The pupæ of the butterflies and *Noctuæ* seek, on the contrary, the air, particularly those which hang themselves freely in the air, that they may enjoy it upon all sides. Those that are affixed may, lastly, be compared with the spiders that float in their webs.

With respect to their internal organisation, the imperfect simple tubular form of the entire intestinal canal, the predominance of the circulation in all parts, as well as the mere rudiments of the sexual organs, evince the analogy of the larvæ to the *Annulata*. The perfecting of the intestinal canal during the pupa state, particularly the formation of the proventriculus at this period, and, lastly, the more distinctly developed sexual organs, although the latter conditionates no significant external difference, still further prove the analogy of the pupa and the *Malacostraca*.

We have thus shown the repetition of the lower grades in the development of insects with a perfect metamorphosis. But this entire repetition has been expressed by Oken in the following words *: " Every fly creeps as a worm out of the egg; then by changing into the pupa, it becomes a crab, and, lastly, a perfect fly."

§ 251.

We have as yet taken no notice of insects with an imperfect metamorphosis, and, indeed, because they are not subjected to the law of repetition or analogy which is so distinctly expressed in insects with a perfect metamorphosis; for moulting is no metamorphosis, although

---

* Naturgeschichte für Schulen, p. 577. 9th Class and pp. 581, 583.

the form of the body is somewhat changed; besides, all other *Arthrozoa* are likewise subjected to this moulting. They differ from the remaining *Arthrozoa*, namely, from those of the third group, merely by the presence of new organs of motion peculiar to them, and the presence of these organs constitutes really their physiological and philosophical character. But insects with a perfect metamorphosis likewise present this character and a second one in addition, namely, the repetition of all the earlier forms of the *Arthrozoa* during their period of development. It is a positive fact, confirmed by the history of the development of all, especially of the vertebrata, that the degree of perfection of an organism or organ is the greater the more numerous the grades of development are which it must traverse to attain its full perfection. If we apply this law to insects, it follows incontestably that insects with a perfect metamorphosis must be placed higher in the series of animal bodies than insects with an imperfect metamorphosis.

We may now ask, why was such a difference of insects from each other necessary? Why could not all develope themselves, and propagate in the same manner? To this we may reply—Nature endeavours to make every possible use of the means which she has conceived allowable for the variation of a determinate type, that is to say, all the forms that are elaborated by the normal progress of development, she absolutely creates and produces as independent creatures. This law, which we find everywhere confirmed, will furnish us with a key to the necessity of a difference among insects with respect to their metamorphosis. I refer for this purpose to the four chief classes of the *Arthrozoa*, each of which is characterised by its place of abode and the possession of peculiarly formed organs of motion, and we already saw above that the presence of wings in any of the *Arthrozoa* suffices to raise it to the class of insects. But we also perceive that Nature, if she will derive differences merely from the organs of motion, possesses no further means to found new variations, for she has already exhausted the forms of these organs. Whence, then, should she obtain means for the attainment of her object of producing the greatest possible variety, if she did not resort to the last, which is the repetition of the earlier forms in a higher grade of perfection? She, therefore, avails herself of this, and allows one portion of insects to be distinguished from all the other *Arthrozoa* merely by the presence of wings, whereas the other portion of already winged insects she raises so above the preceding, that she conducts them, before they arrive at their final stage, through the earlier forms of the *Arthrozoa*, which have remained stationary upon a lower grade, and, at a certain period of their lives, furnishes them with merely pedal warts, then with hooked, short feet, then with branchiæ and natatory laminæ, and, later, in their pupa state, with rudimentary wings, and, lastly, with perfectly developed wings. Thus I conceive to be explained the necessity of both the chief groups among insects.

In insects with an imperfect metamorphosis there cannot, consequently, be a passage through the earlier forms and grades of the animal kingdom; even the analogy which I formerly thought I detected between them and the consecutive classes of the *Gastrozoa*, appears to me now, upon a closer investigation, to be a merely playful endeavour to discover resemblances, and which I consequently no longer value. What I formerly, as a proof of such a repetition, deduced from the successive development of the sexual organs, may, with equal justice, be applied to all insects, or to all *Arthrozoa*, and, indeed, to all animals whatsoever, in as far as in all, the perfecting of the genitalia progresses with the gradual development of the creature.

Nevertheless, all insects, notwithstanding this difference from each other, must be recognised as members of the same class, and, indeed, by reason of the uniformity of the figure of the whole body, that is, by its division into three chief parts. This division of the body, which, among all the *Arthrozoa*, is peculiar to insects alone, is their second most important truly physiological character, which proves the equalisation of the contention between the various organs of the body, and in the limitation of each individual organ to a particular and impassable sphere of action, most clearly illustrates the fixed laws of its type of structure, which is always a predominant character of highly developed and perfected groups. The same law exhibits itself in the structure of the mouth, the antennæ, the wings, and, especially, in the number and articulation of the legs, whence their number, restricted to six, has always been considered as the safest character of insects.

§ 252.

Having thus explained the significance of the insect metamorphoses, it still remains for us to define distinctly the several changes which the insect undergoes during these stages. Indeed, in the anatomical description of the organs of digestion and generation, we have already spoken of the changes they experience during the metamorphosis (§ 114 and § 153); but these changes have not yet been brought into connexion with the other transformations of the body; and, besides, we have not yet at all spoken of the great discrepancy of the form of the limbs, nor even of what is still more important, namely, the addition of new ones. In the explanation of these subjects which we are now entering upon, the insects with a perfect metamorphosis will chiefly occupy us, in so far as in them only does a true transformation take place; whereas we shall speak of the insects with an imperfect metamorphosis only where we take notice of the moulting, and upon our investigations into the sprouting of the wings. We shall here, therefore, have an opportunity of circumstantially referring to that law laid down by Von Bär, that there is visible in the development a perfecting as well by the means of morphological and histological separation as by the progressive forming of a particular figure from one more general.

If an *Arthrozoon*, whose form consists of a longitudinally distended and generally hardened case, composed of limbs and rings, is to enlarge by growth, it must strip off its former covering and clothe itself with a new one, as the old one interrupts the universal distension, and, indeed, makes it wholly impossible. It is only in those *Arthrozoa* which dwell in moist places, so that from their place of abode their integument cannot harden in the air, which, therefore, constantly remains equally soft and flexible, the casting of the external integument is rendered unnecessary, and they therefore do not moult, but even in the higher *Annulata*, for instance, in the leech, a moulting is observed, and still higher, for example, in the *Malacostraca*, it is the necessary condition of growth. In insects, also, this change of skin must likewise take place so long as they grow, and it is this change of skin alone which, in insects with an imperfect metamorphosis, presents itself as the external mark of metamorphosis; but it is also proper to insects with a perfect metamorphosis, among which it indicates, as well as among the preceding, a transition from one stage of life to another.

The earlier physiologists differ in opinion from the moderns upon the mode in which this new skin originates beneath the former. Swammerdamm and Bonnet were of the opinion, in accordance with the general idea of their age of the theory of encasement, that all new skins already existed beneath the old one, and that the latter, without any re-production upon the part of the larva, was merely stripped off. Exclusively of the true object of moulting being overlooked in the adoption of this opinion, the mere observation of the larva having considerably increased in size immediately after the divestment, contradicts it; for if the new skin already existed beneath the old one, must it not there exist in considerably smaller compass rather than in larger? That Kirby and Spence could adopt and explain this opinion as the most correct, distinctly fixes their position in physiology, which, not merely here, but almost everywhere, exhibits itself as an antiquated one. Whereas, according to Herold's * admirable observations, there is not the least trace in the young larva of the new skin, but this first originates towards the end of the first period of the caterpillar's life, a few days only before the old one is stripped off. It is then observed that the mucous and muscular layers of the skin separate all round from the epidermis, and then clothe themselves upon the superior surface with a new epidermis. The development of this new external skin occupies two or three days, during which the caterpillar appears sickly and takes but little or no nourishment. Lastly, the old skin divides longitudinally along the back, and the caterpillar frees itself from its now separated skin by means of contortions and violent motions, first emancipating its head and then drawing the body out. The epidermis, all the external visible organs, and even the mandibles and palpi, remain attached to the old skin. Upon the caterpillar having quitted its old case, it appears very languid, its body is soft and easily injured, so that during its change of skin even a slight pressure is sufficient to kill or wound them, but it speedily resumes its former strength, and it then devours with renewed voracity, as if eager to make up for lost time. Contemporaneously with the formation of the new skin, the intestinal canal has also enlarged, thence after its moulting the quantity of food becomes greater, the digestion more perfect, and the formation of the fatty mass is more rapid and in larger quantities. In general, this first moult takes place about the twelfth day of the life of the caterpillar. The second moulting, which occurs after another lapse of from six to eight days, presents the same phenomena, and has the same effects; and the third also, which takes place after another six or eight days. But its voracity constantly increases, so that a larva does not now merely consume three or four times its own weight of food, but it also increases considerably in corporeal mass; as, for instance, the comparative weight of a full-grown caterpillar of the goat moth to that of the young one just crept out of the egg is, according to Lyonet, as 72,000 to 1. A growing flesh-fly takes in twenty-four

* Entwickelungsgeschichte der Schmetterlinge, p. 26, &c.

hours 150 times its own weight; but the common caterpillar of *Euprepia Caja*, which weighed thirty-six grains, and every twelve hours rejected from fifteen to eighteen grains of excrement, increased only one or two grains in weight in the same space of time *. The increase in weight appears to be much greater in carnivorous larvæ, for, according to Redi †, the maggots of the flesh-flies, which at first weighed one grain, so increased, that each, on the following day, weighed seven grains, which gives a proportion of increase, in twenty-four hours, of from 1 to 200.

After the third moulting, when the larva has acquired its full size, the rudiments of the wings begin to form beneath the skin, upon the first and second segments. They at first present themselves as short viscous leaves, the substance of which greatly resembles that of the mucous tunic, and to which many delicate tracheæ pass, which distribute themselves throughout them. These rudiments increase with the growth of the caterpillar, and betray themselves, even externally, by both the segments of the caterpillar, upon which these rudimentary wings are found, appearing swollen and spotted. Their enlargement probably takes place by the assistance of the blood flowing into them. Simultaneously with the perfecting of these rudiments the intestinal canal increases in compass, and, as a consequence of this increase there is a greater accumulation of the fatty mass. A transformation is also taking place in the anterior feet of the caterpillar, for the larger legs of the butterfly begin to form. But, as a similar transformation is going on in the oral organs, the caterpillar loses its desire to eat and power of mastication, it ceases to receive food, and prepares itself for its last moulting, viz., for its change into the pupa. It seeks for this purpose an appropriate place where it can lie, hang, spin, or attach itself, and it accomplishes this, its last business, the same as its earlier ones, with great care and consideration. After its situation and web are prepared it reposes a few days, then strips off its skin, and now presents itself as a pupa, with the visible limbs of the butterfly.

It is striking that insects, notwithstanding such a great, and, we might almost say, unexampled, capacity of production which is exhibited both in their rapid growth and the increase of the body in mass as well as in the development of new parts and the enlargement of the old ones during the pupa state, display but very slight traces of a power of re-

---

* Kirby and Spence, vol. i.   † De Generat. Insectorum, p. 27.

production. Beckmann * and Goeze † have imparted experiments, the results of which are—that the former, in *Agrion virgo,* and the latter in *Semblis bicaudata,* Fab. (*Perla,* Geoff.), once observed a leg, which was smaller than the rest, whence Goeze concludes that this leg must have been lost, and subsequently replaced by a new one. To these former observations we may add some more recent ones of Heineke ‡, which are absolutely of greater importance. On the 25th of July he cut off both the antennæ of a *Blatta Madeiræ,* after which it moulted on the 8th of August, and now acquired two new, but much shorter ones. He repeated the same experiment in the pupa of a *Reduvius,* where he obtained the same result. In perfect insects also, subject to no further moulting, namely, species of the genera *Forficula, Gryllus, Locusta,* and *Acridium,* he mutilated in the same manner, but even in the space of two months they acquired no new limbs, but cast off the old ones shortly after they were injured. These results entirely harmonise with the reproduction of the spiders; these also renew their lost limbs only so long as they yet moult, whereas after their last moulting they cast off their mutilated ones, but acquire no new ones. We must, therefore, ascribe to insects, at least to those with an imperfect metamorphosis, the power of replacing lost limbs, with these restrictions. It does not appear to be different in insects with a perfect metamorphosis, for mutilated caterpillars are said to obtain new limbs, that is to say, legs, after the next moulting. But it is remarkable that these limbs do not germinate whilst the insect remains in its old case. I think this circumstance is explained by the hardening of the integument, whence it is to be considered as it were dead, and thence I deduce the reason of the known fact, that wounds given to insects cicatrise only upon the next moulting, and consequently never in their perfect state. It must also be attributed in a great measure to the deficiency of blood vessels, for by their assistance cicatrisation and the resupply of flesh is promoted, namely, the constant streaming of the blood to the wounded spot, is the first cause of its subsequent living reconnexion. By means of the blood the lips of the wound are stuck together, and hence is formed the cellular tissue which unites the divided parts. Both blood and cellular tissue are consequently the means which nature makes use of to replace lost or divided animal

* Physinkalisch-œkonomische Bibliothek. vol. viii. p. 20.
† Naturforscher, part xii. p. 221.
‡ Isis, 1801, p. 1359. From the Zoological Journal, vol. iv. p. 422.

parts; and now, as the first stands upon a very low grade in insects, and the second is wholly deficient, consequently a cicatrisation of wounds can never be effected. But if beneath the wounded skin a new one is formed it uninterruptedly covers the wound of the old one, and after moulting the larva appears healed, if the wound be not of a description to affect its life, and thus interrupt all future changes of the skin.

§ 253.

In our representation of the metamorphosis we have omitted one phenomenon which was mentioned in earlier parts of the work (§ 114— 127), namely, the simultaneous moulting of the intestinal canal and tracheæ, with that of the external integument. Bonnet * and Swammerdamm †, the first physiologists of their age, especially with respect to the class of insects, maintained this opinion, and from their works it has passed into those of modern physiologists; whereas Herold, in his history of the development of the butterfly, says, that such a change of the tunic of the intestinal canal never happens, and that in the tracheæ it occurs only in the large main stems ‡. In fact, we must confess that if the stripping of the skin is, as we have above remarked, merely caused by its gradual hardening in the air, and the consequent impossibility of the distension of the increasing body, it does not require that we should thence admit of an equally requisite change of the internal tunic of the intestinal canal, nor even of the tracheæ, except in their large main stems, into which much air passes, and that, therefore, Bonnet's assertion reposes either upon a false observation, or was perhaps wholly invented by him for the support of his theory of encasement. But in opposition to this, independent of the credibility to which a man like Bonnet may lay claim, the testimony of Swammerdamm speaks, and who certainly did not lie, or say more than he saw: he remarks, that at the posterior end of the stripped skin, where it is twisted up and folded, he observed the moulted colon, and that after the moulting of the larva of the rhinoceros beetle the internal tunic of all the tracheæ, even to their most delicate extremities, were visible in the stripped integument §. I have distinctly observed the same in the moulting of the *Libellulæ*; in these, not merely the main stems, but

---

* Contemplations de la Nature, tom. ii. p. 48.   † Biblia Naturæ, pp. 129, 134, 239, &c.
‡ Pp. 34. and 88.   § Biblia Naturæ, p. 129, b.

also many auxiliary ones, were divested of their tunic, and likewise the internal tunic of the colon remained attached to the peeled case. We have likewise above drawn attention to the uniformity of the external epidermis with the mucous tunic of the internal organs, and by a similar pathological phenomenon, shown their affinity. Thus, the observations of equally credible witnesses and the several theories clash together. It is difficult to discover the truth in the midst of such contradictions. To conclude that in one order such a changing of the skin exists, but not in the other, appears inadmissible, as nature in general pursues in its process of development a certain uniformity. Perhaps, however, we may find an outlet if we adopt that in smaller individuals the internal tunic of the intestinal canal is more easily absorbed, whereas in the larger ones, furnished with a coarser mucous membrane, it is rejected. Many observations speak in favour of such an absorption, namely, the absorption of the mucous membrane of the egg-tube at its lower extremity, where it stands in connexion with the oviduct after it has developed the lowest egg at this spot, and then has passed into the oviduct itself (§ 210). But the perfect explanation and determination of this doubt remains still as the problem of careful, prolonged, and comprehensive experiments and observations.

§ 254.

The number of moultings of the larva until its full growth appears to vary considerably in different families and genera. "It may be assumed in general that they change their skin three times. This is the case in all insects with an incomplete metamorphosis. After the first change the larva has merely increased in size, but during this second period of its existence the rudiments of the wings form beneath the skin; consequently, after the second moulting, these incipient wings present themselves externally as small leaves, which cover the sides of the first abdominal segment; these larvæ are called nymphs *," it being analogous to the pupa state of other insects. When this pupa again moults the insect attains its perfect condition; the at first short, soft, thick wings spread in the course of a few minutes to their future full size, then speedily dry in the air, when the at first distinct circulation of the blood in the ribs gradually disappears, and the metamorphosis of the individual is completed. It raises itself with difficulty

* The passage in inverted commas is a MS. alteration from the original, communicated by the author.—Tr.

in the air by means of the first strikings of its wings, which succeed but imperfectly, and it then seeks a more elevated spot whence to exercise its new function with fuller effect.

Some genera, which from their abode in water prior to this period, make a transition to living in the air, form in a remarkable manner a perfect exception to the law, that with the casting of the pupa case the metamorphosis of the individual is concluded. It is universally known of the *Ephemeræ*, that in about half an hour, and indeed frequently only some minutes, after they have quitted the pupa case, again moult, and then only are able to copulate and procreate. This observation may be repeated without the least trouble in July and the commencement of August, when the *Ephemeræ* in watery situations quit the water towards evening by myriads. The just excluded *Ephemera* flutters immediately, although with difficulty, out of the water, and in the course of a quarter or half an hour, but in the smaller species in a shorter space of time, it seeks an elevated object, for instance the stem of a tree, the post of a bridge, houses that are close at hand, and even individuals standing upon the bank, and here clings firmly with extended legs. Speedily afterwards the dorsal case splits in its middle, upon which the insect with violent motion first frees its head and anterior legs from the old skin, which is succeeded by the other legs as soon as the anterior ones have affixed themselves, and then at the same time, but gradually, by the wings and abdomen. Prior to this moulting the creature has not acquired its usual markings and dark colour, which we perceive immediately after the new change of skin; and it is also remarkable, that after this change all the limbs, particularly the longer anterior legs and anal setæ of the male, become both more slender and longer than before. The horny case of the eyes is the only part which does not participate in this moulting. An analogous process is found to take place in the pupa of the *Phryganeæ* and *Semblodes*, which in that state repose without taking food, and are consequently endowed with a perfect metamorphosis, for, according to De Geer [†], it quits its place of repose, beneath the water, and creeping up the sides higher than the surface, there casts its pupa case. I am inclined to surmise from my own, indeed not fully comprehensive observations, that the already perfected insect creeps forth, and then reposing for a time, moults a second time. During this repose the wings especially

---

[†] Mémoires sur l'Hist. des Insectes, tom. ii.

are formed, which in the just excluded insect possess but half their size, but fully develope themselves after this renewed change of skin.

Among insects with a complete metamorphosis the caterpillars of the butterflies moult, according to Kirby and Spence *, frequently; but thrice, according to Cuvier †. After the last moulting they become pupæ, and after the casting of the pupa case butterflies. The caterpillars of the *Noctuæ*, on the contrary, moult four times, but some of the large ones, which live for two years as caterpillars, much more frequently, for instance, *Euprepia villica*, from five to eight times; *Euprepia dominula*, nine times; and *Euprepia caja*, ten times ‡. The time between two moultings also varies much, which appears to depend partly upon the size of the insect and partly upon its length of life. The larger ones require a longer and the smaller ones a shorter period. In general the interval between two moultings varies from eight to twenty days, excepting that those *Lepidoptera* which change into pupæ late in the summer or autumn, then lie the whole winter as pupæ, and are only fully developed upon the following spring. These pupæ change their larva-skin very early, mostly in the course of a few days, whereas others remain long in it. This is the case in the larvæ of the *Tenthredonodea*; even after the pseudo-caterpillar has spun its cocoon, it still remains for some weeks in its old skin, and only shortly before its time of exclusion does it strip off its dried up larva case. This is at least the case in the genus *Cimbex*, but in the smaller *Tenthredos*, for instance in *Lophyrus*, in which the pupa state is of short duration, the larva skin is earlier cast. Some larvæ, namely, the maggots of many of the flies, *Œstri*, *Syrphodea*, and *Notacantha* change into pupæ in their larva-case. All these larvæ likewise possess the remarkable peculiarity that they do not moult, but retain their old skin from the commencement of their existence. It is in connexion with this peculiarity that we observe the stronger folding of their external tunic, as also their abode in damp situations; some larvæ of the *Syrphodea* alone, namely, the larvæ of *Syrphus*, which prey upon the *Aphides*, make an exception to this dwelling-place, whereas on the other side many larvæ moult which live in moist places, namely, all the larvæ of the *Diptera*, with many joints to their antennæ, for instance, those of the gnats and *Tipulæ*, which distinguish themselves from the preceding by the possession of a distinct head. The

---

* Introduction, vol. iii. Nouv. Dict. d Hist. Nat. vol. vi. p. 289; vol. xx. p. 372.
† Leçon's d'Anat. Comp. vol. ii. p. 547.
‡ Kirby and Spence, vol. i. Lyonet, in Lesser Théologie des Insectes, vol. i. p. 167 *).

reason, therefore, why these larvæ do not moult cannot lie exclusively in their damp place of abode; nor that their existence as maggots is but of short duration, as, for example, in the common flesh fly from eight to ten days, but it must be found in other conditions of their organisation which have not yet been discovered. Besides, this phenomenon also proves that the development of insects of different orders, and even of the different families of the same order, can take place in a different manner, and that, therefore, the assertion that the intestine also moults in some orders, whereas in others it does not, is not so wholly gratuitous; but we will nevertheless not decide, having made no observations upon the subject. The determination in another instance is just as difficult, and in which also the observations of several naturalists stand in direct contradiction: this is the case in the maggot of the bee. This, according to Reaumur and Huber's observations [*], like all the apode larvæ of the *Hymenoptera*, consequently in by far the majority, does not moult, but merely gradually grow larger. Whereas Swammerdamm says expressly that he has observed the moulting of the larva of the bee [†], and that he has likewise found the inner tunic of the intestinal canal in the cæcum behind the stomach of the maggot of the hornet [‡]. However the case may be, we prefer adopting the first opinion, as all these larvæ exhibit a very great conformity with those of the *Diptera*, which certainly do not moult. This conformity refers not merely to the larva, but likewise considerably to its mode of life, in as far namely as that the larva of the *Œstri*, as well as the maggots of the pupaphaga, are true internal feeders. But they in so far differ from each other that the hymenopterous larva casts its skin when it becomes a pupa; the larvæ of these *Diptera*, however, change into pupa within their larva skin. In *Stratiomys*, indeed, the shape of the larva remains unaltered, and it was thence that Knoch considered this larva an annulate worm, in which the larva of the *Stratiomys* lived as a parasite [||]: in the rest, however, the soft skin of the larva shrinks up into an egg-shaped, hard, annulated case, in which the pupa is concealed, with its free and visible limbs. The other *Diptera*, which moult as larvæ, cast their larva skin before changing into the pupa state; this is the case, for instance, in the larvæ of the gnats, of the *Asilica*, *Xylophagi*, and many others.

---

[*] Kirby and Spence, vol. iii. [†] Biblia Naturæ, p. 163, a. [‡] Ib. p. 133, a.
[||] Neue Beiträge zur Insektengeschichte, Pl. I.

§ 255.

The changes which take place within the larva during the several moultings are unimportant. But formerly, where we spoke of the changes which the intestinal canal and the sexual organs undergo during the metamorphosis (§ 114 and 143), and which we have since recently referred to, we noticed that the changes of these organs commence only during the pupa state, and that consequently the caterpillar retains the same form of the intestinal canal and the same figure of the sexual germs, and that both merely increase with its growth, in compass and in the structure of their tunic. But, upon the larva passing into the pupa state, a change of the internal organs takes place, as well as of the external figure. These changes we have indicated at the above place, but those undergone by the larva we explained earlier (§ 60); it, therefore, merely remains for us to make a few observations upon the character of these transformations.

With respect to form, by it the law laid down by Von Bär, of a progression from a general to a particular figure during development, receives full confirmation. The intestine of the larva is simple, broad, generally straight, and without many convolutions; its divisions are not strongly marked, but pass gradually into each other. During the pupa state, however, it transforms itself to a longer, much convoluted tube, separated into several divisions, which now exhibit a distinct difference of texture; and indeed new organs are added of which there was formerly no trace, namely, the proventriculus in the *Carabodea*, the sucking bladder and cæcum in the *Lepidoptera*, the villi in the ilium of the flesh eaters, &c. In the flies, in which indeed the intestine upon the whole shortens, each individual division, however, and particularly the ilium, acquires a more determinate form and a more compact structure; the sucking stomach more distinctly separates itself, its orifice lengthens, as also does the œsophagus. In the sexual organs there is a more distinct difference of structure: parts which previously had a great resemblance to each other, namely, the testes and ovaria, from day to day increase in dissimilitude; and other organs, of which before there was no indication, gradually form themselves from simple processes to long convoluted canals; lastly, the pupa itself exhibits a vast discrepancy of form. The larva was a worm composed of equally large rings; the pupa, on the contrary, possesses the entire form of the subsequent insect, and differs, therefore, with respect to the forms of its rings chiefly by the difference of size found between several, namely, those of the thorax and abdomen. This dissimilarity is founded upon the more determinate figure divaricating more from the general one which the three segments of the thorax have adopted, a dissimilarity found to exist not only between them and the segments of the abdomen but also between them individually.

With respect to the second, the histological and morphological separation, the first we have already superficially touched upon. The tunics of the intestine do not indeed become uniformly more compact and firmer by the metamorphosis, but in general only in those cases in which the perfect insect 'takes the same food as the larva, namely, in the *Carnivora*. In the *Lepidoptera* the increased development increases the necessity of better and more delicate nutriment, consequently the butterfly does not require so compact an intestinal tunic as the caterpillar. The latter has to elaborate and extract the entire substance of the plant, the former merely feeds upon the most delicate juices of flowers, namely, their honey. The thick fleshy proventriculus, armed with horny teeth and plates, most perfectly exhibits the histological separation. From the thin membranous cardia of the stomach of the larva during the short pupa state this powerful and muscular organ has been produced; from this same thin tunic processes have arisen, and thus its cavity has distended upon all sides. But in conjunction with this the general cavity of the ilium decreases, the muscular fibres contract, and form a compact firmer membrane than that of the stomach of the larva. And lastly, the morphological separation is even more decided; similar rings transform themselves into the most dissimilar divisions of the body, and in these divisions large muscles grow from small beginnings, new organs of motion are also associated during the pupa state, and the old ones become lengthened generally as well as in their several joints, and, indeed, what was formerly a single joint becomes divided into from four to five, namely, the tarsus; or an organ which consisted of three or four joints now exhibits ten, twenty, and sometimes as many as fifty. Eyes even, the most important of all the organs of the senses, originate; and at a place where previously the situation of the head was indicated, merely by the orifice of the mouth, an entire head is formed with all its requisite organs.

§ 256.

The preceding paragraph shows us that the character of the metamorphosis of insects is found to be now restricted to its progress from a, in every respect, general form to one more particular and determinate. This character displays itself most distinctly in the perfect insect in the separation of the entire body into three particular divisions, each of which comprises its peculiar organs. It likewise stands in the closest connexion with the general ideas of development, and of the higher perfection of organic natural bodies, in as far as by this structure of the body the individual organs are more distinctly separated from each other, and each has acquired its determinate situation and a more artificial composition. The head is the bearer of the organs of the senses, the thorax of those of motion, and in the abdomen the organs of vegetation are placed. That portion of the body, consequently, which in the series of *Gastrozoa* predominated has become in the insect if not the smallest yet the most simple and least developed, whereas that in which all the organs are situated that characterise the *Arthrozoa*, which are the organs of motion, namely, the thorax, is, with respect to its composition and development, the most perfect. But we have above seen (§ 158) that the organs of motion fall into active and passive. But this separation is first found distinctly expressed in the *Arthrozoa*. We certainly find the active ones or muscles universally among the *Gastrozoa*, and also indications of the passive ones are found in the internal bony parts and partial skeleton; but a perfect skeleton of hard parts to which the muscles can be attached is first found in the higher *Arthrozoa*, namely, the *Crustacea* and *Insecta*, and which presents itself as an external ossified or horny integument. The most simple form of this external integument is the ring, all particularities and individual divarications have consequently proceeded from the annular form, and must, therefore, admit of being referred back again to it. The first change, however, which the ring in the progress of development suffers is, that it separates into a superior and inferior half; thus are formed the rings or segments of the abdomen, as well as of many larvæ and caterpillars. Whence the lower half thickens in its centre, and from this spot sends processes inwardly, which also occasionally form into a ring, and thus a smaller ring is inclosed within the larger one, but both of which touch at one spot, namely, where a half diameter drawn from the centre touches the circumference. This inner ring, or the processes which indicate it, receive the nervous cord within it, whereas all the other organs are encompassed by the larger external ring. Thus are formed the most perfect segments, namely, those of the thorax.

If we compare this structure of the parts of the skeleton with those found in the vertebrata we discover a not unimportant uniformity in their fundamental composition. That point namely from which the arch of both rings proceeds is analogous to the body of the vertebra; the bow of the smaller ring presents itself as the foramen medullare, and that of the larger ring those moveable processes which hang attached to the vertebræ, and which are called ribs; the superior and generally smaller half ring, lastly, which unites the two arches of the lower half ring to a whole ring, represents the sternum placed between the ends of the ribs. Hence, thus we obtain as the fundamental form of the skeleton of the insect the vertebræ with their radiations, just the same as these bones form the foundation of the trunk and head-bones of the vertebrata. The difference between both is found only that in the vertebrata the radiations of the vertebræ take an opposite direction, whereas in insects they project on one side only. Besides, this view, which appears to contain so much truth as not to require a proof in detail, is by no means new, but has been advanced by several comparative anatomists, namely, Geoffroy St. Hilaire [*], Robineau Desvoidy [†], and more recently by Carus [‡]. We need, therefore, merely refer to the labours of these learned men, particularly to the last, and those who shall consider this comparison an absurdity, we draw their attention to his detailed representation; it here suffices to have found the result in a simple development.

§ 257.

But that the vertebræ here lie upon the surface, whereas in the *Osteozoa* they are encompassed by soft parts, is grounded upon the entire formative type of the *Arthrozoa*, which is no other than that the skeleton in them is always external, whereas in the *Osteozoa* it has become internal. But why this is so ordained by nature we can only answer when we shall have seen why nature has produced *Gastro-*, *Arthro-*, and *Osteozoa*, and to answer this would be stepping beyond those limits within which human investigation is restricted, especially in its inquiry into final causes; consequently a miscalculation of its capacity. But one thing strikes us with astonishment, namely, that in

---

[*] Annales des Sciences Physic. Part iv. 1820, p. 96—133., whence translated in Meckel's deutschen Archiv für die Physiologie, tom. vi. p. 59.

[†] Recherches sur l'Organisation vertebrale des Crustaces, &c. Paris, 1828. 8vo.

[‡] Von den Urtheilen des Knochen und Schalengerüstes. Leipz. 1830. Folio, with plates.

the *Arthrozoa* the vertebræ lie upon the ventral side, and in the *Osteozoa* upon the dorsal. This arises from the situation of the nervous cord; if this lie upon the ventral side it then attracts the vertebræ to it, for it is the earlier, they being formed around it. The nervous system in general, as well as every individual nerve, seeks the best protected parts, therefore, in the *Gastrozoa*, as well as in the *Arthrozoa*, its main stem lies at the ventral surface, that it may conceal itself beneath the other organs. If, then, the ganglionic ventral cord of the *Arthrozoa* be analogous to the spinal cord, or as others prefer considering it, to the dorsal ganglionic chain lying contiguous to the vertebræ, which may be doubted since the discovery of a distinct *nervus sympathicus* proceeding directly from the brain; then the encompassing parts of the skeleton will necessarily be analogous to those parts of the skeleton of the vertebrata, which inclose that cord. But we prefer considering the ventral cord of the *Arthrozoa* as the true spinal cord, from its passing within the canal formed by the horny skeleton, and not contiguously, as would necessarily be the case upon the adoption of its identity with the dorsal ganglionic chain. According to this representation, therefore, insects run with their back turned forwards, or rather underwards, and what is called back in them is the true ventral side. This idea has been long since suggested, and was immediately, like everything that diverges from common views, strongly disputed; but the proofs cited in opposition do not appear tenable, as will be evinced by what follows in support of our opinion.

The situation of the intestines perfectly confirms our view. That organ which lies most approximate to the vertebral column of the vertebrata is, with the exception of the vessels which are deficient in insects, the œsophagus and the intestinal canal; even so in insects, it lies immediately over the nervous cord, directly upon the inner horny arch when it is closed, or still between its branches. In the vertebrata next to the intestinal canal proceeding from the back towards the belly we find the lungs and the heart in the thorax, in the ventral cavity the intestine touches the ventral surface, in the pelvis the sexual organs namely, the gravid uterus, lie in front of it. We find exactly the same arrangement in insects: the lungs are omitted, as they are universally distributed; in the thorax proceeding from the back towards the breast we find the heart with its large vessels. In the ventral cavity, whither the heart also extends, it is likewise placed externally, and indeed the return of the aorta to the back is indicated in the two main currents passing from the head and proceeding laterally, inclining downwards. Thus also in insects the motion of the blood first proceeds forwards and upwards, and then backwards and downwards. The sexual organs, lastly, lie in front of the intestinal canal, therefore above, immediately beneath the heart. This situation is shown above in the ovaries; in their rudiments also in the caterpillar it was remarked that they lie above the intestinal canal. The orifice only of the sexual organs differs, as in insects it lies beneath the anus, whereas, according to analogy, it should lie above. Nature appears to have pursued a determinate object in this situation, which agrees with that found in fishes, but which could not be subjected to the twisting of the insect body; but what this object is remains undiscoverable. This only is evident, that the genitalia in insects lie as much in front of the intestinal canal, calculating from the spinal cord, as in the mammalia and other animals. A second objection, besides that of the altered situation of the sexual aperture, which could be made to this twisting of the insect's body, might be deduced from the situation of the mouth, which does not lie laterally with respect to the spinal cord, but upon it, like the former. But the twisting of the anterior half of the head occasions this, and that such a twisting is actually the case is proved by the co-relative situation of the cerebrum and cerebellum, both of which, in fact, do not lie upon one side, but upon the opposite sides of the œsophagus, namely, the cerebrum above, on the true ventral side, the cerebellum beneath, towards the true back. This wholly irregular relation of the parts can only be explained by a twisting of the anterior portion of the head. The organs placed upon that part of the head naturally participate in it, and thus the mouth came beneath, whereas properly it should lie above, were it in harmony with the entire structure of the insect. But how is such a twisting consistent with the simplicity of the case of the head? The reply to this question appears difficult, but in fact it is not so when we consider that the head as well as the body consists of vertebræ. Their number is regulated by that of the cerebral ganglia; in the vertebrata there are three, namely, the cerebellum, the posterior lobe of the cerebrum, and its anterior lobe. This anterior lobe, the ganglion of smell, is deficient in insects, as they have no particular organ of smell, and consequently we find in them only two ganglia, namely, the ganglion of sight and the cerebellum. Thus their skull is divided into two vertebral arches. These are also very distinct in the head of the larva; the posterior one, in which the cerebellum lies, is the largest, and consists of the throat as the base, and of the two large temples which meet at the vortex, as the arch. Between them a triangular piece lies anteriorly and above, the clypeus, which has the eyes at its lower angles, and the mandibles at its base; beneath, the chin lies next to the throat, which thus closes the second arch indicated by the clypeus. Both together form the second vertebra; it enlarges during the metamorphosis, and thereby pushes back the arch of the posterior vertebra. The oral organs are attached to it, and it contains within it, the cerebrum, or the ganglion of the eyes. The clypeus is the body, or vertebra itself, the branches of which, or arch, bend downwards to the chin; the chin itself is the upper plate of the vertebral ring, or part corresponding with the sternum. The mandibles hang attached as limbs to this vertebra. The eyes also are situated upon the anterior vertebra, and which indicate posteriorly its limits, in as much as their horny external surface appear, as it were, introduced in the free space between the two vertebræ, or rather have separated them from each other. Thus, therefore, the optic nerve passes just in the same manner between the two vertebræ, as the nerves of the spinal cord pass between the arches of the vertebræ. The posterior of these vertebral arches, namely, that for the cerebellum has, as well as the thoracic vertebræ, its internal processes, or the second ring, which corresponds with the true vertebral arches. It, therefore, originates as a furcate process from the throat, and embraces the cerebellum with its branches. When these branches unite they form the tentorium, or the small band which divides the occipital aperture into two halves. But we do not find anything analogous in the first vertebra; did it exist, it would necessarily proceed from the clypeus or the forehead.

§ 258.

The opinion, therefore, that the trunk of the insect is formed upon the same type as that of the vertebrate animal is thus corroborated: we have exhibited even the same analogy in the head. The chief difference of the two organisations, however, consists in the back in the insect being turned downwards, but in the vertebrate animal upwards. What Von Bär[*] cites as a proof in opposition to this assertion, viz.—that the upper side of insects is the distending side, the lower the bending side, and that, therefore, as in the vertebrata, the

---

[*] Entwickelungsgeschichte der Thiere, p. 246.

former is more densely covered with hair, and more deeply coloured than the latter—does not at all suffice; for, in the first place, in very many insects, particularly in the beetles, the under side is that which makes the greatest bow, and, therefore, the distending side, and often, as in the bees, is the most densely haired, and besides the darker colouring, as the consequence of a greater effect of light, is no proof in opposition. This is evinced by the universally brighter colour of the upper side of the abdomen in the beetles, in which the elytra oppose the effect of light. What also he cites in opposition from the situation and posture of the extremities is also inapplicable; for the extremities proceed precisely from the same side as they do in the vertebrata, namely, from the dorsal side. In all the vertebrata the extremities are attached to particular bones which stand in connexion with the vertebral column. These bones are, for the anterior extremity, the scapulæ, and for the posterior one the ilium, of the pelvis. We refind these portions of the skeleton also in the *Arthrozoa*, at least in the most perfect among them, namely, the beetles; but they do not lie superficially attached to the vertebræ and its arches, but as external cases they are connected with the ring which is formed by the vertebra and its processes, and necessarily at the spot where they properly belong, namely, between the vertebra and the sternum. This approximation of the shoulder-plate to the vertebral column is very distinct in the anterior extremity of the vertebrata, it descending closely contiguous to the vertebræ; in the posterior extremity, however, where the ribs are wanting, it is even traced, in as far as here the ilium borders immediately upon the vertebral column, and when the sternum here, the os pubis is wanting, it presents itself as an arched process, upon the vertebral series of the pelvis. The same is the case in insects; here also the ribs are compressed, and the scapulæ take their place. We, therefore, obtain in insects both a shoulder-blade and a pelval piece; the first is also the plate, called by us the scapula, the latter our parapleura, the ischium of Straus, which, properly, should be called the ilium. The most distinct proof that these pieces merit their names is the fact that the muscles which move the thighs, namely, its flexor, thence proceed, and that consequently the femur is attached to these pieces. In the anterior legs it is the omia which correspond with them in situation and function Analogous to the dorsal and ventral plates these three plates might therefore, be called the promium, mesomium, and metomium, whereas the dorsal plates should now be called pro-, meso-, and metasternum and the ventral plates, pro-, meso-, and metanotum. But why do the thighs articulate with the vertebræ itself?—why not with the shoulder-blade, as it is present? These questions could be suggested only by a superficial observer, with reference to the posterior femur, for upon the anterior and intermediate pairs the shoulder-blade actually forms a portion of the articulating socket*. The posterior femur also, or rather its ball, which is usually called the hip, joins the parapleura above, and this forms a portion of the articulating socket †. Likewise in the downward bent margin of the parapleura the small articulating socket is formed for the round ball of the top of the femur which revolves in the large hip socket. Lastly, the aperture through which the muscles of motion pass into the thorax is always found between the pleura and the sternum, and is partly encompassed by the former and partly by the latter.

Thus the composition of the insect body and the analogy of its individual plates with the bones found in the vertebrata, is fully proved, and we obtain as the result that

The head consists of two vertebræ, the one of which is twisted in opposition to the other ‡.

The thorax consists of three vertebral rings, each of which is subdivided into the true vertebra, the shoulder-blades and a sternum.

The abdomen consists of nine vertebræ, each of which again consists of the true vertebra and its arch, which are either the analogies of the ribs or frequently merely represent the transverse processes of the vertebra and the ventral sternum, the horny ventral covering. The last of these vertebral rings, namely, the anal and sexual vertebra, is also twisted, so that the vertebra with the anus lies above, and the ventral plates with the sexual apertures lie beneath. These abdominal vertebræ have no internal processes; they retain their original most simple larva form, and generally present themselves as simple but more frequently halved rings. In some cases, for instance, in the locusts, from the lateral parts of the half ring other free moveable half arches project into the cavity of the abdomen, which both in situation

---

* See Pl. IX. No. 2. f. 2., No. 3. f. 5.; Pl. X. No. 1. f. 6., No. 3. f. 5.

† Pl. IX. No. 3. f. 5.

‡ This composition of the head from two vertebræ or rings is confirmed by Ratzeburg's observations upon the development of the larvæ of the *Hymenoptera*. See Darstellung und Beschreibung der Arzneithiere, vol. ii. p. 175, Pl. 23, f. 47—50 and f. 88—91.

and function perfectly agree with the ribs. But I have never been able to find a second series of vertebral arches for the nervous cord.

§ 259.

We must now proceed to the comparison and explanation of the limbs. We have shown above that the wings are no limbs, but gills (§ 243). For the completion of this uniformity, which is already exhibited by their structure from two external membranous layers and the currents of blood distributed between them, we have only to show that these gills lie precisely where when present the gills are always found. If we, therefore, commence with the superior groups, we shall find that in them the branchial apertures lie at the anterior part of the neck, and, consequently, upon the ventral side. In some *amphibia*, namely, the *Batrachians*, they are found exactly at the same spot. The same in the fishes. In these they are protected additionally by means of a bony covering which opens posteriorly and beneath, and therefore towards the venter. In the *Mollusca*, the branchiæ lie more or less upon the back, as it is called, but their back is nothing else than the true belly, from the very same reason, that in them also the main nervous mass takes its course along the so called ventral disc.

We thus obtain this general law for the situation of the branchiæ, viz. that they are placed laterally, but inclining to the venter, and thence descend to the venter. The wings have the same position; they originate between the scapula and sternum, consequently upon the external side of the body, and thence descend to the ventral side. In those insects furnished with gills, they also lie at the same part; they always originate at the side where the main stems of the tracheæ lie, and thence rise upwards, either wholly so or partially inclining backwards, as in the larvæ of the *Ephemera* and *Phryganeæ*. As long as the insect dwells in the water, its rudimental wings are true water gills, but so soon as it has quitted the water, they transform themselves into air gills, for in both cases fluids circulate in their vessels, which, doubtlessly, receive oxygen from the air. The beetles exhibit the most perfect conformity, for in the entire hardening of their body the wings also have become horny, and now supplant the place of gill covers. The *Orthoptera* approximate to this structure by their pergamentaceous superior wings, but many *Hemiptera* approach still closer, for in them half the wing is horny. Thence we must remove the wings from the category of limbs, they being merely gills which are occasionally moved in the air, just as the gills are incessantly moved in the water; the insect, therefore, uses them for flight, as the former are used by larvæ for swimming. The endeavour of some naturalists to see arms in the wings, and to indicate in their ribs the arm-bones with their joints and inflexions, cannot therefore be justified. The wings present me with no other resemblance to limbs than that they move and assist the progression of the creature. If this be the sole character of the arm or of the leg, I will then admit that they are either arms or legs, but, otherwise, certainly not.

§ 260

But there is less doubt of the legs being analogous to the extremities; indeed, they have always been considered as such, and the entire leg as well as its individual joints have been thence named. The first question that suggests itself is—Are the legs forms truly analogous to the arms and legs of the vertebrata? To this we may safely reply in the affirmative, for these limbs are similarly situated, and often consist of just as many, and sometimes, indeed, of more divisions. The similarity of situation is shown above, where we have treated of the scapulæ of the vertebra representing the true scapulæ; we have there seen that the legs hang attached to a distinct plate between the vertebra and the sternum, which corresponds with the scapula or the ilium of the pelvis, and that it is from this plate that the majority of muscles come, positive facts which prove an important analogy.

With respect to the division of the limbs, we always find in insects at least five but never more than nine joints; of these, the first and third, with the smallest second, form a joint articulating upwards; the fourth with the third one articulating downwards; the fifth with the fourth one again articulating outwards; the following joints, lastly, sit where they present themselves upon the fifth, and take a straight direction, and also participate in its motion, yet the entire foot can bend downwards and again distend itself. A perfect conformity with the anterior limbs of the superior animals has been supposed to be found in these articulations. It has been endeavoured to explain the first joint, the coxa of entomologists, as the humerus; the second smallest, as the separated olecranon, the analogue of the patella; and the third, the femur of entomologists, as the antibrachium; the fourth joint, the tibia of entomologists, would then be the carpus; the fifth, the metacarpus; and the subsequent ones, the joints of the toes or phalanges. This explanation becomes absolutely necessary, if the legs of insects be considered the analogues of the anterior limbs; but I prefer considering them as the posterior limbs, and, indeed, because those are the least perfect, not only in structure, but also in function. Where, therefore, true limbs first present themselves, there must they be considered as the inferior ones or legs. Both, however, the arm and the leg differ from each other in the angles of their joints, being opposed so that the angle which in the anterior extremities open outwards, on the posterior ones open posteriorly. But these differences are not found in the extremities of insects; the anterior ones are merely distinguished from the posterior ones by their situation, for their corresponding angles all open upon one side. Hence, therefore, the hip is not the thigh, but the hip, and the trochanter and femur form conjunctively the thigh. The hip is the head of the femur, the trochanter its neck, and the femur its tubular body. This division of the femur into three parts is occasioned by the feet being in insects so placed, that they proceed as it were from the lower end, and direct themselves upwards, in which direction they possess considerable power of motion, which was only to be attained by this mode of articulation. If in solitary cases more mobility is required, the trochanter must be divided into several pieces, and this is exemplified in the genus *Pimpla* (§ 83. 2.). If, however, it be the elbow or olecranon, in this instance we must adopt the existence of two successive patellæ, for which there is no analogy; but if a division of the thigh into three parts may be imagined, it is still more possible to conceive its subdivision into four. If now the coxa, trochanter, and femur be the subdivided superior thigh (*femur*), the tibia must necessarily be the lower thigh (tibia). The angles of both joints fully harmonise with this view, in as far as they always open either posteriorly or inferiorly. The first large joint of the tarsus then indicates the metatarsus, as the basal bones are wanting, and the following are then the phalanges. They vary considerably in number; sometimes they are entirely wanting, but never more than four exist.

If after this explanation, which must still appear forced, from the deficiency of the basal bones of the foot, we look around us for an analogy in the higher animals, we find the most perfect conformity in the structure of the foot in birds. In these, also, the basal bones of the foot are deficient, and in them, also, there is a variation in the number (from one to four) of their phalanges. This variation is found in every individual bird, in as far as each of its four toes, commencing inwardly, increase one joint, so that the innermost, generally the posterior one, has one joint, and the three anterior ones, in regular rotation, two, three, and four joints. In insects, on the contrary, this variation is distributed throughout the whole order, so that their one toe of each foot exhibits either one, two, three, or four joints: it is more unusual for some toes to have three and others four joints, as is the case among the beetles, for instance, in the *Heteromera*.

It is hoped that no one, after this comparative view, will take objection to the explanation of the leg joints; he will but find a conformity of insects with birds, to which, in the course of our treatise, we have frequently referred, and he must therefore be necessarily convinced of the correctness of what we have advanced. Birds are in every respect concentrated insects, and insects birds deprived of their internal skeleton.

FOURTH CHAPTER.

OF MUSCULAR MOTION.

§ 261.

THE collective motions of animals are produced by a distinct system of organs, which we call muscles. With respect to the structure and arrangement of these organs in insects, we have already stated all that was requisite in the third chapter of the preceding division; we consequently consider as known both the structure of the entire apparatus of motion as also of its individual parts, and proceed at once to the consideration of their functions.

We obtain as the first and chief difference in motions their subdivision into voluntary and spontaneous.

Under the spontaneous motions we consider all those which are not subject to the influence of the will, and which take place in the insect, from the commencement of its life to its death, precisely in the same manner, and which can never be wholly or for any long period interrupted, so long as life is to proceed uninterruptedly. We know, from what has preceded, that all these organs are encompassed by a peculiar muscular layer, which, by means of compression and distension, produce a certain change in the compass of the vegetative organs, which partly contracts them and partly allows them to relapse to their former compass, and that it is only in consequence of this motion that the functions of every individual part and organ can proceed uninterruptedly. These motions are especially visible in the several parts of the nutritive system, where they present themselves as the peristaltic motion of the intestinal canal, as the respiratory motion of the tracheæ, and, lastly, as the pulsations of the heart. All these motions have been described sufficiently in detail in a former chapter, where we have spoken of the functions of the nutrimental system, and where we discerned in them the true cause of the entire process of nutrition, which commences with the reception of the food. The motions of the sexual organs are less apparent, as they become visible only at certain periods. Yet in the male sex there appears to be, from the moment of puberty, an undisturbed production of semen. This semen, by means of a motion not dissimilar to the peristaltic motion of the intestine, arrives in the vesica seminalis, whence it passes during copulation into the female organs. After this act the activity of the female organs commences, which exhibits itself as a peristaltic motion, both in the egg-tube and in the oviduct, and where it terminates in the production of the collective egg germs.

Upon surveying the common expression of all these motions, we recognise nothing further in them than a spontaneous re-action on the part of the organism to external irritation at least, external in reference to the organ which is moved. This irritation consists in the food, for the intestinal canal, the atmospheric air for the tracheæ, the blood for the heart, the semen secreted by the testes for the male organs, and for the female organs the male semen also which is conveyed into them.

§ 262.

The stimulus, however, which determines the action of the voluntary muscles is the will only of the creature; the insect has but to will, and in the same moment its legs are in motion, and it flaps its wings and hastens away. The common property of both, therefore, consists in their requiring a medium of irritation, the differences we find in the phenomena are that this excitement for the involuntary muscles is physical and corporeal, and that for the voluntary is spiritual. Both descriptions of muscles, however, may be affected in the same manner by one and the same excitement, for electricity effects both a contraction of the heart and the same phenomena in the muscles of the limbs.

The first thing we perceive in the activity of any determinate muscle is a contraction of itself. By means of this contraction its compass enlarges, its texture feels more compact and firmer, and the entire muscle is in a state of excitement. How this excitement is produced we know not, but thus much is ascertained, that the nerves exercise great influence upon the motions of the muscles. But the nature of this influence we must leave undetermined whether, as some physiologists suppose, generation produces the necessary power for acting upon the muscles, or whether, with others, it be to be considered as merely the conductor of the excitement from its point of production to the muscle. We are most fully convinced of the importance of the influence which the nerves exercise upon the motion of the muscles when galvanic electricity is applied to a nerve and a muscle standing in connexion with it, or upon its application to the former alone. Alexander von Humboldt, whose great genius first announced itself in a surprising manner in the illustration of this difficult and then insufficiently-laboured field of physiology, has supplied us with some interesting observations, even in reference to insects [*]. He saw animated contractions in the limbs when the nerves passing to them were touched by the poles of a voltaic pile, re-actions which continued for a space of twenty minutes, and which admitted of being prolonged three times that space upon the nerves being artificially prepared with alkalis and oxidised muriatic acid. He also observed in the thigh of a *Blatta orientalis*, touched with gold and zinc, from two to three successive shocks; indeed "the thigh raised itself up, and held itself some seconds trembling in the air." He further remarks: "Upon galvanising the spinal marrow of a *Blatta orientalis* with silver and well-burnt carbon, I observed its posterior portion move to and fro and press with its feet." Even in the body of a *Vespa crabro*, the head of which had been cut off fourteen hours before, the same admirable observer saw the limbs tremble upon the application of the metallic stimulus.

This trembling of the limbs after the effect of galvanic electricity speaks also in favour of an oscillation of the muscular fibres in insects as well as in the superior animals. This oscillation was formerly denied

---

[*] Ueber die gereizte Muskel-und Nervenfascir. Berlin, 1797. 8vo. vol. 1, p. 273.

in insects, and its deficiency explained from the imperfection of their nervous system. But the muscular and nervous system of insects is as perfect as that of the *Cephalopoda*, and there can be no objection to admit it in the former, since it has been proved to exist in the latter *. We undertand in this oscillation an undulating motion of the fibres, which is seen together with the contraction, and which, for instance, exhibits itself in partially pressed muscles, as a trembling motion which frequently seizes the entire limb. The incessant vibrating motion in many parts of the body of many insects, for instance, the motion of the antennæ in the *Ichneumonodea*, the trembling of the wings in repose, the palpitation of the extremities of the feet in *Chironomus*, &c., appear to be less the result of voluntary muscular motion than of the oscillation peculiar to all perfect muscular substance.

§ 263.

This muscular activity is therefore the foundation of all the motions exercised by insects. These motions may be referred to four principal kinds, namely, walking, jumping, swimming, and flying. But few insects are restricted to the first and most simple of these motions, the majority possess the power of flight in addition; some can only walk and leap, as the flea; some can walk, leap, and fly, as the grasshopper; many can walk, fly, and swim; whereas there are none which possess the power of swimming and flying in conjunction. Many larvæ can only walk and swim, others creep and swim; no perfect insect, however, possesses the last mode of motion exclusively.

If we now investigate the first, most simple, and most universally distributed of these modes of progression, walking, this also may be subdivided into several kinds, from the structure of the motive apparatus. The first, and most simple, which is the progression of maggots, without the help of feet, and is properly merely an advance upon the ventral surface, is a sort of slow creeping. The maggot thus progresses by means of the longitudinal contraction of its body, whereby the distended and, as it were, swollen head is pushed onwards, this then affixes itself by means of the lower and strongly projecting ventral surface of the first abdominal segment, which appears to act something like a sucking cup, and then draws the body as far as possible after it. The posterior extremity, which in general is furnished with distinctly

* K. A. Rudolphi Grundrisz der Physiologie, vol. ii. part i. p. 290, 294.

projecting pedal warts, then likewise attaches itself, and thus the body pushes itself forward by gradual contraction of all the segments, which begins behind. The alternating attachment of the anterior and posterior ends is repeated as long as the maggot is in motion. We find this mode of progression in all the apodal larvæ of the *Diptera*, and they accomplish it better upon uneven, rough surfaces; upon a smooth surface their progress is imperfect, and then frequently the short pedal warts refuse their office. Some of the larvæ of the *Diptera*, whose pedal warts, as well as occasionally the entire body, are covered with short horny spines or bristles, can perform this creeping motion more quickly and securely, but the mechanism is just the same. As an instance of the first kind of creeping we may cite the larva of the blue-flesh fly (*Musca vomitoria*, Pl. I. f. 25.); and, as the representative of the second, the rat-tailed fly, the larva of *Eristalis tenax* (Pl. I. f. 32.).

The motion of larvæ with thoracic feet and one or two pairs of anal prolegs (the geometer caterpillars, Pl. I. f. 35.) next follows. In them the step-like advance is more distinctly performed by means of the attachment of the first and last abdominal segments. The whole of the middle of the body bows itself into an acute arch, so that thereby the anterior and posterior feet are brought closely together; the posterior feet then remain affixed, but the anterior ones are so far pushed forward with the extended body until it lies parallel to the surface; they then also affix themselves, and draw the posterior ones after them by the arching of the body.

The motion of the caterpillars furnished with thoracic, ventral, and anal legs is indeed the same, but it so far differs that all the segments possessing legs participate in the attachment. This attachment is now no longer from behind forwards, but, after the pairs of thoracic feet have advanced and affixed themselves, the ventral feet follow in succession, until the last pair, or the anal prolegs, move forward whilst the ventral feet still further advance. Thus the whole body is producing a constant undulating motion as the raising and attachment of the consecutive series advance in regular progression.

Lastly, the walk of six-legged larvæ very much resembles that of the perfect insect. In both, one of the anterior legs, generally the right one, makes a step which is followed almost simultaneously by the left anterior leg and right intermediate one. Whilst now the right anterior leg is making another step the left intermediate and right posterior ones make the same movement, and thus support it; whereas the left posterior leg makes a simultaneous movement with the left anterior and right intermediate. This contemporaneous motion of the several legs does not generally take place so exactly synchronally, but rapidly in succession, so that all the legs of each side are occupied in a constantly progressive advance. The anterior and posterior legs appear to take the greatest share in this advance, and the intermediate ones seem only to support them. Thus, the anterior and posterior legs of one side and the intermediate of the opposite side appear to progress together. But this successive motion is distinctly visible only in insects walking slowly, but, when running, the interval of time is so short between the movements of each individually that the contemporaneous motion of different legs is scarcely perceptible, and we can only discern an alternating advance and remaining behind of the two legs of one pair as well as the rapidly successive advancing motion of all the legs of one side.

In this motion of the entire leg every joint, each in its particular manner, participates, so that the hips revolve upon their axis, the femur approaches to it, and the angle between the femur and tibia becomes more acute when the leg bends, whereas all lie more in a line when the leg is extended. The anterior legs, however, bend in an opposite direction to the rest, for they are extended when they advance; the others, on the contrary, upon the same movement are bent, whereas, if the posterior ones extend themselves, the anterior pair must necessarily bend. Hence arises the differences in the insertion of the muscles in the hips. The chief object in the anterior pair, namely, is the advancing motion and clinging, but in the posterior pair it is a pushing forward, which is attained by means of extension. Thence the anterior and posterior legs have more extensors than flexors (at least in *Melolontha*, see § 179); whereas the intermediate participate chiefly in the advancing motion of the anterior legs of the opposite side, and have consequently more flexors than extensors: an advance forwards is especially prescribed to them, we therefore find their flexile apparatus more developed than the extensional.

§ 264.

Leaping, also, is in general effected by means of the legs; but, as exceptions, we find peculiar organs and apparatus adapted for the purpose.

When the legs leap it is again the posterior ones which produce the chief motion, and they are then therefore altogether larger, and also some of their joints are more fully developed. This development chiefly affects the thigh; it is not only longer than in the anterior legs but also much thicker, particularly at its lower end when it is very long, or in the middle when it but little exceeds the rest in length. In the first case it is obclavate, and in the last it is either ovate or conical. When, therefore, a leap is to be made, the posterior leg bends at its knee joint as much as possible; usually the femur and tibia then touch each other. The tarsus is also so much bent back that its superior surface touches the tibia, but the entire femur is so depressed that its axis is parallel to the surface upon which the insect rests. In this position, with its anterior legs somewhat withdrawn, the insect stops for some seconds, as it were to collect itself, when it distends all and chiefly the posterior legs with considerable force and rapidity, and by means of which it throws itself from the surface. We therefore perceive that it is chiefly the extensors which produce the leap; they are consequently throughout the whole posterior leg, and particularly the thigh, the strongest and largest, whence it is also that the greater convexity of the thigh is always above, and not beneath.

The line described by the insect in its leap, if, for instance, when winged it should not expand its wings, and by their action supporting the leap continue it by flight, is that of all projectiles, namely, parabolic, which is explained by the gradually increasing gravity of the body, and in consequence its decreasing power of flight. But the extent of the leap depends partly upon the force with which it is made and partly upon the size of the body, but particularly upon the latter, so that we may consider as a law that the larger the body of the leaping insect the less is the extent of its leap, and the flatter is the parabolic line. Both, however, depend upon the flexure and correlative position of the femur and tibia, so that the smaller the bend the shorter and flatter is the leap. Thus every insect regulates both the direction and height of its leap by the position of its feet and the force of their extension.

The power of leaping in insects, from the lightness of their bodies, and the relative strength and size of their muscles in general, is considerable, and doubtlessly greater than in any other animals. No mammal can leap proportionately so high and far as the flea, which of all insects possesses this power most strongly developed, for in one leap it will spring a height exceeding two hundred times the length of its body. The following genera of minute *Coleoptera*, *Hymenoptera*, and *Hemiptera* class themselves with it in this power of leaping, and we place them in the order of the progressive decrease of the function; for instance, *Haltica*, *Orchestes*, *Eupelmus*, *Chalcis*, and other *Pteromalidæ*, *Jassus*, *Aphrophora*, *Chermes*, *Livia*, &c. The larger *Cicada*, grasshoppers, and locusts do not leap so well. We also find a few minute *Diptera* possessing this power; for instance, many species of the genera *Ceratopagon* and *Tachydromia*, in the first the males especially, but in general their activity is but small, which is probably occasioned by their softer integuments, whence the contraction of the muscles is much less, but which also may be partly ascribed to the less perfect development of the muscles themselves.

The two families of insects in which we detect peculiar organs for leaping are the *Elaters* and the spring-tails (*Podura*, *Smynthurus*, &c.)

In *Elater*, the articulation of the pro- and meso-thorax gives them the power of leaping, but it can only be accomplished when the insect lies upon its back, whence, should it by any accident be placed in this position, it could not readily recover itself, owing to its short legs and flat back; nature has therefore supplied it with assistance in the mode of the articulation of the two thoracic segments. For this purpose the mesonotum and mesosternum are prolonged into a projecting tubular process, which is fitted to a cavity in the pronotum and prosternum; upon this process we find in the middle of the anterior margin of the mesonotum a hook-shaped joint, bent upwards, adapted to a cavity in the posterior margin of the pronotum. At the base, close to this hook, there are two smooth flat articulations, which likewise fit two flat cavities in the pronotum. The mesosternum has, on the contrary, exactly in its centre, a deep funnel-shaped groove, into which a conical process of the prosternum fits; upon the anterior margin, close to this large groove, there are two smaller cavities for the reception of two flat processes, which lie at the base, close to the conical process of the prosternum. Their connexion is effected by a tubular membrane, which passes from one segment to the other. If now the insect lie upon its back, by means of the muscles which connect the two dorsal plates together it raises its body upwards, so that the pronotum, moving upon the processes of the mesonotum, bends back upon the dorsal surface of the body. It now suddenly contracts with all its force the connecting muscles of the two thoracic segments, as well as the others which run down from the mesonotum to the prosternum, and it thereby strikes violently with the somewhat raised margin of the pronotum, and the base of the elytra against the ground, which throws it upwards, yet, as this blow does not proceed from the centre of the body, but its anterior portion, this part receives the greater impetus, in consequence of which the body turns over in the air, and it consequently falls with its ventral surface to the ground. It retains itself in this position by the sudden clinging of its legs, and so prevents the effects the concussion would otherwise have of throwing it up again. The dagger-shaped process of the prosternum, which fits into the funnel-shaped groove of the mesosternum, has no other purpose in this motion than to regulate and preserve the direction of the prothorax during the contraction, without participating in the least in the blow.

In the spring-tails a furcate process originates at the ventral plate of the penultimate and ante-penultimate abdominal segments, which in repose lies extended towards the head along the belly, and reaches to about the posterior legs. By the insect striking this process rapidly and with force against the surface it is enabled frequently to make an extensive leap. During this leap the fork is directed posteriorly, but as soon as it again touches the ground it again bends forward. In *Smynthurus*, Lat., De Geer found, besides, a conical process at the sternum, whence the creature projected two long flexible filaments when it wished to affix itself *. Probably these filaments also participate in producing the leap, which is much greater in them than in *Podura*.

§ 265.

In swimming, insects are assisted either by their legs or other organs, which, in conjunction with other functions, exercise also that of fins. Among these organs may be classed the branchial leaves of the larvæ which live in water, of which we have before noticed their incessant motion backwards and forwards, whereby the larva moves and breathes. This is however the case only in those larvæ which have lateral branchial leaves; a portion of the rest, for instance the larvæ of the *Agrions*, move by the serpentine motion of their abdomen, and the leaves at their caudal extremity, which act as a rudder. Thus also do the larvæ and pupæ of the gnats move. Others, again, swim like the leech, by a serpentining of the abdomen; which motion sometimes describes an undulating line, and sometimes, as in the red larva of

---

* Mémoires, tom. vii. p. 20, Pl. III. f. 7, 8.

Chironomus plumosus, it is produced by means of a lateral convolution of the anterior portion of the body, whereby its posterior end strikes forwards.

But all perfect insects, as well as the larvæ of those with an imperfect metamorphosis, which live in water, swim by means of their legs. Among the *Coleoptera* it is the family of *Hydrocantharides* which possess this faculty, for example, *Hydrophilus, Elophorus*, and the whirlwigs (*Gyrinus*); other insects which live in water, as many *Curculios, Helodes Phellandrii, Donacia Zosteræ, Elmis, Potamophilus, Parnus*, cannot swim, but creep about, clinging to different objects. In the other orders we find but a single family of the *Hemiptera* whose limbs are adapted to swim, namely, the genera *Notonecta, Sigara, Naucoris*, and also in an imperfect degree the genus *Nepa*. They all are, like the majority of insects, from the quantity of air contained in their bodies, as well as from the lightness of their constituents, of less specific gravity than water, and consequently float upon the surface without any exertion of their own, when they contract their limbs. The respiration of atmospheric air, to which all these genera are restricted, is thereby facilitated to them. It is thence also that many water-beetles cannot quit the surface when they have remained for some time in the air; the air then exercises so great an attraction upon them that their swimming power is not able to counteract it, and they consequently remain in this condition until they succeed in overcoming it. This may be observed in any *Gyrinus*; it first whirls itself about upon the surface before it can dive. Other beetles have so little specific gravity, that even with all their endeavours they cannot get beneath the water when any accident has removed them from their places of concealment to the surface. This is the case in many of the smaller *Hydrophili*, for instance, in *Hydrophilus orbicularis* and the *Elophori*. These, therefore, never swim, but creep about, clinging to objects beneath the water; if they quit their hold they immediately rise to the surface, and struggle here until they meet with a reed, that serves them as a ladder to descend by. Even the powerful *Hydrophilus piceus* swims very awkwardly, and has great difficulty to continue beneath the water.

The great *Dytici* are the best swimmers, namely, *Dyticus dispar*, or *Rœselii*. The whole form of its body is flat compared with its size, much narrowed anteriorly, and laterally has a sharp edge, which gradually increases in bulk to where its posterior legs are placed, and then again narrowing by degrees, contributes very considerably to facilitate its swimming. The legs also, particularly the posterior ones, are flat, compressed, and either upon one or upon both edges thickly furnished with long setæ or bristles. The first joint of the tarsus has a very free motion, and can so place itself that either the sharp edge or broad flat surface of the entire foot is brought forward and opposed to the pressure of the water. In the first case the motion finds little resistance, and easily cuts through the water, and in the last the pressure of the water acts as a resisting medium against the broad flat surface of the foot, which is increased to about double its width by means of the long fringes, and thus the beetle is enabled to advance. In addition to the repulsion which the rowing of the insect occasions we may also add the pressure exercised by the water itself, occasioned by the specific gravity of the insect. Were the beetle placed horizontally in the water it would thereby be raised upwards, but its posture is not horizontal, its axis forming an acute angle with the surface, and indeed the head is the deepest situated. By means of this position its swimming is much facilitated, as the pressure of the water from beneath, acting against an oblique surface, pushes both sidewards and upwards. The rowing of the beetle therefore has only to overcome that portion of the pressure which urges upwards, and then, without further exertion on its part, the beetle swims forward. If, therefore, it applies more power than is requisite for its swimming direct, it necessarily descends obliquely, and we consequently always observe it to dive in this direction, and never perpendicularly. But its own muscular activity is, however, the chief cause of its motion in water. This muscular motion is exercised principally by the posterior legs, which bend forwards as far as possible, when the narrow edge is directed anteriorly. In their distending motion all the joints bend, but particularly those of the foot, so that their broad surface is opposed to the pressure of the water; at the same time, but probably merely mechanically, by this pressure the stiff marginal fringe is expanded, so that by lying closely contiguous it forms as it were the face of the oar which the insect uses in its posterior legs. The violent extension of the leg to where it meets its opponent of the opposite side, behind the body, then propels it, and a repeated rowing continues the commenced motion.

The genera *Notonecta, Naucoris,* and *Sigara* swim in the same manner, but with this essential difference, that in them the ventral surface is directed upwards, and the keel-shaped back is directed downwards.

§ 266.

Flight, the last of the voluntary motions to be considered by us, is the most difficult to explain of all, as not only the muscles which are attached to the organs of flight, but all those found within the thorax, participate in producing it, and therefore it is not merely the wings during flight but the entire thorax, by means of the motion according to its several plates, which are detected as contributing to effect it. We can consequently distinguish two chief motions which are visible during the flight of an insect, namely, the individual motion of the wings themselves, and the contemporaneous motion of the thorax. The above described respiratory motion of the thorax during flight is identical with the latter, so that the same motion which effects the in- and expiration of the air from the thorax produces also the flapping of the wings.

The motion peculiar to the wings consists in their expansion and bending backwards; the expansion is produced by the extensors and the bending back by the flexors. From § 178 we know that the extensors are by far the largest of these muscles, and that they vary in compass according to the varying size of the anterior and posterior wings. By the contraction of an extensor, therefore, the wing is expanded, and by the continuance of this contraction it is retained in this position. In those orders with four membranous wings or coriaceous anterior wings we find no difference in the position of the wings during expansion. The anterior ones lie in front of the posterior ones, and in one plane with them, sometimes separate and sometimes connected with them by means of a peculiar apparatus. In the beetles, however, in which the anterior wings are transformed to hard elytra, their position is quite different. Sometimes these elytra are not at all expanded during flight, and this is the case in the genus *Cetonia* and in the earwig. In other instances the elytra are expanded it is true, but in a very different direction, namely, perpendicularly upwards; whereas the wings are extended horizontally, as we observe in *Necrophorus*, in the genus *Hister*, and in many *Staphylini*. In many other beetles, lastly, they lie in the same direction with the wings, yet not in general upon the same plane, but a little higher. In all these cases, therefore, the elytra do not participate in the blow of the wing, but they retain the same position and situation during the whole flight.

The remaining muscles of the thorax, but particularly those of the two segments upon which the wings are placed, and which above

(§ 176) we have called the dorsal-, lateral dorsal-, lateral- and furcate dorsal-muscles, are those which act in common for producing the respiratory and volatile motions, and therefore must be examined here more closely as to their effects. One of them, the straight dorsal muscle, which is expanded between the meso- and meta-phragma, acts parallely to the axis of the body; it arches by its contraction those plates within which it lies, and thereby produces the inflexion of the wing. In insects with connate thoracic segments it is assisted in this function by the oblique, lateral dorsal muscles, which likewise sit quite alone upon the dorsal plate and its processes, particularly the metaphragma. By means of it, therefore, the blow downwards of the wing is produced, and as it also arches the entire thorax, and likewise also distends it, it promotes the inspiration of air. In opposition to them the lateral and furcate dorsal muscles act. By their contraction they approximate the dorsal plate to the sternum, draw it down to the latter, and thereby effect the raising of the wing. They also contract the cavity of the thorax, and thereby promote the expiration of the air. By the alternating contraction of these muscles, opposed in their effects, the flapping of the wing of insects is produced. It is therefore the result of a distension and contraction of the thorax, in which naturally its lateral radiations, the wings, must immediately participate; this is another reason for considering the wings as mere continuations of the membrane of the thorax, which, only in consequence of their change of function occasioned by internal respiration, have received their peculiar extensor and flexor muscles.'

If after this very general survey of the mode of flight in insects we look around us for some peculiar divarications of individual orders, we shall find it expressed, especially in the position of the entire body, as well as of its individual limbs. With respect, in the first place, to taking flight, we shall even find some differences in the manner in which this is executed. Those that likewise possess the power of leaping, namely, the *Grylli* and *Cicada*, do it most readily. They raise themselves by a leap from the ground so soon as they may be urged to take flight, then expand their wings already floating in the air, and proceed in the direction already given by the leap. Yet are these insects not good and continuous fliers, with the exception of the migratory locust, but the majority return again to the ground at a very short distance from their place of starting. With the same ease do all other flying insects take wing which bear their wings always expanded, for instance, many flies, butterflies, *Hymenoptera*, and many *Libellulæ*. In the latter, also, they remain in the same position during repose that they are found in during flight; the insect, therefore, does not require to expand and direct them. Thence arises the facility with which these creatures raise themselves into the air; thence, also, as well as from their lightness of structure and small size, the facility of their motion in the air, and the long continuance of their flight. Beetles, and especially the largest ones, have the greatest difficulties to overcome in taking flight. We observe in them distinctly the great exertion not only of the muscles of flight, but all the other organs of the body also labour to support their flight; and the cockchafer in particular, which, doubtlessly, every one of our readers has observed in this occupation, gives us a distinct idea of the great labour these little creatures are obliged to apply to the execution of one of their most ordinary occupations. We see it at first, as it were conscious of its increasing labour, slowly raise itself, expand its antennæ, and, in the endeavour to free itself of a burdensome and hindering load, adapt itself to its purposed course by violent respiratory motions of its abdomen. It has hardly cast this burden from it, when it forthwith commences with considerably increased activity its pedestrian journey, seeking for some elevated spot whence it may commence its aërial expedition; and if it do not speedily find one, its anxiety to fly urges it to endeavour from the plain surface, but this impatience is frequently punished by the failure of its exertions. But, having reached an elevated spot, it raises its elytra during the violent backward and forward bending of its head, then suddenly expands them as well as the wings, and at the same moment makes its first elevating blow, after having, at the same time, compressed the whole abdominal cavity by means of the flexible dorsal integument, and thus driven all the air out of it. Thus, during flight, respiration takes place only in the thorax, and the abdomen resumes that function only when the creature alights after its completed course. But then its first motions are very violent and powerful.

The position of the body during flight in the air in this and other beetles is not the usual, viz. the horizontal, but inclined obliquely towards the horizon, in which inclination the head takes the more elevated, and the anal extremity the lower place. The cause of this oblique position I think may be found in the preponderance of the abdomen, particularly during puberty, owing to the turgidity of the internal genitalia, over the smaller and lighter thorax and head; at least in those insects in which no such preponderance of the abdomen can occur, partly from its smallness, as in the flies, and partly on account of its thinness and lightness, as in the *Libellulæ*, we observe no such obliquity during flight: whereas in other insects in which the abdomen itself is heavier, for instance, in the *Bombi* and wasps, we observe a similar posture, yet its greater weight does not incline the thorax from its horizontal position, but the abdomen alone, which is affixed at one small spot, hangs down. In other insects, again, in which the very long and also heavy abdomen forms by far the most considerable part, it is placed in such a position as not to incline the thorax during flight considerably from its horizontal position. Among these is found the genus *Fœnus*; which raises, during flight, the abdomen with, in the larger species, its very long ovipositor, perpendicularly upwards, or even sometimes bends it forwards, so that the chief pressure is directed towards the centre of the body. But there requires less strength to advance the thus pressing abdomen, than if, stretched directly out, it drew the entire body downwards, and daily experience can teach us how much more easy it is to balance a long stick upon the flat hand or the tip of a finger, than to carry it with an extended arm. Most external organs adapt themselves to the same law, for the legs are in general contracted to the body, and but very rarely stretched out posteriorly. But the antennæ appear always to maintain their extended position during flight, but which position is transformed in the *Cerambycidæ*, furnished with long antennæ, into a gentle curvature inclining outwards and backwards. In this position they contribute much to maintain an equilibrium with the abdomen, that it may not sink still lower.

This inclining posture of the whole body is, however, of no consequence to the execution of flight, but the likewise oblique attachment of the wings to the thorax is especially so. This oblique attachment is distinctly seen if a line be drawn through the direction of their affixion, and this is conceived to lie in the plane of the axis of the thorax when both are found to cut closely behind the thorax, and even sometimes upon its posterior limits [*]. The wings consequently during flight do not move perpendicularly to the body, but on an oblique plane; and are also acted obliquely upon by the pressure of the air, so that upon rising they appear bent upon the posterior margin, and upon sinking they also appear raised. This difference of posture is occasioned

---

[*] See Plates IX.—XIV.

by the irregularity of the nervures, for upon the anterior margin stiff, firm and inflexible nervures are found, but upon the posterior margin there are none, and in its vicinity there are only soft, thin and flexible ones. Also the oblique position of the wing to the direct plane of its motion effects the entire progression in the air; so that by the pressure of the air going obliquely against the surfaces of the wing, it acts like any other power upon an oblique plane which admits of being divided into two so called parallelograms of force, one of which is lost, but the other acts perpendicularly, yet somewhat less effectually than the original force. An equal force, which, like that of the stroke of the wing, presses downwards, presses also upwards in the stroke, which, likewise, may be divided into two forces, one of which is lost. We thereby acquire, therefore, two moving forces, both of which, it is true, stand perpendicularly to the wings, but yet cut each other in their direction, as the posture of the wing is different in its rising and sinking. These two moving forces consequently form, when we add to them their parallels, a third parallelogram of forces, and the diagonal of this parallelogram, drawn through the angles where both forces meet in the horizontal plane fixed by the centre of gravity, describes the line of flight.

Had not nature concurred in all these adaptations, had, for instance, the surfaces of the wings stood at right angles to the plane of motion of the wings, progression in the air could not have taken place, but the insect must necessarily have stopped short in the air upon the very first stroke of its wings, as the pressure from above and beneath would have been opposed in a linear direction, and, in consequence of the rapidity of the motion of the wings, would have neutralised each other. But this is actually the case in some volatile motions, namely, in hovering, or the stopping at one spot in the air. The insect can give voluntarily such a posture to the wings, that the propelling forces oppose each other in a linear direction, and the consequence of which is, that it remains hovering at one spot in the air. But it requires much exertion, whence it is that the strokes of the wings follow each other more rapidly, and the buzz during it is shriller and louder. We particularly observe this capacity of hovering in the *Diptera*, which, in consequence of the narrowness of the base of their wings, possess the power of moving the wings on all sides, and among them again we observe it most perfect in the *Bombylii, Anthracodea,* and *Syrphodea,* likewise in many true genera of flies, viz. *Miltogramma.* This order also is distinguished from the rest with respect to their flying apparatus, by being deficient in posterior wings, instead of which they possess balancers. We have before (§ 168) expressed our opinion of their supplying the place of posterior wings; modern experiments have confirmed this opinion in as far as they anatomically agree with the wings, namely, in consisting of a simple but somewhat more compact neurated membrane, which, as well as the membrane of the wing, is a continuation of the epidermis, and forms a closed, and, in these, a smaller pedunculated bag. Into this peduncle a tolerably thick trachea passes, but which, however, is not more than half as thick as the foot-stalk, and which, as soon as it reaches the knob, ramifies within it in many branches. With respect to the function of this poiser during flight, Schelver[*] has already proved that they are essential to it. He cut off the balancers of several *Diptera;* they indeed still flew, but only short distances. I have convinced myself of the correctness of his assertions by many experiments: every fly which was deprived of these organs had lost the art of flight; they indeed flew a distance of from one to two feet, but then rolled over, and fell to the ground. If then they were urged, they made a fresh endeavour to fly, but which again failed in the same way, as well as in all subsequent ones. To convince myself if any other mutilation of the body would affect the capacity of flight, I now likewise cut off the scales, but the result did not justify my expectations. *Eristalis tenax* flew with the same rapidity and skill after as before the operation, the same as if it had suffered no loss. Schelver, indeed [†], gives a different result to the same experiment, but he errs; I have frequently repeated my experiment, and always with the same consequence. The results to the capacity of flight from the loss of the legs are also not correct, for a *Tipula*, from which I removed every leg but one, flew as well as before the experiment, but the loss of all the legs appears to injure that operation.

§ 267.

Having thus explained the different motions of insects, we still have to make a few general observations upon the force and duration of muscular motion. Both attain a degree in insects which remain to be

---

[*] Beobacktungen über den Flugnnd das Jesumme einiger Zweiflugligen Insekten. Wiedemann's Archiv. vol. ii. Pt. 2, p. 212.
[†] Ib. No. 4.

discovered in other animals, and is probably nowhere surpassed. I think I discover the cause of this, for such small and insignificant creatures, remarkable phenomenon in the preponderance of their respiration; for wherever we meet with the function of respiration, and especially of the respiration of atmospheric air, preponderating, we find in conjunction the faculty of powerful and continuous muscular activity. Thus in this view also there is an affinity between insects and birds, as both classes exhibit the high importance of respiration to the entire organisation, and, as a consequence, the most powerful muscular activity.

The muscular power exhibits itself likewise in each of the four several modes of motion. The rapidity with which certain insects progress on foot is admirable, and presents itself in a very distinguished degree in the last family of the beetles, namely, the *Carabodea*. Their allies also, the *Staphylini*, display very rapid motions both in running and in flight, but especially in the former. Even among the most minute insects do we find rapid runners, for instance, among the flies, in which the genus *Tachydromia* of the family *Empidodea* derive their name from it. But it is not solely in the rapidity of their motions that we recognise the muscular power of insects, but also in their faculty of coursing about upon perpendicular walls and vibrating surfaces. This faculty they especially owe to their sharp claws, and to the clinging organs placed at the extremity of their foot. Many of these, namely, the *pulvilli* of the bees, wasps, and flies, are true sucking cups, which at first lay themselves flatly upon the object, and then by their concavity and rarefaction of the air beneath them clutch closely to it. But yet considerable muscular power is requisite for an animal to continue hanging with its whole body suspended by its own limbs by voluntary muscular force.

Still more admirable is the rapidity with which many insects that prepare for themselves cavities and subterranean dwellings are able to execute them. This rapidity also presumes great muscular power, and especially a great duration of the force. How rapidly, for instance, does not the larva of the ant-lion dig its pit, which can receive within its cavity at least a dozen insects of its own size! How speedily do not the fossorial wasps dig a hole for the reception of their eggs after they have first placed in it a caterpillar as large as themselves, and frequently weighing at least half as much again; and yet the common *Ammophila sabulosa* carries off its prey with the greatest facility! Who has not observed an ant-hill, and admired the industry with which these little creatures labour! Whom has the fact escaped that two or three pismires, or, according to the size of their prey, five or six of them, convey away a large caterpillar, which has by accident come within the limits of their fortifications, and bear it, notwithstanding its violent resistance, to their purposed spot! In such undertakings they frequently work in opposition to each other, and, under such circumstances, the colossus remains for a time immoveable, retained by equal powers acting in opposition to each other. Lastly, the burying-beetle, how quickly does it not bury its corpse! From four to six of them are sufficient to bury a moth several inches deep in the course of a quarter of an hour, and even a single beetle would execute this certainly monstrous labour in the course of an hour. Let us only reflect upon the capability of even a dozen men burying a whale in one hour; and yet the proportions with respect to size are more favourable to the execution of the project in this last case than in the former.

But the force and duration of muscular motion exhibits itself most conspicuously during flight. We admire the continuous flight of the migratory bird and the rapidity of the swallow, and yet the most common insects exhibit the same phenomena. The well-known dung-beetle flies in warm summer evenings with a rapidity which yields in nothing to the swallow, although it is not one-tenth part its size. The *Œstri, Tabani,* and flies which pursue cattle and horses with a voracious thirst for blood, excite by the humming noise of their flight the poor objects of their rapacity to escape by resorting to their quickness, but they do not thereby secure themselves from their persecutors, who, quicker than them, at last discover a suitable place of their body for the exercise of their parasitic occupation. We may frequently convince ourselves of their rapidity when riding upon a horse about to be attacked by an *Œstrus*, upon spurring it to its full speed, for it constantly remains in the vicinity of the animal, at about two or three inches distance from its body, and even at last, when convinced of the impossibility of executing its purpose, it flies away still faster than the rider, preceding him with incredible rapidity upon his own path. The most remarkable instance of this kind is possibly that related by an English traveller *, who was travelling with a steam-carriage that was

* In the Philosophical Magazine.

propelled at the rate of twenty miles an hour. This carriage was accompanied a considerable distance by a humble-bee (*Bombus subinterruptus*, Kirby), not merely with the same rapidity, but even with greater, as it not unfrequently flew to and fro about the carriage, or described zig-zag lines in its flight, in addition to which the wind was against them. Leeuwenhoek relates an instance in which a swallow in a long avenue pursued a *Libellula* of the genus *Agrion* for the space of an hour without catching it *; the little creature continued at least six feet below its pursuer, and at last escaped it. These few instances will convince us of the muscular power of insects. A detailed description of their different modes of flight would lead us too far; we consequently refer to Kirby and Spence's Introduction to Entomology: in the 23rd letter in the second volume will be found an interesting collection of such instances.

We have as yet cited no convincing instances of the duration of muscular motion, but they are in fact of rarer occurrence than those which exhibit the power and rapidity of flight. Certain phenomena, however, namely, the migrations which certain insects occasionally undertake, prove that even in this view the power of insects is not insignificant. As a wandering insect, the migratory locust is most celebrated. We do not here speak of the devastations that this terrible creature frequently produces, but merely of its flight. This is indeed but slow and heavy, for the locust flies but a short space above the ground, unless opposing objects intervene and cause it to rise higher, yet still of not shorter duration. In their migrations, which, in 1774, devastated Siebenburgen and Hungary, and which even advanced as far as Vienna, swarms were observed several hundred fathoms thick, one of which occupied four hours in passing a high tower, and thus long at least must every individual have flown. The intelligence of an American newspaper is still more striking †, which relates that the ship Georgia, upon its voyage from Lisbon to Havannah, upon the 21st of November, was in the vicinity of the Canary Islands, but yet 200 English miles from land. A calm came on, which was succeeded by a light wind from the north-east. Now for the space of a whole hour locusts fell upon the ship and the surrounding sea, which covered its entire surface, yet they were not at all fatigued, but jumped and endeavoured to escape their pursuers. If we even conclude that these

---

* Kirby and Spence, Introd. vol. ii. † Ib. vol. i.

locusts were conveyed even a considerable distance from land by high winds, yet must a great portion of their journey be ascribed to their own continuous muscular power, for otherwise they would have fallen much earlier into the sea, but as the abated wind no longer supported their flight like the violent one, their strength decreased and they fell down. Other instances are found of the continued voyages of *Libellulæ* to considerable distances. We have before mentioned the rapidity of their flight in a case observed by Leuwenhoek. Indeed these little creatures do not more excite our astonishment by the lightness and rapidity with which they fly, than by the duration of their motion. They incessantly swarm and hover about meadows, brooks and ponds, their favourite places of resort, without ever reposing any length of time; and as if they wished to excite still more the rage of their pursuer by their playful motions, they hover in front of him the moment he thinks to capture them, and yet do not allow him to attain his object. Several instances are on record of their migrating in vast multitudes. Kirby and Spence in their classical work * have cited several, and I myself have twice been an eye-witness of such migrations. They proceeded rather low, in innumerable multitudes, in an undulating body over the heads of their astonished spectators, without the least apparent cause of their collection or migration offering. On the evening of the day they dispersed, and on the following day, all the streets of the town over which the swarm passed were animated by the returning members of this numerous society.

We will here conclude our description of the motions of insects. Much that was highly interesting and much that might be still said upon these subjects from the natural history of these creatures, we have necessarily left unnoticed, as our object was but to state the chief results and most general phenomena. The very interesting work of Kirby and Spence contains such a multitude of these details, related in a charming style, that, had we wished to have been more copious, we could but have repeated their animated description. We must consequently refer our readers for what relates to the external relations of insects entirely to the work of those learned and well-informed gentlemen.

* Introduction, vol. ii. p. 12.

FIFTH CHAPTER.

OF THE SOUNDS AND NOISES EMITTED BY CERTAIN INSECTS.

§ 268.

THE investigation into the sounds emitted by insects during their motions does not inappropriately follow the description of these several motions, for the causes of these sounds appear to exist in these motions themselves. It was formerly supposed that the majority of these sounds were produced by the motion of the wings alone, without taking the least consideration of the apertures that are found upon the body of the insect, and through which, upon every respiration, air streams in and out. The mechanical friction of the wings together, or of the latter against the thighs, were considered as the causes of the loud cries of many grasshoppers and locusts, and also the vibration of the air caused by the strokes of the wings was considered as all that produced the hum in the flight of bees, wasps, and flies. If even the friction of portions of the integument together, for instance, of the pronotum upon the face of the mesonotum in many beetles is apparently the sole cause of the noises emitted by them, yet in the majority of other instances a mere mechanical friction is not sufficient to produce so strong and shrill a tone, for it is doubtlessly frequently the air streaming out of the stigma, and thereby putting vibratory bodies in motion, that produces these sounds: and just as easily as this is considered to be the cause of the noises emitted by the *Cicada*, may it also be proved to be that of the humming of the bees, wasps and flies. An experiment of this description is the theme of the present chapter: we therefore pursue the path, in our investigation of this subject, which nature seems to have traced, and shall commence with the sounds produced by mere mechanical friction, which will be followed by the hum heard during flight, and we shall conclude with such noises as are produced by peculiar organs.

§ 269.

By the friction of parts of the integument together, all those sounds are produced which we observe in beetles of the different families. The best known family in this respect, and which also produce the loudest sounds of this description, are the capricorn beetles. Almost all the species of this very extensive group emit, upon being touched, a tolerably loud, chirping, uniform sound, varying only in its intensity, and which is produced by the friction of the posterior margin of the pronotum upon the prolonged anterior portion of the mesonotum which projects somewhat into the cavity of the prothorax. Both the surfaces are very smooth, but not otherwise distinguished, so that the mere mechanical friction of the one against the other must be regarded as the sole cause of the sound produced. Indeed the same sound may be produced after the death of the creature, by rubbing the two parts together. Whether this sound have any determinate purpose, for instance, attraction, cannot be decided with certainty, but thus much is the case, that both sexes equally produce it, and, particularly, only in such situations as affect their free and voluntary motion. I have never found that any *Cerambyx* made it, unless disturbed or touched, and precisely when those restraints were most violent the sound was then loudest; for instance, when impaled by a pin, and he endeavoured with all his limbs to free himself from his thraldom. The same is the case in all other insects which produce sounds by the same means. We also detect similar sounds in the dung-beetles, viz. in *Geotrupes stercorarius, vernalis, Copris lunaris,* and others of the family of *Lamellicorns,* as in *Trox sabulosus.* The only difference is, that these beetles produce it by rubbing the abdomen against the elytra. Of this we may easily convince ourselves by taking such a beetle between our fingers, and turning its belly upwards; we then distinctly see the up and down motion of the abdomen. The sound is also prevented if a pin be introduced between the abdomen and the elytra, so that the former cannot touch the latter. The burying beetle (*Necrophorus vespillo*), the lily beetle (*Lema merdigera,* and another species of this genus), even a swimming beetle (*Hygrobia Hermanni,*) and many others, produce similar sounds in the same manner. Indeed, according to Latreille[*], the *Pimelias* emit similar sounds by rubbing

---

[*] Hist. Nat. tom. x. p. 264.

either their legs together or against the body. Bugs also (viz. *Cimex* [*Reduvius*] *subapterus*, De Geer*) and the *Mutillæ* (*M. Europæa*) produce such sounds upon being touched †, the former by the motion of its head, probably, therefore, by rubbing the occiput against the margin of the prothorax.

Hence, consequently, all these sounds are doubtlessly expressions of pain or displeasure, precisely as many of the higher animals only under similar circumstances make their voices heard, but have otherwise no use for them.

§ 270.

The second kind of sounds which insects produce are those which we hear during their flight, and especially by the *Hymenoptera* and *Diptera*, but also by the beetles, *Orthoptera*, and bugs. That these sounds are not produced solely by the flapping of the wings, we may easily convince ourselves, for if the wings be cut off, the fly produces its former sound, although somewhat weaker. Hence, therefore, the question occurs, Which is truly the organ of sound? The reply will readily suggest itself when we shall have first more closely investigated the conditions under which the noise originates. If any fly, for instance, the very common *Eristalis tenax*, be held by the legs, and the wings left free, it will endeavour by the violent motion of its wings to emancipate itself, and emits a loud buzzing sound. If the wings be half cut off, the vibration of the wings continues, and the sound becomes shriller; but if they be quite cut off, we observe their roots still in motion, and the sound becomes a little shriller, but also weaker than before. Thus, therefore, the presence of the wings has no influence upon the production of the sound, and at most but a trifling one in causing a change of tone. But there are other organs besides the wings upon the thorax which might be the causes of the sound, namely, the scales behind the wings, the poisers, and the spiracles which lie between the meso- and metathorax. If the scales be removed, the sound is not at all affected; it remains unchanged as long as the wings can vibrate. If the poisers, lastly, be cut off, this produces no difference of sound; and a fly deprived of all the external organs which tend to assist the flight, can, so long as the mere stumps of the wings remain to vibrate, produce a distinct but somewhat weaker and higher sound. The spiracle alone remains, therefore, to be considered as the cause and

---

* Mémoires, tom. iii. p. 190. † Kirby and Spence, vol. i.

instrument of the sound. To convince myself of this, I closed both the spiracles with gum, and then urged the fly to vibrate its wings, but it was scarcely to be induced to do so, yet when it occasionally tried it, no sound was produced; only after an interval, when the spiracle was freed from its stoppage by means of violent volatile motions, was the sound renewed. There is no doubt, therefore, that the air streaming from the spiracle is the cause of the sound, and that a body which by this draught of air is brought into vibration, must necessarily stand in connexion with the spiracle. I therefore cut out one of the spiracles, opened it carefully, separating the angles of the incision, and soon found what I sought, namely, the vibrating body, and not one only, but very many. That lip of the spiracle, namely, which lies posteriorly, and also somewhat inwardly, and which is lengthened upon its inner side, that is turned towards the commencement of the trachea, is formed into a small flat half-moon-shaped plate; upon this plate there are nine parallel very delicate horny leaves, the superior free sharp edges of which are bent somewhat downwards, so that the anterior one inclines a little over the rest. They are also higher towards the trachea, and towards the margin of the spiracle lower, and the central one is the largest, from which on each side they gradually become smaller and lower. Upon the air, which is driven with force out of the trachea, touching these laminæ, they are made to vibrate and sound precisely in the same manner as the vibrating of the glottis of the larynx. Thus, consequently, there is no insignificant analogy between the spiracles and the larynx, particularly of birds. To convince myself that it was merely the posterior spiracles of the thorax which emitted sounds, I likewise inspected the anterior ones, but found in them not the least trace of the just-described laminæ at the inner side of the posterior lip*.

We can now comprehend the reason of the change of tone on the loss of the wings. The vibrations of the contracting muscles can no longer be so intense in consequence of the loss of the organs made to vibrate, and in consequence of the weaker contractility, the air cannot be expired with the same degree of force. The tone is therefore weaker than when the wings were present; also, as Chabrier supposes, some air may escape through the open trachea of the wings which are cut off.

* Chabrier, in his Essai sur le Vol des Insectes, p. 45, &c., likewise explains the hum of insects as produced by the air streaming out of the thorax during flight: he also speaks of laminæ which lie at the aperture of the spiracle; but I cannot recognise from his description whether he saw these or others.

Whether the structure and situation of these vibrating bodies be the same in all buzzing insects, I cannot for the present decide. Another work, devoted exclusively to this subject, will impart all the details that I may discover; but for the present, thus much is determined. Delicate laminæ are found at the entrance of the posterior spiracles of the thorax, which are set in vibration by the streaming in and out of air, and which are the cause of the humming noises produced by bees and flies during their flight. In the buzzing-beetles, for instance, the cockchafer, I could not discover such laminæ near the aperture of the thoracic spiracles, and in these, therefore, the outward streaming air must be the sole cause of the tone; physics teach us also that a stream of air made to pass through any aperture with violence will produce a sound. In fact, the tone of the humming-beetles is weaker, proportionately, than that of the much smaller *Diptera*, and we may thence trace the cause of it to the deficiency of the vibratory laminæ.

§ 271.

The sounds that are produced by peculiar organs solely adapted to the purpose are found only in two orders, namely, in the *Orthoptera* and in the *Hemiptera*; in both cases they are in general peculiar to the male sex alone, and the females are then dumb. The male *Orthoptera*, in which we observe such organs of sound, bear them always at the base of the superior wings. Among these the genus *Acheta* and *Locusta* possess them. In both it is a round, flat, shining, very thin plate, seated at the base of the wing, immediately behind the large main nervures, which appear to produce the tone. The following is doubtlessly its mechanism. By means of the violent volatile motions which agitate the whole body, but during which the wings are not expanded, the air is driven out of the spiracles, and especially out of the central ones of the thorax, and thus bounds against the inflected external margin of the superior wing, which is pressed closely to the thorax. It must necessarily, therefore, to find an exit, rise beneath the wing, in order to escape from it beneath the posterior margin. Pursuing this path, it precisely strikes upon the just described elastic field of the superior wing, which vibrates through the pressure of the air, and consequently emits the sound. To corroborate this view I have cut off the wings of several locusts, but they never subsequently made any noise. It is here, therefore, the wings or the vibration of the elastic base of the wings, which produces the sound upon the motion of the wings. The shrill tones of the grasshoppers, locusts, and field crickets are therefore tolerably alike, varying merely in intensity. The tone of the cricket is probably the weakest, and that of the grasshopper perhaps the strongest. According to Kirby and Spence * the mole cricket is said to produce a dull tone resembling that of the goat-sucker, but I never heard it; and in the insect itself I have not been able to find anything analogous to a vocal organ.

In the remaining *Orthoptera* which possess a voice, namely, in the genus *Gryllus*, Fab. (*Acrydium*, Lat.), it is equally found in both sexes. The organs which produce it lie at the base of the abdomen, upon its first segment, one on each side, immediately behind the first abdominal spiracle. Each presents itself as a half moon-shaped cavity, closed at its base by a very delicate membrane, which is sometimes wholly free (*Gryllus stridulus*), and at others half covered by a triangular plate, projecting from the anterior margin. Close to the anterior margin of this fine membrane there is a small, brown, horny spot, upon which internally a delicate muscle is inserted, that runs over to a projection of the external horny plate which lies over and in front of the margins of the spiracle. By means of this small muscle it is made to vibrate, and consequently sound, when the whole body is agitated by the volatile motions. The sound thus produced is increased by a large air bladder, resembling a distended trachea, lying beneath the fine membrane, which re-echoes the sound like a sounding-board. But the tone thus produced is, however, weak, but it is loudest in the thence named *Gryllus stridulus*, and possesses no other differences than in intensity and weakness. Formerly it was thought that the friction of the posterior thighs against the wings was the sole cause of the chirping of these creatures, an opinion founded upon the contemporaneous motion of the wings and hind legs. Indeed, such a friction of the hinder femur against the inflected margin of the superior wing appears to participate in the mechanism of the sound, for even after the death of the creature I could produce a similar but much weaker sound by rubbing those parts together. Thus the allied genus *Acrydium*, F., (*Tettix*, Lat.) appears to produce the weak tone which it emits, for it has no vocal organ like *Gryllus*. The African genus *Pneumora*, Lat., also is said to produce a sharp chirping noise by the friction of the femur against the abdomen, or small ridges seated upon it. De Geer even detected the vocal organ of *Gryllus*, and considered it as such,

* Introd. vol. ii.

but he did not clearly comprehend its true mechanism * during chirping. Joh. Müller has latterly described it as an auditory organ †.

It is in the family of the *Cicada*, namely, the larger ones (*Tettigonia*, Fabr., *Cicada*, Lat.) that the voice attains its highest degree. In these creatures also we find the voice possessed exclusively by the males, and it is produced by an organ that has the greatest resemblance to that of the *Grylli*. In these it is also an elastic membrane, which is longitudinally folded and stretched over an oval horny ring seated immediately behind the first large spiracle of the abdomen, which, by a peculiar muscular apparatus, is made to vibrate. To each of these elastic membranes a strong conical muscle runs, which, with its broad basal surface, is attached to a plate-shaped horny tendon, the short pedicle of which is in connexion with the drum, and which originates at a central, furcate, horny process of the ventral plate of the second abdominal segment, the analogue of the furcate process of the breastplates. This muscle, together with the membrane, constitutes the vocal organ. If the abdomen, by the respiratory motion, be expanded or contracted, this muscle likewise stretches, whereby the membrane is made to vibrate, and consequently resound. The sound is increased, as in the *Grylli*, by means of a large air bladder, which lies at the lateral portion of the abdomen, and which closely covers the muscle as well as the membrane. In this cavity the sound rebounds, and thus proceeds more strongly from the insect. As external organs, there are, in addition to this vocal organ, some other parts which serve as a cover to it, but which are not of importance to the production of the voice, namely, two half circular horny plates, which spring from the margin of the horny integument in front of the drum, and more or less cover it; also beneath the drum in the centre of the ventral plate of the segment behind the coxæ of the posterior legs there are two small, oval, transparent fenestrations filled by a tense membrane, but which likewise appear to stand in no direct causal connexion with the voice. In the female also these little fenestrations are found, although less perfect, as well as the external valves which cover the drum; but there is not the least trace of this itself, nor of the muscle which moves it. The air-bladder the female likewise possesses, but it is smaller than in the male ‡.

* Mémoires, vol. iii. p. 471, Pl. XXIII. f. 2 and 3.

† Zur vergl. Physiol. der Gesichtssinne, p. 438.

‡ Compare, upon this vocal organ, the Treatise of Carus in the Analekten zur Naturwissenschaft und Heilkunde. Dresden, 1829. 8vo. p. 151.

At the close of this description of the several organs whereby insects produce peculiar sounds, we still have to speak of the sound and the mechanism that produces it in a *Lepidopterous* insect, the well-known death's head moth (*Acherontia atropos*, O.), which it emits upon being touched or disturbed. Reaumur and Rossi were both acquainted with the plaintive cry of this moth, and expressed their opinion that it proceeded from the friction of the tongue against the palpi. More recently, the experiments which Passerini has made to ascertain the organ which produces this sound have proved that it must lie somewhere in the head. He found a cavity in the head which has connexion with the false canal of the tongue (or rather, it should be said, with the central canal formed by the application of the two halves of the proboscis together), and about the entrance to which muscles lie which rise and sink alternately, and by these motions drive the air out of it and re-admit it. I do not, however, distinctly see how the mere streaming in and out of air could produce so loud a noise, if at the entrance there be not some body made to vibrate by its passage. Such must therefore be shown to exist, to explain fully the mechanism whereby the death's head moth produces its plaintive cry. I have not yet possessed a living individual of this otherwise not uncommon moth, I can therefore say nothing from my own experience; according to Duponchel*, whom we have to thank for the communication of Passerini's observations, there is a delicate membrane stretched between the eyes and the base of the proboscis, which certainly might be the cause of the sound if we adopt that the above cavity immediately adjoins it, and that it is made to vibrate by the air passing to and fro. Duponchel found this membrane also in *Sphinx Convolvuli*, which, however, produces no such sound; but then the internal cavity may be wanting whereby the faculty of causing the membrane to vibrate, as in the death's head, is lost, and it is consequently dumb. Passerini purposes making his observations public, which will then doubtlessly spread more light over this interesting subject. Thus much, however is certain, that the death's head moth makes a peculiar plaintive cry, which is produced by a particular organ seated in the head.

* See Annales des Sciences Naturelles, tom. xiii. p. 332 (Mar. 1828), and Heusinger Zethshrift für die Org. Phys. vol. ii. part iv. p. 442.

SIXTH CHAPTER.

OF SENSATION AND THE SENSES.

§ 272.

The functions of the nervous system are certainly among the most problematical of all the animal organs. Even in the higher animals, in which observation is more easy, and it has to contend with fewer difficulties, much still remains in impenetrable obscurity, notwithstanding the light that has been given in modern times to this portion of physiology; it will therefore strike us as less singular if the most general phenomena of the functions of the nervous system of the lower animals have not been satisfactorily explained. We move here in a field where simple experience frequently quits us, and a wider space is given to the fancy for its hypotheses and inventions. Yet we will keep ourselves as far as possible from this frequently misguiding conductress, and only endeavour to explain what our own experience and that of others enables us to do satisfactorily.

It accordingly appears confirmed that the nervous system, and chiefly the first chief ganglion or the brain, is the truly animating element which sets all the other organs in activity, and retains them in it. From the nervous system the muscle derives the irritability which puts it in action; by means of the nerves the intestinal canal is excited to digestion, and by the impulse of the same organs the sexual parts exercise the function appointed to them. Lastly, the nerve is the recipient and conductor of all immediate perceptions of external objects, and consequently the seat of sensation in general. Experience corroborates all these assertions. With respect to the effect of the nerves upon the muscles, we know from Rengger's * experiments, that after the nervous cord has been cut through at any part, the portion of the body which lies beyond that spot can exhibit no more motion. Rengger repeated this experiment in different kinds of caterpillars, some of which he cut through at a higher and others at a lower part of the

* Physiologische Untersuchungen, &c. p. 41.

ventral cord, and the same result always ensued. The legs which lay behind the scission no longer executed their function, but appeared as dead. The segments of the body also became flaccid and motionless, and only at isolated spots catchings of the muscles were to be observed. If the caterpillar were now carefully opened it was seen that the posterior portion of the stomach, namely, that which lay beyond the scission, no longer exercised its peristaltic motion, and that its contents no longer passed into the ilium, and also that the indigestible remains contained in this portion, as well as in the colon, were no longer ejected, but that entire part of the intestine appeared lifeless. The anterior portion acted however as usual; the caterpillar still ate and crept about with its anterior legs as if fully enjoying its preceding state, dragging its insensible lamed posterior portion along with it. If, lastly, the scission which separated the nervous cord were very near the head, so that thereby the lamed portion considerably preponderated over that still capable of motion, the latter was likewise hindered in the full exercise of its function, the caterpillar could then no longer crawl, although it exercised the requisite motions with its anterior legs, yet the preponderating lame posterior portion prevented its moving from the spot. Upon the nervous cord being separated at so high a spot the vital system was considerably affected, and the caterpillar soon ceased to live, but the further backwards the cut was made the longer the caterpillar lived, and the less was the exercise of its functions disturbed.

The irritability of the muscles beyond the point of separation was not yet wholly lost by the cutting, they speedily contracted after considerable pressure, but immediately became flaccid upon the removal of the exciting cause. The motion of the stomach also continued at its superior extremity, even when the nervous cord was cut through between the second and third pairs of legs, as this portion of the stomach received its own nerves from the pharynx; but if this nerve running from the pharynx was separated the peristaltic motion of the anterior portion of the stomach likewise ceased, and the entire function of digestion suddenly stopped.

Hence the brain appears the true seat of the animating forces, which are transmitted from it by means of the nerves to the most remote organs. The more distant therefore from the brain the wound takes place, the less is the disturbance that it occasions to the system, but the closer to the brain the more fatal is the operation.

But, to obtain a positive result, Rengger now made his experiments immediately upon the brain itself. He first laid it bare, and by some further incisions he removed it, and carefully closed the wound. The creature made, even during the operation, several convulsive motions of the whole body, which continued for a space of time after the removal of the brain, but then ceased, upon which the body appeared as in a paralysed state; the caterpillar could no longer eat, could no longer walk, but struggled first forwards and then on one side or the other; the peristaltic motion of the stomach disappeared, and only here and there did a fasciculus of muscles still catch. But, just as in the preceding experiments, the muscles retained their individual irritability, and reacted upon the application of stimulants. Rengger, that he might avoid the hemorrhage and other violent effects which necessarily occur in such operations, wounded and removed the brain with a red hot needle, but still the loss was accompanied by the same phenomena.

§ 273.

Treviranus' observations [*], however, do not harmonise with the conclusion deducible from the preceding communications of an important preponderance of the brain over the other ganglia. He saw a *Carabus granulatus* after its head was cut off still run about and seek a way to escape by; even after the removal of its prothorax the creature exercised its former voluntary motions, until, upon the removal of the mesothorax, they died away in irregular catches. The head of *Tabanus bovinus* was cut off, and it was then laid upon its back, when it made every possible endeavour to resume its usual position, and laid hold of a pencil offered it, and thereby crept up. Other insects, which were injured only upon one side, directed their motions towards the unwounded side. Thus an *Orgyia pudibunda*, O., of which the left antenna was cut off, kept running in a circle towards the right side, and continued this motion even when it had lost the entire left side of its head; when, however, the whole head was removed, the creature made violent exertions, running in circles, sometimes on one side, sometimes on the other. The same moth lived three days without its head, and continued to move its wings violently until its death. A different result was however produced when Treviranus removed the antenna of a wasp, for it moved indifferently on both sides. *Æschna forcipata*

---

[*] Das Organische Leben, vol. ii. part i. p. 192.

OF SENSATION AND THE SENSES. 477

also lived four days without its head, and even evacuated excrement during this period, but it could no longer move its wings, and was sensible only to pressure made at its caudal extremity. Treviranus also cites an experiment of Walckenaer, in which *Cerceris ornata* had its head cut off just as it was entering the cells of *Halictus terebrator*, when it still continued its endeavours, and even turned round towards the hole upon being placed in a contrary direction.

§ 274.

To endeavour to harmonise these discordant results, or rather, to ascertain to which the preference was truly to be given, I myself instituted the series of experiments which follow.

Among the *Coleoptera* it was chiefly the water-beetles, viz. *Dyticus sulcatus* and *cinereus*, which I made use of. I first took the male *D. cinereus*, and cut off its head, but the crop and proventriculus were also thereby removed from the body; from the very instant it totally ceased all voluntary motion, but upon pinching the feet severely with a pair of pliers a strong reaction of the muscular irritability was produced; the posterior legs immediately made three or four swimming motions, but they then remained in their preceding lifeless and gently bent position. This reaction continued, but constantly decreasing in force, for about half an hour, after which the severest pinching was not able to produce it.

I opened the breast of a lively female *Dyticus sulcatus*, between the second and third pairs of legs, so that the nervous cord was laid bare. With a pair of pliers I now laid hold of the nervous cord, and removed it; the left posterior leg was immediately lamed, but the right one and all the four anterior legs still exercised their voluntary motions, and the creature could still tolerably swim when thrown into the water. When placed upon its back, the contractions of the muscles were distinctly seen. These continued for about an hour, the posterior legs then lost all motion, and even their irritability, whilst the anterior ones still possessed it, but yet a decrease of animation was clearly seen, and in about three hours afterwards it was completely dead.

In another male *Dyticus sulcatus* I separated the nervous cord close to the soft connecting membrane between the pro- and meso-thorax; in the course of a few seconds the motion of the four posterior legs ceased, whilst the anterior ones retained their perfect mobility, but signs of irritability still presented themselves. The anterior legs, even after four hours, still exercised their voluntary motions, although with less vivacity, but in the evening the insect was dead.

In a fourth perfectly animated male *Dyticus sulcatus*, by an incision which removed the horny integument of the head, I laid the brain bare. Immediately much yellowish brown green blood streamed forth; it was perfectly clear and viscid, and covered the entire wound, and stood upon the naked part like a drop of water. I thus allowed the insect to go; it retained its complete motion, but moved all its limbs slowly and convulsively as if severely injured. I now removed the brain by means of pliers; the insect immediately became motionless as dead, and did not move a single joint as long as it lay upon its belly. Upon my teasing it, after about a minute it endeavoured to cling with its legs, but this motion appeared to proceed rather from the irritability of the muscles than from its own volition. I now laid it upon its back, and it directly made its usual swimming motions, during which, as when swimming, the anterior pair were drawn closely up to the breast. These motions lasted uninterruptedly as long as the insect lay upon its back; if I laid it upon its belly they ceased, and the insect again moved no limb. I now cast it into the water, when it swam upon the surface with the greatest rapidity, impelled by incessant natatory strokes, striking all its comrades that it met on one side by the violence of its motions, and continued thus uninterruptedly for about half an hour. It did not, however, descend to the bottom, nor did I see any respiratory action in its abdomen. After this, upon the gradual decrease of the force of its strokes, it lay upon the surface with distended legs, but displayed irritability upon the legs being pinched; lastly, towards evening, the experiment having been made about 11 a. m., all life had vanished.

The brain was similarly laid bare in a female *Dyticus sulcatus*, but the incision passed obliquely through the right eye, and wounded its right hemisphere, whereby the insect lost the voluntary motion of the left posterior foot. I now removed the brain entirely, and the insect became instantly lifeless, but in the course of a few seconds the legs recovered their motion, but not to the same extent as in the preceding experiment. Cast into the water, this female did not swim like the former insect, but lay with extended legs, moving with a catch some of its joints; these motions could be perceived, even after an hour, upon effective excitement, but towards evening, as in the preceding experiment, the beetle was perfectly dead.

With grasshoppers I have made the following experiments.

A small *Gryllus* (*Acrydium*, Lat.) I opened in the breast, between the intermediate and posterior thighs, and removed the large ganglion lying there. The insect thereby immediately lost the mobility of the posterior extremities, and was also very much enfeebled, but yet crept about by means of its four anterior legs. Having accidentally soiled its antennæ, it made stroking motions towards them with its left anterior leg to cleanse them, and upon my taking it up by them, it made very active exertions with the anterior legs to free itself. I now made an incision in the same individual through the membrane of the neck, whereby the nervous cord was separated, but the œsophagus not injured. The creature at first still moved its anterior legs, and in them there was a powerful reaction upon pressure, and it trembled for a time afterwards, but otherwise exhibited few signs of life; it lay lifeless upon one side; it did not even lie upon its belly; but yet there were still catchings in the feet when nipped with the tweezers, but not in the large posterior thighs. In ten minutes the motion of the legs considerably decreased, and in half an hour the animal was entirely dead.

A second somewhat larger and also very active *Gryllus* I again cut through the membrane of the neck; the insect, immediately after the incision, made violent movements with its thighs, which cast off one of its posterior legs; the other legs exhibited irritability as often as I pinched them, but, after the lapse of a minute, it lost all voluntary motion, it could no longer walk, and remained quietly lying upon its side when so placed. In half an hour it was dead.

I have besides made experiments in *Diptera*, namely, in some species of *Eristalis*.

I separated the nervous cord of a lively *Eristalis nemorum*, closely in front of the middle legs; those legs immediately lost their motion as well as the right posterior leg, but it still crept about by means of its anterior legs and left posterior one. These motions continued, but its course was not straight, but inclining obliquely to the left. I now made the incision deeper, to be perfectly convinced that I had thoroughly separated the nervous cord. The left posterior leg now lost its motion, but the fly still crept with its anterior pair, but it could no longer fly, as was the case upon the first incision. I now cut off its head; immediately all the motion of its anterior legs ceased, but the proboscis of the separated head still throbbed when I drew it from the cavity of the mouth. These catchings continued for a quarter of an hour, but the body was entirely dead.

In another lively *Eristalis nemorum* I made an incision transversely through the eyes, and seriously injured the brain; the insect, however, still retained the perfect mobility of all its legs, and crept about, although but slowly; shortly, however, its strength decreased, it reposed quietly, and but slightly moved upon excitement; in an hour it was quite dead, but still displayed slight irritability of the muscles upon violent external excitement.

§ 275.

From these experiments, and those communicated by Rengger, we may deduce the conclusion, that after the separation of the nervous cord at any part, the voluntary motion of the organs seated beyond the point of incision is lost, but that the irritability of the muscles, that is to say, their power of re-action upon external excitement, is retained by these organs as long as life is still present, but that it disappears with it. It thence consequently follows that the nerve passing to the muscle supplies the place of external excitement, and that therefore the will can act upon the muscles only through the medium of the nervous system. These experiments also confirm the assertion so frequently repeated, that the brain is the principal of all the ganglia, and that the causes of all the vital phenomena exist in it, and proceed from it. The instance in which the male *Dyticus* swam about a considerable time after the removal of its brain appears to contradict this conclusion, but I am still very strongly inclined to perceive nothing but irritability in the rowing of the feet. The entire uniformity of the motion speaks strongly in favour of this opinion, as well as the circumstance likewise that the beetle deprived of its brain did not execute these motions so long as it lay upon its belly on a dry surface. We may also deduce from these experiments, that still for a short time after the removal of the brain, not merely signs of life but even proofs of voluntary motion present themselves, which are the stronger the more imperfect the injury to the brain may be. We may here class also the experiments made by Treviranus, but I doubt their entire accuracy. How could a beetle seek ways to escape when all the organs whereby it might perceive such opportunities were removed from it? Walckenaer's observation is more probable, that the *Cerceris* repeated several times its preceding endeavours after the loss of its head; it was merely a continuation of the undertaking resolved upon previously to the mutilation, but which, however, could only continue as long as the remainder of the nervous cord still conveyed the excitement impressed upon it by the will; that, however, after the alteration of the direction of the motion the wasp absolutely resumed its previous position, I very much doubt, it is improbable in every case, and my experiments do not tend to substantiate it. Treviranus' remark also, that the *Orgyia* lived for three days after the loss of its head, excites just suspicion, for in all similar experiments of mine life had perfectly vanished in the course of a few hours. But I am acquainted with other instances in which the *Noctuæ*, after having been killed with red hot needles, and extended upon the setting-board for a week, have not only moved the abdomen upon the application of an excitement, but still also continued to lay eggs. I think the reason of this may be found in the independent irritable life of the sexual organs, which, excited by the continual stimulus of the eggs contained within them, continue laying them, and as long as eggs exist within them display signs of irritability. To this class, consequently, the instance cited by Treviranus may be placed; life no longer truly existed, but merely the reactive power of the sexual organs, and they did react when excited by external stimulants, but I consider the observed motion of the wings as very doubtful; for the needle thrust through the thorax and the other red hot one would doubtlessly have had the same effect as removing the ganglion situated in the thorax; the red heat would doubtlessly have deprived it of its activity, and thereby the motion of the parts with which it supplied nerves would necessarily have been destroyed. We frequently observe in insects thus mutilated a still continued motion, for instance, in the antennæ and the parts of the mouth, when the legs and wings have entirely lost theirs.

§ 276.

The influence which the nervous system exercises upon the several organs of the body may thus therefore be generally stated; we have still to consider more closely the nerves as the recipients of external excitement, in short, as the organs of sensation in particular. It would be difficult to obtain a satisfactory result upon this subject by experiments upon insects, for, although we perceive that they are sensible to external excitement, yet we cannot distinctly prove that they receive these sensations through the nerves. We can maintain nothing further with certainty than that in insects similar organs are found, to those whereby the higher animals, and particularly man, feels, and that therefore, by means of these organs, insects likewise perceive the presence and quality of the external objects which their body touches. But we know, upon the other side, by means of direct observations, that insects do feel, and we may therefore deduce from the preceding opinion, founded upon analogy and these observations, that the nerves of insects are likewise the organs of sensation.

Observations confirmatory of the presence of sensation in insects daily offer; we have but to look at some creeping insect, and observe how it convinces itself of the presence of an object by touching it with its antennæ, and then carefully avoiding it; and besides, insects that are reposing are disturbed from their repose by any ungentle touch, and upon a repetition of the disturbance quit the spot; and lastly, pupa, upon the least touch, and by their rapid and serpentine motions, instantly evince a feeling of displeasure. In many pupæ the sensation of inimical influence is so delicate as scarcely to be credible; the mere opening of a box in which they may have been placed disturbs them, and, indeed, some of the slightly clothed pupa of the *Coleoptera*, whose natural situation is beneath the earth or in dark situations, instantly move, and with considerable force, if a ray of light be allowed to fall upon them, but they are peculiarly sensitive to bright sunshine.

But we are most distinctly convinced of the sensation of insects upon impaling them for the collection. Even the mere pressure of the pin produces unpleasant sensations, which the insect expresses by the rapid and painful motion of its limbs; upon its point proceeding still further the expression of disagreeable feeling increases by its more rapid and unnatural contortions, and I have frequently observed, that at the moment when probably the pin passed through the ganglion, and when the insect appeared as it were suddenly lamed by its excessive pain, it extended all its limbs, and even its oral organs, and then ceased for some seconds all motion. This motion continues for some space of time, frequently from a week to a fortnight, as long as the insect is teased, but it does not appear to happen in repose, or if the insect be enclosed in a dark situation, at least I have observed many instances in which, under such circumstances, the insect did not move. Hence, as well as from the subordinate sensibility of the nervous system of the lower animals, we may conclude that insects thus impaled no longer feel any pain, and that their motion is produced merely by their endeavours to free themselves from a disagreeable restraint. In favour of the adoption of this opinion the deficient formation of the blood in insects speaks, in consequence of which no inflammation and suppuration can take place. Inflammation, however, or the immediate touching of the nerve laid bare, by the air or other extraneous bodies, occasions our feeling pain from a wound, and as long as this irritable condition does not occur no pain is felt. This irritable condition, however, can never take place in insects, they having no blood-vessels and cellular membrane, through which the irritable matter may transude, but merely a lymph, circulating freely in the body. This lymph encompasses the extraneous body, the pin, coagulates around it, and thus perfectly protects the nerves from its influence. According to this view the majority of impaled insects die of hunger, and not by mechanical wounding; if, for instance, the thoracic ganglion or the nervous cord be not separated; for so serious an injury to the nervous system the preceding experiments have shown must speedily produce death; but yet I would not be understood as approving of that certainly very unnecessary torture to which poor captured insects are exposed by the young and old, as objects of their pleasure. In support of this opinion we may still mention that many impaled insects still continue the exercise of their most usual corporeal functions; for instance, still eat, still evacuate excrement, creep about with the pin through them, and sometimes even fly, and lastly, the *Lepidoptera* even copulate in this state, and, a still more common occurrence, is their continuing to lay eggs.

§ 277.

Upon passing from these introductory observations upon the functions of the nervous system in general to the senses themselves, we may maintain, in reference to these, that insects are not deficient in any important one found in the superior animals. At the end of the preceding division we described the organs of the several senses, but we yet found only one certain organ of sense, which, with few exceptions, is discoverable in all insects, and this was the eye. We, nevertheless, endeavoured to discover the other organs of the senses, proceeding from determinate observations which prove that insects have perceptions which can only be received by senses of touch, taste, smell, and hearing, and we then found several organs, each individual one of which admitted of being referred to some one of these senses, either from analogous situation or structure to that of the same organ of sense in the higher animals, and partly from the deficiency of a satisfactory proof of a different function of the organ. Thus we recognised in the palpi organs of touch, in the tongue the seat of taste, in the mucous membrane of the tracheæ the sense of smell, and in the antennæ, lastly, we discovered the instruments of hearing. The mode whereby the insect receives perceptions through these organs will certainly not divaricate from that found in the superior animals. Touch, taste, and smell require the direct application of the investigating organs to the investigated object, and so soon as this takes place the insect perceives. We have convinced ourselves by experiment that an insect feels objects all over with its palpi which it wishes to inspect for food or other purposes, but that the tongue tastes, and the mucous tunic of the tracheæ smells, can only be made probable. With respect to the latter, it is contradictory to the views of very learned naturalists, namely, Kirby and Spence * and Treviranus, who both adopt as the organ of the sense of smell a peculiar one standing in connexion with the mucous tunic of the mouth. With respect to its situation above the mouth, it has certainly the analogy of all the other animal classes in favour of it, and their opinion would even on that account merit entire approbation if absolutely the organ of which these authors speak could there be found. But this is not the case, and even Treviranus convinced himself by multitude of experiments of its absolute deficiency, and so suggested the opinion that the mucous tunic of the mouth was likewise the organ of smell, and that therefore the sense of smell was especially to be ascribed to haustellate insects only. Kirby and Spence, however, to whom the striking contrary proof exhibited in the extremely keen smell of the burying beetle was probably present, decide absolutely in favour of a peculiar organ of this sense, lying beneath the clypeus, and which they call the nose, and which borders upon the mucous tunic of the mouth. In the burying beetle they say they have discovered this organ in the form of two circular fleshy cushions, which are covered by a beautiful and finely transversely striped membrane; the same also in *Dyticus marginalis*, in which it is further provided with a pair of warts; as also in *Œschna viatica*. But the investigations of other anatomists do not confirm these discoveries. If such an organ really existed at the spot indicated, Straus would certainly have seen it in the cockchafer; and I believe I may assert, that in several endeavours

* Introduct. to Entom. iv. Letter xlv.

I made expressly for the purpose in *Dyticus marginalis* and *Calosoma sycophanta*, *Hydrophilus piceus*, and *Scarabæus vernalis* that it must have shown itself if it had been present at the spot mentioned. In freshly opened insects I could discover really nothing of the kind, and in those which had been long immersed in spirits I saw the space in front and between the clypeus and the most approximate organs filled with nothing but coagulated blood. I cannot therefore determine in favour of Kirby and Spence's opinion, but prefer the earlier hypothesis, that the internal surfaces of insects receive smell, and supply the place of an organ especially devoted to that sense.

The majority of modern physiologists and entomologists agree in explaining the antennæ as organs of hearing, as we have already remarked. Kirby and Spence's representation, whose names were inadvertently omitted to be mentioned there as the authorities for our opinion, conveys so much conviction that we may almost consider it as settled, although we must at the same time admit that all the difficulties are not yet solved: we have already indicated above that the real perception of sound may possibly depend upon the trembling produced by the vibration of the air in organs so easily moved as are the antennæ, and we here repeat this opinion as the explanation of the mode by which insects hear. According to Kirby and Spence, Wollaston suggested this opinion, and even supposed that insects could perceive much more delicate tones than our ears are capable of distinguishing, from their very much greater irritability. This irritability, however, in consequence of the much harder integument in which insects are enveloped, can be possessed only by the antennæ, which are so easily moveable, and which, indeed, in many insects are in a constant state of motion; even the slightest vibration of the atmosphere must be sufficient to put into motion an organ of the structure of the antennæ of a gnat, and thereby apprise its possessor of the approximation of some occurring change; this is equally the case with the delicate and easily moveable antennæ of the *Grylli*, and indeed of all insects furnished with long antennæ; the same with the short fan-shaped flaps, as well as with the delicately haired joints forming a knob in the antennæ of other insects; the very structure of all betrays the possibility of very delicate perception. Organs of touch they cannot be, for their surface is too hard and horny, and besides, all insects have for this purpose organs furnished with a very delicate touching surface. Hence the mode whereby insects hear will necessarily differ from the hearing of the superior animals, and in reference to it we may possibly be allowed to surmise that they do not possess the power of distinguishing tones; but in opposition to this, it may be mentioned, that their females would not be able to distinguish the luring tones of the males from any other sounds, and consequently their possession of a means of indicating their presence would not much serve them; and also the signs of recognition among the bees, to which we shall have occasion to return below, is opposed to it. There are also other instances of a mode of communication among insects, by means of peculiar sounds.

§ 278.

The way in which insects see by means of their eyes will be best explained by Joh. Müller's investigations [*]. With respect to simple eyes, we know, partly from their structure and partly by the direct observations of Reaumur [†] and Hooke, who closed these simple eyes, and then never detected the creatures moving in the direction of these eyes, and that they only then flew whither their compound eyes could survey their path, that these vertical points are actually eyes. Joh. Müller has made it probable, from the structure of these eyes, that their refraction must be very great, in as far as each ray of light suffers a fourfold refraction, the first of which is produced by the convex cornea, the second by the anterior convex surface of the lens, the third by the posterior convex surface of the lens, and the fourth, lastly, by the convex surface of the glassy body itself. This disposition presumes an indistinct distant sight, as the object is thereby too great to be distinctly seen, but a well defined and distinct short sight. And, indeed, we find in all the *Arthrozoa*, which have merely simple eyes, for instance, in the *Arachnodea*, the power of sight agreeing with this view, for it is only closely that spiders can see accurately, at a distance the object appears to vanish from them. If we apply this to the simple eyes of insects we shall find in them, likewise, that the function of their simple eyes is adapted for a distinct close sight, and particularly for small objects, which are difficult for the large field of vision of the compound eyes to survey. They hence appear to make most use of their simple eyes in narrow spaces, and as these simple eyes, as well as compound eyes, are almost exclusively found in those insects which feed upon the

---

[*] Zur Vergleichenden Physiologie des Gesichtssinnes, p. 332, &c.
[†] Mémoires pour servir à l'Hist. des Insectes, tom. v, part i, p. 363.

juices of flowers or other vegetable substances, they may probably be of especial service to them for the discovery of this pabulum, particularly to those which thrust themselves into the flowers themselves, and there seek the nectaries.

The compound eyes of insects appear constructed for vision at greater distances, and to embrace a wider horizon, and yet by means of these only are they enabled to have a distinct close sight. They are so composed that each individual facet can survey but a small space of the entire field of vision, so that each contributes to the perception of all the objects comprised within that field ; but each separate one does not at the same time see all such objects, whence the insect must receive as many forms of objects in its eye as there are individual facets to the eye. This consequence of a common and yet subsidiary vision of these facets springs partly from the immobility of the eyes, and partly it arises from the circumstance that only those rays of light which fall in a right line upon a facet of the eye, which itself forms the segment of a circle, can reach the optic nerve of this facet, whereas all others are withheld by the pigment which partly separates the individual glass lenses* from each other, and partly circularly surrounds the margin of the crystalline lens beneath the cornea. Hence it results that the nearer the object is, the more obliquely do all but the perpendicular rays of light fall upon the facet, and therefore contribute so much the less to the production of the image; the object

---

* Treviranus, even in his latest work (Gesetze und Erscheinungen des Organischen Lebens, neu dargestellt, vol. ii. Pt. 1, p. 77), denies the presence of this glass lens in the eyes of all insects. Joh. Müller has so far modified his earlier assertion that the *Diptera* in lieu of it exhibit beneath the cornea a transparent crystalline layer, which beneath each facet of the cornea stands in connexion with a filament of the optic nerve, but that in all insects there is either a true crystalline lens or something analogous. According to Treviranus, the lenses serve "to shorten the distance of the concentrated rays from the divisions of the cornea to the extreme ends of the filaments of the optic nerve, there where the light, owing to these divisions, is but slightly refracted, and the refracted rays form a very long arch." But, according to Joh. Müller, their object appears to be rather to concentrate into one point the rays falling in a right line.—But the observation communicated by Treviranus is more important, namely, that the filaments of the optic nerve proceed at first from the clavate optic nerve itself in large stems, whence subsequently radiating branches divaricate, as has been figured by Straus in the cockchafer (Pl. IX. f. 6). In *Œschna forcipata* he even saw the nerves run parallely to the plate which forms the inner circumference of the eye, and thence proceeded the filaments destined to supply the divisions of the cornea.

consequently is most clearly seen closely, and more indistinctly at a distance. If now each facet of the eye can survey but one small portion of the field of vision, yet will the entire eye be able to survey a field the larger in proportion to the size of the segment of the circle it forms and to the convexity of its arch. Therefore, the larger the eye is, and the more convex, the wider will be its horizon. The various structure of the eyes of insects agrees also with this. Males, which are appointed by nature to seek the female, have larger eyes than the latter. Insects which live in and upon their pabulum itself, have small and flat eyes, like all parasites; others, again, which have greater difficulties to contend with in procuring their food, as those insects which live upon prey, like the *Carabodea, Dytici, Libellulæ,* &c., have either large or greatly convex hemispherical eyes. The position of the eyes also corresponds with their size and convexity; flat eyes, which are able to survey but a short space only, are always more approximate and placed more anteriorly than laterally, and are frequently contiguous, as in the male *Syrphi.* Spherical and very convex eyes are placed laterally, and their axis is frequently directly opposite, but they yet harmonise by their greater convexity with their field of vision, as is distinctly observable in the large *Carabi.* But the fields of vision of the two eyes do not affect each other, there still remains a free space between the eyes, which the insect can only survey by turning its head. Sometimes, to compass a still wider field of vision, a complete divarication from the usual form becomes necessary, as in *Gyrinus,* a division of each eye, the one half of which lies upon the vertex, and the other half is placed at the lower surface of the head; the latter is for the discovery of food which the insect finds in the water, and the former to secure it from its enemies which approach out of the water; or, as in some male *Ephemeræ,* in which two large flat eyes lie upon the vertex, and two smaller but more convex ones are found at the margin of the head.

Joh. Müller appends to his beautiful and apparently perfectly successful explanation of the sight of insects, the result of which we have condensed above, some other more general observations, which we cannot forbear briefly introducing here. Thus the relative proportions of the distinctness of the image in various eyes increases, according to him, in proportion to the size of the sphere of which the surface of the eye forms a segment, with the number and smallness of the facets, and with the length of the transparent lens. Whereas the power of sight at a distance or close does not depend upon the structure of the eyes; every compound eye which distinctly discerns objects at a distance, produces also closely a clear image of it. But the larger the individual facets are, and the smaller the spheres formed by them, and the brighter the pigment deposited between the lenses, the more indistinct does the image of the object seen become, and in such a structure a better image is formed of distant objects, but a worse one is seen of approximate objects, for the rays are more diverging in consequence of their proximity, whereas they run more parallely from every point of an object at a distance; in the former case, therefore, it passes through the brighter pigment into the contiguous glass lenses, and renders obscure the image that should be there formed upon the retina.—The apparent size of the object seen corresponds only with its true size when the convexity of the eye is perfectly spherical and concentrical with the convexity of the optic nerve; in every other case the apparent size of the image will not correspond with its true size, and the image must therefore appear distorted. Hence all elliptical or conically arched eyes wil see worse than those forming the segment of a circle.—As the structure of the eye does not differ in water insects and those which avoid the light from that of day insects and those which live upon the land, namely, the pigment is by no means brighter in the former, as Marcel de Serres affirms, consequently their sight must fully correspond with the sight of day insects.

With respect to the difference of structure of the eyes in larvæ to those of the perfect insect, in insects with an imperfect metamorphosis, it consists especially in the relative size of their compound eyes. These are always smaller in larvæ, but continue increasing with every moult, until they at last attain their full size. In the large eyes of the larvæ of the *Cicada* no facets are observed; these, therefore, gradually distinctly develope themselves. The cornea of the eye is changed also with the change of skin, which very well admits of a transformation. Whereas simple eyes are never found in larvæ with an imperfect metamorphosis; they present themselves only as bright spots where they are subsequently to appear.—The majority of larvæ of insects with a perfect metamorphosis have merely simple eyes, and, indeed, exactly where the compound eyes afterwards appear; many entirely want eyes, and a few, as the larvæ of the gnats, have already compound eyes. With respect, therefore, to the development of the eyes during the metamorphosis, it appears to take place especially during the pupa state, and, indeed, by the compound eyes being gradually developed from the simple ones. Pupæ, however, have the entire cornea immediately after stripping off their larva-skin; and in the pupa of *Stratiomys* Joh. Müller found beneath it the glass lens and the layer of pigment yet but slightly coloured. If now this composition of compound eyes from simple ones actually takes place, which cannot very well be doubted, it may serve as a guide to the explanation of the parts of the compound eye, which I would thus explain: the glass lens corresponds with the glassy body, the lens with the thick cornea, and this latter with a superficial thin layer of the entire cornea, which it likewise is, and which is peeled off during the metamorphosis. After the last moult this layer grows to the lens, and they then both appear as identical, but, in relation to the other parts, merely as a thick layer of the cornea. Hence the compound eyes of insects consist of the same parts as the simple eyes.

SEVENTH CHAPTER.

THE LUMINOUSNESS OF INSECTS.

§ 279.

THE peculiar light which many insects, but chiefly beetles, display, is a very remarkable phenomenon. We have deferred its consideration to the end of somatic physiology, as it does not appear to stand in direct connexion with either of the four chief functions of the animal body, but may be considered rather as the result of an entirely peculiar vital phenomenon, the cause of which has been by no means thoroughly ascertained. We will defer communicating the results of the experiments made upon this highly interesting subject to the end of this chapter, and first mention those insects in which this peculiar luminousness has been observed.

The majority of them belong to the *Coleoptera*, and indeed to two families which also in other respects present a tolerable affinity. These families are the *Elaters* and the *Lamprodea*. Among the *Elaters* we know as luminous the *E. noctilucus, E. ignitus, E. lampadion, E. retrospiciens, E. lucidulus, E. lucernula, E. speculator, E. Janus, E. pyrophanus, E. luminosus, E. lucens, E. exstinctus, E. cucujus, E. lucifer,* and *E. phosphoreus**. In all of these there are two bright oval, convex spots upon the thorax, which, after death, are of a greenish yellow, and whence light, whilst living, streams forth, and in addition to which there are two other spots upon the abdomen that are luminous, and which, during repose, are concealed beneath the elytra. Indeed, the whole inside of the body is luminous, but it is concealed by the impenetrable integument, and only sometimes upon the very great expansion of the abdomen is it perceptible through the divisions of the segments. All the named species are found in tropical America, and, according to Sloane, repose during day in dark shady places, and only fly during dusk and at night, when they betray themselves by their light; but, according to Sieber, they also fly at noon in the sunshine, but then exhibit no light. Their light is of a bright blue-white colour, and in the larger species, for instance, in *E. noctilucus*†, it is so strong, that, by its aid, small writing may be read at night if the luminous spots be passed regularly over the lines. Some naturalists who have had the opportunity of observing the insect in its native country (Spix) assert that they have found beneath the luminous spots a yellowish glandular mass, to which a multitude of branches of the tracheæ are distributed from the approximate main stems. These are the true luminous bodies whence the light streams forth either brightly or dully, according to the quantity of air the insect admits to them by respiration. It is also said that the insect can prevent the emission of all light by, according to Spix, preventing the admission of any air. Amongst the natives, all these insects are called *Cucujos* or *Cucujii;* they use them as ornaments for their dresses by night, and they are worn by the females especially as ornaments to the head-dress, and the Indians are said to bind them to their feet on a journey, to enable them to discern their road more distinctly. According to Piedro Martire ‡, the inhabitants of Saint Domingo keep the luminous *Elaters* in their rooms

---

* See Illiger in the Magazin der Geselsch. naturf. Freunde zu Berlin, vol. i. p. 14.

† See Curtis in Zoological Journal, 1827, No. 2, p. 379. Heusinger Zeitschrift, vol. iii. Pt. 1, p. 137.—Thons Archiv. vol. ii. Pt. 2, p. 63.

‡ In Kirby and Spence, vol. ii. p. 462.

at night, which destroy the gnats that would otherwise disturb persons sleeping; but this tale does not merit belief, as the *Elaters* are well known not to be carnivorous, but feed upon nectar and pollen. Yet by the light they distribute they may probably chase away the gnats.

§ 280.

The European *Lampyri* were known as luminous earlier than the *Elaters*. The ancients were acquainted with this faculty*. The Romans called them *cicindelæ*, the Greeks λαμπυρίδες; but it does not appear that they distinguished several species; and, as in southern Europe, the *Lamp. Italica* is the luminous species, it is doubtlessly upon this that they made their observations. Besides this, there are three other species in Europe, *L. noctiluca*, *L. splendidula*, and *L hemiptera*, the second of which is common with us (Germany), the first is found in more northern countries, and the third in southern ones. The last is not deficient in the phosphoric light, as Illiger first thought, and, probably, it is also present in the numerous extra-European species of this genus. The most recent experiments upon their luminousness have been made chiefly upon the *L. noctiluca*, which is common in the south of England and in Sweden, by J. Murray †; upon *L. splendidula* by Macartney ‡ and Macaire§; and upon *L. Italica* by Carus ||. *L. hemiptera* was observed and described in detail by Müller ¶, and he also first discovered its luminousness, although the light was but feeble. Both sexes are luminous, as also are the *Elaters*, but the light is strongest in the female. In the *Lampyri* it does not stream from the thorax, but from the posterior extremity of the abdomen, where also, even after death, there are spots which are brighter than the rest of the integument, and it is these especially which shine. Besides the difference of light in the two sexes, there are others between them even in their external form. In *L. noctiluca*, the largest of the European species, the male, which has wings and elytra, is of a uniform brownish grey, with a reddish grey margin to the pronotum : the apterous female has a similarly shaped back, which is, however, of

* Plinii Hist. Nat. Lib. 18. c. 66. 2.—Aristot. Hist. An. 1. 3.
† Experimental Researches, Glasgow, 1826.
‡ Schweigger's Jour. &c. vol. x. p. 409.—Gilbert's Annal. vol. lxi. p. 113.
§ Gilbert's Annal. vol. lxx. p. 265.
|| Analekten zur Naturw. u Heilkunde, p. 169.
¶ Illiger's Magazin. vol. iv. p. 175, &c.

but one colour, and it has a yellow-white, thin-skinned fat abdomen. In both, the luminous spots present themselves as four bright points, two of which are upon the antepenultimate abdominal segment, ad two upon the next one. In the smaller *L. splendidula*, the male, which is also winged, and is of a brown grey, has a bright glassy spot upon the convex margin of the pronotum : the female, which is entirely of a whitish yellow, and is brown only on the centre of the pronotum, has very short oval elytra, which merely cover the margin of the mesonotum, but it has no wings. In both the luminous parts are two transverse bands on the ventral side of the two penultimate abdominal segments, yet in the female the whole abdomen distributes but a weak light. With respect to size, *L. Italica* is between both; it is black, with a red prothorax and legs ; two large white spots on the penultimate and antepenultimate abdominal segments display the light. In this species the female does not differ externally from the male; both are winged ; yet some entomologists, as Rossi, Illiger, Carus, speak of apterous females, but they have certainly mistaken the larva for the female [*]. In *L. hemiptera*, the male has truncated elytra and the female none. It is also the smallest of all, being scarcely four lines in length, entirely of an opaque black, but which is lighter in the female, and the ventral plates of the penultimate and antepenultimate abdominal segments are whitish. But these do not emit the light, which is confined to two round spots on the penultimate segment. In *L. splendidula*, I have discovered the larvæ to be luminous. Müller was acquainted with the larva of *L. hemiptera*, but he does not say whether it gives light. The *L. splendidula*, *noctiluca* and *Italica* conceal themselves during the day, and only appear at night-fall, when, upon warm damp evenings, the male flies about, whereas the female sits tranquilly among the hedges and shrubs, betraying her situation to the male by her much brighter light. *L. hemiptera* creeps about also by day, but generally in damp weather ; it also appears earlier in the year, namely, towards the end of April, whereas *L. splendidula* about the end of May and the beginning of June, and *L. noctiluca*, on the contrary, is found chiefly towards the end of the summer.

Their light is of a bluish white, and sometimes also of a greenish

---

[*] Touss. de Charpentier, Horæ Entomologicæ, p. 192. Pl. VI. f. 5 and 6. He also separates the larger specimens, as *L. Lusitanica*, and the smaller ones with a black spot upon the pronotum are, according to him, the true *L. Italica*.

or quite bright colour; it is strongest in the female, and shines uniformly, as in *L. noctiluca* and *L. splendidula*, but in *L. Italica* and in others * it varies in intensity in rhythmical vibrations; during the day it is not observed, and can be momentarily suppressed by night at the will of the insect. This they appear to do in moments of danger, at least I have often observed that those which I have caught with my hat during flight immediately ceased shining, and so frequently deceived me by my fancying that I had missed the creature, but I afterwards discovered it in my hat, when it again shone. The light is increased during motion as well as during exciting corporeal action, for instance, during copulation and in great heat, but which must not be much higher than 40° R.; cold, however, speedily destroys the faculty, and even at 10° beneath zero. If the insect be kept some days in the dark it entirely loses its luminousness, but regains it upon being again placed in the sunshine. After its death the light still lasts some hours and even days, and even afterwards can be re-produced by warm water or acids. All poisonous gases, which speedily kill the insect, destroy just as quickly its light; even in pure oxygen the light was indeed at first brighter, but disappeared at the death of the insect. In heated water, on the contrary, the light long continued in a temperature not exceeding 50° R., but immediately disappeared upon the application of greater heat, and also by degrees as the water cooled. Electricity has no influence upon the strength of the light, nor did it produce any luminousness in insects already dead, whereas galvanic electricity occasioned a much brighter light, and even re-produced the luminousness in dead insects which no longer exhibited it. But these effects are not produced in vacuum, nor if the creature be covered with oil. Upon anatomical inspection there was found at the shining spots a whitish, transparent, granulated mass, intersected by tracheæ, and which mass did not appear to be very different from the fatty substance. This mass shines also for a time when removed from the body of the insect, particularly in warm water, but it loses its light upon drying, but regains it for a short time upon being remoistened.

Among other beetles we find the *Scarabeus phosphoreus* named as luminous, and upon which Lüce has communicated some observations†.

---

* See Carus, at the above cited place, and in the Isis, 1824, vol. ii, p. 245, where it is related, that according to Long, a New Holland species also exhibits this rhythmical luminousness.

† Rozier, Journ. de Phys. vol. xliv. p. 300.

According to him, the insect which is found in the department du Var, in the vicinity of Grosse, in May and June, but which, with respect to its situation in the system, is no farther known, distributes a phosphoric light from its abdomen, that disappears when the beetle contracts it, but which remains with the juices pressed from the creature so long as they continue moist. *Paussus sphærocerus* also, which is found on the coast of Guinea, and is remarkable for the singular globular form of its antennæ, its discoverer, Afzelius, observed likewise to emit a weak phosphoric light from the globe of the antennæ * ; the same is supposed of *Chiroscelis bifenestrata*, Lam., a beetle belonging to the family of the *Melanosoma*, which is provided with two oval, hairy, reddish spots upon its second ventral segment, and it is from these that the light issues †. From a communication of Latreille ‡ the large yellow spot is luminous upon the elytra of *Buprestis ocellata*, a very beautiful insect, native of China.

§ 281.

Instances of luminous insects not of the class of beetles are great rarities. Kirby and Spence observe that it is to be seen sometimes in the eyes of some nocturnal *Lepidoptera*, for instance, in *Noctua psoi* and *Cossus ligniperda*, and also relates an instance in which the common mole cricket (*Acheta Gryllotalpa*, Fab.) is said to have been luminous; but this faculty can present itself merely as an exception, for no other observations have ever been made upon it. Perhaps they had been in contact with rotten wood, which is also sometimes luminous, or with other rotting substances, and the light with a portion of the substance still adhered to them. The luminousness of the Brazilian lantern-fly appears more credible, from the positive assertion of Mad. Merian §. In this insect, which belongs to the family of the *Cicada* among the *Hemiptera*, the light is said to be produced from the large clavate frontal process, and to be so strong that a single specimen is sufficient to admit of reading very clearly by it in the dark. But this observation is not supported by the testimony of any modern traveller. Count Hoffmannsegg, supported by the communications of Sieber, was the first to attack as groundless this tale of Mad. Merian ||, and subse-

* Trans. Lin. Soc. vol. iv. p. 261.   † Ann. du Mus. d'Hist. Nat. No. XVI. xxii. 2.
‡ Kirby and Spence, vol. ii. p. 471.
§ Mar. S. Merian de Generat. et Metam. Insect. Surinamensium, p. 49.
|| Magaz. der Gesellsch. Naturforsch, Freund Izu. Berlin, vol. i, p. 153.

quently the Prince of Neuwied * confirmed this contradiction, having never observed the least trace of a peculiar light in the *Fulgora laternaria*, Fab., which is by no means a rare *Cicada* in the Brazils.

§ 282.

These, therefore, are the collective instances hitherto known of a peculiar light emitted by insects. There are many opinions of the causes which produce this faculty, one of which lays most stress upon the influence of the nervous system, another upon the respiration, and a third upon the circulation. Others, but chiefly chemists, speak of a substance resembling phosphorus secreted by peculiar organs, and whence the light is emitted. Treviranus, however, who has anatomically inspected *Elater noctilucus*, as well as the *Lampyri*, say there is no organ anywhere situated that secretes the luminous substance, not even at the luminous spots, and that this quality proceeds from the fatty substance. This appears, as is confirmed by Macaire's investigations, to consist, in luminous insects, of a great portion of albumen, and to this some ascribe the faculty of being luminous, but it requires the peculiar quality, according to Macaire, of being semi-transparent. We know no instance of albumen itself being luminous, but must conclude that some other substance is incorporated with it, and that either this substance alone, or by its connexion with the albumen, is the cause of the light produced. The best known substance that produces light is phosphorus, which is abundantly present in animal bodies, and we therefore might ascribe the luminousness of insects to the phosphorus intermixed with their fatty substance. Phosphorus alone does not shine, but only gas charged with phosphoric vapour when coming into contact with oxygen, or if this be the saturated gas when this meets with hydrogen or azote, and this kind of mixture is only to be exhibited in luminous insects to explain the faculty peculiar to them. This, therefore, admitted, for a convincing proof of its presence has not yet been produced, it follows, as Treviranus accurately says, and observation has confirmed, that the insect is luminous not merely at its brightly coloured spots, but throughout its interior † wherever the luminous phosphoric combination is found; the brighter coloured or rather colourless spots, for the subjacent fatty substance is the cause of the whitish yellow colour, serve only to give a free passage to the light.

* Reise nach Brasilien, vol. ii, p. 111.
† See Treviranus, Biologie, vol. v. p. 475.

The observations that have been made under a variety of circumstances also tolerably harmonise with the conditions under which phosphorus is luminous, in so far as its light disappears in irrespirable gases, increases by warmth, but is destroyed, also like phosphorus, by cold, immersion in oil, alcohol, acids, saturated solutions of salts and alkalis, as also in vacuo.

If, therefore, phosphorus appears to be the substance which produces the light in insects, it may be asked, as phosphorus is not luminous in itself, what may be the conditions under which phosphorus is luminous? To this the above remarked differences of opinion especially refer. As phosphorus can only become luminous by contact with oxygen, if, therefore, we imagine it combined with the fatty substance, or with its albumen, respiration gives it luminousness; by means of respiration oxygen is deposited in the corporeal substance, and each inspiration therefore makes the beetle shine. Now, as we have before noticed, respiration being strongest during flight, it necessarily follows that the emission of light will also then be most powerful. In opposition to this the wingless state of the female might be urged, yet her short thicker body must contain more of the fatty substance, and must therefore emit a stronger light than that of the male. Next to respiration the circulation of the blood appears to have considerable influence upon the light, for we know that the substance emits the light only when moist. As, now, the blood flows all round upon the fatty substance, this may be considered as the moisture, which helps to support the luminousness. Carus has also observed that upon each pulsation, and consequently upon each fresh wave of blood, the light shines brighter. He refers to this also the brighter shining of the female, as she constantly dwells in dark, damp places. Thirdly, the nervous system may exercise a certain influence upon the production of the light, for as it is the chief agent of all the voluntary actions of the body, it will also necessarily exercise an influence upon the voluntary suppression of the light if the insect stops this influence by checking respiration in the way in which it causes the nerve to act upon the muscle in muscular motion. That it possesses this faculty of checking the respiration we know, but that this cannot be long protracted lies in the very nature of the thing, and thus by both causes the momentary cessation of light which is frequently observed, and which we have mentioned before, may be produced. Upon respiring anew the beetle would necessarily become again luminous.

SECOND SUBSECTION.

PSYCHOLOGICAL PHYSIOLOGY.

§ 283.

AFTER the consideration of the corporeal functions of insects there still remains a whole series of phenomena which are not the pure results thereof, but are superior intellectual functions, which may be exercised apparently at the will of the insect. Similar phenomena naturalists have observed, not in insects only but likewise in the higher animals, and in them very especially, and have found therein the analogies of the intellectual powers of man, yet with the essential difference that these phenomena in animals must necessarily ensue, whereas man, superior to the compulsion of nature, has the means of resisting this necessity by his volition. Hence the idea of freedom. Were the enjoyment of this freedom, and indeed especially of moral freedom,—for external freedom is merely the result of internal or moral freedom,—given to man by nature with restrictions, his intellectual superiority would then completely vanish, as he would then necessarily exercise all his functions within certain limitations, and never remain within these limits nor ever surpass them. His freedom then would also be merely apparent, and he, as well as all animals, would then be curbed by the chain of certain instincts, the satisfying of which would become a necessity. But man is free, that is to say, he has the faculty of in so far subjecting his natural instincts to other relations, either voluntary on his part, or introduced by social life, as the law of self preservation will admit, and may satisfy them at his own discretion; whereas the animal is not free, it exercises all, both corporeal and intellectual functions, from a determinate necessity, from which it has not the power of emancipating itself. Thence the entire greatness of man consists in his freedom, and in it consists the faculty of his progressive development or perfection, as well as the possibility of his degeneration, and which would place him beneath the animal. The animal is equally perfect in all its individuals; men are distinguished from each other as perfect or imperfect, according to the exercise of their freedom towards good or evil.

§ 284.

The phenomena thus characterised bear in animals the general name of instinctive impulses, and that which urges their exercise we call instinct; in man we call them intellectual phenomena, and their stimulant mind or soul. Instinct in animals, therefore, is the analogue of the soul in man; a soul differing only from the human soul by the necessity with which it does everything, whereas the human soul is independent of necessity, and freely resolves upon its actions. From this necessity, with which the instinctive impulses of animals act, ensues their determinate restriction in every species. The instinct of every animal is enclosed within a circle, which it cannot pass, and all the phenomena within this circle are repeated by every individual in the same manner. In them, therefore, there is no teaching or progressive perfection, but the young just born individual exercises all its instincts just as its mother did, without being in the least taught to do so. This unconscious execution of the first occupations harmonises with the desire of the infant for the mother's breast, and with its innate power of suction, that we cannot forbear considering both as quite analogous phenomena. But it is only during his nonage that man exhibits himself as an animal with innate skill; these disappear so soon as he becomes older and more developed, whereas they remain with the animal during its whole life. The celebrated wisdom of many animals is founded solely upon the faculty by necessity present in them, and what we admire is nothing more than the general law of nature, that for the attainment of their object they always select the best and most serviceable means. Necessity and suitableness are therefore as inseparable phenomena in the instinctive functions of animals as in the physical world are the ideas of life and action; they cannot be parted, one conditionates the other; for a necessary unsuitableness would destroy itself, whilst man, by the insight gained through experience and custom, is led to new endeavours, upon an ascertained unsuitableness, which at last conducts to the suitable accomplishment of his object. But the animal makes no essay, what it undertakes it succeeds in, and indeed with the least trouble, and with the least expense of force, as it seeks the easiest and surest way to its object. Yet this apparent choice is no choice, but iron necessity, which rules the life of all organisms, and which endeavours to dominate in the life of man, wherein it at first indeed acts promotive, but subsequently chiefly obstructive and restrictive.

§ 285.

But we, nevertheless, observe phenomena in many animals, and also in insects, which appear to be the result of a free and rational consideration, and of a certain degree of reflection; indeed experience, recollection, and memory are likewise perceived in them.

The reflection of insects consists in the choice of the best means to attain the object. There is nothing remarkable or astounding in this when we admit that nature for the exercise of every function of the insect has prescribed to it the way, and that we therefore observe all insects invariably follow this prescribed path. But there are facts which cannot be made to harmonise with this prescribed course. For instance, it is well known that when bees in the construction of their combs meet with objects that obstruct their progress in a right line, they avoid them by the change of its direction, before the comb touches the object, therefore by the immediate cessation of the continuation of the work in that direction. Darwin observed a sand-wasp (*Sphex sabulosa*) which wished to carry off a large fly that it had caught, but as it violently fluttered with its wings, and so hindered her own progress, she bit off its wings, and then flew off with it unimpeded. We must in these cases,—as in the organs of the body and their functions there is exhibited a certain faculty of adaptation to a determinate purpose, as, for example, the alternating secretion of one instead of the other, of the intestine instead of the skin, in rheumatic affections, &c.,—admit also of an adaptation of the instinct to new purposes, which expresses itself in the recognition of the necessity of a change of the function yet in action before the obstruction which obligates it absolutely obtrudes. It is evident that this recognition is a purely intellectual activity, which appears to contradict the prescribed necessity in the functions of animals. But this contradiction is only apparent, for nature has also prescribed the choice of the most serviceable means to the end, and this choice presumes a knowledge of difficulties and hindrances. Hence the instinct of the animal is competent to a partial quitting of the prescribed circle as soon as extraneous phenomena intrude into the actions of insects, which likewise lie beyond the circle of their usual functions, and this transit, this voluntary adaptation, still more convinces us that the instinct of animals corresponds to the soul of man, and that reason, which has been considered as the exclusive characteristic of man, is not wholly wanting in them.

The proof that insects acquire a certain experience, and are capable of combinations of what they have experienced, many bees exhibit to us, which lick with their long tongues the honey glands of flowers, and fly industriously around from one to the other. Thus, humble-bees, which cannot reach with their proboscis the nectaries placed at the bottom of the long tubular flower, open it at the side with their mandibles, and now passing their tongue through the aperture, imbibe the honey previously inaccessible to them. According to Ch. K. Sprengel, those flowers which contain nectaries are often decorated with radiating markings, generally red, which serve the insect as a mark of recognition. If such a recognition actually take place, experience which the insects have gained can be the sole instructor. According to Reaumur, the ants that have formed a dwelling in the vicinity of a bee-hive never enter it so long as it continues occupied by the bees, but laboriously collect their nectar from the *aphides* dispersed upon plants; but if a hive, of which the bees have been destroyed, be placed in the situation of the former one, they speedily visit it in large troops, and enjoy the honey undisturbed. Here, therefore, we again detect experience, viz. that the bees immediately destroy all visiters that intrude into their dwelling, as the warning instructress of the cautious reserve of the ants.

To the faculty of collecting experience, a second is superadded, which gives this experience its value, namely, memory. The experience gained must remain in constant recollection if it be to yield a constant advantage, and it is made so by a quality of the soul which we call memory. This quality is also attributable to the instincts of insects. The same as the swallow and the stork yearly return to their former dwellings, so does the bee each spring revisit her former collecting places, and the very same tree whence she gathered honey the preceding year. Among the many hives which may possibly be placed together, each bee accurately recognises her own when she returns from her journeys, and we never observe the neuters flying around other hives for the purpose of discovering theirs. This is not a mere recognition of the same hive from its external marks, but the bee exactly knows the spot where it is to be found, for if another have been put in its place, it will prepare within it, in conjunction with all its returning comrades, a new dwelling, supposing that the preceding one has been lost in the interim *. Kirby and Spence relate another still more striking instance of the memory of these creatures, in which a swarm from an old hive occupied a hole in the roof of a house, but were again removed by its possessor. Every year the envoys of the new swarms of the same hive regularly returned to this hole to convince themselves of its existence and suitableness, certainly a distinct proof of the remembrance of the discovered place among the older members of the hive. There are many instances of the memory of insects, which all, more or less, prove it to be a quality of their instinct. Thus, the *Odyneri*, which have found a hole for the dwelling-place of their young, constantly return back exactly to it when they quit it to fetch the young ones' provisions. If it be closed during their absence, on their return they seek about upon the wall, yet without entering other holes; if they again find it, they remove the obstacles and pursue their previous labours.

But the power of communicating to their comrades what they purpose is peculiar to insects. Much has been talked of the so-called signs of recognition in bees, which is said to consist in recognising their comrades of the same hive by means of peculiar signs. This sign serves to prevent any strange bee from intruding into the same hive without being immediately detected and killed. It however sometimes happens that several hives have the same signs, when their several members rob each other with impunity. In these cases the bees whose hive suffers most alter their signs, and then can immediately detect the enemy. But in what these signs consist is not known. The wasps also apprise their comrades of the place whence they fetch the materials of their nests, whence it happens that some always fetch the same material, for example, rotten wood; others a different material; and others, again, coloured substances.—The ants, also, can inform their own citizens of the presence of a choice morsel, for Kirby and Spence relate an instance where a pot filled with treacle was suspended from a ceiling, and which being discovered by one, she fetched a whole host of her comrades. In places distant from their abode, ants touch each other with their antennæ, so to recognise their friends and enemies, and, after having satisfied themselves, they pursue their journey. A remarkable instance of such a communication is related in Illiger's Magazine ‡, in which a

---

* Kirby and Spence, Introduction, vol. ii. p. 590.
† Germar's Magazin, vol. iii. p. 425.   ‡ Vol. i. p. 488.

traveller observed *Gymnopleurus pilularius* prepare its ball of dung. This ball happened by accident to fall into a hole whence the insect could not remove it by all its exertions. It therefore apparently gave it up, but speedily returned with three comrades, and their united labours succeeded in accomplishing it. This instance is so remarkable, that we might be inclined to doubt its veracity were it solitary, but those above communicated are so analogous, that we cannot help considering it as true. They therefore prove that insects possess the power of communicating their objects to their fellows without the intervention of language, and that the imparting of determined objects must be classed with the qualities of insect instinct. We have thus found four important functions which are considered as the qualities of the human soul to exist even in insects.

§ 286.

If we now survey the several phases of the instinct of insects, we shall find that all refer either to the preservation of the individual or to the conservation of the species, and, consequently, stand in close connexion either with the several functions of insects, to provide themselves with subsistence, or with the suitable depositing of their eggs, the provision of their young, and their undisturbed development, &c. Between these two groups other phenomena present themselves which refer to both, we mean their connexion in large societies, which is peculiar to certain species, and which precisely furnish us with the most animated and comprehensive picture of the several intellectual activities of which insects are capable. We will, therefore, more closely inspect these chief functions of the instinct of insects, and, in the first place, those referring to self-preservation; then those referable to the conservation of the species; and, lastly, the societies and unions which have been observed in certain genera and species.

EIGHTH CHAPTER.

OF THEIR SELF-PRESERVATION.

§ 287.

The means which insects make use of for self-preservation are of two kinds, as they refer to their mode of procuring food and to their means of defence against their enemies. They both evince in so many instances an amount of sagacity, that we feel astonished at the apparent high degree of reflection and consideration announced by it; indeed they would absolutely convince us of a freer activity of the mind, did not the same phenomena of necessity and a want of freedom exhibit itself in as far as that every individual repeats the same processes in the same manner and in perfect concordance even to their minutest details, without having learnt it from its predecessors.

I. Means of Defence.

§ 288.

The means insects have received from nature for their defence may also be viewed under two aspects, namely, first, as a passive means derived from the form and structure of their bodies, and, secondly, as an active means of defence derived from the free exertion of strength on the part of the insect.

Passive means of defence are derived chiefly from the form and colour of the body, by their giving insects such a resemblance to the objects in or upon which they dwell, that upon superficial observation it is not easy to distinguish them from it. To give examples of this, we might remind our readers of the similarity of colour of many beetles to the ground upon which they are found. This is strongly exemplified in the large family of *Curculios*, in which the majority of the species of the genera *Thylacites, Sitona, Trachyphlæus, Cleonis*, &c. are of an earthy grey or yellowish, like the sand or loamy soil where they creep. *Thylacites incanus* is of a brownish yellow, like that of the colour of the earth of the woods covered with fallen pine leaves. *Thylacites geminatus*, in many districts a very injurious enemy to young vines, is of the same yellowish brown grey colour as the soil of vineyards. *Cleonis sulcirostris, Cl. glauca, Cl. marmorata*, &c., are greyish, like the dry light earth upon which they crawl. The resemblance is still more striking in those beetles which dwell upon a slippery clay soil, and which from their rough integument are unwillingly soiled with this clay, as, for instance, *Asida grisea, Brachycerus algirus, Meleus variolosus, Trox arenarius, Opatrum sabulosum,* and many others. Others, again, like our native tortoise-beetles (*Cassidea*) are generally of the bright green colour of the plant upon which they dwell. But the resemblance of insects in other orders to lifeless things is still more remarkable, namely, in the *Orthoptera*, in which many species of the genus *Mantis* resemble fallen and green leaves, both in form and colour, as *Mantis siccifolia, M. oratoria, M. phyllodes*, &c. The locusts also, which dwell chiefly amongst high grass and upon green plants, are usually of a bright grass green; others, as *L. Ephippium* and the *Grylli*, which prefer dry hedges and fields, are, like these, of a grey streaky colour and sculpture. This is also the case with many bugs, which, as they are deprived of all other means of defence, would necessarily become the easy prey of all enemies if they did not, as in the species of the genus *Aradus*, resemble the bark of trees where they dwell, or were they not, like the *Corei*, difficult to discern upon fields and hedges where they are found, from their grey colour. The same means of defence is possessed by many of the moths which, as it is well known, repose tranquilly during the day, and only fly at dusk. Many conceal themselves in the slits of the bark, and, consequently, from their conformity of colour, are easily overlooked. The caterpillars also of many *Lepidoptera* possess in their form and colour means to prevent their being observed, many of them being green, like the leaves upon which they live. Others, namely, the *Geometers*, so closely resemble the young twigs of trees, that even upon a strict inspection they are difficult to be recognised as caterpillars, particularly if they, as they not unusually do, stretch themselves straight out, holding only by their posterior legs, when they perfectly resemble a young leafless twig. I was myself once thus deceived by the caterpillar of *Ph. quercinaria*, Borkh (*Eunomus Erosaria*, Tr.), mistaking it for a small dry twig, upon wishing to break off a small twig of oak, but I subsequently observed its motion, and then, upon a closer inspection, recognised it as the caterpillar of this moth. The caterpillars also of *Gastrophaga quercifolia*, of *Catocala Fraxini*, O. &c., very much resemble the dry twigs of trees, and the moth of the first also closely resembles a dry fallen leaf, and may thus easily conceal itself when it reposes motionless by day, as is the case with most moths.

As, in all the above instances, form and colour are the means of defence, in others, it is provided by the external integument and peculiar habits. Thus the caterpillars of most of the butterflies and the larvæ of the tortoise-beetles have a skin covered with simple or ramose spines, which clothing gives them a formidable appearance, and thereby partly, and partly by the pain which the spines give to the œsophagus, disqualify them for being the food of birds. Others are protected by their thick hairy clothing both against the prejudicial influences of the elements as well as from the attacks of insectivorous birds. The cuckoo alone, which likewise, from its other habits, is a most remarkable bird, not deterred by this fur from swallowing such caterpillars, and it is thence that its stomach is frequently covered inside with hair, an occurrence that has occasioned much dispute, as some naturalists maintain that this accidental clothing is the constant structure of the stomach. Among the habits which many insects find a protection from their enemies, we include that of many larvæ covering themselves with their own excrement, as is the case with the larva of *Lerma merdigera* and some others. They then resemble little lumps of dirt, and are certainly also regarded as such by many of the enemies of insects.

Other insects secrete peculiar fluids, in which they partly envelope themselves and partly thereby secure themselves from the attacks of their enemies. The *Aphrophora spumaria* is one of these, which envelopes itself in a thick white frothy fluid, that comes out of the anus. This cuckoo-spittle is found during summer upon almost all shrubs, and particularly willows; within it is seated the larva of that *Cicada*, which undisturbedly sucks its nutriment from the plant, constantly the while secreting fresh bubbles. The perfect-winged insect has no longer the frothy covering. We find other coverings in the *Aphidæ* and tortoise-beetles, which envelope themselves with a white woolly or fibrous substance, the origin of which we are not yet acquainted with, but it appears likewise to be produced by a peculiar secretion of the skin. Other insects, as the *Cantharides*, burying-beetles, carrion-beetles, carrion-flies, wasps, &c., emit, upon being touched, such a nauseous stench, that this must prevent every insectivorous bird from using them as food.

Another peculiarity which may be also classed among the passive means of defence is their tenacity of life, and for which they have to thank, in the first place, an organisation adapted to all possible circumstances, and, secondly, their hard exterior integument. The latter acquires in many insects, particularly the beetles, such hardness, that it is with difficulty that their elytra can be pierced. This is especially the case with the large *Curculios,* for instance, the species of the genus *Cleonis, Lixus, Otiorhynchus,* &c., then in the *Histers,* which have so firm an integument, that, upon any but a stony surface, they may be trod on with impunity, and are more easily pressed into the ground than crushed. This is partly the case also with the *Byrrhi.* This hard clothing is not found exclusively among the beetles; in the otherwise soft *Diptera* there is an instance of the kind, namely, in the louse-fly of the sheep (*Melophagus ovinus*), which cannot be crushed between the fingers; and the smaller parasites, as the louse and the flea, are difficult to crush in this manner. Respecting the tenacity of life with which they, even wounded or mutilated, resist death, we have before cited instances. Impaled insects will live thus for several weeks, and at last appear to die less from the effect of the injury than from hunger. I myself have kept *Blaps mortisaga* for three months without food; and Rudolphi mentions, in his " Physiology," an instance which Schüppel communicated to him, of an insect of the same family which this skilful entomologist received from the South of France, which, although impaled, arrived alive in Berlin, and here even continued still to live for some time. Other cases, in which beetles have been enclosed in wood for years without any food, have been communicated by other writers; and instances of insects remaining torpid in spirits of wine for several hours, and indeed days, and yet be re-aroused from their sleep upon being brought into the air, I have previously mentioned. They still longer retain their life in water. According to Lyonet, the caterpillar of *Cossus ligniperda* will live nearly three weeks beneath water; and according to Curtis, the plant lice will survive for sixteen hours in that element, but die if continued for twenty-four. Kirby and Spence relate, after Reeve, instances in which in warm fountains, the temperature of which was about 205° Fahr., he has found the larvæ of *Tipulæ;* and Good has observed little black beetles, probably

Colymbetes, in the hot sulphur baths of Albano, and which died when, placed in cold water. He himself found a specimen of *Lyctus Juglandis* Fab., in the warm dung of a hotbed, and cast it into hot water to kill it; after it had been some time there it was removed, and appeared dead, but speedily again moved, and entirely recovered. Reaumur and De Geer also relate instances of the larvæ of the gnats being found frozen in ice, and which revived when the ice melted. One of my acquaintances saw a *Dyticus latissimus* enclosed in ice, he took it out, and found it alive; and Alex. v. Humboldt found insects upon the Cordilleras above the limits of snow, which, although not natives of this altitude, yet retained their vivacity at this temperature.

§ 289.

The active means of defence which we find in insects are more numerous and more striking to the eyes. Some appear merely defensive, in as far as insects which use them can only protect themselves by attitude and appearance: among them we class the sudden torpidity aped by many insects in a moment of danger. Thus the minute *Agathidia* roll themselves up, and appear dead; thus the *Byrrhi* and *Anobia* contract their limbs, and pretend death so long as they are in the hands of their enemies. Others stretch out their limbs, as *Geotrupes stercorarius,* and thus imitate dead insects. Among the *Hymenoptera* the ruby-tails (*Chrysodea*) adopt the first plan of deceiving their enemies, by rolling themselves up when caught, and only arouse themselves upon the departure of their enemy. Others, particularly the tortoise beetles and *Curculios,* endeavour to secure themselves upon the approach of an enemy by suddenly falling down from the leaves upon which they were seated, that they may thus conceal themselves among the leaves and blades of grass; if they are found here they simulate death, but not with the obstinacy of the species of the preceding genera. Those active means of defence which may likewise be used as defensive weapons are very numerous, and partly consist in large mandibles and other pinching instruments, and partly in concealed stings. All the carnivorous beetles are furnished with the first kind of arms, namely, the *Carabi, Cicindelæ, Dytici, Staphylini,* &c. In general, however, the bite of these creatures is not injurious, and with the exception of the pain occasioned by the mechanical injury, the bite has no prejudicial consequences. Among the vegetable feeders also there are many, as the *Dynastes, Lucanus Cervus,* many capricorn beetles, and others, furnished, some with really large mandibles and others with processes upon the head and prothorax, which, like the mandibles, can meet like tongs, and thus serve as a weapon. This is asserted of the *Hercules* and its large comrades. Pincers of a different kind, as in the earwig, are likewise doubtlessly arms, but in general their possessors are too weak to wound the larger animals or man with them. The generally known means of defence of the bomb-beetle (*Brachynus crepitans*) is of a peculiar description: it consists in its ejecting from its anus against its enemy a vapoury moisture accompanied by a slight sound, and which vapour has great resemblance to the gas of aquafortis. It is not yet distinctly known what organ secretes this fluid; according to some it is the anal glands, which we have considered as kidneys; and according to others, on the contrary, the ejected gas is nothing else than the air accumulated in the colon. This opinion seems to be the most correct, for in the former we cannot distinctly see how the fluid contained in the bladders could so immediately be transformed into gas. Another mode of defence, which we have before mentioned, is allied to this, namely, the ejection of the corrosive juices of the stomach, which we observe in many of the larvæ of the *Lepidoptera*, in almost all *Carabodea*, and in the grasshoppers. It has evidently for object to deter their enemies, for it is only in moments of danger that insects eject it, and therewith soil their enemies, as in the *Grylli*, or project it against them, as in the rest. The sharp stinking urine of the *Dytici*, and the other secretions which we have before mentioned, are cast forth in the moment of danger to check the enemy.

We have before noticed some peculiar organs of secretion in several larvæ, as, for instance, in that of *Pieris Machaon*, which are projected at the approach of danger: they appear, in fact, to be glandular organs which partly secrete odours and partly liquids, for the purpose of chasing the enemy. In *P. Machaon* the furcate organ lies in the neck, between the head and prothorax, and the same in *Doritis Apollo*. In the larvæ of *Harpya vinula* it projects from the tail, in the form of a filament; and in the larvæ of the *Tenthredonodea* they lie between the five anterior pair of ventral feet, and are wart-shaped, transpierced protuberances, which project only during danger, and then emit a peculiar odour. In other larvæ they lie upon the back, as in the caterpillar of *Lip chrysorrhea*. Among the beetles similar organs are found in the genera *Cantharis* and *Malachius*, which in these are seated at the sides of the thoracic and ventral segments, and are likewise projected in times of danger. It is remarkable that these organs in all the preceding instances are of a red colour: it might be thence concluded that the substances which they secrete or contain are very rich in acids. The larva of *Chrysomela Populi* has likewise secreting organs upon its back, in the form of two conical knobs on each segment, whence, at a time of danger, a white, milky, and strongly scented fluid issues, which may also serve chiefly as a means of defence. In the processionary caterpillar, according to a recent discovery of Dr. Nicholai, the whole external surface of the skin secretes a sharp juice, which is distributed over the body in a farinaceous form, and which acts very prejudicially upon all organisms that inspire it; therefore workmen who are occupied in woods where this caterpillar is numerous sicken very rapidly. Bechstein knew that the processionary caterpillar was prejudicial to the touch, but he ascribed their effects to the hair that was removed by it.

Other larvæ, which have not received means of defence in such organs of secretion, nor in the thick hairy coat that envelopes them, construct cases for themselves, into which they retire upon the approach of danger. We find such among the larvæ of the *Coleoptera*, namely, in the larva of *Clythra*, which all dwell in cases formed by themselves, and in which they change into pupæ. Among the *Lepidoptera*, the remarkable genus *Psyche* forms such cases of morsels of wood, and there change into the pupa, and even the naked apterous female still continues to dwell in it. Besides these, the family of the *Phryganea* are furnished with this means of defence; their larvæ live in the water, and form cases of small stones, pieces of wood, shells, &c., which they also close with a distinct lid when they change.

The sting is the chief weapon of offence. The majority of insects furnished with a sting as a means of defence belong to the order of the *Hymenoptera;* it is but recently that a stinging lepidopterous insect has been found, and which we have before mentioned. It is always the female which possesses the sting, or else the neuters; the males never have it. We refer to the anatomical division of this work for its structure, and we can only say of the way in which it is used as a weapon, that the insect upon the approach of danger projects it from the abdomen, and thereby endeavours to wound its enemy with it. It is not so much the mechanical injury that occasions the pain as the poison which is injected into the wound. There are solitary instances of two or three stings being present at the same time, and which also wound in conjunction, namely, among the wasps, and in the genus *Onyderus*. I have hitherto neglected to inspect more closely the structure of this threefold sting, but I surmise that in this case the several setæ of which the simple sting consists are more remote from each other, and therefore project separately from the abdomen.

The stings of the *Diptera* are not weapons of defence, but organs whereby they may imbibe their nutriment. They are therefore only used for this purpose, and not as a means of defence. Among the *Hemiptera*, which likewise possess organs of puncture in the mouth, the latter may not be affirmed, for the *Notonecta* defend themselves with their proboscis, and their puncture, as was before mentioned, is very painful.

II. INSTINCT OF NUTRITION.

§ 290.

The food which insects take is more important to their self preservation than all these means of defence. We have before classed their chief kinds, and can here only make a few observations upon the way in which they procure it.

In the majority of insects this takes place without much art or exertion, in as far as the insect in its most helpless state, namely, as a larva, finds itself generally in a place where its food is very abundant. It has to thank its mother's care for this, for she lays the eggs mostly where there is food for the larva, or else provides it with food in its cell, in which she has enclosed the egg. But these instances do not properly belong here, but to the following chapter, where we shall speak of the means provided for the conservation of the species, and only such facts, as convince us of the instinct of the insect for its independent supply of food, shall here be mentioned. Among our native beetles the larvæ of the *Cicindelæ* exhibit these instincts. They dwell in sandy places, where they dig a cylindrical hole by means of their feet and mandibles, wherein they sit. They watch from this place of concealment all insects that pass by, and which heedlessly venture to the margin of the hole, when they fall in, and are then devoured by the larva. Miger, who first observed this larva *, has given a detailed account of its economy. The plan adopted by the larva of the genus

* Annales du Museum d'Hist. Nat. v. 14.

Myrmecoleon, in the order of the *Neuroptera,* is very similar to this, which is also found abundantly in sandy places, and here excavates a funnel-shaped cavity, at the bottom of which it lies concealed with its mandibles projecting, and it likewise seizes and sucks all insects which by mischance fall in, and then throws away the empty case by placing it on its head and giving it a jerk. These two larvæ are, however, almost the only ones in which we observe such striking and exceedingly sagacious methods of procuring their food, the majority of the rest of the carnivorous larvæ hunt about like the beetles for prey. The larvæ of the *Carabodea* are found especially in the earth, beneath stones, and in other nooks, where they prey upon the vegetable-devouring larvæ, which seek a place of safety. It does not, however, appear that the law that carnivorous animals shall not destroy other carnivora is strictly obeyed, for indeed the larvæ of one species frequently devour those of another, which Miger states of the voracious larvæ of the *Cicindelæ*. The black larva of *Calosoma sycophanta* devours with appetite the caterpillar of the *Lepidoptera,* especially that of *Liparis dispar;* consequently, where this caterpillar is abundant they are also abundantly found. They are then observed to pursue their food even by day, and knowing that the caterpillars are found especially upon trees, they themselves climb up and there attack them. It is chiefly in the morning about sunrise that they are to be found there; I have also detected the perfect insect in the same pursuit. We cannot, however, maintain that other larvæ possess peculiar instincts for obtaining their food. The vegetable feeders are deposited in the egg state by the mother in the vicinity of plants, where they find their food. This is likewise the case with the perfect insect. The *Lepidoptera* and *Hymenoptera* fly from flower to flower, visiting at pleasure now this and now that; insects which devour vegetable substances dwell in the vicinity of the plants which serve them as food, or if less particular in their choice, they feed wherever it presents itself; a few undertake wider migrations for theirs, as the locust, and devour every vegetable they meet with. But it is not a migratory insect in the same sense as in birds, but it is found almost all over Germany, sometimes singly and sometimes in bodies, but sometimes their numbers are so great that one district is no longer able to support them, and they then undertake their devastating expeditions. Other species of this genus also seem to possess this wandering propensity, at least the South

African migratory locust is specifically different from the European one. Whether the migrations of the *Libellulæ* have the same object cannot be ascertained with certainty, but it is improbable, as they are carnivorous.

NINTH CHAPTER.

OF THE CONSERVATION OF THE SPECIES.

THE SEXUAL INSTINCT.

§ 291.

THE impulses which nature has implanted for the conservation of the species are more evident than those for the preservation of the individual. We have before hinted that all the several conditions of insect life appear to have for their chief object the conservation of the species, and we have also ascertained that the life of the individual terminates with its sexual activity, it having thereby fulfilled the object nature contemplated through its means, and it may then quit the stage. If now, therefore, we collectively comprise together the several phenomena which refer to the sexual functions, we shall find them to consist of two chief divisions, under which the various functions may be classed. These are, the impulse which brings the sexes together, the copulative impulse, and that which urges the impregnated female to take such care of her eggs and young that they may thrive under favourable circumstances, an impulse which admits of comparison with the maternal love of the human race, and which in insects also exhibits itself in the anxiety of the parent for her progeny.

I. COPULATIVE IMPULSE.

§ 292.

This impulse presents itself in insects so soon as they have attained their perfect state, and it henceforward predominates throughout the life of the individual. The duration of the lives of insects depends upon their copulation, for the majority die speedily after its accomplishment, and only those which have been prevented from the act can survive longer. Hence copulation is the object for which Nature produces individuals, and she must necessarily be anxious for its most easy and securest attainment. We find several arrangements to promote this object, which facilitate the mutual meeting of the sexes, some of which are merely corporeal, and others are called forth by the instinct. In the majority of cases it is in the male that this impulse first becomes active, and it is therefore they especially which seek the female. When difficulty attends this, Nature has often provided peculiar organs to render it more easy. One of the most usual means consists in the males being more numerous than the females; indeed it is not possible to give the exact proportions of the sexes, but it is, according to De Geer's calculation, among the *Phalenæ*, about three to one; or, according to Lyonet, about four to one. Among the bees there are several hundred males and only one fertile female. Another means is the greater activity of the male. They are generally smaller in size, have longer wings, longer antennæ and legs, or have wings in many instances when the female is without them, as in *Lampyris, Symbius, Psyche,* many *Phalenæ (Acidalia brumata,* &c.), the *Mutillæ, Methoca, Myrmosa,* &c. Sometimes, also, the females have peculiar marks of distinction, as in *Lampyris,* in the female of which the light emitted is considerably brighter than that produced by the male. A reversed relation occurs in the *Achetæ, Locustæ,* and *Cicadæ,* in which the males are furnished with a vocal organ not found in the females. We observe the same phenomena also in the singing birds, among which the males only are the songsters. Thus Nature wished, by furnishing the males with distinguishing characters, to place them in a condition to lure the females from their hiding places, which in most of the mentioned instances it is their habit to resort to. Others, as the nocturnal *Lepidoptera,* have received for this purpose a very developed sense of smell, by means of which they can discover the female at considerable distances, to whom they immediately flock. I have myself observed males of *Liparis salicis* fluttering around my breeding-cage, in which there were several just developed females of the same species; upon my letting them into the cage they immediately copulated. This instinctive impulse, the satisfying of which nature has thus facilitated, is most conspicuous also in the *Lepidoptera.* The males of many *Noctuæ* will even copulate with impaled and half dead females, and the excitement of other insects occasionally urges them to an intermixture with individuals of a different species, and even of a different genus. Several such instances have been observed; Rossi*, for instance, detected a connexion between *Cantharis melanura* and *Elater niger*, the former the male, the latter the female; Müller, of Odenbach, observed a connexion between *Chrys mela graminis* and *Chry. polita*, and of *Attelabus coryli* and *Donacia simplex*, in both instances the first was the female; and Heyer, of Lüneberg, saw a female *Cantharis rufa* actually connected at the same time with two males. Treviranus† mentions other cases of such commixture, namely, one between a male *Melolontha agricola* and a female *Cetonia hirta*; and two others, observed by O. F. Müller, in which *Chrysomela Ænea* was connected with *Galleruca alni*, and *Papilio Turtina* with *Papilio Janira*. It is uncertain whether such mixtures have been productive, but, from the analogy of the superior animals, we might say no; should, however, the copulation of closely allied species actually produce young, these would not be able to unite productively, as is proved by the general rule of analogous instances in the superior animals, yet this, even, is not without exception. Hence Gravenhorst's opinion, that from such bastard copulations of allied species many intermediate forms originate, must be totally rejected, exclusively of the view that in case of such a course in nature, its beautiful regularity and order would speedily terminate in illimitable confusion, of which, however, there is not the least proof.

II. Affection for the Young.

§ 293.

The chief business of the male terminates in copulation; but it is this which first excites in the female the impulse that stimulates her to the completion of her most important occupation. This impulse henceforth exhibits itself to us in her affection for her progeny, it is the cause of her activity after copulation, and in aid of which her most distinguishing and remarkable instincts are developed. We will now survey these in detail in the several orders.

In the beetles this instinct presents itself almost solely in the suitable depositing of their eggs. Just as the birds of prey are not distinguished by any artificial preparation of their nests, so we may maintain of the predaceous beetles, that they, as those birds place their nests on elevated inaccessible situations, deposit their eggs in concealed

* Germar's Magazin, vol. iv. p. 404. † Vermischte Schriften, vol. i. p. 22.

and retired places safe from the attacks of their enemies; it is, therefore, very rarely that we find not merely their eggs, but even their young larvæ. Nor do we know whether the mother furnishes them with food for their first supply, yet it is much to be doubted, as many of their larvæ, which as remarkable exceptions do not feed upon animal matter, as, for instance, the larva of *Zabrus gibbus*, immediately find in their vicinity a sufficiency of food in the young roots of corn *. Thus, also, the eggs of the water beetles may be deposited, without any particular care on the part of the mother, at the bottom of ponds and pools in which the beetles are, for the young larvæ will find in the water a sufficiency of other larvæ to feed upon. The modes of life vary considerably in the *Staphylini* in their perfect state, but the majority live upon animal substances. But the larvæ are rarely found, and least likely to be so there where we discover the perfect insect; we may therefore conclude that they also live beneath the earth, where they find their food in concealment. The larvæ of the carrion beetles are more visible, they are frequently observed in the society of their parents, and we may therefore conclude that the female deposits her egg in the carrion, where the young immediately find nutriment. In the large family of the *Lamellicornia* there exists a great difference both in the nature of the food and in their mode of depositing their eggs. The vegetable feeders lay their eggs in the earth, where we find the larvæ feeding upon roots, or even upon the soil; the excrement feeders, on the contrary, likewise dig holes in the earth, wherein to deposit their eggs, but they supply their larvæ with food, by rolling up balls of excrement, in which they envelope their eggs. We therefore occasionally find the beetle occupied in carefully pushing this ball along, as we have recently related of *Gymnopleurus pilularius*. *Copris lunaris*, which prefers the dung of sheep, is said to use the individual lumps of it as balls for her eggs, depositing a single one in each, and then burying them. Examples exhibiting greater skill are rare among the *Coleoptera*, yet *Hydrophilus piceus*, according to Miger, forms a little boat of substances which it fixes together by means of some viscid fluid, and herein depositing the eggs, closes it, leaving it to its fate. The capricorn beetles, and bark beetles, which busy themselves with the destruction of dead trees, lay their eggs in and upon them, generally beneath the bark, and it is their larvæ which gnaw the wood in all directions. The same is the case

* Germar's Magazin, vol. i. part i. p. 1, &c.

with the *Anobia* and the *Ptini*, but these prefer dry manufactured wood, paper, &c.; they consequently produce, in their larva state, the same injury to furniture and libraries. The fur beetles and fur moths also are destructive only in their larva state, and it is by the care of the mother that they are deposited in furs and wool, which they use as food. The *Chrysomelæ*, as larvæ, live upon leaves, and are deposited upon them in their egg state by the mother; the *Curculios*, which prefer especially the seeds of plants, are deposited in flowers as eggs, and during the development of the fruit they devour its substance, for which purpose nature produced them, and then, instead of a shell producing a kernel, it produces a beetle.

All the other orders furnish us with similar instances of the affection of the parent for her progeny. It would lead us too far were we thus to go through them individually to show their consimility by adducing instances; we will merely remark, that the large order of the *Lepidoptera*, throughout all its members, exhibits the same anxiety and care in depositing their eggs. Almost all caterpillars feed upon leaves, and therefore almost all eggs are deposited upon the plants themselves, or in their proximity. The majority are much exposed, and are therefore enveloped by peculiar coverings, which the mother, precisely as among the birds, procures from her own body. Others have, instead, a hard glue-like case, over which a second woollen covering is spread. The fruit moths deposit their eggs upon ripening fruit, unripe fruit they will not touch.

The eggs of the *Orthoptera* are deposited in general in the earth, usually in particular holes dug expressly for this purpose by the female, and which are again closed so soon as she has placed all her eggs therein. As the young immediately after their development seek the light, and feed upon leaves of all kinds, provision furnished by the parent was here also unnecessary; whereas the *Diptera* and *Hemiptera* lay their eggs generally in such places as the developed larva can immediately find food. We thus find the eggs of the *Syrphodea* among the plant lice, which the larva devours, or in the nests of the bees and wasps, whose honey they help to devour. The eggs of the true flies (*Muscæ*) are laid by the mother in dung or carrion, which substances constitute the food of the larvæ. The gnats let their eggs fall into the water; here the larvæ are developed, and one species of them devours the other with as much voracity as they themselves are again seized by the larger larvæ of the water beetles. The eggs of the bugs we find upon the leaves and stems of plants, the juices of which the larvæ imbibe; the same in the plant lice and *Cicada*, which select the same materials as food. The water bugs live as larvæ also in the water, and feed upon prey. We there find their eggs, but generally placed in rows affixed to the stems and leaves of plants growing beneath the water.

§ 294.

But the maternal care is exhibited most strikingly in the order of the *Hymenoptera*, and here presents itself in such a variety of forms that we cannot refuse ourselves a detailed description of this attractive subject.

The *Tenthredonodea*, whose larvæ, like the caterpillars of the *Lepidoptera*, feed upon fresh vegetable substances, cut with their saw-shaped ovipositor the surfaces of leaves, and in these incisions deposit their eggs. Here the larvæ develope themselves, and subsequently feed upon the same leaves. Thus their care for their progeny perfectly corresponds with that of the majority of other insects. The *Ichneumons* also are not distinguished by a greater anxiety from the rest; they deposit their eggs in other larvæ, particularly in the caterpillars of the *Lepidoptera*, and for this purpose they bore a hole with their pointed ovipositor in the skin of the caterpillar, through which the egg passes into its body. In the gall-flies the egg is also deposited in the parenchyma of the leaf, but steeped in a corrosive moisture, which occasions a powerful influx of the juices to the wounded part. This thereby grows gradually into a cellular body, the so called gall-nut, in the inside of which the larva lives, feeding upon the juices; it changes here into the pupa, and also into the perfect insect, in which state it pierces through the dwelling nature prepared for it through the care of the mother, and then first sees the light of day. But this care is still more striking in the fossorial wasps, all of which dig subterranean cavities, whither they convey insects which they have caught and killed, and in which they deposit an egg; the body serves the young larva as food, and the hole is a secure dwelling. We have before admired the strength and patience which many species of this family apply to the attainment of their object, and we then cited the large *Ammophila sabulosa* as the best known and most striking instance. During the summer we continually observe her incessantly employed in this labour; we may also admire her sagacity in the selection of a suitable soil, neither too loose nor too firm, and feel astonished at the apparent toil to which she must so repeatedly subject herself. But all the allied genera are subjected to the same. *Pompilus* and *Pepsis* proceed in the same way. *Pelopæus* constructs sinuous passages in old timber; *Trypoxylon* and *Crabro* seek such holes in walls and palings, and into which they convey the larvæ they have seized, and where also they lay their eggs. *Cerceris* and *Philanthus* likewise dig holes in the ground, but they select a loose soil, whence they are found most frequently in sandy situations. *Philanthus apivorus* is notorious as a dangerous enemy to bees, as it only makes use of the honey bee as food for its larva, and which it seizes wherever it finds them *.

Many wasps and bees have similar habits. The majority, however, excavate themselves the holes in which they deposit their eggs, and which they line with peculiar substances, either made by themselves or obtained elsewhere. But they are nevertheless distinguished from the former by their not in general supplying their larvæ with other insects or their larvæ †, but either with the pollen or the nectar of flowers, either in its raw state or previously prepared by them. Among the wasps this custom is found in the genera *Odynerus, Eumenes, Pterocheilus,* &c. They construct separate dwellings for their larvæ in clay walls or clay banks, and sometimes even form a tubular entrance to it, still further to prevent the intrusion of unwelcome guests. The egg is then deposited in the cavity, and provided with a lump of pollen intermixed with honey. Among the bees, the whole group of *Andrenæ* form such nests, yet not in walls, but perpendicularly in the firm earth. The depth of these shafts, which generally descend in a direct line, is not trifling, it frequently exceeding a foot; at the end of the shaft lies the egg, or larva, embedded, as it were, in a quantity of pollen and honey. Many true bees construct them similarly, but the dwellings of their larvæ are generally more artificially formed. Thus the *Megachiles* envelope both egg and pollen in the leaves of plants, which they cut off in pieces, and have gradually wrought together; the *Anthidia* furnish their entire cells with the woolly clothing of many plants, for instance, of the several species of *Stachys*. They thus form in the

* See a paper of mine upon this subject in the first part of the Trans. of the Entom. Society of London.—Tr.

† According to Müller's observations (Germar's Mag. vol. iii. p. 61.), the hornet supplies its young with the bodies of bees, both neuters and drones, as well as with the honey of flowers.

structure of their dwellings a tolerable transition to the elaborate dwellings of the social bees and wasps.

§ 295.

This indication shows that the nests of the wasps and bees which live in society are nothing more than dwelling-places for their progeny. This is their first and chief purpose, and all others which they at the same time execute proceed necessarily from this. If we examine this more closely, we shall find that among the wasps and the humble bees it is always the female which lays the foundation of such a dwelling. The impregnated wasp seeks a place where she can deposit her eggs, when she finds it she constructs a cell, and deposits an egg in it. Instead now of seeking another spot, like the solitary wasps, she remains where she commenced, and adds another cell to the first; thus the first layer is formed. In the interim the first eggs have become larvæ; these larvæ are now carefully fed by the mother until the time of their change into pupæ, when each closes its cell, becomes a pupa, and speedily appears as a perfect insect, which immediately participates in the labour, both in the structure of the nest and in feeding of the larvæ, and upon the increase of the number of those to be fed, by reason of the increasing fertility of the first female, the number of the nurses and labourers also increases, until at last from small beginnings a numerous society is formed. That the first born young wasps may immediately participate in feeding the younger larvæ, they are, as it were, placed in a maternal situation, and it is therefore that they are made barren by being prematurely ripe, and the one female function, that of conception and production, they sacrifice for the other, the feeding and nursing of the young, and it is hence that they are abortive females. Experience has proved that this abortion is produced by the defective feeding of a truly female larva.

If, now, we more closely inspect the several social communities of insects, the object of all of which is the nourishment of the young, the most imperfect of all presents itself in the society of ants. It consists of winged males and females, and apterous abortive females, called neuters, or workers, which are besides distinguished from the rest, especially from the females, by their smaller size. The dwellings in which we find these three members of a society of ants are found in the earth, and consist of passages which lead to larger vacant spaces, all of which again stand in connexion, and which generally have several outlets. The hollow spaces lie in several stories over each other, and are used only as rooms for the larvæ; the ants do not make a provision of food, but hybernate within their dwellings, from which they arouse upon the approach of spring. Their food consists of sweet animal and vegetable juices, which they convey also to the larvæ; they are particularly fond of the juice that exudes from the tubes upon the abdomen of the plant lice; they therefore not merely pursue these creatures, but also retain them in their dwelling. Their pairing time is August; immense multitudes of both sexes then quit their dwelling, and copulate in flight, especially towards evening, about which time they frequently fly up and down in the air in myriads. The males die quickly after copulation, whereas the females are either brought back by the neuters to their former dwelling, or else, either singly or in society, they found new dwellings, which they speedily populate with their own progeny. It is remarkable, that before the commencement of their new labours they purposely deprive themselves of their wings. The young, which pass but a short time in the larva state, during which they are fed by the mother, do not quit the egg before the following spring; and if neuters, they immediately after their development participate in the labours of the mother, they feed the larvæ, increase the dwelling, leaving nothing for the old parent of the nest to do: whereas in the old colonies, to which impregnated females return, or therein pair with the males, the eggs are not laid until the spring, until which time no young progeny is to be found in the nest. Thus the entire society of neuters, with the few impregnated females among them, and without any young ones, hybernate. As soon, however, as the first warm sunshine of the spring rouses them they re-commence their labours, they mend their dwelling, seek food, and convey nutriment also to the female. These then lay eggs, from which the larvæ soon creep, the whole development of which, from the egg to the imago, is so rapid that it is completed in twenty-three days. The males and females now present themselves, but they remain in the dwelling until the middle of the summer, and then quit it for the purpose of pairing. When this is fulfilled the whole series is repeated in the nests founded by the young impregnated females. In the progress of the several occupations exercised by the different members, and especially by the neuters, the ants develope striking art and proofs of the great perfection of their instinct. They always select sunny but not too dry places to lay the foundations of their nests, but they always avoid moist situations, and give considerable preference to the foot of a hollow tree, or its interior when it has but small accesses. They here labour with considerable industry in laying the foundations of the nest, each assisting the other, and in the course of a few days we perceive a structure rise having several outlets. If the nest be upon the ground there are generally affiliated colonies in its vicinity, which are in a constant animated intercourse with the parent state. This intercourse is facilitated by the construction of particular roads, which in a loose soil are tolerably deeply furrowed, and upon these roads we observe innumerable neuters incessantly coursing to and fro. All the obstructions that may here interrupt them are removed, each lends its assistance, and if there be at first too few for the purpose, by means of signs they urge other comrades to participate in the labour. Along these roads they convey into the dwelling the food for the larvæ, which consists in captured insects, caterpillars, small earth worms, and other, mostly animal, substances. We have before related that the ants possess the faculty of communicating their views to their comrades; all that requires the labour of many immediately occupies several, and to this participation they urge each other. Huber *, to whom we are indebted for the most interesting observations upon the economy of the ants, has observed them go out in troops to enjoy some dainty repast when such has been communicated by a compatriot, whither also more and more proceed, until at last nearly the entire population of the nest is found there. Once, upon separating a portion of the community, which he kept in a closed place for several months and then brought them back to the garden where the nest was, he observed their former fellow-citizens gradually emancipate them, after their dwelling had been discovered by some stray ones. But still more remarkable than all this is the warlike and predatory excursions which *Formica rufescens* and *F. sanguinea* undertake upon losing their young progeny of neuters. They then proceed in hosts to the nests of other ants, master its entrances, and convey away their young. These then grow up as helots in the foreign community, execute all the labour necessary for the advance and preservation of the state; they seek food, increase the building, sun the larvæ and pupæ, convey them back into the nest, and assemble with their subduers without recalling their disgrace. Thus originate the variously coloured and intermixed communities.

* P. Huber, Recherches sur les Mœurs des Fourmis Indigenes. Paris et Genève, 1810. 8vo.

§ 296.

The economy of the remaining social *Hymenoptera* differs from that of the ants by their constructing an artificial nest for the reception of the society, and not merely excavating cavities in the earth for this purpose. The wasps, which most closely agree with the ants in their societies, build some their nests in holes in the ground, and others pendant from the boughs of trees. The material they use is wood, either fresh or rotten, which they grind to a fine powder by means of their powerful mandibles, and then moisten it with a viscid liquid, which is probably the secretion of the salivary glands, when they prepare it into thin pasteboard surfaces. The size of the nest varies considerably; in *Polistes gallica* it consists of about twenty roundish cells, open beneath, which form a small convex comb, and which is attached to some object at its highest point; *Vespa holsatica* affixes a second larger, and sometimes a third smaller comb to the first, which are connected together by many perpendicular, tolerably thick pillars, and the whole nest is enclosed by two or three ovate cases, the lowest of which alone envelopes all three combs, each of the succeeding ones being about one-third shorter. The entrance to the interior is in the pendant apex of the first envelope. In the nest of *Vespa vulgaris*, which is placed in a large hole in the ground, the external case consists of a thick, tolerably strong pasteboard, formed of several layers, and the combs are more numerous, the central ones larger, and the entire nest attains about the size of a moderate melon. Others, for instance, the exotic species (*Vespa tatua*, Lat.), build a very large but similarly pendant nest, the entrance to which is also beneath, and the superior surface is covered with a multitude of conical knobs. *Vespa crabro* (the hornet) prefers the cavities of trees for her nest: it differs from that of the common wasp both in size, which is that of a moderate gourd, and also that the external envelopes are separated from each other by the space of at least half an inch, whence passages lead from the exterior to the interior; it therefore appears upon the first glimpse to be covered with large scales. The much smaller nest of *Vespa Germanica* is very similar, but it is placed in the earth, at about six inches from the surface; the form of the cells is originally, as also in the humble bees and bees, that of a cylinder, which subsequently, by the pressure of the rest, take that of a hexagon. This last regular form of the cells has ever been considered one of the most extraordinary things, and its precise repetition in all the societies of the *Hymenoptera* as a proof of the great skill of these insects; but nothing is more natural and necessary in the whole economy of the bees and wasps than this form of their cells; if, for instance, large soft tubes are to be so placed side by side that they may occupy the least space, the form conditionated by the point of contact, and the equal pressure upon all sides must necessarily be that of an hexagonal prism, as may be proved by mathematical demonstration. The bees and wasps consequently, from the innumerable multitudes inhabiting a nest, or hive, must necessarily apply the smallest space possible to their structure, that they may be enabled to introduce a greater number of cells, and hence they become hexagonal: nature also only aims at what is necessary, and not at what is superfluous, and there would have been a waste had she allowed the bees to construct their cells independent of each other, for much unappropriated space would have remained. Besides, each cell is by no means so determinate an hexagonal prism, but rather a cylinder pressed flat by its contact with six other cells; no sharp angles are found inside, and the sides where the angles of three cells meet are thicker than where two cells lie contiguously with their flat surfaces. Among the humble bees, in consequence of the smaller number of the inhabitants of their nests, so strict an economy of space was not requisite, the cells but loosely touch each other, retaining their original round form flattened only at their extremities.

The inhabitants of a wasp's nest likewise consist of three distinct groups, namely, of males, females, and neuters, which last are also abortive females. The foundation of the community is laid by the female, and indeed very early in the spring. The impregnated female hybernates during winter in suitable places, without laying her eggs, and she first seeks, on the approach of spring, after being aroused from her winter torpidity, a place adapted to the structure of her nest, which she begins as soon as she has found such a situation. When the first cells, or the first and smallest comb is completed, she lays in each an egg, whence in the course of a few days a young larva creeps. These she feeds with the juices of other insects, especially of *Hymenoptera*, until they change into pupæ, when the larva closes the lower aperture with a web of silk. In the course of eight or ten days the young wasp presents itself, which, like all the following ones, is a neuter, and consequently a worker, which immediately proceeds with feeding the larvæ and increasing the nest. When all the neuter wasps are thus developed, the development of the male and female eggs which the old mother has laid in the interim is proceeding, while the neuters continue to increase the nest. The perfect males and females remain for some time in the nest, and it is only towards the end of the summer that they quit it. They now pair, after which the males die, but the females prepare for their hybernation. After the males and females have quitted the nest the community appears to have lost its importance, the neuters disperse, and soon die for want of food; the nest itself then loses also its consequence, its community is dispersed never to return again, and it falls to pieces like a deserted ruin. The skill and instincts which the wasps develope during their lives refer therefore almost exclusively to the preparation of their indeed very artificial nest; combined undertakings like those we observed among the ants, we do not detect in them, yet they nevertheless appear to possess a power of communication, for many of the neuters assemble if an enemy appear before their entrances, and endeavour to beat him to retreat by their desperate attacks. These troops are said to be assembled for battle by the guards placed to watch the entrance.

§ 297.

Among the social bees, the society of humble bees is the least perfect. It also consists of males, females, and neuters; and it owes, like that of the wasps, its first foundation to a female. For this purpose the impregnated female, which has lain torpid throughout the winter, seeks in the spring a place suitable to lay the foundation of her nest. She in general seeks shady places concealed among bushes and tufts of grass, where, with much labour, she digs a cup-shaped but yet very slight cavity, over which she spreads an arch, formed of light dry moss. The internal surface of this arch she clothes with a thin layer of wax, and attaches to it the first comb, consisting of large, oval, waxen cells, very loosely connected together. The entrance to the nest is beneath where the arch joins the margin of the hole, but in general a long vaulted passage leads from the exterior to it, that the entrance of enemies may be rendered more difficult. When the first cells are completed the female lays eggs in them, and then fills them with pollen and some honey, for the nourishment of the young. If this does not suffice she also feeds them. These larvæ merely produce workers, which immediately after their birth assist to feed the younger members, for which purpose they especially collect pollen and honey. The development of the neuter larvæ then proceeds, until all are perfected; when the old female lays male and female eggs in the new or cleansed cells. The neuters are chiefly occupied with feeding the larvæ thence disclosed; they are continually collecting honey, which they convey to the larvæ: this honey is also their sole nutriment, for they do not receive pollen, like the larvæ of the neuters. More honey is conveyed into the empty cells. These consist, singularly enough, not of wax, but of the web spun by the larvæ, which has previously transformed into the pupa state within the cell. When this web is completed the workers convey away the wax encompassing it to form new cells, and subsequently use the web as a jar for the honey. Towards the end of the summer the young of both sexes quit the nest, and pair at large; the males die, but the females return to the nest, where they hybernate in cells prepared by themselves, and filled with moss, and some occupy the succeeding spring the old nest, whilst the remainder go forth to form new ones. The neuters and the hybernating females live in the interim upon the collected honey.

Many writers speak of smaller females among the humble bees, as well as among the wasps, which only lay male eggs, and which appear either with the neuters or immediately after them. These are evidently neuters which have not wholly sacrificed their sexuality, and which are consequently capable of procreation. I doubt whether their existence be absolutely necessary, and also, notwithstanding the uniform assurance, that they lay only male eggs. Perhaps the female maggots, either as being superfluous or less perfect, by proceeding from a weaker mother, are killed, and only the males reared.—Among the bees we also occasionally observe fertile workers, or smaller females.

§ 298.

The society of the bees is doubtlessly the most perfect of all, and it differs also in many respects from those already described. It likewise consists of the same members, namely, of males or drones, and females or the queen, and the neuters or workers; we find a multitude of the first and of the last, but of females only one old one, and, according to the differences of season, two or three young ones.

The first founding and structure of the nest of a community of bees, which is called the hive, originates indeed with the female, but is executed by the neuters. If, for instance, an old hive be provided in the spring with a multitude of youthful progeny, so numerous that the old abode can no longer retain them, a great portion of the neuters, led by a single female, migrates or swarms, and proceeds to form a new colony. This swarming is repeated several times even in one hive, which may thus give rise to as many as four other colonies. The first swarm quits it about the middle of May, and the following ones from week to week, until the middle of June. The first that migrate consist chiefly of the older inhabitants of the hive, and their queen is also the old one who had hybernated with them; the subsequent swarms are led by young impregnated females. The swarm quitting the parent hive has at first no dwelling place, but the queen, after a short flight, settles at some spot, and all the workers accompanying her do the same around her; single neuters now fly forth to seek a place which the swarm can inhabit. They in general select for that purpose hollow trees, or other dry situations that they may meet with; when such a cavity is found the entire swarm, with the queen, immediately occupy it. So soon as the swarm has taken formal possession of the dwelling the neuters commence their labours: they first investigate all the entrances, and close all excepting one, which forms the true entrance, which is in general of but small compass, but which is decreased to the requisite size if it be too large. The material with which they close the entrances, and also cover the interior surface of the cavity, is called propolis, metys, pissoceros; it is a resinous substance, which they collect from the clammy and resinous buds of the birch, the sallow, poplars, chestnuts, &c: it differs from wax by its peculiar balsamic smell, by its combustibleness, and its resinous components. They do not appear to prepare it, but apply it to their purpose just as they find it. Their second building material, but of which the cells alone are made, is wax, which is a peculiar secretion of the bees; of the organs which prepare it we have before spoken. The tablets secreted between the ventral segments are removed as soon as a bee wishes to build, then crumbled and dissolved by means of the alkaline saliva into a pap, when it is applied to the construction of the cells. These cells they do not construct like the wasps and humble bees, in horizontal combs, but in perpendicular ones, which run from the summit of their dwelling to its base; both sides also of these combs are occupied by cells, and not, as in the former insects, the lower side only. The cells are of a roundish, slightly hexagonal form, and terminate at their base in triangular points bordered by indistinct rhomboidal surfaces, each of which borders a third of the opposite cell: thus each cell rests upon three of the opposite ones, and their centre meets exactly where the edges of the three cells join. This phenomenon, however skilful it appears to be, has but the object of saving all space, which could be attained by this and no other means, and which admits of being mathematically demonstrated. We here find another proof of the wisest adaptation to the purpose so constantly observed in nature; but the choice of means for attaining it must not be ascribed to the free intellectual power of the creature that employs it; it is but the expression of the eternal necessity and uniformity to which the instinct of the creature is subjected. The number of combs in a hive depends upon the space; the central one is first constructed, and brought down to the ground, on each of which others then follow at the distance of about half an inch from the first; thus by degrees the whole hive is filled with combs. The size of the cells also varies, the smaller ones serve for the reception of the neuters and the provisions, the larger ones contain the male maggots; for the royal maggots, of which there are from three to four in each hive, distinct cells are formed upon the margin of the comb, but which, however, never touch the walls of the nest. They are in the form of a very large, spacious, ovate cell, which is not horizontal, like the others, but perpendicular, opening beneath. The aperture is smaller than the body of the cell, and increases with the larva, for the neuters increase both the cell and the aperture upon the growth of the larva.

Being thus acquainted with the structure of a young bee-hive, we shall now pass to the examination of its inhabitants and their several occupations. After the workers of a young colony have built a requisite number of cells, others then busy themselves with filling them with honey; thus a portion of them are constantly occupied with enlarging the dwelling the while another portion are busied in collecting provisions. This gathering continues the whole remainder of the spring and summer, and is carried on even late in the autumn, and they do not cease until the flowers cease blossoming. The substance they collect is honey, a thick yellowish fluid, consisting of crystallising sugar, liquid sugar, and a peculiar viscid substance insoluble in alcohol, which the neuters imbibe by means of their long tubular tongue from the nectaries of plants, and conserve in their sucking stomach, which thus supplies the place of a crop; hence it is thrown up when the bees wish to get rid of it, when probably it does not repass through the tube of the proboscis, but through the aperture of the mouth, beneath the valve of the œsophugus, or second tongue.

During this time the true stomach receives no honey for digestion, but we invariably find in it a crumbly mass called bee bread, consisting of pollen, which constitutes the true food of the bees, and which alone is given to the larvæ as food. This mass of pollen does not appear to be received through the canal of the proboscis, but through the true aperture of the œsophagus. As soon as the colder season interrupts the collecting of honey the bees gradually become more inactive, when a few alone loiter about the entrance of the hive, whereas the majority are preparing for their hybernation within. They then so constrict the opening that one bee only can pass through at a time, they cling together in the hive, and appear to have lost much of their former vivacity; but they do not become absolutely torpid, but feed temperately upon the honey collected in the summer.

During this whole time the queen reposes quietly in the nest, enjoying the respect shown to her by the neuters. As soon as some of the small cells are completed for the workers she commences laying her eggs, impregnated by the preceding year's pairing, notwithstanding having previously laid many in the old hive; or if she be a young queen she will have been impregnated by the drones of the old hive prior to her quitting. In the course of three days after laying the egg the young larva is disclosed, which is full grown in five days more; the larvæ then close the cells themselves, in three days more they become pupæ, and in the course of seven days and a half the perfect bee comes forth, thus its development is completed in the twentieth day after the laying of the egg. A great number of workers being thus born, the queen begins to lay male eggs in the larger cells, and from three to four female ones in the royal cell. When the old queen has laid all her eggs she dies, and the hive is without a head until the young royal larvæ are developed. This the bees bear very quietly, whereas the loss of the queen without the survivance of a royal progeny produces the total dissolution of the society. But if the young royal maggots are developed whilst the old queen still lives she kills them, which the neuters freely allow; it will therefore sometimes happen that a swarm, after the female has laid all her eggs, is without a royal successor. This evil it is said the neuters remove by transferring a one-day old maggot from the cells of the neuters to the royal cell, where they rear it with superior food, whence a queen is developed. The correctness of this assertion, which is however supported by many direct observations, has been doubted, and Treviranus has endeavoured to deny it, but it has so much analogy in its favour, and is related by such credible observers, that it may really be considered as a fact. Thus, therefore, the hive receives a new queen when the old one dies. This new queen quits the dwelling, in company with the drones, in the middle of summer, pairs with some of them, and then returns impregnated to the hive; she is here then treated with greater respect than before, she is stroked with the antennæ, licked with the tongue, and they on all sides offer her honey. Forty-six hours after pairing she lays her first egg, and then continues uninterruptedly until the 1st of November, from whence until April she ceases, but which she again resumes in April, upon the return of fine weather, when the workers again collect. Now, after having laid none but the eggs of neuters, she lays about 2,000 male eggs, whence, at their appointed time, the drones proceed. From this time until their pairing with the female they live undisturbedly in the hive; they fly out for food and again return, but they do not form cells or collect honey, and do nothing else than go out to feed for their own support. At the time of pairing, which takes place in June, a great multitude of them fly out with the queen, and return again after she has paired with one of them, for which it sacrifices its life; for, according to Huber and Audouin, the penis torn off remains for some time in the vagina of the female, fixed in the neck of the spermatheca. The remaining drones quietly rest until August, even after the remaining young queens which lead out the subsequent swarms have been impregnated by them, but at this period the general slaughter of the drones commences, in which, in the course of three days, all the males are destroyed by the neuters, and even whilst still living are cast from the hives. Thus, without males, and provided with one female, who is however impregnated, and without any progeny for males and females, the inhabitants of the hive hybernate as well as the young maggots of the workers, all subsisting upon the collected provisions. It is then also the time to destroy the hive, to remove the bees, and to take their honey.

The instincts developed by the bees during their life are extremely remarkable and surprising. Their attachment to the queen, their endless anxiety for her welfare, the affection and self sacrifice with which they rear the young, have ever excited the greatest admiration, and also well merit it. No individual bee cares for herself, her whole anxiety is for the entire community, and so long as she perceives that her labours do not miss their aim—the preservation and prosperity of the hive, she is contented with her fate. But as soon as by the death of the queen this prospect is obstructed, by there being no possibility of obtaining a new queen, she becomes depressed, without courage, ceases her work, and is lost in the conviction of having lost her labours. We cannot here relate in detail the several phases and very special facts which exhibit the comprehensiveness of her instinct, and they are the less necessary as other works fully show them; we therefore refer to the Introduction of Kirby and Spence, as well as to the admirable work of Huber *. As willingly as we could wish to refer the actions of the neuter bees to reflective powers, we yet feel ourselves obliged to deny them this reasoning; they act rather from eternal invariable laws, for they have added nothing to it in so many thousand generations, nor have they lost anything, which therefore announces their want of freedom, as well as the other side the endless wisdom of nature is clearly exhibited in the consistency and suitableness of all their proceedings. They are but the wheels and instruments in a higher hand, imperceptible to us, and still more so to them, which holds the universe; and to which science must always refer, but which is depicted to the fancy in a beautiful and attractive image. What Johan von Müller † has expressed to be the result of his researches into the history of the human race we may apply to the life of bees, to the actions of the rest of the world of insects, and indeed to the great effects of organic nature in general. The whole is an infinite machine, to whose eternal motion every individual, be it plant, animal, or man, must contribute, and he who of all that can obey this law is wantonly deaf—he is judged.

§ 299.

There are two orders, namely, the *Neuroptera* and *Dictyotoptera*, to whose care for their young we have as yet paid no attention, and to which we now therefore proceed. Among the first, the young larvæ of the *Semblodea* and *Phryganea* live in water, and without any especial care on the part of the mother, are confided to this element. We are still ignorant of where the eggs and larvæ of the *Panorpæ* are to be found, for their larvæ are as yet unknown. The larvæ of

* F. Huber, Nouvelles Observations sur les Abeilles; addressées à M. C. Bonnet. Genève, 1792. 8vo. Nouvelles Observ. sur les Ab. Paris et Genève, 1814. 8vo. 2 vols.

† Vier und Zwanzig Bücher Allgemeiner Geschichte, vol. iii. p. 532.

Raphidia live in the stems of pines, and here hunt up their food, which consists in other insects; we might doubtless find their eggs there also, and presume that they are deposited by the mother at suitable places upon the stem. The larvæ of *Myrmecoleon* and *Ascalaphus* live in the sand, the first, as we have before mentioned, in pitfalls made by itself, where it watches for prey; the mother doubtlessly therefore conveys her eggs there, and deposits them in suitable places, sheltered from the weather and from enemies.

The same is doubtlessly the case among the *Dictyotoptera*. The parasites, or *Mallophagi*, deposit their eggs at the base of the feathers or hair of those animals upon which they dwell, and upon which their young are to reside. It is not yet known where the eggs of the *Thysanura* are placed. The eggs of the *Ephemeræ* and *Libellulæ* are deposited in the water, where the young also dwell, and they are laid singly, the mother the whilst fluttering over the water. To conclude, the last families of *Psoci* and *Termites* differ considerably from each other in their modes of life. The majority of the species of the genus *Psocus* live in the old stems of trees, and here appear to hunt for prey: *Ps. pulsatorius* is a voracious enemy to collections of insects, and it will devour dry animal substances, namely, the smaller soft-winged *Diptera*; it doubtlessly, therefore, deposits its eggs in the vicinity of such things, and there leaves them to their fate. This the *Termites* do not do, but they build dwellings similarly to the *Hymenoptera*, where they lead a still more artificially regulated social life. We indeed possess several treatises upon the remarkable economy of these insects, distributed between the tropics (two species are found in the South of France), and especially an early one by Smeathman*, but still their complete economy is not fully illustrated, in as far as these tracts contain so much that is striking and divergent that it cannot well be compared with the social life of other insects. Their community is said to consist of five different members, namely, winged males and females, apterous neuters, or soldiers, which have large heads furnished with strongly projecting mandibles, unwinged pupæ, having a smaller head and the rudiments of wings only, and lastly, of similarly formed larvæ, or workers, differing from the latter only in wanting the rudiments of wings. The last of these construct the dwelling, in which they are assisted by the

---

* Phil. Trans. vol. lxxi. 1781, completed from more recent observations in Kirby and Spence, vol. ii.

pupæ; the neuters are the guards at the entrances, and defend the nest against enemies; the males and females are inactive, and remain until they pair in the nest, they then fly forth, pair, and a single couple of them are conveyed back again into the nest by the workers, and here kept prisoners; the rest die or are destroyed, losing immediately their wings, when they are quite helpless.

If we receive this description as true, particularly as the *Termites*, according to general assertion, belong to the tribes with an imperfect metamorphosis, and therefore might be active and industrious in their larva state, yet the circumstance of its being without any analogy in the whole animal world may be urged against it; we have no other instance of the young still undeveloped labouring for the old, and which as larvæ and pupæ they must necessarily be. Besides, the assertion that the neuters are apterous is not correct, for I have had the opportunity of dissecting winged *Termites*, through the kindness of the Privy Councillor Klug, the Conservator of the Royal Berlin collection, and I did not find the least trace of either external or internal genitalia: nor had they the large head with projecting mandibles, but one perfectly corresponding with that of the males and females. But these *Termites* readily lost their wings upon the least touch, and retained but a small triangular basal piece at the thorax. There is, namely, at the base of the wing, close to its root, an apparent joint, in front of which the wing is horny, but behind it soft and membranous, and provided only upon its anterior margin with ribs. The wing is easily broken off at this joint, and therefore the neuters very speedily lose their wings, but they are not, as maintained by writers, wingless. Nor do I see why the neuters should be merely the defenders, as these among all other social insects are the true workers. If it may be allowed to start hypotheses upon subjects that can only be satisfactorily explained by experience, we might also, with reference to the society of the *Termites*, admit of the community consisting of merely males, females, and abortive females, or neuters, and that the latter were likewise winged, but from external causes speedily lost their wings after their development. To these might be added the larvæ and pupæ which would intermix with the swarms of neuters, but not participate in the labours; they have no wings, and consequently resemble the neuters when the latter have lost them, thence has sprung the assertion that the larvæ are workers. The larvæ and the pupæ, in consequence of their much greater voracity, may especially contribute to the destruction of furniture, as well as of all other dead vegetable substances, and are therefore, as well as from their being necessarily the most numerous portion of the community, the most dangerous members of the society. For instance, the *Termites* have a habit of gnawing all dead vegetable and animal substances which they can reach, and so vexatiously to mankind that they merely destroy its interior, leaving the external form unchanged. They thus bore the balustrades of houses, excavate the planks of the floors, tables, chairs, and all kinds of household furniture, and they frequently leave so very slight a case remaining that the whole falls to pieces upon the least touch. Man has therefore much difficulty in defending himself from these concealed enemies, and finds his only means of escape in leaving those parts inhabited by *Termites* unoccupied. The *Termites* gnaw these objects chiefly to obtain thence the materials for their buildings, or even also for food. The building that they construct is often of the shape of a sugar-loaf, and about twelve feet high, which gradually grows from several small towers of the same description. When, for instance, they have raised a small cone of about one or two feet high, they lay around the foundations of several similar cones, which are contiguous at their base; these are then connected together by a thick wall, which is continued by degrees in an oblique direction, until a cone of the given size is thence constructed. Whilst they are still building, the original small community inhabits the interior of the central cone; this has in its middle an arched cell about an inch thick, which is on the same plane with the ground, and in which the old male and female live. In the circumference of this cell there are many smaller ones for the soldiers, and around these again others for the eggs and provisions, which consist of collected drops of gum, pieces of wood, and other substances which they have found upon their desolating forays. When the large arch is completed they remove the apex of the first cone, the entire surface of the described cells is flattened, and here, as well as upon the walls of the arch, new cells are constructed for the provisions. Passages which run along the wall of the arch lead to their upper cells, and bridges are sometimes constructed, which spring from the surface above the royal cell, and extend to the internal wall of the arch. The materials of which they form this structure is clay and earth, which they artificially combine together, it then speedily dries in the sun and becomes a hard, firm covering, that in time is covered with grass, and will easily bear the weight of a man; the internal cells, especially those for the eggs and provisions, are doubtlessly constructed of splinters of wood fastened together with gum. All these cells are connected by means of small apertures, and several apertures also open from the surrounding spaces into the central royal cell; the exterior outlets are not perceptible, they lie at the foundations of the house, and consist in passages, which also pass beneath the earth, and only at distant points open to the surface. At these the *Termites,* which pass in and out, present themselves.

The following is the economy of the state:—At the termination of the hot season, when the moderated temperature of the rainy period announces itself by cooler winds, the young males and females disclosed in the nest quit it, and appear upon the surface of the earth; here they swarm in innumerable hosts, and pair. The busied workers then convey a pair back into the dwelling, and imprison them in the central royal cell, the entrances to which they decrease and guard. Through these apertures the imprisoned pair then receive the nutriment they require. The male now, as among all other insects, speedily dies after copulating, but the female commences from this period to swell considerably from the development of the eggs; this swelling continues until the time of her commencing to lay them, when her abdomen is about 1,500 or 2,000 times larger than the rest of her body. During the period of this swelling the workers remove the walls of the royal cell, uniting the nearest cells to it, so that in proportion to the increase of the body of the queen the size of the cell she inhabits is also increased. She now commences to lay eggs during the constant undulating motion of her abdomen, which exhibits the peristaltic motion of the egg-ducts. The eggs are conveyed away by the workers as they are laid, and conveyed to the distant rearing cells. It is impossible to give the exact number of the eggs laid, but it must be enormous, which is proved as well by the size of her abdomen as by the long time she is laying them, as well as by the number she lays in a minute, namely, sixty. In these nursery cells the larvæ are first fed by the workers, they afterwards intermix among the workers, and participate in their destructive expeditions, which they make without any impediment, by means of their subterranean passages to the vicinity of the substance they purpose to destroy. Thus far extends the information of naturalists who have travelled. They are silent upon the mode in which a new colony is founded, and what induces the old ones to their formation, and we may, if we will not remain wholly dark upon the subject, start the hypothesis that the communities of *Termites,* at the time when the number of the inhabitants of a nest is too numerous to admit of its accommodating them all, swarm in a similar manner to the bees. But such a swarm would only consist of workers and soldiers, which select at the time of pairing a couple from the numerous royal pairs, and raise them to be the lords of the colony.

We terminate here with the consideration of this family, in which the interesting facts of the earlier ones are again repeated, the description of the intellectual impulses that have appropriately been designated as instinctive phenomena, as perfectly as a short outline will admit. As anxious for self-preservation, and therein exhibiting especially its intellectual functions, the insect steps forth into the series of independent organic beings, and as still anxious for the conservation of the species, it again quits this large community. It was requisite to illustrate this result, already expressed in the introduction to the second chief division, as concisely as possible, and therefore all facts which remain more or less isolated were necessarily omitted. This we could the more satisfactorily do, as another work, to which we have here frequently referred, as well as below, has endeavoured to give a similar solution to the same problem, yet with infinitely greater detail; we mean Kirby and Spence's Introduction to Entomology, a book which, for the animation of its description, fidelity of portraiture, and fulness of facts, vainly seeks its equal, and will with difficulty be surpassed. We will therefore refer our readers to it, who may here have observed many defects, and none, we can assure them, will quit it undelighted or without regret.

THIRD SUBSECTION.

RELATIONS OF INSECTS TO THE EXTERNAL WORLD.

§ 300.

We have now become acquainted with both the corporeal and intellectual natures of insects, and might therefore consider their general natural history as concluded; but having as yet left untouched one portion of the history of the lives of these creatures, namely, their relation to the rest of organic nature, we will therefore appropriate a few pages to the investigation of this subject. That the whole of organic nature stands in close connexion together must be evident to every one who has paid the least attention to the subject. When the plant dies it becomes the parent of a thousand others, all chiefly indeed of lower station; the animal supports itself by deriving its nutriment from the vegetable kingdom, and then itself supplies other animals, which are not appointed to feed upon vegetables, with means of preservation. This relation of insects to the vegetable kingdom and to other organisms will form the immediate subject of our present investigation; we shall here class the conditions under which the insect continues in the external world, in so far as it is only by this favourable relation that that first object is attained, and these we distinguish as the places of resort and the distribution of insects; their geographical division should form a component part of this chapter, and we may then devote our attention to the insects of a past creation, concluding their general history with this last inquiry.

TENTH CHAPTER.

INSECTS IN RELATION TO OTHER ORGANIC BEINGS.

§ 301.

It is a proved fact that all animal bodies derive their nutriment originally from the vegetable kingdom. In no class of animals is this more evident to us than among insects. We have before seen, where we spoke of the food of insects, that vegetable substances constitute their chief subsistence, and that entire orders, as, for instance, the *Lepidoptera*, from the first moment of their existence, feed upon nothing but plants and their juices. In the innumerable multitudes of different species, and the hosts of individuals of one species, this might eventually prove injurious to the vegetable kingdom, if also many insects did not likewise aid to promote the growth of plants. This observation leads us to recognise the true relations of the insect to the vegetable world, and whilst discovering this we perceive at the same time the precise object nature accomplishes in its capacious economy by means of insects. It is double; in the first place to set a limit to the preponderating increase of plants, and also, as such a relation might easily degenerate into their total destruction, it is also careful, by another course, of preserving the vegetable kingdom.

The first object is attained by means of those insects which derive their nutriment from vegetable substances, consequently by means of those which devour leaves, flowers, wood, fruits, and their seeds. These organs provide for the continuance of plants as individuals or species, and every plant would more or less suffer if one or all of them were totally destroyed by insects. Let us examine this more closely in individual instances.

§ 302.

With respect to those insects which destroy the roots of many plants, and thereby restrict their superfluous growth, we must remark, that it is generally larvæ only which feed upon that part. Among the *Carabodea* the larva of *Zabrus* belongs to these, for in the spring of the year 1812, in the vicinity of Halle, whole corn-fields were devoured by their voracity *. During the day it buries itself six inches deep in the earth, and towards evening it comes to the surface, and then eats into the pith of the roots, biting off the blade closely above the ground. Thus in the above year twelve hides of wheat, rye, and barley were destroyed. As the genus *Amara*, which is closely allied to *Zabrus*, has in its perfect state a very similar mode of life, particularly the division of it known by the name of *Leirus*, we may conclude that their larvæ also live upon the roots of grass. We may perhaps also class here the larva first described by Walfrod, and which he considered as a wire worm (the larva of *Elater segetis*, Gyll.). Kirby and Spence † consider it as the larva of a *Staphylinus*, but this is contradicted by the difference of the mode of life of the other individuals of this tribe. It lives, namely, at the roots of wheat, devours the just germinating grain, and in older plants it consumes the root only. According to Sir J. Banks the same larva destroys turnips, and sometimes from forty to fifty individuals are found in one root.

In addition to these it is especially the larvæ of many of the *Elaters* which attack the roots of corn and other plants. We know that the wire worm, which is the larva of *Elater segetis*, Gyll., (*E. lineatus*, Lin., *E. striatus*, F.), feeds upon the roots of corn, as well as that the larva of the allied *Elater obscurus*, Lin., (*E. variabilis*, Fab.) feeds upon the roots of almost all kinds of garden plants and culinary vegetables, and sometimes, in places where they have much increased, produce great injury.

The majority of the larvæ of those *Lamellicornes* which in their perfect state feed upon leaves, as the *Melolonthæ* and *Cetoniæ*, devour, in that state, the roots of plants; these thick, fat, yellowish white larvæ are well enough known to farmers, and frequently produce great injury to corn. Multitudes of the larvæ of *Melolontha ruficornis* actively participated in the devastation committed by the larvæ of *Zabrus gibbus* in the vicinity of Halle. The more numerous and more generally distributed larvæ of *Melolontha vulgaris*, the common cockchafer, are not less injurious, particularly as they pass several years as larvæ, and every year new ones are produced. An instance occurred near Norwich, in

---

* Germar's Mag. vol. i. part i. p. 1, &c.
† Introduct. to Entom. iv. Letter xlv.

which all the fields of a farmer were entirely destroyed, and he and his labourers collected eighty bushels of them. The larvæ of *Hoplia pulverulenta*, *H. graminicola*, and *H. argentea*, dwell in humid meadows, where they destroy the roots of the different grasses. Some few years ago I myself discovered all the blades of high grass of this description completely covered with the perfect *H. argentea*.

It is especially among the *Curculios* that we find larvæ which are destructive to roots; but less so among the other families, yet the larva of *Lathridius porcatus*, according to Kyber[*], feeds at the roots of *Rhaphanus sativus*, and especially in that of the variety known by the name of the radish. Kirby and Spence reared from a small larva that was found in the root of *Sinapis arvensis* the *Curculio contractus*, Msh., and the *Rh. assimilis*, Fab., two species of insects belonging to the genus *Ceutorhynchus*, which, even as perfect insects, like all their congeners, attack the young shoots of plants.

Besides the above larvæ of the beetles, many of the maggots of the *Diptera* are fond of the roots of plants. Thus the maggot of a fly has been found in a carrot (the root of *Daucus carota*), but it was not reared; in the radish (the root of *Rhaphanus sativus*) the maggot of *Anthomya radicum*, Meig.; and in onions a similar maggot, which produced a fly that Kirby and Spence call *Scatophaga ceparum*. Other dipterous larvæ Reaumur[†] found in the bulbs of the narcissus, and reared from them a fly belonging to the family of the *Syrphodea*, which Meigen calls *Merodon equestris*. The root also of the cauliflower feeds the maggots of flies; in that, as well as in the other varieties of the cabbage, is found the maggot of the *Tipula oleracea*, Lin.

Although the majority of the caterpillars of the *Lepidoptera* feed upon the leaves of plants, yet there are some which prefer their young roots; thus the caterpillar of *Noctua* (*Episema*, Tr.) *graminis*, Fab., which consumes the tender roots of the softer grasses, and spares the elder harder ones, for instance, those of *Alopecurus pratensis*, Lin., as well as those of corn and of the *Trifolium pratense*, Lin.[‡]

§ 303.

Those insects, however, are more numerous which either bore into the stems of plants or into the woody trunks of trees; but their pre-

---

[*] Germar's Mag. vol. ii. p. 1, &c.   [†] Mémoires, vol. iv. part xxxiv.
[‡] Ochsenheimer Schmetterlinge von Europa fortges. von Treitschke, 5 t. part i. p. 122.

sence does not in general so speedily occasion the death of the plant, as the stem is a larger and less easily wounded organ than the root.

Among the beetles we may place here the several boring and bark beetles that form the family of *Deperditores* (*Xylotrogi*, Lat.) and *Bostrychodea* (*Trogositariæ*, Lat.), as well as the large family of the *Cerambycina*. The majority, however, destroy the woody substance of the stem in general only when the tree is felled or already prepared for manipulation, in the latter case especially it is attacked by those of the *Deperditores*, which belong to the genera *Ptinus* and *Anobium:* they appear to be created more for the dispersion of dead vegetable substances than for the destruction of living plants. As Nature produces the more rapid dissolution of corrupt animal matter, by means of the onthophagous and carrion beetles, so it appears that she accomplishes the same object with respect to the dead stems of plants, through the agency of these insects. The larvæ also of the *Buprestodea* and of many *Elaters* live in the stem, for instance, the larva of *Buprestis biguttata* in the stem of oaks, *Elater rufus* in the stem of pines, and both especially in the remaining stumps of felled trees. There also do we particularly find the larvæ of the capricorns, and living trees they do not appear to care for, yet the larva of *Saperda linearis* lives in the pith of the young twigs of the stem of the hazel (*Coryllus avellana*), and that of *Lamia amputator* in the pith of tropical plants [*], that of *Callidium bajulus* in timber, rafters, and roofs. But the family of the bark beetles (*Bostrychodea*), thus named from their dwelling-place, beneath the bark, are most destructive to woods, especially to those consisting of firs, pines, and oaks, for example, the genus *Platypus*. The commoner species, namely, *Bostrychus typographus*, *B. laricis*, *Hylesinus piniperda*, *Hylurgus ater*, &c., occasionally so much undermine the bark that it becomes quite loosened from the stem, and the tree, having lost in its liburnum its nutritive layer, dies. Formerly many instances occurred of whole forests of pines being thus destroyed in the Harz, in Franconia, and in Silesia, and it was called the (wurmtrocknisz) worm dry rot. Tropical trees are also visited by such guests, for instance, the stems of palms by the *Calandra palmarum*, but they are chiefly found in felled trees lying in the woods, and which they speedily destroy through the great size they attain. It is thus also that the large larvæ of exotic capricorns live, as those of *Prionus cervicornis*, *Pr.*

---

[*] Lansdown Guilding in Linnæan Trans. vol. xiii.

damicornis, Lamia tribulus, &c., which live in the stems of Brazilian or tropical plants, particularly those of the genus *Bombax.*

The stems of corn also serve as a dwelling-place for many larvæ; thus we find the maggot of a fly belonging to the genus *Mosillus*, of Latreille, subsisting in the blade of wheat. Another, known by the name of the Hessian fly, also lays its eggs in the blade of wheat, and thus frequently destroys entire fields, from the increasing maggot devouring all the leaves. *Musca pumilionis,* Lin., lays its eggs in the heart of young rye, and the larva destroys the shoot, commencing with the germen and then consuming the leaf. *Pyralis sicalis* attacks in a similar manner the blade of barley, depositing its eggs in a cavity bored between the leaf and stem. Exotic grasses also are destroyed by enemies which consume their pith. An ant (*Formica analis,* Latr.) makes its dwelling in the interior of the sugar-cane, and feeds upon its sweet pith; another (*F. saccharivora,* Lin.), takes up its abode between the cellular roots of the same plant, and thus destroys it by drying it up. In the fortieth year of the preceding century this ant had so much increased in the island of Granada that every plantation was destroyed by it, and every means applied to remove the evil was fruitless. The larvæ also of the *Elater noctilucus*, of which we have already spoken, lives in the pith of the sugar-cane, and feeds upon it [*].

The larvæ of many *Lepidoptera* live in the interior of the stems and of the twigs, or beneath the bark, and thereby prevent the growth of the plant: thus, for instance, we find the caterpillars of several moths, as that of *Tinea corticella,* Fab., beneath the bark of trees; and another caterpillar, that of *Tortrix Weberana,* F., is the cause of great injury to fruit trees, by boring through their bark. The caterpillar of *Thyris fenestrina,* O., lives in the annual twigs of the common *Sambucus niger*, L., and of *Arctium lappa*, and destroy their soft pith. But the caterpillars of the genus *Sesia* are well known as borers of the stems of trees, but from their small number we have never heard of extraordinary devastations committed by them. Thus the caterpillar of *Sesia apiformis* lives in the stems of all kinds of poplars, as does that of *S. asiliformis* in the young stems of *Populus dilatata*, L.; *S. spheciformis* in the stems of the elders and birch trees; *S. hylæiformis* in the branches of *Rubus idæus*, L.; *S. culiciformis* in the bark of plum and apple trees; *S. formicæformis* in the branches of

---

[*] Humboldt, Essai sur la Geographie des Plantes, p. 136.

different willows, for instance, of *Salix alba* ; *S. tipuliformis* in the pith of the stem of the red currant (*Ribes rubrum*, Lin. *). It is, lastly, very generally known that the caterpillar of the goat moth (*Cossus ligniperda*) lives for several years in the stems of old willows, where by degrees it transforms the internal dead part into powder.

Among the other orders we are acquainted with the family of the *Sirices*, which all live as larvæ in the stem partly of pines and partly of oaks, and there change into pupæ, as well as individual genera of bees, for instance, *Xylocopa*, which bores into wood, especially door-posts and gates, and there forms cells for its young *. The same in the *Dipterous* family of the *Xylophagi*, the larvæ of which live in stems beneath the bark.

§ 304.

The leaves of plants and their young germens or eyes are more universally destroyed by insects. Among those which make the just developing eyes their dwelling place are the larvæ of the *Tortrices* and the skip-jacks (*Hatticæ*). Many plants are absolutely infested by these inimical guests, and we frequently hear the gardener and farmer complain of these terrible enemies of their fruit harvest, when they have resumed their activity in the destruction of the young buds. The larvæ of the *Tortrices* fold up by their webs the just developed leaves, and thus obstruct the younger ones, and then conveniently eat away the innermost core of the eye, which in fruit trees consists especially of the blossom buds. They do not appear to have any particular preference among the different kinds of fruit, but attack all at the same time or successively. The skip-jacks do not weave the leaves together, but merely devour the young shoots. Among these also no species appears to be especially restricted to one and the same plant, but choose them at caprice. Yet *H. oleracea* and *H. nemorum*, being the most common species, are the most notorious. The first especially attacks young culinary plants, particularly those belonging to the family of the *Cruciferæ*, namely, cabbage, turnip, mustard, rape, &c. *H. concinna* lives in the young shoots and buds of the hop; *H. nemorum* in the turnip; and the remaining numerous species in the buds of wild uncultivated plants.

The host of insects that destroy the leaves of vegetables is so innu-

* Ochsenheimer Schmetterlinge von Europa, vol. ii. p. 121, &c.

merable, that even a superficial account of our native plants, and the insects that dwell upon them, would fill a volume: we will therefore limit ourselves to the enumeration of the chief families that consume leaves, and cite from them the most interesting genera. Among the beetles we find the large family of the *Chrysomela*, both as larva and imago, select leaves for their food, and they are therefore usually found upon plants. Thus we find *Galleruca tanaceti* upon the *Tanacetum vulgare*; *G. viburni* upon *Viburnum opulus*; *G. nymphea* upon water plants *Nymphea, Alisma, Sagittaria*; *G. Alni* upon *Alnus glutinosa*; *Chrysomela pallida* upon *Sorbus aucuparia*; *Chr. varians* and *Chr. centaurei*, F., upon *Hypericum perforatum*; *Chr. Sophiæ* upon *Sisymbrium Sophia* L.; *Chr. vitellinæ* upon *Salix vitellina*; *Lema Asparagi* and *L.* 12-*punctata* upon *Asparagus officinalis*; *Lema merdigera* and *L. brunnea* upon *Lilium martagon*, &c. All these beetles and their larvæ have the peculiarity of not in general consuming the leaf from its margin, like the caterpillars of the *Lepidoptera*, but they bite a hole into the substance, around which they continue to eat. Thus both these destroyers may be distinguished from each other by the appearance merely of the leaf that has been attacked. Other families of beetles do not restrict themselves so exclusively to leaves, yet many, for example, the *Malacoderma, Melolonthodea, Vesicifica*, the *Cassidæ* (particularly the larvæ) and other genera devour leaves by preference.

Of the remaining orders it is, especially in that of the *Hymenoptera* and among the family of saw-flies (*Tenthredonodea*), that we find leaf-devouring insects. The pseudo caterpillars of these insects, deposited even by the mother as an egg in the parenchyma of the leaf, devour the leaves with incredible voracity, and thereby frequently destroy entire plantations. Thus the large larva of *Cimbex variabilis* lives chiefly upon willows, of *C. lucorum* upon the birch, of *Hylotoma rosæ* upon roses, of the different species of *Lophyrus* upon different pines and firs, *L. pini*, for instance, upon *Pinus silvestris*, of *L. laricis* upon *Pinus larix*, &c. The true saw-flies (*Tenthredo*) are the most numerous of all, and destroy cherries (*Prunus cerasus*), alders (*Alnus glutinosa*), willows (*S. alba, S. capræa*, and many others), roses (*Rosa canina*), and many other plants. Where they are numerous upon a tree they speedily destroy all the leaves, and the tree, already sickly from the loss of its organs of respiration, dies. Thus, one known by the name of the slug-worm, living upon the plum, some few years ago destroyed whole districts of orchards, as Peck has related in a distinct treatise *. The larva of *Lyda pratensis* also, which lives upon the fir, a short time since, in the vicinity of Muskau, in Silesia, committed dreadful devastation, according to the communication of K. Hapf †.

But in no order are leaves used so universally for food as among the *Lepidoptera*, of which the majority as caterpillars consume them. We imagine we shall give a sufficient proof of this by mentioning some of the numerous trees and plants indigenous with us, and which are eaten by caterpillars. The oak, in the first place, feeds innumerable caterpillars, for instance, *Gastropacha quercus, Smerinthus quercus, Harpya Milhauseri, Notodonta camelina*, innumerable *Noctuæ*, and *Geometers;* according to a calculation of Roesel's, this tree supports in its several parts and organs about two hundred distinct species of insects, whence it will be easy to deduce their relation to the rest, as well as of insects to the vegetable kingdom in general. Thus every forest tree has not merely one, but three, four, and even as many as a dozen caterpillars which feed upon its leaves, and which often seriously injure them. We will merely refer to the destruction occasioned by *Liparis dispar* to poplars, *L. salicis* to willows, *L. chrysorrhea, L. nudibunda, L. fascelina* to different fruit trees, *L. monacha* to the fir, and a multitude of others, which are known as tree and forest destroyers. The number of injurious forest caterpillars is so large that we cannot wonder at the great devastation we so frequently hear committed by them. Thus there are found upon the pine, besides those already enumerated, *Gastropacha pini, G. pityocampa, Sphinx pinastri, Noctua (Trachea,* Tr.) *piniperda, Lithoria quadra, Geometra (Fidonia,* Tr.), *piniaria, G. (Ellopia,* Tr.) *prasinaria, G. (Ell.* Tr.) *fasciaria ; Tinea resinella*, which occasions the escape of rosin from the young twigs of the fir ; *T. dodecella, T. strobilella, T. pinella,* &c., which dwell partly in the young buds, and partly in the eyes of the firs. We will not extend this list to other forest trees, but refer at once to Bechstein's ‡ Natural History of Injurious Forest Insects, where there is ample detail. We will only further mention that many of our fruit trees support their peculiar enemies, among which the cater-

---

* W. Peck, Natural History of the Slug-worm. Boston, N. A., 1799. 8vo.
† Bemerkungen über Raupenfrass v. K. Hapf. Bamberg. in Aschaffenberg. 1829. 8vo.
‡ Bechstein's Naturgeschichte der schädlichen Forstinsekten. Leipzig, 1805, 3 vols. 4to.

pillars of *Gastropacha neustria* and *Episema cæruleocephala* are the most common and the most dangerous.

The different kinds of corn, as well as the grasses in general, are less attacked by leaf-devouring caterpillars, yet the caterpillar of *Episema graminis* has been observed to destroy them *. The numerous members of the order of the *Orthoptera* feed very generally upon these plants, but they do not despise even others. Thus the grasshoppers can be fed with all kinds of leaves, but they seem to prefer those of grass to all others. One insect of this order, the migratory locust, has acquired a widely dispersed notoriety from the devastating expeditions it undertakes in immense hosts, and it has thence been unjustly considered as an introduced insect. This it is certainly not, it being indigenous with us (Germany), and it is only occasionally that it appears in vast hosts, which quit their birth-place from having there destroyed all their vegetable food, and they proceed further to seek fresh. We will refer to Kirby and Spence for a full account of their mode of migrating, as well as for the details of their several excursions, and merely mention that an instance of this occurred in June, 1832, near the Bavarian town Weissenburg. They passed from east to west over the town, in some places but a few ells above the surface, and their number was so great that it took three quarters of an hour for the entire swarm to pass. Wind and rain, which speedily came on, adds the informant, prevented further observation †.

These remarks sufficiently prove how many insects derive their food from leaves, and how great the destruction is when their numbers disproportionately increase: we will now proceed to notice those insects which attack by preference the fruit and stem.

§ 305.

Upon returning to the order of the *Coleoptera*, we immediately find a large family among them which are chiefly occupied with the destruction of the seeds of plants, namely, the *Curculios* (*Rhynchophora*). The majority of the species have their peculiar plants upon which they live, and in the fruits of which they are found as larvæ. In the large genus *Bruchus*, which is the nearest allied to the *Curculios*, all the species whose transformations we are acquainted with live as larvæ in seeds.

---

* Germar's Mag. vol. iii. p. 433.
† Vossische Berliner Zeitung for the 21 June, 1832.

Thus, in the pulse of the pea (*Pisum sativum*) the larva of *B. granarius* dwells, devouring the seed. In North America the same plant is attacked by another species, which is also sometimes found with us, namely, *Br. Pisi*. A third, the *Br. pectinicornis*, destroys peas in China. And a fourth species, perhaps *Br. scutellaris* F., attacks the seed of a pulse (*Phaseolus* or *Dolichus*) in India, which is called by the natives *Koloo*, and by the English *Gram*. A very large species, native to South America, *Br. ruficornis*, Germ., lives in the kernel of the cocoa-nut, and is sometimes even found in it in Europe *; and *Br. nucleorum*, according to Fabricius (*Br. bactris*, Hbst.), is found in the same fruit. Another genus, *Apion*, Hbst., has the same habits. We find the numerous species of this genus upon the plants in the seeds of which the larva lives, for instance, *Apion flavofemoratum*, Kirb.; upon *Trifol patense*, Lin.; *Ap. Ulicis*, Kirb.; upon *Ulex Europæus*, *Ap. vernale*; upon *Ballota nigra*, L., and *Lamium album*, L. *Ap. æneum*; upon *Alcea rosea*, Lin. *Ap. frumentarium* in the seeds of corn. The larva of this beetle, known by the name of the red corn worm, frequently causes great injury in granaries: it consumes the farinaceous portion, and leaves the case untouched. But the black larva of *Calandra granaria*, which is frequently found in houses, granaries, &c., is even more injurious. A second species of this genus *Cal. Oryzæ* we frequently find among rice. The third enemy to corn warehouses, known by the name of the white worm, belongs to the order of the *Lepidoptera*, and is the larva of *Tinea granella*. We might considerably enlarge this list were we to enumerate all the *Curculios* injurious to seeds, but we will merely remark that it is particularly the smaller species which appear to prefer this food. Thus the genera *Balaninus* and *Anthonomus* are known as attacking nuts and stone fruits. The larvæ of *B. nucum* live in the common hazel nut, and that of *A. druparum* in the stones of the sour cherry. The smaller *Ceutorhynchi* all dwell upon plants, and doubtlessly feed upon their seeds or leaves. The *Cioni* attack the species of the genus *Verbascum*, and live in the stem beneath the epidermis. Very many other *Curculios* live similarly in the substance of plants. Thus, the larva of *Lixus paraplecticus* lives in that of *Phellandrium aquaticum*, and of *Cryptorhynchus Lapathi* upon *Rumex hydrolopathum*, Lin. &c.

Among the other orders it is especially the *Lepidoptera* and *Diptera*

* Germar's Mag., vol. iii. p. 1, &c.

which, as larvæ, live upon fruits. Among our fruits, the plum, apple, and pear are attacked by a small moth, *Tinea* (*Carpocapsa*, Tr.) *pomona*, and which, although it does not destroy the propagative powers of the seed, yet it renders the fruit disagreeable to us. Thus another caterpillar of a moth attacks the fruit of the chestnut (*Castania vesca*), and destroys, by causing the fruit to fall before it is ripe, a rich and profitable harvest. The date also is destroyed by a larva which Haselquist observed, and refers it to the genus *Dermestes*, but certainly incorrectly. Another larva of a moth, *Pyralis fasciana*, F., lives in grapes, and destroys the most beautiful and largest grapes. But not this only attacks the vine, but many other insects in different countries. *Pyralis vitana*, F., as larvæ, devour the leaves. In the Crimea, the larva of a *Zygæna* attacks the young shoots as well as the larva of *Eumolpus Vitis*, F., and of *Rhynchites Bacchus*, Herbst. In Silesia, in the vicinity of Grünberg, where the vine is extensively cultivated, *Thylacites geminatus*, Germ., is a destructive enemy to young shoots, as it entirely consumes them immediately upon the budding. *Lethrus cephalotes* does the same in Hungary. In southern countries where the vine is cultivated, a species of *Coccus* sometimes destroys the entire vintage by sucking the young shoots. A caterpillar also lives in the fruit of the olive, which destroys the kernel and produces *Tinea oleella*, F. A second larva lives in the same plant, that of *Oscinis oleæ*, Lat., an insect belonging to the family of the flies, whose nearest ally, namely, *Dacus Cesari*, and the species of the genus *Tephritis*, follow a similar mode of life. *Tephr. cardui* especially attacks thistles and burdocks, and partly lives in the pith of the stem and partly in the fruit and flower which it then distorts. Other dipterous maggots distort plants by gall-shaped excrescences, for instance; the genera *Cecidomya*, *Lasioptera*, &c. One of these maggots especially attacks the ripening ears of corn, and thereby occasions great destruction. Kirby has described this fly by the name of *Tipula tritici* [*].

§ 306.

We will now drop the thread of our inquiry into those insects which are injurious to plants or which restrict their superabundance, convinced that the instances adduced above sufficiently prove a strong relation between plants and insects. We must now prove, on the opposite side,

---

[*] Lin. Trans., vol. iii. p. 243—245; vol. iv. p. 224—239; and vol. v. p. 96—110.

that very many insects quite unconsciously promote the growth and advance of them.

If we inspect the organisation of those parts of plants upon which its further existence as a species depends, namely, the sexual organs, we shall speedily observe that their position is such, that, without extraneous means, the male seed could not reach the female organ. Thus, therefore, in all plants which, without such assistance, could not be impregnated, the procreation of new individuals by the planting of a ripe seed is rendered almost impossible, and would also in fact but seldom occur, were it not for the intervention of insects. A great number of insects, therefore, namely, all the *Lepidoptera*, the bees, wasps, ichneumons, the majority of *Diptera*, and many beetles find their food either in the pollen itself of the plants or in the honey juices secreted by the nectaries, and for this purpose they visit flowers to procure their food from them. In these visits made without care for disturbing the parts of flowers, or mixing them together, they convey the farina which has burst from the anthers to the stigma of the female pistil, and thereby cause impregnation. This relation, for the observation of which we are indebted to the venerable Ch. K. Sprengel[*], perfectly explains to us the relative connexion existing between plants and insects. To obtain at some period this object, the plant, by great self-sacrifice, and, indeed, with sometimes the loss of its own life, has nurtured the insect within its bosom, and fed it with its own juices, and, what it is not enabled to attain individually, being destroyed by its enemy which it reared as a friend, it conveys over to its congeners. We may possibly be misunderstood in thus speaking of the reciprocal relation existing between plants and insects, as insinuating a species of consciousness of their calling and a recognition of their duties; for it is not the plant or insect that thinks or reflects, but Eternal Wisdom has felt and thought for them, and has so strengthened their mutual attachment, that the human mind in explaining it may well illustrate it as affection and friendship, and as a recognition of what the one is indebted to the other, and what it may thence expect in return, thereby exhibiting the infinite love distributed throughout the universe[†]. But we are diverging from the path of facts, to which we shall

---

[*] Das Entdeckte Geheimnisz im Baue und der Befruchtung der Blumen. Berlin, 1793. 4to.

[†] See Burdach's Physiologie, tom. i. p. 322 and p. 399, &c.

therefore return, further explaining this reciprocal relation in individual instances.

Very many, indeed we may say the majority of plants are furnished with nectaries which secrete a honey, which many insects, particularly the *Lepidoptera* and bees, seek very greedily. To procure this honey, those insects fly, some by day in the sunshine, and others in the twilight from flower to flower, visit each, and here for a time imbibe the freshly-secreted juices. They cannot avoid sweeping off the farina that has just escaped from the anthers with their rough hairy bodies, and which they bring into contact with the stigma, for both organs must frequently be pushed on one side by the insect visiting the flower before it can reach the nectaries. Some observers have remarked that insects are very particular in the selection of flowers, and at one flight visit but the blossoms of one kind of plant. This, according to Ch. K. Sprengel, occasions the impregnation of flowers, for in the majority of flowers the anthers and stigma have not the same degree of ripeness, but either the one or the other is the earliest. As insects visit only flowers of the same species, they now meet with those that have ripe anthers and now with those with ripe stigmata, and cause impregnation by bringing the ripe pollen into contact with the ripe stigma. Also, as Kölreuter has already remarked, and later observations have tended to confirm, the majority of flowers cannot be impregnated by their own pollen, but require that of other individuals, just as the hermaphrodite *Mollusca* require a mutual connexion, and cannot impregnate themselves; and if this law be general, which, however, does not appear to be the case, insects alone can be the means by which nature attains the full object of plants, namely, their impregnation and formation of seed.

If in many cases by other means, namely, by wind and rain, both of which shake the flowers, and thus bring the pollen into contact with the stigma, impregnation is effected, yet in very many it appears to be possible only through the assistance of insects. This is the case in diœcious plants, namely, in the sallows and poplars, which blossom early in the year. In these also the male flowers are the earliest, the female ones the latest; both contain nectaries, and are therefore much visited by bees and flies. It is only thus that the female flowers can be impregnated by means of the pollen hanging to the insect. This is the case also with the diœcious palms, namely, in *Phœnis dactylifera*, the male of which is the rarest in its country, and is frequently at many miles distance from the female. Also many monœcious plants, in which, as in *Ricinus*, the female parts are above the male ones, can therefore be only thus impregnated. The same in the whole family of orchideous plants, in which indeed the anthers are placed above the stigma, but frequently consist of a viscid waxy mass, whence the pollen, upon the shaking of the plant, cannot fall upon the stigma, but only by means of insects which visit the plant, and who smear themselves with this clammy substance, can it be rubbed upon the stigma. The *Aristolochia clematitis*, in which there is also observed a growing together of the filaments with the style, is impregnated by a little fly peculiar to it, the *Tipula pennicornis*, Lin., and which belongs to Meigen's genus *Ceratopogon*. This little creature creeps through the tubular portion of the flower into the lower cavity where the nectaries are placed, but cannot return back,—hairs placed in that direction preventing it. Whilst it now flutters about for several days until the flower fades, it brings the pollen into contact with the stigma, and thus causes impregnation. It appears also that other plants require certain species of insects to facilitate their impregnation; and it may originate thence that so many exotic, and especially tropical, plants, produce no seed in our hot-houses, as they have not the peculiar insects requisite to promote it. This appears to be confirmed by the observations made upon indigenous plants, namely, upon *Nigella arvensis*, *Iris xiphium*, and the species of *Antirrhinum*, that they are also visited by insects of only one species or of one genus, and therefore more frequently remain unproductive than others to which many insects resort, as the *Umbellatæ, Syngenistæ*, &c. Many insects, namely, bees which live solitary, and especially the males, pass the night also in flowers, for instance, *Chelostoma truncorum*, Labr., which reposes in the large *Campanulæ* with pendent flowers. In these visits they likewise must bring the pollen into contact with the stigma. The *Syngenistæ*, in which the stigma in general projects far above the coronet of anthers, are visited by innumerable small beetles, particularly *Nitidula ænea* and the *Thripes*, which creep down into the recesses of the flower, and naturally upon their return touch the stigma with their body covered over with pollen, whence arises, as we have before remarked, the great fertility of these flowers.

These remarks may suffice as a proof of the reciprocal relation between plants and insects. A more detailed account of it may be found in the book that we have before referred to of Ch. K. Sprengel.

§ 307.

With respect to their relation to other animals, it is probable that none takes place between them and the lowest in the scale, as the majority of the latter dwell in water, whereas insects are air-animals. The lower animals also are especially found in the sea, which no insect inhabits. The lower fresh-water animals are partly too small to supply insects with sufficient food, and partly again too large to be conquered by the rapacious water insects. Yet I have sometimes observed leeches (*Hirudo vulgaris* and species of *Clepsini*) in the power of the large *Dytici*. We may also admit that these water animals exercise the right of retaliation, and also devour small insects, at least those among them which are appointed to feed upon animal matter; yet they would doubtlessly offer but little nutriment to the leeches, as these seek the blood of the vertebrata. Nor do insects appear to stand in any very near relation to the *Mollusca*, particularly as the majority of these inhabit the sea. The larvæ of many insects may serve fresh-water snails as food, whereas the land snails, which feed upon vegetable substances, are attacked by many insects which as larvæ live parasitically upon them. Mielzinsky first discovered the larva and apterous female of *Drilus flavescens* in the shells of snails in the vicinity of Geneva, and described it under the generic name of *Cochleoctonus*. Subsequently Victor Audouin and Desmarest made further observations upon this parasite, which is not rare upon *Helix nemoralis*, and explained its development to the perfect insect *. The larvæ also of the *Lampyri*, which are closely allied to the genus *Drilus*, live parasitically in snails, as Audouin has communicated †. A third insect, the maggot of a small fly, the perfect state of which, however, is not known, is said to live as a parasite in the body of the garden snail, and even to show itself in its feelers. These are the only instances hitherto known of insects living as parasites upon *Mollusca*.

But we find the relation of insects to other articulata, namely, to the *Arachnodea* and to other insects, much more common. The *Crustacea* almost all live in the sea, and are therefore secured from the attacks of insects, and no parasitic insects have yet been found upon the *Myriapoda* and wood lice. The spiders are also free from their

---

* Annales des Sciences Nat., tom. i. p. 67; tom. ii. p. 129 and 443.
† Ib. tom. vii. p. 353.

attacks, but not insects from the spiders, for almost all of the latter feed upon insects only. Indeed there are no parasitic spiders, for they are all absolutely animals of prey, which capture insects either by cunning or by nets, they then kill them, and suck out all their nutrimental juices. A great portion of the *Acari*, however, are parasitic upon insects, and not, indeed, as we find the parasitic *Acari* upon birds and *Mammalia*, beneath the epidermis, but upon it, and chiefly where a delicate connecting membrane binds two plates together. We thus find *Gamasus coleoptratorum* especially upon the dung and carrion beetles, namely, *Necrophorus*, *Scarabœus*, and the Histers; several of the *Trombidia* upon different winged insects, namely, *Libellulæ*, gnats, aphis, &c., and *Ocypeta rubra*, as a small cochenille spot, upon several also often very small *Diptera*, and, lastly, the genus *Aclysia*, even upon the water-beetles. They dwell also upon their connecting membrane, and are besides enveloped in a peculiar case, whence through a particular aperture the creature projects its mandibles, and bores into the skin of the beetle *.

Much more numerous are the relations, considered from our present point of view, in which insects of different families stand to each other. We might assert that the predaceous beetles and those which live upon animal substances, carry on as it were a war against those which feed upon vegetables, and upon which they feed with the same voracity as the latter do upon plants. Some, as the *Carabodea*, *Dytici*, and *Staphylini*, do this, particularly in their perfect state, hunting down the larvæ of the herbivorous ones, and devouring all that they can catch; whereas others, and these especially are the most dangerous enemies, seek to lay their eggs in the bodies of the larvæ, thus presenting their young with food in the body of a living creature. We find this habit among the Ichneumons and the *Tachinæ*. Both select for this purpose almost exclusively the caterpillars of *Lepidoptera*, and as a caterpillar thus pierced must sooner or later die, they therefore considerably restrict the influence such caterpillars have, by the destruction of plants, upon the advance of the vegetable kingdom. The larvæ of the minute *Pteromali* live in a similar manner in the bodies of the *Cocci* and *Aphides*, the influence of which is not less upon the decrease of the vegetable kingdom than that of the caterpillars of the

* Vict. Audouin in Mém. de la Soc. d'Hist. Nat. de Paris, tom. i. p. 98, Pl. V. f. 2.
—Dict. des Sc. Nat. Art. *Aclysia*.

Lepidoptera. Many of them also live in the caterpillars of several butterflies. We cannot yet determine with certainty whether these enemies of the vegetable feeders are as select in the choice of particular insects as the latter are in the choice of their vegetable nutriment; yet this appears to be the case among the larger Ichneumons. Thus, for instance, *Ophion amictus,* Fab., lives upon the caterpillars of *Sphinx pinastri, Ichneumon lapidator* in those of *Noctua Typhæ.* The large families of *Sphecodea* and *Crabronea* also destroy the larvæ of *Lepidoptera* to use them as food for their young, as we have frequently before mentioned. It is remarkable that all these enemies of other insects belong to the order of the *Hymenoptera,* of which we already know that its members, by visiting flowers, contribute directly to the advance and increase of the vegetable kingdom. We have now, therefore, also seen that they even go still further in promoting this, as they destroy and remove insects inimical to plants. This double function we perceive also in the majority of the *Diptera,* in as far as these in their imago state visit blossoms, but as larvæ thrive frequently in or upon insects that feed upon vegetables. These two orders it is, therefore, especially, which exhibit to us the closest connexion of insects to the vegetable kingdom, as they in a double manner promote the increase of plants.

§ 308.

With regard to the relation of insects to the vertebrata, we may observe, that the same holds good with respect to fishes as what we have observed upon the *Mollusca.* By their living especially in water and in the sea, they are removed from the direct influence of insects, and only those fishes which inhabit fresh water appear to lie in wait for the larvæ of the *Ephemeræ, Semblodea, Libellulæ,* and gnats, and use them as food. It has not yet been observed that insects are parasitic upon fish, yet the larger *Dytici* and other water-beetles doubtlessly feed upon the spawn of fishes, and even *Dyticus latissimus,* as well as its larger congeners, attack small fishes and eat out their eyes.

Nor do the reptiles either supply insects with food or serve them to dwell upon, unless, which is very probable, the spawn of frogs is frequently consumed by the large predaceous water beetles. These beetles also frequently devour the little tadpoles, whereas insects supply the reptiles that live upon land, namely, the frogs, salamanders, lizards, and small snakes, with their sole and favourite food.

The relation between insects and birds is somewhat different. This class, which we have found analogous to insects in their type of organisation, overlooking their internal skeleton, stand in the closest relation to insects. This relation is double, as we find insects deriving their food from birds, and birds again feeding upon insects. With respect to the first, there is probably not a single bird which is not inhabited by one or even several clearly distinct species of parasitic insects, and which even sometimes belong to distinct genera. All these insects form a peculiar large group among the parasites, which Linnæus classed with the lice, but which De Geer, from their mandibulate oral organs, separated by the name of *Ricinus*, from the lice (*Pediculus*), and Nitzsch, lastly, collected together in a separate family which he called *Mallophaga* (fur destroyers), and classed with the *Orthoptera*. Their most correct situation is perhaps amongst the *Dictyotoptera*, with which we formerly placed them. This group falls into four very natural genera, of which *Philopterus* and *Liotheum* are the most numerous, and are distributed among all species of birds; *Trichodectes* and *Gyropus* are the smallest in number, and are found only upon the mammalia, namely, upon beasts of prey, the *Glires* and the *Ruminantia*, they dwell between the softer down or woolly hairs, and feed upon that and not upon the blood of the animal, at least Nitzsch found in all those which he anatomically investigated portions of down in their stomach *. Besides this large group there are smaller genera and species, which likewise live as parasites upon birds, especially upon young nestlings, particularly the genus *Carnus*, discovered by Nitzsch, upon young starlings, a form allied to the *Conopica*, as well as the genera *Ornithomya*, Lat., and *Strebla*, Wied, both of which belong to the pupiparous family of the *Diptera*, which are found upon other young birds, especially swallows.

Insectivorous birds are those chiefly which belong to the *Passerines* and the *Cuculines*. The *Laniadæ* feed almost exclusively upon insects, but some are said also to prey upon small warm-blooded vertebrata. The *Coraces*, or crows, devour chiefly carrion, but also very many feed upon insects, namely, the jays and blackbirds; some also eat fruits, which we find likewise in the true singing birds. The genera *Fringilla*, *Emberiza*, *Tanagra*, and *Euphone* eat fruits and seeds; *Sylvia*, on the

* See Nitzsch über die Familien und Gattungen der Thierinsekten. In Germar's Magazine, vol. iii. p. 261.

contrary, *Motacilla, Anthus, Certhia, Muscicapa,* and *Hirundo,* devour insects only, namely, flies and larvæ. Among the *Cuckoos* it is especially the large genera of *Cuculus* and *Picus* which attack insects, and *Upupa, Epimachus, Merops,* and many exotic ones; whereas the genera *Rhamphastus, Buceros,* and *Psittacus* prefer vegetable food, particularly fleshy fruits, to insects, and therefore feed chiefly or exclusively upon them. We besides find among the snipes many genera which feed upon insects and preferably upon their larvæ, for instance, *Charadrius, Œdicnemus, Scolopax, Tringa,* and *Totanus,* particularly their smaller species; the other waders and water birds prefer to insects as food the amphibiæ, molluscæ, fishes, and other marine animals.

§ 309.

We find a similar relation between insects and the mammalia. Many of them are inhabited by parasitic insects, which either belong to the already mentioned genera *Trichodectes* and *Gyropus* among the *Mallophagi,* or come under the genus *Pediculus,* peculiar to the mammalia. The genus *Pulex* also lives principally upon the mammalia. Among these also may be classed the pupiparous genera of the *Diptera,* which family is also distributed upon both classes, yet only upon individual species, and lastly, the family of the *Œstrodea,* which is peculiar to the mammalia. *Trichodectes* and *Gyropus* likewise devour the soft woolly hair of the mammalia, and perhaps also their epidermis; whereas the lice, by means of their hooked proboscis, which they thrust through the integument, suck their blood. Many species of them are found upon very many mammalia, for instance, upon the *Glires, Ruminantia,* and swine, but not upon all. The genus of the flea is parasitic only in its perfect state, as a larva it lives in putrid substances, especially in dirty sleeping apartments, in the stalls of animals, &c. The flea lives upon men, bats, beasts of prey, *Glires,* and they have even been found upon pigeons and swallows; they were all formerly classed under one species, which Linnæus called *Pulex irritans,* but they have since been correctly separated into several species [*], and characterised, as is usual among parasites, according to the animal they inhabit. I have myself only yet closely examined the flea of the rat, and I have found it distinct from that of man. Among the *Pupipara,* the genus *Hippobosca (Nirmomya,* Nitz.), of which only one species, the *H. equina,* is

[*] J. F. Stephens' Catalogue of British Insects. Lond., 1829. 8vo. Part 2, p. 328.

known, inhabits the horse, particularly beneath the tail and in the softer parts; the genus *Melophagus*, Lat. (*Melophila*, Nitzsch), is also only known by one species, the *M. ovinus*, which inhabits the sheep, among the downy hair; the only species of the genus *Lipoptena*, Nitz. (*Melophagus*, Autor.), namely, *L. Cervina* (*Pediculus cervi*, Autor.), frequents the different species of deer, and the genus *Nycteribia* the bats, particularly the membrane of the wing.

The remarkable family of *Œstrodea*, of which we have before made frequent mention, live in their larva state parasitic upon the hoofed quadrupeds, especially the *Ruminantia*, and they quit the animal when they change into pupæ: this takes place in the earth; but the flies, which must be numerous, to judge from the multitude of larvæ, are seldom visible; and we are as yet ignorant upon what they live. But the parasitic larvæ are deposited by the fly upon the skin of the animal as eggs, and bore through it when, as is the case with *Œstrus bovis* and *Œ. tarandi*, they live beneath the epidermis; or if they live in the viscera of the animal they are conveyed in either by suction or licking. The animals most subject to them are oxen, whose skin this fly pierces and deposits its egg therein, the larvæ here cause swollen excrescences, from which their tails project, that they may respire. Another species, the *Gastrus pecorum*, lives, according to Fabricius, in the intestines of oxen. The sheep is still more tormented, which receives a species (*Œstrus ovis*) into its nostrils and temporal cavities. The giddy sickness of sheep, which has been attributed to this larvæ, may doubtlessly be more correctly ascribed to the worm (*Cœnurus cerebralis*) living in its brain, whereas these larvæ are the cause of the sneezing, from which many sheep suffer in summer. But the horse is chiefly annoyed by these parasites: one species, the *Gastr. nasalis*, dwells in its œsophagus; a second, *G. equi*, and third, *G. salutarius*, in its stomach; a fourth (*G. hæmorrhoidalis*) even in the colon. The larvæ hang here, holding by means of their hooked mandibles, in rows, and look like thick, blunt, long cones, which are surrounded at the apex by many rows of spines, and at the base have two kidney-shaped horny laminæ at their stigmata. The deer besides is tormented by the *Œstri*; one species, *Œstrus tarandi*, lives beneath the skin of the rein-deer, like *Œ. bovis* in the ox, whereas *Œ. trompe* inhabits the temporal cavities of the rein-deer. This fly is also found in Saxony, so that it is probable that it also inhabits other species of deer. It is certain that *Œstrus lineatus*, Meig., which, according to Schrank, hangs from the superior gums of the deer, as well as *Gastrus nasalis*, attacks, besides the horse, likewise the ass, mule, deer, and goats. Beyond Europe we also find several species, one of which, *Trypoderma cuniculi*, Wied, (*Œstrus cuniculi*, Clark) lives beneath the skin of North American hares and rabbits. *Œstrus buccatus*, Fab., and *Musca Americana*, Fab., likewise belong to this genus, established by Wiedemann, and without doubt live in a similar manner. The genus *Colax*, Wied., which is native to the Brazils and Java, admits of presuming a similar mode of life, from its affinity to them.

The mammalia, which feed upon insects, are less numerous than the insectivorous birds. We will enumerate as such the smaller *Makis*, for example, the genera *Stenops*, *Otolicnus*, the last of which lives especially upon grasshoppers; the majority of indigenous bats, the shrew, the hedgehog, mole, and the other genera belonging to the *feris insectivori*. Besides, very many of the *Edentata*, namely, *Dosypus* and *Manis*, feed upon insects. The species of the allied genus *Myrmecophaga*, devour only ants, which they lick up with their long vermiform tongue, like the woodpecker among the birds.

§ 310.

There still remains, as the subject of a short notice, the relation existing between insects and man. The human body, like that of the mammalia, serves as a residence for several parasitic insects. The best known and most generally distributed parasites are the lice, four species of which man nurtures in different parts of his body. The most numerous of these is the head louse (*Pediculus capitis*), which lives in the hair of the head of many children, and of such adults who are not clean, where it pierces the skin and sucks the blood. It prefers the inclined parts of the head, and especially the back of the head, where it deposits its eggs (nits), which are little pear-shaped bodies, which it fastens to the base of the hair by means of a clammy substance. The clothes louse (*Pedic. vestimenti*, De Geer), which differs from the head louse by its larger size, more slender form, and by having black spots upon the sides of its body, dwells upon the whole surface of the body, but not upon the head, preferring particularly the breast and back, and is less general than the former, and only found in very dirty people among the lowest classes; it is exceedingly abundant in Poland and Russia. It lays its eggs at the base of the small hairs of the skin, and conceals itself upon the skin and in the folds of the vestments. A third species, the louse of Phthriasis (*Ped. tabescentium*), which is the nearest to the two preceding, has longer antennæ, a larger and more distinctly separated thorax, and an indistinctly ringed abdomen, especially at the sides; at its apex there are four strong setæ. It only originates with Phthriasis, and lives like the former upon the skin at parts where folds are formed and much perspiration collected. It has been recently observed by Alt, in Bonn. * The fourth, or *Ped. pubis*, Lin., has a contracted body, a very broad thorax, short thick legs, and a two-pointed abdomen, it being emarginate at its apex. It is found amongst the hair of the arm-pits and of the pubis, and sometimes even in the eyebrows, and is also found only amongst dirty people. According to Fabricius † the louse of the Negro is a fifth specifically different species peculiar to mankind. It is black, and has a large, flat, triangular head, two-pointed in front, and a wrinkled uniformly black abdomen.

Next to the louse the flea is the most general parasite upon man; yet, as we have already mentioned, it is parasitic only in its perfect state, and accompanies man by day and by night, tormenting him with its painful punctures. Children and girls are particularly annoyed by it. That the flea of man is of a peculiar kind recent observations have made probable. A second species of the genus *Pulex*, the *chique, pique, jigger, nigua, tungua* (*Pulex penetrans*, Lin.), is found in America, and nestles in the flesh beneath the nails of the toes, where it deposits its eggs. It thus speedily raises such swelling and irritation that if the dangerous enemy be not speedily removed inflammatory swellings originate, which quickly affect the whole limb. If, as some observers have remarked, this creature does not pass through a perfect metamorphosis, it will, notwithstanding its resemblance to the flea, not belong to the genus *Pulex*, but must form a distinct genus of the *Hemiptera*, in the vicinity of the lice. *Pediculus ricinoides*, of Fabricius, is, without doubt, the same creature, and, from the information he had received of its imperfect metamorphosis, was placed by him among the lice ‡.

Besides the flea, the bed bug (*Acanthia lectularia*, Fab.) is known as a parasite of man. It is found in the joints of bedsteds, and is not rare, especially in large towns, and when once they have nestled

---

* Alt Dissertatio de Phthriasis. Bonnæ, 1820. 4to.
† Systema Antliatorum, p. 240. 2. ‡ Ibid., p. 341. 4.

themselves it is but with the greatest trouble and cleanliness that they can be removed. All day long they repose tranquilly, and it is only at night that they attack mankind. Towards morning they retire into their retreats, and do not, like the flea, accompany man also by day, secreting themselves between the clothes and the body. They are sensible of all kinds of odours, for example, citric acid, the sweat of horses, assafœtida, sulphur, &c. will drive them away for a time.

Besides these constant parasites there are a multitude of other insects which as blood suckers annoy man by their punctures: such are the gnats (*Culices*), the genera *Ceratopogon* and *Simulia* (to which, according to all probability, the mosquitos belong, if this name be not applied without distinction to all kinds of small puncturing *Diptera*, and which thence comprises in different countries very different insects), the *Tabani* (especially *Chrysops* and *Hæmatopota*), and the *Stomoxys*. It is usually said of the true gnats that the females only sting, but this is incorrect; it is true that the males are observed less frequently, as they die immediately after pairing, yet do they sting as well as the females, as I have myself observed.

Many larvæ are also classed among the true parasites of man, as they have been found in isolated instances in his evacuations. Kirby and Spence relate several instances in their classical work in which larvæ were either cast up or down. Thus the larvæ of *Tenebrio molitor*, of *Dermestes* (*lardarius ?*), and of butterflies; and even perfect beetles, for instance, *Meloë*, have been rejected. According to Azara there is a brown moth in South America which glues its eggs to the skin of sleeping persons; the young larvæ bore into the skin, and here live for a time, until they betray themselves by the pain they occasion, and when they are pressed out. If this be true it can be referred only to the genus *Œstrus*. Indeed it is said that there is a species of this genus (*Œstrus hominis*[*]) the larva of which resides beneath the skin of man, as is confirmed by Humboldt's more recent enquiries[†]. That maggots of the flies are sometimes evacuated is a frequently occurring fact known to all physicians, and indeed one instance came under my own observation during the short period I practised. The maggots were of the size of the half grown maggots of the flesh fly, and corresponded with them; but they were dead when I saw them, other-

---

[*] Gmelin Systema Naturæ, vol. i. p. 5. page 2811, No. 10.
[†] Essai sur la Geographie des Plantes, p. 136.

wise I should have endeavoured to rear them. There is no Scolechiasis, as Kirby and Spence call it, in opposition to Phthriasis, but the instances in which sick people have evacuated the larvæ of insects have been accidentally occasioned.

The advantages which, on the other side, man derives from insects are also not insignificant. We cannot indeed maintain of any individual insect that it forms a very important and necessary food to man, but there are instances of insects being used as food, and indeed as delicate dishes. The *Cossus* of the Greeks and the Romans, which at the time of the greatest luxury among the latter was introduced at the tables of the rich, was the larva of a large beetle that lives in the stems of trees; and was, according to Keferstein[*], the larva of a large species of *Calandra*, a native of Persia and Mesopotamia. In the Brazils, also, the larva of the large *Calandra palmarum* is eaten, and even considered by many as a choice morsel. The grasshoppers are said to furnish good food to the Bedouins of Egypt. The ancients were likewise acquainted with this food of the Africans, and they distinguished a particular tribe by the name of *Acridophagi*. Even among the natives of Senegambia and the negroes of the coast of Guinea we find locusts used as food. The *Cicada*, which are in many respects closely allied to the locusts, were eaten by the ancients, especially the fat gravid females; the males were less so, as they, from their large air-bladders, were considered as empty. Amongst the *Hymenoptera* there are two families, whose economy has been already described, which yield food, namely, the ants, which, from their agreeable sour flavour, are eaten by several Brazilian tribes; and the bees, whose collected provision consists of honey, of which mention is made as food even in the earliest records, and which is everywhere used as such at the present day. Manna also, which is the juice of an Arabian plant, the *Tamarix mannifera*, dried in the sun, is caused to flow by the puncture of a small species of *Coccus*, and is an agreeably flavoured substance, frequently used in the East as food. If the pleasant taste of these substances readily explains their adoption as articles of food, it is, therefore, the more incomprehensible how certain tribes, for instance, the *Adyrmachidæ*, according to Herodotus, the Hottentots and the South American Charruels, can devour as delicacies their own vermin, a fact related and confirmed by many travellers.

[*] Über den unmittelbaren Nutzen der Insekten. Erfurt, 1829. 4to. P. 8—10.

As insignificant as all these insects are in point of the supply of food with which they furnish man, yet many others are extremely important medicinally. The chief place among these is doubtlessly occupied by the true Spanish fly (*Lytta vesicatoria*), a beetle belonging to the family of the *Vesicifica*, the majority of the members of which more or less possess the same quality. They are applied, when dried, pulverised, and spread upon wax or salve, as blisters against rheumatic affections and the inflammation of the internal organs, and thereby occasion an external attraction. It is for this purpose, not only the most universal, but also the most powerful and effective means. The ancients knew this blistering property, but they did not apply our beetle, but a species of the allied genus *Mylabris*, to effect this. This beetle they called κανθαρὶς, a name applied by Linnæus to a genus of beetles of a different family, whence Latreille, supporting himself by the authority of the ancients, calls Fabricius's genus *Lytta*, *Cantharis*, which, however, is not to be justified, as properly our genus *Mylabris* contains the *Cantharis* of the ancients. In different countries, however, different species of the genus *Lytta* are used for this purpose; thus *L. atomaria*, Fab., in the Brazils, *L. gigas*, Fab., in Guinea and the East Indies, *L. violacea*, Brandt and Ratzeb.*, likewise in the East Indies, *L. vittata*, F., in North America, *L. marginata*, F., also in North America, particularly in Maryland, *L. atrata*, F., the same, *L. cinerea*, F., in Pennsylvania, *L. rufipes*, Illiger, in Sumatra and Java. Besides, the following insects of this family have been used for blistering, *Lydus trimaculus*, Fisch. (*Mylabris trim.*, F.), in the East and in Southern Europe, *Mylabris Cichorei*, F., in China. The species used by the ancients appears to have been *Mylabris Füeslini*, Panz., it is sometimes found in Germany, and is very abundant in the south of Europe. Another genus of this family, namely, *Meloe*, has been used for a somewhat different purpose. There are twenty-seven species of this genus distributed over the earth; all, as far as they are known, secrete a peculiar yellow fluid, which flows from between the joints of the legs, which, like all the parts of the *Cantharides*, has a sharp blistering effect, and, as this consists of the camphor of *Cantharides*, it has been therefore applied as a remedy against the bite of mad dogs and the consequent hydrophobia, sometimes with success, and at others without any effect whatsoever, yet modern physicians strongly recommend it.

* Arzneithiere, vol. ii. p. 121, &c.

No other insects that have been used as medicines, for instance, the ladybird (*Coccinella*), against the toothach, have exhibited such general utility, nor are there any insects in any of the other orders which have shown themselves as useful or important as medicines. Formerly the formic acid was used as a volatile stimulant, whence it was applied to paralytic affections, but it does not appear to have exercised much influence upon it. The tannin of galls, produced by the punctures of many small hymenopterous insects belonging to the genus *Cynips*, has been applied as an astringent.

Among those insects which either in themselves or in their productions present man with materials which his skill has converted into clothing or articles of luxury, the first place is occupied by a lepidopterous insect, namely, the silk-worm (*Liparis mori*). The web in which this caterpillar encloses itself upon its change into the pupa is the raw silk, from which, after passing through several preparations and manipulations, the most beautiful material which human skill ever produced is woven. Originally a native of China, this material was early conveyed to the Greeks under Alexander, and subsequently to the Romans, who also knew the mode whereby it was obtained from a caterpillar * ; but this itself remained unknown to them, until, lastly, some monks, in the reign of Justinian (about 550 after Christ), brought the first cocoons to Constantinople. From here the cultivation of the silk-worm spread about 1150 to Sicily and Italy, whence, under Charles the 8th and Henry the 4th, the French transplanted it to France; since this period silken raiments have become more general and cheaper. Even in Germany its cultivation has been attended with success, but which does not appear to be profitable. Upon the Rhine, in Wurtemberg, and in Westphalia, it is still cultivated, where the silk is manufactured as a native produce. Thus the worth of silk has infinitely fallen, and consequently its use has increased in the same ratio. Other allied caterpillars also produce silk, especially the species of the genus *Attacus* and some South American *Papilios*, which are no further known. In Peru, even in the time of Montezuma, materials were manufactured from the silk, known by the name of *misteka*, of these caterpillars.

* See Dr. J. F. Brandt and W. F. Erichson, Monographia generis Meloes. In Nova Acta Cæs. Leop., t. xvi. part ii. p. 101, &c.

† See Keferstein upon the Bombyx of the ancients, in Germar's Magazin, vol. iii. p. 8, &c.

We may class with the silks, among the useful materials produced by insects, and which is almost of greater importance, the red colouring matter that several species of the genus *Coccus* present us with. Many of these insects contain within their whole body a very beautiful red colour, which is extracted by acids; and these admit of being used as a colouring matter for all materials. Among the German species there is one called *Coccus Polonicus*, which is abundant at the roots of *Scleranthus perennis*, and which was universally sought, prior to the introduction of the cochineal, as a red colouring matter. Since the introduction of the cochineal, however, which is a species of this genus, known by the name of *Coccus cacti*, Lin., and which lives upon the leaves of the *Cactus coccinellifer*, the Polish cochineal has lost its importance. A third species also, which is native to the South of Europe, the *Coccus Ilicis*, which is found upon the branches of the *Quercus coccifera*, Lin., and which in the middle ages was especially used by the Arabians, who applied the still used name of *Chermes* to it, has likewise, owing to the more useful Mexican cochineal, been discontinued. A fourth species of this genus, the *Coccus ficus*, Fab. (*C. lacca*, alior.), which dwells in the East Indies upon *Ficus Indica*, *F. religiosa*, and *Mimosa cinerea*, and which, by puncturing the young twigs of these plants, occasions the exuding of the clammy resinous substance which when dry is known by the name of lac, or gum lac, likewise produces a red colour, which is most concentrated in the eggs, and the use of which has recently increased so much as to threaten equalling that of the cochineal.

Lastly, the tannin contained in gall-nuts, and which we have above mentioned as a medicament, has been used as a colouring matter, as it forms with iron a black precipitate, that is admirably adapted to this purpose. The ink also, which to the learned is a very important article, is made by the assistance of this acid. The species of galls used for this purpose are of two kinds; one, the true gall-nut, proceeds from the *Cynips gallæ tinctoriæ*, which pierces the leaves of *Quercus infectoria*, Oliv., which causes those smooth spherical excrescences upon them; the second kind, which are distinguished by being rugose, and of an angular form, are found on the fruit of *Quercus ægylops*, and are either the fruit itself distorted by the puncture, or merely the scaly cup, which is developed into a gall. The insect which pierces it is, according to M. von Burgdorf, *Cynips quercus calycis*. Both are found in southern countries, the latter in Greece and in the islands of the Archipelago, and the former in Asia Minor.

ELEVENTH CHAPTER.

THE HABITATS OF INSECTS.

§ 311.

When the question is asked where are insects found, we may unconditionally reply everywhere except in the sea, for there is no spot upon the earth accessible to organic beings that is not inhabited by insects. In this universality of their abode it will appear desirable to class them under several heads, that we may be thereby enabled to combine them more closely together; we may therefore consider this subject under the differences of elements, the differences of season, and lastly, the differences of climate, the last of which has usually been called their geographical distribution, and which, although it has been already elaborated by several entomologists[*], is as yet laid down in a very meagre outline. The materials we have collected for the completion of this subject are as yet too imperfect to submit them to the public, and which we therefore defer to another opportunity, and shall here consequently only examine them with reference to their abode, as respects the elements and seasons.

§ 312.

As regards the elements, we have already in several places indicated that insects are animals of the air, and are referred especially to live in that element. Yet this means only that the majority of them possess the power of raising themselves in the air, and there moving at will for a time, and not that they exclusively dwell in it. The air is absolutely necessary to every organic being, and in so far every animal is an air animal; for although many live in the water, they even here make use of the air intermixed with it for the preservation of their lives. But there is yet a certain difference between the different classes of animals with respect to this necessity, and if insects do not belong to those ani-

---

[*] P. A. Latreille, Considerations sur la Geographie des Insectes. Mém. du Mus. 1815.—W. S. M'Leay, Horæ Entomologicæ. Lond. 1819—21. 8vo. vol. i. p. 1.—Kirby and Spence, Introd. to Entom. vol. iv. p. 486, &c.

mals which can least bear the withdrawal of air, as some instances cited above prove their great tenacity of life, they are yet doubtlessly the animals in which respiration of atmospheric air is most perfectly developed, and may therefore especially lay claim to the distinction of air animals. If now, proceeding from another point of view, we should characterise those groups among insects which of all chiefly reside in the air, they are doubtlessly the *Lepidoptera*, to which succeed in the order of their respective claims the *Hymenoptera*, *Diptera*, and *Libellulæ* (compare §§ 125, 126).

There is not a single species among the *Lepidoptera* which dwells in the water or exclusively upon the ground, all seek the air, and flutter about in it, with the exception of a before-named apterous female. Even their larvæ, more than the larvæ of any of the other orders, seek a place in the air, and are best contented in this element. There is but one caterpillar of a moth (*Botys stratiotalis*) as yet observed to be an inhabitant of the water, whereas the caterpillars of some of the *Noctuæ* (*Noctua graminis*, &c.) are found among stones, or at the roots of grass, others in the stems of plants (*Noctua typhæ*, &c.), or in fruits (*Tinea* (*Carpocapsa*) *pomona*, &c.) Similar habitats in concealed places less accessible to the air are peculiar to several of the inferior families of the *Lepidoptera*, whereas the more perfect ones, for instance, the butterflies and crepuscular moths, all live in the open air upon plants. The perfect insects of each family, lastly, are constantly in motion during that portion of the day in which the time of their growth as larvæ falls, and then only occasionally repose: thus the butterflies are found on wing in the sunshine during day, the crepuscular moths and *Noctuæ* in the twilight; the *Tinea*, again, chiefly by day, but especially towards the afternoon.

The *Hymenoptera* are, the next to these, the principal air insects; they also, in their perfect state, are never found in the water, and as rarely as larvæ; yet at this early stage of their existence they considerably diverge from aërial life, and live chiefly in confined close places, for instance, in holes in the ground, in nests, in the excrescences of plants, in their stems, and parasitic within other larvæ. The pseudo-caterpillars of the saw-flies only seek the air, and dwell in it openly upon leaves. The perfect insects possess excessive motion, are constantly flying about in the air and sucking flowers, and the females only of some of them as well as the neuter ants are deprived of the power of flying.

Among the flies, or *Diptera*, there are several which live as larvæ in the water, as, for instance, the gnats, many *Tipulæ*, and the *Stratiomyda*, but no perfect insect of this order dwells in this element. The other larvæ, like those of the *Hymenoptera*, all seek dark remote places, removed from the air, and come but seldom, and as exceptions, into day-light.

The same is the case with the *Libellulæ*, for as much as these in their perfect state are aërial insects, so strictly as larvæ are they confined to the water.

In the other orders the habitat differs more and more, until among the beetles it attains its greatest degree of dissimilitude. If we examine in the first place the *Hemiptera*, the majority of them are indeed aërial insects, but also very many are inhabitants of the water. The family of the lice live parasitic upon mammalia, they therefore live, although in the air, for the water mammalia have no lice, yet in places secured from its free access. The *Aphides*, or plant lice, partly live in a similar manner, namely, in the excrescences of plants formed by themselves, but partly also in the open air upon leaves and young twigs. The *Cocci* and *Chermes* have similar places of abode. The true bugs are chiefly found upon the ground, in the grass, or on trees, or lastly, upon leaves; but few are apterous, and these must necessarily crawl about upon the ground; some genera (*Hydrometra, Velia*, &c.) run upon the surface of the water, or dive into it. One genus of this group, namely, *Halobates*, Eschsch., courses about upon the surface of the sea between the tropics, and is the only insect that that has familiarised itself with the sea. The true water bugs (*Hydrocorides*) live exclusively in the water, exactly as the *Cicadaria* course about exclusively in the air, upon the leaves of plants and on their twigs.

All the *Neuroptera* in their perfect state live in the air, where they fly tolerably constantly and rapidly about, yet their larvæ are found partly in the water, as among the *Phryganeæ* and *Semblodea*, and partly in sand, as in *Myrmecoleon* and *Ascalaphus*, or in the air upon plants, where they hunt down other insects, as is the case with *Rhaphidia* and *Hemerobius*.

The *Orthoptera* have received as their chief dwelling-place the earth itself; here they are found concealed among grass and plants, and a few, as *Locusta viridissima*, upon the elevated parts of plants. They are therefore especially animals of the earth, which is still more strongly expressed by the habits of some of the genera, for instance, of

Acheta and *Gryllotalpa*, which excavate holes for their dwelling-places. Some, as the cockroaches (*Blattaria*), are true nocturnal animals, which conceal themselves during the day, and only at night run about upon the ground.

The habitats of beetles are as different as their entire organisation. Large families, as the *Melanosomata* and *Helopodea*, are strictly fixed to the earth, and scarcely ever quit it. The majority of the *Melanosomata* have consequently lost the organs of flight with its capability. Others, as the capricorns, *Chrysomelæ*, ladybirds, and cockchafers, are found only upon plants, and consequently seek the air, although they, and chiefly the former, but seldom fly. The *Curculios* are partly fixed to the earth, as *Brachycerus, Plinthus, Meleus, Cleonis, Thylacites, Sitona*, &c.; others live upon plants, as *Ceutorhynchus, Cionus, Orchestes, Phyllobius, Apion, Rhynchites*, &c.; a few, as some species of *Bagous, Hydronomus, Alismatis,* Schön., &c. are found also in the water upon roots, but they do not swim. The true water beetles are the *Dytici, Gyrinus, Hydrophilus, Helophorus, Elmis,* and the other *Macrodactyli*. The larvæ of these also are found only in the water, whereas the larvæ of the preceding families, as far as they are known, seek remote and concealed places, for instance, the earth and the interior of plants. The larvæ of the *Chrysomelæ* and *Coccinellæ* live chiefly upon plants, partly from which they support themselves, and partly from the plant lice found upon them. Many insects also seek dark remote places removed from the open air; some therefore live in dung, as the *Coprophagi*, some in carrion, as the *Peltodea*, or in both substances, as the *Brachyptera* : their larvæ also live partly in these substances or in the earth in their vicinity. Some perfect beetles likewise, as the genera *Heterocerus* and *Prognathus*, live in the earth, particularly in the moist sand of the sea coast, but towards evening they quit these places of abode, and fly about in the dusk. The majority of the small *Carabodea* do the same, seeking for prey, although they but rarely quit the earth during the day. The larger ones are for ever fixed to the earth, for they have no wings, although the genus *Calosoma* forms an exception, the species of which are winged, and frequently fly. The last family of the beetles, the *Cicindelacea*, live chiefly upon sand, but the majority of them can fly as well as they can run, and immediately exercise this faculty when in danger or if pursued.

§ 313.

With respect to the several seasons of insects, in cold and temperate climates, they first present themselves during the warm days of spring, but, in hot climates, it is during and immediately after the rainy season, which there supplants winter, that they are seen. We know but little of the appearance of insects in the highest latitudes. Otto Fabricius mentions in his "Fauna Grœnlandica" sixty-two species of insects observed by him in Greenland, of which eleven were beetles, nine *Lepidoptera*, two *Hymenoptera*, nineteen *Diptera*, seventeen *Dictyotoptera* (one *Libellula*, seven *Podurœ*, and nine *Mallophagœ*), two *Neuroptera*, and two *Hemiptera* (lice), the most of which he caught in the months of July and August. But we may readily admit that many escaped him, as may be presumed from Zetterstedt's "Fauna Lapponica," where very many more are enumerated. In temperate climates the number of species increases considerably, for in Europe only there are doubtlessly more than 20,000 species, at a moderate calculation. Their time of appearance varies considerably, yet the time of their greatest activity is the summer: during the whole of winter there are but few insects in the open air. The reason of this we may, with Kirby and Spence, consider to be the deficiency of their aliment, for although many insects do not feed upon vegetable substances, yet the majority of the flesh feeders obtain their nutriment from the herbivorous ones, and whose existence is thus therefore bound to the vegetable kingdom. It therefore thence happens that winter, by putting aside the green vesture of the earth, likewise chases the insects that feed upon it. If we examine this more closely we shall find that this relation of insects to plants is very absolute, for the majority of those insects which hybernate in their perfect state are flesh eaters, which find food even in the young larvæ just escaped from the egg-shell, whilst the latter are feeding sparingly upon the just developed leaves. If we look to those insects which pass through their earlier stages during the winter, we may assert generally that all insects likewise exist during the winter, but in very different states. Some hybernate as eggs only, others as larvæ, others again, and perhaps the majority, as pupæ, and the fewest doubtlessly as perfect insects. From all these very different states they all assemble as perfect insects in the summer, and this also is truly the season in which insects are consequently most active.

As eggs, insects of all orders hybernate, yet these are but few in comparison with their collective numbers. The reason of this is, that many young larvæ, if they were disclosed from the egg early in the spring, would not find their necessary food; and other eggs are deposited in substances which are found only in the summer, as leaves of plants, the larvæ of other insects, &c. But we may maintain as a general fact that those insects especially hybernate as eggs, which develope in the course of one year two or three generations, as we have already mentioned of the plant lice; most of these do not hybernate, except as eggs. Those also hybernate as eggs whose development as perfect insects takes place very late in the year, as most of the *Orthoptera*, for instance, *Acheta, Gryllotalpa, Locusta, Gryllus*. They can therefore pair only very late in the year, so that the young, should any be disclosed, would no longer find food during the same year. The females consequently excavate holes in the earth and bury their eggs therein, when they die, as the males have before done. The same is the case with the second autumnal generation; in this instance also the larvæ would no longer find food, the eggs are therefore disclosed in the spring. Amongst the *Lepidoptera, Gastrotropacha, Neustria*, and *Liparis dispar* hybernate as eggs. In each case the mother deposits her eggs on the twigs, and never on the leaves, of such trees the leaves of which the caterpillars feed on. *Geometra grossulariata*, on the contrary, is disclosed the same year, and hybernates as a larva. It is remarkable that only those *Lepidoptera* whose caterpillars live upon perennial plants hybernate as eggs or as caterpillars, and the rest chiefly as pupæ, a phenomenon which even Roesel observed, and which finds its natural cause in that the leaves of all annual plants appear later than those of perennial ones. The pupæ consequently are developed later than the eggs, because the imago finds food only in the flowers, whereas the caterpillars find it in the leaves. The degree of cold that exposed eggs can endure is not trifling. Spallanzani placed the eggs of the silkworm in a temperature of 38° Fahr., and yet larvæ were disclosed from them, as well as from others that had been exposed to a temperature of 56° Fahr.

Many insects are found as larvæ also during the winter, namely, all such which pass more than one year in this state, as, for instance, *Melolontha vulgaris, Oryctes nasicornis, Lucanus cervus*, the large capricorns, many *Elaters, Buprestes*, and a multitude of *Lepidoptera*, namely, *Euprepia matronula, Cossus ligniperda*, &c. Many of them are said to form a sort of dwelling, for example, *Cossus*, in which they pass the winter in a species of torpidity. The rest creep into slits, holes, or between fallen leaves, where they also fall into a lethargic state. But this kind of hybernation is the least usual, as the majority of larvæ live but one year, and most of them, even during the summer, pass into the perfect state. Those larvæ which hybernate can, in their lethargic sleeping state, bear a high degree of cold. Lister says that he has seen frozen caterpillars, which, upon falling upon hard substances, rebounded like stones, and yet, after thawing, return again to life. Although Reaumur was unsuccessful in this experiment, Kirby and Spence assure us that the larvæ of *Tipula oleracea* have come to life again after thawing. Bonnet also has observed the same in the caterpillars of the common white butterfly.

Those insects which hybernate in the pupa state are chiefly the *Lepidoptera*, nine-tenths of which, according to Kirby and Spence, do so. As their entire pupa state is a species of lethargy, it must be very easy for them to hybernate in it, and consequently endure severe cold, yet the majority of pupæ are nevertheless protected by particular coverings and places of repose from this influence of the cold. Many lie tolerably deeply in the ground, in cavities which have been previously excavated by the caterpillar. Others which hybernate merely between fallen leaves, as the pupæ of *Deilephila Galii*, *D. Euphorbiæ*, *D. Elpenor*, &c., weave these by means of their web into a covering; others, as the caterpillars of the *Noctuæ* and *Bombyces*, weave a perfect cocoon, which inside is covered with a glue-like substance. The lethargy of these pupæ continues also frequently towards the commencement of the summer, for the imago only appears when the plants are in blossom. The larvæ also, which live several years, pass their last winter generally in the pupa state; we therefore find the perfect insect, as, for example, the cockchafer, early in the spring.

Perfect insects, which hybernate as such, prepare themselves early in the autumn for this purpose, especially in the warm days of October. They consist chiefly of beetles, but also of individuals of all the other orders, which, like these beetles, have not yet paired. They then run in troops in every direction, seeking places where they can pass the winter. These are the apertures and holes of trees, especially those between the bark and stem of old ones still existing only as stumps. Here they may be found during winter in multitudes. We especially find all such insects there, which, as larvæ or as perfect insects, inhabit wood, as the genera *Lyctus*, *Colydium*, *Rhyzophagus*, with their allies.

Also *Nitidula, Engis, Allecula*, and the *Securipalpa*. Also the smaller *Carabodea*, as *Lebia* and *Dromius*, and many others. Some *Hymenoptera* also, as the *Ichneumons* and *Diptera*, we likewise find in such situations. Others, as the *Harpali, Amaræ,* and *Feroniæ*, prefer lying beneath stone, generally in small holes, chiefly with their backs turned downwards, clinging to the stones with their legs. Others, again, at the foot of trees, in woods, amongst the moss, sometimes in holes prepared for the purpose, like the large *Carabi*, the *Elaters*, the *Silphæ*, &c. We in general find them alone in such situations, but sometimes they lie in multitudes collected together, as *Brachinus crepitans*, and other *Carabodea*. Between leaves the *Curculios* delight, and we find the *Staphylini* under grass. Some *Lepidoptera* also hybernate at suitable places in granaries, &c., as *Vanessa Urticæ*, O., *V. Polychloros, V. Cardui, V. Io*, also *Colias Rhamni*, and many *Noctuæ*. These, therefore, appear very early in the year, as soon as they are aroused by the warm sunshine. All, especially those which creep beneath bark, are said to place themselves on the south side, and never, or very seldom, on the north. Whilst remaining in these hiding-places, they are generally, unless excessive cold intervenes, pretty lively, and they are even lured during warm days to quit their retreats, as for instance, the *Carabi, Aphodii*, and *Staphylini*, which then, even in winter, are seen swarming upon the snow. At what degree of cold torpidity is produced cannot be easily determined, and it also differs considerably in different insects. According to Huber, the ants become torpid at $-2°$ Reaum., and previously lay themselves as closely as possible together: this may happen also earlier or later. In others, its degree also is very different, according to the temperature. That such a torpid state is actually found in insects, we may easily convince ourselves by seeking them in their hiding places, and bringing them by degrees into a warmer temperature, when we see them gradually arouse themselves and become active. The flies also, which give us their society even during the winter in our apartments, are active near the fire-place, whereas at the windows they appear weak and inert.

Some few insects do not appear to become torpid, but even in winter present themselves. This is well known of *Geometra (Acidalia) brumata*, which appears towards the end of the autumn, and flies about in orchards, to which, as larva, it is very injurious, until late in the winter. Others become torpid on cold days, but present themselves on mild ones, and again gnaw the buds, as the caterpillar of *Noctua fuliginosa*. This is also the case with the *Trichocera hiemalis*, Meig., for it is not rarely that we find it upon clear sunny winter days, dancing its choral round in the air over the snow. Others, again, present themselves only with and upon the snow, as *Boreus hiemalis*, Lat., a genus allied to *Panorpa*, but wingless, which is not rare in woods upon warm winter days; as also the *Podurœ*, which swarm like black dust sometimes upon the surface of the snow; and, lastly, the equally apterous *Chionea araneoides*, which belongs to the *Diptera*, with many jointed antennæ, and which Dalman* has described, and which, according to him, is found in Sweden upon the snow at a temperature of 2°—3° (of the scale divided into a hundred).

If we now cast a glance upon the time of appearance of tropical insects, the information we have yet received upon this subject is so imperfect, that scarcely anything satisfactory can be deduced from it. According to the letter of Westermann to Wiedemann†, at Kiel, which is so interesting from the intelligence it gives us of the habits of many tropical insects, insects are found in Java, Bengal, and at the Cape, only during the rainy season, during which the whole tropical vegetation is in its highest luxuriance, and they then swarm upon flowers and leaves, seeking nutriment. Where they conceal themselves during the hot season is not yet known with certainty, yet they doubtlessly seek places of retreat similar to those sought out by our own during winter. Thus the hot temperature of a tropical summer has the same effect upon insects as the cold of winter with us, and what lures them from their hiding places with us, drives them there into their concealed places of resort. Yet it is the same law which is in force, and by which insects are especially bound to the luxuriant increase of the vegetable kingdom, for it is only during the warm rainy season that tropical plants are in blossom, and they are then visited by insects of all descriptions.

* Analecta Entomologica, p. 33. † Germar's Magazin, vol. iv. p. 411, &c.

TWELFTH CHAPTER.

INSECTS OF A FORMER WORLD.

§ 314.

Since, in modern times, more attention has been paid to the organic remains of a former world, communications have occasionally been made of insects of this description, but this class has not yet received all the elaboration that has been given to the others. The reason of it may be that insects are not generally found in those formations where the remains of the other classes are so abundant, namely, in the calcareous strata of the tertiary period, but are chiefly imbedded in a vegetable resin known by the name of amber, and which is cast up by the Baltic, or found in the more recent strata. This substance is found at places, which, although not lying beyond the limits of scientific cultivation, yet where the study of a destroyed organisation is not heeded, either from their remains not presenting themselves, or in very solitary instances; and amber, which is the sole substance in which the remains of organised beings have been frequently found there, is generally applied to mercantile purposes, and it seldom happens to fall into the hands of learned men or the there very isolated naturalists. But within these few years the incentive to the investigation of native productions has very much increased, and attention begins to be paid at home to what the country's produce has previously only advanced abroad. We cannot however deny that the study of destroyed organic beings has been much stimulated and promoted in and by France, especially by Cuvier's immortal works. Hence have originated also the labours upon destroyed insects which are found in other formations, namely, in calcareous marl, by Marcel de Serres [*], who, in a distinct treatise, has characterised the insects found in it. Berendt has promised a detailed description of the insects found in amber, and his prefatory remarks upon the existence

---

[*] Annales des Sciences Nat., tom. xv. p. 18.

and origin of amber are already published *. From these preludatory labours and our own investigations, which we have been enabled to make in the academical collection at Greifswald and Berlin, the following summary is drawn.

§ 315.

Upon commencing with insects which are found in amber, as the organic remains belonging to an earlier formation, namely, to brown-coal, we may assert there is not the least doubt that amber is a vegetable resin, which must have originated like the present copal, that exudes from the stem of a North American tree, namely, the *Rhus copalina*, Lin. The tree which produced amber was doubtlessly lost with the vegetables whose remains form the strata of brown-coal, and, therefore, amber is still found in isolated masses in this formation. It more frequently occurs, as I have above mentioned, amongst the rejectamenta of the Baltic, and imbedded in the recent strata of its southern coasts, especially in moory peaty places, where the ground still continues covered with woods, namely, on the Prussian coasts in Pomerania, upon the coasts of the peninsula Dars, which partly forms the frontiers towards Mecklenburg. I have there myself frequently found it in the situations above described. The way in which insects have been enclosed in this amber can be no other than that they stuck to the resin when this was in a fluid state, and were enveloped in it by what continued to exude. According to the rapidity with which this took place, depends the condition of the enclosed insect. Those which were quickly enveloped are perfectly well preserved with their natural colours, but those which first died and remained for a time exposed to the open air, are more or less injured, and are surrounded upon the surface with a white mouldy covering, and which has occasionally obscured and disfigured the approximate resin. I have observed this mould in many insects of the Berlin Museum, which came from Prussia, and which are enclosed in a dark bubbly amber, whereas I have never observed it in the bright yellow Pomeranian amber. We might thence conclude that the latter was originally more fluid and the former slower in exuding, and thence building a further hypothesis that the two kinds proceeded from different trees.

With respect to the families, genera, and species of insects which

* Die Insekten in Bernstein von Dr. G. C. Berendt. Danzig. 1830. 4to.

are thus found in amber, we may repeat what has been observed by earlier inquirers, that they present a conformity, in the majority of instances, with existing forms, and even an identity of species can be shown; but this yet remains undecided, and, in many instances, is not the case. Among all the amber insects that I have seen, I have rarely found a completely new or very dissimilar form, but I have in general immediately recognised still existing genera. I must also agree with the earlier observers, that the insects found in amber are not those which belong to our latitudes, yet there are many forms which perfectly agree with ours. This may especially be said of the smaller flies and gnats; but particularly in the cockroaches, many beetles, and the majority of the *Hymenoptera*, the resemblance to exotic forms is still greater. The number of different species of insects that have been found in amber is not inconsiderable, and convinces us that the class of insects in a former world, as even now, must have been the most numerous in species; but we find in amber only the members of those families which are found in woods or trees, and scarcely ever water-beetles, whence, from the abundance of these, we may draw conclusions as to the multitudes of all the rest.

§ 316.

After these prefatory remarks, we may proceed to the consideration of the enclosed insects themselves. I shall, however, only give what I have myself observed, merely mentioning the orders, families, and frequently also the genera of insects that I have detected in amber, and reserve their detailed description for another distinct work. I have been induced to this by the work announced by Berendt of the amber insects observed by him, and for the appearance of which I shall wait.

In the order of the *Coleoptera* I have never detected an individual belonging to the *Cicindelæ*, and of the *Carabodea* I have only observed a small *Dromius* in the collection at Greifswald, whereas Germar * has discovered another, which he has described and called *Lebina resinata*. I have never yet met with a *Staphylinus;* it is not improbable that they, especially the *Aleochara*, may be found in amber. Nor have I observed any carrion-beetles nor any pentamerous beetles with clavate or capitate antennæ. I have detected several *Elaters*, for example,

* Magazin der Entomologie, vol. i. Pt. 1, p. 13.

one very similar to the *Elater cylindricus*, Gyll., and many smaller species, but I have not found a single *Buprestis*, although these might readily offer. The *Deperditores* are, however, not rare, namely, forms resembling *Anobium pertinax* and *An. rufipes*. Desmarest found, also, an *Atractocerus* in amber. A *Cantharis* very like *C. nigricans*, Fab., I have seen in the Berlin collection. Among the *Heteromera* I have hitherto only observed a small *Opatrum* allied to *Op. sabulosum*. Germar has described a *Mordella* (*M. inclusa*). Of the *Tetramera*, I detected, in the collection at Greifswald the leg of a capricorn-beetle, but no other insect of this family except a little creature very like the *Obrium testaceum*. The *Chrysomelæ* are more numerous. I saw a small purple shining *Haltica*, several *Crioceris*, and a few *Gallerucæ*. The *Bostrychodiæ* are very numerous, but I could not determine one with certainty. In Greifswald I met with a species of *Platypus*, and in Berlin with several true *Bostrychi* and *Apata*. The *Curculios* also are tolerably abundant, particularly species of the genera *Phyllobius*, *Polydrusus*, *Thylacites*, &c., and some forms allied to exotic groups, which I could not more closely determine. I have never observed any of the smaller *Curculios*, as *Ceutorhynchus*, *Cionius*, or *Apion*.

The *Hymenoptera* are very abundant, but I have never observed a *Tenthredo* or a *Urocerus*, although both families live especially in woods and feed upon vegetable substances, and the latter, as larvæ, bore the stems of trees. But in the Berlin Museum there are several *Ichneumonodea*, whose generic affinities I have not yet been able to determine satisfactorily. One of them has antennæ swollen in the middle like *Bassus* (*Euceros*) *Crassicornis*, Grav. An *Evania* also, allied to *Evania minuta*, Fab., is at Berlin and Greifswald. I have not yet observed a *Cynips* in amber, although I have seen a *Sphex* that certainly belonged to the genus *Pepsis*, but which is entirely faded, so that it is impossible to determine the species. It is of about the size of *Pepsis lutaria*, Fab. (*Ammophila*, Kirby), but the thorax is more slender, and the abdomen has not so long a petiole, whence it resembles the American and particularly the African species. *Crabros*, *Scolias*, *Mutillas*, and wasps, I have not found, but I saw a small form of bee, which appears to belong to the South American genus, *Trigona*, Lat. The ants are the most numerous in this order, particularly true *Formicæ* and *Myrmicæ*, which have frequently a close resemblance to our native ones. The majority are apterous neuters, which have fallen into the fluid resin in their excursions. I have also observed in the Greifswald collection a peculiar form of ant, which I consider new, as it appears to be no longer existing, at least I know no allied form among the still living ones.

Amber *Lepidoptera* are amongst the greatest rarities. I have never seen one yet. Berendt mentions a large *Sphinx* in his collection, and several caterpillars, which also have never occurred to me.

The *Diptera*, on the contrary, are extremely numerous, and, indeed, of all the families. Berendt mentions amber *Tabani* and *Bombylii*, none of which have I seen; whereas in the Berlin collection there is an *Anthrax* of the size of our *A. semiatra*. Besides, I there saw two of the genus *Leptis*, not dissimilar in size and figure to the *L. aurata*, several *Empes*, and several species of the genus *Tachydromia*. Besides, there are in both collections innumerable small *Muscaria*, and, among the larger ones, species of the genera *Musca*, *Anthomya*, *Scatophaga*, &c. I observed a great number of individuals of the family *Dolichopodea*, and, among them, the genera *Dolichopus*, *Medeterus*, *Porphyrops*, and *Rhaphium*. *Diptera* with multiarticulate antennæ are even more numerous, especially the *Bolitophagi*. I found species of *Boletophila*, *Mycetophila*, *Leia*, and *Sciara*, frequently perfect, and with all their colours preserved. I think I have also observed *Bibios*. True *Tipulæ* are more rarely seen, but I detected one resembling the *T. pratensis*, several *Limnobiæ*, some small, like *L. pulchella*, and others larger. There is also an abundance of gnats, particularly species of *Psychoda*, *Lasioptera*, *Cecidomya*, *Ceratopogon*, even some *Tanypus* or *Chironomus*, but a true *Culex* I have never discovered.

Next to these the *Neuroptera* are probably the most numerous. Berendt possesses the larva of a *Myrmecoleon*. I myself have seen but a small *Hemerobius*, like *H. hirtus* or *fuscatus*, a *Semblis* about the size of *S. marginata*, as well as a larva of this family, which is the more remarkable, as they all live in water; and innumerable *Phryganeæ* of various sizes.

Among the *Dictyoptera* I observed two individuals of the genus *Ephemera* in the Berlin collection, as well as two specimens of *Machilis polypoda*. According to Berendt, *Libellulæ* are also found in amber. The most numerous of this order are the *Termites* in both collections. I saw several pieces completely filled with them. The winged ones as well as unwinged larvæ and neuters with large heads are found in it. Germar's *Hemerobius antiquus* is a true *Termites*, which

I know from my own inspection of the identical piece of amber in the collection at Halle. In the Greifswald collection I observed two distinct species of *Psoci*.

In the order of the *Orthoptera*, the *Blattaria* are the most numerous. Berendt assures us that he has distinctly detected some American forms; those which I saw had a greater resemblance to our own native *Blatta Germanica*, which is not rare in woods. To these we may add some *Achetæ*, particularly small not fully developed individuals. The Berlin collection possesses a piece of amber with an insect of this family, that is distinguished by having short filiform antennæ composed at most of sixteen joints, gradually increasing in size, and a short straight ovipositor. It is of the size of *Forficula minor*, but is still a larva. According to Berendt, there are larger grasshoppers. I have myself only seen a small locust in the Berlin collection.

In the last order, the *Hemiptera*, we frequently observe *Cicada* preserved in amber, for example, in the Berlin collection there are several specimens of a *Flata* allied to the *F. cunicularia*. In Greifswald I also saw several species of *Jassus*. I have never discovered bugs, but Berendt and Marcel de Serres have both observed them. Even a *Nepa* the former found enveloped in amber. That species of *Chermes*, *Aphis* and *Coccus* would necessarily occur in amber, might be absolutely supposed, yet have I never fallen upon any forms belonging to these families.

§ 317.

Passing hence to the fossil insects that have been discovered in recent formations, we will first mention the impressions noticed by Knorr[*] in the Œnningen calcareous formations, and which chiefly represent the larvæ of *Libellula* and other water-insects. Impressions of cockchafers have also been observed in them. Van der Linden likewise describes a *Libellula* found in this formation[†]. The most complete list of fossil insects has been given by Marcel de Serres, in the above treatise. According to him, they are found in calcareous marl, which separates the several strata of gypsum in the quarries of

[*] G. W. Knorr. Lapides, Diluvii univers. Testes, &c. Norimb. 1755—1773, folio, vol. i. p. 151, Pl. XXXIII. f. 2—4.

[†] Notice sur une Empreinte d'Insecte renfermée dans un Echantillon de Calcaire schisteux. Brux. 1827. 4to. av. f.

Aix, in Provence, and, consequently, belong to a still more recent formation. They are accompanied by impressions of different plants, but never by fish, the impressions of which are also found in distinct strata. The majority of the insects enclosed by this marl have preserved their horny integument, and mere impressions are more rarely found; but their colour appears to be gone, as they are of a uniform brown or black. They are chiefly such insects which live upon a dry sandy or clay soil, and which partly still are found in the vicinity of Aix, as *Brachycerus undatus, Forficula parallela,* and *Pentatoma grisea.* The list given by the above author includes the following forms.

1. *Coleoptera.* A *Harpalus* of moderate size; a *Dyticus* also of moderate size; a small *Staphylinus*; a *Melolontha*, remarkable from its deep furrows on the elytra; a *Buprestis* of the form of *Trachys nana*, Fab.; several *Melanosoma*, among which one like *Asida grisea*, also a *Chrysomela* like *C. cerealis;* two species of *Cassida*, one like *C. viridis;* many bark-beetles; one *Apate*, allied to *A. capucina;* an *Hylurgus*, a *Scolytus*, and a *Trogosita* like *T. cerulea;* lastly, innumerable *Curculios*, two *Brachyceri*, one like *Br. nudatus*, Dej., the other like *Br. algirus*, Fab.; several species of *Cleonis*, one like *Cleonis distincta, Larinus*, Germar (*Rhinobates*, Meig.); several *Meleus*, the still living form of one species; then *Hyperæ, Naupacti,* one like *N. lusitanicus,* Dej., and one *Cionis*, like *C. Scrophulariæ.*

2. *Hymenoptera.* Three species of *Tenthredos*, one smaller than *T. viridis*, the second larger, and a third of moderate size; an *Ichneumon;* an *Agathis*, Lat.; two *Polistes*, one species like *P. Gallica*, the second like *P. morio*, Fab.; several *Formicæ*, some larger, some smaller like *F. subterranea.*

3. *Lepidoptera.* One butterfly of the genus *Satyrus*, from the communication of another party; a *Zygæna*, a *Bombyx*, perhaps a *Cossus* of moderate size.

4. *Diptera.* An *Empis* like *E. tesselata*, a *Nemestrina* like *N. reticulata,* an *Oxycera* of the size of *Stratiomys chamæleon,* and one allied to *Xylophagus ater;* a *Microdon* and an *Ochthera.* Of *Diptera* with multiarticulate antennæ, there are several *Bibios*, two *Penthetriæ,* some minute *Sciaræ*, and one *Platyura* like *P. cingulata.*

5. *Neuroptera* there are none.

6. *Dictyotoptera.* Many *Libellulæ*, some as large as *Æschna grandis*, and their larvæ are tolerably abundant.

7. *Orthoptera.* One *Forficula*, like *F. parallela;* several *Achetæ*, one like *A. italica*, Fab., one like *A. campestris*, a third very small, a small *Gryllotalpa*, perhaps the larva of our species; a *Xya*, Ill., allied to the *Xya variegata*, Ill.; a *Gryllus*, like *Gryllus cærulescens*, F.

8. *Hemiptera.* Bugs especially of several genera, for instance, two *Pentatomæ*, one like *P. grisea*, the second like *P. oleracea;* two species of *Coreus*, from ten to twelve different species of *Lygæus*, a small *Syrtis*, F., three species of *Reduvius*, of moderate size, a very characteristic species of *Hydrometra*, F., a small *Gerris*, Lat., a *Nepa* smaller than *N. cinerea*, a *Cicada* like *Cicada plebeja* (*Tettigona plebeja*, Fab.).

FOURTH SECTION.

TAXONOMY.

FIRST CHAPTER.

GENERAL IDEAS.

§ 318.

TAXONOMY, which is the last division of the general portion of Entomology, has to exhibit the means whereby the large host of insects may, according to certain principles, be classed in divisions and groups, and also the connexion of these groups together. The necessity of this grouping and subdivision is not so evident in any class of animals as the present, as the number of their different forms is very great, and doubtlessly greater than those of the entire vegetable kingdom. A computation of the known species has not been indeed latterly made, and can scarcely be so, as all the known forms are nowhere yet brought together, or even described, yet a tolerable result may be deduced by comparing the number of known species of any country with its indigenous plants, and then forming a comparative computation with that of all known plants. There are, for instance, in Germany, including the *Cryptogamea,* at most 6000 different plants, but certainly more than 12,000 insects, so that if this proportion be constant, which may be admitted, the number of known insects, according to the 60—70,000 known plants, will evidently rise to 120—140,000 species. If, now, in concordance with the estimation of the latest and most successful botanists, we say that about one-third of the collective species of plants are known, then the number of insects inhabiting the earth would amount to from 360—420,000 species, or, in round numbers, we may say 400,000. But this number has neither been collected nor described. Even were we to calculate all that are preserved in the large museums of Paris, London, Berlin, and Vienna, the number of known species would scarcely extend to one-fourth of this. M'Leay and Latreille consider 100,000 to exist already in cabinets, yet I much doubt whether a positive calculation of them would give so many species. Count Dejean in Paris, whose collection is known to be the richest private one, calculates the number of his beetles at 21,000, and in the Berlin collection, according to a general computation, there are about 28,000 beetles. The beetles stand in proportion to all the other insects in the ratio of two to three, consequently the Berlin Museum should therefore possess about 78,000 species, a number which is not, however, attained, because, as every one knows by experience, the beetles are more anxiously sought by travellers than the other insects. Hence I believe the number of known species in collections may be considered at 80,000, which is certainly not too few, but many more would not certainly be found. Of these there may be 36,000 beetles, 12,000 *Lepidoptera*, 12,000 *Hymenoptera*, 10,000 *Diptera*, 4,000 *Hemiptera*, 1,000 *Orthoptera*, 1,000 *Neuroptera*, and 2,000 *Dictyotoptera*, including the parasitic *Mallophaga*. Taxonomy instructs us in the division, determination, and the description of these species, as well as furnishes us with the history of all preceding arrangements.

§ 319.

Every division and grouping of natural bodies has for object the easier survey of the whole, and thus to facilitate the knowledge of all by a course easier than the study of the separate individuals. Proceeding from a somewhat different point of view, their division has for object to render the discovery of any individual more easy from certain determinate and essential characters, and this can be attained only by the arrangement of the characteristic marks found in all natural bodies. We thus obtain a classification which commences with the most general characters, whence, proceeding to other more limited characters, the groups are formed, which must be strictly exclusive, if the utility of the subdivision is to be preserved. By means of such generally-opposed groups, the list then gradually descends to the lowest of all, the species, and with the definition of which its purpose is fulfilled. We call a division made upon these principles artificial or an artificial system, yet unjustly so, for a system can never be artificial, but must be necessary and natural. A second point of view proceeds from the idea that in nature there is a concatenation of beings in every direction, and it seeks in their arrangement to express this interlinking in their subdivision, and, thereby to produce the proof of the correctness of the opinion. It thus creates a system which therefore must be natural, that is to say, such as appears expressed in nature itself. This system can, however, only be constructed, when not only all the forms, but also all the ideas which express themselves in these forms, are known, and when it is seen that every form has absolutely a thought as its foundation, and that it is not an accidental but a necessary one. But the idea to which the study of natural bodies leads is their gradual development, to exhibit which is the proposition of the systematist.

Both subdivisions, for the system is also a subdivision, have this in common, that they form groups, the members of which possess certain characters, and by collecting these groups together by means of still more general characters, a survey of the entire contents is effected. They nevertheless sometimes lead to very different results, by separating a division that connects the rest, and *vice versâ*. But system has the advantage of not regarding solitary characters only, but all collectively, and can therefore only separate and connect where nature itself has marked a separation and connexion.

§ 320.

The methods whereby both attain the goal are different, for artificial subdivision proceeds from the characters of the last group, which we generally call species, and collects similar species under one common character, and thence forms the genus; the characters common to genera give those of the higher groups, the orders and their common characters combine to form those of the classes. It depends, therefore, upon every classifier how far he will proceed in separation and subdivision. Indeed, much difference of opinion exists upon the determination of the groups between the species and the order, whence have arisen the several definitions of sub-genus, genus, and tribe. In fact, opinions will never harmonise upon the claims of genera, because no universal principle for the structure of genera in an artificial subdivision can be given. This principle is in itself exceedingly capricious, and if one maintains thus far a genus extends, and another thus far, both are certainly right, if only every group which they distinguish as genera are distinguished by similar and exclusive characters.

The natural system, the object of which is to discover analogies and affinities, does not proceed from characters, but from the idea expressed in each group, and forms from these, according to the laws of thought, a philosophical structure. It is requisite, as well for the discovery of the conception and its formation into an idea, as for the constructing of the system, to be thoroughly acquainted with all forms, both in their external and internal characters, for it is these which express the concealed idea: when these ideas are found, their arrangement offers of itself, if we but keep in view the object of the natural system, namely, the discovery of analogies and affinities. This concealed idea is properly the true character, and which is expressed in a natural group, and so distinguishes it; if we have the idea, the character is conveyed with it. These ideas are expressed in the history of the development, or in the manner in which the individual has evolved itself from its origin; then in the form and composition of the internal organs; then in the figure, structure, and number of its external organs; and, lastly, in its functions, both external, and more particularly those of the internal organs. Where there is a resemblance or similarity in all these relations, there is found a perfect affinity; but where only some resemble and others differ, there it is only partial, and it is the greater the more and more perfectly the several determinate causes harmonise together. We hence distinguish several kinds of affinity, namely, the following *:—

1. Gradational affinity. This is founded upon the resemblance of the several organs in the grades of development, for example, upon a conformity in the development of the organs of the mouth, whether these are mandibulate or haustellate; upon a conformity in the metamorphoses, &c. Insects which present these resemblances in their organs, and the development of these organs, are brought together in the same group.

2. Parallel affinity. This is expressed in the mutual relation of the developed forms of individual organs to the rest. It may happen that whilst the remaining organs have acquired a tolerably equal development, one passes through several, either higher or lower, forms of development. Thus are produced:

a. Changes of external form in the same grades of organisation, for instance, beetles with elongate proboscideal mouths imitate the mouths

---

* See Schulz natürliches System der Pflanzenreiches. Berlin, 1832. 8vo. p. 132, &c.

of haustellate insects, although their oral organs are formed as in all beetles.

b. Repetition of the same form in different grades, for example, a resemblance between genera of different orders, namely, *Tipula* and *Bittacus*, *Mantis* and *Mantispa*, &c.

c. A change of form in individual organs, with a general resemblance in the rest, for instance, clavate antennæ of *Hellwigia* among the *Ichneumons*, filiform antennæ in *Anthribus* among the *Curculios*, &c.

3. Typical affinity.—It will be found that in general all forms and grades of organisation in a natural group stand in a certain degree of resemblance to each other, which relation is considered as the type or characteristic expression of the group ; where this resemblance is found there is typical affinity. This can present itself as

The generic type—if the species of a genus agree in form, sculpture, and colour.

The family type,—if, for instance, the oral organs, antennæ, legs, or the entire form resemble each other in the genera of a family ; and as

The type of the order—if the grades of metamorphoses or the construction of the body evince a certain conformity, as is very evidently the case in the *Coleoptera*.

These three kinds of affinity separate and connect at the same time the several groups. Gradational affinity presents the characters of the classes, orders, and higher groups ; typical affinity distinguishes the natural limits of the lower groups. Parallel affinity again connects the several groups together. Thus, upon the similitude and dissimilitude of all the qualities and characters is the natural system founded.

§ 321.

It may now be asked what course does the natural system follow in the consecutive arrangement of the groups ? In reply to this, we can scarcely say more than that it arranges the groups according to their affinities, and this series regulated by affinities is the course of the system. Nevertheless we can, proceeding from the essence of the natural system, characterise its course *à priori.* It is also the task of the natural system to show the developments which a group has passed through from its simple beginning to its extreme perfection. These developments are shown to us by physiology, and therefore every natural system must proceed upon physiological principles.

The physiological principles whence the natural system proceeds are:—

1. That the entire organisation takes its origin from a most simple beginning, whence by the development of this into several organs, it elevates itself to its most perfect form. This development exhibits itself partly in the internal and partly in the external organs, and almost throughout presents itself in antitheses, for instance, insects with a metamorphosis and insects without a metamorphosis; the former are again divided into those with a perfect and those with an imperfect metamorphosis, &c. The more these antitheses are divided the more do they seek to re-unite, in the first place, to preserve their original unity, and in the second place to produce a new antithesis, as, for instance, both groups into insects with haustellate oral organs and with mandibulate oral organs, each of which again strives to approach the other. Thus lower groups with individual superior organs stand opposite in equal value to the lower groups of the superior grades.

2. This equivalent value produces the mutual relations of the groups, which re-produces their more intimate concatenation.

Thus we find insects with an imperfect metamorphosis possessing mandibulate organs, which, from their second degree of development, strive to rise above those with a perfect metamorphosis and haustellate oral organs, as, for instance, the *Orthoptera* are placed by the majority of systematists above the *Diptera* and *Lepidoptera*, which, however, is inadmissible, from their imperfect metamorphosis.

3. The external organisation can attain a higher grade, while the internal remains stationary, and thus mark the prefiguration of a superior group in one that is inferior. It thence happens that the natural system does not ascend in a direct line from the most simple to the most complex group, but sends forth on all sides lateral branches, which, proceeding from a lower grade, strive to attain the highest.

According to these principles, which we have thus made to harmonise with the views of modern systematists, was the system sketched that we formerly published*, and which we shall have an opportunity of presenting, in the historical survey of systems.

Upon passing from these general observations upon the nature and difference of both divisions to the groups characterised in both, we shall find them to consist of the following:—

---

* De Insectorum systemate naturali. Halæ, 1829. 8vo.

§ 322.

I. IDEA OF SPECIES.

A species is that group of natural bodies which agree together in all their essential, unchangeable characters. The idea of species comprises in it a congruency, that is to say, not a mere conformity, but also a resemblance of its individuals.

A species is the lowest of all the systematic groups, and consequently the most fixed and conformable; no further differences are observable amongst its individuals, all have consisted from the commencement of this form, and continue so by the propagation of new and congruent individuals. Yet differences in less essential characters may occur, for example, in colour, and even in size, and such forms have been called varieties. They originate from accidental circumstances, which cannot be predicted. Others, which have been called sub-species, exhibit a greater conformity together, but which differ in some characters from the type of the species, and these differences are continued through all subsequent generations, which is not the case in mere varieties. But they yet announce themselves as true individuals of the species by a conformity in essential unchangeable characters, and therefore cannot, notwithstanding these differences, be separated from it.

§ 323.

One important character which especially identifies the sub-species with the species is, that they are fertile together. This is a very definite character, and which is subjected to no divarication; for howsoever much the several sub-species of *Coccinella variabilis*, Ill., differ from each other, so much so that Fabricius considered them as forming several species (viz. *C.* 10-*punctata*, *C.* 13-*punctata*, *C.* 10-*pustulata*, &c.), we however find them in reciprocal connexion, and there is consequently no doubt that they are all one species. Truly distinct species never regularly *, or at least but rarely, intermix in a state of nature, and certainly not fruitfully, although bastards (*species hybridæ*), that is, new intermediate ones originating from the intercourse of two species, produced in a state of captivity, or in a state of life differing from their original natural state, is not rare among the superior animals. In reference to this, we may therefore say that sub-species and varieties

---

* See above, § 292.

are met with pre-eminently among such insects as are found in the proximity of mankind, and there in great multitudes, as, for example, in the recently mentioned *Coccinella*, in the cockchafer (*Melolontha vulgaris*), the garden chafer (*Anisoplia horticola*), &c. It is also possible that the influence the universal cultivation of the country has had upon even the nutrimental plants, has extended also to them, and has united together several originally distinct species, as may with much probability be asserted of the sub-species of the domestic dog.

§ 324.

Many differences of sub-species and varieties depend also upon the nature of the country and of the climate. Several of our recently established species have originated from such circumstances, and must therefore be re-arranged with their original species, as has also been occasionally done by several authors. *Carabus arvensis*, F., for example, is found not so much in fields as in sub-alpine situations, and here presents itself in its usual form; *C. pommeranus*, Oliv., a native of the north of Germany, is one of these sub-species, which is distinguished by its less brilliant colour and less distinct sculpture; *C. Harcyniæ*, St., also is a sub-alpine variety of the *C. catenulatus*, F., which is found in the woods of plains; and there are doubtlessly many new described species of the *Carabodea* which stand in the same relation to old and long-known ones.

We must also enumerate with the sub-species the smaller individuals of many of the *Lamellicorns*, which have long been separated as true species under a distinct name, for example, the smaller variety of *Lucanus cervus*, or *L. capreolus*, of many writers. I think it very possible that these smaller individuals have originated from a deficiency of food or of a less nutritive quality in the larva state [*], and that in the larger insects this variety must be greater than in the smaller ones, as the former require more for their support, and are more exposed to the effects of temperature than the latter, the duration of whose lives besides is limited in general to one year, whereas the larger ones pass several years in the larva state. We find smaller, and indeed sometimes very small, individuals of almost all the larger, and especially of the very large beetles; and the *Lamellicorns* particularly exhibit this variety, for instance, *Oryctes nasicornis*, *Scarabæus stercorarius*,

---

[*] This idea I find suggested also in Meckel's vergleichenden Anatomie, tom. i. p. 335.

Typhæus, and many exotic species. A striking instance of the influence which good or bad nutriment has upon the development of the larva is exhibited to us in the practice of the bees rearing queens from the larvæ of the neuters.

These facts show that the establishment of a true species is not so easy an affair, and that it requires very comprehensive tact. Good specific characters however may be derived from the general form, the form of individual parts, especially of the head and thorax, the sculpture or markings of the external integument; after which the size and the relative proportions of different parts; and lastly, also even colour.

The specific character, or sum of all the essential characters that define the species, serves for the distinction of a species.

§ 325.

II. IDEA OF A GENUS.

Above the species stands the group, which has been called the genus. A genus is composed of several species, which agree in certain qualities of essential parts or organs; its idea consequently comprises that of conformity.

This, in itself correct definition, admits however of a variety of interpretations, according to the object aimed at in the foundation of the system. Artificial classification divides where it observes divarications and differences in the organs adopted as the basis of the subdivision; whereas the natural system regards the harmony of all the organs, and only forms divisions where divarications of decided importance are observed in those organs. An example will speedily illustrate this. Fabricius, whose classification, founded upon the oral organs, is evidently artificial, divided the *Chrysomelina,* according to the structure of the parts of their mouths, into several genera, and referred to these genera all those leaping beetles which Geoffroy and Illiger united in the one genus *Haltica,* according as the parts of the mouth, or even merely the external form, appeared to agree with the characters of this or that family; the most prominent character, that of leaping, he left quite unnoticed, keeping merely the principles of his system in view. Latterly, however, and even indeed formerly, as soon as it was wished to form natural genera, the greatest attention has been paid, and justly, to this power of leaping, and it has consequently been considered as the chief characters of these creatures, and indeed they appear to be particularly distinguished by it.

§ 326.

The method whereby we pass through several qualities and characters which constitute groups, down to the genus, is analytic. The last group before the species is generally considered the genus. But it is possible that one or the other of such determinate genera may be still further subdivided by divarications in isolated characters: are now such groups to be raised to positive genera? In general this must be negatived, for as the higher groups were defined by the simultaneous differences of all the organs, and the peculiarities deduced from them, so must the genera of a family, besides a decided difference in the generic characters, exhibit likewise a general transformation in shape. If this be not the case the genera will necessarily be of unequal value, and it will therefore never be possible to settle the contest upon the generic rights of any determinate group. Every discussion and dispute upon any subject rests upon principles; if upon these a difference of opinion prevails all further argument is useless, and no satisfactory result can ever be obtained until one of the contesting parties can be convinced of the falseness of their principles.

§ 327.

In the structure of new genera there are two wrong roads to be avoided; the one is too circumstantial a dividing, and the other is the unnatural connexion of absolutely different groups.

The first is most easily followed, when, upon the increase of the number of the species of a genus, the survey of the whole is rendered difficult. Hence has proceeded in modern times the host of genera which are in general deficient in all fixed characters, and are frequently exceedingly superficial, being constructed merely from the external form and general impression. A distinction, as, for instance, that which has been used for the separation of *Ophonus* and *Harpalus*, namely, the deeper punctures of the superficies in the former, whereas in the latter it is smooth, must indeed be regarded when it is extensive; but it never justifies the construction of a genus, and can at most serve for a subdivision of the species within the limits of the genus. Another instance is exhibited likewise in the same family, namely, the *Carabodea*, in the genus *Feronia*, the former subdivision of which into distinct genera was founded chiefly upon the form of the prothorax, and which modern writers have very justly, from its being untenable, re-united into one genus. If, for example, genera might be formed from mere outline, we might readily form new genera in the large family of the *Elaterodea*, from the figure of the prothorax, which would be equally inadmissible. There are, in fact, among the *Elaters*, as well as among their close allies the *Buprestes*, several natural genera, but we much doubt whether the many genera of *Elaters* recently constructed by Eschscholz *, from the form of the tarsal joints, may be considered as natural.

§ 328.

The second by-way we find to have been pursued chiefly by the older entomologists; but it originated in the nature of the thing when but few species were known, and thence their family characters were adopted as generic characters. Thus all the Linnæan, and many of the Fabrician genera have become families, and the divarications they were either not acquainted with, or did not regard, have never supplied the characters of genera.

§ 329.

It may be asked how are these by-ways to be avoided?

It has often been considered that exactitude and acuteness were the qualities that gave a right to found genera. Indeed, every naturalist who is deficient in these qualifications will vainly endeavour to form new genera, and never produce anything useful: but, on the opposite side, is every considerate and acute observer competent to found new true genera? We should even here doubt constant success. A judicious eye corrected by experience, an equally secure feeling of the value of the discovered differences, as well as the conviction that only natural genera may be admitted, are the qualifications that combine to form the happy talent in which we may repose unconditional confidence in the formation of genera. This talent, which, by the exercise of years, may be extraordinarily increased, was especially and distinctly exhibited in Fabricius and Illiger, but in the former it decreased with increasing age, whence many of the genera he last constructed are devoid of naturalness; whereas Illiger rejoiced in its complete perfection throughout the whole of his indeed short but very active career. This happy talent, or, as it may be called, judicious tact, is

---

* See Thorn's Archiv., vol. ii. part i. p. 31, &c.

never doubtful of the characters requisite to the formation of a genus. Fabricius could not have made a better choice for the determination of genera than of characters deduced from the oral organs and the antennæ, as these organs are of the greatest importance to the existence of the insect, both for procuring its nutriment and in its economy. Their structure is regulated by the former, and they instruct us upon the latter. If, indeed, much may be said against this selection, from the difficulty of their investigation and observation, yet it affords no sufficient ground entirely to reject them. Industry and patience overcome much, and the excellent labours of many modern entomologists, for instance, of Savigny, prove that a new era in the history of entomology may be dated from his comparative representation of the oral organs, and especially from his inquiries into the mouth of the *Lepidoptera* *.

When such an important point is discovered the definition of the genus is no longer difficult ; it is only necessary to inspect, if the other parts of the body present the same differences as the organs of the mouth ; if this be the case the genus is natural, if not it is artificial and superfluous. This is likewise the case in the introduction of the neuration of the wing for the determination of genera. In many families the divarication is in such close connexion with the structure of the entire body that a mere view of the wing suffices to show us the difference of genera ; but this is often not the case, and to separate the genus *Rhamphomyia*, Meig., from *Empis*, because it has one nervure less at the apex of the wing, is very artificial, and cannot consist with the principles of a natural system. These differences can only be used to characterise the divisions within the boundaries of a genus, and thus to facilitate the discovery of a species among a multitude, as Meigen himself has done in the genus *Limnobia ;* but the divarication in the neuration of the wing cannot be raised to the character of a true genus. But let all entomologists who occupy themselves with the formation of new genera remember the dogma of Linnæus,—" It is not the character which forms the genus, but the genus, constructed by nature, brings forth the character."

§ 330.

Little that is universally applicable can be said upon the value of certain organs for the determination of genera, for even the oral organs are

* See his Mémoires sur les Animaux sans Vertèbres. Paris, 1816. 8vo., with figures, vol. i.

sometimes exactly alike in truly different genera; but the stability of genera depends in many instances much more upon the judicious balancing of all the parts of the body, and their differences, in which case it is only the above mentioned happy tact that can securely guide the observer. For, however fixed the number of the joints in the antennæ, for example, may be in certain families, yet instances occur in which they are subjected to much variety. The genus *Cimbex* is a case in point, the antennæ of which consists sometimes of six, sometimes of seven joints, of which sometimes one, or two, or three of them are swollen into a knob. If we compare with this the number of the joints in the antennæ in the whole family of the saw-flies, we shall speedily perceive that genera formed merely from the number of those joints cannot absolutely be considered as natural. This number is still more variable in the genus *Forficula*, in which almost every species has a different number, and which likewise is not even uniform in the individuals of the same species; and yet Leach has formed distinct genera founded on these differences.

§ 331.

The sum of the characters adopted for the definition of the genus forms the generic character, which is either natural when deduced from all the organs, or artificial when it merely refers to the characters admitted as the basis of the classification. This again constitutes the essential character when it merely cites the distinguishing marks of the genus. The generic description refers neither to the natural nor to the artificial generic character, but presents the entire form, even to its most minute divarications; it is, as it were, a figure in words, whereas the characters depict in words particular organs only.

III. IDEA OF THE SUPERIOR GROUPS.

§ 332.

It is from characters of greater generality, especially from resemblances in form, or the similar structure of certain parts, as the feet, wings, &c., which yield no generic characters, that the genera group themselves into superior divisions. This grouping must follow the principles adopted in characterising genera, if no violence is to be done to nature. We must here also strive for an equality of value in the groups formed.

The division immediately above a genus is usually called a family It is peculiar to the natural system, and by this only is it called forth Linnæus and Fabricius, who formed artificial classifications, had no families.

The characters which distinguish the families are derived not only from their resemblances in structure in general, but also frequently from their economy. Thus the allied families of the *Carabodea* and *Hydrocantharides*, which both live upon prey, are distinguished, as well from their dwelling-place, and a very definite and easily recognisable form of the body, and also by a very marked difference in the structure of their posterior legs, whereas the organs of the mouth and the antennæ agree in the types. Were we to deduce the characters of families from such relations, it could be defined only as one of resemblance; in the similar structure of certain parts in several genera lie the characters of a family.

§ 333.

We sometimes also remark within the boundaries of a family, especially of a very comprehensive one, subdivisions, which bear the same relation to the families as do the subdivisions of a genus to the latter. Such groups have been indeed called sub-families. They are as useful for the easier discovery of the genera, as the former for facilitating the discovery of the species, and they are therefore more artificial than natural groups. But it depends much upon their mode of division, for this does not admit of being said of the sub-families of the large family of the *Ichneumonodea*, and as little of many others. For the sake of an example, we may be allowed to state that those three sub-families differ in the structure of their palpi. The genuine *Ichneumonodea* have five-jointed maxillary palpi, and four-jointed labial palpi; the *Braconodea* five-jointed maxillary and three-jointed labial palpi; the *Bassina* six-jointed maxillary and four-jointed labial palpi. Similar groups, founded upon analogous relations, are found in the families of the *Carabodea, Lamellicornia, Rhynchophora, Vespacea, Apiaria, Muscaria*, &c.

§ 334.

The chief group above the family is the order; it does not so much depend upon a similarity of individual parts, as upon the entire body, for instance, whether the thorax be divided in its three segments, or whether these are closely jointed together; upon the form and structure of the larva; upon the type upon which the oral organs are formed, whether mandibulate or haustellate; or upon the fundamental form in the structure of the wings. All these relations, indeed, produce an external resemblance, but these resemblances are the result of physiological divarications. The orders are properly families of greater compass, yet with the distinction that the family characters are founded upon a similarity of form of individual limbs, as the feet, antennæ; whereas the characters of orders are derived from a similarity of form of the body.

There are likewise other subdivisions between an order and its families, as between a family and its genera, which have been called sub-orders, or tribes. The characters of such groups generally consist in the different form of a certain organ, but which differences, from their wider distribution, admit neither of being applied to family divisions nor to generic divisions. Thus the *Coleoptera* are divided into tribes from the number of their tarsal joints, the *Diptera* according to the number of the joints of the antennæ, the *Hymenoptera* according to the structure of the sting, &c. Yet such tribes are more artificial than natural, which admits of being demonstrated in the three examples cited; they can merely serve to facilitate finding the families, and are not to be considered as natural groups.

§ 335.

The classes, lastly, are the highest groups of animals; which, like the orders, are founded upon the differences of an otherwise uniform grade of structure, and consequently repose upon the differences of the grades of organisation. An equal structure and form of the organic systems and the thence produced very general conformity of external figure, a similarity of periods of development, and other similar relations are the characters which justify the formation of classes. All insects collectively form one class, in as far as they actually agree with each other in the above characters.

The objects forming classes consequently neither require to be congruent nor equal, nor even externally to resemble each other, as these qualities are deduced from a conformity of external figure, but they must all, physiologically considered, be of equal value; they must all, to make use of a mathematical illustration, be pure geometrical inconstant magnitudes, and not at the same time likewise algebraical constant magnitudes, both of which are virtually different.

§ 336.

Some naturalists admit, and certainly correctly, still further divisions, which comprise several classes, but which have no name. They also are founded upon similarities in the structure of the organs and of the organic system. The four above explained (§ 88) organic systems, stand in three different relations to each other; namely, in the first group they retain their vegetable character, with the mere addition of the animal character of voluntary motion; in the second and third groups the animal character predominates; so that in the second, motion, and in the third, sensation, are especially developed. We thus obtain the chief types under which all animal forms may be arranged.

SECOND CHAPTER.

HISTORY OF THE CHIEF ENTOMOLOGICAL CLASSIFICATIONS AND SYSTEMS.

§ 337.

THE earliest essay to group animals in general, and consequently insects, is that of Aristotle (about 330 B. C.). In his works, one of which is exclusively devoted to Zoology, he indeed nowhere gives a complete system of animals; but from hints here and there expressed, it appears that he separated the *Crustacea* as a particular group (Μαλακόστρακα) from other insects ("Εντομα). A further division of insects is deduced from their wings, and from their presence or absence they fall into "Εντομα πτιλωτὰ and "Εντομα ἄπτερα; both again consist of several groups, which are partly perfectly natural. The divisions of Aristotle are in general so successfully made, that we are perfectly astonished at his vast genius, which whithersoever it directed itself, always found the right, and he maintained in everything he attempted an equal greatness.

The labours of his successors are very different. Pliny's " Natural History" is merely a systematised Encyclopædia, in which all those works are abridged that the author had read in the course of a life devoted to science, and which was sacrificed in the contemplation of a magnificent natural phenomenon. Much is therefore collected without any criticism; what was new was not at all introduced, and the old frequently distorted by the mode of communication.

Ælian's " Natural History of Animals" properly contains merely anecdotes and characteristic features of individual animals, and no zoological description, and may be therefore merely noticed.

§ 338.

Since Aristotle, nothing of any consequence, either in antiquity or in the middle ages, was done for the natural history of animals; so that we leap over a space of more than 1800 years, and with Conrad Gesner re-commence our historical detail.

He, a poor but industrious Swiss (born in 1516), collected everything that was known relative to the history of animals; he filled up many gaps by his personal observations, and thus filled five large folios with merely the natural history of the vertebrata. Before he reached insects, death carried him off (1558). His posthumous papers upon this subject fell into the hands of the well-known Joachim Kamerarius, of whom they were purchased by an Englishman, Dr. E. Wotton, who sent them to Thomas Penn, in London, to be published; he, however, did not fulfil the commission, but these papers fell, when he died, into the hands of Thomas Moufet, who incorporated them with his " Theatro Insectorum," and they were thus imparted to the world about a century after their origin (1634).

Gesner is justly considered as the restorer of natural history; it was by means of his extraordinary industry that long lost treasures were again made known to that age, which was thus stimulated to further researches; had he not existed the world would doubtlessly have still much longer slept.

His influence, however, did not so much exhibit itself in the natural history of insects from the above causes, and it was still several lustres before they were independently and satisfactorily elaborated.

Ulysses Aldrovandus was the first who took notice of these forgotten creatures, and described them and their natural history in seven books. We here find the first division of insects into land and water dwellers, two chief groups, which were still further divided according to the structure of their legs and wings.

After a commencement was thus made to the study of entomology several amateurs speedily collected. The imperial court painter, Hoefnagel, figured insects very beautifully; Franciscus Redi observed their origin and propagation; M. Malpighi made a masterly dissection of the silkworm; and Swammerdamm, lastly, investigated insects in the several stages of their existence, and formed the first essay towards a natural system. His arrangement of insects was this:—

I. Insects without a metamorphosis.

They, indeed, change skin, but retain their original form. Spiders, lice, woodlice, and *Myriapodæ*.

II. Insects with a metamorphosis.

1. The creature moves throughout all the stages of its existence: in the first it is wingless, in the second (pupa) it obtains the rudiments of wings, and in the third entire wings.

    Here are arranged the *Neuroptera, Orthoptera*, and *Hemiptera*, but he did not separate them into distinct groups.

2. The creature, in its central grade of development, is motionless, but has limbs.

    Here the *Hymenoptera, Coleoptera*, and as appendix, the *Lepidoptera*.

3. In its central stage of development the creature has neither motion nor wings, but appears as an ovate pupa.

    Here the *Diptera*.

In the author's Book of Nature, " Biblia Naturæ," which was published after his death, which took place in 1685, this system was illustrated with examples, and the anatomy of insects especially is admirably presented.

The now increasing writers upon entomology offered each his own arrangement, and according to which their subject was presented, but system still remained subordinate to observation. Thus Joh. Gœdart wrote upon the metamorphosis. Sybilla Merian observed the development of the *Lepidoptera*, and, from affection to the science, went herself to Surinam, to continue there her observations. Ant. von Leuwenhoek made microscopic experiments; and Antonio Vallisnieri pursued the path trodden by his predecessors, of describing the metamorphoses of insects: works which are still worthy of regard as well as of emulation.

§ 339.

The first true systematist was an Englishman, John Ray; the following is the arrangement published by him in his "Method. Insectorum." Lond. 1705, 8vo.

I. *Ametamorphata* (insects without a transformation).
  1. *Apoda* (annulate worms).
    a. Terrestria.
    b. Aquatica.
  2. *Pedata.*
    a. Hexapoda.
      α. *Terrestria* (lice).
      β. *Aquatica.*
    b. Octopoda (spiders).
    c. Quatuordecempoda (lobsters and crabs).
    d. Polypoda.
      α. *Terrestria* (centipedes, woodlice).
      β. *Aquatica* (*Amphipoda* and *Isopoda*, Lat.).

II. *Metamorphota* (insects with transformation).
  1. *Larvis et pupis agilibus* (*Orthoptera, Hemiptera*).
  2. *Pupa immobili.*
    a. Coleoptera (beetles).
    b. Aneloptera.
      α. *Alis farinaceis* (*Lepidoptera*).
      β. *Alis membranaceis.*
        † *Diptera, bipennia* (flies).
        †† *Tetraptera, quadripennia* (*Hymenoptera*).

III. *Metamorphosi simplici e vermiculo in animalculum volatici, interposita aliqua quiete* (dragon-flies).

A posthumous manuscript of his, containing a detailed history of insects, Martin Lister published after Ray's death (1707), at the command of the Royal Society of London (Historia Insectorum, ed. M. Lister. Lond. 1710-11), and at the same time appeared a new classification, which we will also subjoin. It is the following:

I. *Insecta ex ovis sphæricis, quæ nullam subeunt metamorphosim.*
    a. Pedibus senis (lice).
    b. Pedibus octonis (spiders).
    c. Pedibus plurimis (crabs, wood-lice, centipedes).
    d. Pedibus nullis (worms).

II. *Insecta ex ovis longiusculis, quæ metamorphosim subeunt.*
   a. *Coleoptera.*
   b. *Anelytra.*
      α. *Pennis quatuor nudis.*
      β. *Pennis quatuor farinaceis.*
      γ. *Pennis duabus.*

This arrangement is in fact nothing more than a mere modification of that already given by Ray, and only differs in that its author has brought Ray's third chief group under the second, and unites it with the *Anelytris pennis quatuor nudis.*

§ 340.

From Ray to Linnæus, nothing extraordinary took place for the arrangement of insects. But when this master of natural history published his System of Nature, in the year 1735, in three folio sheets, in which he gave a complete survey of all the then known groups of animal bodies, insects also were placed by him in a new order, which he skilfully determined according to the form and structure of their wings. The following is his division.

The fifth class of his animal system, which comprises those with a simple heart, white blood, and jointed antennæ, contains within it all the insects and *Crustacea.* Both together, therefore, form a single chief group (*Insecta*), which is thus subdivided:

I. Insects with four wings.
   1. The anterior ones horny. 1. *Coleoptera.*
   2. The anterior ones half horny and half membranous. 2. *Hemiptera.*
   3. The anterior and posterior membranous.
      a. All covered with scales. 3. *Lepidoptera.*
      b. All naked. The nervures.
         α. Reticulated. 4. *Neuroptera.*
         β. Ramose. 5. *Hymenoptera.*
II. Insects with two wings. 6. *Diptera.*
III. Insects without wings. 7. *Aptera.*
   1. With six feet (louse, flea, and some others).
   2. With more than six feet.
      a. Head connected with the thorax (spiders, crabs, &c.).
      b. Head free (centipedes, wood-lice, &c.).

It is not to be denied that by this arrangement many natural, and therefore, very constant groups, were formed, but, s often the case, when, in the arrangement of natural bodies, only one principle of division is adopted, others comprise, in every instance, very different animals. This deficiency must necessarily be recognised upon continued inspection, and, therefore, an anxiety must exist to remove it as much as possible. Above all, the order of the *Hemiptera* is subject to many objections, for, in the first place, the character attributed to it is not found in many of its members, for instance, in many *Cicada*, the *Aphides*, the genus *Chermes*, &c., as they possess four perfectly membranous wings, and, secondly, there are insects united in it, which exhibit the greatest differences in their oral organs.

These circumstances caused the next systematist after Linnæus, who was also a Swede, namely, De Geer, to separate the Linnæan *Hemiptera* into several equivalent groups, as well as to the adoption of a new system, which is the following:

I. Insects with wings. *Alata.*
  A. *Gymnoptera.*
    1. *Lepidoptera.*
    2. *Elingula* (*Ephemeræ,* &c.).
    3. *Neuroptera* (*Libellulæ* and other Linnæan *Neuroptera*).
    4. *Hymenoptera.*
    5. *Siphonata* (*Aphides* and *Cicada*).
  B. *Vaginata.*
    6. *Dermaptera* (bugs and water-bugs).
    7. *Hemiptera* (cockroaches and grasshoppers).
    8. *Coleoptera* (beetles).
  C. *Diptera.*
    9. *Halterata* (*Linnæus, Diptera*).
    10. *Proboscidea* (the genus *Coccus*).

II. Insects without wings. *Aptera.*
  D. *Saltatoria.*
    11. *Suctoria* (the genus *Culex*).
  E. *Gressoria.*
    12. *Aucenata* (the genera *Lepisma, Podura, Termes, Pediculus,* and *Ricinus*).
    13. *Atrachelia* (the spiders and crabs).
    14. *Crustacea* (the *Isopoda, Ampiphoda,* and *Myriapoda* of Latreille. See below).

This system, which cannot be called a purely artificial one, as it is founded upon several principles of division, is yet deficient in its object as a natural one; the second and third orders are falsely separated, although a division of the Linnæan *Neuroptera* was desirable; the fifth must be again united with the seventh, and the tenth belongs as an integral portion to both; the twelfth and thirteenth, however, are both an intermixture of the most distinct creatures, and the fourteenth cannot make claim to be very natural.

§ 341.

Twelve years (1764) after De Geer's subdivision, a French naturalist of the name of Geoffroy stepped forth as a systematist, where hitherto Englishmen and Swedes had for half a century alone presented themselves. Indeed, the French had not been idle during this time, to prove which we have merely to refer to the labours of Reaumur; but they had not yet presented themselves as systematists, which is the more remarkable, as their countrymen subsequently have been most active in this branch of natural inquiry. Geoffroy's system, which, exclusive of other points, is important from the introduction of the joints of the tarsi as points of division, has fewer groups than any of the earlier ones, namely, only the following six.

I. *Coleoptera*. Mandibles and hard anterior wings. They are divided into
  1. Those with hard entire elytra.
  2. Those with hard half elytra. And
  3. Those with soft membranous elytra (the *Hemiptera* of De Geer).
     Each of these groups is subdivided from the number of the joints of the tarsi, in four or five lower groups.
II. *Hemiptera*. Sucking oral organs and half hard anterior wings.
III. *Lepidoptera*. Same as Linnæus.
IV. *Tetraptera*. Four naked membranous wings.
  a. Feet three jointed (*Libellula, Semblis*).
  b. Feet four jointed (*Rhaphidia*).
  c. Feet five jointed (*Ephemera, Phryganea, Hemerobius, Myrmecoleon*, and the *Hymenoptera* of Linnæus).
V. *Diptera*. The same as Linnæus.
VI. *Aptera*. The same as Linnæus.

From whatever point of view we regard this system, it is equally unna tural, and worse than any of his predecessors. In the second group of beetles we find the genera *Staphylinus, Forficula, Meloë,* and *Necydalis.* De Geer had already shown that the earwig does not belong to the beetles. But, indeed, if cockroaches, grasshoppers, and locusts are to be classed among the beetles, as Geoffroy has done, the earwig may very well be placed there. What a mixture is not the fourth order even! It was very necessary that an active mind should occupy itself to separate all these errors from the truth, and to raise entomology from its existing state of childhood to its age of manhood.

§ 342.

This genius was found amongst the Germans; it was John Christian Fabricius, who was born in 1748 at Tondern, in the Grand Duchy of Sleswig: he died upon the 3rd of March, 1808, as Professor at Kiel. It was indeed time that the Germans should exhibit themselves as a people that loved science and knew how to promote it, for all their neighbours had preceded them with celebrated examples; but it soon displayed itself in a manner superior to any of the rest, as the most comprehensive, active, profoundest, and most zealous for science.

His division, which was first published in the year 1775, in his Systema Entomologiæ, followed quite a new path, the groups of it being founded upon organs which had never yet been used by authors as the principles of subdivision. These were the oral organs. Fabricius defined the orders (which he incorrectly called classes) by their differences, and in the course of his progressive investigation he established thirteen equivalent groups. Both his first and last subdivisions we will here subjoin.

His first classification was given in 1775, in the Systema Entomologiæ.

I. Insects with biting oral organs.
  1. Four or six palpi at the *maxillæ* and *labium.*
     a. *Maxillæ* free, uncovered. 1. *Eleutherata* (*Coleoptera* of Linnæus).
     b. *Maxillæ* covered. 2. *Ulonata* (*Hemiptera* of De Geer; a portion of the *Hemiptera* of Linnæus).
     c. *Maxillæ* connate with the *labium.* 3. *Synistata* (*Neuroptera, Hymenoptera,* and some *Aptera* [*Monocul. Onisc. Lepisma, Podura*] of Linnæus).
     d. No *maxillæ.* 4. *Agonata* (lobsters and scorpions).

2. Only two *palpi*, and indeed upon the *maxillæ*. 5. *Unogata* (*Libellulæ*, centipedes, and spiders).

II. Insects with suctorial mouths.
  a. With a spiral tongue. 6. *Glossata* (Linnæus's *Lepidoptera*).
  b. With valvular proboscis consisting of *setæ*. 6. *Rhyngota* (the remaining *Hemiptera* of Linnæus).
  c. With fleshy setiferous proboscis. 7. *Antliata* (Linnæus's *Diptera*).

Howsoever meritorious the undertaking of Fabricius was to discover a new principle of subdivision, whereby all groups of insects could be determined, yet this first division by no means answers the requisitions that a strict classification is justified in making. It therefore at first found but little favour, and the difficulty of the investigation also impeded it, and in many cases indeed doubt was entertained of the possibility of the process. In fact, this work was but the first essay of a new method, and, as such, certainly praiseworthy, in as far as the attention of entomologists was drawn to parts which had not previously been regarded, and which, however, as was evident from this representation, were of the greatest importance for the distinction of groups, and especially of genera. Fabricius has not therefore acquired an immortal name in science so much by the establishment of his system, as exactly like Linnæus, by the path he pursued. All that was distorted and false that originated with him, time in the progress of the science has removed, and his system is put aside; but he is the founder of this mode of arrangement, for which he will never be forgotten, for this he stands forth as a model to succeeding generations.

The changes to which he gradually subjected his system are manifold. New orders were established, old ones more correctly restricted, and the whole was raised to a superior scientific completion. Thus almost in the evening of his days he proposed the following division in the supplementary volume to the second edition of his System of Insects.

I. Insects with biting mouths.

A. Two pairs of mandibles.
  a. The lower ones having *palpi*.
    1. Free without covering.   1. Class. *Eleutherata* (beetles).
    2. Covered.   2. —   *Ulonata* (*Orthoptera*).
    3. Connate with the *labium*. 3. —   *Synistata* (*Neuroptera*).
    4. Distended, thin, coriaceous. 4. —   *Piegata* (*Hymenoptera*).

5. Horny, strongly toothed, labium without *palpi*.	5. Class. *Odonata* (*Libellulæ*).
b. All without *palpi*.	6. — *Mitosata* (*Scolopendra*).
B. A pair of *maxillæ* resembling scissors.	7. — *Unogata* (scorpions and spiders).
C. More than two pair of *maxillæ*.	
1. Within the *labium*.	8. — *Polygonata* (*Isopoda*).
2. Outside the lip closing the mouth.	9. — *Kleistagnatha* (short-tailed crabs).
3. Outside the lip, but covered by the *palpi*.	10. — *Exochnata* (long-tailed crabs).
II. Insects with suctorial mouths.	
1. In the mouth a spiral tongue.	11. — *Glossata* (*Lepidoptera*).
2. In the mouth a horny proboscis, surrounded by jointed sheaths.	12. — *Rhyngota* (*Hemiptera*).
3. In the mouth a soft unjointed proboscis.	13. — *Antliata* (*Diptera*).

We perceive from this division that Fabricius had no idea of a natural grouping, but that he separated from solitary characters when he could. Thus forms the most allied were torn from each other, and very different genera were forced into the divisions from one-sided views; thus for instance, the flea stands among the *Rhyngota*, with which it has nothing in common but its suctorial mouth, whereas we find the lice among the *Antliata*, although they pass through no metamorphosis. The character of the *Odonata* is erroneous, for the *Libellulæ* have one jointed labial palpi, and the character of the *Synistata* does not agree with all, but merely with some genera.

§ 343.

Nevertheless, the system of Fabricius had many followers, especially because by means of it the genera were more correctly determined than had previously been the case; yet its being so unnatural and artificial displeased many, and, therefore, Illiger * proposed uniting both systems, that of Linnæus with the latter, a proposition which he himself executed in the following manner:—

---

* In the Appendix to his Käfer Preussens, vol. i. Halle, 1798. 8vo.

1. *Coleoptera*, Lin., without *Forficula* — *Eleutherata*, Fab.
2. *Hemiptera*, Lin. . . . — $\begin{cases} a. \text{ } Ulonota, \text{ F.} \\ b. \text{ } Rhyngota, \text{ F.} \end{cases}$
3. *Lepidoptera*, Lin. . . — *Glossata*, F.
4. *Neuroptera*, Lin. (to which *Termes*, *Lepisma*, and *Podura* are added) — $\begin{cases} a. \text{ } Odonata, \text{ F.} \\ b. \text{ } Synistata, \text{ F.} \end{cases}$
5. *Hymenoptera*, Lin. . . . — *Piezata*, F.
6. *Diptera*, Lin. (with *Pediculus* and *Acarus*) — *Antliata*, F.
7. *Aptera*, Lin. (without the above-named apterous genera) . . — $\begin{cases} a. \text{ } Unogata, \text{ F.} \\ b. \text{ } Agonata, \text{ F.} \\ c. \text{ } Mitosata, \text{ F.} \\ d \text{ } Kleistagnatha, \text{F.} \\ e. \text{ } Exochnata, \text{ F.} \end{cases}$

According to this grouping, which, indeed, removes several of the deficiencies of that of Fabricius, the large Helwig-Hoffmannseggian collection was to be arranged, and thus made the basis of a detailed elaboration of entomology, but its execution was prevented by political events.

Clairville * published almost contemporaneously with this essay of Illiger's a subdivision of insects, which, although it had no influence upon the progress of the science, yet merits a short notice. It was the following:

I. Insects with wings. *Pterophora*.

A. With mandibulate oral organs.
   1. Anterior wings horny.   1. Ord. *Elytroptera* (beetles).
   2. . . coriaceous.   2. — *Deratoptera* (*Orthoptera*).
   3. Wings with reticulated nervures.   3. — *Dictyoptera* (*Neuroptera*).
   4. Wings with ramose nervures.   4. — *Phleboptera* (*Hymenoptera*).

B. With haustellate oral organs.
   1. Wings and halteres.   5. — *Halteriptera* (*Diptera*).
   2. . . covered with scales.   6. — *Lepidoptera*.
   3. . . variously constructed.   7. — *Hemimeroptera* (*Hemiptera*).

II. Insects without wings.

1. With suctorial oral organs.   8. — *Rhophotera*.
2. With mandibulate oral organs.   9. — *Pododunera*.

* Entomologie Helvétique. Zur. 1798—1806, 2 vol. 8vo.

§ 344.

These were the systems of the preceding century. But the whole science of zoology, and consequently, therefore, entomology, was involved in a great and advantageous revolution, promoted by the general impulse towards a natural system, and which was especially stimulated by anatomical studies. Blumenbach, by the publication of his comparative anatomy, had conducted naturalists to this we may almost say new field, and its elaboration was now commenced with zeal. Hence was developed the zootomical tendency of zoology, and which possessed in Cuvier its most distinguished and universally revered representative. It took, lastly, a physiological direction, which did not, like the former, merely regard form, but inspected the entire essence of which form is merely the expression. The latter consequently reposes upon the zootomical, and without which it cannot be brought to bear, but its tendency to secure us from one-sidedness, to which the latter so easily leads, is its very greatest advantage. It is also called the philosophical system, and justly, for the path it pursues is more philosophical, in as far as it seeks to explain the composite from the simple, and endeavours to refer the former back to this. But its foundation being physiology, it justly merits its first name. Oken and his system are the representatives of this method.

§ 345.

The first new division of animals was proposed about this time by Cuvier (George Leopold Christian Frederick Dagobert, born 1769 at Mümpelgarde, in Alsatia, died at Paris in 1832), and actually executed in his 'Traité Elementaire'. Insects are here still treated according to the system of Linnæus, but yet the subsequent divisions are indicated in the grouping of the orders. The first of these divisions, namely, the separation of insects into two equivalent classes, was executed some years later in the Tables appended to his Comparative Anatomy, where he separated those with distinct blood-vessels as *Crustacea*, but left all the rest united as *Insecta*.

In the interim, another French naturalist, who afterwards acquired the highest fame in entomology, namely, P. A. Latreille (born 1762 at Brives) published a new division of insects*, which differs from

---

* Precis des Caractères Génériques des Insectes. Brives, 1796. 8vo.

the Linnæan merely in establishing the *Orthoptera* as an order, and the separation of the *Aptera* into seven equivalent orders. The following are the seven new orders:

1. *Suctoria* (the genus *Pulex*).
2. *Thysanura* (the genera *Lepisma* and *Podura*).
3. *Parasita* (the lice, with *Ricinus*, De Geer).
4. *Acephala* (*Unogata*, F., spiders, scorpions, and *Acari*).
5. *Entomostraca* (the genera *Cypris*, *Daphina*, &c.).
6. *Crustacea* (*Kleistagnatha* and *Exochnata*, F.).
7. *Myriapoda* (*Mitosata*, F., the genera *Scolopendra*, *Iulus*, *Oniscus*, and allies).

The author professes to have sought their natural arrangement, and to have founded his divisions less upon a single character than the general expression of the whole; but the mode in which he has formed his system scarcely supports his proposition, for many unnatural separations still remain. He, however, claims the positive merit of having introduced the natural families.

The next arrangement published by Latreille we find in his 'Genera Crustaceorum et Insectorum,' Paris, 1806, 4 vols. 8vo. He here divides, with Cuvier, Linnæus's *Insecta* into two equivalent groups, *Crustacea* and *Insecta*, the former of which he characterises by the possession of a heart and bronchial respiration, and the latter by respiring through tracheæ. The class of insects which alone here concerns us is divided in the following manner:

I. Insects without wings. *Aptera.*
  A. With segments bearing seven or more pairs of legs.
    a. Head separated from the thorax.
      a. a. Four antennæ. Last segments of the body without legs. 1. Legion. *Tetracera.*
      b. b. Two antennæ. All the segments except the last with legs. 2. — *Myriapoda.*
    b. Head connected with the thorax. No antennæ. 3. — *Acera.*
  B. With three segments bearing legs. 4. — *Apterodicera.*
II. Insects with wings. 5. — *Pterodicera.*
  A. With elytra and wings. *Elytroptera.*
    a. With mandibles. *Odontata.*

       a. a. Wings folded transversely.   1. Ord. *Coleoptera.*
       b. b. . . . longitudinally,   2. — *Orthoptera.*
     b. With haustellate mouth. *Sipho-*   3. — *Hemiptera.*
       nostomata.
   B. Without elytra, with wings. *Gymnoptera.*
    a. With mandibles. *Odontata.*
      a. a. Nervures reticulated.   4. — *Neuroptera.*
      b. b. . . ramose.   5. — *Hymenoptera.*
    b. With haustellate mouth. *Siphonostoma.*
      a. a. Four wings covered with scales.   6. — *Lepidoptera.*
      b. b. Two wings and two halteres.   7. — *Diptera.*
      c. c. No wings or halteres.   8. — *Suctoria.*

We may oppose to this arrangement, which, as it does not regard the entire being of insects, is still merely artificial, that it is not sufficiently strict, for the order of the *Suctoria* is as an apterous group, not in its right place among the *Insecta pterodicera*. And also the groups which are here considered as equivalent to the *Tetracera, Myriapoda, Apterodicera,* and *Pterodicera,* are by no means of equal value, but the two first and two last are most closely allied; the former are the subordinate members of a higher group, and the latter also could at most be placed as equivalent to the orders of the *Insecta pterodicera*. Latreille published shortly afterwards a new grouping of insects in his ' Considerations Générales,' &c. (Paris, 1810), his attention having been aroused by Lamarck's division of invertebrate animals; and he here differed from his former work, by subdividing Linnæus' insects into three equivalent groups. The first of these, the *Crustacea*, remained as before; the second, the *Arachnides,* comprised all the *Insecta aptera* of the former system; the third, the *Insecta*, included the earlier *Insecta pterodicera*, containing the same orders in the same series, whereas the second had received some alteration by the separation of the *Insecta apterodicera* into two orders, the *Thysanura* and the *Parasita*. Later alterations, which Latreille repeatedly made, convince us that, even this arrangement, which is so far superior to the former, neither satisfied the author nor the demands of judicious criticism. In his own discontent with the result, and his endeavours to correct it where possible, and to take advantage of everybody's views, which, indeed, he has nowhere expressed, yet which is but too apparent from all his subsequent works, he evinces a deficiency of all the principles which should have guided him in his systematic labours, and he thereby exposes their being untenable. Thus we find in his next grouping, published in Cuvier's Règne Animal (Paris, 1817, 4 vol. 8vo.), the *Insecta* of Linnæus again divided into three groups, but these differently limited. The first, the *Crustacea*, has received an addition in the order *Tetracera*, whereas the second, *Arachnides*, is made to sacrifice not only this, but also the *Myriapoda*, *Thysanura*, and *Parasita*, which are placed in the third group among the *Insecta*. This also received a new order in the *Strepsistera*, discovered and established by Kirby, so that it now consisted of twelve orders. His next division (Familles Naturelles du Règne Animal, Paris, 1825, 8vo.) raises the *Myriapoda*, after Leach, to a distinct class, and divides the *Insecta* into eleven orders, which remain as before established: the *Annulata* collectively, which form Linnæus' *Insecta*, are here first called *Condylopa*. In the new edition of Cuvier's Règne Animal (Paris, 1829, 5 vols. 8vo.) the class *Myriapoda* is again reduced to an order among the insects, and their number again raised to twelve orders, whereas in his latest system (Cours d'Entomologie, Paris, 1832, 8vo.) they are again made into a class and placed between the *Arachnides* and insects, the loss of which in the number of the orders is made up by the establishment of *Forficula* as a distinct one. The following is this system, which is the last published by its author:

I. *Apiropoda.*   *Condylopes* with more than six legs.
  1. Class. *Crustacea.*
  2. — *Arachnides.*
  3. — *Myriapoda.*
II. *Hexapoda.*   *Condylopes* with six legs.
  4. Class. *Insecta.*
    A. Insects without wings.
      a. Without metamorphosis.
        * With mandibulate organs.   1. Order. *Thysanura.*
        ** With suctorial mouths.   2. — *Parasita.*
      b. With a perfect metamorphosis. 3. — *Siphonoptera.*
    B. Insects with wings.
      a. *Elytroptera.* The anterior wing
         covers the posterior like a
         sheath.

> * Mandibulate mouth.
>> Cases horny. Perfect metamorphosis.   4. Order. *Coleoptera.*
>>
>> Cases horny. Imperfect metamorphosis.   5. — *Dermaptera,* the genus *Forficula.*
>>
>> Cases coriaceous. Imperfect metamorphosis.   6. — *Orthoptera.*
>
> ** Suctorial mouth.   7. — *Hemiptera.*
>
> *b. Gymnoptera.* Wings alike.
>> * Four wings.
>>> † Mandibulate oral organs, at least distinct mandibles.
>>>> Wings with reticulated nervures.   8. — *Neuroptera.*
>>>>
>>>> Wings with ramose nervures.   9. — *Hymenoptera.*
>>>
>>> †† Suctorial mouth, mandibles abortive.   10. — *Lepidoptera.*
>>
>> ** Two wings.
>>> † Two distorted moveable processes on the prothorax.   11. — *Strepsiptera.*
>>>
>>> †† Poisers behind the wings.   12. — *Diptera.*

We have not space here to enter into the merits of this system, and we can only remark that the author has made divisions upon mere external characters, and that, therefore, the naturalness of his grouping, which he chiefly aimed at, was necessarily lost. This may be asserted also of the families within the orders; they are also frequently deficient in a natural connexion and a natural arrangement.

§ 346.

Whilst Latreille was elaborating the natural system during a space of thirty-six years, other countrymen of his were busied with the same subject. Lamarck is the first among these. He first proposed the separation of the *Arachnides* as a class, and he separated the *Insecta* of Linnæus into the three equivalent groups, *Crustacea, Arachnides, Insecta.* The *Insecta* he subdivided into eight orders, as follows:

I. Insects with suctorial mouths.
1. Order. *Aptera* (merely the genus *Pulex, Suctoria,* Lat.).
2. — *Diptera* (besides the *Diptera,* the order *Rhiphiptera,* Lat., also belongs here, but which differs by a mandibulate mouth).
3. — *Hemiptera* (the same as Latreille).
4. — *Lepidoptera* (the same as Linnæus).
 II. Insects with mandibulate mouths.
5. — *Hymenoptera* (like Linnæus and Latreille).
6. — *Neuroptera* (do. do.).
7. — *Orthoptera* (like Latreille, but with the addition of the order *Dermaptera*).
8. — *Coleoptera* (like Linnæus and Latreille).

All other apterous insects Lamarck places among the *Arachnides* and *Crustacea*. Then the *Thysanura,* (*Lepisma, Podura,*) *Myriapoda,* (*Scolopendra,*) *Julus* and the parasites (*Pediculus, Ricinus*) among the *Arachnides,* with the scorpions, spiders, and *Acari ;* the *Crustacea* are the same in Cuvier and Latreille.

§ 347.

Another French naturalist, Dumeril, to whom we are indebted for a, in some degree, peculiar division of insects, in so far differs from the opinion of his compatriots, that he places insects in the series of animals above the *Mollusca ;* his arrangement, with this exception, is but a slight modification of the Linnæan. He forms two classes of Linnæus' insects, namely, *Crustacea* and *Insecta,* the former of which comprises all the crabs, and the latter, on the contrary, all the six-legged insects, spiders, scorpions, wood-lice, and *Myriapoda*. They are thus brought into eight orders

I. Insects with wings.
  A. Four wings.
   a. Mouth with mandibles.
    a. a. Wings unequal, the anterior horny.
     * The posterior transversely folded. 1. Order. *Coleoptera*.
     ** The posterior longitudinally folded. 2. — *Orthoptera*.
    b. b. Wings equal.
     * With reticulated nervures. 3. — *Neuroptera*.
     ** With ramose nervures. 4. — *Hymenoptera*.

614   TAXONOMY.

    b. Mouth without mandibles.
        a. a. Without a bent proboscis.   5. Order. *Hemiptera.*
        b. b. A spirally rolled proboscis.   6.   —   *Lepidoptera.*
   B. Two wings.   7.   —   *Diptera.*
II. Insects without wings.   8.   —   *Aptera.*
   a. Six legs.
      a. a. Mouth a proboscis.   1. Family. *Rhinaptera*
                                   (lice and six-legged *Acari*).
      b. b. Mouth with mandibles, ab-   2. Family. *Ornithomyzæ*
          dominal apex without setæ   (genus *Ricinus*, De
          and appendages.   Geer.
          Mouth with various append-   3. Family. *Nematuræ*
          ages.   (*Lepisma, Podura*).
   b. Eight legs. No antennæ.   4. Family. *Acera.*
   c. More than eight legs.
      a. a. Body with many segments, each
          bearing a pair of legs.   5.   —   *Myriapoda.*
      b. b. Body with fewer segments,   6.   —   *Polygnatha*
          fourteen pairs of legs.   (*Oniscus* & *Armadillo*).

The author, besides, endeavoured to reunite more naturally, and by other principles, the families that had been so monstrously subdivided, and to reduce, especially, the host of genera, which, as his work was to serve as a general introduction to the natural history of insects*, is very much to be praised.

§ 348.

The whilst these systems were being sketched by the French, English naturalists likewise occupied themselves with entomology. Among these there are especially three which well merit mention, namely, Leach, Kirby, and Macleay. The system of the last is founded upon philosophical principles, and which we will therefore examine last. Leach sketched the following system †.

I. Insects without a metamorphosis. *Ametabola.*
   A. Abdominal apex with setæ.   1. Order. *Thysanura.*
   B. . . . without setæ.   2.   —   *Anoplura*
                                          (*Parasita*, Lat.).

---

* Considerations Générales sur la Classe des Insectes. Paris, 1823. 8vo. av. fig.
† Zoological Miscellany, vol. iii. p. 57—60.

II. Insects with metamorphosis. *Metabola.*
  A. With mandibles and wing cases.
    a. Metamorphosis imperfect (perfect).
        Wings folded transversely.   3. Order. *Coleoptera.*
    b. Metamorphosis half perfect.
        Wings folded longitudinally and
          transversely.   4. — *Dermaptera*
                                                 (*Forficula*).

        Wings folded longitudinally.
          With a straight suture.   5. — *Orthoptera.*
          Crossed at the apex.   6. — *Dictyoptera*
                                                 (*Blattaria*).
  B. With setiform mandibles for puncturing.
        Wings crossing at the apex.   7. — *Hemiptera*
                                                 (bugs).

        Wings straight, contiguous.   8. — *Omoptera*
                                                 (*Cicada*).
  C. With setiform mandibles and without wings.   9. — *Aptera*
                                                 (*Suctoria*, Lat.).
  D. With indistinct mandibles, connate at the base.
        Wings covered with scales.   10. — *Lepidoptera.*
        Wings generally hairy.   11. — *Trichoptera*
                                                 (*Phryganea*).
  E. With mandibulate mouths, but without wing cases.
    a. With simple foot claws.   15. — *Diptera.*
    b. With divided foot claws.   16. — *Omaloptera*
                                                 (*Diptera pupipara*).

The subdivision of insects into many orders, which the English are especially fond of, certainly merits no recognition; only where nature has set true limits let them be divided, and let us not wilfully destroy the beautiful picture of harmony she everywhere presents us with. How, for instance, will the author justify the separation of the *Orthoptera* into three orders; and how the separation of the *Trichoptera* and *Neuroptera* by these principles; and how the division of the

Omaloptera from the *Diptera* ? What business has the genus *Nycteribia*, which forms for him a separate order, *Notostoma*, in this company, and which should be among the *Acari* with the *Aracknides* ?

§ 349.

William Kirby, who, together with William Spence, has earned an immortal fame in entomology, by their Introduction to this science, has inserted in their fourth volume the following system.

I. Insects with mandibles. *Mandibulata.*
    1. Order. *Coleoptera* (like Linnæus and Latreille. *Eleutherata*, Fab.).
    2. — *Strepsiptera*, Kirb. (*Rhiphiptera*, Latr.).
    3. — *Dermaptera*, Leach (Family *Forficula*, Latr.).
    4. — *Orthoptera* (like Latreille, but without *Forficula*).
    5. — *Neuroptera* (like Linnæus and Latreille, but without the *Trichoptera*).
    6. — *Hymenoptera* (like Linnæus and Latreille).

II. Insects with suctorial mouths. *Haustellata.*
    7. Order. *Hemiptera* (like Linnæus and Latreille).
    8. — *Trichoptera* (Leach).
    9. — *Lepidoptera* (Linnæus and Latreille).
    10. — *Diptera* (like Linnæus and Latreille).
    11. — *Aphaniptera*, Kirby (*Suctoria*, Latr.).
    12. — *Aptera* (all apterous insects breathing through tracheæ).
       * *Hexapoda* (*Ametabola*, Leach, *Thysanura* and *Parasita*, Latr.).
       ** *Octopoda* (*Arachnides, Tracheales*, Latr.).
       *** *Polypoda* (*Myriapoda*, Leach, Latr.).

That many of the orders here partly adopted from Leach cannot be justified upon principle, must be speedily discovered by every one upon a close inspection. To separate the earwigs from the *Orthoptera*, on account of the structure of their wings, is as wrong as it would be to raise those beetles which have but half elytra into a distinct order. Both principles of division are merely family characters. The same may be said of the order *Trichoptera*, which has been equally capriciously separated from the *Neuroptera*. If even the *Phryganea* imbibe their food, yet are their oral organs formed upon the type of mandibulate mouths, and by the same right the beetles and *Hymenoptera*, which suck the juices of flowers and plants, for example, the *Lucani*, many *Lamellicorns*, and the wasps and bees, should be removed among insects with suctorial organs.

§ 350.

Upon now passing to the physiological or philosophical systems, we find their originators to have consisted chiefly of Germans. Proceeding from the view that organic nature is to be considered as one great whole, which exhibits in its several members progressive grades of development up to its very fullest perfection and evolution, the philosophical system endeavours to characterise these grades of development as classes, and then further strives to prove their gradual perfection in the order of each class. After this idea had been started hypothetically in Schelling's school, Oken sought to transfer it to natural history, and there practically to apply it. He thence obtained thirteen classes among animals, each of which is represented by a successively added organ. Insects occupy the ninth of these classes, and are characterised as lung-animals. The following * is their division :

  I. Order. Germ flies (Keimfliegen).

Insects with imperfect metamorphosis.

  1. Tribe. Bugs (*Hemiptera*, Latr.).
  2. — 'Schricken' (*Orthoptera* and *Dermaptera*, Latr.).
  3. — 'Bolde' (*Neuroptera*, Latr.).
  II. Order. Sexual flies.

Insects with perfect metamorphosis and equal wings.

  4. Tribe. 'Mücken' (*Diptera* and *Suctoria*, Latr.).
  5. — 'Immen' (*Hymenoptera*, Latr.).
  6. — 'Falter' (*Lepidoptera*, Latr.).
  III. Order. Lung-flies. Beetles (*Coleoptera*, Latr.).

Insects with perfect metamorphosis, elytra, and wings.

  7. Tribe. 'Kirner' (*Coleopt. tetramera*, Latr.).
  8. — 'Schruppe' (*Coleopt. heteromera*, Latr.).
  9. — 'Runke' (*Coleopt. pentamera*, Latr.).

We may object to this arrangement, which tolerably distinctly exhibits the gradual development of the insect world, that the three

---

* Naturgeschichte für Schulen. Leipzig. 1821. 8vo.

chief groups of beetles, which are here made equivalent to the other tribes, are much more closely allied together, and should properly form but one tribe; besides that in the tribe *Neuroptera* there are insects with perfect and imperfect metamorphoses, which is opposed to the principles of the system. Many objections might also be made to the arrangement of the families within each group, but this would lead us too far.

The systems of other German naturalists, which are founded upon philosophical principles, merely diverge from that of Linnæus in the consecutive arrangement of the orders: we will therefore no longer dwell upon them, but only cite Goldfuss and Wilbrand as their projectors.

§ 351.

We now come to the system of M'Leay[*]. The following are the principles which guided him in the distribution.

1. All natural groups of the kingdom of nature return within themselves, and, consequently, present themselves in the form of circles.

2. Each of these circles contains five other circles, which are connected together in the same way.

3. Where these circles join, there are intermediate groups by means of which they are still more closely connected.

4. The members of each circle, which are at the points where the circles meet, exhibit analogies.

According to these principles, organic nature is divided into two large circles, one of which comprises the vegetables and the other the animals. Each consists of five circles, which, in the animal kingdom, are the following: *Acrita* (*Infusories* and *Polypes*), which are bordered on the one side by the *Mollusca*, and on the other by the *Radiata* (*Medusa* and *Echinodernia*); next to the *Radiata* stand the *Annulosa* (*Crustacea*, insects), and to the *Mollusca* the *Vertebrata*, which pass over to insects by means of the fishes, and to the *Mollusca* by the *amphibia*. The *Annulosa*, which chiefly concern us here, again consist of five principal groups, which have the following characters and boundaries.

[*] See his Horæ Entomologicæ. Lond. 1821. 2 vol. 8vo., and Linnean Transactions, vol. xiv. p. 46, &c.

1. *Crustacea.* (According to Cuvier, Latreille, &c.) they are contiguous to the *Radiata*, and especially the *Echini.* Upon one side they join the

2. *Arachnida.* (The spider-like annulosa, according to Latreille, Lamarck, &c.) On the other side the *Crustacea* border upon the

3. *Ametabola.* Insects without a metamorphosis, namely, the *Myriapoda*, *Thysanura*, and *Parasita* of Latreille.

4. *Haustellata.* Six-legged insects with wings and suctorial mouths. They join the *Arachnida*, metamorphose, and therefore form with the following group the true insects.

5. *Mandibulata.* Six-legged insects with wings and mandibulate mouths. Their place is between the *Haustellata* and *Ametabola;* the latter form the transition to the fishes.

Here, therefore, only three orders will occupy us, namely, the *Ametabola, Mandibulata,* and *Haustellata.*

Hitherto but three groups of the *Ametabola* have been found, viz., the *Myriapoda*, which join the *Crustacea;* the *Thysanura* and the *Anoplura* (*Anopl.,* Leach, *Parasita,* Lat.), which approach the *Mandibulata.*

The division and affinities of the *Mandibulata* and *Haustellata,* which are called *Insecta ptilota,* in contradistinction to the *Ametabola,* as apterous insects, is represented in the following table:—

Ptilota.

Mandibulata.	*Haustellata.*
Larvæ with feet, pupæ obtectæ.	
Trichoptera.	*Lepidoptera.*
(*Semblodes, Phryganea,* &c.)	
Larvæ apods, pupæ exaratæ.	
Hymenoptera.	*Diptera.*
Larvæ varying, pupæ free and quiet.	
Coleoptera.	*Aptera.*
	(*Suctoria,* Lat.)
Metamorphosis semi-complete, larva resembles the imago.	
Orthoptera.	*Hemiptera.*
	(*Hemip. Heteroptera,* Lat.)
Larvæ with six feet, metamorphosis varying.	
Neuroptera.	*Homoptera.*
	(*Hemip., Homopt.,* Latr.)

These circles, which the *Mandibulata* and *Haustellata* form, are contiguous to each other in the *Trichoptera* and *Lepidoptera*, especially the genus *Mystacides*, Latr., of the former, makes the transition to the genus *Aglossa*, Latr., in the latter. M'Leay considered the following families as the connecting links between the two orders of

Mandibulata and *Haustellata*.

Bomboptera.
(*Tenthrenodea*, stand between the *Trichoptera* and *Hymenoptera*.

Strepsiptera, Kirb.
(Between *Hymenoptera* and *Coleoptera*.

Dermaptera, Leach.
(Between *Coleoptera* and *Orthoptera*.

Dictyoptera, Lea., Kirb.
(Between *Orthoptera* and *Neutera*.

Megaloptera.
(*Semblodes* between *Neuroptera* and *Trichoptera*.

Genus *Psychoda*.
(Between *Lepidoptera* and *Diptera*.

Homaloptera.
(*Diptera pupipara*, Lat., between *Diptera* and *Aptera*.

Genus *Aphis*.
(Between *Aptera* and *Hemiptera*.

Family *Hydrocorides*, Latr.
(Between *Hemiptera* and *Homoptera*.

Genus *Aleyrodes*, Latr.
(Between *Homoptera* and *Lepidoptera*.

It is not to be denied that in this arrangement there are many affinities, but just as many appear forced and unnatural. The opinion that has also been expressed by Goldfuss and other German naturalists appears indeed true, that animals in general, and consequently insects, do not ascend in a consecutive series from the most simple to the most perfect, but the several groups touch each other in different parts, thereby receiving other forms, and are frequently interlinked by true groups of transition. If, now, the determinate adoption of five chief groups appears forced, and without a sufficient reason, if also we cannot detect in what relation the osculant groups stand in the system of the author to the chief ones, whether they are equivalent or subordinate, and if, lastly, the *Hemiptera* are incorrectly divided into two orders, and the entire order of the *Trichoptera* must be considered as artificial, as the *Phryganeæ, Semblodes,* and *Tenthredonodea* are united, we must yet admit that the author has exhibited considerable skill, correct judgment and knowledge of the whole, and that his system as an essay to arrange the animal world from this point of view, must not be considered as without its use, or wholly unsuccessful, although his propositions are not fully solved.

§ 352.

We have still to explain the system which we have ourselves sketched, and which we communicated partially in the introduction. To do this we refer to the chapter upon the metamorphoses, where we gave our arrangement of the entire animal kingdom, and the relation of insects to other animals. We there discovered that its physiological character was its organisation as a motive animal, that is, its division into segments and joints, but which were, however, collected into three chief divisions. We do not find this division into three parts in any other annulose animal; and as we again find a similar separation in the most perfect of the *Vertebrata*, we may conclude that insects are the most perfect of all the *Annulosa*. To attain this most perfect grade insects require a gradual development, which displays itself in their transition through the earlier animal forms and organisations. This we denominate their transformation, or metamorphosis. The more marked the transformation the more heterogeneous is the individual in the several stages of its existence; and as all insects proceed from the same point, those, necessarily, whose metamorphosis we call complete must attain a higher grade than the rest, which transform themselves incompletely. We thus obtain two chief groups among insects, which we distinguish as *Insecta ametabola* and *Insecta metabola*, but in a different sense to that understood by Leach. Both commence a new development in the organisation of the mouth, as they at first exhibit to us abortive setiform oral organs, only adapted to suction, but in the higher grades these suctorial organs develope themselves into free mandibles, with a lip covering them. Thus each group has *Insecta haustellata* and *Insecta mandibulata*. Each of these groups may then be further subdivided according to the form of the larva, the structure of the wings, and the entire internal organisation and these divisions constitute their orders. We thus obtain an arrangement, the principles of which are deduced from the idea of the entire insect, and which, as this idea becomes separated according to its several characters and constituents, it consequently necessarily and spontaneously forms itself by the philosophical laws of thought. It is the following:—

I. *Insecta ametabola.*

The larva resembles the perfect insect, yet it wants wings if the perfect insect be winged; the pupa in this case have their rudiments; it runs about and eats.

    a. With sucking mouths, which consist of four fine setæ, lying in a sheath; palpi are wanting; four biliary vessels, and generally a free prothorax.

1. Order *Hemiptera.*

    b. With mandibulate mouths: mandibles and maxillæ distinct, the latter having palpi, and generally distinct large superior lip.

        a. Four unequal wings; the anterior ones leathery or parchmenty, the posterior ones folded longitudinally and also once transversely; prothorax always free; many biliary vessels.

2. Order *Orthoptera.*

        β. Four, generally equal, more rarely unequal wings, never folded, or sometimes none at all: in the first case the nervures are usually reticulated, and generally many biliary vessels; in the last case four biliary vessels, attached to the intestine; prothorax sometimes free, sometimes not.

3. Order *Dictyotoptera.*

II. *Insecta metabola.*

The larva is a worm, consisting of thirteen segments, either with or without legs; the pupa is quiet, or if it moves it does not eat.

    a. Four equally large or equally long wings, with reticulated nervures; mandibulate mouths; few, four or eight, biliary vessels, rarely more; prothorax always free.

4. Order *Neuroptera.*

    b. Wings always unequal, the posterior ones sometimes wanting, rarely all.

        a. Mouths adapted to sucking.

            a. a. Instead of posterior wings there are pediculated knobs, yet the wings are sometimes wholly wanting; four biliary vessels; larvæ apods; a soft proboscis in the mouth, with several setæ and a pair of palpi; prothorax not free.

5. Order *Diptera.*

  b. b. Four wings, generally covered with scales; six biliary vessels; larvæ with feet and a distinct head; the maxillæ forming a spiral tongue; prothorax not free, but small, and closely connected with the mesothorax.
6. Order *Lepidoptera*.
 β. Mouths with distinct, biting mandibles.
  a. a. Four naked wings traversed by ramose nervures; larvæ generally without head and feet, but sometimes with both; many biliary vessels; prothorax not free.
7. Order *Hymenoptera*.
  b. b. Anterior wings, horny elytra; larvæ with head, with or without feet; four or six biliary vessels; prothorax always free.
8. Order *Coleoptera*.

 Our system is not acquainted with an order *Aptera*, which we have found in the majority of the others, as in every case it is artificial, and must embrace insects of the most dissimilar orders. The most distinct proof in support of this assertion is furnished by the circumstance that we find in the same family winged and apterous genera, contiguous together, and, indeed, in many genera which we have before enumerated, the males winged, and the females apterous. From the principles of the system we might expect a group containing insects without any metamorphoses, but there cannot be such an one, as the idea of an insect would be thereby annulled. All true insects whose metamorphosis has been denied by other entomologists belong to the group with an imperfect metamorphosis, and were only considered as deficient in it, because in them the organ is wanting in which we detect the imperfect metamorphosis. If, for instance, an insect remains apterous throughout its whole life, it loses the organ by which we distinguish the imperfect metamorphosis, but in other respects its development is conformable to those with an imperfect metamorphosis. We have therefore applied the name given by Leach to those apterous insects, to all with an imperfect metamorphosis, for in fact there is no difference in the processes of development in each. This is the guide to the correct estimation of our system.

 A difference of opinion may exist upon the application of the Linnæan names to our orders; as many orders contain entire families to which those names do not apply, for instance, apterous insects. But I think it better to retain an old characteristic name, than by means of new ones, formed upon new principles, to increase the already innumerable host of names. Groups that are so multiform as are the higher ones of a natural system can scarcely be distinguished by one name, and composed of many, as would be requisite in the present instance; as, for instance, *Insecta ametabola haustellata* or *Insecta metabola mandibulata elytroptera* appear still less appropriate; we have therefore retained Linnæus, as the most ancient, but have applied them to differently determined groups.

THIRD CHAPTER.

OF NOMENCLATURE.

§ 353.

System has not only to attend to the division, but also to the naming of natural bodies; this is important, as names serve us as the means of distinguishing groups which differ from the rest by certain characters and qualities. Thus the names of insects are as important to the entomologist as the words of his mother tongue to man in general; were there no words there could be no communication of ideas, for they are the means to express and characterise them. Without the groups being named, naturalists could not communicate together, and without a distinction of the known and discovered all would speedily return to its former obscurity: there is, consequently, in natural history a distinct chapter, which treats of the doctrine of naming, and which is technically called the nomenclature. Nomenclature propounds the laws whereby names must be formed, and investigates the correctness of existing ones, by the principles of grammar and language. Linnæus is the originator of this division of natural history; he was the first to introduce systematic names into natural history: before him it was customary to call animals according to their vulgar name, or by that imposed by the ancients. By the introduction of these scientific, fixed, and universally valid names Linnæus has doubtlessly acquired his greatest merit in science, and if everything else should be forgotten that he has done, this, which is wholly his work, will secure his name from forgetfulness.

§ 354.

The groups to be distinguished by separate names are those of which we have treated in the first chapter of this section; for every species, genus, and higher group has its distinct name. With respect to the form of these names, Linnæus determined that the names of genera, and of all the higher groups should be substantives, whereas those of species must be adjectives which should refer to the substantive name of the genus. This mode of distinction has the advantage of requiring fewer substantives than if all the species were to be named by them; and also the same distinguishing adjective can be applied in many genera, which would not be the case if substantives were used. It is indeed also allowed to use substantives as the names of species, but then they are proper names, and are not to be understood without the addition of the genus. Thus Linnæus distinguished most of the butterflies by giving them mythological or historical names, for example, *Papilio Priamus*, *P. Hector*, *P. Hecuba*, &c.

§ 355.

The structure of the generic name, as the chief word for the distinction of the lowest groups, will first occupy us. The most appropriate name for a genus would certainly be that which at the same time characterises it. Fabricius, indeed, maintained *optima nomina, quæ omnino nil significant*, but we do not participate in this opinion; a name that expresses a character is in every case better than an absolutely foreign and unmeaning one. But every one in this may follow his own opinion, and he who has discovered a genus has the privilege of naming it, be it by cities (*Edessa*), rivers (*Halys*), or heroes (*Polyphemus*), and maidens (*Daphnia, Cypris*). If, however, the name expresses the character, and is formed for this purpose by composition, this must follow the laws of grammar and language, and is not allowed the same caprice as the choice of the name itself; here choice can make but the first step, all the rest are subject to immutable laws. By not following these laws compound words have been recently formed, which scarcely bear the least trace of what they should properly be, and words have been made which neither Greeks nor Romans would admit to be theirs, although they have been published as derived from the Greek and Latin. Fortunately, entomology is less encumbered with these monstrosities than other portions of zoology, for instance, ornithology, and yet we should have to sweep long before we cleansed away all the rubbish. We must therefore be satisfied with stating some of the laws by which such names should be formed.

1. The words intended to compose the name must be of the same language. There were many delinquencies against this natural law even formerly, for instance, *Monoculus, Insectology*, &c. It would require too many innovations to remove all such hybrid words; but let no new ones be thus formed, for it is opposed to the fundamental laws of language.

2. A Latin word cannot receive a Greek termination, nor can a Greek word a Latin one, but entire Greek words may be transmuted into Latin. Grammar teaches the modifications the word undergoes in this case; its explanation would here lead us too far. *Cicindeletæ* is erroneous, for *Cicindela* is Latin, and *eta* is doubtlessly from the Greek termination ιτης; it should therefore be *Cicindelina*.

3. New words may be formed either out of two substantives or a verb and substantive, or an adjective and substantive, or a preposition and a substantive.

In every case the rule is that the chief idea stands behind, appended to the root of the first word, and generally with an inserted vowel. In Greek words this vowel is *o*, and in Latin words *i*. If the second substantive in Greek commence with a vowel, the *o* is contracted, or cut off, in Latin the *i* is omitted. But this rule does not obtain in every case; exceptions are sometimes admitted, which analogies determine, for example, *Glossotheca* is derived from γλῶσσα and θήκη; the root, after rejecting the termination, of the genitive, is γλωσσ, therefore γλωσσοθήκη in Greek. *Fissipes* comes from *fissus* and *pes*; *fiss* is the root, thence *fissipes*. Linnæus's word *Myrmeleon* is wrong, as it comes from μύρμηξ and λέων, it should therefore be called *Myrmecoleon*, for μύρμηξ is the root, and not μυρμη. Latreille incorrectly writes *Melasoma*, whereas it should be *Melanosomata*, for μέλας has in the genitive μέλανος, and therefore μελαν is the root, not μελα.

In prepositions the connecting vowel remains away if they terminate in a vowel, for instance, *Metathorax* from μετὰ and θῶραξ. Even this vowel is rejected if the following word commences with a vowel.

If the second word in composition be a verb there is appended to the root, in Greek words, the terminations ος, ε, and ον, which are transformed in Latin into *us*, *a*, and *um*. Many verbs also in this composition transmute a vowel of the root, for instance, φέρω does not form φέρος, but φόρος, thence *Aspidiphorus*. In Latin verbs *us* is appended similarly, for example, *Carnivorus*, derived from *caro*, gen. *carnis*, root, *carn* and *vorare*, root *vor*, thence *vorus*, the *i* is the inserted vowel, whence we have *carnivorus*.

4. New generic names are formed chiefly from Greek words, partly because Greek compounds are more harmonious, and partly because the Greek is richer in words, and more flexible than the Latin.

§ 356.

The laws are the same for the composition of the names of groups. With respect to the form of the generic name itself, it can only be altered when urgent circumstances demand it, for the name is sacred, and no one dare touch it with impunity. Two circumstances only, namely, false construction and previous application, warrant its alteration. The sex of the generic name is optional, and may be left wholly to the taste of the originator, but within certain groups, wherein a certain sex has been introduced for the genera, it is as well to continue it for the sake of uniformity. The genera *Carabus, Anthia, Calosoma, Bembidium* stand together in one family, notwithstanding their difference of sex. But if a new genus be separated from an old one the sex must be left unaltered, else it may too easily occasion confusion and misunderstanding in the specific names.

Generic names consisting of two separate words, as we find them in the older writers, Fabricius justly rejects, for example, Ray's *Vespa Ichneumon* for *Ichneumon*, or Petiver's *Musca apiformis* for *Bombylius*, &c. Whereas Fabricius goes too far when he wishes to reject words composed of two Latin substantives, as *Gryllotalpa*, Lin. Generic names that sound badly, or are too long (*nomina sesquipedalia et enuntiatu difficillima*) must also be avoided, as well as such as have objectionable double meanings [*].

If a new genus be separated from an old one, the best known and commonest species must be left with the old name, and a new one must be invented for the rarer ones: hence Linnæus's *Scarabæus stercorarius*,

---

[*] Fabricius, Philosophia Entomologica, p. 115. § 32.

is more appropriately called in Fabricius *Scarabæus*, than in Latreille *Geotrupes*, for, next to the cockchafer, it is the commonest of all Linnæus' *Scarabei*.

§ 357.

Family groups were deficient in the older systems, and therefore also family names; but as the families have been chiefly formed from the external resemblance of their individuals, it appears appropriate to express this conformity in the name, and they are therefore called after the best known genus. Thus Jussieu proceeded when he devised names for his natural families of plants. They took the form of an adjective, as the substantive *planta* was tacitly understood; all therefore required the feminine gender, for example, *Malvaceæ, Gramineæ*, &c.

Latreille, the first founder of families among insects, selected also generally the adjective form, but he did not consider that the word *insectum* was to be understood, and that, consequently, they should be neuter. The gender of these names appeared to him indifferent, and we thence find in the same order every possible form, for example, *Cicindeletæ, Carabici, Malacodermi, Pimeliariæ, Melosomæ, Bruchelæ, Rhyncostoma*, &c. But all adjectives must necessarily, even when they stand alone, refer to an understood substantive, which in this case can be no other than *insectum* or *insecta*, and therefore all generic names must, according to the first grammatical rule that the predicate shall agree with its subject in gender, number, and case, be in the neuter. Latreille's family names must therefore be corrected by this and the previously instituted laws. Let us examine more closely the way in which he and others have constructed the names of families.

§ 358.

Four different paths have been followed in the structure of family names.

The first is that pursued by Jussieu in botany, namely, to form an adjective name from the chief genus of a family for its distinction, and by means of this name to indicate its resemblance with a known form. This process appears to be the best, in the first place, because we can never be at a loss for a family name, and secondly, because these adjectives are easily formed, and merely the knowledge of the derivation of the generic name, whether it be from the Latin or the Greek, is required. But then regard must be had to the form of the termination of the adjective, as this is always determinate for certain purposes. The termination of adjectives derived from animals is always εως in Greek, and in Latin *inus;* it is, consequently, with these terminations that generic names must be formed into family names. Thus, for instance, from *Syrphus* we must form the family name *Syrphea*, because the ει in its transit into Latin becomes long *e*, as in *Pythagoreus*, derived from Πυθαγόρειος. From the Latin word *Cicindela* we should make, according to this rule, *Cicindilina*, and not with Latreille, *Cicindeletæ*. The terminations *aceus, a, um*, which Jussieu introduced into the families of plants, express the resemblance to the object of the root of the word, and could therefore be perfectly correctly applied also in Latin generic names, yet the termination *inus* should be preferred, as it is the most usual and common to indicate a derivation from animals, as *Asininus, Equinus, Ovinus*, &c.

§ 359.

A second adjective termination for family names is that which has originated from the composition with εἶδος, which the Greek termination οειδης or ωδης gives. It also expresses a resemblance with the idea of the root, but can only be united with such words as originate from the Greek. We nevertheless find in Linnæus errors against this rule, for example, *Curculionides* derived from *Curculio*. Error has frequently happened from appending this termination to the nominative, as it, which is the case in all compounds, should be added to the root, consequently to the genitive upon the rejection of the genitive termination. The Romans, as far as I know, have received no Greek word thus formed into their language, and we can therefore merely decide by analogy upon the transmutation that must take place upon this transition. In Greek they are of the common gender, and are declined by the third contracted declension, consequently, upon their transition into Latin, they would most appropriately follow the third declension also, and their inflexions be made analogous to original Greek words. I have thus treated these names, but have left the uncontracted Greek form always in the neuter, for the sake of distinction, as *Carabodea* instead of *Caraboda*. It is still doubtful whether we should use *oides* or *odes*, as both forms exist in the classics, for instance, in Aristotle καραβοειδης and καραβωδης. Buttman gives the form *oides* as the most correct, because ειδος has in the ancient language the digamma; but I have chosen the contracted form, as it is shorter, and because it is more frequent in Aristotle.

§ 360.

Besides these adjective forms substantives have been used to distinguish families; latterly, namely, Greek patronymics have been applied to the construction of family names, but these also can only be formed of true Greek words. If in the Latin poets forms such as *Romulidæ* exist, prose absolutely rejects them, and the language of naturalists is no poetry, but a scientific and consequently pure prose. If, on the contrary, they be applied to Greek names, they must be declined according to the first declension; upon transition into Latin all are then true masculines.

Other substantives originate by the compounding of two words, according to the above rules. Names like the following are false, *Melosoma, Taxicornes, Myrmeleonides;* they should be *Melanosomata, Taxocera* (for *cornu* is Latin and ταξις Greek), *Myrmecoleontoides.*

The substantive termination *ites*, which Latreille so frequently applies to family names, is Greek, and therefore can be appended only to such words as are of Greek origin. It is always of the masculine gender, and distinguishes some relation, and therefore a resemblance with the object represented by the root. It may therefore be unquestionably used for the structure of substantive family names; but names like *Curculionites, Crabronites,* are erroneous, as *Curculio* and *Crabro* are of Latin origin.

§ 361.

The names of the higher groups of the tribes and orders are in general formed of two words, generally substantives, compounded according to the above rules. It is seldom requisite to form new names for such groups, as those existing are sufficient, and, at least in insects, the orders were determined very naturally even by Linnæus. Although our system proceeds from different views to the Linnæan, we have yet retained the names of his orders, as they are everywhere known, and everybody already connects an idea with them. The names of classes also have been already correctly distinguished by early naturalists, and even by the common man in his mother-tongue, so that we scarcely require them; but it is only among the lower animals that new ones are necessary, yet those already existing well enough suffice to distinguish even them. But if new ones are to be formed they must be constructed by the above rules. It is also endeavoured, even in the higher groups, to express their character in their names.

§ 362.

Specific names (*nomina trivialia*) are formed in three ways: they are either pure adjectives or substantives, in apposition to the generic name, or the genitive of the predicate, which expresses a relation to the thing whence the name is derived.

The adjectives are usually deduced from the most remarkable and striking quality of the insect, and refer to form, colour, general clothing, sculpture, size, &c. &c. It is scarcely possible to give general rules for their imposition, it must be left to the tact of every one who names species to select appropriate names. This is a subject in which the naturalist can exhibit much skill, and we cannot in this respect sufficiently admire the talent of the immortal Linnæus: Fabricius has also in general invented good names. Comparative names, however, are not adapted as specific names, as we do not always know whether the species which we distinguish as the smallest is actually the smallest; but when once applied we must leave them where we find them, if they do not become incorrect by the discovery of one surpassing them. Fabricius endeavours also to discountenance specific names derived from the time of appearance, &c., but in this he probably goes too far; if the field be too much contracted we shall ultimately find no adjectives for specific names. Some insects likewise frequent very determinate places, and why then should they not be named after it? It however sometimes happens that animals have names that are not at all appropriate to them, for instance, the genus *Euphone* among the birds, the species of which, travellers say, do not sing at all.

§ 363.

Specific names formed of substantives refer either to the resemblance which insects have to the object represented by its name, be this expressed in form, colour, or any other quality; thus is *Amphicoma vulpes* rough, like a fox, and of the same yellowish colour. Or they express a significant comparison, and are the sports of the fancy of the namer, for instance, *Cerambyx heros*, *Geotrupes Hercules*, &c.

Thus Linnæus has wished to indicate the beauty of the butterflies by giving them names from the mythology and the mythic history of the Greeks, and restored the heroes and gods of the infancy of the human race in them; we here again find Apollo and the Muses, Jason and his companions, and the vigorous warriors of the plains of Troy.

The genitive of the predicate is also of a double kind. In the one case it exhibits the locality of the insect, either in its larva or perfect state. In this case the substantive is either the name of the plant or animal upon which the insect lives as a parasite, or parts of them, when they dwell only on certain parts, for example, *Apion Ulicis, Ceutorhynchus Echii Balaninus nucum, Œstrus ovis, Gastrus equi, Pediculus capitis,* &c. The second kind of genitives of the predicate consists of the names insects have received in honour of meritorious entomologists, the person imposing the name wishing thereby to express his estimation for such individuals, for their scientific exertions. Thus we have *Carabus Linnei, C. Fabricii, C. Germari, C. Schönherri,* &c. But latterly there has been too much liberality in thus naming after individuals, for mere collectors, known to nobody but the namer himself, have been thus immortalised. In these instances the idea spontaneously suggests itself, that the namer has thereby wished to raise his friend to the rank of those entomologists who have promoted the science by their study and industry, and consequently thus express the esteem in which he holds their works. But he who cannot distinguish between the merits of a naturalist and a collector had better be silent, lest, by uttering a word, he should betray himself.

THE END.

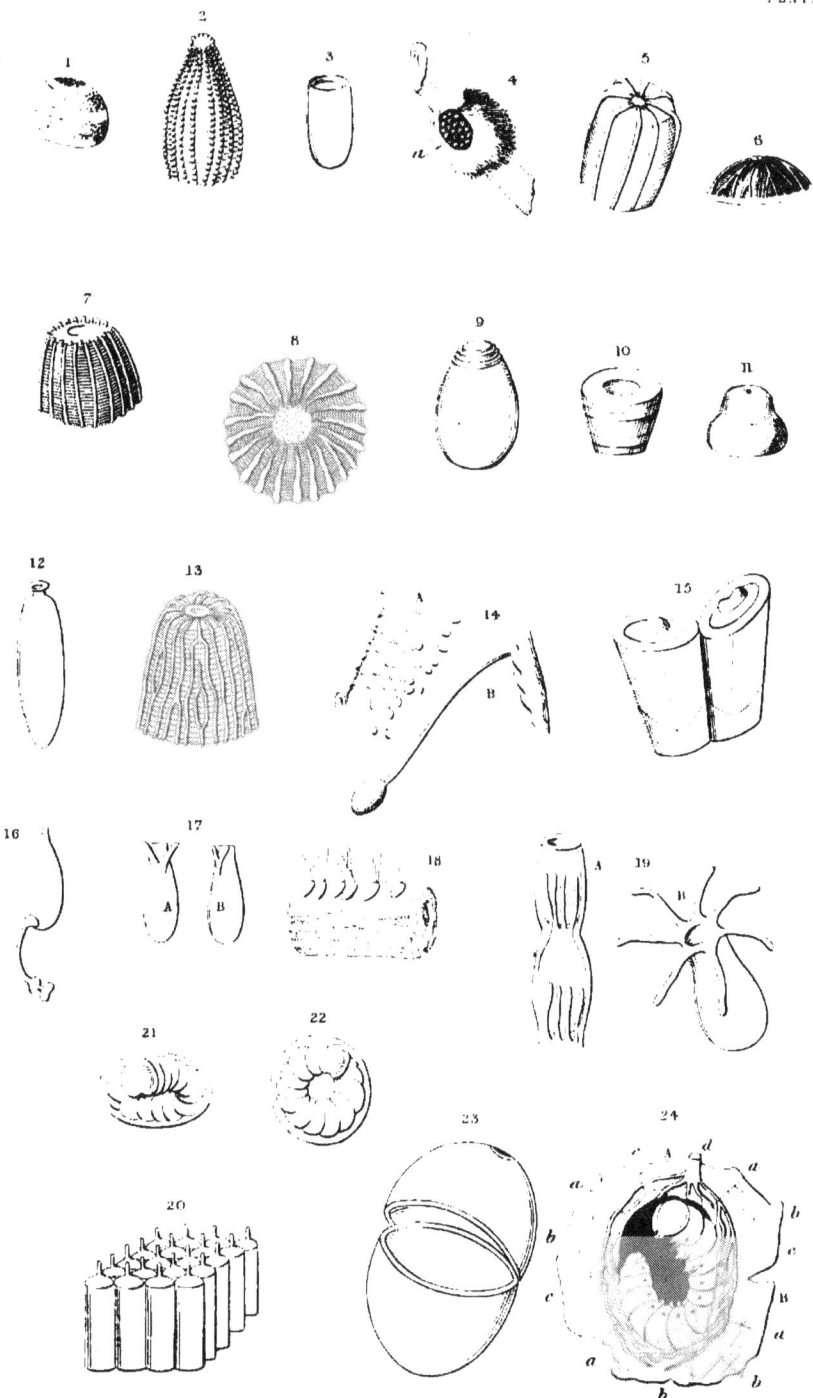

PLATE

PLAT

Larva of phryganea with the case in which it dwells
as of ephemera. a.a. lateral branchial leaves.
rudiments of wings.
larva of Culex, a, air tube. b, anal tube
Pupa of do a.a. air tube
larva of chironomus. a.a. air tubes at
b air tubes at breast.
Pupa of Chironomus a,a, Branchial feelers on the thorax
Larva of corethra. a Branchial fasciculi
at the tail. b, first c. second pair of
ms which stand in connexion with the intestine
d. mandible. e, antennae
pupa of corethra. a.a. air tubes b.4
c leaves. Fig 9. lar. Simulia. a.a fasciculi
head, perhaps palpi. b.b, antennae. c air tube in
vrax. d, d, indicated spiracles. 2,2 Anal air tubes
Pupa of simulia a.a, branchial fasiculi. b.b,
sheaths. c, head. d, thorax from the back e,
run.
head of carabus glabratus from above. A. Skull. a,
B. frons. b, Sinciput. C, clypeus I labrum,
mandibles. y.y. first joints of antennae. a.a eyes —
under view. D. Gula. d, under margin of the same. G.
t. I mentum. o.a mandibles. P P maxillae —
lateral view. S. Facies. E, cheek. F. temple. y, socket of
mae. The other letters as before

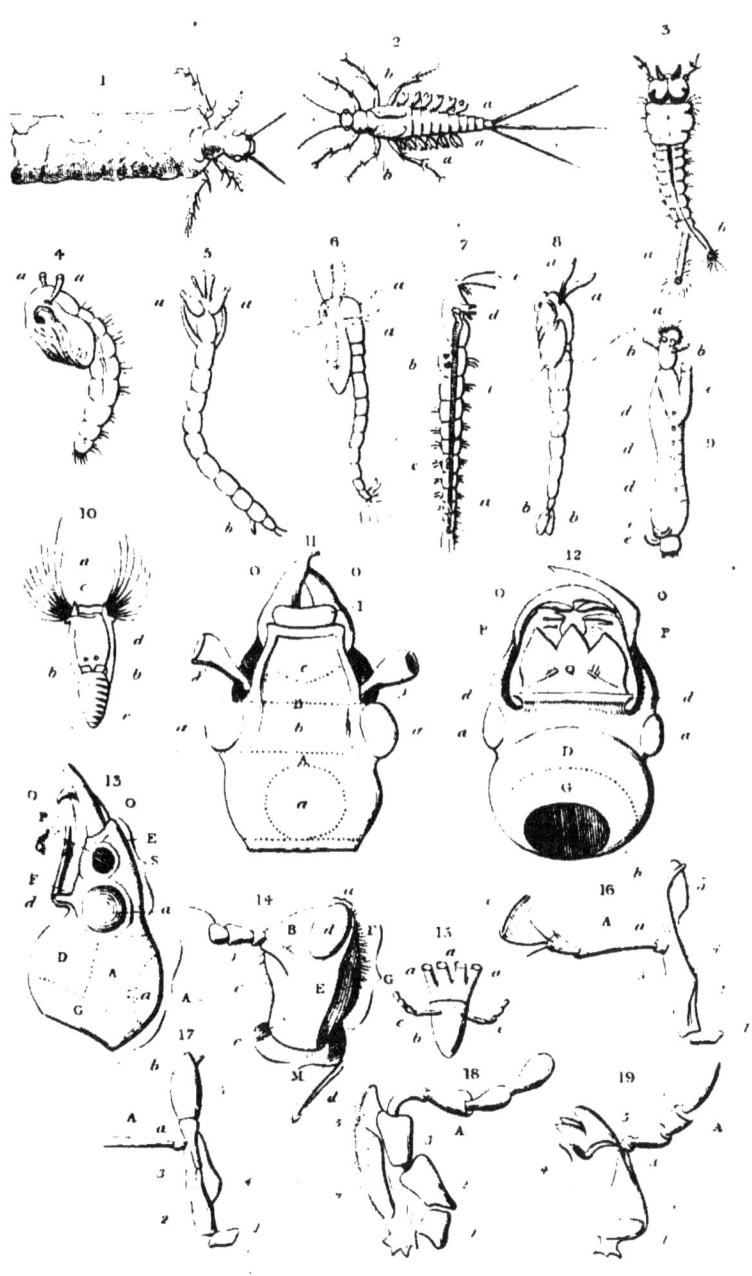

THE NEW YORK
PUBLIC LIBRARY

ASTOR, LENOX AND
TILDEN FOUNDATIONS.

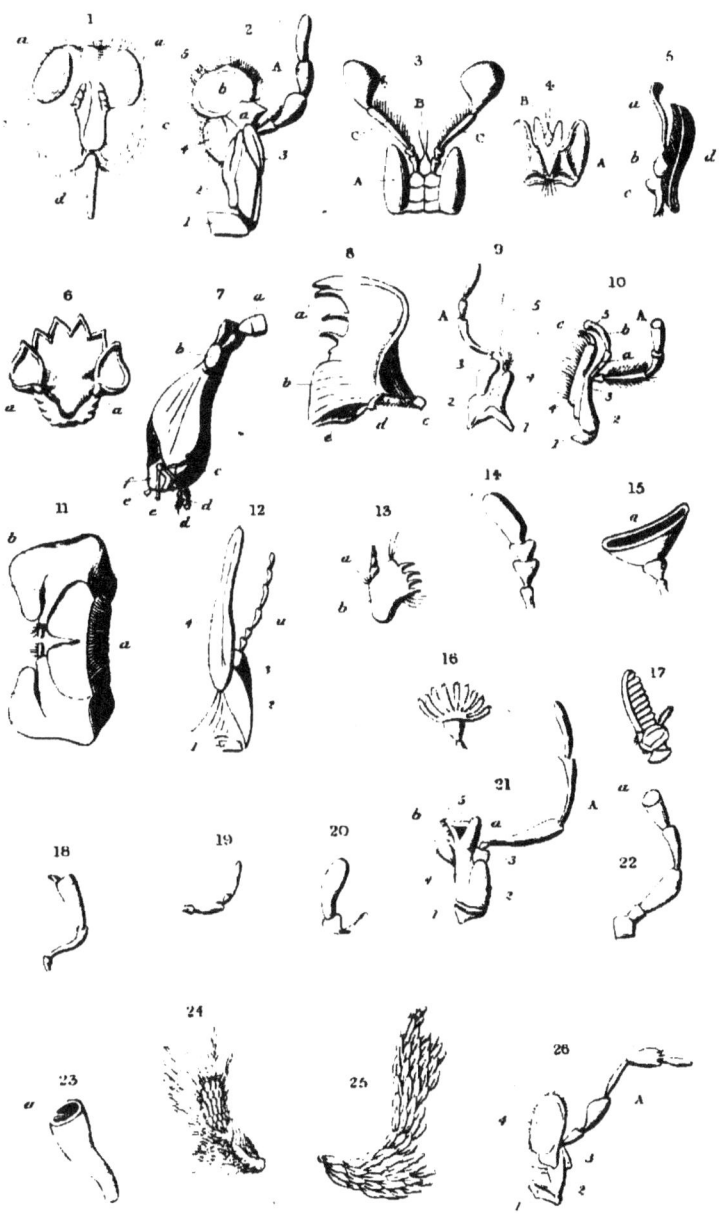

PLATE I.

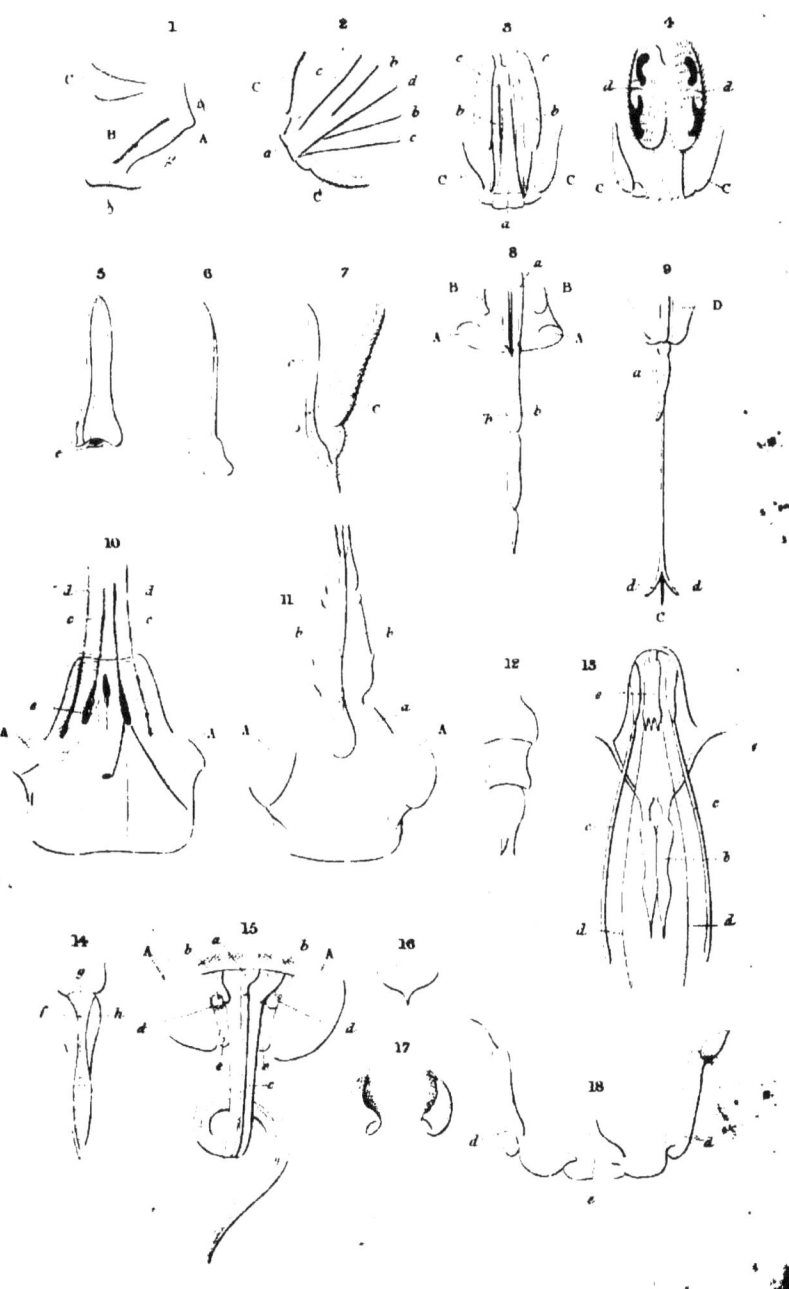

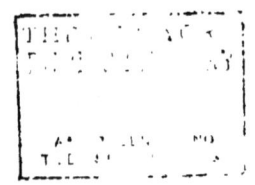

PLATE 6

PLATE 7.

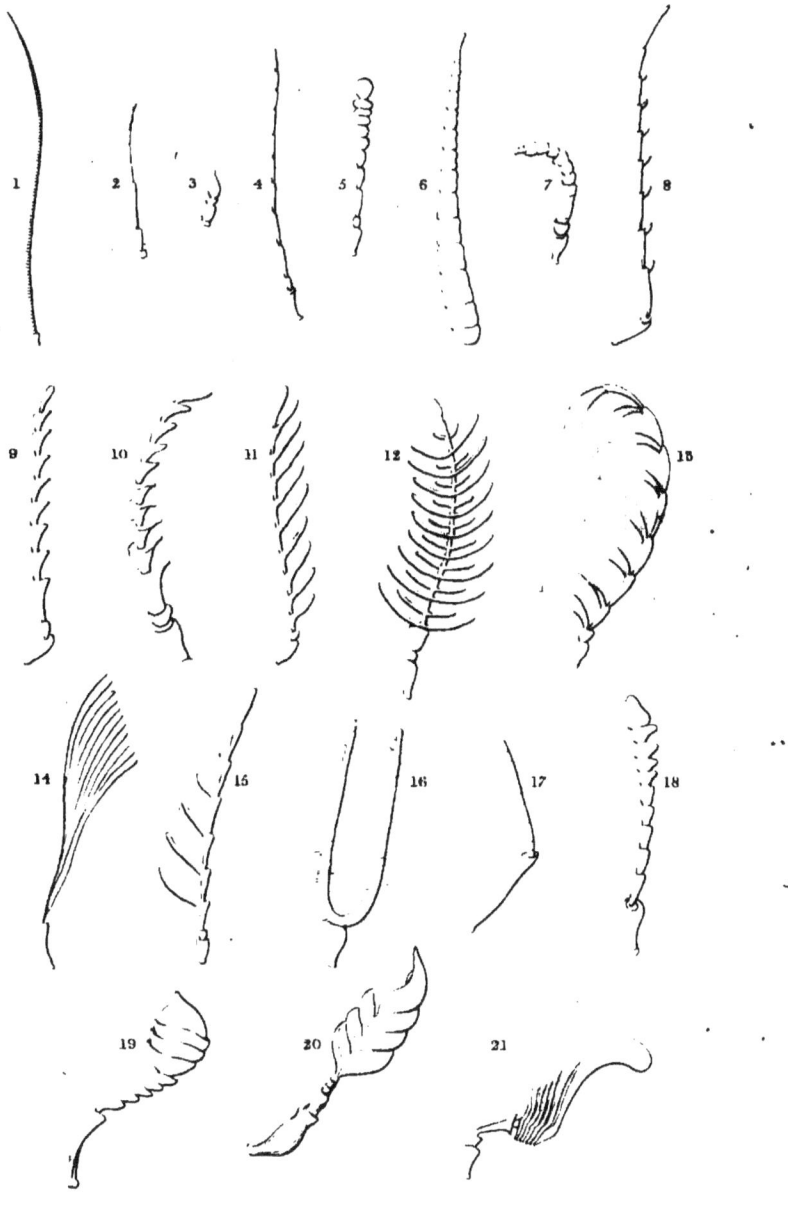

THE NEW YORK
PUBLIC LIBRARY

ASTOR, LENOX AND
TILDEN FOUNDATIONS.

PLATE 8.

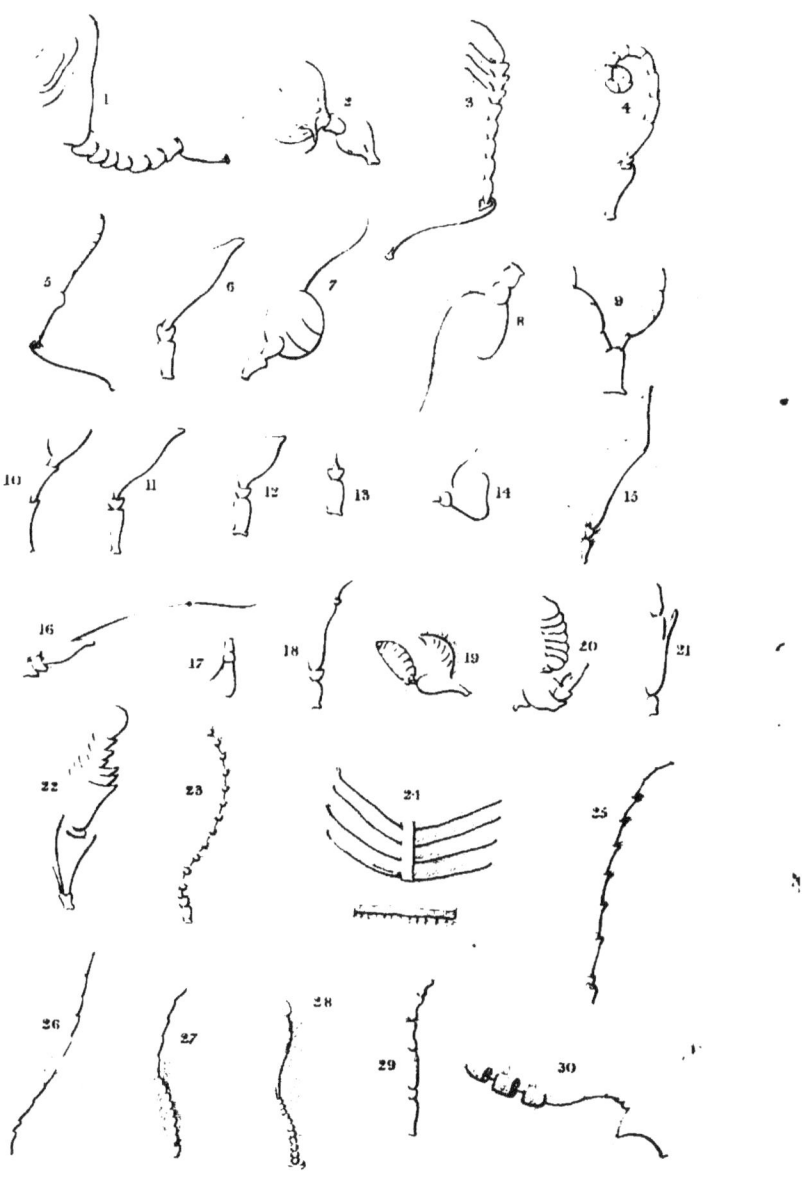

PLATE 9.

THE NEW YORK
PUBLIC LIBRARY

ASTOR, LENOX AND
TILDEN FOUNDATIONS.

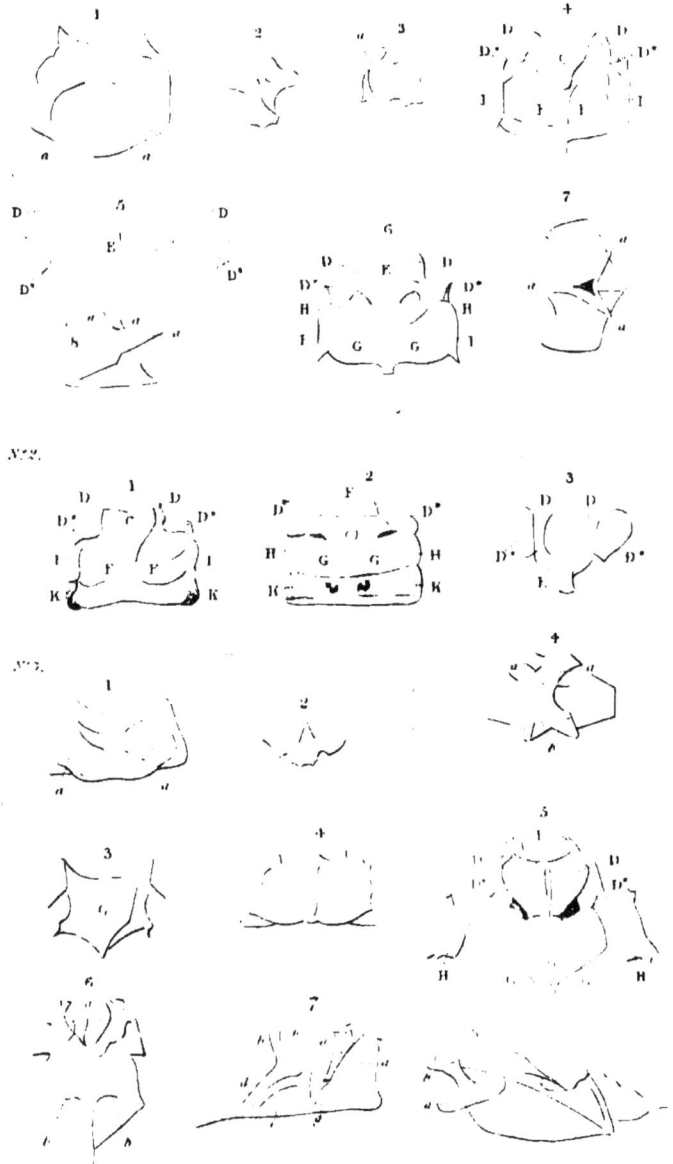

PLATE II

PLATE 12

THE NEW YORK
PUBLIC LIBRARY

ASTOR, LENOX AND
TILDEN FOUNDATIONS.

PLATE 13.

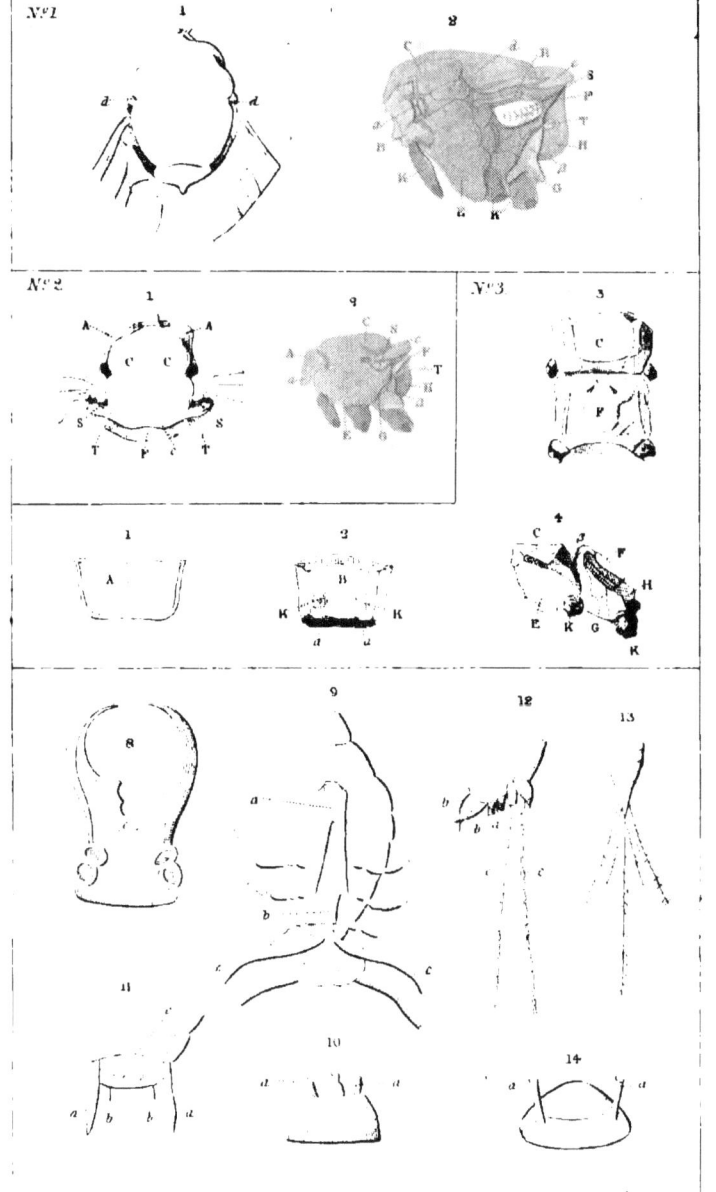

PLATE 14.

ASTOR, LENOX AND
TILDEN FOUNDATIONS.

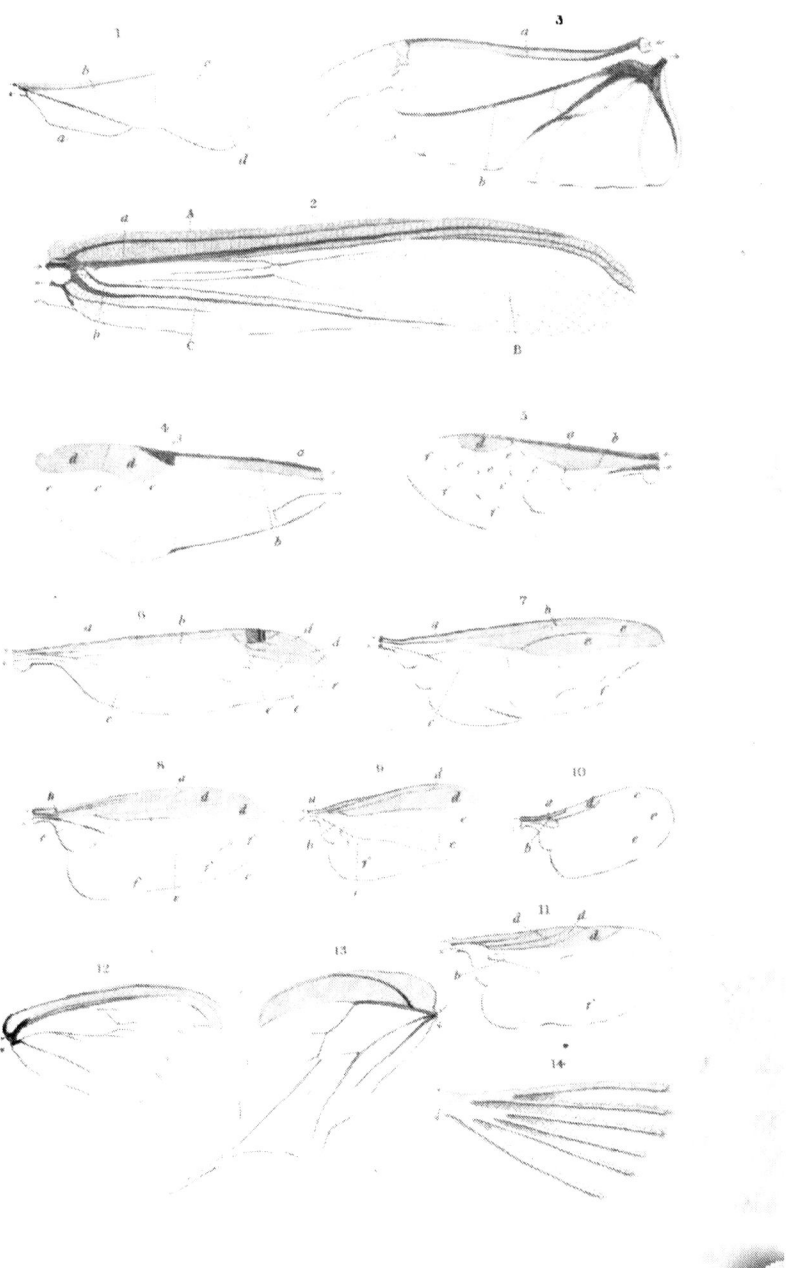

PLATE 15.

PLATE 16

PLATE 18

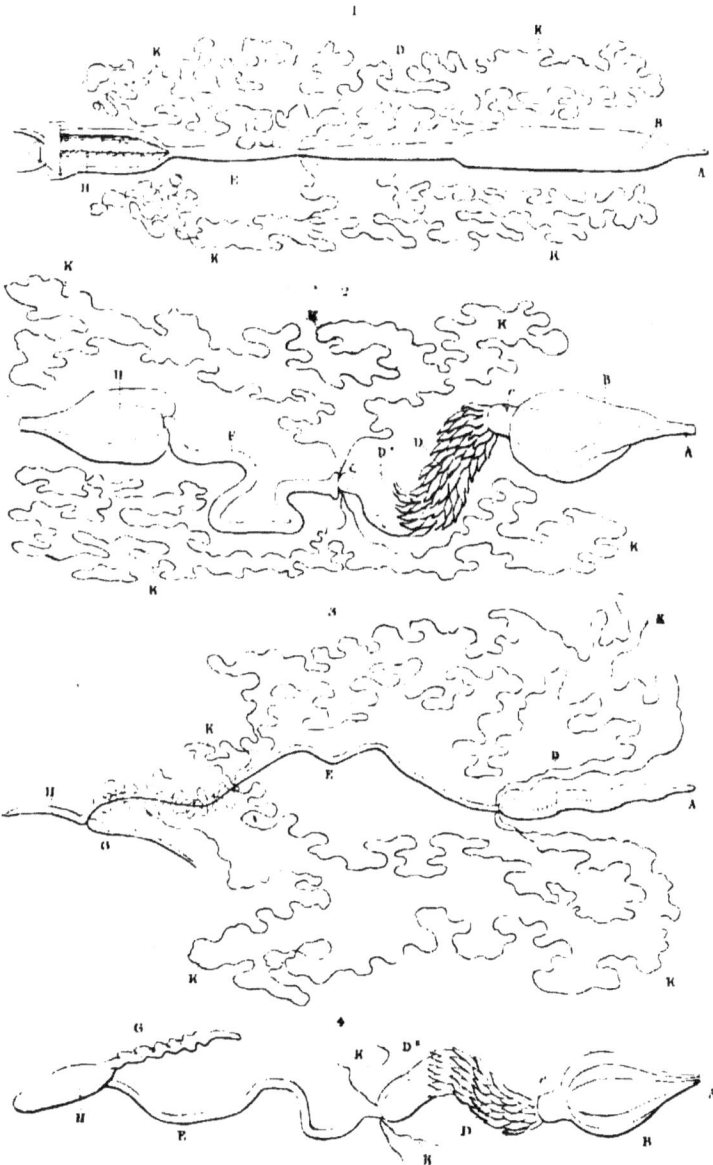

PLATE 19

THE NEW YORK
PUBLIC LIBRARY

ASTOR, LENOX AND
TILDEN FOUNDATIONS.

PLATE 20

PLATE 22

THE NEW YORK
PUBLIC LIBRARY

ASTOR, LENOX AND
TILDEN FOUNDATIONS.

PLATE 23.

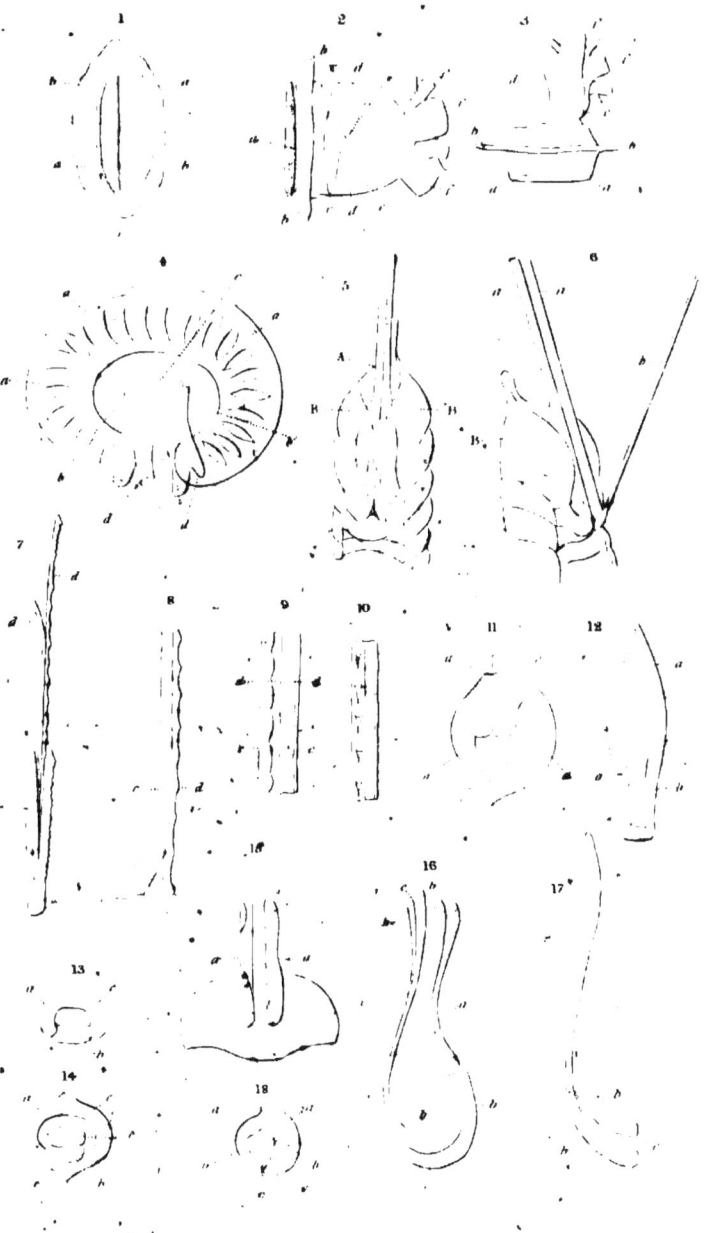

PLATE 24.

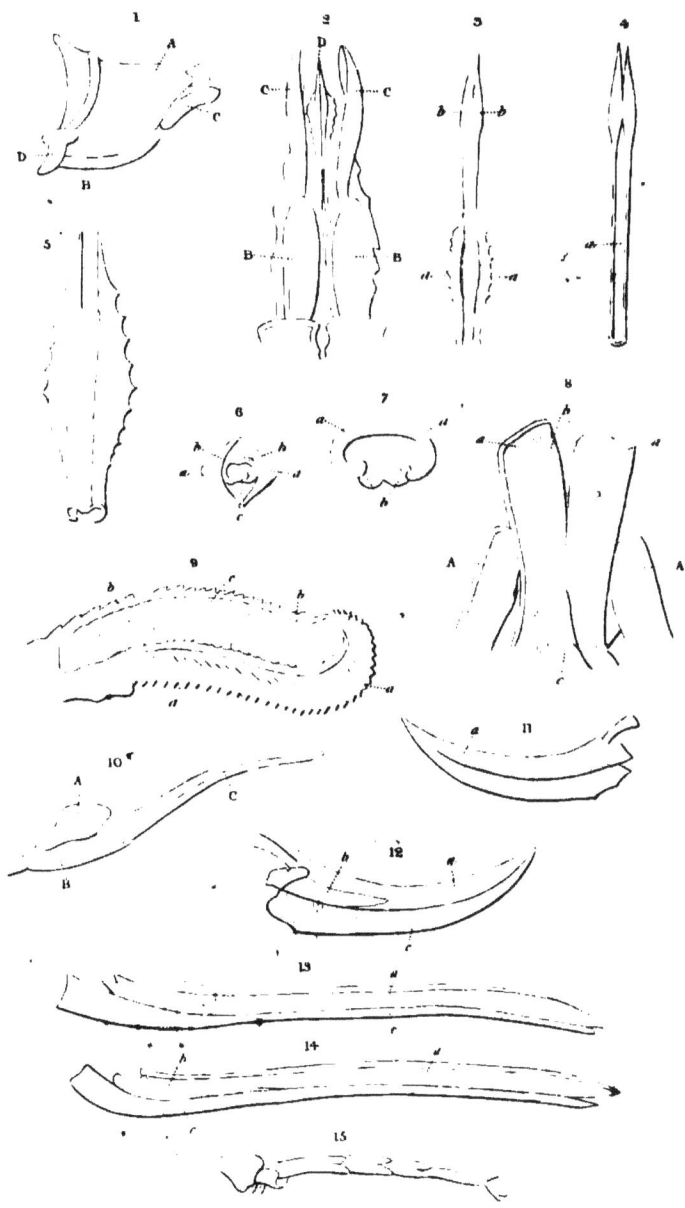

PLATE 25.

THE NEW YORK
PUBLIC LIBRARY

ASTOR, LENOX AND
TILDEN FOUNDATIONS.

PLATE 36

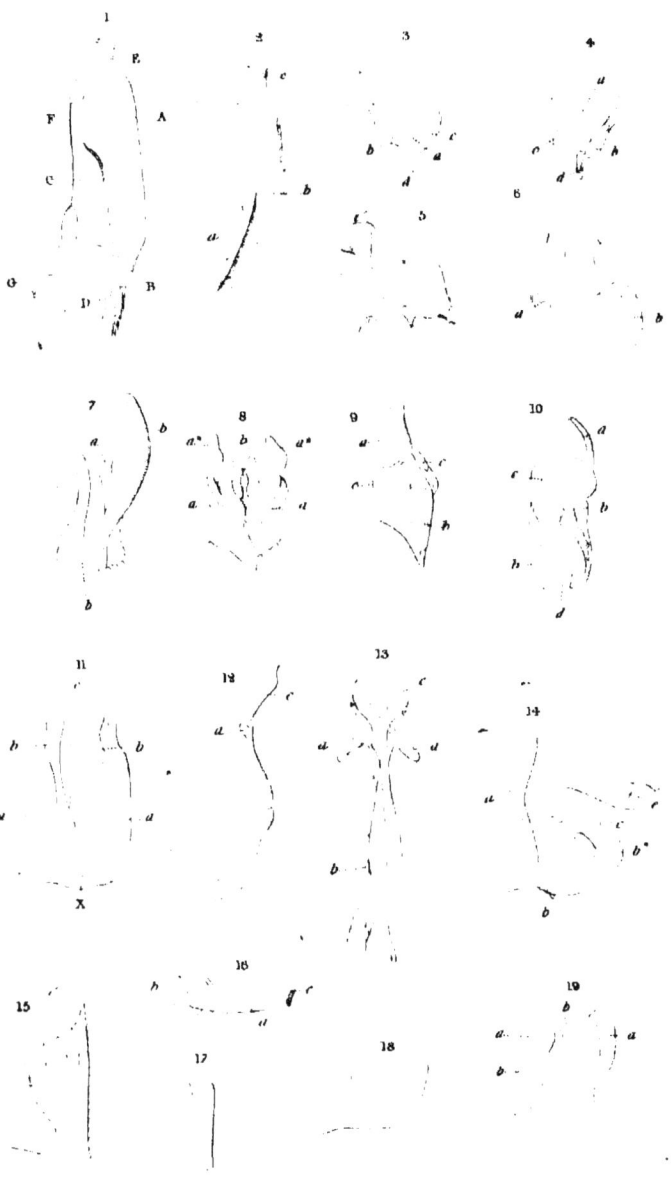

PLATE 27

THE NEW YORK
PUBLIC LIBRARY

ASTOR, LENOX AND
TILDEN FOUNDATIONS.

PLATE 28

THE NEW YORK
PUBLIC LIBRARY

PLATE 29

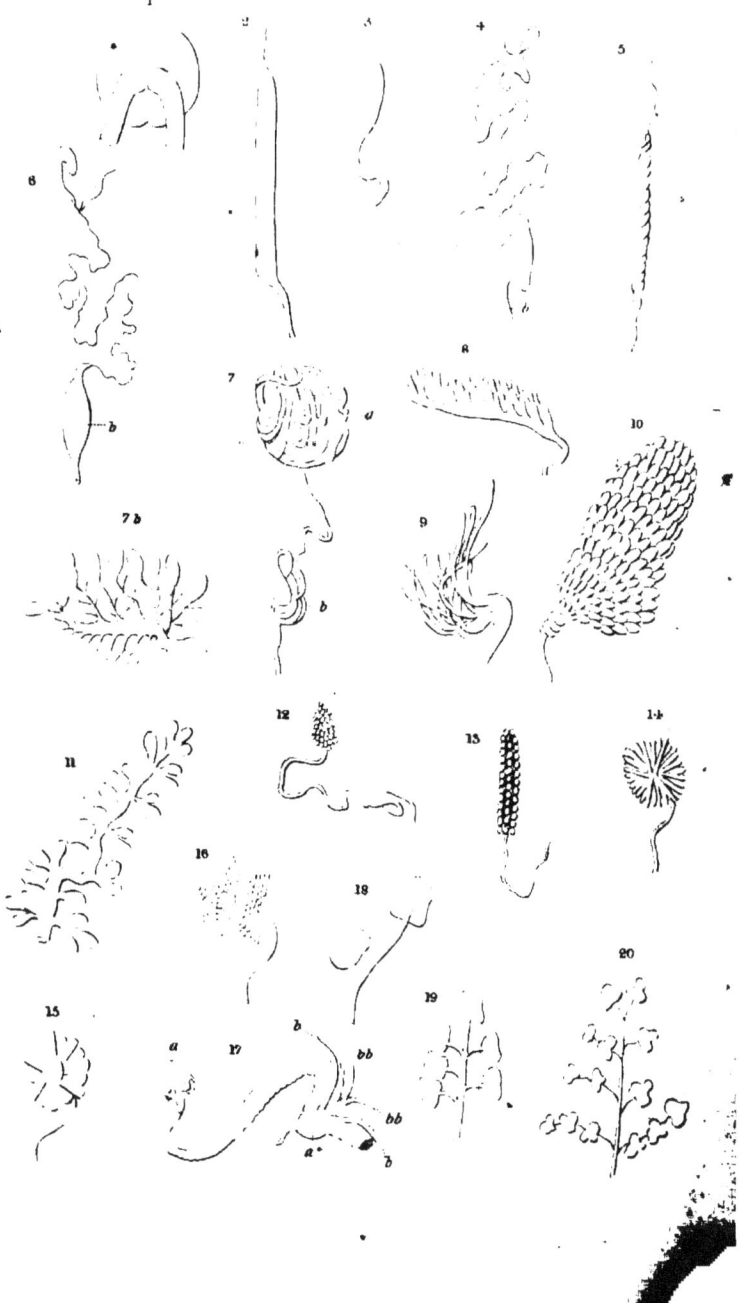

THE NEW YORK
PUBLIC LIBRARY

ASTOR, LENOX AND
TILDEN FOUNDATIONS.

PLATE 30

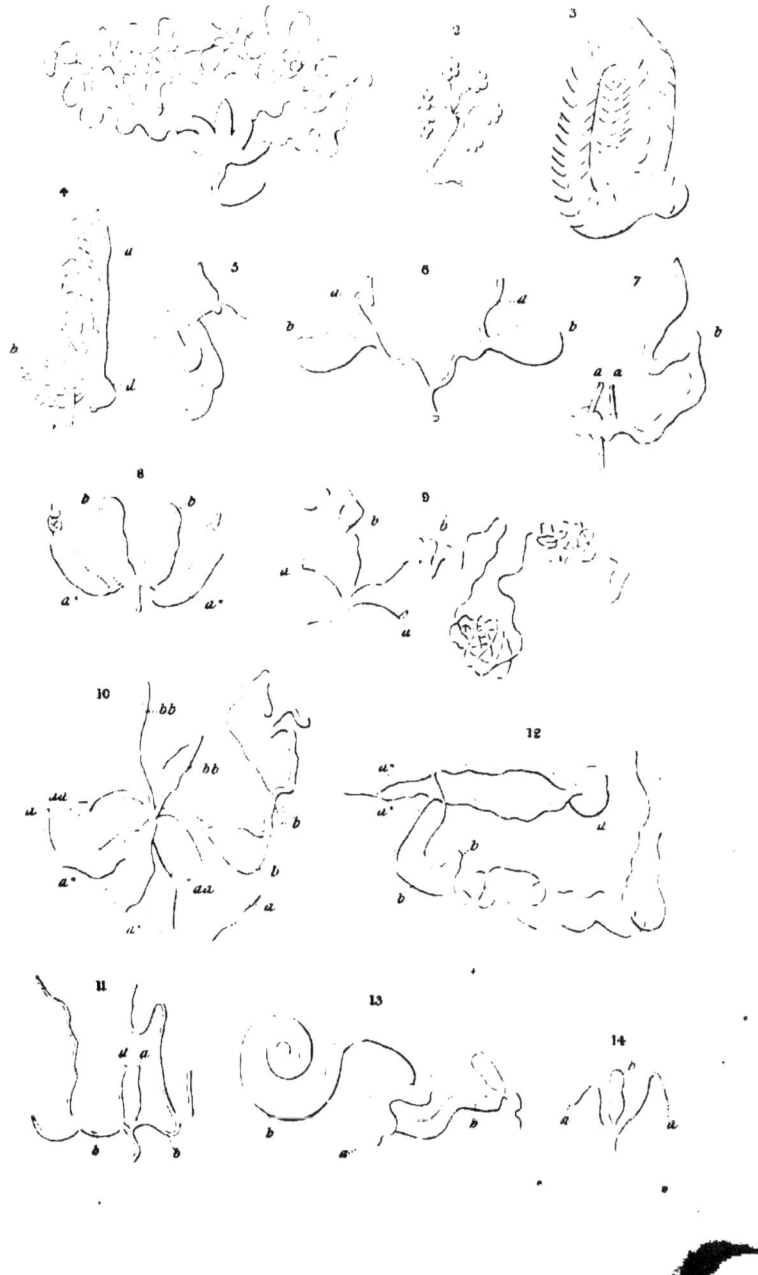

THE NEW YORK
PUBLIC LIBRARY

ASTOR, LENOX AND
TILDEN FOUNDATIONS.

PLATE 31

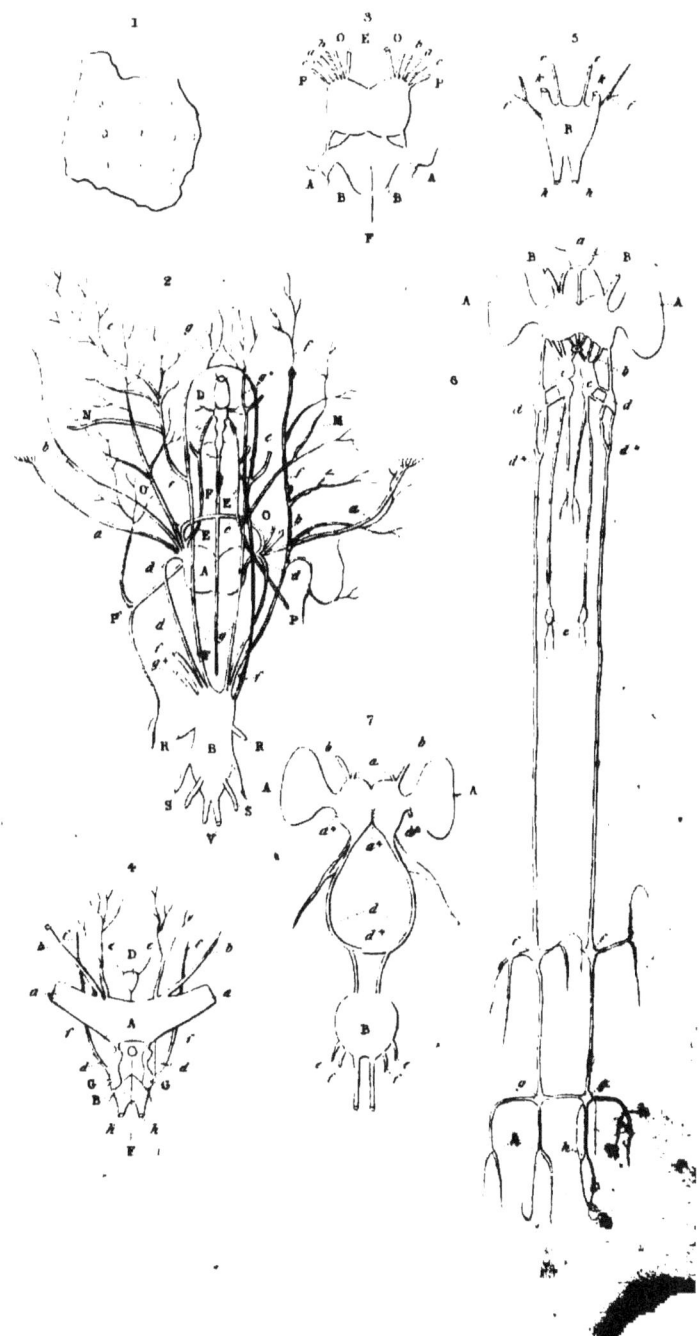

PLATE 32

THE NEW YORK
PUBLIC LIBRARY

ASTOR, LENOX AND
TILDEN FOUNDATIONS.

DESCRIPTIONS OF PLATES.

FRONTISPIECE. 1, *Carabus nitens*, F. 2, *Enceros crassicornis*, Grav. 3, *Hemerobius concinnus*, Steph. 4, *Polyommatus Adonis*, Lat. 5, *Anomoia Gaedii*, Walk. 6, *Blatta Germanica*, L. 7, *Acrida varia*, Kirb. 8, *Corizus Hyoscyami*, Fall.

[*All the above insects are British, and all but No. 3 in my own collection.*—Tn.]

*** All the figures to which no authority is placed are from the author's drawings.

Plate I. Figure 1, Hemispherical egg of *Gastropacha dumeti* (Knoch). Fig. 2, Conical egg of *Pontia Napi* (Sepp.) Fig. 3, Cylindrical egg of *Gastropacha everia* (Knoch). Fig. 4, Hairy egg of the same, *a*, spot where the hair is removed, and the eggs exposed to view. Fig. 5, Tun-shaped egg of *Vanessa Urticæ* (Sepp.). Fig. 6, Lenticular egg of *Noctua psi* (Sepp.). Fig. 7, Convex and ribbed egg of *Hipparchia Tithous* (Sepp.). Fig. 8, Flat lenticular ribbed egg of *Noctua Orion* (Sepp.). Fig. 9, The egg of *Phalena prunata*, with an apparent cover (Sepp.). Fig. 10, Cup-shaped egg of *Orgyia antiqua* (Sepp.). Fig. 11, Turban-shaped egg of *Lycæna Betulæ* (Sepp.). Fig. 12, Flask-shaped egg of *Culex pipiens* (Reaumur). Fig. 13, Thumbstall-shaped egg of *Argynnis Lathonia* (Sepp.). Fig. 14, Petiolated eggs of *Hemerobius perla* (Reaumur). A, Natural size. B, One enlarged. Fig. 15, Contiguous eggs of *Gastropacha Neustria* (ib.). Fig. 16, Petiolated egg of *Ophion luteus* (Kirby and Spence). Fig. 17, Eared egg of *Scatophaga putris* (Reaumur). A, From the front. B, From the side. Fig. 18, Tailed egg of *Ranatra linearis* (Geoffroy). Fig. 19, Crowned egg of *Nepa cinerea*. A, Two eggs as they hang together (Kirby and Spence). B, One with the distended crown (Rösel). Fig. 20, Cylindrical, pointed egg of *Sialis lutarius* (Suckow). Fig. 21, Elliptical egg, with the larva seen through, of *Sphinx Ligustri* (Sepp.). Fig. 22, Globose egg, with the larva shining through, of a *Noctua* (Sepp.). Fig. 23, Egg shell of the egg of *Gastropacha Pini* (Suckow). Fig. 24, Embryo with the membranes of *Gastropacha Pini* (Suckow). A, Head of the embryo, with the already visible eye points. B, Its body. C, Space in which the amnion is contained. *a a a*, The amnion. *b b b*, The chorion. *c c*, Tracheæ, which distribute themselves upon the superior surface of the amnion. *d*, Main stem of the trachea, which lies beneath the germen.

Pl. II. Fig. 1, Headless maggot of *Musca vomitoria*. A, *a*, The hook-shaped setæ projecting from the mouth. B, The flat tail. *a a*, The two stigmata. *b b*, The coronet of fringe surrounding them. *c c*, The pedal warts. Fig. 2, The caterpillar, with anal feet only, of *Œcophora Rajella* (De Geer). Fig. 3, Maggot with a head of *Vespa vulgaris* (*ib.*). Fig. 4, Larva of *Lixus paraplecticus*. *a*, Head. *b*, Setiform feet. *c*, Anal propellers (*ib.*). Fig. 5, Pseudo-caterpillar with five pair of ventral feet, and one anal proleg of an *Hylotoma* (*ib.*). Fig. 6, Larva of *Cetonia aurata* (*ib.*). Fig. 7, Pseudo-caterpillar of *Cimbex* (*ib.*). Fig. 8, Rat-tailed maggot of *Eristalis tenax*. *a a*, Anterior air tubes. *b*, Anus. *c*, External sheath of the tail. *d*, Internal tube. *e*, Setiform crown at the apex. *f*, Mouth with furcate mandibles. Fig. 9, Caterpillar of *Pieris Machaon* with the tentaculæ of the neck extended. Fig. 10, Caterpillar of *Plusia gamma* (Sepp.). Fig. 11, Geometer caterpillar of *Phalæna betularia* (De Geer). Fig. 12, Caterpillar without anal proleg of *Harpyia vinula* (Sepp.). Fig. 13, Caterpillar's head with its organs. *a*, Upper lip. *b b*, Upper mandibles. *c c*, Lower maxillæ. *d*, Under lip with the spinneret. *ff*, Antennæ. *g g*, Eyes. Fig. 14, Under lip of the caterpillar of *Cossus ligniperda* seen externally (Lyonet). *a*, Spinneret. *b b*, Sheath surrounding the base of the spinneret. *c c*, Maxillary palpi. *d d*, Labium. Fig. 15, Head of the caterpillar of *Vanessa prorsa*. Fig. 16, Head of the caterpillar of *Apatura iris*. Fig. 17, Feet of the caterpillar of *Cossus ligniperda* (Lyonet). *a*, Part of the ventral membrane. *b*, Coxa. *c*, Trochanter. *d*, Femur. *e*, Tibia. *f*, Tarsus. *g*, Claw. Fig. 18, Ventral or proleg of the same caterpillar with a double coronet of hooklets (*ib.*). Fig. 19, Pupa of *Sphinx Ligustri*. *a*, Head-case. *b*, Eye-case. *c*, Tongue-case. *d d*, Leg-cases. *e*, Antenna-case. *f*, Case of the prothorax. *g*, Case of the mesothorax. *d*, Of the metathorax. *i i*, Of the ventral segments. *k k*, Spiracles. *l l*, Kirby and Spence's *adminicula*. *m*, Case of the superior wings. *n*, Of the under wings. *p*, Cremaster. Fig. 20, Pendent pupa of *Hipparchia Egeria* (Sepp.). Fig. 21, Enclosed pupa of *Musca vomitoria*. Fig. 22, Cremaster of the pupa of *Noctua dissimilis* (Knoch). Fig. 23, Cremaster of the pupa of *Noctua lucipara* (*ib.*). Fig. 24, Pupa of neuter bee (Swam.). Fig. 25, *a*, Cremaster of the pupa of *Harpya Fagi* (Knoch). *b*, Cremaster of the pupa of *Euprepia mendica* (*ib.*). Fig. 26, Bound pupa of *Pontia Cratægi*. Fig. 27, Larva case of *Stratiomys chameleon* (Swamm.). *a*, Head. *b*, Coronet of setæ around the spiracle at the tail. *c c*, The pupa shining through.

Pl. III. Fig. 1, Larva of *Phryganea*, with the case in which it dwells (De Geer). Fig. 2, Larva of *Ephemera*. *a a*, Lateral branchial leaves. *b b*, Rudiments of wings (*ib.*). Fig. 3, Larva of *Culex*. *a*, Air tube. *b*, Anal tube (Swamm.). Fig. 4, Pupa of *Culex*. *a a*, Air tube (*ib*.). Fig. 5, Larva of *Chironomus*. *a a*, Air tubes at tail. *b*, Air tubes at breast (Reaumur). Fig. 6, Pupa of *Chironomus*. *a a*, Branchial fasciculus on the thorax (*ib*.). Fig. 7, Larva of *Corethra*. *a*, Branchial fasciculus at tail. *b*, First, and *c*, Second pair of bladders, which stand in connexion with the intestine *f*. *d*, Mandible. *e*, Antennæ. Fig. 8, Pupa of *Corethra*. *a a*, Air tubes. *b b*, Anal leaves (*ib*.). Fig. 9, Larva of *Simulia*. *a a*, Fasciculi on the head, which are perhaps palpi. *b b*, Antennæ. *c*, Air tube in the thorax. *d d*, Indicated spiracles. *e e*, Anal air tubes (Verdet). Fig. 10, Pupa of *Simulia*. *a a*, Branchial fasciculi. *b b*, Wing sheaths. *c*, Head. *d*, Thorax from the back. *e*, Abdomen (*ib*.). Fig. 11, View from above of the head of *Carabus glabratus*. A, Skull. *a*, vertex. B, Frons. *b*, Sinciput. *c*, Clypeus. I, Labrum. O O, Mandibles. γ γ, First joints of the antennæ. *a a*, Eyes. Fig. 12, Under view of the same. D, Gula. *d*, Swollen margin of the same. G, Occiput. Q, Mentum. O O, Mandibles. P P, Maxillæ. *a a*, Eyes. Fig. 13, Lateral view. S, Facies. E, Cheek. F, Temples. γ, Socket of the antennæ. The other letters as before. Fig. 14, Lateral view of the head of *Myopa testacea*. B, Frons. *a*, Vertex. E, Cheek. F, Temples. G, Occiput. M, Mouth. *c*, clypeus (*hypostoma*, Meig.). *d*, proboscis. *e*, Whisker. γ, Antennæ. Fig. 15, Labium of *Vespa vulgaris*. *a a*, Glandular points of the four-lobed tongue. *b*, Chin. *c c*, Palpi (Treviranus). Fig. 16, Maxilla of *Cychrus rostratus*, from above. 1, Cardo. 2, Stipes. 3, Squama. 4, Mando. 5, Palpus maxillæ internus, or galea. *a*, Basal joint. *b*, Apical joint. A, palpus maxillaris. *e*, The groove. Fig. 17, The same from beneath. Fig. 18, Maxilla of *Spondyla buprestoides*, with the same lettering. Fig. 19, Maxilla of *Melolontha vulgaris*, with the same lettering.

Pl. IV. Fig. 1, Anterior view of the head of *Myopa testacea*. *a a*, Eyes. γ γ, Antennæ. *c c*, Hypostoma. *d*, Proboscis. Fig. 2, Maxilla of *Copris lunaris*, with the lettering as in fig. 16 of preceding plate. Fig. 3, Labium of *Cychrus rostratus*. A, Mentum. B, Ligula. C C, Palpi. Fig. 4, The same from within. A, Mentum. B, The bilobed tongue. Fig. 5, Lateral view of the labium of *Locusta viridissima*. *a*, Superior lobe of the mentum, forming the true mentum. *b*, Basal joint of the left palpus. *c*, Basal portion of the mentum. *d*, The loose tongue. Fig. 6, Head of *Ateuchus sacer*. *a a*, The eyes (Sturm). Fig. 7, Head of *Truxalis nasutus*. *a*, Root of antenna. *b*, Eye. *c*, Labrum. *d d*, Maxillary palpi. *e e*, Labial palpi. *f*, Labium. Fig. 8, Mandible of *Hydrophilus piceus*. *a*, Incisor teeth. *b*, Molar process. *c*, Lower joint ball. *d*, Superior bent joint ball. *e*, Situation of the third internal process, where the flexor muscle is inserted. Fig. 9, Maxilla of *Lucanus cervus*. 1, Cardo. 2, Stipes. 3, Squama. 4, Mando. 5, Penicillate lobe. A, Palpus (Sturm). Fig. 10, Maxilla of *Cicindela campestris*. As far as 4 the same as above, the latter internally beset with teeth, and with a superior moveuble tooth. *c.* 5, Internal maxillary palpus. *a,* Basal joint. *b,* Apical joint. A, External maxillary palpi. Fig. 11, Labium of *Libellula. a,* The true labium. *b b,* The lateral lobes, which appear to be modified labial palpi, 2 2. These would then be the second joints of the labial palpus. Fig. 12, Maxilla of *Sphex (Ammophila) arenaria.* 1, Cardo. 2, Stipes. 3, Squama. 4, Mando, here forming the membranous sheath of the tongue and labium. *a,* Filiform palpus. Fig. 13, Maxilla of *Barynotus obscurus. a,* Conical palpus. *b,* The maxilla, with four teeth on its inner edge (Germar). Fig. 14, Maxillary palpus of *Melandrya.* Fig. 15, Labial palpus of *Oxyporus. a,* The groove which exhibits after the death of the insect the palpal surface. Fig. 16, Maxillary palpus of *Lymexylon navale.* Fig. 17, Maxillary palpus of *Atractocerus necydaloides* (Kirby and Spence). Fig. 18, Maxillary palpus of *Bembidion* (Sturm). Fig. 19, Ditto of *Trechus (ib.).* Fig. 20, Ditto of *Trox sabulosus.* Fig. 21, Maxilla of *Hydrophilus piceus.* 1, Cardo. 2, Stipes. 3, Squama. 4, Mando. 5, External lobes, consisting of *a,* the basal joint, and *b,* the hooked, hairy, apical joint. A, Palpus, Fig. 22, Maxillary palpus of *Gryllotalpa vulgaris. a,* The swollen palpal surface. Fig. 23, Terminal joint of the same palpus with the dried up surface, *a.* Fig. 24, Labial palpus of *Noctua libatrix* (Savigny). Fig. 25, Ditto of *Lithosia pulchella* (*ib*). Fig. 26, Maxilla of *Banchus falcator.* The figures the same as in fig. 21.

Pl. V. Fig. 1, Proboscis of a *Musca.* A, The fleshy lip. *a,* The peduncle. β, A portion beyond the knee. γ, The knob. B, The seta within the channelled excavation of the lip. C C, The one-jointed palpus. Fig. 2, Setæ which lie in the fleshy lip of *Tabanus. a,* Labrum. *b b,* Mandibles. *c c,* Maxillæ. *d,* Tongue. C C, Two-jointed maxillary palpi. Fig. 3, Proboscis of *Tabanus* seen from above; the letters as before. Fig. 4, The same from beneath. *d d,* The halves of the knobs of the labium. C C, Palpi of the maxillæ. Fig. 5, Labrum from beneath (Savigny). Fig. 6, Mandible (*ib.*). Fig. 7, Maxilla (*ib.*). *c,* Maxilla. C, Two-jointed palpus. Fig. 8, Head of *Cimex rufipes* seen from beneath. A A, Eyes. B B, First joints of antennæ. *a,* Labrum. *b b,* Four-jointed sheath of the proboscis produced by the growing together of the labial palpi. Fig. 9, Clypeus of the same, with the rostral seta extended. *a,* Labrum. *c,* Mandible still united. *d d,* Maxillæ (Savigny). Fig. 10, Head of *Cimex rufipes,* in which the upper integument is removed. A A, The eyes. *c c,* The mandibles, with the muscle which affixes each to the occiput. *d d,* Maxillæ attached by muscles to the tongue. *e,* Tongue. Fig. 11, Head of *Nepa cinerea* seen from above. A A, Eyes. *a,* Labrum. *b b,* Sheath of the proboscis or labium. Fig. 12, The three-jointed sheath of the proboscis seen from beneath. Fig. 13, Proboscis of *Nepa cinerea* separated (Savigny). *b,* Proboscideal sheath. *c c,* Mandibles. *d d,* Maxillæ. *e,* Tongue, at the base of which is the entrance to the œsophagus. Fig. 14, Labrum of *Nepa cinerea* seen from beneath (Savigny). *g,* Clypeus from within. *h,* Reflexed margin of the labrum. *f,* Internal passage for the reception of the maxillary setæ. Fig. 15, Head and oral organs of *Noctua libatrix* (Savigny). A A, Eyes. *a,* Labrum. *b b,* Mandibles. *c,* The maxillæ partially united and forming the proboscis. *d d,* Maxillary palpi. *e e,* Articulating cavities for the labial palpi in the reflexed labium. Fig. 16, Labrum of the same moth separate *(ib.).* Fig. 17, Both of the mandibles of the same moth *(ib.).* Fig. 18, Labium of the same moth *(ib.).* *c,* Labium. *d d,* Labial palpi divested of their hair and scales.

Pl. VI. Fig. 1, Maxilla of the same moth *(ib.).* *a,* The filiform portion. *b,* The palpus. 1, The cardo. 2, The stipes. 3, The squama. 4, The mando. Fig. 2, Section of the proboscis *(ib.).* *a a,* Ridges which close the central canal of the proboscis above. *o,* The central canal. *p p,* The canals in each half of the proboscis. Fig. 3, Head of *Galleria cereana (ib.).* A, Eye. B, Antenna. *d,* Labial palpus. *e,* Projecting proboscis. Fig. 4, Parts of the mouth of the same moth. *f,* The proboscis, consisting of two halves. *g g,* Palpi of the proboscis. *d d,* Labial palpi. *e,* The labium. Fig. 5, Head of a neuter *Apis mellifica* seen from beneath. *a,* Mentum. A, Fulcrum. *b,* Tongue (a pierced sucking tube). *g g,* Paraglossæ. *c c,* Four-jointed labial palpi attached to the tongue close to the fulcrum. *d d,* Pergamentaceous maxillæ. *h h,* One-jointed maxillary palpi. *f f,* Mandibles. *n n,* Horny ridges in the articulating membrane of the parts of the mouth. *m.* Occipital aperture. Fig. 6, Mouth of the same insect similarly marked. *e,* The valve of the œsophagus, the second tongue according to Treviranus. 1, 2, 3, 4, 5, The several horny bones which lie in the articulating membrane. Fig. 7, Lower portion of the proboscis (tongue). *b,* With the paraglossæ *a a,* (Brandt). Fig. 8, Anterior view of the head of *Apis mellifica.* A A, Eyes. B, Stemmata. C C, Antennæ. D, Clypeus. E, Labrum. *f f,* Mandibles. *d d,* Maxillæ. *c c,* Labial palpi. *b,* Proboscis or tongue. Fig. 9, Head of *Phryganea grandis* seen in front. A A, Eyes. *a a,* Mandibles. *b,* Labrum. *c c,* Maxillæ. *d d,* Maxillary palpi. *e e,* Labial palpi. *f,* Spoon-shaped Labium. Fig. 10, Labium seen from above. *c c,* Maxillæ. *e e,* Maxillary palpi. *d,* The channel of the under lip which leads to the orifice, *g,* of the œsophagus. Fig. 30, Labium from beneath. *f f,* Labial palpi. *e e,* Basal joints of the maxillary palpi. *g,* Fulcrum.

Pl. VII. Fig. 1, Setiform antenna of *Locusta.* Fig. 2, Ditto ditto of *Cicada.* Fig. 3, Bodkin-shaped ditto of *Leptis.* Fig. 4, Filiform ditto of *Carabus.* Fig. 5, Moniliform ditto of *Tenebrio.* Fig. 6, Sword-shaped ditto of *Truxalis.* Fig. 7, Sickle-shaped ditto (Kirby and Spence). Fig. 8, Dentate ditto of *Stenochorus.* Fig. 9, Serrate ditto of *Elater.* Fig. 10, Imbricate ditto of *Prionus coriarius,* male. Fig. 11, Pectinated ditto of *Ctenocerus.* Fig. 12, Doubly-pectinated ditto of *Ctenophora* (Meigen). Fig. 13, Curled antenna (Kirby and Spence). Fig. 14, Fan-shaped ditto of *Prygmatocerus* (Perty). Fig. 15, Ramose ditto of *Cladius difformis*. Fig. 16, Furcate ditto of *Schizocerus*. Fig. 17, Geniculated ditto of *Apis mellifica*. *a*, Scapus. *b*, Flagellum. Fig. 18, Clavate ditto of *Silpha*. Fig. 19, Capitate ditto of *Necrophorus*. Fig. 20, Ditto of *Hydrophilus*. Fig. 21, Lamellate ditto of *Melolontha fullo*, male.

Pl. VIII. Fig. 1, Tunicate antenna of *Lethrus*. Fig. 2, Inflated antenna of *Paussus* (Sturm). Fig. 3, Fissate antenna of *Lucanus*. Fig. 4, Uncinate ditto of *Odynerus*, male. Fig. 5, Nodose antenna of a *Curculio* (Kirby and Spence). Fig. 6, Angustate ditto of *Asilus* (Meig.). Fig. 7, Setigerous ditto of *Sargus* (ib.). Fig. 8, Plumose ditto of *Volucella* (ib.). Fig. 9, Both of *Ceria conopsoides* seated on a process of the frons (ib.). Fig. 10, Antenna of *Chrysotoxum* (ib.). Fig. 11—13, Ditto of *Bombylius* (ib.) Fig. 14, Of *Lophosia* (ib.). Fig. 15, Of *Rhaphium* (ib.). Fig. 16, Of *Sybistroma* (ib.) Fig. 17, Of *Gonia* (ib.). Fig. 18, Mucronate ditto of *Empis* (ib.). Fig. 19 and 20, Auriculate ditto of *Parnus* and *Gyrinus*. Fig. 21, Ramose ditto of *Nepa*. Fig. 22, Irregular ditto of *Cerocoma*. Fig. 23, Ditto of *Psychoda* (Meig.). Fig. 24, A portion of the antenna of *Gastropacha trifolii*. *b*, A portion of the branch to exhibit the fine ramose hairs which form the fringe, the one strongly, the other slightly magnified. Fig. 25, Fasciculate antenna of *Callichroma alpinum*. Fig. 26, Antenna of a small Brazilian *Saperda*. Fig. 27 and 28, Feathery antennæ of *Ceratopogon* and *Tanypus* (Meig.). Fig. 29, Portion of an antenna with kidney-shaped joints of *Nephrotoma* (ib.). Fig. 30, Irregular clavate antenna of *Agaon paradoxum* (Dalman).

Pl. IX. N.B. In Plates IX.—XIV., which explain the composition of the thorax in the different orders, for the sake of distinction the prothorax is coloured *red*, the mesothorax *blue*, the metathorax *yellow*, and the coxæ *green*. In all the figures, A indicates the pronotum, B the prosternum, *b* the omium, C the mesonotum, D the scapula of anterior wing, D* of posterior wing, E the mesosternum, F the metanotum, G the metasternum, H the parapleura, I the pleura, K the coxæ (generally of the posterior legs). All the figures are original, and from drawings by the author.

[No. 1] exhibits parts of the thorax of *Carabus glabratus*. Fig. 1, Prothorax from above. Fig. 2, Ditto from beneath. Fig. 3, Prosternum from the inner surface, to exhibit the situation of the two weak internal processes. Fig. 4, The omium. *b*, The external surface. *b**, The reflexed margin which is attached to the inner surface of the pronotum. Fig. 5, Lateral view of the prosternum. *c c*, Its two internal scale-shaped processes, between which the nervous cord lies. Fig. 6, Meso- and Metathorax seen from above. R R, The rudimentary wings. *b*, The same from beneath. S S, The first abdominal segment. S* S*, The second ditto. K K, Coxæ of the posterior legs T T, Trochanters. Fig. 7, Anterior view of the mesosternum to exhibit the two processes *f*, which form the fork, and between which the nervous cord lies Fig. 8, Anterior wings of the scapula seen from the surface. *b*, The reflexed margin which lies against the posterior wings. Fig. 9, Posterior wings of the scapula seen from the surface. *b**, The reflexed margin which lies against the margin of the anterior wing, and forms the suture in which both meet together.

[No. 2,] Parts of the skeleton of *Dyticus*. Fig. 1, View of the internal portion of the head after the removal of the upper integument. *a a*, The two ridges which proceed from the throat and enclose the cerebellum between them. *c*, The tentorium or the transverse band of connexion between the two ridges. *d*, A second deeper-seated band, consisting of two halves, upon which the anterior portion of the cerebellum rests. *e e*, Two hooked processes, which proceed from the superior margin of the bands, and encompass the œsophagus in front of the cerebrum. They serve for the insertion of small muscles which retain the œsophagus. *f f*, A horny ridge which runs beneath the frons from one side of the head to the other, and to which the labrum is attached. *g*, The labium, or, rather, its superior fleshy part, the tongue. *h*, A horny semicircular bone, to which the tongue is attached; it lies free in the flesh, and does not come in contact with the integument of the head. *b b*, The orbits. Fig. 2, The prothorax seen from beneath. *b b*, The omia. Fig. 3, The prosternum from behind. *a a*, The jugularia which lie in the membrane of the neck, and upon which the head revolves. *b b*, Internal processes of the prosternum which encompass the nervous cord. Fig. 4, The omium seen from the surface. *b*, The external surface. *b**, The reflexed margin which lies against the surface of the pronotum. Fig. 5, Prosternum from the side. *b*, The internal processes. Fig. 6, Coxæ, trochanters and femur of the intermediate leg, to show the free articulating process. *a*, Audouin's trochantinus. Fig. 7, Meso- and metathorax from above. Fig. 8, The same from beneath. Fig. 9, Mesosternum separated from the parapleura, with its internal processes. This gives the most perfect representation of the vertebra of an insect. E is the body of the vertebra whence the arches proceed which encompass the nervous cord. *b b* are the transverse processes. *a* forms the processus spinosus, consisting of two halves. At the superior transverse process of the body the scapulæ articulate; they correspond to the articulating surfaces of the ribs in the vertebræ. Fig. 10, Anterior wing of the scapula (D). Fig. 11, Posterior wing of the scapula (D*). *b*, The reflexed margin which forms the suture with that of the anterior wing. Fig. 12, The connate coxæ seen from the front to exhibit the process springing from them. It ascends in a forwardly inclined direction from the suture of both coxæ, and then divides into four processes, the two posterior of which again furcate. *b b,* The anterior processes. *a a,* The posterior with their furcate branches **.

[No. 3,] Portions of the skeleton of *Buprestis mariana.* Fig. 1, Prothorax from beneath. A A, Reflexed margin of the pronotum. B, Prosternum. *b b,* The small round plates which correspond to the anterior wings of the scapulæ in *Carabus* and *Dyticus.* Fig. 2, The same from the front. *a a,* The jugularia which lies in the membrane of the neck. Fig. 3, Prosternum from the side. The internal processes are small, and stand forwards. *g,* The same from within, *a a,* these processes. Fig. 4, Upper view of the meso- and metathorax. Fig. 5, The same from beneath. Fig. 6—8, Mesosternum and scapulæ in their natural situation. *b,* Mesosternum (E E). Fig. 7, Anterior wings of the scapulæ (D D). Fig. 10, Metathorax from within to exhibit the quadridentate process. *b b,* The anterior teeth. *a a,* The posterior. Fig. 11, The same from the side. Fig. 12, Meso- and metathorax of *Hister cadaverinus* seen from beneath. S, First abdominal segment. Fig. 13, The same from above.

Pl. X. [No. 1,] Fig. 1, Parts of the skeleton of *Geotrupes nasicornis.* Fig. 1, Pronotum from beneath, the prosternum is removed. *a a,* The reflexed margin. Fig. 2, Prosternum from beneath. Fig. 3, The same from the side. *a,* The internal processes. Fig. 4, Meso- and metathorax from above. Fig. 5, Mesosternum with the scapulæ. E, Mesosternum. D D, Ala anterior scapulæ. D* D*, Ejusd. ala posterior. Fig. 6, Meso- and metathorax from below. Meso- and metasternum are here connate. Fig. 7, Mesosternum from within. *a a a,* The three points of the processus internus. Fig. 8, The internal process from the side. *a a a,* The three points. [No. 2,] Skeleton of *Cetonia aurata.* Fig. 1, Meso- and metathorax from above. Fig. 2, The same from beneath. Fig. 3, Prosternum and scapulæ seen from the front. Fig. 4, The connate sternum from within. *a a,* Proc. intern. mesosterni. *b,* Proc. intern. metast., each consisting of two divaricating lamellæ, between which the nervous cord lies. [No. 3,] Skeleton of *Hydrophilus piceus.* Fig. 1, Pronotum from beneath. Fig. 2, Prosternum ditto. Fig. 3, Mesonotum from above (the letter G is here wrong). Fig. 4, Metanotum from above. Fig. 5, Sternum from without. Fig. 6, The same from within. *a,* The internal processes of the mesosternum which ascend to the scapulæ. *b b,* Wings of the processus internus metasterni. Fig. 7, The same from the side. *a a,* The pro. int. mesost. ascending as far as the scapulæ. *b b,* Both wings of the processus internus metast. *d,* This process itself. *e,* A thin horny lamella which lies beneath the proc. *g,* An externally visible aperture which indicates the point of division between the two parts of the connate sternum. Fig. 8, Parapleuræ from the inner surface, with the tendon of the large extensor of the wing. *a,* The plate-shaped distension.

b, The central petiole which is affixed to the anterior main nervure of the wing.

Pl. XI. [No. 1,] Skeleton of *Gryllotalpa vulgaris.* Fig. 1, Pronotum from above. Fig. 2, Prothorax from beneath. *a a*, The two stigmata which lie in the membrane behind the prothorax. *b*, Aperture of the neck, being the entrance to the prothorax. *c*, Posterior aperture. *d d*, Cavities for the coxæ. Fig. 3, Internal skeleton of the prothorax. A, Pronotum. B, Prosternum. C, Descending keel of the pronotum, which divides into two furcating lamellæ, the anterior and posterior points of which are at E E and F F. With the anterior ones, the T-shaped anterior distension of the sternum articulates, and with the posterior ones, which again unite, the posterior apex articulates at *. Besides which, two processes, D D, spring from the sides of the pronotum, which meet at the anterior angles of the central carina near E E. A process, G, springs on each side backwards from the posterior angles of the central carina, both of which are retained by a bone upon which the crop rests, and which is connected by muscles at * * with them. Fig. 4, Meso- and metathorax from above. Fig. 5, Mesosternum from the side, lying free internally upon the external plate E, the point bending backwards. Fig. 6, The same from beneath with the backwards directed processes, the points are cut off. Fig. 7, The mesonotum seen from the front to exhibit the prophragma, in which, at *a*, the aperture to the aorta is found. Fig. 8, Lateral view of the meso- and metathorax. β, Stigma upon the limits of the meso- and metathorax. [No. 2,] Skeleton of *Gryllus migratorius.* Fig. 1, Head from beneath, with the aperture of the mouth distended anteriorly to exhibit the radiating tentorium (*c c c*). *a a*, Basal joints of the antennæ. *b b*, The eyes. Fig. 2, Prothorax from front, natural size. *a a*, The horny arch springing from the sides, which bow over the acetabulæ of the coxæ. Fig. 3, Meso- and metathorax from above, with distended but cut-off wings. *c c*, Prophragma. Fig. 4, The same from the side. *a a*, Rudiments of the base of the wings. *c*, Prophragma. β, Second spiracle of the thorax. Fig. 5, The same from beneath. Fig. 6, Mesothorax alone seen from behind. C, Mesonotum. D D, Scapulæ. E, Mesosternum. *a a*, Remains of the wing. *c*, Mesophragma with the aperture *p* for the aorta. *d d*, Internal ridges, which indicate the suture of the wings of the scapulæ. *e e*, Horny arch spanned over the acetabulæ. [No. 3,] Skeleton of *Libellula.* Fig. 1, Entire thorax from above, with the remains of the wings. Fig. 2, The same from the side. *c*, The free prophragma. β, Second thoracic spiracle. Fig. 3, The same from beneath. Fig. 4, Prehensile organ upon the second and third ventral segments of the male *Libellula.* *a a*, Two moveable hooks which encompass the points * * of the processes *b b.* *c c*, Processes of the second division of the prehensile organ, between which the hook *d* lies. *e*, Third division of that organ. Fig. 5, The same from the side. Fig. 6, Third division of the prehensile organ, consisting of a large swollen knob, *a*, which at *d* is excavated, and at the anterior ridge of which the hook *b* hangs by two joints. Fig. 7, Central division of the prehensile organ. *a a*, The processes. *b*, The hook between them raised. Fig. 8, First division of the same organ, consisting of the anterior pieces, *a a*, which articulate at *d d* with the posterior ones, *b b*, and the hooks *c c*. Fig. 9, Apex of the abdomen of a male *Libellula*. Fig. 8, 9, 10, The same ordinal joints of the abdomen. *a*, The aperture to the sexual organs.

Pl. XII. [No. 1,] Skeleton of *Cimbex variabilis*. Fig. 1, Lateral view of the thorax. *a*, Tegula which covers the first thoracic spiracle. *d*, Patagium analogous to the anterior wing of the scapula. *c*, Scutellum. β, Second spiracle. Fig. 2, View of the thorax from above. γγ, Cenchri. Fig. 3, Mesonotum alone. *a*, Prophragma. *d d*, Patagia. *c*, Scutellum. Fig. 4, Prosternum seen from behind, to show the internal processes *a a*. *b b*, Cavities of the coxæ. Fig. 5, The same from the side. Fig. 6, Mesosternum with its lateral ascending wings. *a a*, Internal process divided into two points. *b b*, Cavities of the coxæ. *c*, Hook-shaped process, which originates from the side of the sternum, and serves the muscles of the coxæ for insertion. [No. 2,] Skeleton of *Scolia flavifrons*. Fig. 1, Thorax from above. *d d*, Patagia. *c*, Scutellum. β β, Second spiracles. Fig. 2, The same from the side. *a*, First spiracle. β, Second. *d*, Patagium. *c*, Scutellum. Fig. 3, The same from beneath. * Aperture through which the tendon passes which holds the abdomen. Fig. 4, Metanotum with the process to which the muscle is attached, which, with the tendon proceeding from it, holds the abdomen. Fig. 5, The same from the side. Fig. 6, Prosternum from behind. *a a*, Acetabulæ of the coxæ. *b b*, Internal processes. Fig. 7, Cavity, A, in the metathorax, for the reception of the apex of the abdomen. *a*, Hole through which the tendon passes. *b b*, Ball joints. Fig. 8, Cavity in the base of the abdomen, which inserts itself in the cavity of the metathorax. *a a*, Sockets. *b b*, Ball joints. *c*, Process to which the tendon is attached. Fig. 9, First segment of the abdomen seen from the side. *a*, Process to which the tendon is affixed. *b*, Socket for the reception of the ball joint of the metaphragma. *c*, Ball joint which is inserted in the socket of the metaphragma.

Pl. XIII. [No. 1,] Thorax of *Methoca ichneumonides*, Lat. Fig. 1, Thorax seen from above. A, Pronotum. *c*, Scutellum. F, Metanotum. Fig. 2, The same from the side. B, Prosternum. E, Mesosternum. G, Metasternum. β, Second spiracle. [No. 2,] Thorax of *Myrmosa melanocephala*, male. Fig. 1, From above. Fig. 2, From the side, marked as above. [No. 3,] Superior view of the thorax of *Chrysis ignita*. A, Pronotum. C, Mesonotum divided by two furrows into three fields. *c*, Scutellum. *d d*, Patagia. F, Metanotum. [No. 4,] Thorax of *Cossus ligniperda*. Fig. 1, View from above. *e*, Mesonotum. D*, Patagium. *d d*, Frenum. *c*, Scutellum. F F, Metanotum. K K, Coxæ

of the posterior legs. Fig. 2, Lateral view. A, Scale-shaped pronotum.
B, Prosternum. *a*, Cavity in which the first spiracle lies. C, Mesonotum.
c, Scutellum. D*, Patagium. D, Scapula. E, Mesosternum. β, Cavity
of the second spiracle. F, Metanotum. G, Metasternum. K K K, Coxæ.
[No. 5,] Thorax of *Cicada Fraxini*. Fig. 1, View from above. A, Pronotum.
C, Mesonotum. *c*, Scutellum. *d d*, Frenum. F F, Metanotum. Fig. 2,
View from beneath. B, Prosternum. E, Mesosternum. G, Metasternum.
β β, Scales beneath each of which the second spiracle of the thorax lies.
[No. 6,] Thorax of *Lygæus equestris*. Fig. 1, Prothorax from above. Fig. 2,
The same from beneath. Fig. 3, Meso- and metathorax from above.
C, Mesonotum. *c*, Scutellum. Fig. 4, The same from beneath. E, Mesosternum. β β, Cavities covered by scales, beneath which the spiracles lie.
G G, Metasternum.

Pl. XIV. [No. 1,] Thorax of *Tabanus bovinus*. Fig. 1, View from above.
d d, Protrusions which take the place of the patagia. Fig. 2, View from the
side. *a*, First spiracle, indicating the boundary of the prothorax. B, Situation
of the prosternum. C, Mesonotum. *c*, Scutellum. *d*, The patagium.
E, Mesosternum. R, Base of the wing. S, Scale. F, Metanotum.
G, Metasternum. T, Poiser. β, Second spiracle. H, Metaphragma.
K K K, Coxæ. [No. 2,] Thorax of *Myopa testacea*. Fig. 1, View from above.
A A, Protrusions which indicate the prothorax (humeri of entomologists).
C C, Mesonotum. *c*, Scutellum. S S, Scales. T T, Poisers. F, Metanotum. Fig. 2, Lateral view. A, Humerus. *a*, First spiracle. C, Mesonotum. *c*, Scutellum. E, Mesosternum. S, Scale. F, Metanotum.
G, Metasternum. T, Poisers. β, Second spiracle. H, Metaphragma.
[No. 3,] Thorax of *Semblis bicaudata*. Fig. 1, Prothorax from above. Fig. 2,
The same from beneath. B, Prosternum. *a a*, Place of the first spiracle.
K K, Acetabulæ. Fig. 3, Meso- and metathorax from above. C, Mesonotum.
F, Metanotum. Fig. 4, The same from the side, with the same indications.
Fig. 8, Pincers of a *Forficula* (De G.). Fig. 9, A *Smynthurus* seen from
beneath (De G.). *a*, The fork which produces the leap. *b*, Process upon the
mesosternum whence the filaments proceed. Fig. 10, Apex of the abdomen of
Staphylinus erythropterus. *a a*, The hairy styli. Fig. 11, Apex of the abdomen
of *Blatta orientalis*. *a a*, The circi. *b b*, Two other processes which proceed
from the ventral plate. *c*, The male organs withdrawn. Fig. 12, Apex of
the abdomen of a male *Ephemera*. *a*, The penis. *b b*, The two fangs which
are seated on the ventral plate. *c c*, The jointed fila proceeding from the
dorsal plate, the half of which is cut off. Fig. 13, Apex of the abdomen of
Machilis polypoda (Dumeril), with the hairy setæ. Fig. 14, Apex of the
abdomen of *Aphis*. *a a*, The siphunculi.

Pl. XV. N. B. The two arrows at the base of the wings indicate the course of the current of the blood. Fig. 1, Wing case of *Nepa cinerea*. *a*, Clavus. *b*, Hemielytrum. *c*, Appendix. *d*, Membrana. Fig. 2, Wing case of *Gryllus migratorius*. A, Marginal cell. *b*, Vena radialis. B, Central cell. *c*, Vena cubitalis. C, Sutural cell. Fig. 3, Wing of *Dyticus*. *a*, Vena marginalis or radialis. *b*, Vena cubitalis or postcosta, also nervus internus.— The marginal space is in this and in all the following wings indicated by red, and the sutural space by yellow. The former is bounded by the vein through which the current of blood streams, and that of the latter by the one through which it returns. Fig. 4, Wing of a *Tenthredo*. *a*, Vena radialis. *b*, Vena cubitalis. β, Stigma, carpus. *d d*, Cellulæ radiales. *e e e*, Cellulæ cubitales. Fig. 5, Wing of a bee. *a*, Marginal vein. *b*, Discoidal vein. *d*, Marginal cell. *e e*, Cubital cells. *c c*, Discoidal cells. *f f f*, Incomplete cells. Fig. 6, Wing of a *Tipula*. Fig. 7, Wing of a *Syrphus*. Fig. 8, Wing of a *Tachina*. Fig. 9, Wing of one of the smaller *Muscidæ*. Fig. 10, Wing of a *Phora*. Fig. 11, Wing of *Hippobosca*. All these figures are marked like 5. Fig. 12, Anterior wing of *Platypterix*, ala falcata. Fig. 13, Posterior wing of *Papilio Podalirius*, ala caudata. Fig. 14, Anterior wing of *Orneodes hexadactyla*, ala digitata.

Pl. XVI. Fig. 1, Anterior leg of *Carabus*. *a*, Coxa. *b*, Trochanter *c*, Femur. *d*, Tibia. ♃♃, Calcaria. *e*, Tarsus. Fig. 2, Anterior leg of *Ateuchus sacer*. *e*, The terminal spine supplying the place of a tarsus. Fig. 3, *a*, Intermediate leg of a butterfly. *b*, Abortive leg of the same. Fig. 4, Swimming leg of *Dyticus dispar*. Fig. 5, Leaping leg of *Haltica*. Fig. 6, *a*, Prehensile leg of *Mantis religiosa*. *b*, Prehensile leg of *Nepa cinerea*. Fig. 7, Digging leg of *Gryllotalpa vulgaris*. The tarsus is three jointed. Fig. 8, Fringed femur of an *Andrena*. Fig. 9, Supporting trochanter of *Carabus*. Fig. 10, Double-jointed trochanter of a *Pimpla*. Fig. 11, Lamellate tibia of a *Lygæus*. Fig. 12, Scutellate tibia of *Crabro cribrarius, a*. *e*, The five-jointed tarsus. Fig. 13, Brush-like tibia of *Apis*. *e*, Planta. Fig. 14, The sole of *Carabus* fringed with spines. Fig. 15, Cordate tarsal joint of *Timarcha tenebricosa*. Fig. 16, Triangular tarsal joint of *Copris lunaris*. Fig. 17, Quadrate tarsal joint of *Buprestis mariana*. Fig. 18, Bilobate tarsal joint of *Cullidium violaceum*. Fig. 19, Furcate tarsus of *Xya*. *a*, Spines on the tibia. *e e*, The furcate tarsus, consisting each of one joint. Fig. 20, Tarsus with three distended joints of *Cicindela campestris*. Fig. 21, Tarsus with four distended joints of *Calosoma sycophanta*. Fig. 22, Tarsus with one distended joint of *Hydrophilus piceus*. Fig. 23, Anterior tarsus of *Dyticus dispar*, *a*, from above, *b*, from beneath. *p p*, The large patellulæ. Fig. 24, Claw joint of *Carabus*, equal claws. Fig. 25, Claw joint of *Anisoplia fructicola*. Fig. 26, Claw joint with very large unequal claws of *Rutila*. Fig. 27, *b*, Furcate claw of *Meloë* divided near the surface. *a*, Furcate claw of *Anisoplia horticola*, divided near the ridge.

N. B. It is only the external larger claw that is thus divided, and not, as the drawing indicates, the smaller one also. Fig. 28, Dentate claw of *Melolontha*. Fig. 29, Dentate claw of *Ornithomya*. Fig. 30, Serrate claw of *Cistela*. Fig. 31, Claw joint of *Lucanus cervus*. *a a*, The large claws. *b*, The pseudo claw. Fig. 32, Claw joint of *Tachina fera*. *a a*, The serrate claws. *b b*, The plantulæ. Fig. 33, Claw joint of *Laphria flava*. *a a*, The claws. *b b*, The plantulæ. *c*, The pseudo claw. Fig. 34, Tarsus of *Xenos*, without claws, but with soft plantulæ. Fig. 35, Hairy plantula of *Lamia*. Fig. 36, Plumose plantula of *Zabrus*. Fig. 37, Spongy plantula of *Timarcha tenebricosa*. Fig. 38, Tarsus cryptopentamerus of *Cerambyx heros*. 1, First tarsal joint (metatarsus); 2, second tarsal joint (phalanx prima); 3, third bilobate tarsal joint (phalanx secunda); 4, abortive fourth tarsal joint (arthrium); 5, claw joint. Fig. 39, Tarsus cryptotetramerus of *Coccinella*. 1, First tarsal joint; 2, second deeply excavated foot joint; 3, arthrium; 4, claw joint.

Pl. XVII. Fig. 1, Internal structureless folded tunic of the ilium of *Hydrophilus piceus*. Fig. 2, Second tunic of the ilium of the same beetle beset with ridges, teeth, and stars. Fig. 3, Third or muscular tunic, with the ventral glands, which lie in a transparent case, of the same. Fig. 4, Third or muscular tunic of *Dyticus marginalis*. Fig. 5, Second tunic of the crop of the same beset with horny ridges that form regular meshes. Fig. 6, Transverse section of the membrane of the crop of the same. *a*, Internal layer beset with ridges. *b*, Muscular tunic. Fig. 7, Tunic of the œsophagus of the same with undulating horny ridges. Fig. 8, Proventriculus of the same. It is excavated in the form of a tunnel, and supplied with four teeth, which are broad above and narrow below. 3, Intestinal canal of the larva of *Vespa crabro* (Suckow). A, Œsophagus. D, Ventriculus. H, Cæcum. K K, Biliary vessels. Fig. 10, Intestinal canal of *Vespa crabro* (*ib*.). A, Œsophagus. C, Crop. D, Transversely striated ventriculus. E, Ilium with four longitudinal stripes. H, Colon with horny rings.

Pl. XVIII. Fig. 1, Intestinal canal of *Aphrophora spumaria* (*ib*.). A, Œsophagus. D, Crop. D*, First division of the ventriculus. D D**, Second division, which returns to the crop. E, Ilium. H. Colon. K K, Biliary vessels. Fig. 2, Intestinal canal of the maggot of *Musca carnaria* (*ib*.), marked the same as above. N N are the salivary vessels with their simple outlets, O. Fig. 3, *a*, A portion of the biliary vessel much magnified. Fig. 3, Intestinal canal of the perfect fly (*ib*.). Fig. 4, Intestine of the caterpillar of *Gastropacha Pini* (Suckow), marked similarly. F is the clavate gut. O O are the spinning vessels. Fig. 5, Intestinal canal of *Pontia Brassicæ* (Herold). C, The sucking stomach. G, The cæcum. The rest as before.

Pl. XIX. Fig. 1, Intestinal canal of the larva of *Calosoma sycophanta* (original), marked as before. H is the internally longitudinally folded colon to which the last segment of the larva is still attached. Fig. 2, Intestinal canal of the perfect beetle (Suckow). D is the ventriculus, the anterior half of which is covered with the pancreas, and the posterior portion, D*, with glands. Fig. 3, Intestinal canal of the larva of *Dyticus marginalis* (orig.), marked the same. Fig. 4, That of the perfect beetle, as before, the ventriculus anteriorly covered with the pancreas.

Pl. XX. Fig. 1, Intestinal canal of *Cetonia aurata* (Ramd.). D, The pancreas covers the ventriculus with three coronets. F, The clavate gut. Fig. 2, Ditto of the perfect insect (*ib.*), as before. Fig. 3, Ditto of *Cimex rufipes* (Trevir.). *a a* and $\beta \beta$ are the setæ of the proboscis whence the vessels $\gamma \gamma$ originate which open into the commencement of the ventriculus. *b b*, The salivary vessels and glands. D, The first stomach with the two-folded bodies (? ?) at its orifice (this supplies the place of a crop). D*, The second stomach (supplying the place of a proventriculus). D**, The third stomach, forming, as it were, a second crop in front of the true ventriculus. D***, The ventriculus, consisting of four contiguous tubes. The rest as before.

Pl. XXI. Fig. 1, Intestinal canal of *Gryllus migratorius*. Lateral view. *a a*, Four of the six blind tubular appendages at the orifice of the stomach (pancreas). *n*, Nervus sympathicus. Fig. 2, The same opened. B, The crop with the rows of teeth. **, Spot where the blind appendages open. D, Ventriculus. ****, Spot where the biliary vessels open; the rest the same as before. Fig. 3, *a b*, Two rows of teeth which are found within the crop much magnified. Fig. 4, Raised longitudinal ridges beset with teeth within the lower portion of the crop. Fig. 5, The processes, *b b*, of the internal tunic of the stomach, *a a*, which thrust into the blind appendages and their cavities, and open at C C into the intestine. Fig. 6, The portion of the intestine where the blind appendages open, *a a*, their apertures; these cut off, to show their internal volume. *c c*, V-formed horny teeth, which form the proventriculus Fig. 7, Œsophagus and crop of *Gryllotalpa vulgaris* (J. Müller). A, Œsophagus. B, Crop. C, Continuation of œsophagus. D, Proventriculus. E E, Blind bags which open into the commencement of the ventriculus. G, Ventriculus. *a*, Cerebrum. *b b*, Nervous cords which form the first ganglion, *c*, of the sympathic system. *d d*, The sympathic nerves. *e*, Branch of it for the crop. *f*, Second or connecting ganglion. *g*, Branch for the proventriculus. Fig. 8, Transverse section of the proventriculus of *Termes fatalis*. *a a*, Projecting horny plates. *b b b*, Six fasciculi of muscles which close it. Fig. 9, Lateral view. *a*, Space before the proventriculus, crop. *b*, The proventriculus seen through the contracted orifice of the ventriculus. *d*, Ventriculus. Fig. 10, Opened proventriculus of *Termes fatalis*. *a a*, Twelve horny plates, which are alternately supplied with strong fasciculi of muscles, *b b*, which unite to form the sphincter of the stomach. Fig. 11, Orifice of the stomach of *Lamia ædilis*. *a a*, Four teeth, which have two fine horny ridges. *b b*, Ridges of the crop. *c*, Ventriculus. Fig. 12, Salivary vessels of *Locusta viridissima*. *a*, Tongue from beneath. *b b*, Outlets of the glands. *c c*, Glands. Fig. 13, Mandibles and salivary vessels of the caterpillar of *Gastropacha Pini* (Suckow). *a*, Mandible. *b*, Gland, aperture of the salivary vessel. *c*, Muscle of the mandible. *d d*, Salivary vessel. Fig. 14, Urinary organ of *Dyticus marginalis*. *a a*, Secreting vessel, kidney. *b*, Urinary bladder. *c*, Evacuating duct. Fig. 15, Salivary vessels of *Reduvius personatus* (Ramd.). *a*, Œsophagus. *b*, Duct of the salivary glands. *c c*, Longitudinal glandular bodies. Fig. 16, Salivary vessel of *Pulex* (Ramd.), vesicular glands. *b*, Excretory duct.

Pl. XXII. Fig. 1, Single salivary vessel of *Nepa cinerea* (Ramd.). *a*, Duct. *b*, Glands. *c*, Glandular vessel. Fig. 2, Second salivary vessel of ditto (*ib.*). *a b*, Double duct of the auxiliary gland. *d*, Auxiliary gland. *e e*, Chief gland. Fig. 3, Salivary vessel of *Blaps* (Leon Duf.). Fig. 4, Ditto of *Tabanus* (Ramd.) Fig. 5, Ditto of *Cicada* (Leon Duf.). Fig. 6, Ventral salivary glands of *Leptis* (Ramd.). *a a*, The two glandular bags. *b*, Œsophagus. *c*, Outlet of the sucking stomach. *d*, Commencement of the ventriculus. Fig. 7, Ventral salivary glands of *Bombylius* (*ib.*), the same. Fig. 8, Ditto of *Chrysotoxum* (Ramd.), the same. Fig. 8*, Lateral view of the heart of *Melolontha vulgaris* (Straus-Durck.). *a a*, Orifices of the heart, 12. *g*, Ventriculi. B, End of the heart. C, Aorta. Fig. 9, Commencement of the heart, with the muscular wings (*ib.*). *a a*, Muscular wings. *b b*, Orifices in them, in front of each aperture of the heart. Fig. 10, Spiracle of the abdomen of *Dyticus marginalis*. Fig. 11, Portion of a trachea. *a a*, External tunic. *b b*, Spiral filament which forms the second tunic. *c c*, Third, or mucous tunic. Fig. 12, A portion of the tunic of the air-bag of *Musca vomitoria*, very much magnified.

Pl. XXIII. Fig. 1, Spiracle of *Oryctes nasicornis*, seen from the front. *a a*, The projecting margin. *b b*, Horny plates, which form its lips. *c*, Aperture. Fig. 2, The same, removed from the contiguous parts, and seen from the side. *a*, Projecting margin. *b b*, The separated integument in the vicinity of the spiracle. *c c*, Posterior projecting margin of the spiracle. *d d*, The two horny triangles, which lie on one side of the main stem of the trachea, which join at *, and are moved by the broad muscle, *e*. *f f f*, Branches of the tracheæ. Fig. 3, The same, from beneath. *a a*, External projecting margin. *b b*, Separated integument. *c*, Spot where the apex of the lower triangle articulates with the margin of the spiracle that projects inwardly. *d*, The lower horny triangle. *f f f*, Stems of the tracheæ. Fig. 4, Spiracle of the larva of *Cetonia aurata*. *a a*, The external darkly-coloured margin, which is decorated with paler elliptical spots. *b b*, The central paler horny plate. *c*, The raised margin of the true aperture. *d d*, Branches of tracheæ. Figs. 5—11, Ovipositor of *Sirex juvencus*. Fig. 5, Last abdominal segment, with the ovipositor, A. B B, Lateral margins of the last largest segment. Fig. 6, Apex of the abdomen, from the side. The ovipositor, *b*, projects from the two valves, *a*. Fig. 7, Apex of the ovipositor, seen from above. *c*, The divided dentate apex of the sheath. *d d*, The two dentate setæ within the sheath. Fig. 8, The ovipositor, from the side. *c*, The upper channel. *d*, The single lower seta. Fig. 9, From beneath. *c c*, Sheath. *d d*, Setæ. Fig. 10, One seta, to exhibit the shape of the teeth upon it. Fig. 11, Transverse section of the ovipositor. *a a*, The external valves. *c*, The sheath. *d d*, The setæ. *e*, Central free channel. Figs. 12—14, Ovipositor of *Pimpla*. Fig. 12, Apex of the organ, covered with short teeth. *a*, The upper channel. *b*, The fine seta. Fig. 13, Section of the mere ovipositor. *a*, Channel. *b*, Seta. *c*, Canal. Fig. 14, Section of the ovipositor, with the valves. *a*, Channel. *b*, Seta. *c c*, Valves. *e*, Canal. Figs. 15—18, Ovipositor of *Cynips quercifolia*. Fig. 15, Last bent segment, with the two hairy processes originating from the internal surface. Fig. 16, The ovipositor. *a a*, Valves. *b b*, External channel of the setæ. *c*, Central finer seta. Fig. 17, The external, *b b*, and the central seta, *c*, alone. Fig. 18, Section. *a a*, Valves. *b b*, External setæ. *e*, Central one.

Pl. XXIV. Figs. 1—7, Ovipositor of *Cicada Fraxini*. Fig. 1, Apex of abdomen. A, Last dorsal segment. D, Last ventral segment. B, Basal joint of the sheath of the ovipositor. C, Terminal joint. Fig. 2, Ovipositor with the valves from beneath. B B, Basal joints of the valves. C C, Terminal joints. D, The ovipositor. Fig. 3, Apex of the ovipositor from beneath. *a a*, Superior distended sheath, with teeth on the margin. *b b*, The lower setæ pushed upwards, so that they project beyond the apex of the sheath. Fig. 4, Setæ from the inner side, to show the central channel. Fig. 5, Apex of the sheath from above, toothed on the margin, furrowed in the centre, emarginate at the apex to receive the points of the setæ, which form the true apex of the ovipositor. Fig. 6, Section. *a a*, The valves. *b b*, The sheath. *c*, The setæ. Fig. 7, Section of the mere ovipositor. *a a*, Sheath. *b*, Seta. Figs. 8, 9, Ovipositor of *Cimbex variabilis*. Fig. 8, The valves opened from beneath. A A, The last dorsal segment. *a a*, External valves. *b b*, Internal valves, or saws. *c*, Central short process. Fig. 9, An internal valve, or saw, from its external surface. *b*, Furrow, by means of which the external surface is divided into two halves. *a*, Lower more finely serrated. *b*, Superior more coarsely serrated surface. Figs. 10—15, Ovipositor of *Locusta*. Fig. 10, Apex of the abdomen of *Locusta viridissima*. A, Last dorsal segment. B, Last ventral segment. C, Ovipositor. Fig. 11, One half of the sheath seen from the exterior of *Locusta ephippiger*. Fig. 12, The same from the inner surface. *a*, Superior half of the valve. *c*, Lower half. *b*, Central, smaller, inner valve of the same side. Fig. 13, External view of the apparatus of *Locusta viridissima*. *a*, Upper half. *c*, Lower half. Fig. 14, The same from within. *a*, Upper half. *c*, Lower half. *b*, Internal valve, indicated here only as a projecting ridge, Fig. 15, the jointed ovipositor of *Chrysis* (Kirby and Spence).

Pl. XXV. Figs. 1—4, Male organs of *Carabus glabratus*. Fig. 1, Prepuce from above, as taken from the ventral cavity. *a*, The horny ridges which distend the bag of the prepuce. *b*, The process of the prepuce, in which the penis lies. *c*, Apex of this process, into which the vasa deferentia extends. *d*, Last dorsal segment. Fig. 2, The same from beneath. *a a*, The horny ridges of the prepuce. *b*, The horny plate which lies in the lower portion of the prepuce. *c*, Process in which the penis lies. *d*, Last dorsal segment. Fig. 3, Penis from above, with *a*, lateral moveable process, *b*, in which muscles are inserted. Fig. 4, The same from beneath. *a*, Aperture of the penis, whence the sperm flows. Figs. 5—10, Male organs of *Dyticus marginalis*. Fig. 5, View of them beneath, with the last divided ventral plate. A A, The two halves of the ventral plate. B B, Muscles whereby they are affixed to the preceding one. C C, Horny ridges, which partly serve these for insertion. D D, Muscles which unite the transverse ridge with the ventral plates. *a*, A horny ring lying beneath in the prepuce. *g g*, Muscles that move the penis. *f*, Vasa deferentia. Fig. 6, Penis and prepuce separated from the last ventral plate, seen from beneath. *a*, A horny ring that distends the prepuce. *b*, Horny plate which lies in it. *i*, Membranous portion of the prepuce. *d*, Sheath of the penis. *e*, Penis. *g g*, Muscles which move the penis. *f*, Vasa deferentia. Fig. 7. The same from above. *a a*, Horny ring of the prepuce, running at the margin, and connected with the penis by muscles, *h h*. *i*, Membranous portion of the prepuce. *k*, Horny plate lying in the upper part of the prepuce. *l*, Horny scale to which the ends of the horny arch of the prepuce are attached. *e*, Penis. *g g*, Muscles which move the penis, *f*, Vasa deferentia. Fig. 8, The same seen from the left side. *a*, Horny ring of the prepuce. *b*, Horny scale lying in the lower portion. The rest as in the preceding. Fig. 9, The penis, after the removal of the prepuce. *a a*, Membranous portion of the prepuce, which is drawn back by horny ridges, *b*, which are connected with the horny ring of the prepuce *c c*, by means of muscles, at its upper margin. *d d*, Valves of the penis. *e*, Penis. Fig. 10, Penis, quite free. *a*, Ridge which lies in the penis, and closes its aperture. *b*, Lower channel, in which the ridge or bone lies. Figs. 11—14, Male organs of *Hydrophilus piceus*. Fig. 11, Prepuce from above. M, The removed colon. *d d*, Last dorsal segment, with three fenestrations. *b b*, Horny ring which distends the prepuce. E E, Sheaths of the penis. F, Penis. *f*, Vasa deferentia, surrounded by the membranous portion of the prepuce. Fig. 12, The same, from beneath. *a*, Horny plates, which lie in the lower portion of the prepuce, whence the ridges proceed which affix themselves to the apex of the last ventral plate, *e e*. *c c*, Other horny ridges, which proceed from the horny arch. *b b*, As fig. 11. *d d*, Last dorsal segment. E.E, Sheath of the penis. F, The penis. Fig. 13, The free penis, from above, more magnified than fig. 12. A A, Reflexed margins of the horny plate. A, As in fig. 14. B, Membranous portion of the penis. E E, Sheaths of the penis, consisting of horn. F. Penis, provided in the middle and on the margin with horny ridges. Fig. 14, Free penis, from beneath. A, A cordiform horny plate, to which the sheaths are attached. E E, The sheaths of the penis. F, Penis, with the aperture X, which is surrounded by a horny arch, whence a ridge proceeds.

Pl. XXVI. Figs. 1, 2, Sexual organs of *Callichroma moschatum*. Fig. 1, A, Prepuce, supported by a horny ridge, C, which distends into a horny plate, B, upon the upper surface of the prepuce. D, Penis. E, Vasa deferentia. F, Ridge, by means of which the penis is pushed forwards. G, Last ventral segment. Fig. 2, Free penis, seen from the left side. *a*, Lower horny tip of the penis. *b*, Upper ditto. *c*, Vasa deferentia. Figs. 3—7, Male organs of *Blatta orientalis*. Fig. 3, View from above. *a*, Superior horny plate covering them. *b*, Left. *c*, Right. *d*, Penis. Fig. 4, The same from beneath. *c*, Right horny plate. *b*, Left. *a*, Upper. *d*, Penis. Fig. 5, The superior covering plate, consisting of several horny pieces, and provided with a hooked process. Fig. 6, The right covering plate, composed of two pieces, *a* and *b*. Fig. 7, The left covering horny plate, with the penis. *a a*, Ridges, which enclose the penis between them. *b*, The upwards bent penis, furnished at the end with a hook. Figs. 8—10, Male organs of *Cimbex variabilis*. Fig. 8, From below. *a a*, The external sheaths, each consisting of a lower (*a*) horny and a superior (*a**) membranous portion. *b b*, The penis, likewise consisting of two valves. Fig. 9, The left half of the sexual apparatus, seen from without. *a*, Horny basal portion of the sheath. *b*, Membranous appendage. *c c*, Halves of the valvular penis. Fig. 10, The same from within, marked similarly. *d*, Outlet of the vasa deferentia. Figs. 11—13, Male organs of *Vespa Germanica*. Fig. 11, Seen from beneath. *a a*, External sheaths. *b b*, Internal sheaths of the penis. *c*, Penis. X, Aperture for the vasa deferentia. Fig. 12, Penis, from the side, distended like a spoon, anteriorly, *c*, with a barb, *a*, by which it hangs attached during copula. Fig. 13, The same, from above, marked similarly. *b*, Internal passage of the penis. Figs. 14—17, Male organs of *Deilephila Galii*. Fig. 14, Lateral view of the whole apex of the abdomen. *a a*, Horny ring to which the external sheath is affixed. *b*, External sheath of the left side, with the hooked appendage (*b**). *c*, Penis. *d*, Horny process, into which the colon passes. *e*, Anus. Fig. 15, Sheath of the right side seen from within. Fig. 16, Free penis, *a*, with the aperture *c*, and the muscles *b b*, which attach it. Fig. 17, Anterior aperture of the penis, seen from above.—Figs. 18, 19, Male organs of *Cercopis vulnerata*, Ill. Fig. 18, The sexual apparatus, enclosed in valves, seen from the left side. Fig. 19, The opened sexual apparatus, seen from above. The external valves are removed. *a a*, The internal valves. *b b*, The horny penis, consisting of two parts, bent outwards.

Pl. XXVII. Fig. 1, Ovaria of *Ephemera marginata.* Fig. 2, Of *Phasma gigas* (Müller). Fig. 3, Ditto of *Gryllus migratorius.* Fig. 4, Ditto of *Meloe proscarabeus.* Fig. 5, Ditto of *Gryilotalpa vulgaris* (ib.). Fig. 6, Ditto of *Lepisma* (Trev.). Fig. 7, Internal sexual organs of *Hippobosca* (L. Duf.). *a a,* Ovaries. *b,* Uterus. *c c,* Conducting vessels. Fig. 8, Ovary of *Anthidium* (Suckow). Fig. 9, Ditto of *Tinea Evonymella* (ib.). Fig. 10, Ditto of *Musca carnaria* (ib.). Fig. 11, Ditto of *Aphrophora spumaria* (ib.). Fig. 12, Ditto of *Lucanus parallelopipedus* (ib.). Fig. 13, Uterus without appendage of *Tipula crocata* (ib.). Fig. 14, Ditto, with an appendage of *Anthidium manicatum.* *a,* The spermatheca (ib.). Fig. 15. The same of *Hydrophilus piceus* (ib.). *a,* The spermatheca, into which the serpentine gum-vessel evacuates. Fig. 16, The same of the *Melolontha vulgaris* (ib.). *a,* Spermatheca. *b,* gum-vessel. The pockets are at the end of the sheath, into which the knob of the penis inserts itself. Fig. 17, The same of *Xylocopa* (ib.). *a,* Spermatheca. *b,* Gum-vessel. Fig. 18, The same of *Sirex* (ib.). *a,* Spermatheca, with the two ears. *b,* Gum-vessel. Fig. 19, The same of *Harpalus ruficornis.* *a,* Sack-shaped distended sheath. *b,* Gum-vessel.

Pl. XXVIII. Fig. 1, Uterus of *Lucanus* (Suckow). *a,* Spermatheca. *d d,* Double gum-vessel. Fig. 2, Ditto of *Gryllotalpa vulgaris* (ib.). *a,* Spermatheca. *b b,* Gum-vessels. Fig. 3, Ditto of *Lepisma* (Trev.). *b b,* Gum-bags. Fig. 4, Duct of the internal genitalia, with its appendages, of *Gastropacha Pini* (Suckow). *a,* Spermatheca, with its narrow duct. *b b,* Glue-vessel, forked above, beneath distended into a bladder. *c c,* Second secreting vessel, probably a urinary organ, corresponding to the poison vessel of the *Hymenoptera.* *a,* Colon and cœcum. Fig. 5, Poison-vessels of *Vespa crabro* (ib.). *a a,* Secreting vessels. *b,* Poison-bladder. Fig. 6, The same of *Apis mellifica* (Swamm.). *a a,* Secreting vessels. *b,* Poison-bladder.

Pl. XXIX. Fig. 1, United testes, with the two outlets, of *Pontia Brassicæ* (Herold). Fig. 2, Testes of *Libellula* (Suckow). Fig. 3, Ditto of *Aphrophora spumaria* (ib). Fig. 4, Ditto of *Tipula crocata* (ib.). Fig. 5, Ditto of *Ranatra linearis* (ib.). Fig. 6, Half of the poison vessel of *Apis mellifica.* Fig. 7, Testes of *Dyticus marginalis.* *a,* Large knob. *b,* Small knob of the duct. Fig. 7, *b,* Testes of *Silpha obscura* (L. Duf.). Fig. 8, Ditto of *Hydrophilus piceus* (Suck.). Fig. 9, Ditto of *Trichodes* (ib.). Fig. 10, Ditto of *Locusta viridissima.* Fig. 11, Ditto of *Staphylinus* (L. Duf.). Fig. 12, Ditto and duct of *Musca deviens* (Suckow). Fig. 13, Ditto of *Semblis bicaudata* (ib.). Fig. 14, Ditto of *Apate* (L. Duf.). Fig. 15, Ditto of *Œdemera* (ib.). Fig. 16, Ditto of *Pimelia* (*ib.*). Fig. 17, Ditto and duct of *Lytta vesicatoria* (Brandt). *a*, Testes. *b*, First gum-vessel. *b b*, Second ditto. *a**, Bag-shaped distension at the connecting point of the duct. Fig. 18, Testes of *Lamia ædilis*. Fig. 19, Ditto of *Prionus* (L. Duf.), Fig. 20, Ditto of *Cicada* (*ib.*).

Pl XXX. Fig. 1, Testes of *Nepa cinerea* (Swamm.). Fig. 2, Ditto of *Melolontha vulgaris* (Suckow). Fig. 3, Auxiliary testes of *Hydroph. piceus* (*ib.*). Fig. 4, Ditto of *Locusta viridissima*. *a*, Superior fasciculus of vessels. *b*, Retainer, clothed on the surface with small processes, into which the duct, *c*, opens. *d*, Sperm bladder. Fig. 5, Ducts of the genitalia of *Donacia aquatica* (Suckow), without appendages. Fig. 6, Ditto of *Phryganea oleracea*. *a*, Vasa deferentia. *b*, Vesica seminalis. Fig. 7, The same of *Dyticus marginalis*, marked the same. Fig. 8, The same of *Apis mell.* (Brandt). $a^* a^*$, Vesica seminalis. *b b*, Clavate gum-vessels. Fig. 9, The same of *Melolontha vulgaris* (Suckow). *a a*, Ducts of the vesica seminalis. *b b*, Gum-vessels, with their distension. Fig. 10, The same of *Hydrophilus piceus* (*ib.*). *a a*, Vasa deferentia. $a^* a^*$, Vesica seminalis. *a a*, Ends of the auxiliary testes. $b^* b^*$, The first furcate gum-vessel. *b b*, The second simple ones. Fig. 11, The same of *Lamia ædilis*. *a a*, Vesica seminalis. *b*, Furcate gum-vessel, with unequal branches. Fig. 12, Organs of *Vanessa Urticæ*, male (Swamm.). *a*, United testes. $a^* a^*$ Vasa deferentia, into which the gum-vessels, *b b*, open. Fig. 13, Gum-vessel of *Calosoma sycophanta* (Suckow). *a*, Vasa deferentia of one side, which opens into the gum-vessel (*b b*) of the side, that of the other side and the ductus ejaculatorius is cut off. Fig. 14, Ducts of the genitalia of *Tipula crocata* (Suckow). *a a*, Vasa deferentia. *b*, Gum-vessels.

Pl. XXXI. Fig. 1, A portion of the hard membrane of the brain of *Dyticus marginalis*. Fig. 2, Brain of the caterpillar of *Cossus ligniperda* (Lyonet). A, Cerebrum. B, Cerebellum. *a a*, Nerves of the eyes. *b b*, Of the antenna. *c*, Cord round the œsophagus, proceeding from the cerebrum. *d d*, Cord connecting the cerebrum and cerebellum. *e e*, Nerves of the mandibles, the branches of the second nerve of the lip (*g g*), whence a branch for a muscle, N, originates. *f f*, Nerves of the maxillæ. *g g*, Second connecting nerve of the labium, of which the nerve of the mandible is a branch. $g^* g^*$, First nerves of the labium, which give off a branch, M, to the muscles of the maxillæ. O O, Nerves of the muscles of the mandibles and antennæ. P P, Nerves of the muscles of the mandibles. R R, Nerves that distribute themselves at the posterior portion of the skull. S S, Nerves of the muscles of the neck, which pass into the thorax. V V, Connecting cords of the cerebellum and first thoracic ganglion. D, The frontal ganglion, formed of the two branches, E E, whence the sympathic nerve, F, originates. Fig. 3, Cerebrum of the same caterpillar (*ib.*). E E, Branches to the frontal ganglion. O, Nerve of the muscles of the mandibles. *b b*, Nerves of the antennæ. *a a*, Nerves of the eyes. *c c*, Cord of the œsophagus. P P, Nerves of muscles. A A, Small ganglion of the sympathic nerve. B B, Branches to ditto. F, Nervus sympathicus (which Lyonet did not discover here). Fig. 4, Brain of *Melolontha vulgaris* (Straus). A, Cerebrum. B, Cerebellum. *a a*, Optic nerves. *b b*, Nerves of the antennæ. *d d*, First ganglion of the sympathic system. G G, Second ganglion. D, Frontal ganglion. *e e*, Nerves of the mandibles. *ff*, Nerves of the maxillæ. Fig. 5, Cerebellum alone (*ib.*). *e e*, Nerves of mandibles. *ff*, Ditto of maxillæ. *k k*, Connecting cord with the cerebrum. *h h*, Connecting cords to the first thoracic ganglia. Fig. 6, Cerebrum of *Gryllus migratorius*, with the sympathic system seen from above. A A, Optic nerves. B B, Nerves of the antennæ. *a*, Frontal ganglion. *b*, First ganglion, in which the odd (unpar.) nerve terminates. *c c*, The large ganglia. *ee*, The small ditto, whence the sympathic nerve originates by two branches, which again unite at *d** and *d**. *e e*, Small ganglia upon the œsophagus. *ff*, First ganglion upon the crop. *g g*, Second, which lies at the end of the crop. *h h*, Nerves which pass between the blind appendages. Fig. 7, Brain of *Gryllus migratorius*, seen from the front. A A, Optic nerves. *a a*, Nerves which pass to the frontal ganglion. *b b*, Nerves of the antennæ. *a* a* a**, Nerves to the ocelli. *d d*, Connecting cords between the cerebrum and cerebellum. *d**, The connecting cord of these. B, Cerebellum. *e e*, Nerves of the mandibles. *ff*, Nerves of the maxillæ.

Pl. XXXII. Fig. 1, Brain of the larva of *Calosoma sycophanta*. A, Cerebrum. *a a*, Optic nerves. *b b*, Nerves of the antennæ. *d d*, Branches to the frontal ganglion. D, Frontal ganglion. F, First ganglion of the sympathic system, the posterior one I have not discovered. B, Cerebellum. *e e*, Nerves of the mandibles. *ff*, Nerves of the maxillæ. *g g*, Nerves of the labium. Fig. 1, B, Commencement of the ganglionic ventral cord of the same larva. *k*, Cerebellum. *h h*, Auxiliary connecting cord, with the first thoracic ganglion. *n n*, Auxiliary ganglia. A A, Nerves of the anterior legs. L, First thoracic ganglion. *i i*, Auxiliary connecting cords of the first and second ganglia, forming small ganglia, *m m*. *k k*, Auxiliary connecting cords between the second and third ganglia. M, Second thoracic ganglion. N, Third. O, Fourth. *p p*, *q q*, *r r*, *s s*, Nerves of muscles. B B, Nerves of the intermediate legs. C C, Nerves of the posterior legs. Fig. 2, The ventral cord of *Dyticus marginalis*. A A, Nerves of the anterior legs. B B, The intermediate ones. C C, The posterior ones. Fig. 3, Ventral cord of the larva of *Eristalis tenax*. Fig. 4, Ventral cord of the fly *Erist. tenax*. *a a*, Connecting cords with the cerebellum. A A, Nerves of the anterior legs. B B, Of the intermediate. C C, Of the posterior. *b b*, Branches of the muscles which pass into the abdomen. *d*, First abdominal ganglion. *c c*, Branches of it. *e*, Second abdominal ganglion. *ff*, *h h*, *g g*, Branches of it to the genitalia and other internal organs. Fig. 5, Cerebrum of *Vespa Germanica*. *a a a*, Nerves to the ocelli. A A, Optic nerves. B B, Nerves of the antennæ, cut off. *c*, Branch to the cerebellum. Fig. 6, Cerebrum and sympathic system of the caterpillar of *Liparis Mori* (Brandt). A A, Nerves of the eyes. B B, Nerves of the antennæ. C C, Hemispheres of the cerebrum. *a a a a*, Nerves which originate from the frontal ganglion and its branches. b^* b^*, First ganglion of the œsophagus. b^{**} b^{**}, Second ganglion of the œsophagus. *f*, Nervus sympathicus. *d*, Its first ganglion. *e*, Its second ganglion. Fig. 7, The same in the developed moth, similarly marked. Fig. 8, The same of *Meloë proscarabeus* (Brandt), similarly marked.

THE END.

www.ingramcontent.com/pod-product-compliance
Lightning Source LLC
LaVergne TN
LVHW021648131225
827696LV00038B/770